Combat and Genocide on

By 1944, the overwhelming majority of the German Army had participated in the German war of annihilation in the Soviet Union and historians continue to debate the motivations behind the violence unleashed in the east. Jeff Rutherford offers an important new contribution to this debate through a study of combat and the occupation policies of three frontline infantry divisions. He shows that while Nazi racial ideology provided a legitimizing context in which violence was not only accepted but encouraged, it was the Wehrmacht's adherence to a doctrine of military necessity which is critical in explaining why German soldiers fought as they did. This meant that the German Army would do whatever was necessary to emerge victorious on the battlefield. Periods of brutality were intermixed with conciliation as the army's view and treatment of the civilian population evolved based on its appreciation of the larger context of war in the east.

JEFF RUTHERFORD is Assistant Professor of History at Wheeling Jesuit University.

Cambridge Military Histories
Edited by:
Hew Strachan
Chichele Professor of the History of War
University of Oxford, and Fellow of All Souls College, Oxford

Geoffrey Wawro
Professor of Military History, and Director of the Military History Center
University of North Texas

The aim of this series is to publish outstanding works of research on warfare throughout the ages and throughout the world. Books in the series take a broad approach to military history, examining war in all its military, strategic, political, and economic aspects. The series complements Studies in the Social and Cultural History of Modern Warfare by focusing on the 'hard' military history of armies, tactics, strategy, and warfare. Books in the series consist mainly of single author works – academically vigorous and groundbreaking – which are accessible to both academics and the interested general reader.

A full list of titles in the series can be found at:
www.cambridge.org/militaryhistories

Combat and Genocide on the Eastern Front
The German Infantry's War, 1941–1944

Jeff Rutherford
Wheeling Jesuit University

CAMBRIDGE
UNIVERSITY PRESS

CAMBRIDGE
UNIVERSITY PRESS

University Printing House, Cambridge CB2 8BS, United Kingdom

One Liberty Plaza, 20th Floor, New York, NY 10006, USA

477 Williamstown Road, Port Melbourne, VIC 3207, Australia

314-321, 3rd Floor, Plot 3, Splendor Forum, Jasola District Centre, New Delhi - 110025, India

79 Anson Road, #06-04/06, Singapore 079906

Cambridge University Press is part of the University of Cambridge.

It furthers the University's mission by disseminating knowledge in the pursuit of education, learning and research at the highest international levels of excellence.

www.cambridge.org
Information on this title: www.cambridge.org/9781107652736

© Jeff Rutherford 2014

This publication is in copyright. Subject to statutory exception and to the provisions of relevant collective licensing agreements, no reproduction of any part may take place without the written permission of Cambridge University Press.

First published 2014

A catalogue record for this publication is available from the British Library

Library of Congress Cataloging in Publication data
Rutherford, Jeff.
Combat and genocide on the Eastern Front / Jeff Rutherford.
   pages cm. – (Cambridge military histories)
Includes bibliographical references.
ISBN 978-1-107-05571-1 (Hardback)
1. World War, 1939–1945–Campaigns–Eastern Front. 2. World War, 1939–1945–Atrocities–Eastern Front. 3. Germany. Heer–History–World War, 1939–1945. I. Title.
D764.R9558 2014
940.54′217–dc23   2014006668

ISBN 978-1-107-05571-1 Hardback
ISBN 978-1-107-65273-6 Paperback

Cambridge University Press has no responsibility for the persistence or accuracy of URLs for external or third-party internet websites referred to in this publication, and does not guarantee that any content on such websites is, or will remain, accurate or appropriate.

Table of contents

List of illustrations   *page* vii
List of figures   ix
List of maps   xi
List of tables   xii
Acknowledgments   xiii

    Introduction   1

1   The Wehrmacht and German society   34

2   Preparations for war   56

3   "Attack with a ruthless offensive spirit and … a firestorm of destruction": the opening phase of Operation Barbarossa   84

4   "Will the continuation of this attack be worth it?" The drive on Leningrad   115

5   "It is only a question of where, not if, civilians will starve": the 121st Infantry Division and the occupation of Pavlovsk   151

6   The failure of Operation Barbarossa: the fusion of ideology and military culture   197

7   The Soviet winter offensive, 1942: Demiansk and the Volkhov river   217

8   "The population … shouted out to the interpreter that one would rather be shot instead of being left to starve": the evolution of military necessity   240

9   "From one mess to another": war of attrition in northwest Russia   280

10   "We need to fight to the end, *so oder so*": combat and the reconstruction of Army Group North   305

11	A more rational occupation? The contradictions of military necessity	330
12	"As miserable representatives of the miserable twentieth century, we burned all of the villages": the scorched-earth retreat to the Panther Line	357
	Conclusion	374
	Bibliography	389
	Index	415

Illustrations

Illustration 3.1	German troops confidently advance towards Leningrad in the summer of 1941. Bundesarchiv, Bild 101I-209-0090-31. Photographer: Zoll	*page* 106
Illustration 4.1	German infantry units fight north of the Luga Line during the advance. Granger 0322603	118
Illustration 4.2	The radicalization of German anti-partisan policy led to the increasing use of public hangings in the fall of 1941. bpk, Berlin/Art Resource, NY 467884	137
Illustration 5.1	In September 1941, the local population was forced to register with German authorities at Pavlovsk Palace. bpk, Berlin/Hans Hubmann/Art Resource, NY 467883	157
Illustration 5.2	The ravages of battle and German occupation policies doomed thousands of Soviet civilians to starvation. bpk, Berlin/Hans Hubmann/Art Resource, NY 467882	188
Illustration 6.1	German military cemeteries in northwest Russia testified to the intensity of combat in 1941. Bundesarchiv, Bild 121-1470. Photographer: unknown	199
Illustration 7.1	After the establishment of the Demiansk pocket, supplies could only be delivered to the encircled German troops by air. Bundesarchiv, Bild 101I-003-3445-33. Photographer: Ullrich	226
Illustration 7.2	During the 1941–2 winter crisis, the German Army increasingly utilized civilians for labor. bpk, Berlin/Bayerische Staatsbibliothek/Heinrich Hoffman/Art Resource, NY 467881	233

viii   List of illustrations

Illustration 8.1	A German soldier navigates the swampy terrain during the battle for the Volkhov pocket. bpk, Berlin/Art Resource, NY 443233	242
Illustration 8.2	The 121st Infantry Division's commander stated, "the world's asshole begins here," when describing the muck and mud in the Volkhov theater. bpk, Berlin/Georg Gundlach/Art Resource, NY 467880	247
Illustration 8.3	German troops deployed in the devastated Volkhov region. bpk, Berlin/Bayerische Staatsbibliothek/Heinrich Hoffman/Art Resource, NY 467877	253
Illustration 8.4	The food situation in the Demiansk pocket led civilians to find sustenance wherever possible. Bundesarchiv, Bild 101I-004-3650-09. Photographer: Richard Muck	262
Illustration 9.1	Fighting in the Ladoga region resembled that of the Western Front during the First World War. bpk, Berlin/Art Resource, NY 467879	286
Illustration 10.1	The 123rd Infantry Division's withdrawal from the Demiansk pocket included the evacuation of the civilian population. bpk, Berlin/Art Resource, NY 467878	313
Illustration 10.2	Fighting in the Ladoga region often pitted Soviet armor against German infantry. Granger 0114021	317
Illustration 10.3	Trenches in the Volkhov theater highlight the shift to attritional warfare in northwest Russia. Granger 0072985	326
Illustration 11.1	German anti-partisan and labor policies in 1943 were characterized by the forcible evacuations of entire villages. Bundesarchiv, Bild 101I-151-1798-03. Photographer: Götzke	334
Illustration 12.1	Exhausted German troops retreat to the Panther Line. bpk, Berlin/Etzold/Art Resource, NY 467876	365
Illustration 12.2	The German scorched-earth retreat to the Panther Line left numerous villages burning in its wake. Bundesarchiv, Bild 146-1971-059-20. Photographer: Jarolin	372

Figures

Figure 6.1	Casualty numbers for June–September 1941	*page* 200
Figure 6.2	Casualty figures for October–December 1941	201
Figure 6.3	Total casualties and replacements, 1941	203
Figure 6.4	Origin of replacements. Note: while specific numbers regarding the origin of the 121st ID's replacements are unknown, it is clear that the majority came from Military District I.	205
Figure 6.5	Personnel changes in 1.I/405th Infantry Regiment and 1.I/407th Infantry Regiment, 121st Infantry Division, 1941	206
Figure 6.6	Personnel changes in 1.I/422nd Infantry Regiment and 2.I/424th Infantry Regiment, 126th Infantry Division, 1941	207
Figure 6.7	Personnel changes in 1.I/415th Infantry Regiment and 1.I/416th Infantry Regiment, 123rd Infantry Division, 1941	208
Figure 8.1	Divisional casualties and replacements during the winter crisis, mid-December 1941–April 1942	274
Figure 8.2	Company casualties and replacements during the winter crisis, January–April 1942. Note that records for the 1.I/415th are available only for January and April 1942 and that the 1.I/416th only has documentation for replacements from April 1942	277
Figure 9.1	121st Infantry Division manpower, May/June–December 1942	296
Figure 9.2	126th Infantry Division manpower, June–December 1942	298
Figure 9.3	123rd Infantry Division manpower, June–December 1942	298
Figure 9.4	Company manpower, June–December 1942	300
Figure 10.1	121st Infantry Division manpower, 1943	321

Figure 10.2   126th Infantry Division manpower, 1943   321
Figure 10.3   123rd Infantry Division manpower, 1943   322
Figure 10.4   Company manpower, 1943   324

Maps

Map 3.1	The drive on Leningrad	*page* 89
Map 5.1	The Leningrad siege line	154
Map 7.1	The Soviet winter offensive, January 1942	220
Map 8.1	The Volkhov pocket	243
Map 8.2	The Demiansk pocket	256
Map 9.1	Operation Michael	282
Map 9.2	The first Ladoga battle	285
Map 10.1	Withdrawal from the Demiansk pocket	311
Map 10.2	The second Ladoga battle	318
Map 12.1	Army Group North's retreat to the Panther Line, 1944	362

Tables

Table 8.1	415th Infantry Regiment's deployment, January–July 1942	*page* 258
Table 8.2	418th Infantry Regiment's deployment, August 1941–June 1942	258
Table 11.1	123rd Infantry Division's expected agricultural production, summer 1943	342

Acknowledgments

The completion of this manuscript would have been impossible without the support of numerous institutions and individuals. Funding granted by the German American Exchange Service (DAAD) in 2004–5 allowed my family and myself to spend ten months in Freiburg and Berlin, where I completed the bulk of my research. Several Foreign Language and Area Study (FLAS) grants gave me the opportunity to learn Russian during my graduate study at the University of Texas, while a West Virginia Humanities Council fellowship supported my writing.

I wish to thank the archivists and staffs at the Bundesarchiv-Militärarchiv, Freiburg im Breisgau; the Bundesarchiv Berlin-Lichterfeld; the Feldpostarchiv in the Berlin Museum für Kommunikation; the Deutsche Dienstelle, Berlin; the Geheimes Staatsarchiv Preußischer Kulturbesitz in Berlin; the Bibliothek für Zeitgeschichte, Stuttgart; the National Archives and Records Administration, College Park, Maryland; and the United States Holocaust Museum and Memorial Archive, Washington, DC. Everyone I worked with was extremely helpful in answering questions and facilitating my research.

Material in this book has appeared in different forms in various publications. I thank Rochester University Press for granting me permission to use information from "The Radicalization of German Occupation Policies: The Wirtschaftsstab Ost and the 121st Infantry Division in Pavlovsk, 1941," in Alex J. Kay, Jeff Rutherford, and David Stahel (eds.), *Nazi Policy on the Eastern Front, 1941: Total War, Genocide, and Radicalization* (Rochester, NY, 2012); Palgrave Macmillan for material from "'One Senses Danger from All Sides, Especially from Fanatical Civilians': The 121st Infantry Division and Partisan War, June 1941–April 1942," in Ben Shepherd and Juliette Pattinson (eds.), *War in the Twilight World: Partisan and Anti-partisan Warfare in Eastern Europe, 1939–45* (Basingstoke, 2010); and Cambridge University Press for information from "Life and Death in the Demiansk Pocket: The 123rd Infantry Division in Combat and Occupation," *Central European History* (41) 2008, pp. 347–80.

I have been fortunate to study under numerous talented historians during my undergraduate and graduate career. These include Kenneth Straus and the late George H. Stein at Binghamton University; H. Peter Krosby and Dan White at SUNY Albany; and Charters Wynn, W. Roger Louis, Tracy Matysik, and Jim Boyden at the University of Texas. The most important person in guiding me through the labyrinth of graduate school and academia has been David Crew. His advice and encouragement were indispensable to completing the project. He was everything a dissertation adviser should be and I am privileged to now call him a friend.

At Wheeling Jesuit University, Leslie Liedel, Donna Simpson, and Dan Weimer have provided a welcoming professional home and Dan in particular has encouraged my research. The Wheeling Jesuit librarians, particularly Barb Julian, have done yeoman's work in locating books I requested through interlibrary loan.

At Cambridge University Press, I thank my editor Michael Watson for his assistance in completing this project; his early encouragement as well as his patience in answering my numerous queries has not been overlooked. The two reader reports and that of the Cambridge Editorial Board were extremely useful in forcing me to sharpen my argument and their criticisms and suggestions have hopefully made this a much stronger work.

Four other individuals have been instrumental in completing this study. I had the privilege of working with two outstanding scholars in Alex J. Kay and David Stahel on another project and each of them provided trenchant commentary on the sections of my manuscript that they read. Both are model historians and discussions over the years with each of them have helped me formulate my ideas. Ben Shepherd gave me my first opportunity to present my research and has been enormously supportive of this project. His valuable criticisms and suggestions have greatly improved the final version in innumerable ways and I am extremely grateful for his assistance. Adrian Wettstein has been my closest professional collaborator over the past decade; his encyclopedic knowledge of German military history and his intellectual rigor have challenged my assumptions and forced me to rethink numerous issues. Of course, all errors remain my responsibility.

A special debt of gratitude is owed to my family. My father first piqued my interest in the Second World War and both he and my mother have always encouraged me in my career. Pursuing a career in the humanities in this era is neither financially profitable nor socially valued; their shared belief in the importance of education and knowledge, however, sustained me during my studies. I cannot thank them enough. My son Ryan was six months old when we moved to Germany for my initial research and my daughter Rachel was born as I was completing the dissertation. Both have grown up with this project and their laughter and joy have provided cheerful distractions from its grim topic. Finally, my wife Bridget has listened to more discussions about the German infantry than any person should have to endure. Her patience and support cannot be measured; I dedicate this book to her in love and gratitude.

Introduction

I. The infantry's war

"This campaign is the infantryman's war. He wins and holds territory. He combs through the forests, he secures the supply lines, he wins the war." So wrote Lt. Schmidt, a member of the East Prussian 121st Infantry Division (ID) in early August 1941.[1] His appraisal of Operation Barbarossa as an infantry campaign was certainly correct: while the overall success of the operation primarily hinged on the performance of the elite motorized and mechanized tip of the Wehrmacht,[2] 107 of the 139 divisions that invaded the Soviet Union marched towards their objectives overwhelmingly dependent on horse-drawn transport for their supply needs.[3] The declaration highlights the importance of the individual *Landser* to the German war effort: despite contemporaries'

---

[1] Tagebuchartige Aufzeichnungen des Lt. Schmidt-Btl. Adjutant, 2.8.41, Bundesarchiv-Militärarchiv Freiburg im Breisgau (hereafter BA-MA), RH 37/3905; emphasis in original. German data protection laws prevent the naming of the following types of individual: those still alive, those who died within the previous thirty years, those of whom no proof regarding death exists and who were born within the past 110 years. For this reason, each soldier in this study who falls into one of these categories has been given a pseudonym.

[2] Strictly speaking, the Wehrmacht (Armed Forces Command) included the Heer (Army), Kriegsmarine (Navy) and the Luftwaffe (Air Force). Within the context of the German military and the war of extermination waged in the east, however, the term Wehrmacht is generally used to describe the army and it is in this sense that the term will be deployed in this study.

[3] For a breakdown of the German order of battle on 22 June 1941, see Burkhart Mueller-Hillebrand, *Das Heer, 1933–1945: Entwicklung des organisatorischen Aufbaues*, vol. II, *Die Blitzfeldzüge 1939–1941: Das Heer im Kriege bis zum Beginn des Feldzuges gegen die Sowjetunion im Juni 1941* (Frankfurt am Main, 1956), pp. 188–91. On the armored units' importance to the invasion's success, see David Stahel, *Operation Barbarossa and Germany's Defeat in the East* (Cambridge, 2009). On the preponderance of infantry divisions in the German order of battle, see R.L. DiNardo, *Mechanized Juggernaut or Military Anachronism? Horses and the German Army of World War II* (Westport, CT, 1991), p. 38; and Rolf-Dieter Müller, "Von der Wirtschaftsallianz zum kolonialen Ausbeutungskrieg," in Horst Boog et al., *Das Deutsche Reich und der Zweite Weltkrieg*, vol. IV, *Der Angriff auf die Sowjetunion* (Frankfurt, 1996), pp. 141–245, here pp. 209–27.

fixation on the armored units that were racing across the steppes of the Soviet state – a fixation that has indeed persisted until the present day – it was the German infantryman who shouldered the bulk of the fighting, especially with the constant attrition suffered by armored divisions that left them severely weakened by the conclusion of the year.[4] Lt. Schmidt did not, however, merely focus on the traditional military aims of destroying enemy forces and seizing territory. Due to the German High Command's massive gamble that the Soviet state would crumble after only several weeks of fighting, he and other foot soldiers found themselves carrying out tasks normally set aside for rear-area formations: the securing of communication and supply lines between the front line and their logistical tails as well as apprehending thousands of scattered Red Army soldiers dislocated by the advancing German armor.[5]

Such irregular warfare plagued the invaders from the very beginning of the campaign, as Lt. Schmidt's diary makes clear. On the second day of the operation, he raged against guerilla forces who "seemingly shot out of every house" in the village of Vilkoviszki. Members of his 405th Infantry Regiment responded in the heavy-handed, yet traditional, manner called for by the German High Command: "as every house from which the devious guerillas shot was set on fire, nearly the entire town was burning by evening."[6]

When examined in the overall context of the invasion, these two diary entries illustrate the dual nature of the invasion of the Soviet Union for the German infantryman: on the one hand, the particular circumstances of this campaign forced him to assume numerous other roles in addition to his primary, and extremely arduous, task of fighting the Red Army, while on the other hand, his own political and military leadership considered him "a bearer of an inexorable racial value" in its ideological

---

[4] Nearly every major study of Operation Barbarossa written in the first forty-five years after the war, particularly in English, places heavy emphasis on armor operations; see, for example, Albert Seaton, *The Russo-German War, 1941–1945* (Novato, 1993); Alan Clark, *Barbarossa: The Russian–German Conflict 1941–1945* (New York, 1985); and Matthew Cooper, *The German Army, 1933–1945* (Chelsea, 1990). One of the primary causes of this preoccupation with armor divisions lay in the postwar popularity of memoirs written by German armor commanders; see, among others, Heinz Guderian, *Panzer Leader* (New York, 1996); Erich von Manstein, *Lost Victories* (Novato, 1994); Hans von Luck, *Panzer Commander* (New York, 1989). For a detailed examination of these types of historical and popular writing, as well as the memoirs themselves, see Ronald Smelser and Edward J. Davies II, *The Myth of the Eastern Front: The Nazi–Soviet War in American Popular Culture* (Cambridge, 2008), pp. 73–156.

[5] Rolf-Dieter Müller, *Der letzte deutsche Krieg 1939–1945* (Stuttgart, 2005), pp. 81–90; Christian Hartmann, "Verbrecherischer Krieg – verbrecherische Wehrmacht?" in *Vierteljahreshefte für Zeitgeschichte* (52) 2004, pp. 5–10.

[6] Tagebuchartige Aufzeichnungen des Lt. Schmidt, 23.6.41, BA-MA, RH 37/3905.

war that demanded any and all means to destroy the "Jewish–Bolshevik system."[7] In many ways, these two entries penned by the lieutenant encompass the German infantry's war in the Soviet Union.

Historians have provided excellent coverage and analysis of the Wehrmacht during the period stretching from the opening of hostilities to the conclusion of the 1941–2 winter crisis, examining the various operational, ideological, and economic facets of the war.[8] Unfortunately, the remainder of the war in the Soviet Union has not received the same type of dedicated investigation and the twists and turns of army policy and behavior from 1942 through 1944 are much more difficult to bring into focus.[9] The tasks faced by the German infantry only multiplied as the war dragged on. Certainly combat remained its first and most important responsibility, but as the conflict transformed from one of movement to one of grinding defensive battles, frontline combat units found themselves burdened with occupying cities, towns, and villages for extended periods of time – and these were tasks that no one within the army had even remotely planned for before the invasion due to the general belief that the campaign would be over in mere months. Now questions such as "improving ... the hopeless food situation for evacuated Russian civilians" became ones wrestled with by combat divisions as they surveyed the misery – that they themselves had caused – in their midst.[10] This more complicated relationship with civilians that emerged after the conclusion of the winter crisis in early 1942 and which evolved up until the scorched-earth retreats of late 1943–early

---

[7] The cited phrases are drawn from Field Marshal Walther von Reichenau's infamous order issued to his Sixth Army on 10 October 1941; as the order corresponded to Hitler's own conception of the campaign, it was later circulated to other units of the Ostheer. The order is printed in Gerd Ueberschär and Wolfram Wette (eds.), *Der Deutsche Überfall auf die Sowjetunion 1941: "Unternehmen Barbarossa"* (Frankfurt am Main, 1997), pp. 285–6.

[8] Several recent and important studies that approach Operation Barbarossa from various perspectives include Christian Hartmann, *Wehrmacht im Ostkrieg: Front und militärisches Hinterland 1941/42* (Munich, 2009); Johannes Hürter, *Hitlers Heerführer: Die Deutschen Oberbefehlshaber im Krieg gegen die Sowjetunion, 1941/42* (Munich, 2006); Felix Römer, *Der Kommissarbefehl: Wehrmacht und NS-Verbrechen an der Ostfront 1941/42* (Munich, 2008); Alex J. Kay, Jeff Rutherford, and David Stahel, *Nazi Policy on the Eastern Front, 1941: Total War, Genocide and Radicalization* (Rochester, NY, 2012); and David Stahel's three volumes on German operations during the summer and fall of 1941: *Operation Barbarossa*; *Kiev 1941: Hitler's Battle for Supremacy in the East* (Cambridge, 2011); and *Operation Typhoon: Hitler's March on Moscow, October 1941* (Cambridge, 2013).

[9] The most recent and comprehensive study of the entire war from the German perspective is Stephen Fritz's excellent work *Ostkrieg: Hitler's War of Annihilation in the East* (Lexington, 2011), though Fritz is more concerned with the activities of the upper levels of command than with the war on the sharp end.

[10] Gruppe Rauch, Abt. Ib, Nr. 194/42 geh., Betr.: Ernährung der Zivilbevölkerung, 2. Mai 1942, BA-MA RH 26-123/205.

1944 underlined the fundamental contradiction facing the *Ostheer* (Eastern Army) during the second half of the war: while Nazi propaganda portrayed the Soviet population as an inchoate mass of subhumanity that needed to be scrubbed from the pages of history, the German Army's only chance to achieve victory lay in mobilizing this same population behind the German war effort.

Both forced-labor roundups and anti-partisan operations highlighted this contradiction within the Wehrmacht's occupation policy and the interplay between these two issues set into motion an accelerating violent spiral in which the Germans responded with increased brutality and ruthlessness against Soviet civilians, indiscriminately devastating large swaths of Soviet territory, which in turn led to more people fleeing their homes and joining the resistance. Working under slogans such as "where the partisan is, the Jew is, and where the Jew is, there is the partisan," German anti-partisan policies were frequently indistinguishable from other genocidal policies and smoothly elided into their later scorched-earth retreats.[11] Thus, by 1944, the overwhelming majority of the German Army had participated in some way or another in the German war of annihilation in the Soviet Union.[12]

The primary question confronting all historians of not only the Wehrmacht but also the Third Reich is *why* did German soldiers engage in such behavior? How important a role in motivating individuals did an identification with Nazi racial ideology play?[13] Did other concerns, be they economic or a desire to conform, lead Germans not only to support the Nazi regime but to actively work for it both at home and abroad?[14]

---

[11] Cited in Jürgen Förster, "Die Sicherung des 'Lebensraumes,'" in Boog et al., *Der Angriff auf die Sowjetunion*, pp. 1227–1287, here p. 1240.

[12] Christian Hartmann concludes his analysis of five German formations on the Eastern Front in 1941–2 by stating that all "were guilty of war and often even of NS-crimes during the first year of the German–Soviet war." Hartmann, *Wehrmacht im Ostkrieg*, p. 792. Christoph Rass writes in his examination of the 253rd Infantry Division that "the soldiers of the 253rd Infantry Division had taken part in a large number of crimes connected" to the war of annihilation; see his *"Menschenmaterial": Deutsche Soldaten an der Ostfront. Innenansichten einer Infanteriedivision 1939–1945* (Paderborn, 2003), p. 410.

[13] For our purposes, Nazi racial ideology will be defined as a belief system that held that the Aryan, German *Herrenmensch* not only were justified in reorganizing the racial structure of eastern and central Europe due to the alleged inferiority of Slavs and other "racial" groups but also righteously demanded the elimination of the mortal Jewish enemy. For more detailed discussions of Nazi ideology and its application, see Eberhard Jäckel, *Hitler's World View: A Blueprint for Power* (Cambridge, 1981); Claudia Koonz, *The Nazi Conscience* (Cambridge, 2005); and Michael Burleigh and Wolfgang Wippermann, *The Racial State: Germany 1933–1945* (Cambridge, 1991).

[14] For a controversial examination of materialism as an important bond between Nazi state and society, see Götz Aly, *Hitler's Beneficiaries: Plunder, Racial War, and the Nazi Welfare State* (London, 2009). On the function of conformity in stabilizing the state, see Peter

The infantry's war 5

For soldiers in the Wehrmacht, such issues are complicated not only by situational factors during their violent existence on the Eastern Front but also by the institutional practices of the organization that dominated their lives: the army itself.[15]

This study will look at three frontline infantry divisions – the 121st, 123rd, and 126th Infantry Divisions – and their combat and occupation practices in an attempt to understand not only what policies and practices the army and its soldiers carried out in the Soviet Union but also why they did so. These units were chosen for several reasons. First, all three divisions were mobilized in the eleventh wave in October 1940 and saw their first action during Operation Barbarossa.[16] Each formation was constructed around cadres drawn from pre-existing units originating from the same military districts and was then filled out by new recruits. None of these divisions could be considered elite, with the majority of the enlisted men consisting of civilian recruits – or "ordinary men" – who seem representative of the communities that they called home.[17]

Second, each division attempted to recruit men from specific regions within the German Reich. East Prussia, Berlin-Brandenburg, and Rhineland-Westphalia were home to the 121st, 123rd, and 126th IDs respectively. These areas significantly differed from one another in economic development, confessional allegiance, and political orientation, and recruiting territorially from such varied regions had two possible consequences. First, these divisions became microcosms of their geographically and culturally distinct areas, with the rank and file carrying a distinct cultural baggage with them into the service; such different backgrounds could help explain differences in the behavior of the units. Second, the various experiences of the home front during the war affected the soldiers and their conduct at the front

---

Fritzsche, *Life and Death in the Third Reich* (Cambridge, 2009); on its role in the carrying out of mass executions, see Christopher Browning, *Ordinary Men: Reserve Police Battalion 101 and the Final Solution in Poland* (New York, 1993).

[15] For an outstanding examination of this issue, see Rass, *"Menschenmaterial"*, pp. 205–330.

[16] On mobilization, see Mueller-Hillebrand, *Die Blitzfeldzüge 1939–1941*, pp. 76–81; and Bernhard Kroener, "The Manpower Resources of the Third Reich in the Area of Conflict between Wehrmacht, Bureaucracy, and War Economy, 1939–1942," in Bernhard Kroener et al., *Germany and the Second World War*, vol. V/I, *Organization and Mobilization of the German Sphere of Power* (Oxford, 2000), pp. 966–1000.

[17] The phrase was first coined by Christopher Browning in his groundbreaking study *Ordinary Men*. This is a major drawback of Omer Bartov's highly influential work. In his two monographs, *The Eastern Front 1941–1945: German Troops and the Barbarization of Warfare* (London, 1985) and *Hitler's Army* (Oxford, 1992), Bartov focuses on two first-wave divisions and one which rapidly attained the level of an elite division, and this emphasis limits the applicability to the rest of the army.

in diverse ways and this also helps explain the range of behaviors displayed by the three divisions.[18]

Third, each unit fought for the majority of the war in Army Group North, with the 121st ID and the 126th ID capitulating in Latvia as part of Army Group Kurland in May 1945 while the 123rd ID was sent to Ukraine in fall 1943, where it disintegrated during the fighting of early 1944. Of the three army groups that invaded the Soviet Union, Army Group North has been the least well served by historians. Both Army Groups Center and South won more spectacular successes and suffered more devastating defeats than their northern counterparts and have consequently received the lion's share of scholarly and popular attention. With the exception of the siege of Leningrad, the operational and occupational practices of the northernmost army group have received very little attention in comparison with the two army groups engaged to its south.[19] While Army Group North's campaigns contained no decisive battles, such as Moscow, Stalingrad, or Kursk, and nor did the military occupation authorities find themselves responsible for a large Jewish population, the nature of Army Group North's war sheds light on an important and relatively neglected topic: the occupation practices and policies of frontline troops and their interactions with Soviet civilians.

The experiences of Army Group North offer the most important examples of long-term occupation by combat soldiers in the Soviet Union due to the nature of war in this theater. With the exception of the six-week advance through the Baltic states in the summer of 1941,

---

[18] This theme will be discussed in more detail below.
[19] Studies of the siege include Harrison Salisbury, *The 900 Days: The Siege of Leningrad*, 2nd edn (New York, 1985); Leon de Goure, *The Siege of Leningrad* (Stanford, 1962); Antje Leetz and Barbara Wenner (eds.), *Blockade: Leningrad 1941–1944. Dokumente und Essays von Russen und Deutschen* (Reinbek, 1992); Peter Jahn (ed.), *Blockade Leningrads – Blockada Leningrada* (Berlin, 2004); Jörg Ganzenmüller, *Das belagerte Leningrad, 1941–1944: Die Stadt in den Strategien von Angreifern und Verteidigern* (Paderborn, 2005); and, most recently, Anna Reid, *Leningrad: The Epic Siege of World War II, 1941–1944* (New York, 2011). The only full-length operational treatment of the campaign, albeit based primarily on Russian-language sources, is David Glantz, *The Battle for Leningrad 1941–1944* (Lawrence, KS, 2002). Johannes Hürter examines Eighteenth Army and the encirclement of Leningrad; see Hürter, "Die Wehrmacht vor Leningrad: Krieg und Besatzungspolitik der 18. Armee im Herbst und Winter 1941/42," *Vierteljahrshefte für Zeitgeschichte* 49 (2001), pp. 377–440; for a brief overview of German occupation practices in northern Russia, see Gerhart Hass, "Deutsche Besatzungspolitik im Leningrader Gebiet 1941–1944," in Babette Quinkert (ed.), *"Wir sind die Herren dieses Landes": Ursachen, Verlauf und Folgen des deutschen Überfalls auf die Sowjetunion* (Hamburg, 2002), pp. 66–81. Jürgen Kilian has recently produced a comprehensive examination of German rear-area practices; see his *Wehrmacht und Besatzungsherrschaft im russischen Nordwesten 1941–1944: Praxis und Alltag im Militärverwaltungsgebiet der Heeresgruppe Nord* (Paderborn, 2012).

positional warfare (which often closely mirrored the style, if not the intensity, of combat on the Western Front during the First World War) became the norm in Army Group North's area of operations for some two and a half years. From the fall of 1941 to January 1944, the army group administered an area that essentially remained the same throughout the duration of the occupation.[20] German troops controlled the same industrial suburbs of Leningrad, the same communities along the Volkhov river, and the same villages and towns in the Demiansk region for two to three years, and this provides a prism through which to examine the development of Wehrmacht occupation practices on the local level in an amount of detail hitherto missing in the historiography. An examination of these three divisions and their combat and occupation practices will allow for a more precise reconstruction of how frontline German infantry divisions behaved during their years of occupation and, just as importantly, why.

This study will argue that while Nazi racial ideology provided a legitimizing context in which violence was not only accepted but encouraged and that it frequently complemented the army's own attitudes, it was the Wehrmacht's adherence to a doctrine of military necessity which proves most useful in explaining how and why the German Army and its soldiers fought the war in the Soviet Union. Variously described as "military utilitarianism" or "pragmatism," the concept of military necessity provides the necessary flexibility in understanding the development of policies on the ground in the Soviet Union.[21] Military necessity should not be understood as a rigid concept, however. At its essence, it meant that the German Army would do whatever was necessary to preserve its combat efficiency and emerge victorious on the battlefield, though how to achieve victory could be understood by various units in different ways. While previous analyses have emphasized an increasing brutalization of German behavior due to the inculcation of Nazi ideological values within the ranks, or have focused on the continual radicalization and application of German violence during the war, these approaches are unable to completely explain the contradictory turns of the army's policy, specifically with regard to occupation as periods of brutality were intermixed with periods of conciliation.

---

[20] Hass, "Deutsche Besatzungspolitik im Leningrader Gebiet 1941–1944," p. 66.
[21] Timm C. Richter uses the former term in his introduction to his edited volume; see Richter (ed.), *Krieg und Verbrechen. Situation und Intention: Fallbeispiele* (Munich, 2006), p. 15; Mark Edele and Michael Geyer deploy the latter term in "States of Exception: The Nazi–Soviet War as a System of Violence, 1939–1945," in Michael Geyer and Sheila Fitzpatrick (eds.), *Beyond Totalitarianism: Stalinism and Nazism Compared* (Cambridge, 2009), pp. 345–95, here p. 377.

In contrast to historiographical approaches that emphasize the ideas of ideology or situation in explaining the attitudes and actions of the Wehrmacht, the notion of military necessity has been rather sparsely utilized. Two exceptions to this trend are studies that examine the activities of army-level formations in the Soviet Union. Johannes Hürter's examination of German policy towards the city of Leningrad in 1941 and the subsequent occupation of the surrounding area emphasized the idea of military necessity, or a "vague military utilitarianism," in explaining both Army Group North and Eighteenth Army's practices.[22] While ideology served as a necessary ingredient in the "merciless occupation policies of Eighteenth Army," the "most important motivating force was a military utilitarianism that wanted success in this particular theater of war at any price and by all means."[23] The army viewed the intentional starvation of Leningrad's occupants and the forced deportations of the hungry, poverty-stricken population in the area ringing the city as necessities to ensure "sufficient food and permanent shelters" for German troops and thereby to "save their combat strength."[24]

Manfred Oldenburg's comprehensive examination of Eleventh Army's occupation policies in the Crimea and those of Seventeenth Army in the Donets basin and the Caucasus in 1942 similarly illustrates the centrality of military necessity to the command structures of these armies and their participation in war crimes.[25] Oldenburg persuasively argues that the Wehrmacht fundamentally transformed its behavior towards the surrounding civilian population due to the army's need for both security and supplies; in other words, due to the worsening strategic situation, the Germans enacted more conciliatory policies towards the sections of the civilian population that neither resisted nor fell into categories deemed ideologically dangerous. Such reasoning led to Eleventh Army's active complicity in the murder by the SD (Sicherheitsdienst, or Security Service) of 14,500 Jews in Simferopol in December 1941; here, military necessity – providing food for civilians in order to lessen any resistance and consequent threats to the army's security – smoothly functioned alongside the regime's desire to exterminate Soviet Jewry.[26]

The approaches of both Hürter and Oldenburg allow for a more nuanced examination of the Wehrmacht's behavior and actions not by

---

[22] Hürter, "Die Wehrmacht vor Leningrad," p. 440.   [23] Ibid., pp. 418, 423.
[24] Ibid., p. 439.
[25] Manfred Oldenburg, *Ideologie und Militärisches Kalkül: Die Besatzungspolitik der Wehrmacht in der Sowjetunion 1942* (Cologne, 2004).
[26] Ibid., pp. 79–87.

exploring just one approach, but instead by analyzing the interplay between ideology, situation, and the concept of military necessity. Despite their immense importance to the general historical debate, both of these works focus on the headquarters of the respective armies and offer little to no discussion of how frontline troops interacted with Soviet civilians.[27] This study intends to fill this gap not only by looking at how German soldiers experienced the sharp end of war, but, by integrating their roles as warrior and occupier into one narrative, it also looks to examine the totality of the German infantry's war in northwest Russia.

An examination of the 121st, 123rd, and 126th IDs clearly illustrates that their policies towards civilians underwent dramatic changes during the course of the war. Operation Barbarossa – the initial invasion of the Soviet Union – was marked by a callous neglect of the overwhelming majority of civilians, who, when thought of at all, were viewed as potential partisans. German behavior towards these very same individuals underwent a dramatic radicalization during the 1941–2 winter crisis when not only victory, but even survival, seemed in doubt; now the divisions ruthlessly exploited civilians for food, clothes, and labor. Following the stabilization of the situation, each of the three divisions began to rethink its occupation policy. The realization that military victory could only be achieved against a larger, increasingly better-armed force through a mobilization of all resources, including civilians, led to the implementation of more conciliatory policies by the Germans.[28]

While such a revision of occupation practices is only comprehensible through the framework of military necessity, the same focus on military victory led the Wehrmacht to carry out policies that not only contradicted its more agreeable new course, but frequently completely negated their intended effects; here the toxic effect of Nazi racial ideology reinforced more violent interpretations of military necessity, ensuring that hard-line policies remained very much in the mix. The final stage in the evolution of German policy occurred in different phases across the front of Army Group North between 1943 and 1944. As the German Army began its long, arduous, and bloody retreat back to the Reich,

---

[27] For example, Oldenburg devotes a mere three pages to the activities of frontline troops; ibid., pp. 116–19.
[28] The contention made by Edele and Geyer that "this more pragmatic approach also turned out to be a far more radical one" is true in one sense as the final development of this policy turned exceedingly violent. During the second half of 1942 and stretching well into 1943, however, the measures enacted by these three divisions under examination proved to be far less violent and arbitrary than previous German practices. See Edele and Geyer, "States of Exception: The Nazi–Soviet War as a System of Violence, 1939–1945," p. 375.

scorched earth and the creation of "dead zones" became the order of the day in an attempt to limit the military potential of the Red Army. As this brief overview shows, the German war in the east, while certainly influenced by both Nazi ideological beliefs and situational factors, is best explained through the idea of military necessity. But how has the war been understood in the historiography? A brief review of the primary themes and controversies follows.

II. Explaining the German *Vernichtungskrieg*

The Wehrmacht's criminal activities across occupied Europe have been public record since the various postwar Nuremberg trials.[29] Recent work has examined the German armed forces and their behavior across the continent, including France,[30] Greece,[31] Italy,[32] and Yugoslavia.[33] Events on the Eastern Front, however, have correctly received the bulk of the attention concerning this issue during the past thirty-five years. Despite this focus, several questions remain open.

Three of the thornier issues include the scale of the Wehrmacht's participation in the war of annihilation, what types of unit carried out what types of crime, and the motivations behind such atrocities. The explosive 1995 Hamburg Institute for Social Research's Vernichtungskrieg: Verbrechen der Wehrmacht 1941–1944 (War of Extermination:

---

[29] *Trials of the Major War Criminals before the International Military Tribunal at Nuremberg, Germany*, 42 vols. (Nuremberg, 1947); *Trials of War Criminals before the Nuernberg Military Tribunals under Control Council Law No. 10: Nuernberg Oct. 1946–April 1949*, vol. XI, *The High Command Case* (Washington, DC, 1950).

[30] Raffael Scheck, *Hitler's African Victims: The German Army Massacres of Black French Soldiers in 1940* (Cambridge, 2008); Thomas Laub, *After the Fall: German Policy in Occupied France, 1940–1944* (Oxford, 2008); Peter Lieb, *Konventioneller Krieg oder NS-Weltanschauungskrieg? Kriegführung und Partisanenbekämpfung in Frankreich 1943/44* (Munich, 2007).

[31] Mark Mazower, "Military Violence and the National Socialist Consensus: The Wehrmacht in Greece, 1941–1944," in Hannes Heer and Klaus Naumann (eds.), *War of Extermination: The German Military in World War II, 1941–1944* (New York, 2000), pp. 146–74; more generally, see his outstanding study of the German occupation of Greece, *Inside Hitler's Greece: The Experience of Occupation, 1941–1944* (New Haven, 1993).

[32] Gerhard Schreiber, *Deutsche Kriegsverbrechen in Italien: Täter, Opfer, Strafverfolgung* (Munich, 1996); Michael Geyer, "Civitella Della Chiana on 29 June 1944: The Reconstruction of a German 'Measure'," in Heer and Naumann, *War of Extermination*, pp. 175–216; and Carlo Gentile, *Wehrmacht, Waffen-SS und Polizei im Kampf gegen Partisanen und Zivilbevölkerung in Italien 1943–1945* (Paderborn, 2012).

[33] For different approaches to occupied Yugoslavia, see Walter Manoschek, *"Serbien ist judenfrei": Militärische Besatzungspolitik und Judenvernichtung in Serbien 1941/42* (Munich, 1995); Klaus Schmider, *Partisanenkrieg in Jugoslawien 1941–1944* (Berlin, 2002); and Ben Shepherd, *Terror in the Balkans: German Armies and Partisan Warfare* (Cambridge, 2012).

Crimes of the Wehrmacht 1941–1944) exhibition staked out an extreme position.[34] It claimed that "the Wehrmacht did not wage a 'normal, decent war', but rather a war of annihilation against prisoners of war, Jews, and other civilians, a war with millions of victims."[35] German prewar directives were "tantamount to a declaration of war against the entire civilian population," and the process of radicalization that began at the outset of the invasion culminated in 1943 with the formulation of a new war aim: "To wage war against an entire people with the goal of annihilation ... the Wehrmacht of 1943 had finally become [Hitler's] Wehrmacht."[36] Ideology was the driving force behind the army's behavior and this found its most horrific expression in the army's complicity in the Holocaust: "when it came to murdering Jews, one could count on the Wehrmacht."[37] Its director, Hannes Heer, maintained that somewhere between "60 to 80 percent" of German soldiers committed crimes during the war with the Soviet Union.[38]

Perhaps the most influential contributions to the debate have been written by Omer Bartov. In a pioneering examination of German combat divisions on the Eastern Front, Bartov demonstrated that they carried out various war crimes due to their attraction to Nazi ideology.[39] Expanding his analysis to the Wehrmacht as a whole, he argued that the "troops at the front were the firmest of Hitler's followers, and the

---

[34] Hamburger Institut für Sozialforschung (ed.), *Vernichtungskrieg: Verbrechen der Wehrmacht 1941–1944*, Ausstellungskatalog (Hamburg, 1996). Among the numerous books that examined the exhibition's reception in Germany and its accuracy, see Hamburger Institut für Sozialforschung (ed.), *Besucher einer Ausstellung* (Hamburg, 1998); Hans-Günther Thiele (ed.), *Die Wehrmachtsausstellung: Dokumentation einer Kontroverse* (Bremen, 1997); as well as the citations given in Omer Bartov, "The Wehrmacht Exhibition Controversy: The Politics of Evidence," in Omer Bartov, Atina Grossman, and Mary Nolan (eds.), *Crimes of War: Guilt and Denial in the Twentieth Century* (New York, 2002), pp. 270–1, nn. 1–4. Several falsely captioned pictures led to the eventual closure of the exhibition in 1999; following a revision of the exhibition, it reopened two years later. For Heer's take on the closing of the exhibition, see *Vom Verschwinden der Täter: Der Vernichtungskrieg fand statt, aber keiner war dabei* (Berlin, 2004), pp. 12–66; see also Bartov, "The Wehrmacht Exhibition Controversy: The Politics of Evidence," pp. 41–60.

[35] Hamburger Institut für Sozialforschung (ed.), *The German Army and Genocide: Crimes against War Prisoners, Jews and other Civilians, 1939–1944* (New York, 1999), p. 19. This is a translation of the original catalog, *Vernichtungskrieg: Verbrechen der Wehrmacht 1941–1944*.

[36] Ibid., pp. 152, 170.

[37] Hannes Heer, "Killing Fields: The Wehrmacht and the Holocaust in Belorussia, 1941–1942," in Heer and Naumann, *War of Extermination*, pp. 55–79, here p. 55. His analysis is based on the actions of Wehrmacht Security Divisions and the infamous 707th Infantry Division in the rear of Army Group Center.

[38] "Abrechnung mit Hitlers Generälen," in *Spiegel-Online*, 27 November 2001. Heer claims he was misquoted; see Hartmann, "Verbrecherischer Krieg – verbrecherische Wehrmacht?" p. 2, n. 4, for a further discussion of this issue.

[39] Bartov, *The Eastern Front 1941–1945*.

least cynical about his ideology."[40] It was this "ideological conviction of the troops" that led to the Wehrmacht's tremendous staying power in combat, as well as to a policy of unrestrained brutality towards Soviet prisoners of war and civilians in the occupied areas.[41] In combination with a vicious system of military justice, the internalization of Nazi propaganda led the Wehrmacht to wage a war of extermination against Soviet soldiers and civilians alike, and it "finally [became] Hitler's Army" in the east.[42]

The contention that combat units were inextricably entwined with war crimes has been buttressed by Christoph Rass's extremely detailed institutional history of one combat infantry division.[43] He argued that

> the analysis of the combat practices of an *ordinary infantry division* has made clear that a differentiation between a conventional war at the front and a war of extermination in the rear cannot be made … Nearly all elements of National Socialist warfare and extermination policies coincided in the world of these soldiers.[44]

Rass also found the overwhelming majority of war crimes committed by soldiers, such as thefts of livestock or goods or the physical abuse of civilians, to have been "frequently insignificant, unspectacular and marginal," but "in their connection and totality, they characterized the everyday occurrences of the war of extermination on the front."[45]

Other scholars, however, claim that combat units, far from being racial warriors, were not actively involved in crimes at the front. Both Stephen Fritz and Rolf-Dieter Müller have claimed that less than 5 percent of German combat soldiers personally committed crimes in the Soviet Union.[46] Arguing that a new orthodoxy has taken hold which portrays "Wehrmacht soldiers as politically motivated warriors in a racial war," Müller claims that this is based on several isolated studies then

---

[40] Bartov, *Hitler's Army*, p. 169.
[41] Omer Bartov, "Brutalität und Mentalität: Zum Verhalten deutscher Soldaten an der 'Ostfront'," in Reinhard Rürup and Peter Jahn (eds.), *Erobern und Vernichten: Der Krieg gegen die Sowjetunion 1941–1945* (Berlin, 1991), pp. 183–97, here p. 184.
[42] Bartov, *Hitler's Army*, p. 28. Clarifying his position, Bartov writes (p. 144), "This does not mean every individual solider was a committed National Socialist; rather, it is to say that the vast majority of troops internalized the distorted Nazi presentation of reality, and consequently felt that they had no other alternative to fight to the death."
[43] Rass, *"Menschenmaterial"*. [44] Ibid., p. 410. Emphasis in original.
[45] Rass, "Verbrecherische Kriegführung an der Front: Eine Infanteriedivision und ihre Soldaten," in C. Hartmann, J. Hürter, and U. Jureit (eds.), *Verbrechen der Wehrmacht: Bilanz einer Debatte* (Munich, 2005), pp. 80–90, here pp. 89–90.
[46] "'Gegen Kritik immun.' Der Potsdamer Historiker Rolf-Dieter Müller über die Wehrmacht im Zweiten Weltkrieg und die Thesen des Hamburger Instituts für Sozialforschung," *Der Spiegel* (23) 1999, pp. 60–2; Fritz, *Ostkrieg*, p. 482.

generalized to the remainder of the army.[47] Dismissing ideology as the primary cause of the barbarization of war in the Soviet Union, he called for a more nuanced approach that examines the "military situation, patterns of behavior, [and] motives of Wehrmacht units and soldiers."[48] Concurring with an approach that downplays the importance of ideology, Sönke Neitzel and Harald Welzer have recently written that "the majority [of the men] had little interest in ideology, politics, world order and the like; they didn't fight the war out of conviction, but rather because they were soldiers and combat was their job."[49] They argued that "abstract issues such as the 'Jewish world conspiracy,' 'Bolshevik subhumanity' or even the 'National Socialist Racial Community' only marginally played a role. These soldiers were no ideological warriors as most were completely unpolitical."[50]

The responsibility of combat troops for war crimes has also been challenged by Fritz and Christian Hartmann. Fritz concludes that while the German Army's success created the preconditions necessary for the war crimes that defined the Third Reich, "relatively few of the active perpetrators were *front troops*":

the worst of the crimes with which the *Ostheer* was associated – the murder of the Jews, the shooting of political officials, the systematic starvation of prisoners of war, the colonial exploitation of food and raw materials, and participation in forced labor roundups – were largely perpetrated by occupation and security units.[51]

Hartmann's exhaustive analysis of three frontline and two rear-area divisions through early 1942 argues that frontline troops simply had neither the time nor the opportunity to wage a criminal war of extermination. Since the tasks of "forward" combat soldiers centered on waging war this meant that the criminal undertakings of "mass murder, forced recruitment [of workers] and the exploitation of the land ... were not genuine tasks of [these] troops" and instead were carried out by rear-area units as well as SS formations and other civilian agencies.[52] While several "crimes of the front" – such as implementation of the Commissar Order – did occur,

---

[47] Rolf-Dieter Müller, "Die Wehrmacht: Historische Last und Verantwortung. Die Historiographie im Spannungsfeld von Wissenschaft und Vergangenheitsbewältigung," in Rolf-Dieter Müller and Hans-Erich Volkmann (eds.), *Die Wehrmacht: Mythos und Realität* (Munich, 1999), pp. 3–35, here pp. 18, 11.
[48] Ibid., p. 12.
[49] Sönke Neitzel and Harald Welzer, *Soldaten: Protokolle vom Kämpfen, Töten und Sterben* (Frankfurt, 2011), p. 14.
[50] Ibid., p. 393.   [51] Fritz, *Ostkrieg*, p. 481.
[52] Hartmann, *Wehrmacht im Ostkrieg*, pp. 466, 467; Christian Hartmann, "Wie verbrecherisch war die Wehrmacht?", in Hartmann, Hürter, and Jureit, *Verbrechen der Wehrmacht: Bilanz einer Debatte*, pp. 69–79, here p. 74; Hartmann, "Verbrecherischer Krieg – verbrecherische Wehrmacht?", p. 47.

14   Introduction

Hartmann argues that either the number of victims was relatively small or the patterns of behavior were too varied to implicate all soldiers in a war of extermination.[53] Similarly to Fritz, his argument transfers the overwhelming majority of the army's guilt onto rear-area security and occupation formations.[54]

Two important studies which examine rear-area units, but nonetheless deal with issues germane to this study, are Theo Schulte's analysis of a rear-area command and Ben Shepherd's investigation of security divisions. Schulte argued that "continued participation in the war [by German soldiers] was often in spite of rather than because of Nazi ideology."[55] Though Shepherd places more weight on the importance of ideology, both emphasize tangible factors, such as the training of the soldiers, their lack of firepower, or their lack of manpower, in explaining why these units committed atrocities.[56] Here, situational factors – i.e. the use of terror as a means of pacification when faced by superior numbers and firepower – proved more powerful in motivating German actions than did ideology. Clearly, the questions of combat-unit participation in war crimes and the motivations for it remain open.

III. Continuities in German history: the Prusso-German Army and "military necessity"

As this historiographical discussion indicates, most historians have looked to the immediate Nazi period in trying to unravel the army's participation in the war of annihilation. This is a result of recent trends which have highlighted the ruptures and breaks in the history of the German nation-state, especially within the context of the twentieth century. The rise of cultural, linguistic, and postmodernist thought effectively ended the idea of constructing an all-encompassing narrative of German history. Such new approaches to history led Konrad Jarausch and Michael Geyer to contend that the "instability of the German condition" needs to be made "the pivotal concern of historical reconstruction."[57] In order to do this,

such an approach needs to break through the crust of a single narrative to recover the multiple subjects that make up a national history. Dissolving

---

[53] Ibid., p. 47.   [54] Hartmann, "Wie verbrecherisch war die Wehrmacht?", p. 73.
[55] Theo Schulte, *The German Army and Nazi Policies in Occupied Russia* (Oxford, 1989), p. 294.
[56] Ibid., pp. 264–84, the quoted sentence is from p. 267; Ben Shepherd, *War in the Wild East: The German Army and Soviet Partisans* (Cambridge, 2004), pp. 226–8.
[57] Konrad Jarausch and Michael Geyer, *Shattered Past: Reconstructing German Histories* (Princeton, 2003).

the single overarching story of the nation into multiple histories permits the recovery of a sense of the nation's fractures and of the labors in joining and orchestrating them.[58]

This emphasis on the conflicts and fissures in recent German history, however beneficial for understanding the contradictory impulses and development of Germany during the tumultuous twentieth century, runs the risk of divorcing the Nazi period from earlier periods of German history.[59]

Recent work has suggested that the past century needs to be kept in the context of the *longue durée* of the earlier epochs of German history. "Ideas, institutions, and politics" have existed "across significant political ruptures" throughout German history and it is the continuities that thread their way through the Prusso-German Army and its development, thinking, and practices during the existence of the unified Reich that are essential in understanding the behavior of the Wehrmacht during the war in the east.[60] An examination of the army from 1870 to 1945 is a necessary complement and, in some ways, corrective to the recent historiographical trends that center on the importance of ideology and situational factors and have pushed other possible explanations for the German Army's participation in the war of annihilation to the side. A more profitable avenue of investigation would be one which looks not only at the war itself but also at the institutionalized practices of the German Army as they developed during its history; here, the issue of "military necessity" looms large.

German military thought evolved in reaction to the new demands of war that emerged during an age of volatile nationalism, mass armies, and industrialized warfare. Small, professional armies no longer decided matters amongst themselves on the battlefield; warfare had evolved into one between warring societies. The German experience between 1870 and 1945 highlighted the Prusso-German Army's increasing intervention in matters that had once remained far outside its purview. The Franco-Prussian War confronted the Germans with the reality of irregular warfare while the Third Supreme Army Command's virtual seizure of power during the last years of the *Kaiserreich* highlighted the army's attempt to mobilize society behind the war effort. The creation of the Ober Ost military state (named after the title *Oberbefehlshaber Ost*, the supreme

---

[58] Jarausch and Geyer, *Shattered Past*, p. 17.
[59] See Helmut Walser Smith's contributions to the forum "The Long Nineteenth Century," *German History* 26 (2008), pp. 72–91.
[60] Helmut Walser Smith, *The Continuities of German History: Nation, Religion, and Race across the Long Nineteenth Century* (Cambridge, 2008), pp. 9–10.

German commander in the east) in the occupied Baltic states during the First World War involved the army in an unprecedented project of constructing a new, "civilized" and "Germanized" state.[61] Events on the Eastern Front during the Second World War dramatically illustrated the much more far-reaching power and aims of the German Army; here, "the administration, security and exploitation of the occupied territories became increasingly important within the conduct of war in the age of 'total war.'"[62] Military victory thus hinged not only on battlefield performance, but also on controlling civilian populations and mobilizing them behind the war effort; thus the notion of military necessity retains real importance in explaining the German Army's behavior.

General Julius von Hartmann, a former cavalry officer, provided perhaps the most precise and useful definition of military necessity in the aftermath of the Franco-Prussian War. Hartmann believed that all military logic pointed to the "great, final purpose of war: *the defeat of the enemy's power, the overcoming of the enemy's energy, the overwhelming of the enemy's will*. This *one* goal commands absolutely, it dictates law and regulation. The concrete form of this law appears as *military necessity*."[63] In other words, the absolute importance of achieving victory on the battlefield overrode all other considerations: triumph was to be attained at any cost. This led Hartmann to claim that "modern war targets the entirety of the military character and includes general damage to the enemy ... misery and torment should not be spared the enemy – they actually serve to break his energy and conquer his will."[64]

The growing importance of society in conflict – as the Franco-Prussian War made abundantly clear – meant that any irregular resistance needed to be immediately quashed. Drawing upon the experiences of Wellington and Napoleon with guerilla warfare, Hartmann wrote that "both men resorted to terrorism as soon as people's war increased."[65] He thus believed that civilian

> excesses can only be reined in when their paroxysm is met with drastic means. If individuals are hit hard, as warning examples to others, that is certainly

---

[61] Vejas Gabriel Liulevicius, *War Land on the Eastern Front: Culture, National Identity and German Occupation in World War I* (Cambridge, 2000), p. 54.
[62] Hürter, "Die Wehrmacht vor Leningrad," p. 384.
[63] Julius von Hartmann, "Militärische Notwendigkeit und Humanität," *Deutsche Rundschau* 13 (1877), pp. 453–4, quoted in Isabel Hull, *Absolute Destruction: Military Culture and the Practices of War in Imperial Germany* (Ithaca, 2006), p. 123. Hartmann's emphasis.
[64] Quoted in ibid., p. 124.
[65] Quoted in Manfred Messerschmidt, "Völkerrecht und 'Kriegsnotwendigkeit' in der deutschen militärischen Tradition," in Manfred Messerschmidt (ed.), *Was damals Recht war ... NS- Militär- und Strafjustiz im Vernichtungskrieg* (Essen, 1996), pp. 190–229, here p. 195.

deeply regrettable, but this harshness is a healthy and preserving good deed for the whole. Where there is popular uprising, *terrorism* becomes a necessary military principle.[66]

For Hartmann, the necessity of victory legitimized the use of any and all means due to the "elemental character of war."[67]

Hartmann's rather pitiless discussion of anti-partisan measures reflected the experiences of the Prusso-German Army during the Franco-Prussian War. Following the defeat of the French Army at the battle of Sedan, French irregulars sprung up throughout the country and began harassing German troops. This affront to the Prusso-German Army's professionalism led to the implementation of drastic measures designed to smash the *francs-tireurs* (guerilla) movement. Helmuth von Moltke the Elder, Chief of the Prussian General Staff, noted that "experience has established that the most effective way of dealing with this situation [guerilla activity] is to destroy the premises concerned – or, where the participation has been general, the entire village."[68] Moltke also ordered the taking of hostages as a deterrent to sabotage activities.[69] The use of collective measures – the punishment of a community or hostages when the actual perpetrators could not be identified – became the basis of German anti-partisan policy at this time and remained so up through the Second World War. Though the Germans resorted to terror tactics of this type during the Franco-Prussian War, on the whole, the army nonetheless maintained a relatively "disciplined restraint" in their dealings with French civilians.[70]

After the war, Moltke wrote that "their [*francs-tireurs*] gruesome work had to be answered by bloody coercion. Because of this, our conduct of war finally assumed a harshness we deplored, but which we could not avoid."[71] Such actions could not be averted because Moltke believed that modern war demanded measures directed against all of an enemy's resources to achieve a quick and decisive victory, including "finances, railroads, food and the prestige of the government."[72] In other words,

---

[66] Quoted in Hull, *Absolute Destruction*, p. 124. Hartmann's emphasis.
[67] Messerschmidt, "Völkerrecht und 'Kriegsnotwendigkeit'," p. 196.
[68] Quoted in Michael Howard, *The Franco-Prussian War* (New York, 1991), p. 378.
[69] Hull, *Absolute Destruction*, pp. 118–19.
[70] Examples of German collective measures are found in Geoffrey Wawro, *The Franco-Prussian War: The German Conquest of France in 1870–1871* (Cambridge, 2003), pp. 238, 264–5, 279. For further instances of German behavior towards civilians suspected of guerilla activity, see Mark R. Stoneman, "The Bavarian Army and French Civilians in the War of 1870–1871: A Cultural Interpretation," *War in History* 8 (2001), pp. 273–93, here pp. 271–8. The judgment on the Prusso-German Army's general behavior is from Howard, *The Franco-Prussian War*, p. 379.
[71] Daniel J. Hughes (ed.), *Moltke on the Art of War: Selected Writings* (Novato, 1993), p. 32.
[72] Messerschmidt, "Völkerrecht und 'Kriegsnotwendigkeit'," p. 195.

Moltke himself converted to the belief that war had transformed into a "struggle for existence," one that men could not regulate as it was part of God's divine order.[73]

As Isabel Hull has so brilliantly detailed, the policies enacted on the spur of the moment during the Franco-Prussian War were both institutionalized into the army's official doctrine and kept alive through "memory and myths" in the officer corps and the enlisted ranks.[74] While many of these practices enshrined in army policy actually contradicted existing international law, the majority of the military leadership believed that "the exceptionality of war rais[ed] it above law," and, due to this, military professionals should be allowed to wage war to a victorious conclusion, no matter the cost, without outside interference.[75]

Such thinking was encapsulated in a 1902 General Staff publication on the laws of war entitled "Customs of War on Land."[76] The document began with the following statement:

> A war led with energy cannot simply be directed against the combatants of the enemy state and his fortifications; rather, it must try to destroy the entire spiritual and material resources thereof in the same way. Humanitarian claims, i.e. the protection of people and goods, can come into question only insofar as the nature and goal of the war allow.

It continued by stating that "immersion in the history of war will protect the officer from excessive humanitarian notions, as it will teach him that war cannot be waged without certain severity; rather, the one true humanity often lies in its ruthless application."[77] "Leniency" towards civilians was a type of "cruelty against one's own troops" as it only increased the length of the war and consequently led to higher casualties.[78] So already at the turn of the twentieth century, segments of the German military leadership demanded a ruthless waging of war against not only the enemy's armed forces, but its society as well. Each individual strand of this set of policies would be utilized in increasingly radical fashion in the occupied Soviet Union during the 1940s; clearly, a real continuity wove its way through the Prusso-German Army's thinking during its existence.

The evolution of the army's antiguerilla policies outside the bounds of international standards was only radicalized during the opening days of the First World War by the "*franc-tireur* myth."[79] John Horne and Alan

---

[73] Ibid.   [74] Hull, *Absolute Destruction*, pp. 119–30, the cited phrase is from p. 119.
[75] Ibid., p. 123.
[76] Quoted in Messerschmidt, "Völkerrecht und 'Kriegsnotwendigkeit'," p. 193.
[77] Ibid., pp. 194–5.   [78] Richter, *Krieg und Verbrechen*, p. 11.
[79] John Horne and Alan Kramer, *German Atrocities, 1914: A History of Denial* (New Haven, 2001), p. 94.

Kramer have painstakingly re-created this myth as it spread throughout the ranks of the Imperial German Army during its advance in the summer and fall of 1914 in Belgium and northern France. The memories and myths of guerilla activities during 1870–1 had been passed down to the soldiers of Kaiser Wilhelm II, and when invading German troops were faced with tense or unexplainable situations they lashed out at the civilian population.[80] Unlike the Franco-Prussian War, however, collective measures became the order of the day during the opening months of the war in the west, despite the fact that there appears to have been no *franc-tireur* activity during this time period.[81] In the east, German behavior towards popular resistance during the occupation of present-day Ukraine proved strict but relatively benign.[82] Occupation practices in both Belgium and the Baltic region, however, pointed towards the future development of the army's occupation policy. In the west, German practices led to a rapacious exploitation of the Belgian economy, with well over 100,000 Belgians deported for labor in either Germany or the army.[83] Actions in Lithuania, however, proved far more comprehensive. Instead of merely administering the area as an occupying power, the army attempted to construct "a monolithic military state"; in other words, German officers "aimed to impose their own form and order on the lands, then to use the lands to the fullest extent towards the final, long-range goal of progressively making over the territory."[84] At the root of this program, however, stood the notion that "the interests of the army and the German Reich always supersede the interests of the occupied territory."[85] The attempt to extract the area's resources led to a "statistical psychosis" as the Germans tried to requisition all the goods

---

[80] The deep impression made on the German Army by the irregular war of 1870–1 led at least one Reserve Bavarian Infantry Regiment during the First World War to hand out ropes to every third man in its platoon for hanging expected *francs-tireurs*; see Thomas Weber, *Hitler's First War: Adolf Hitler, the Men of the List Regiment and the First World War* (Oxford, 2010), p. 27.

[81] Horne and Kramer, *German Atrocities, 1914*, pp. 435–9, identify some 130 incidents of ten or more civilians being killed for alleged partisan attacks. For an analysis of the German invasion of the west in 1914 that integrates German treatment of civilians into the narrative of military events, see Holger Herwig, *The Marne 1914: The Opening of World War I and the Battle That Changed the World* (New York, 2009).

[82] For a brief overview of German occupation policy in the east during the First World War, see Dieter Pohl, *Die Herrschaft der Wehrmacht: Deutsche Militärbesatzung und einheimische Bevölkerung in der Sowjetunion 1941–1944* (Munich, 2008), pp. 25–34. On Ukraine, see Stefan Karner and Wolfram Dornik (eds.), *Die Besatzung der Ukraine 1918: Historischer Kontext – Forschungsstand – wirtschaftliche und soziale Folgen* (Graz, 2008); and Winfried Baumgart, *Deutsche Ostpolitik 1918: Von Brest-Litowsk bis zum Ende des Ersten Weltkrieges* (Munich, 1966).

[83] Hull, *Absolute Destruction*, pp. 230–42.

[84] Liulevicius, *War Land on the Eastern Front*, pp. 7, 54.   [85] Ibid., p. 66.

necessary for the army's well-being.[86] Though this "military utopia" failed to come to fruition due to the crumbling of the *Kaiserreich*, the example of Ober Ost certainly served as a model for later German occupation policies in the east.[87]

Once the war ended, however, the chaos and confusion in the east that followed led to a round of brutal fighting between German troops; Freikorps units; Baltic, Polish, and Russian nationalists; and Soviet sympathizers.[88] German complaints about the communists who acted as "barbarians" and utilized "insidious combat methods" resulted in "numerous massacres by the Freikorps against real and alleged communists in the conquered Baltic cities and areas in which thousands of victims fell."[89] Here, the Prusso-German Army's traditional means of applying maximum violence to quash irregular warfare contributed to a merciless struggle on Germany's eastern borders, and this proved to be an important way station on the road to the unrestrained use of force that characterized the German Eastern Front during the Second World War.

Both during and after the war, Allied propaganda made much use of the atrocities committed in the west. In response, the German Army vigorously defended its policies, which had the effect of "reaffirm[ing] its doctrine of the illegality of enemy irregular warfare" during the interwar period and providing "one strand of its descent into lawlessness and barbarity during the Third Reich."[90] In the period stretching from 1870 to 1920, violent anti-partisan policies that stood outside accepted international law became enshrined in German military thinking. Such developments in the "military culture" of Wilhelmine Germany need to be considered when examining the behavior of the Wehrmacht in the Second World War.[91]

The implications of military necessity therefore led to the development within the Prusso-German Army of a ruthless attitude towards guerillas

---

[86] Ibid.   [87] Ibid., p. 7.
[88] On the Freikorps and their activities in the German east, see Liulevicius, *War Land on the Eastern Front*, pp. 227–43; Hagen Schulze, *Freikorps und Republik 1918–1920* (Boppard am Rhein, 1969), pp. 101–201; Robert L. Waite, *Vanguard of Nazism: The Free Corps Movement in Postwar Germany, 1918–1923* (Cambridge, 1969); and Annemarie H. Sammartino, *The Impossible Border: Germany and the East, 1914–1922* (Ithaca, 2010), pp. 45–70.
[89] The first quotation comes from Heinz Guderian, the second from Hermann Hoth, and the third from the historian Johannes Hürter. See his *Hitlers Heerführer* for all three quotes, pp. 89–90. The German Army's determination to use all means to destroy communist enemies on its frontiers was complemented by its policies directed towards internal communist movements. The use of military force against revolutionaries in the immediate postwar period is examined by Dieter Dreetz, Klaus Gessner, and Heinz Sperling, *Bewaffnete Kämpfe in Deutschland, 1918–1923* (Berlin, 1988). I thank Adrian Wettstein for suggesting this line of thinking.
[90] Horne and Kramer, *German Atrocities*, p. 425.
[91] Hull, *Absolute Destruction*, pp. 93–8.

and the civilian society from which they arose. Military necessity also had ramifications for the army's operational performance. As it attempted to secure Germany's position in a seemingly hostile Europe, the army increasingly focused on achieving military victory through a decisive campaign predicated on speed and concentrated aggression that utterly devastated the opponent. Robert Citino has termed this quest for the *Vernichtungsschlacht* (battle of annihilation) as "the German way of war."[92] According to Citino, a quick victory was seen as desirable due either to the diplomatic situation at the time or to the balance of forces opposing the German Reich. These "front-loaded" wars would allow the German Army to conceal its relative weakness and crush its enemies before their weight could be brought to bear on the battlefield.[93] Such thinking certainly did not materialize overnight in the post-1870 period – as evidenced by the battles of Königgrätz in 1866 and Sedan in 1870 – but the German Army increasingly fixated on *the* decisive battle as the solution to all of its problems following the ascension of Alfred von Schlieffen to Chief of the Great General Staff in 1891.[94] Under Schlieffen's command, the army prepared to knock France out of the war immediately following the opening of hostilities before turning to deal with the Russian colossus to its east.[95] The seeming necessity of quickly dispatching the French on the battlefield also played a role in the use of terror against any perceived resistance: in order to ensure that its ambitious timetable was met, the army mercilessly dealt with any hindrances.[96] The all-consuming desire to achieve a Cannae-style victory

---

[92] Robert M. Citino, *The German Way of War: From the Thirty Years' War to the Third Reich* (Lawrence, KS, 2005).
[93] Ibid., p. xiii; Hull, *Absolute Destruction*, pp. 174–8.
[94] On Prussian planning for the war with Austria, see Geoffrey Wawro, *The Austro-Prussian War: Austria's War with Prussia and Italy in 1866* (Cambridge, 1996), pp. 20–1; on the Franco-Prussian War, see Wawro, *The Franco-Prussian War*, pp. 41–64; Howard, *The Franco-Prussian War*, pp. 43–4; more generally, see Arden Bucholz, *Moltke, Schlieffen, and Prussian War Planning* (Providence, 1993); and Jehuda Wallach, *The Dogma of the Battle of Annihilation: The Theories of Clausewitz and Schlieffen and Their Impact on the German Conduct of Two World Wars* (Westport, 1986).
[95] While Terence Zuber has challenged the notion of a defined Schlieffen Plan, the existence of a military doctrine that could have fostered such an aggressive plan remains unchallenged. For opposing viewpoints on the Schlieffen Plan, see Terence Zuber, *Inventing the Schlieffen Plan: German War Planning 1871–1914* (New York and London, 2003); and Hans Ehlert, Michael Epkenhans, and Gerhard P. Groß, *Der Schlieffenplan: Analysen und Dokumenten* (Paderborn, 2006). See also Jack Snyder, *The Ideology of the Offensive: Military Decision Making and the Disasters of 1914* (Ithaca, 1984), pp. 107–56, as well as Hull's penetrating analysis, *Absolute Destruction*, pp. 159–81.
[96] Hew Strachan, "Time, Space and Barbarisation: The German Army and the Eastern Front in Two World Wars," in George Kassimeris (ed.), *The Barbarization of Warfare* (New York, 2006), pp. 58–82, here p. 68.

influenced not only German planning on the continent but also its colonial operations in Africa.

The narrow focus on military triumph triggered a genocidal campaign against the native population in German Southwest Africa in 1904.[97] Hull has convincingly argued that the army's need to maintain its professional reputation led it to brush aside any political attempts at ending the revolt. Instead, it insisted on achieving a battle of annihilation in the field that not only led to unnecessary German casualties but also resulted in the near total extermination of the Herero and Nama tribes. Decisive operations had become such a critical component of both German military operational thought and its institutional culture that all other considerations – especially the treatment of rebellious civilians – merited no thought.

The unprecedented totality and violence of the First World War transformed the notion of military necessity within the German officer corps, particularly amongst those junior and field-grade officers who would later command Hitler's army in the Soviet Union. "A new understanding that the scale and severity of this war made unusual demands" emerged which the "traditional 'trade of war'" no longer sufficed to explain. In the place of older forms of thinking, a newer notion of military necessity arose, one which "appeared to legitimize itself with the renunciation of earlier practices in this existential war between peoples."[98] According to Johannes Hürter,

> the new image of war was determined by the use and consumption of all resources of the warring nations. To balance these efforts, it seemed that the occupied territories demanded exploitation. Considerations towards the foreign civilian population needed to retreat behind "military necessity."[99]

The advent of this type of warfare not only helped usher in a new, more radical notion of military necessity, but also forced the army to significantly modify its own practices in hopes of achieving total victory.

Fulfilling the requirements of military necessity not only meant that the German Army single-mindedly strove for victory on the battlefield; it also meant that when faced with the threat of professional failure, the army would undergo fundamental transformations to ensure a successful outcome. Nowhere is this more apparent than during the First World War when the nature of the fighting forced the army to modify significantly its institutional structure. During the first decade of the twentieth

---

[97] For the most concise examination of this theme and a solid discussion of the campaign in Southwest Africa, see Hull, *Absolute Destruction*, pp. 5–90.
[98] Hürter, *Hitlers Heerführer*, p. 84.   [99] Ibid., p. 85.

century, sections of the German officer corps realized the necessity of expanding the army in order to keep pace with French and Russian rearmament, but the majority of the officer corps blanched at such a prospect, preferring to maintain the officer corps's aristocratic nature.[100] Due to unprecedented numbers of casualties as well as the need for a more technologically literate officer corps, the German High Command forfeited the noble exclusivity of the officer corps, opening the doors to thousands of middle-class candidates, even though they did not originate from the "desired classes."[101] The quest for final victory was deemed important enough, however, for the officer corps to weaken its collective standing within the state.

Not only did combat in the Great War force the army to dilute the aristocratic nature of its officer corps, but it also caused it to embrace what has been termed "a military machine-culture."[102] Having suffered horrifying losses during the first two years of war, Hindenburg and Ludendorff's Third Supreme Command radically reconfigured German doctrine; now "the optimal use of weapons alone shaped command and deployment ... [and] even organized the co-ordination and co-operation among units."[103] In this new understanding of war, "machines (machine guns and artillery) were the bearers of combat," not the man.[104] Michael Geyer notes that "the formation of a military machine-culture and the instrumental organization of units undermined the very essence of the Prusso-German military institution and profession, traditionally based on uniformity, hierarchy and

---

[100] Holger Herwig argues that the army's decision not to expand by two or three army corps in 1912–13 was due to a "fear that this would undermine the social cohesion of the officer corps"; see his *The First World War: Germany and Austria-Hungary, 1914–1918* (New York, 1997), p. 19. See also Martin Kitchen, *The German Officer Corps, 1890–1914* (Oxford, 1968), p. 31. For the classic look at the Imperial German Army as a reactionary force more concerned with political and social power than with military efficiency, see Bernd F. Schulte, *Die deutsche Armee 1900–1914: Zwischen Beharren und Verandern* (Düsseldorf, 1977). For a powerful challenge to this perspective, see Dieter Storz, *Kriegsbild und Rüstung vor 1914: Europäische Landstreitkräfte vor dem Ersten Weltkrieg* (Hamburg, 1992).
[101] The phrase is German war minister General von Heerigen's, quoted in Holger Herwig, "Strategic Uncertainties of a Nation-State: Prussia–Germany, 1871–1918," in Williamson Murray et al. (eds.), *The Making of Strategy: Rulers, States and War* (Cambridge, 1994), pp. 242–77, here p. 262.
[102] Michael Geyer, "German Strategy in the Age of Machine Warfare, 1914–1945," in Peter Paret (ed.), *The Makers of Modern Strategy: From Machiavelli to the Nuclear Age* (Princeton, 1986), pp. 527–97, here p. 543; Gerhard P. Groß, "Das Dogma der Beweglichkeit: Überlegungen zur Genese der deutschen Heerestaktik im Zeitalter der Weltkriege," in Bruno Thoß and Hans-Erich Volkmann (eds.), *Erster Weltkrieg, Zweiter Weltkrieg: Ein Vergleich* (Paderborn, 2002), pp. 143–66, here p. 149.
[103] Geyer, "German Strategy in the Age of Machine Warfare, 1914–1945," p. 541.
[104] Groß, "Das Dogma der Beweglichkeit," p. 149.

24 Introduction

subordination."[105] This new focus on machines and the soldiers who operated them "gave unprecedented freedom of action to soldiers and non-commissioned officers, and an extraordinary independence to the lower echelons of front officers."[106] Local officers of middling rank – not those located far to the rear of the front – were given the responsibility and initiative to launch their own counterattacks, a striking departure from the traditional practice of the army.[107] The initiative displayed by these lower-level officers and NCOs drove the 1918 spring offensive and this command situation "decreased the influence of the middle and higher leadership as much on the battle as on the troops" and "reduced the possibilities for influence and control over the soldiers."[108]

Once again, the German Army demonstrated the importance of military necessity – the drive for victory no matter the cost – within its military culture. In an attempt to defeat the Allied powers on the battlefield, the Prusso-German Army willingly restructured not only its officer corps but also its fundamental approach to combat. These sweeping changes resulted in the army transforming from a bastion of aristocratic power to one that emphasized the initiative of junior officers and non-commissioned officers and increasingly exploited the technological know-how of the middle class. In other words, the need for victory overrode all political and social considerations.

This emphasis on military necessity continued during the early years of the Weimar Republic when some officers began thinking about the necessity of a *levée-en-masse* defense with all of its revolutionary implications. Fearful that a Polish or French invasion could not be stopped by conventional means, "Young Turk" planners explored "harnessing the powers of society" and fighting a *Volkskrieg* (people's war) in its most complete and horrifying sense.[109] These officers realized that the small, aristocratic, and mobile Reichswehr created by Colonel-General Hans von Seeckt within the constraints of the Versailles Treaty could not successfully wage a professional, offensive war in Germany's strategic situation.[110] Joachim von Stülpnagel instead advocated unleashing German society in a large-scale guerilla war against the invaders, hoping that the attrition suffered by the enemy would allow the smaller German Army to then defeat it on

---

[105] Geyer, "German Strategy in the Age of Machine Warfare, 1914–1945," p. 543.
[106] Ibid., p. 544.   [107] Groß, "Das Dogma der Beweglichkeit," p. 149.
[108] Ibid., p. 152.
[109] Geyer, "German Strategy in the Age of Machine Warfare, 1914–1945," pp. 557–64.
[110] For a recent and persuasive examination of this issue, see Gil-Li Vardi, "Joachim von Stülpnagel's Military Thought and Planning," *War in History* (17) 2010, pp. 193–216.

the field of battle.[111] While these ideas never became doctrine in the interwar army, they do highlight how at least some important officers believed that even the most cherished beliefs traditionally held by the army – such as the professional nature of war – could be sacrificed in the name of military necessity.

During the age of total war, the notion of military necessity proved decisive in determining the army's structure and thought. In order to achieve victory against more powerful adversaries, the army developed a doctrine based on the application of overwhelming force in rather limited campaigns, and this guided its conduct during the wars of unification, in the colonies, and through the opening rounds of the First World War.[112] When irregular opposition proved threatening to German goals, the army responded with ruthlessness in an attempt to terrorize the local population into submission, as the experiences of the Franco-Prussian War, the Herero Revolt, and the First World War demonstrated. Once the army's rather antiquated social structure proved unable to master the challenges posed by machine warfare, it dramatically reworked both its social hierarchy and its tactical doctrine so that it could triumph on the battlefield. And finally, the contradictions between the army's traditional beliefs and the reality of the interwar situation led some prominent officers to suggest the unthinkable: a German people's war. As these examples indicate, the concept of military necessity remained the foundation of all Prusso-German military planning.

The focus on speed and daring only increased during the interwar period and the Second World War itself, when new technologies, such as the tank and tactical aircraft, emerged as a possible means to minimize Germany's very real economic and numerical weakness vis-à-vis its enemies.[113] The invasions of Poland and especially France amply demonstrated the potential of technology when skillfully exploited, as German troops dislocated and destroyed the enemy's armed forces at an unprecedented rate of speed. It was during these operations that the emphasis on mobility reached new, unheard-of proportions: instead of units operating according to a systematic plan, the advance frequently degenerated

---

[111] Ibid., pp. 199–200.
[112] For an incisive examination of this theme, see Dennis Showalter, "From Deterrence to Doomsday Machine: The German Way of War, 1890–1914," *Journal of Military History* (64) 2000, pp. 679–710.
[113] Robert Citino, *Path to Blitzkrieg: Doctrine and Training in the German Army, 1920–39* (Boulder, 1999); Geyer, "German Strategy in the Age of Machine Warfare," pp. 584–7; Williamson Murray, *The Change in the European Balance of Power* (Princeton, 1984); James Corum, *The Roots of Blitzkrieg: Hans von Seeckt and German Military Reform* (Lawrence, KS, 1994).

into a competition between ambitious field commanders, who continually drove their units ahead without any regard for their superior orders.[114]

The planning and actual course of operations for the invasion of the Soviet Union witnessed the merging of these two separate, yet related, issues, or, as Michael Geyer has so succinctly written, "Barbarossa showed the fusion of technocracy and ideology in the context of competitive military planning."[115] A military culture that demanded victory at all costs was now charged with defeating a much larger country, both in terms of population and land mass, in an extremely short period of time. In order to achieve this victory, the Wehrmacht jettisoned any considerations that could interfere: these ranged from rational military planning to humane treatment for civilians and prisoners of war.[116] Therefore, the operation was based on a "conduct of war that encouraged the uninhibited, strictly achievement-oriented use of force, unconstrained by the rules of war."[117] This campaign witnessed the culminating developments in both military culture and doctrine in the Prusso-German Army. In order to achieve victory, the army was prepared to use any and all means against the Red Army and Soviet society as a whole. The evolution of this particular technocratic military mind-set ensured that war against the Soviet Union would have been fought as a particularly savage affair even without the influence of National Socialism. The fact that the Nazi regime not only encouraged but demanded a brutal campaign radicalized already present tendencies within the army; ideology injected venom into an already bubbling cauldron, ensuring the army's complicity in the war of annihilation.

IV. The Wehrmacht and the Third Reich

The German Army's place within Nazi state and society existed on two levels, one of which has been well served by historians and one of which

---

[114] Michael Geyer, "Restorative Elites, German Society and the Nazi Pursuit of War," in Richard Bessel (ed.), *Fascist Italy and Nazi Germany: Comparisons and Contrasts* (Cambridge, 1996), pp. 144–5. These themes of competition, insubordination, and the emphasis on speed all clearly emerge in what is perhaps the finest example of operational history in print: Karl-Heinz Frieser, *The Blitzkrieg Legend: The 1940 Campaign in the West* (Annapolis, 2005).

[115] Geyer, "German Strategy in the Age of Machine Warfare, 1914–1945," p. 587.

[116] The literature on German planning for the invasion of the Soviet Union is enormous; three of the more important contributions are Ernst Klink, "Die Landkriegführung," in Boog et al., *Der Angriff auf die Sowjetunion*, pp. 246–328; Robert Cecil, *Hitler's Decision to Invade Russia 1941* (London, 1975); Stahel, *Operation Barbarossa and Germany's Defeat in the East*, pp. 33–104.

[117] Michael Geyer, "War, Genocide, Extermination: The War against the Jews in an Era of World Wars," in Jarausch and Geyer, *Shattered Past: Reconstructing German Histories*, pp. 111–48, here p. 138.

requires further investigation. In terms of the former, the relationship between the officer corps and the state has received a tremendous amount of attention and will not be covered here.[118] The breadth and depth of coverage devoted to this aspect of the army's relationship with the Nazi state has not been equaled by an examination of the Wehrmacht as a conscript army, or, in other words, its relationship with Nazi society. Any work that grapples with understanding and explaining the actions and, more importantly, the attitudes of German soldiers during the war with the Soviet Union needs to be mindful of the larger context of the Nazi state.[119] The men who filled the ranks of the Wehrmacht during the Second World War were not, by and large, long-term professional soldiers but were instead civilians drafted into the army during the late 1930s and early 1940s. Some attempt therefore needs to be made to examine German society during the Nazi regime and the effect the state had on both society and individuals. As previously mentioned, German mobilization practices tied formations to one specific *Wehrkreis*, or military district, and this allowed the division to retain a sense of *Heimat*, that untranslatable word that refers to a community, ranging in size from a small village to a region or even a nation, that shares a particular set of traditions and values, which the area's inhabitants believe set them apart from neighboring communities, regions, or states.[120]

As James Sheehan has argued, Germany was actually a rather decentralized state before the Nazi *Gleichschaltung* of the 1930s and the constituent parts of the Reich continued to celebrate their own unique cultural differences even following Nazi attempts to centralize and homogenize the state.[121] Thus the soldiers who fought in the Wehrmacht

---

[118] The two fundamental studies of this relationship remain Manfred Messerschmidt, *Die Wehrmacht im NS-Staat: Zeit der Indoktrination* (Hamburg, 1969); and Klaus-Jürgen Müller, *Das Heer und Hitler: Armee und nationalsozialistisches Regime 1933–1940* (Stuttgart, 1969). A recent overview of this topic is found in Hürter, *Hitlers Heerführer*, pp. 123–55. Other important works that touch on various aspects of the Wehrmacht leadership's relationship with the Nazi state during the early 1930s include Michael Geyer, *Aufrüstung oder Sicherheit: Die Reichswehr in der Krise der Machtpolitik 1924–1936* (Wiesbaden, 1980); Klaus-Jürgen Müller, *The Army, Politics and Society in Germany, 1933–1945* (Manchester, 1987), pp. 16–53; Wolfram Wette, "'Rassenfeind': Antisemitismus und Antislawismus in der Wehrmachtspropaganda," in Walther Manoschek (ed.), *Die Wehrmacht im Rassenkrieg: Die Vernichtungskrieg hinter der Front* (Vienna, 1996), pp. 55–73; and MacGregor Knox, *Common Destiny: Dictatorship, Foreign Policy, and War in Fascist Italy and Nazi Germany* (Cambridge, 2000).

[119] A point made by Gerhard Weinberg at the Southern Historical Association's 2009 meeting.

[120] For discussions of *Heimat*, see Celia Applegate, *A Nation of Provincials: The German Idea of Heimat* (Berkeley, 1990); and Alon Confino, *The Nation as Local Metaphor: Württemberg, Imperial Germany, and National Memory, 1871–1918* (Chapel Hill, 1997).

[121] James Sheehan, "What Is German History? Reflections on the Role of the Nation in German History and Historiography," *Journal of Modern History* (53, 1) March 1981,

certainly considered themselves Germans, but they also had strong, if not stronger, ties to their regional identities.[122] The relationship between home and front did not end following a soldier's entry into the Wehrmacht. In the age of total war in which the home front and the military front increasingly worked in a symbiotic relationship, events on one necessarily influenced those on the other, with letters between the two fronts serving as the primary link.

The effectiveness of German replacement policy during the war is intimately connected to this issue of the army's regional construction. Effectively functioning during the first two years of the Second World War, the system is widely viewed to have been permanently crippled by the 1941–2 winter crisis, as the army was simply too hard pressed to ensure the delivery of troops from home regions to specific divisions.[123] Divisional records suggest, however, that while the system did nearly collapse during Operation Barbarossa, it generally had regained its equilibrium by the second year of war and functioned more or less as it had been intended up through early 1944. Certainly in terms both of absolute numbers of men and of their regional origin, variations among the three divisions clearly emerge, yet the overall trends that can be identified point to a more robust system of troop replacement than has previously emerged in the literature.

At the basis of the army's appreciation of its own situation on the Eastern Front was its actual strength: how many men could it put into the field? Would the needed replacements be trained to a standard at which they produced value or would they merely serve as cannon fodder? This issue has also become an important one in the literature, with the prevailing wisdom centering on the continual weakening of the Wehrmacht due to manpower limitations. While this general trend is certainly correct, an analysis of these three divisions revises this view. During the course of 1941, each unit received far fewer replacements than casualties and it appeared that the entire system would shatter. During the course of 1942, however, recruits began to arrive in ever greater numbers at the front, a trend that continued on through early 1944. These fresh recruits were complemented by an increasingly large

---

pp. 1–23. Sheehan notes, at p. 21, n. 45, that "Germany, Europe's most fragmented polity, is treated as if it were a cohesive entity" during its period as a unified nation-state from 1871 to 1945.

[122] This is confirmed by the emphasis placed on a unit's social composition by German authors of popular military history such as Paul Carell and Werner Haupt.

[123] The most powerful statement of this position is found in Bartov, *Hitler's Army*, pp. 29–58, especially pp. 41–3. See also Kroener, "The Manpower Resources of the Third Reich," pp. 1001–28.

number of convalescents who returned to their former units, leavening the green newcomers with real experience in fighting the Red Army. The quality of these replacements also appears to be higher than previously thought as the army made real attempts to provide them with proper training before throwing them into battle. In other words, these men were not generally sent to the front like the hastily constructed and poorly trained *Volksgrenadier* divisions of 1944–5 but instead they received intensive instruction immediately behind the front established at either divisional or corps level. The infantry divisions that faced the Red Army in 1944, while certainly not rising to the level of those that had invaded in 1941, nonetheless remained potent formations, especially on the quieter northern section of the front where the Red Army remained dependent on its own foot soldiers.

V. Methodology

In an attempt to understand how both the army as an institution and the individual soldier understood and waged war in the Soviet Union, sources of several different types have been used. For the institutional view, the extensive collection of the Bundesarchiv-Militärarchiv in Freiburg im Breisgau was utilized. Here, divisional, as well as corps- and army-level, records were examined. These files allow for a detailed reconstruction of both operational experiences and practices of occupation during the war in northwest Russia. The most important source for analyzing the division's military situation are those produced by the Führungsabteilung (Operations Section), or Ia, as these files contain the war diary as well as the various orders the division passed on to its subordinate units. Materials generated by the ranking intelligence officer – Abteilung Ic (or Section Ic) – deal with the division's anti-partisan policies, propaganda, and troop morale, among other duties, and those of the Quartiermeisterabteilung (Quartermaster Section), or Ib, contain information regarding the division's supply situation as well as its policies regarding Soviet civilians and prisoners of war; in combination these allow for a piecing together of occupation policy. Finally, Abteilung IIa (Section IIa) was responsible for both tracking casualties suffered by the division and recording the integration of recruits into the formation.

Despite the obvious utility of such sources in re-creating the day-to-day existence of the divisions and their men, they are inherently problematic. First, the different diarists for the operations, intelligence, and quartermaster sections followed only a general set of guidelines for keeping their respective diaries. This led to situations in which one diarist describes daily occurrences in fine detail while another would devote only a vague sentence or two in recapitulation of the day's events. A further problem with the war diaries is that while all events – including negative ones – were supposed to be recorded in the war diary, the fact that the diaries also served as an "evaluation of the commander and the unit" led to a "conflict of interest" for the diarist; clearly, some developments never found their way into the war diary.[124] Finally, official German documentation necessarily skews the historical record. The seemingly complete and comprehensive Wehrmacht records frequently omit mention of atrocities; according to Wolfram Wette, an "awareness of wrongdoing" kept officers from fully recording events such as mass shootings and other war crimes in the official logs.[125] This "cleansing" of the records continued after the war when document collections were tampered with by former Wehrmacht officers, including the former Chief of the General Staff, Franz Halder, who proceeded to weed out documents that painted the Wehrmacht in an unfavorable light while working under the purview of the United States Army Historical Division.[126] Obviously, Wehrmacht records need to be vetted with care.

The Wehrmacht was not the only German organization present in northwest Russia. Both Hermann Göring's sprawling Four-Year Plan complex and Heinrich Himmler's SS-Police empire had representatives in the occupied east. Wirtschaftsstab Ost, or the Economic Staff East, was established by Göring to extract raw materials and foodstuffs from the occupied territories and both feed the *Ostheer* and transport the

---

[124] For excellent discussions of war diaries and their inherent problems, see Adrian Wettstein, "Operation 'Barbarossa' und Stadtkampf," *Militärgeschichtliche Zeitschrift* (66) 2007, pp. 21–44, here p. 24; and Römer, *Der Kommissarbefehl*, pp. 25–51.

[125] Wolfram Wette, *Die Wehrmacht: Feindbilder, Vernichtungskrieg, Legenden* (Frankfurt, 2002), p. 200.

[126] Wette describes the entire process of sanitizing the army's documents as "cleansing"; see his discussion in *Die Wehrmacht*, pp. 197–201. It is improbable that this practice worked its way down to the division level; the literal mountains of documents generated by the army at the levels of the High Command and the Army Group would have left little time for an examination of divisional-level files. On lacunae in Wehrmacht records, see Heer, "Verwischen der Spuren: Vernichtung der Erinnerung," in Heer, *Vom Verschweigen des Täter*, pp. 67–104; on efforts by Halder to present a view of the war favorable to the Wehrmacht see Bernd Wegner, "Erschriebene Siege: Franz Halder, die 'Historical Division' und die Rekonstruktion des Zweiten Weltkrieges im Geiste des deutschen Generalstabes," in Ernst Willi Hansen, Gerhard Schreiber, and Bernd Wegner (eds.), *Politischer Wandel, organisierte Gewalt und nationale Sicherheit: Beiträge zur neueren Geschichte Deutschlands und Frankreichs* (Munich, 1995) pp. 287–302; Wette, *Die Wehrmacht*, pp. 225–9; Smelser and Davies, *The Myth of the Eastern Front*, pp. 64–73; Gerd Ueberschär, *Generaloberst Franz Halder: Generalstabschef, Gegner und Gefangener* (Göttingen, 1991), pp. 92–101. According to Ueberschär, on p. 95, former General Geyr von Schweppenburg confirmed that "one or another of incriminating documents that could have been used in the Nuremburg Trials disappeared."

remaining surplus back to Germany.[127] Its long-term goals of ensuring continued production from the eastern occupied territories brought it into constant conflict with the army, whose short-term policy of living off the land played havoc with rational economic planning. The sometimes quite critical reports issued by this institution contain compelling and detailed accounts of army policies and their effects on civilians.

SS and SD units, organized as *Einsatzgruppen* and other police formations, also sent frequent reports back to Berlin. Local branches of the SD established headquarters and posts throughout the areas occupied by Army Group North and their communications not only highlight the institutional co-operation between the army and the SS; they also provide a different perspective on Wehrmacht policies than either the Economic Staff East or the army itself produced as their goals both overlapped and contradicted those of the other institutions. In sum, the combination of military, economic authority and police reports allows for not only a precise re-creation of what the Reich's agencies hoped to achieve in northwest Russia but also the reality of these policies once implemented.

This institutional – or "above" – perspective is both complemented and supplemented by sources from "below." Any analysis of the attitudes and beliefs of the soldiers themselves is dependent on diaries, letters, and interviews of the men as these are rarely discussed in Wehrmacht records. Diaries are especially invaluable as they trace the development of a soldier's thought across time. The most readily available source generated by soldiers themselves are the estimated 30–40 billion *Feldpostbriefe*, or letters which passed between the front and *Heimat*.[128] Numerous collections of letters have appeared since the end of the Second World War but it is only within the past fifteen years that scholars have made a concerted effort to analyze the contents of this rich source.[129] The first Wehrmacht Exhibition utilized excerpts from letters

---

[127] For more on the Economic Staff East, see Christian Gerlach, *Kalkulierte Morde: Die deutsche Wirtschafts- und Vernichtungspolitik in Weißrußland 1941 bis 1944* (Hamburg, 2001), pp. 150–6; Müller, "Von der Wirtschaftsallianz zum kolonialen Ausbeutungskrieg," pp. 172–7; Jeff Rutherford, "The Radicalization of German Occupation Policies: The *Wirtschaftsstab Ost* and the 121st Infantry Division in Pavlovsk, 1941," in Kay, Rutherford, and Stahel, *Nazi Policy on the Eastern Front, 1941*, pp. 147–84, here pp. 148–53.

[128] Klaus Latzel, "Feldpostbriefe: Überlegungen zur Aussagekraft einer Quelle," in Hartmann, Hürter, and Jureit, *Verbrechen der Wehrmacht*, pp. 171–81, here p. 171.

[129] Earlier collections include Anatoli Bolovchansky et al. (eds.), *"Ich will raus aus diesem Wahnsinn": Deutsche Briefe von der Ostfront 1941–1945* (Wuppertal, 1991); Orwin Buchbender and Reinhold Stertz (eds.), *Das andere Gesicht des Krieges* (Munich, 1982); W. Bähr and H.W. Bähr (eds.), *Kriegsbriefe gefallener Studenten 1939–1945* (Tübingen and Stuttgart, 1952).

and diaries to a great extent and this focus on the war of extermination continues to be the primary theme in published collections of letters.[130]

The primary methodological problem with such collections, however, concerns the question of representativeness. Is it possible to extrapolate the ideological belief of one soldier, or the content of even one letter, to the rest of the Wehrmacht as a whole? Does the use of a Nazi slogan in a message to a parent indicate that the soldier was inculcated with Nazi ideology? How representative of a soldier's mind-set is one letter? Only by examining a series of letters from one soldier or a collection of letters from specific, defined, and limited groups can scholars draw sound conclusions.

In an attempt to locate letters and diaries written by soldiers of the 121st, 123rd and 126th Infantry Divisions, several archives in Germany, including the Bundesarchiv-Militärarchiv, the Feldpostarchiv in the Museum für Kommunikation in Berlin, and the Bibliothek für Zeitgeschichte in Stuttgart have been utilized. While some source material was unearthed, it did not adequately present a clear picture of how these men viewed and understood the war. The analysis was therefore expanded to include other infantry divisions who not only originated in East Prussia, Rhineland-Westphalia and Berlin-Brandenburg, but who also fought under the command of Army Group North.[131] By keeping the variables of unit origin, combat experience, command structures of the army group, armies, and corps, and environmental factors such as terrain and climate relatively equal, the use of letters written by members of these additional divisions should provide a strong supplement to understanding the mentalities of the infantrymen under investigation.

Chapter 1 examines the relationship between the Nazi state and German society. Special attention is paid to the three *Wehrkreise* under examination, East Prussia, Berlin-Brandenburg, and Rhineland-Westphalia, and their cultural, political, economic, and confessional trends. Chapter 2 is concerned with the military, ideological, and

---

[130] See Hannes Heer (ed.), *"Stets zu erschießen sind Frauen, die in der Roten Armee dienen": Geständnisse deutscher Kriegsgefangener über ihren Einsatz an der Ostfront* (Hamburg, 1996); Walter Manoschek (ed.), *"Es gibt nur eines für das Judentum: 'Vernichtung'": Das Judenbild in deutschen Soldatenbriefen 1939–1944* (Hamburg, 1995); Walter Manoschek, "Der Holocaust in Feldpostbriefen von Wehrmachtsangehörigen," in Hannes Heer, Walter Manoschek, and Alexander Pollak (eds.), *Wie Geschichte gemacht ist: Zur Konstruktion von Erinnerungen an Wehrmacht und Zweiten Weltkrieg* (Vienna, 2003), pp. 35–58.

[131] The additional letters and diaries to be examined were written by members of the 1st, 21st, 61st, 206th, and 217th Infantry Divisions from East Prussia; the 23rd, 93rd, and 218th Infantry Divisions from Berlin-Brandenburg; and the 11th, 69th, 227th, 253rd, and 254th Infantry Divisions from Rhineland-Westphalia.

Methodology

economic planning for Operation Barbarossa and how the three newly raised divisions understood their missions. Chapters 3 and 4 analyze the divisions' advances during the summer and fall of 1941, while Chapter 5 provides a detailed discussion of the 121st ID's occupation of Pavlovsk during the 1941–2 winter. The discussion of Barbarossa concludes in Chapter 6 which examines the failure of the Wehrmacht to defeat the Soviet Union in one campaign.

Chapter 7 examines the radicalized behavior of the 126th and 123rd IDs during their fight for survival during the winter crisis. The shift in Wehrmacht occupation policy is the focus of Chapter 8, and Chapter 9 further details the development of a more conciliatory policy. Chapters 10 and 11 investigate Wehrmacht replacement policy and the major contradictions that existed within the concept of military necessity, while Chapter 12 looks at the dislodgement of the Germans from their positions around Leningrad to the abandonment of the Panther Position in July 1944, as German scorched-earth retreat signaled a new and all-encompassing expansion of the war of annihilation.

1 The Wehrmacht and German society

I. Nazi state and society

Perhaps the most important and vexing question regarding the Third Reich centers on the German population's support for and identification with the regime and its objectives: in other words, how successful was the state in constructing a *Volksgemeinschaft*, one united behind the regime and committed to realizing its goal of a wide-ranging ethnic restructuring of central and eastern Europe? Such an issue is certainly important when attempting to gauge how and why the Wehrmacht waged a war of extermination against the Soviet state and society; unfortunately, it is also difficult to ascertain. Scholarship stretching back five decades has reached contradictory conclusions regarding the German population's attitude towards the Nazi state. While an examination of this charged issue is neither feasible nor desirable in this study, some discussion of Nazi society is absolutely necessary to understanding the institution and its men who waged the *Vernichtungskrieg* against the Soviet Union.[1]

The notion of a "violent society," first formulated by Christian Gerlach, provides a solid starting point for understanding the relationship between Nazi state and society. Gerlach argues that within Nazi Germany, "a variety of policies and forms of mass violence were utilized against victim groups," and that while many of the perpetrators saw themselves as "functionaries of the state," this was a rather loosely

---

[1] For examinations of Nazism and German society, see Ian Kershaw, *The Nazi Dictatorship: Problems and Perspectives of Interpretation*, 4th edn (New York, 2000); David F. Crew (ed.), *Nazism and German Society, 1933–1945* (London, 1994); Lisa Pine, *Hitler's "National Community": Society and Culture in Nazi Germany* (New York, 2007); and Frank Bajohr and Michael Wildt (eds.), *Volksgemeinschaft: Neue Forschungen zur Gesellschaft des Nationalsozialismus* (Frankfurt, 2009). For more focused examinations of German society and the war, see Jörg Echternkamp, "Im Kampf an der inneren und äußeren Front: Grundzüge der deutschen Gesellschaft im Zweiten Weltkrieg," in Echternkamp, *Das Deutsche Reich und der Zweite Weltkrieg*, vol. IX/I, *Die deutsche Kriegsgesellschaft 1939 bis 1945: Politisierung, Vernichtung, Überleben* (Munich, 2004), pp. 1–76; Armin Nolzen, "Die NSDAP, der Krieg und die deutsche Gesellschaft," in ibid., pp. 99–193; and Jill Stephenson, *Hitler's Home Front: Württemberg under the Nazis* (London, 2006).

defined group that included far more than just members of the SS-Police or state administrations.[2] The most "stunning" find here, however, "is not the dominance of one specific group of those responsible, but just the diversity of backgrounds, experiences, education and age groups."[3] This broad range of individuals, prepared to utilize varying degrees of violence against targeted individuals and groups, suggests that "mass violence originates from complex processes deeply rooted in the society in which they happen or by which they are generated; they are not merely based on state policies and a rogue regime."[4] In other words, the Nazi state's use of violence resulted not merely from the government's policies but was rather an expression of the German population's attitudes and values.

Gerlach examines the widespread diffusion of violent beliefs in society by analyzing the Nazi campaign against "asocials" – a vaguely defined group of nonconformist citizens. This operation was waged by

> a small army of police and municipal authorities, public welfare officials, labor authorities, social scientists, pedagogues, and journalists [who] supported the regime's policies: mass arrests; reeducation programs, labor camps, restrictive labor legislation, and various policies addressing undesired migration, the "exploitation" of welfare services, and criminality.[5]

This example emphasizes the "broad and diverse support, which [was] based on a variety of motives and agendas that cause[d] violence to spread in different directions in varying intensities and forms."[6] Ideologues looking to rid the state of biological threats, police forces wanting to clamp down on crime, members of the intelligentsia attempting to solve society's problems, and regular citizens who wanted the "work-shy" or "vagrants" out of their neighborhoods all approached the issue from different perspectives but nonetheless worked towards the same goal. "Mass violence" became "the passion of the democratic age" and, simultaneously, "a peculiarly German passion."[7] These popular passions led to a "participatory" aspect of the violence endemic to the Nazi state, as the overwhelming majority of its population participated in the violence against various minority groups during its twelve-year existence.[8]

---

[2] Christian Gerlach and Nicholas Werth, "State Violence – Violent Societies," in Michael Geyer and Sheila Fitzpatrick (eds.), *Beyond Totalitarianism: Stalinism and Nazism Compared* (Cambridge, 2009), pp. 133–79, here pp. 134–8.
[3] Christian Gerlach, "Extremely Violent Societies: An Alternative to the Concept of Genocide," *Journal of Genocide Research* (8, 4) 2006, pp. 455–71, here p. 456.
[4] Ibid., p. 458.   [5] Gerlach and Werth, "State Violence – Violent Societies," p. 173.
[6] Gerlach, "Extremely Violent Societies," p. 460.
[7] Michael Geyer, "The Stigma of Violence, Nationalism and War in Twentieth-Century Germany," *German Studies Review* (15) Winter 1992, pp. 75–110, here p. 77.
[8] Gerlach, "Extremely Violent Societies," p. 462.

Such violence – first against communists and "asocials" and later against a multitude of groups, including the mentally and physically disabled, homosexuals, and Jews – was quite public. Nazi policies against especially communists and asocials were in fact predicated on appealing to traditional German notions of order and correctness and thereby they won not only support but even assistance in their implementation.[9] Knowledge of the "re-education" of asocials and communists was also broadly publicized in the Third Reich; the German press constantly referenced the concentration camps and their attempts to both reform wayward Germans and end the internecine street fighting that had plagued the country since the late 1920s.[10] This public awareness constituted an integral piece of violence inherent to Nazi society: intimidating the remainder of German society into conforming to the behavioral norms set by the state.[11]

What motivated ordinary Germans to participate in – or at least acquiesce to – life in a violent society? Two different, though at times interrelated, themes served as the popular basis for the Third Reich: ideological congruence and a broadly defined notion of conformity. Centered on the social Darwinist notion of a continual struggle between races for survival, Nazi ideology envisioned the Aryan German race waging a pitiless racial war against other inferior groups (such as the Slavs of eastern Europe) and eliminating Jewry, which it viewed as the most diabolical and threatening race.[12] While certain segments of German society agreed with such a Manichean view of the world, the regime recognized that the remainder of the country required additional convincing. This realization led to a multifaceted campaign designed to cultivate the "Nazi conscience" within the German population. The Nazi state "extolled the well-being of the ethnic community as the benchmark for moral reasoning"; in other words, a truly moral and ethical German living in the Nazi racial state would intuitively understand the necessity and righteousness of eliminating Jews and other undesirables from the body politic.[13] In order to transform the collective conscience of the German population, the state utilized the media, schools, youth and professional organizations, and academic research as the means of

---

[9] Robert Gellately, *Backing Hitler: Consent and Coercion in Nazi Germany* (Oxford, 2001), p. 91.
[10] Ibid., pp. 51–69; Detlev Peukert, *Inside Nazi Germany: Conformity, Opposition and Racism in Everyday Life* (New Haven, 1987), pp. 198–9.
[11] Gerlach and Werth, "State Violence – Violent Societies," p. 150.
[12] The best examination of Hitler's ideology remains Jäckel, *Hitler's World View*.
[13] Koonz, *The Nazi Conscience*, pp. 2–3.

disseminating its message.[14] This resulted in "expelling Jews collectively from moral consideration as human beings."[15] While such attitudes did not always lead to genocidal mentalities, the ideological saturation of the German population certainly resulted in the social death of the country's Jews.[16]

Bombarded by ideological messages and surrounded by true believers who worshipped at the altar of Nazism, many Germans simply "converted" and supported the regime with varying degrees of support, ranging from enthusiastic to resigned.[17] The desire to conform played an extremely important role in this process of conversion. The "appearance of unanimity" supplied the Nazi movement with its power and this same apparent unanimity "overwhelmed nonbelievers and prompted them to scrutinize their own reservations."[18] Most Germans, no matter their political inclinations, found something appealing about the new Nazi state, its national revolution, and, more tangibly, its promise to provide a better standard of living – even if the latter was based on redistributing goods to those the regime considered valuable from excluded groups at home and abroad.[19]

The interaction of these developments led to "the astoundingly fast and pervasive establishment of a 'National Socialist morality' that served as a 'benchmark' to 'define moral conduct' as well as other 'social values and norms.'"[20] The construction of this new value system ensured that violence – a central plank of the radical ideologies of the early twentieth century and in particular that of Nazism – was readily accepted by large sections of German society, including those age groups that would serve within the Wehrmacht's ranks during the Second World War.

---

[14] Burleigh and Wippermann, *The Racial State*.   [15] Ibid., p. 213.
[16] On the struggles to create the Nazi conscience in Bavaria, see Ian Kershaw, *Popular Opinion and Political Dissent in the Third Reich* (Oxford, 1991), pp. 224–77, 358–72. One of the most poignant and detailed books on the ostracizing of German Jewry is found in Victor Klemperer's diary, published in two volumes as *I Will Bear Witness: A Diary of the Nazi Years, 1933–1941* (New York, 1999) and *I Will Bear Witness 1942–1945: A Diary of the Nazi Years* (New York, 2001).
[17] Fritzsche, *Life and Death in the Third Reich*, pp. 36–7.
[18] Ibid., p. 24. The remainder of this discussion is based on this study unless otherwise noted.
[19] Geyer, "The Stigma of Violence, Nationalism and War in Twentieth-Century Germany," p. 98; Felix Römer, "Volksgemeinschaft in der Wehrmacht? Milieus, Mentalitäten und militärische Moral in den Streitkräften des NS-Staates," in Harald Welzer, Sönke Neitzel, and Christian Gudehus (eds.), *"Der Führer war wieder viel zu human, viel zu gefühlvoll": Der Zweite Weltkrieg aus der Sicht deutscher und italienischer Soldaten* (Frankfurt am Main, 2011), pp. 55–94, here pp. 63–8; Aly, *Hitler's Beneficiaries*.
[20] Neitzel and Welzer, *Soldaten*, p. 56.

II. *Heimat* and German regionalism

Despite this general acceptance of violence by large segments of German society during the 1930s, German state and society were fragmented along various lines when Adolf Hitler assumed the chancellorship of Germany on 31 January 1933. Politically, the sixty-two-year-old Reich was the culmination of Prussia's absorption of numerous states whose own political and cultural traditions dated back hundreds of years.[21] The settlement that resulted in the creation of the German Empire was one that devolved much authority upon the various kingdoms and duchies that were amalgamated into the new state, with the royal leaders keeping their positions following the proclamation of the Second Empire.[22] A rather weak federal system emerged at the top and while it dominated matters of foreign policy and war, regional power structures played a much larger role in the day-to-day lives of the German population.

The *kleindeutsch* solution to the German question, however, did not result in the creation of a unified German people who all subscribed to the same cultural norms and traditions. While the state certainly attempted to create "Germans" during the late nineteenth and early twentieth centuries, its efforts were complemented and, more importantly for our purposes, countered by a new cultural trend, known as the *Heimat* movement, which sprung up in various localities throughout Germany. The historian Alon Confino has described the *Heimat* idea as one "representing the permanent identity of the local and the national communities, the immutable in the ups and downs of German history, the core of existence in every German."[23] He adds that

> as one of Germany's responses to modernity, the *Heimat* idea was a memory invented just when German society was rapidly changing, as a bridge between a past and a present that looked uniquely dissimilar. *Heimat* looked to the past for reassurances of uniqueness on the local and the national level in times of political, economic, and cultural homogenization: it emphasized the uniqueness of a locality with respect to national standardization, and the uniqueness of Germany with respect to European and North American standardization.[24]

---

[21] Sheehan, "What Is German History?," pp. 18–20. For an outstanding examination of the development of smaller German states during the nineteenth century, see Abigail Green, *Fatherlands: State-Building and Nationhood in Nineteenth-Century Germany* (Cambridge, 2001).

[22] David Blackbourn and James Retallack, "Introduction," in David Blackbourn and James Retallack (eds.), *Localism, Landscape and the Ambiguities of Place: German-Speaking Central Europe, 1860–1930* (Toronto, 2007), p. 5.

[23] Confino, *The Nation as Local Metaphor*, p. 97.   [24] Ibid., p. 98.

The historic regions of Germany – ones "that took their identity from some combination of geography, topography, history, religion, dialect and economics"[25] – experienced a dual process of centralization and a celebration of their own uniqueness during the Wilhelminian period. The outbreak of the First World War temporarily led to a shared feeling of German nationalism among the general population; as the war slogged on, however, German society showed signs of fraying and the subsequent revolution and Peace of Versailles suggested that Bismarck's Reich was now a piece of history.[26]

This regionalism manifested itself even within the constituent federal German states. During the Weimar period, Prussia still remained the most important state, even if it failed to dominate the remainder of Germany as it had during the entirety of the imperial period.[27] In contrast to the popularly held notion that Prussian militarism was the state's most defining characteristic, the Prussian state actually proved to be the most vociferous advocate and defender of democracy in the fledgling Republic.[28] Subsumed under this vibrant support for democratic ideals and practice, however, the various regions within Prussia approached the Republic from very different vantage points, ones determined by their historical, economic, and cultural development.

III. "The bleeding frontier": the eastern provinces of East Prussia and Brandenburg-Berlin

While the silencing of the guns on 11 November 1918 theoretically ended the "War to End All Wars," events throughout central and eastern Europe, from the Baltic to the Adriatic and Black Seas already made a

---

[25] Blackbourn and Retallack, *Localism, Landscape and the Ambiguities of Place*, p. 13.
[26] On Germany and the First World War, see, among others, Roger Chickering, *Imperial Germany and the Great War, 1914–1918* (Cambridge, 1998); and Herwig, *The First World War*.
[27] For concise overviews of the Prussian state during the Weimar Period, see Horst Möller, "Preußen von 1918 bis 1947: Weimarer Republik, Preußen und der Nationalsozialismus," in Wolfgang Neugebauer (ed.), *Handbuch der preussischen Geschichte*, vol. III, *Vom Kaiserreich zum 20. Jahrhundert und große Themen der Geschichte Preußens* (Berlin, 2001), pp. 149–316; and Christopher Clark, *Iron Kingdom: The Rise and Downfall of Prussia, 1600–1947* (Cambridge, 2006), pp. 619–50.
[28] Dietrich Orlow, *Weimar Prussia, 1918–1925: The Unlikely Rock of Democracy* (Pittsburgh, 1986); Clark, *Iron Kingdom*, pp. 630–40; Hagen Schulze, "Democratic Prussia in Weimar Germany, 1919–1933," in Philip G. Dwyer (ed.), *Modern Prussian History, 1830–1947* (Harlow, 2001), pp. 211–29.

mockery of such phrases.[29] The bulk of the violence occurred in the areas formerly ruled by the Ottoman, Austro-Hungarian, and Russian Empires, but Germany's eastern borders also were sucked into the vortex of war. As the Great Powers worked in Paris to create new national boundaries in eastern Europe, the German government rushed troops, including Freikorps, to defend its now fluid eastern borders against the encroachments of the new national states of Poland and the Baltic region as well in an attempt to halt the spread of Bolshevism to the West.[30] The two most important political decisions reached at the Paris Peace Conference for the eastern provinces of Germany concerned the loss of chunks of previously German-controlled territory to both Poland and Lithuania. In addition to these territorial losses, the establishment of the famed "Polish Corridor" led to the isolation of East Prussia from Germany proper. The often violent and chaotic atmosphere that surrounded these border modifications at the local level led Germans from all walks of life and political orientations to view the entire region as a "bleeding frontier," a notion loudly propagated by the some 750,000 refugees of the former eastern Germany forced to head west.[31]

Certainly the shifting borders and emergence of new – and despised – nations to the east left a lasting mark on the psyches of all Germans in both East Prussia and Brandenburg. Political matters, however, proved only of secondary importance in determining the realities of everyday life during the Republic; here, the relative economic backwardness of the region asserted itself. Economic struggles were due in large part to the "area's peculiar structure."[32] Though German industrialization and urbanization had proceeded at an accelerated pace since the mid-nineteenth century, this process occurred unevenly across the Reich and the provinces of East Prussia and Brandenburg – with the significant exception of Berlin, which will be discussed below – remained traditional, agricultural societies with all that that implied.

Brandenburg was the largest province not only in Prussia, but also in the Reich as a whole, while East Prussia comprised the third-largest Prussian province and fourth-largest in the country.[33] Neither region

---

[29] For a survey of the violence that swept over this area as newly founded nation-states rose from the ashes of now defunct multiethnic empires, see Benjamin Lieberman, *Terrible Fate: Ethnic Cleansing in the Making of Modern Europe* (Chicago, 2006), pp. 118–58.
[30] Schulze, *Freikorps und Republik, 1918–1920*, pp. 101–201.
[31] Richard Bessel, *Political Violence and the Rise of Nazism: The Storm Troopers in Eastern Germany, 1925–1934* (New Haven and London, 1984), p. 6.
[32] Ibid., p. 7.
[33] Statistischen Reichsamt (ed.), *Statistisches Jahrbuch für das Deutsche Reich, 1932* (Berlin, 1932), p. 5.

possessed a large population, with East Prussia containing 2.25 million inhabitants and 2.59 million calling Brandenburg (exclusive of Berlin) home.[34] To put this into perspective, these two regions combined had only some 600,000 more inhabitants than Berlin alone.[35] Such low population numbers in these expansive provinces led to extremely low population densities: only sixty-one people per square kilometer in East Prussia while the Brandenburg population density was not significantly higher.[36] These numbers spoke to a society that functioned according to a more traditional rhythm of life, or, in the words of Ingo Materna, "Much that was old, traditional, which would have been regarded as museum-like long before the [First World] War in the large city, continued to thrive in the provinces."[37]

Agriculture remained the foundation of the economic and thus political and social structures of both states. In Prussia as a whole, less than 30 percent of the population toiled in the fields; the East Prussian agricultural workforce nearly doubled this accounting, for almost 56 percent of its working population, and 41 percent of Brandenburg's inhabitants, labored on the land.[38] Consequently, the majority of the population in both areas lived in small villages and towns; in East Prussia, over 60 percent of the population, and just under half of Brandenburg's population (excluding the Berlin metropolis), lived in communities numbering less than 2,000 inhabitants.[39]

What distinguished agriculture in the eastern sections of Germany from those in the west concerned the size of estates. While small-scale farmers not only existed but even prospered during the 1920s in southern and western Germany (especially during the hyperinflation), large-estate owners dominated eastern agriculture. In East Prussia, farms that consisted of 50–250 acres numbered 19,449, and those of 100-plus acres totaled 3,440. Brandenburg followed a similar trend even if its agricultural concentration failed to reach the level of East Prussia,

---

[34] Ibid., p. 15.
[35] More than 4.2 million people lived in Berlin in 1933; see Laurenz Demps, "Die Provinz Brandenburg in der NS-Zeit (1933 bis 1945)," in Ingo Materna and Wolfgang Ribbe (eds.), *Brandenburgische Geschichte* (Berlin, 1995), pp. 619–76, here p. 624.
[36] Statistischen Reichsamt, *Statistisches Jahrbuch für das Deutsche Reich, 1932*, p. 11.
[37] Ingo Materna, "Brandenburg als preußische Provinz in der Weimar Republik (1918 bis 1933)," in Materna and Ribbe, *Brandenburgische Geschichte*, p. 607. Shelley Baranowski, *The Sanctity of Rural Life: Nobility, Protestantism, and Nazism in Weimar Prussia* (Oxford, 1995), p. 67, cites one contemporary observer who noted that "the predominantly agricultural district shows a strong adherence to traditional customs."
[38] For Prussia as a whole see Möller, "Preußen von 1918 bis 1947," p. 225; for East Prussia and Brandenburg, see Statistischen Reichsamt, *Statistisches Jahrbuch für das Deutsche Reich 1942*, p. 18.
[39] Ibid., p. 15.

with 15,730 farms of between 50 and 250 acres and 2,025 possessing more than 100 acres. Such concentration led to tremendously large estates; in Brandenburg, for example, 35 estates controlled over 2,470 acres apiece.[40]

With such an emphasis on agriculture, it follows that the eastern provinces possessed a "relatively underdeveloped industrial base."[41] Outside of the significant exception of Berlin, the cities of the eastern provinces paled next to the size of the urban and industrial concentrations in western Germany. In East Prussia, only the capital, Königsberg, which some 296,000 people called home in 1931, and Tilsit, with its 57,000 inhabitants, numbered among the 100 largest cities in the Weimar Republic. In Brandenburg, the urban areas of Berlin, Potsdam, Brandenburg, and Frankfurt an der Oder all numbered over 60,000 people, though the latter three failed to reach the ranks of the largest cities in the Reich.[42] Some 35 percent of the Brandenburg workforce was, nonetheless, employed in industry, while a mere 19 percent of East Prussians labored in industrial concerns; the latter especially fell far below the 41 percent average for the German state as a whole.[43]

These economic realities proved fundamental in determining "a corresponding social mentality, which in combination with rural tradition and confessional orientation, influenced the political options for voting behavior or for membership in a political party."[44] The largest beneficiaries of this resulting atmosphere were the members of the large landowning aristocracy – the famous *Junker* class – that dominated East Prussia. With the central government's 1918 decision to postpone land reform in the region, the aristocracy maintained its traditional supremacy and this continued during the early years of the Weimar Republic.[45]

This social mentality has been aptly described as a "striking combination of militarism, austere sense of duty, religiosity, rootedness and patriarchalism [that] defined the society that surrounded it."[46] From a confessional perspective, Protestantism predominated in both East Prussia and Brandenburg, with some 84 percent of the former's population and 92 percent of the latter's registered to the Evangelical Church.[47]

---

[40] Materna, "Brandenburg als preußische Provinz in der Weimar Republik," p. 586.
[41] Bessel, *Political Violence and the Rise of Nazism*, p. 7.
[42] Statistischen Reichsamt, *Statistisches Jahrbuch für das Deutsche Reich, 1932*, p. 7.
[43] Ibid., p. 18.   [44] Möller, "Preußen von 1918 bis 1947," p. 226.
[45] Detlev Peukert, *The Weimar Republic: The Crisis of Classical Modernity* (New York, 1989), p. 30.
[46] Baranowski, *The Sanctity of Rural Life*, p. 14. While Baranowski's analysis is on Pomerania, her conclusions seem applicable to other similar regions.
[47] Statistischen Reichsamt, *Statistisches Jahrbuch für das Deutsche Reich, 1932*, p. 15.

"The bleeding frontier": Prussia's eastern provinces 43

A strict religious observance proved extremely important to the aristocracy as, according to the historian Shelley Baranowski, "their authority quite simply came from God."[48] Religion was interwoven into the daily lives of the elite and this filtered down the regions' social hierarchies, providing a strong cohesive bond between the various levels of society.[49]

This religious glue, in the words of a former East Prussian aristocrat, made the region's society "more paternalistic – or more servile – but at the same time it was closer and more personal, and there was greater interdependence; the parallel age groups of the upper and lower levels knew each other fairly well and this made for a peculiar amalgam of formality and familiarity." Baranowski notes that "reaching out to their social inferiors comprised one of the Christian duties that those of a higher station performed for those beneath them."[50] Such close links between the two groups led to correspondingly close political attitudes – here, an "unpoliticized conservatism" predominated among the majority of those Germans who worked on the great estates.[51]

Not surprisingly, politics in these two regions followed a consistently conservative course during the majority of the Weimar Republic. The old Conservative Party, former bedrock of the *Kaiserreich*, transformed into the German Nationalist People's Party (Deutschnationale Volkspartei), or the DNVP, after the war. While it included the traditional groups that supported the old Conservative Party – agricultural landlords, civil servants, army officers, and some captains of heavy industry – the party's message also focused on capturing the vote of the disaffected old *Mittelstand*.[52] Religious factors also proved important in elevating the DNVP to the position of power it enjoyed. The collapse of the monarchy not only removed the king as a political figure, but also swept away the leader of the Protestant Union Church.[53] This, in combination with the rise of the Catholic Center Party to a position of real power in the Republic, led many easterners to support a Protestant party that opposed the "Weimar system" and its attack on traditional values. For old elites as well as numerous members of the middle and lower classes of rural eastern Germany, the DNVP was the logical choice for their support as it

[48] Baranowski, *The Sanctity of Rural Life*, p. 68.
[49] One native of East Prussia recalls that numerous religious observances occurred each day; see Marion Countess Dönhoff, *Before the Storm: Memories of My Youth in Old Prussia* (New York, 1990), p. 17; Baranowski, *The Sanctity of Rural Life*, p. 68.
[50] Dönhoff, *Before the Storm*, p. 135; Baranowski, *The Sanctity of Rural Life*, p. 66.
[51] Baranowski, *The Sanctity of Rural Life*, p. 66.
[52] Thomas Childers, *The Nazi Voter: The Social Foundations of Fascism in Germany, 1919–1933* (Chapel Hill, 1983), pp. 40–1. The following discussion of the DNVP is based on Childers unless otherwise noted.
[53] Clark, *Iron Kingdom*, p. 638.

provided a vehicle for opposition to the Republic and its despised political and economic programs.[54]

In East Prussia, the DNVP consistently received the highest vote up through the late 1920s. In the Reichstag elections in December 1924, nearly 40 percent of the population voted conservative, and while this dropped considerably to 31 percent in 1928, it still received more support than any other party in East Prussia.[55] Voters in Brandenburg also gave the DNVP more support than any other party, with it receiving 32.5 percent in the December 1924 elections.[56] By 1928, the DNVP had fallen behind the Social Democratic Party (SPD), gathering 24.6 percent of the vote, a full eight percentage points behind the Socialists, but it still remained the second-largest party in Brandenburg.[57]

Nineteen twenty-nine proved to be the turning point for Nazi electoral support in East Prussia and eastern Germany as a whole.[58] As recently as May 1928, the National Socialist German Workers' Party (NSDAP) received just over 8,000 votes – a mere 8 percent of the total cast in East Prussia.[59] During the Provincial Parliamentary elections of November 1929, however, the party gathered approximately 40,000 votes and its size had expanded from some 200 party members in September 1928 to over 8,300 by the end of 1929.[60] This upward trend peaked in 1932 when the NSDAP became the largest party in East Prussia, grabbing 47 percent of the vote. Since the SPD finished second in the vote, one spot ahead of the DNVP, it is clear that the bulk of new Nazi voters were former supporters of the Conservative Party.[61] In the three Brandenburg electoral regions, support failed to reach such high levels, but the NSDAP nonetheless finished first with nearly 40 percent of the vote.[62]

Support for the NSDAP in East Prussia and Brandenburg did not result from a sudden identification with Nazi ideology; rather the structural economic crisis that plagued the large rural estates of eastern Germany

---

[54] Rainer Pomp, "Brandenburgischer Landadel und die Weimarer Republik: Konflikte um Oppositionsstrategien und Elitenknozepte," in Kurt Adamy and Kristina Hübener (eds.), *Adel und Staatsverwaltung in Brandenburg im 19. und 20. Jahrhundert: Ein historischer Vergleich* (Berlin, 1996), p. 185; Andreas Kossert, *Ostpreussen: Geschichte und Mythos* (Munich, 2005), p. 211.
[55] Statistischen Reichsamt (ed.), *Statistisches Jahrbuch für das Deutsche Reich, 1924/25* (Berlin, 1925), pp. 390–3; Statistischen Reichsamt (ed.), *Statistisches Jahrbuch für das Deutsche Reich, 1928* (Berlin 1928), pp. 580–1.
[56] Statistischen Reichsamt, *Statistisches Jahrbuch für das Deutsche Reich, 1924/25*, pp. 390–3.
[57] Statistischen Reichsamt, *Statistisches Jahrbuch für das Deutsche Reich, 1928*, pp. 580–1.
[58] Bessel, *Political Violence and the Rise of Nazism*, p. 21.
[59] Statistischen Reichsamt, *Statistisches Jahrbuch für das Deutsche Reich, 1928*, pp. 580–1.
[60] Lagebericht 31.12.1929, GSta, XX HA Rep. 240B, Nr. 9.
[61] Statistischen Reichsamt, *Statistisches Jahrbuch für das Deutsche Reich, 1932*, pp. 542–3.
[62] Ibid.

finally reached boiling point. As Baranowski has perceptively noted, "Economic hardship, which achieved disastrous proportions in the late 1920s and early 1930s, transformed the Prussian east's ingrained antidemocratic conservatism into a virulent and radical anti-republicanism that estate owners especially articulated."[63] The agricultural crisis of the 1920s squarely hit the eastern regions of Germany, causing both rapidly escalating numbers of forced auctions and spiraling debts for farmers.[64] When the German government failed to alleviate these economic problems, numerous voters saw themselves as thrown to the wolves by the state and looked for other alternatives.[65] The NSDAP appealed to these frustrated and allegedly betrayed landowners for several reasons. First, the antidemocratic ethos of the Nazi Party nicely gibed with a region that had always found democracy inherently unnatural.[66] Second, the Nazis' apparent understanding of the importance of agriculture and its associated issues – including the social stability of the region – led many former conservatives into the NSDAP's fold.[67] Finally, in the wake of Weimar's weakness in protecting German interests in Europe, the Nazis and their aggressive and shrill nationalism seemed more willing to defend both East Prussia – a German "enclave" in a sea of Slavic peoples – and the eastern borders of Brandenburg.[68] Nazism won support in the eastern, rural sections of Germany by exploiting the concerns that characterized daily life in the region, not by leading an ideological revolution in the area.

While the issues that affected Brandenburg and East Prussian society were strikingly similar, those affecting another piece of Wehrkreis III – the German capital of Berlin – dramatically differed. Unlike East Prussia and Rhineland-Westphalia, Berlin remained free from the incursions of foreign troops during the immediate postwar period. Dramatic internal upheavals, however, marked Berlin's history during the Weimar Republic. The birth of the Republic was proclaimed on 9 November

---

[63] Baranowski, *The Sanctity of Rural Life*, p. 6.
[64] Bessel, *Political Violence and the Rise of Nazism*, p. 8; Clark, *Iron Kingdom*, p. 640.
[65] Kossert, *Ostpreussen: Geschichte und Mythos*, p. 212. In an attempt to maintain German agricultural production in the face of competition from the newly founded countries of eastern Europe, the Reich and Prussian governments instituted programs known as the Eastern Aid Program (Osthilfe) and the East Prussian Assistance Program (Ostpreußen-Hilfe) during the 1920s. In terms of stimulating the economy, these programs proved relatively ineffective. They did serve, however, to strengthen the position of the landowning aristocracy. See Hans Mommsen, *The Rise and Fall of Weimar Democracy* (Chapel Hill, 1996), pp. 229, 286–7; and Peukert, *The Weimar Republic*, p. 121.
[66] Pomp, "Brandenburgischer Landadel und die Weimarer Republik," p. 218.
[67] Baranowski, *The Sanctity of Rural Life*, p. 150.
[68] Geschichte der 21. Inf. Div. Von Dieter Stein, BA-MA Msg 2/2779.

1918 by the socialist leader, Philipp Scheidemann, from the Reichstag building, the first round fired in what would be a tumultuous battle between the radical right, far left, and moderate middle for control over the city and, by extension, the nation.[69] By January 1919, the latent tensions between these various groups had exploded into open civil war in the capital, with Spartacist-backed workers rising up against a government forced to turn to the rightist Freikorps in hopes of quelling the unrest.[70] The unrestrained brutality of these freebooters culminated with the savage murders of the communist leaders Rosa Luxemburg and Karl Liebknecht on 15 January.

Another stage of class warfare opened up in Berlin in mid-March when a general strike and political violence initiated by the radical left led to yet more brutal repression at the hands of the Freikorps.[71] The balance shifted in favor of the moderate and the more radical left following a successful general strike that ended any chances of success for the Kapp Putsch, a Freikorps attempt to take control of the state.[72] Once the Republic stabilized during its so-called golden years, tensions in the city failed to flare up as frequently or as violently as they had during the early crisis years. It was during this period of relative political and economic calm that Berlin's social and cultural history radically diverged from that of the surrounding countryside. Instead of the reimposition of conservative power after the defeat and upheaval of 1918–19 that marked the experiences of East Prussia and Brandenburg, developments in Berlin led to it becoming the "capital of modernism."[73]

While Berlin had certainly been among the most culturally progressive cities in prewar Europe, the trauma of war and revolution unleashed a "cultural rebirth" that accelerated the avant-garde tendencies of the late imperial period.[74] A vibrant cabaret culture emerged that challenged traditional conventions of state and society while women defied prevailing gender norms.[75] New forms of media – especially film

---

[69] Gordon Craig, *Germany, 1866–1945* (Oxford, 1978), pp. 401–2.
[70] See Mommsen, *The Rise and Fall of Weimar Democracy*, pp. 20–50, especially pp. 33–40.
[71] Craig, *Germany, 1866–1945*, pp. 409–10.
[72] Peukert, *The Weimar Republic*, pp. 68–70.
[73] Alexandra Richie, *Faust's Metropolis: A History of Berlin* (New York, 1998), p. 325. For an overview of the topic, see Peter Gay, *Weimar Culture: The Outsider as Insider*, 2nd edn (New York, 2001).
[74] On Berlin's prewar culture, see Modris Ekstein, *Rites of Spring: The Great War and the Birth of the Modern Age* (New York, 1989), pp. 55–94; for the quoted text, see Richie, *Faust's Metropolis*, p. 326.
[75] Peter Jelavich, *Berlin Cabaret* (Cambridge, 1996), pp. 118–227; Katharina von Ankum (ed.), *Women in the Metropolis: Gender and Modernity in Weimar Culture* (Berkeley, 1997).

and radio – opened up different vistas for communication and thought.[76] Ideas associated with Walter Gropius's Bauhaus school soon manifested themselves in Berlin as the artists linked with this architectural movement began melding form and art into one insoluble whole in areas as diverse as housing and stage props. Perhaps the most famous of all Berlin artists during this period was Bertolt Brecht, whose plays' proletarian themes sharply criticized capitalist society.

Berlin differed from East Prussia and Brandenburg not only in terms of political events and cultural developments, but also in terms of size and ethos.[77] On 1 October 1920, the province of Brandenburg gave up 2 percent of its territory – the districts of Charlottenburg, Köpenick, Lichtenberg, Neukölln, Schöneberg, Spandau, and Wilhelmsdorf – and a consequent 44 percent of its population and, in combination with Berlin's six inner city districts, Greater Berlin was created.[78] With a population some four times greater than that of Hamburg, Germany's second-largest city, Berlin's nearly 4.3 million people dwarfed the number of inhabitants in all other cities in the Reich.[79] Despite the expansion of the city's boundaries, its population density remained the highest in the country, averaging more than 4,550 inhabitants per square kilometer.[80] Just as the low population densities of the eastern provinces spoke to an agricultural foundation, so Berlin's contrasting statistics pointed towards a much more industrial basis for the economy.

By the end of the 1920s, Berlin was an "industrial and trading metropolis of the very first range."[81] More than half of the Berlin workforce toiled in industrial concerns, making it the second-largest working class by percentage and the largest in absolute numbers in the entirety of the Reich.[82] What distinguished the Berlin working class from others concerned its radical nature. The largest branch of the German Communist Party (KPD) existed in Berlin, with one out of every ten members of the party calling the city his or her home.[83] In fact, one author has claimed

---

[76] Peter Jelavich, *Berlin Alexanderplatz: Radio, Film, and the Death of Weimar Culture* (Berkeley, 2009).
[77] In fact, the only real similarity between Berlin and the surrounding rural areas was their shared religious beliefs. Some 72 percent of Berlin's population was registered as Protestant. Statistischen Reichsamt, *Statistisches Jahrbuch für das Deutsche Reich, 1932*, p. 15.
[78] Materna, "Brandenburg als preußische Provinz," pp. 570–2.
[79] Statistischen Reichsamt, *Statistisches Jahrbuch für das Deutsche Reich, 1932*, p. 7.
[80] Ibid., p. 7.
[81] Christoph Kreutzmüller, "Die Wirtschaft Berlins," in Michael Wildt and Christoph Kreutzmüller (eds.), *Berlin 1933–1945* (Munich, 2013), pp. 83–96, here p. 83.
[82] Statistischen Reichsamt, *Statistisches Jahrbuch für das Deutsche Reich, 1932*, p. 18.
[83] Eve Rosenhaft, *Beating the Fascists? The German Communists and Political Violence* (Cambridge, 1983), p. 13.

that "after Moscow, Berlin was the largest Communist stronghold in the world," and while one may quibble with this assertion, that of one former KPD member who described the city as "the reddest of all cities outside the Soviet Union" seems utterly convincing.[84] This radicalism was reflected in the city's voting patterns. During the 1924 elections, support for the SPD and KPD totaled over 42 percent of the vote.[85] The Berlin electorate continued to migrate to the left during the 1920s and in the 1928 elections the SPD and KPD won nearly 64 percent of the vote, with the former gathering 34 percent and the latter just under 30 percent of all votes cast.[86] Berlin's politics became increasingly radical following the onset of the Great Depression and its shattering effect on the city's life. Unemployment ballooned from 31,800 in 1929 to an estimated 700,000 by April 1932 and this resulted in real growth on the radical fringes of political life.[87] While the NSDAP stunningly broke through in the 1932 national elections, its performance in Berlin lagged behind, as it finished third within the city at 24.6 percent of the vote. The KPD received the most votes – 33.4 percent of the total and majorities in nine working-class districts– with the SPD dropping to 27.9 percent.[88] Even at the height of the NSDAP's electoral success, one predicated on the Great Depression and the Weimar regime's inability to solve the crisis, six out of every ten people in Berlin voted for some variation of a leftist party.

When first offered the position of Nazi *Gauleiter* of Berlin, Joseph Goebbels famously described it as both a "morass of dying culture" and a "sink of iniquity."[89] He nonetheless took on the challenge of transforming "Red Berlin" into a National Socialist stronghold.[90] The result of this political assault was a headlong descent into mass street violence that marked daily life in the city's proletarian districts during the early 1930s; in many ways, the revolutionary fighting that characterized the early days of the Republic in Berlin was resurrected during its protracted death. The struggle evolved from one in which individuals brawled in pubs or beer gardens to raids designed to end in murder. A communist document from the period captures the violent polarization

---

[84] Richie, *Faust's Metropolis*, p. 386; KPD member quoted in Rosenhaft, *Beating the Fascists?*, p. 13.
[85] Statistischen Reichsamt, *Statistisches Jahrbuch für das Deutsche Reich, 1924/25*, pp. 390–1.
[86] Statistischen Reichsamt, *Statistisches Jahrbuch für das Deutsche Reich, 1928*, pp. 580–1.
[87] Richie, *Faust's Metropolis*, p. 391.
[88] Statistischen Reichsamt, *Statistisches Jahrbuch für das Deutsche Reich, 1932*, pp. 542–3; Rosenhaft, *Beating the Fascists?*, p. 14.
[89] Cited in Ralf Georg Reuth, *Goebbels* (New York, 1993), pp. 76–7.
[90] A micro-level examination of this development centered on the Stettiner Bahnhof area is found in Oliver Reschke and Michael Wildt, "Aufsteig der NSDAP in Berlin," in Wildt and Kreutzmüller, *Berlin 1933–1945*, pp. 19–32.

of grassroots politics in the city: "we must intensify this action against the Nazi barracks so far that it is possible for us, through our struggle and through the organizing of a mass-assault, which must develop into a mass-terror-action, to drive the SA-troops out of their murder dens."[91] The Nazis responded with calls to end the "Red Terror" and to destroy the "Red murder squads."[92] Even after the 1933 Nazi *Machtergreifung*, certain "worker districts" in Berlin, such as Wedding, Neukölln, and Friedrichshain, existed as red "islands" within the brown city and remained a thorn in the side of the Nazi regime well into the 1930s.[93] Clearly, individuals socialized within Berlin would bring far different understandings and perspectives to war than those from the rural areas of Brandenburg and East Prussia.

IV. The Catholic fortress: Rhineland-Westphalia

Just as the inhabitants of the eastern regions found their lives dramatically affected by the conclusion of the First World War and the Treaty of Versailles, so too did the population of Military District VI, Rhineland-Westphalia. In fact, the historian Klaus Pabst has argued that "more so than in the remainder of Germany, the peace treaty caused a decisive alteration of all political and economic living conditions, ones that still left their traces long after the withdrawal of the occupying powers."[94] These changes were due to French strategic concerns; fearful of a possibly resurgent Germany and wanting to maintain an offensive threat to Germany's industrial heartland – the Ruhr region – the French occupied the left bank of the Rhine.[95] Military control of the area, however, only scratched at the surface of French political goals in the region.

Along with various French politicians, Ferdinand Foch, the commander in chief of the French Army, supported the creation of a Rhenish state, independent from Germany proper.[96] Such machinations received real support from the inhabitants of the region. The divide between what the region's inhabitants viewed as "the politically progressive industrial, commercialized, urban and substantially Catholic west and the

---

[91] Cited in Rosenhaft, *Beating the Fascists?*, p. 15.
[92] Cited in Richie, *Faust's Metropolis*, pp. 386, 393.
[93] Rosenhaft, *Beating the Fascists?*, p. 13; Detlef Schmiecken-Ackermann, *Nationalsozialismus und Arbeitermilieus* (Bonn, 1998), pp. 70–1; Reschke and Wildt, "Aufstieg der NSDAP in Berlin," p. 32.
[94] Klaus Pabst, "Der Vertrag von Versailles und der deutsche Westen," in Kurt Düwell and Wolfgang Kölmann (eds.), *Rheinland-Westfalen im Industriezeitalter*, vol. II, *Von der Reichsgründung bis zur Weimarer Republik* (Wuppertal, 1984), pp. 271–90, here p. 271.
[95] Ibid., p. 275.   [96] Ibid., p. 274.

'Asiatic steppe' of Prussian East-Elbia" stretched back to the founding of the Reich and the turbulent years after the war seemed to offer an opportunity to break free from Prussian control.[97] Pabst notes that

> fear of socialist revolution in Germany, hopes for territorial or financial concession in the coming peace treaty, a strong opposition to the antireligious education policies ... in Berlin, and also the rekindling of the general resentment of Prussia and the influence of the otherwise French-bribed *Kölnischen Volkszeitung* led above all the civil service, farmers and portions of Catholic community to call for "Away from Prussia!"[98]

The most prominent German associated with this movement was Konrad Adenauer, the mayor of Cologne. While Adenauer never favored the idea of a completely independent state, he does appear to have advocated for an autonomous Rhenish state within the larger German nation.[99] Local Rhenish Republics, however, were declared in Aachen, Trier, Wiesbaden, Bonn, and Mainz in October 1923 and fighting between French-backed separatists and German forces was reported.[100] In the end, these dreams of an independent Rhineland fizzled out, but the popular support behind such a notion provided vivid confirmation that the German state still contained some rather deep political and social fractures.

The civil war that marked the daily lives of Berliners during the immediate postwar years also erupted in the Ruhr region in 1920. As mentioned above, a general strike was called by the political left that effectively ended the reactionary Kapp Putsch in Berlin. Emboldened by this success, workers in the Ruhr pressed home their attempts to secure the revolutionary gains of 1918–19 by organizing themselves in the Red Army of the Ruhr. This "last cry of despair of increasingly discouraged workers" was unceremoniously crushed by Freikorps units sent to the region who executed thousands of victims in their wake.[101]

French policies again intersected with German domestic issues in the region during the opening months of 1923. On 11 January 1923, French and Belgian troops marched into the Ruhr due to Germany's failure to fulfill several provisions of the Treaty of Versailles.[102] The population responded by implementing a policy of passive resistance. A general

---

[97] Clark, *The Iron Kingdom*, pp. 562–3.
[98] Pabst, "Der Vertrag von Versailles und der deutsche Westen," p. 279.
[99] Charles Williams, *Adenauer: The Father of the New Germany* (New York, 2000), pp. 152–6.
[100] Ibid., p. 152; Mommsen, *The Rise and Fall of Weimar Democracy*, p. 145; Richard Evans, *The Coming of the Third Reich* (New York, 2004), p. 76.
[101] Mommsen, *The Rise and Fall of Weimar Democracy*, p. 86; Evans, *The Coming of the Third Reich*, p. 74.
[102] Conan Fischer, *The Ruhr Crisis, 1923–1924* (Oxford, 2003).

strike, which the national government financed, complemented the inhabitants' opposition to the foreign troops.[103] It was soon apparent to Berlin that both policies were failures. On the one hand, the government's financing of the strike was an important factor in the rise of the hyperinflation that devastated Germany in 1923, dramatically worsening the lives of workers in the region; on the other, it was clear that continued confrontation with France would eventually lead to an independent Rhineland detached from the German state.[104] In the end, French troops withdrew from the Ruhr in 1925 and from the Rhineland in 1930. The left bank of the Rhine was only brought under German military control in March 1936 when Wehrmacht troops marched across the Rhine bridges in a blatant violation of the Versailles Treaty.[105]

Inhabitants of Rhineland-Westphalia therefore shared some experiences with those living in East Prussia and Brandenburg-Berlin. The imposition of the Versailles Treaty and the events of the German revolution and their reverberations affected Germans all across the Reich. Despite these overarching similarities, however, Rhineland-Westphalia significantly differed both culturally and socially from the eastern provinces. As the preceding discussion suggests, the areas within Military District VI were heavily industrialized and urbanized: "the existence and expansion of metropolitan conurbations and the continual urbanization" of Rhineland-Westphalia marked the region's existence during the first half of the twentieth century.[106] In stark contrast to the low population density of East Prussia and the Brandenburg countryside, Rhineland-Westphalia was one of the most industrialized regions on the globe, averaging 267 people per square kilometer.[107] While East Prussia contained only one city within the top twenty-five most populous in the Reich in 1932, Rhineland-Westphalia was home to eight of the nineteen most heavily populated urban areas.[108] Over 40 percent of the population lived in cities of 100,000 or more and a further 43 percent

---

[103] Peukert, *The Weimar Republic*, p. 60.
[104] On the deteriorating conditions facing the Ruhr working class, see Klaus Tenfelde, "Zur Sozialgeschichte der Arbeiterbewegung im Ruhrgebiet 1918 bis 1933," in Düwell and Kölmann, *Von der Reichsgründung bis zur Weimarer Republik*, pp. 333–48, here pp. 339–41.
[105] Craig, *Germany, 1866–1945*, p. 689.
[106] Heinz Günter Steinberg, "Die Bevölkerungsentwicklung Nordrhein-Westfalens bis 1970," in Kurt Düwell and Wolfgang Kölmann (eds.), *Rheinland-Westfalen im Industriezeitalter*, vol. III, *Vom Ende der Weimarer Republik bis zum Land Nordrhein-Westfalen* (Wuppertal, 1984), pp. 21–34, here p. 23.
[107] Statistischen Reichsamt, *Statistisches Jahrbuch für das Deutsche Reich, 1932*, p. 5.
[108] Ibid., p. 7. Of the ninety-eight cities in Germany with a population over 50,000, twenty-four were located in Military District VI.

lived in communities of between 2,000 and 100,000. A mere 17 percent lived in towns and villages with less than 2,000 inhabitants.[109]

Since the Ruhrgebiet lay within the boundaries of Wehrkreis VI, it is not surprising that a majority of all employees in the region – 52 percent – worked in industry or that over 51 percent of the working population was classified as blue-collar.[110] This concentration of workers ensured that the region experienced the so-called "golden years" of Weimar stability between 1925 and 1929 in different ways than did other Germans. Ulrich Herbert has noted that for the region's working class, "almost without exception, the years between entry into work during the 1920s and the beginning of rearmament in the 1930s were a period of poverty, described above all as a period of instability and insecurity."[111] The "immediate food emergency" that directly affected workers during the 1920s was survived in part due to the deep-rooted social milieus that served as a "counterweight to unstable relationships and future prospects."[112] Such milieus are familiar to labor historians and the growth of a workers' subculture in imperial Germany has certainly received a fair amount of scholarly attention. Developments here, however, differed from those in other areas of the Reich.

Working-class milieus that developed according to a top-down model have been generally identified with efforts of the SPD and its affiliated trade unions; in Rhineland-Westphalia, however, the SPD was "late in establishing itself."[113] Instead of the socialists, the KPD proved to be the largest workers' party in the region, drawing heavily on the younger generation of workers.[114] By the end of the 1920s, it had become the second-largest party in the region.[115] In Rhineland-Westphalia, however, religion proved to be much more effective in serving as political cement, binding large numbers of people together.

---

[109] Ibid., p. 11. [110] Ibid., p. 18.

[111] Ulrich Herbert, "Zur Entwicklung der Ruhrarbeitergeschaft 1930 bis 1960 aus erfahrungsgeschichtlicher Perspektive," in Lutz Niethammer and Alexander von Plato (eds.), *"Wir kriegen jetzt andere Zeiten": Auf der Suche nach der Erfahrung des Volkes in nachfaschistischen Ländern*, vol. III, *Lebensgeschichte und Sozialkultur im Ruhrgebiet 1930 bis 1960* (Berlin and Bonn, 1985), pp. 19–52, here p. 20.

[112] Tenfelde, "Zur Sozialgeschichte der Arbeiterbewegung im Ruhrgebiet 1918 bis 1933," p. 341; Herbert, "Zur Entwicklung der Ruhrarbeitergeschaft," p. 22.

[113] Alexander von Plato, "'Ich bin mit allen gut ausgekommen,' oder War die Ruhrarbeiterschaft vor der 1933 in politische Lager zerspalten?", in Lutz Niethammer (ed.), *"Die Jahre weiß man nicht, wo man die heute hinsetzen soll": Faschismuserfahrungen in Ruhrgebiet*, vol. I, *Lebensgeschichte und Sozialkultur im Ruhrgebiet 1930 bis 1960* (Bonn, 1961), pp. 31–65, here p. 31.

[114] Herbert, "Zur Entwicklung der Ruhrarbeitergeschaft," p. 23.

[115] Plato, "'Ich bin mit allen gut ausgekommen,'" p. 32.

Unlike the overwhelmingly Protestant eastern provinces, nearly 62 percent of the Rhenish-Westphalian population followed Catholic teachings and their religious beliefs played an important role in determining their political affiliation.[116] Political Catholicism was organized behind the Zentrum, or Center Party. Steeled during the *Kulturkampf* waged by Bismarck and Prussian liberals against Catholicism, the Center Party continued to represent the majority of the region's Catholic population up through the collapse of the Weimar Republic.[117] During the Republic's existence, the Center Party was the "dominant political grouping" within the region as it was able to draw upon individuals from a variety of "cultural associations, the Catholic-dominated multiconfessional Christian union, their youth organizations and, above all, parishes which were the most important 'cultural strongholds.'"[118] These Catholic organizations, including elementary schools, were absolutely vital in creating "the continuity and stability of a political culture required for continual nurturing."[119]

Most importantly for the electoral success of the Center Party, it was able to capture the support of a significant number of workers in the region. Just as trade unions funneled workers to the SPD, so did the two largest confessional unions in the region – the Catholic Workers' Union and the Christian Union – direct workers to the Center Party.[120] While both saw their membership decrease during the course of the 1920s, several hundred thousand men nonetheless belonged to the two unions during the Weimar Republic and membership in the former made it nearly "unthinkable" to join or support a political party other than the Center.

Of course, Military District VI was not one industrialized metropolis. The region was home to a relatively prosperous and stable peasantry that, in contrast to the large landed estates to the east that produced grain for export, depended on cattle and dairy sales within the local area

---

[116] Statistischen Reichsamt, *Statistisches Jahrbuch für das Deutsche Reich, 1932*, p. 15.
[117] Ulrich von Hehl, "Zum politischen Katholizismus in Rheinland-Westfalen, 1890–1918," in Düwell and Kölmann, *Von der Reichsgründung bis zur Weimarer Republik*, pp. 56–69, here p. 57; Robert Moeller, *German Peasants and Agrarian Policy, 1914–1924: The Rhineland and Westphalia* (Chapel Hill, 1986), p. 7.
[118] The first judgment is Karsten Ruppert's; see his "Der politische Katholizismus im Rheinland und in Westfalen zur Zeit der Weimarer Republik," in Düwell and Kölmann, *Vom Ende der Weimarer Republik bis zum Land Nordrhein-Westfalen*, pp. 76–97, here p. 76. The description of the Center Party's social and political reach is Alexander von Plato's; see his "'Ich bin mit allen gut ausgekommen,'" p. 34.
[119] Ruppert, "Der politische Katholizismus," p. 83.
[120] Ibid., pp. 83–5.

for their livelihood.[121] These farmers experienced the revolutionary events of the immediate postwar era in a very different way than did workers in the same area. Fearful of the socialist government in Berlin and its policies that seemingly favored urban populations, the political attitudes of the peasantry and its political associations continued to radicalize during the 1920s. Despite this rural–urban split within the region, the leading agrarian organizations in Rhineland-Westphalia remained wedded to the Center Party, a product of what historian Robert Moeller has termed "residual Catholicism."[122] This "emphasis on confessional ties, combined with a fundamental reluctance to allow political conflicts within the Center to reach clear-cut resolution, allowed the party to remain many different things to a highly diverse electorate."[123] Such an all-encompassing approach to its constituency allowed the Center Party to maintain its position as the predominant mass party in Rhineland-Westphalia during the Weimar Republic's existence.

Within the five voting districts in the Rhineland-Westphalia region, the Center Party's vote ranged from 22.5 percent to 48.5 percent of the vote in 1924, averaging nearly 35 percent of the total vote.[124] This share of the vote dropped to approximately 31 percent in 1928, with the SPD generally benefiting most from this switch in voter loyalties, though the KPD received the most support in the East Düsseldorf district.[125] This number held fairly firm even after the Nazis' electoral breakthrough in 1932 as the Center Party captured just over 30 percent of the vote. It was still the largest party in three out of the five districts, with the NSDAP and KPD each triumphing in one area. Hitler's movement, however, had now replaced the SPD as the second-largest party in the region as a whole.[126] While the Center Party remained the region's largest following the last free election in Germany, its continued electoral power was due to "the party's complete retreat behind its confessional standard"; the "Center Fortress" now primarily existed merely as the party whose political goals were too vague and general to inspire its constituency without being wrapped in the shroud of Catholicism.[127]

---

[121] Moeller, *German Peasants and Agrarian Policy, 1914–1924*, p. 4. The remainder of this discussion is based on this source unless otherwise noted.
[122] Ibid., p. 123. [123] Ibid., p. 137.
[124] Statistischen Reichsamt, *Statistisches Jahrbuch für das Deutsche Reich, 1924/25*, pp. 390–1.
[125] Statistischen Reichsamt, *Statistisches Jahrbuch für das Deutsche Reich, 1928*, pp. 580–1.
[126] Statistischen Reichsamt, *Statistisches Jahrbuch für das Deutsche Reich, 1932*, pp. 542–3.
[127] Moeller, *German Peasants and Agrarian Policy, 1914–1924*, p. 153.

V. Conclusion

The men who served in the Wehrmacht during the Second World War were heirs to two different legacies that both complemented and challenged each other. On a general level, these men predominantly were socialized during the tumultuous era of the Weimar Republic and the much more repressive and violent Third Reich. With many working their way up through various Nazi organizations and institutions, they clearly recognized the starkly presented view of good and evil that stood at the heart of the Nazi movement. While not each and every German became a fully fledged convert to the racist ideology propagated by the NSDAP, the violence inherent in the Nazi system engulfed all of German society and it became part of the everyday routine of numerous Germans. The ruthlessness and brutality that manifested themselves on the various fronts throughout Europe during the war were first revealed throughout Germany during the 1930s.

Underneath this larger identity as a "German," however, regional identities continued to flourish, especially during the crisis-filled years of the Weimar Republic. The experiences of the interwar years, ones filled with political, social, and economic upheavals, combined with the particular traditions and practices of a region to provide possible alternative identities to soldiers from these areas. In the case of East Prussia, an overwhelmingly Protestant and agricultural region, the population was more closely linked with traditional values, such as political and social conservatism. Rhineland-Westphalia, on the other hand, was a heavily industrialized and urbanized area where the predominance of the Catholic faith was mirrored by the political dominance of the Catholic Center Party. Brandenburg-Berlin fell somewhere in between these two regions, with its rural areas closely mirroring the social, political, and confessional patterns of East Prussia, and Berlin's industrial nature tipping it towards Rhineland-Westphalia. This combined with the region's Protestantism to give the SPD and the KPD the upper hand in elections. The importance of these various regional identities, practices, and cultures and whether they survived integration into the Wehrmacht and the experiences of the war on the Eastern Front are issues that will be explored in the following chapters.

2 Preparations for war

In the summer of 1940, Nazi Germany triumphantly stood astride the European continent at the apex of its power. Following the defeat of Poland, Germany turned west and, in remarkable campaigns that lasted a mere ten weeks, conquered Denmark, Norway, and the Low Countries, and defeated the "hereditary" enemy of France while forcing the British into two humiliating retreats from the continent. The beginnings of the Battle of Britain took shape following the conquest of France and, as summer moved into fall, the Luftwaffe rained destruction down on British cities. To the east, Hitler's newfound ally – the Soviet Union – seemingly worked with Berlin in dividing eastern Europe into spheres of influence, while simultaneously providing Germany with the delivery of much-needed raw materials and foodstuffs.

Despite this favorable military position, the German imperium still faced various threats. First, the determined resistance emanating from Whitehall ensured that Great Britain and its empire would remain in the war; such an eventuality gave second thoughts to those who remembered Great Britain's decisive contribution to German defeat during the First World War. Second, the Soviet Union pursued an increasingly aggressive foreign policy in the Balkans that clashed with German interests.[1] Finally, a progressively worsening food situation within continental Europe as a whole and in Germany more specifically undermined the Reich's actual power. Fixated on the experiences of the First World War – one characterized by the notion of total war – the Reich's military and political leadership paid special attention to the German home front. The trauma of 1918 in Nazi and German collective memory caused Hitler and his coterie to increasingly focus on the population's morale, an issue they closely linked to food

---

[1] Gabriel Gorodetsky, *Grand Delusion: Stalin and the German Invasion of the Soviet Union* (New Haven, 1999), pp. 23–114.

consumption.[2] It became clear to economic and military experts that one potential way of solving both the strategic and the economic issues facing Germany was to invade the Soviet Union, eliminate it as a potential ally of Great Britain, and exploit the country's abundant agricultural resources and raw materials.[3] This, however, was not planned as the conventional wars fought in the west; rather, the war against the Soviet Union was planned as a literal war of annihilation, one in which the Soviet state would be destroyed and its population severely decimated.

I. The German infantry's campaign

German strategic planning against the Soviet Union began during the late summer of 1940 after it became clear that the invasion of Great Britain would have to be at least temporarily shelved.[4] Hitler first spoke to Colonel-General Walther von Brauchitsch, commander in chief of the German Army, on 21 July 1940, about such an eastern operation, stating that its primary goal would be "to smash the Russian Army" with a two-pronged attack, with the northern force advancing through the Baltic states and the southern pushing into Ukraine.[5] Now having Hitler's general conception of the campaign, the army began its operational planning. The literature on this topic is extremely well developed and has analyzed the evolution of German planning in great detail.[6] The following discussion, therefore, will focus on the role envisioned for Army Group North, under which the 121st, 123rd, and 126th IDs were deployed, within the larger context of the invasion.

---

[2] Fritzsche, *Life and Death in the Third Reich*, pp. 39–40; Fritz, *Ostkrieg*, pp. 40–1, 359–60; Alex J. Kay, *Exploitation, Resettlement, Mass Murder: Political and Economic Planning for German Occupation Policy in the Soviet Union, 1940–1941* (New York, 2006), p. 40.

[3] Andreas Hillgruber, *Hitlers Strategie: Politik und Kriegsführung 1940–1941*, 3rd edn (Bonn, 1993), pp. 519–20. For an excellent analysis of the military-strategic reasoning behind Hitler's decision-making process, see Ian Kershaw's chapter "Berlin, Summer and Autumn 1940: Hitler Decides to Attack the Soviet Union," in his *Fateful Choices: Ten Decisions That Changed the World, 1940–1941* (New York, 2007), pp. 54–90.

[4] Gerd Ueberschär, "Hitlers Entschluß zum Lebensraum Krieg im Osten," in Ueberschär and Wette, *Der deutsche Überfall auf die Sowjetunion*, pp. 28–9; Jürgen Förster, "Hitlers Entscheidung für den Krieg gegen die Sowjetunion," in Boog et al., *Der Angriff auf die Sowjetunion*, pp. 27–68, here pp. 38–42.

[5] Franz Halder, *Kriegstagebuch: Tägliche Aufzeichnungen des Chefs des Generalstabes des Heeres 1939–1942* (ed. Hans-Adolf Jacobson) (Stuttgart, 1962–4), 3 vols. (hereafter *Kriegstagebuch*), vol. II, 22 July 1940, p. 32.

[6] In addition to the works cited in notes 3 and 4 above in this chapter, see also Stahel, *Operation Barbarossa*, pp. 33–138; Klink, "Die Landkriegführung," pp. 246–328; Barry Leach, *German Strategy against Russia, 1939–1941* (Oxford, 1973).

The fundamental problem within German planning for Operation Barbarossa concerned the *Schwerpunkt* of the campaign. From the perspective of the Army High Command and particularly that of Chief of the German General Staff, Colonel-General Franz Halder, Moscow needed to be the focus of the campaign. Initial studies commissioned by the Oberkommando des Heeres (OKH, Supreme Command of the Army) and Oberkommando der Wehrmacht (OKW, Supreme Command of the Armed Forces) all worked under the assumption that "Moscow constituted the economic, political, and spiritual center of the USSR. Its conquest would destroy the co-ordination of the Russian state," and therefore this should be the campaign's primary goal.[7]

Such views were not shared by Hitler. During a meeting with the army leadership on 5 December 1940, he declared that the central German force advancing on Moscow should be prepared to detach "considerable forces" to the north to assist in the destruction of Soviet troops in the Baltic and Leningrad regions.[8] Hitler's view of Moscow as a secondary objective with the real emphasis placed on the flanks was further clarified with the issuing of Directive 21 on 18 December 1940.[9] The directive called for a "quick campaign" to defeat the Soviet Union, one in which the mass of the Red Army would be defeated in no more than six to eight weeks before it could withdraw into the spacious hinterland of the Soviet state. The advancing Wehrmacht was divided into three army groups, with two located north of the expansive Pripet Marshes region. Army Group Center, the strongest of the German formations due to its potent contingent of armored and motorized units, was charged with clearing Belarus. Following this, "powerful sections of the mobile troops" were to turn north and assist the northernmost army group – Army Group

---

[7] The cited phrase comes from Major-General Erich Marcks; see his "Aus dem Operationsentwurf des Generalmajors Marcks für die Aggression gegen die Sowjetunion, 5. August 1940," in Erhard Moritz (ed.), *Fall Barbarossa: Dokumente zur Vorbereitung der faschistischen Wehrmacht auf die Aggression gegen die Sowjetunion (1940/41)* (Berlin, 1970), Document 31, p. 122. For the other key studies, see "Operationsstudie des Gruppenleiters Heer in der Abteilung Landesverteidigung im OKW für die Aggression gegen die Sowjetunion (Loßberg-Studie), 15. September 1940," in ibid., Document 32, pp. 126–34; Stahel, *Operation Barbarossa*, pp. 55–60; and Klink, "Die Landkriegführung," pp. 285–7.

[8] Percy Schramm (ed.), *Kriegstagebuch des Oberkommandos der Wehrmacht 1940–1941* (hereafter *KTB OKW*) (Munich, 1982), vol. I, 5 December 1940, pp. 201–9; Halder, *Kriegstagebuch*, vol. II, 5 December 1940, pp. 211–14; "Aus der Niederschrift über die Vorträge des Oberbefehlshabers und des Generalstabchefs des Heeres zur Operationsplanung gegen die Sowjetunion und die Stellungnahme Hitlers, 5. Dezember 1940," in Moritz (ed.), *Fall Barbarossa*, Document 34, p. 138.

[9] "Weisung Nr. 21: Fall Barbarossa," in Walther Hubatsch (ed.), *Hitlers Weisungen für die Kriegführung* (Frankfurt am Main, 1965), pp. 96–101. The following discussion is based on this document unless otherwise noted.

North – in destroying enemy troop concentrations in the Baltic states before moving on to secure both the important naval base of Kronstadt and the Leningrad metropolis. Only after completing these tasks were Army Group Center's mobile forces to be redeployed to the central axis of the front for the culminating drive on Moscow.

For Hitler, therefore, Leningrad was a high-priority target. Not only did it fit neatly into an apocalyptic vision of the struggle between Nazism and Bolshevism – as the birthplace of the 1917 Revolution, it possessed a certain fascination for the Nazi leadership – but it was also an important industrial center, an exceedingly important consideration in an era of mechanized warfare.[10] From his perspective, "Moscow was not very important" in comparison.[11] This, however, ran diametrically counter to Halder's strategic predilections and the two viewpoints were never reconciled.[12] Rather, the German Army that invaded the Soviet Union in 1941 was pulled in different directions by these divergent beliefs, with important implications for the course of the campaign. This tension between Hitler's and Halder's viewpoints proved especially problematic for Army Group North and its operations during the course of Operation Barbarossa, as will be detailed in the following chapters.

What both Hitler and the OKH unanimously agreed upon was the need for a quick, decisive campaign. Due to a strained war economy, German authorities placed a premium on speed during the planning for the invasion. Achieving such a victory, however, was not deemed an especially troubling issue by the German command; in fact, Berlin viewed the operation as mere "child's play."[13] This overconfidence rested on several factors. The euphoria of victory resulting from the stunning defeat of the French and British Armies during the spring of 1940 created an atmosphere of unbridled optimism that centered on the absolute battlefield superiority of the Wehrmacht. Complementing this belief, the military performance of the Red Army during its 1939 occupation of eastern Poland and the 1940 Winter War against the Finns seriously called into question its ability to wage a modern war.[14] Soviet

---

[10] On the ideological importance of the city, see Gerd Ueberschär, "Der Angriff auf Leningrad und die Blockade der Stadt durch die deutsche Wehrmacht," in Barbara Wenner and Antje Leetz (eds.), *Blockade: Leningrad 1941–1944. Dokumente und Essays von Russen und Deutschen* (Reinbek, 1992), pp. 94–105, here pp. 94–5. The Germans estimated that 16 percent of the Soviet armament industry was located in the city's environs; see Halder, *Kriegstagebuch*, vol. II, 18 December 1940, p. 236.
[11] Halder, *Kriegstagebuch*, vol. II, 5 December 1940, p. 211.
[12] For an outstanding analysis of this struggle over operational goals and Halder's willful deception of Hitler, see Stahel, *Operation Barbarossa*, pp. 70–95. See also Hürter, *Hitlers Heerführer*, pp. 222–47.
[13] Müller, *Der letzte deutsche Krieg*, p. 82.   [14] Klink, "Die Landkriegführung," p. 252.

operational difficulties seemingly highlighted the disastrous effects of Stalin's purges of the Red Army that culminated in 1937–8; some 47,000 officers were "repressed," including the overwhelming majority of its leadership down to the corps level, and this was observed by Hitler himself, who noted that "the Russian Army possesses no leadership."[15] Finally, at an individual level – both officer and rank and file – the Germans deemed the Red Army as strikingly inferior from a racial perspective.[16] Facing a military force that Colonel-General Alfred Jodl, chief operations officer of the OKW, described as "a pig's bladder, prick it and it will burst," the German High Command reckoned on a blitz campaign that would lead to the subjugation of European Russia in some two months' time.[17] The "old stereotype of a 'colossus with clay feet' ran like a red flag" throughout the documents generated by the Wehrmacht during the planning period and this feeling of superiority was woven into German conceptions of the upcoming campaign.[18]

Speed therefore formed the essence of the invasion, with the fate of the war largely pinned to the fortunes of German armor. The accompanying infantry, however, needed to keep pace with the panzer formations as they drove into the Soviet interior. Such was the task of the 121st, 123rd, and 126th Infantry Divisions, all of which were subordinated to Sixteenth Army, which in turn belonged to Army Group North. Commanded by Field Marshal Wilhelm Ritter von Leeb, Army Group North was charged with destroying the Red Army in the Baltic states, capturing the region's vital port facilities, maintaining contact with the northern wing of Army Group Center, and, most importantly, seizing Leningrad.[19] Leeb deployed his forces in accordance with these three tasks – Colonel-General Georg von Küchler's Eighteenth Army, situated

---

[15] For the effects of the purges on the Red Army, see David Glantz, *Stumbling Colossus: The Red Army on the Eve of World War* (Lawrence, KS, 1998), pp. 27–33; und Roger Reese, *Stalin's Reluctant Soldiers: A Social History of the Red Army, 1925–1941* (Lawrence, KS, 1996), pp. 132–62. For Hitler's appraisal of the Red Army, see Schramm, *KTB OKW*, vol. I, 9 January 1941, p. 258.

[16] For more on the German Army's view of the Soviet Union, the Red Army, und the individual Red Army soldier, see Hans-Heinrich Wilhelm, "Motivation und 'Kriegsbild' deutscher Generale und Offiziere im Krieg gegen die Sowjetunion," in Jahn and Rürup (eds.), *Erobern und Vernichten*, pp. 153–82; Andreas Hillgruber, "Das Russland-Bild der führenden deutschen Militärs vor Beginn des Angriffs auf die Sowjetunion," in Hillgruber, *Die Zerstörung Europas: Beiträge zur Weltkriegsepoche 1914 bis 1945* (Frankfurt am Main and Berlin, 1988), pp. 256–71, and Wette, *Die Wehrmacht*, pp. 14–34, especially pp. 32–4.

[17] Walter Warlimont, *Inside Hitler's Headquarters, 1939–1945* (Novato, 1964), p. 140.

[18] Hürter, *Hitlers Heerführer*, p. 229.

[19] "Aufmarschweisung OKH vom 31.1.1941: Barbarossa," printed in Halder, *Kriegstagebuch*, vol. II, pp. 463–9.

on the left flank of the army group, was to drive through the Baltic states while on the right flank, Colonel-General Ernst Busch's Sixteenth Army was given the responsibility of advancing on Novgorod and Staraia Russa while preserving a common front with Army Group Center. Most importantly, each infantry army needed to provide flank support for Colonel-General Erich Hoepner's Panzer Group 4 and its push on Leningrad while simultaneously dealing with the Red Army units bypassed or scattered by the advancing armor.[20] Küchler, in fact, instructed his division commanders that only a "blitz victory" could be considered a success and therefore "Russian resistance needed to be broken quickly."[21] To accomplish its mission, the army group placed high demands on its marching infantry divisions. In order to fulfill these tasks, the German infantry required both steadfast leadership and reliable equipment as well as young, motivated soldiers prepared to suffer the hardships of a blitz campaign.

When war broke out in 1939, a German infantry division officially consisted of 17,734 men.[22] In a 1941 manual for reserve officers and officer candidates, the division was defined as

the smallest piece of the army that, based on its own composition, is capable of operational combat activity. The infantry division of modern military powers is ordinarily composed of: 3 infantry regiments, 1 anti-tank section, 1 light and 1 heavy artillery regiment, 1 reconnaissance section, 1 engineer battalion, 1 communications section, [and] complementary units. To these belong the rear-area services: the supply service, consisting of columns and parts; medical service, consisting of medical companies and motorized ambulances; a veterinary service with horse hospitals; administrative service; and security forces.[23]

As this breakdown of the division's structure makes clear, combat remained its paramount function:

the combat divisions of the Wehrmacht were so organized that nearly everything concentrated on its one task, on the bringing about of a military decision. Everything else stood behind this. Even functions that a military system was actually dependent upon, functions of an economic or political type, were at least for average German combat divisions reduced to only the bare necessity.[24]

---

[20] Klink, "Die Landkriegsführung," p. 550.
[21] "Notizen des Oberbefehlshaber der 18. Armee, Generaloberst von Küchler, für eine Vortag vor seinen Divisionskommandeuren am 25. April 1941," in Hans-Heinrich Wilhelm, *Rassenpolitik und Kriegführung: Sicherheitspolizei und Wehrmacht in Polen und in der Sowjetunion 1939–1942* (Passau, 1991), pp. 133–9, here pp. 135–6.
[22] Hartmann, *Wehrmacht im Ostkrieg*, p. 32.
[23] Quoted in Rass, *Menschenmaterial*, p. 48.
[24] Hartmann, *Wehrmacht im Ostkrieg*, p. 42.

This striking emphasis on combat operations meant that the German Army's "teeth-to-tail ratio" stood at 89.4 percent in 1939 and 89.7 percent in 1944.[25] Due to such a focus on operations, frontline divisions' "center of gravity" remained steadfastly based on their three infantry and one artillery regiments.[26]

While maintaining its traditional role as the "'primary branch' of the German Army" following the First World War, the infantry arm was now integrated into a much larger combined-arms force that served as the basis for German operations during the Second World War.[27] The *Truppenführung* (Unit Command), published in two parts in 1933 and 1934, highlighted the emphasis on mobility that characterized German operations during the Second World War.[28] Infantry divisions were required to be mobile on both the offensive and defensive and, as German "blitzkrieg" tactics developed during the campaigns that subjugated Poland, France, the Low Countries, and finally Yugoslavia and Greece, the ability to keep pace with armored formations became an increasingly important piece of their operational tasks. As a consequence, infantry divisions became increasingly mobile and equipped with more powerful weapons up through the opening years of the war.[29] The expansion of hostilities into North Africa and especially the Soviet Union, however, stretched the resources of the German Reich to their breaking point and infantry divisions found themselves increasingly underequipped in comparison to their adversaries. This was certainly true in the case of antitank weapons and air defenses.[30] Perhaps the largest structural weakness of the German infantry during the Second World War was its overwhelming reliance on horses to drag its supplies and artillery.[31] Since an infantry division consumed some 170 tons of supplies a day, ranging from food to ammunition, this dependence on horse-drawn supplies clearly limited its speed and mobility, thus rendering its tasks increasingly difficult to complete.[32]

A final point needs to be made concerning German infantry divisions. While divisions established before the war tended to fill out at nearly 18,000 men and carried the full complement of subunits, those formed during the conflict failed to reach these heights. Christian Hartmann's

---

[25] Martin van Creveld, *Fighting Power: German and U.S. Army Performance, 1939–1945* (Westport, 1982), pp. 53–4.
[26] Hartmann, *Wehrmacht im Ostkrieg*, p. 32.
[27] Ibid., p. 34; Mattias Strohn, *The German Army and the Defence of the Reich: Military Doctrine and the Conduct of the Defensive Battle 1918–1939* (Cambridge, 2011), pp. 188, 193.
[28] Strohn, *The German Army and the Defence of the Reich*, p. 191.
[29] Hartmann, *Wehrmacht im Ostkrieg*, p. 34.   [30] Ibid., p. 35.
[31] Müller, *Der letzte deutsche Krieg*, p. 84.   [32] Hartmann, *Wehrmacht im Ostkrieg*, p. 39.

analysis of five German divisions on the Eastern Front clearly shows the differences in striking power between infantry divisions. While the 45th Infantry Division, formed in April 1938 and characterized as a "professional, average combat division," came extremely close to meeting the requirements of a prewar division, the 296th Infantry Division constructed in February 1940 did not.[33] Despite possessing some 17,000 men, it lacked several important subunits, including a reconnaissance section and an engineer battalion. More importantly, the few vehicles that it did possess were of British and French origin; locating spare parts for such vehicles when they broke down would prove to be near impossible.[34] Clearly, those divisions created in later mobilization waves would find it even more difficult to meet infantry division guidelines.

The 121st, 123rd, and 126th Infantry Divisions were three of the ten total divisions created on 10 October 1940 during the eleventh mobilization wave that itself was a piece of a much larger construction process for a 180-division-strong army needed for the invasion of the Soviet Union.[35] Each division initially consisted of approximately two-thirds men with prior service and one-third green recruits, totaling some 13,000 men one month later.[36] In terms of age, however, eleventh-wave formations were older than units previously mobilized, reaching a maximum age of thirty-two for reservists integrated into the unit. Obviously, the addition of older men to combat units was viewed unfavorably by professional officers as these men tended to be married with children and therefore were considered to be much less interested in dying for their country.

The quality of the fresh recruits and called-up reserves joining these infantry divisions consequently varied considerably. The commander of the 121st ID noted that "the composition of I[nfantry] R[egiment] 405 and I[nfantry] R[egiment] 407, including officers, NCOs as well as the men appears to be especially good. Very young, good-looking officer

---

[33] Ibid., p. 54.   [34] Ibid., p. 55.
[35] Oberkommando des Heeres, Chef H Rüst und BdE, AHA Ia (I) Nr. 2891/40 g.k., 2.10.1940, Betr.: Aufstellung von Divisionen 11. Welle, BA-MA RH 26–123/172. See also Georg Tessin, *Verbände und Truppen der deutschen Wehrmacht und Waffen SS 1939–1945*, vol. VI, *Die Landstreitkräfte 71–130* (Onasbrück, 1972), pp. 286–7; 298–9; 313–14.
[36] 126 ID, Zustandsbericht, 15.11.40, BA-MA, RH 26–126/3. Eleven days after its establishment, the 123rd ID reported that 7,907 men had previously served in the ranks; 123 ID, Abt. Ib–Az. Aufst., 16.10.1940, BA-MA RH 26–123/3. The 121st ID noted that two-thirds of its men were of prior service; see Stellv. Generalkommando X (Wehrkreiskommando X), Abt. Ib, mob Nr. 4150/40 g., 16.10.40, Betr.: Aufstellung der 121. Inf. Division, BA-MA RH 26–121/2.

corps. Young, strong men, without exception." In the case of the third infantry regiment – the 408th – however,

> the '*Menschenmaterial*' of the men appears to be somewhat worse. There are more older men than in the other regiments. There is, in addition, only a very small percentage that truly desire to see action. The reason for this lay in the sending of poor replacements from the *Ersatz* troop section during the establishment of the division.[37]

The 126th ID's commander also reported some problems with his recruits. While he characterized the enlisted men "as young, fresh and in good spirit" and his NCOs as "good," he received two artillery officers who were more than fifty years old; such a situation was "intolerable." He also complained that the officers for one of his infantry regiments simply did not meet a high enough standard.[38]

The concerns that the 126th ID commander had about the quality of officers assigned to his division reflected a larger problem that afflicted the Wehrmacht as a whole. The seemingly endless expansion of the army since 1935 had produced a diluted officer corps and this process had only worsened with the outbreak of war: over 37,000 new officers had been created between September 1939 and September 1940. The establishment of a further ten divisions in October 1940 exacerbated an already strained system, and consequently increasing numbers of lesser-trained officers entered the army's ranks. While the mechanized and motorized divisions perhaps suffered the most from the lack of a well-trained and technically competent cadre, infantry divisions further down the hierarchy were forced to make do with reserve field officers whose last term of service had been during the Great War.

In addition to problems with leadership and poorly motivated recruits, all three infantry divisions' equipment compared quite unfavorably to some of their sister formations. Rolf-Dieter Müller has aptly described the German *Ostheer* as resembling a "European military museum" as the Germans utilized vehicles and other equipment from the armories of occupied Europe.[39] Five panzer divisions that took part in the initial invasion of the Soviet Union in June 1941 were primarily outfitted with Czechoslovakian 38(t) tanks; if even the elite panzer arm was forced to go to war with foreign equipment, it comes as little surprise that eleventh-wave infantry divisions also made do with such vehicles.[40] Not

---

[37] 121st ID, Kriegstagebuch (hereafter KTB), 3.6.41, BA-MA RH 26–121/3.
[38] 126 ID, Zustandsbericht, 15.11.40, BA-MA RH 26–126/3.
[39] Müller, *Der letzte deutsche Krieg, 1939–1945*, p. 84.
[40] Müller, "Von der Wirtschaftsallianz zum kolonialen Ausbeutungskrieg," p. 226; Mueller-Hillebrand, *Das Heer, 1933–1945: Entwicklung des organisatorischen Aufbaues*, vol. II, p. 170.

surprisingly, each of these units was entirely equipped with French armored cars, trucks, and a sprinkling of tracked vehicles for the antitank units; such a development made locating sufficient spare parts extremely problematic during the campaign.[41]

Despite the cannibalization of prostrate European armies for its own benefit, the Wehrmacht proved unable to properly arm all of its units. By February 1941 (the last date for which complete data exists), only one division – the 121st ID – was considered "fully prepared for action" despite possessing "considerable gaps" in terms of personnel and matériel as well as its training status; such a positive assessment only highlighted the relative weakness of other units from the same wave.[42] The German High Command considered both the 123rd and 126th IDs "unprepared for action," with the latter suffering a crippling shortage of equipment. It was with divisions that suffered both personnel and matériel deficiencies that the Wehrmacht went to war in June 1941.

While the Wehrmacht faced deep-rooted problems in terms of equipment and manpower, it consciously attempted to ease the psychological burden on its soldiers by constructing units from specific regions and thereby re-creating an ever-present, if admittedly muted, feeling of *Heimat* in the ranks. Building on the lessons of the First World War, but also paying close attention to the real regional differences that existed in Germany, the army tied units to military districts in hopes that a shared political, social, and cultural background would help to insulate the troops from the rigors and horrors of industrial war.[43]

Between 1935 and 1941, the army called up its classes of recruits from a specific *Wehrkreis* and, after providing them with a basic training course, sent them to the divisions via march battalions. Commanded by either officers of the division sent to pick up the march battalions or by previously wounded men returning to their home unit, these units, initially numbering 1,000 men, provided a sense of security as well as a type of introduction for the recruits to their new military home.[44] Maintaining the regional homogeneity of each unit proved increasingly

---

[41] Müller, "Von der Wirtschaftsallianz zum kolonialen Ausbeutungskrieg," pp. 225–6; Klink, "Die Landkriegführung," p. 314.
[42] See the table "Stand der Einsatzbereitschaft der Divisionene der Heeresgruppe C (Reich) zwischen dem 20.11.1940 und 20.3.1941," in Kroener, "Die personellen Ressourcen," p. 852. The remainder of this discussion is based on this source unless otherwise noted.
[43] Creveld, *Fighting Power*, p. 45; Christoph Rass, "Das Sozialprofil von Kampfverbänden des deutschen Heeres 1939 bis 1945," in Echternkamp, *Die deutsche Kriegsgesellschaft 1939 bis 1945: Politisierung, Vernichtung, Überleben*, pp. 641–741, here pp. 680–2; Stephen Fritz, *Frontsoldaten* (Lexington, 1996), pp. 157–8.
[44] Creveld, *Fighting Power*, p. 75.

difficult during the war due to increasing casualty rates and other demands made on the Reich's human resources, but it nonetheless remains an important component in explaining the combat effectiveness of German divisions.

Of the three divisions, only the 121st ID documented its regional composition. In February 1941, the division commander reported that 80 percent of the division hailed from East Prussia, while an additional 15 percent called Rhineland-Westphalia home.[45] In order to get some sense of who filled the ranks of the 126th and 123rd IDs, company-level records are needed. In the case of the 126th ID, the first battalions from the first companies in the 422nd and 424th Infantry Regiments contained a total 372 men, with well over half originating from Wehrkreis VI, the division's primary area of recruitment.[46] Of the 372 men in the first companies of the 415th and 416th Infantry Regiments' first battalions, 46 percent originated in Wehrkreis III, by far the majority within the two companies.[47] In all three cases, therefore, each unit was centered on one dominant regional group and this acted as "a positive influence on the cohesion and both the performance and ability to suffer [*Leidensfähigkeit*] of the soldiers."[48]

While the Wehrmacht recognized a fundamental utility in creating regionally homogeneous units, it is also clear that such feelings of solidarity were extremely important to the men themselves.[49] One member of the East Prussian 21st ID expounded on what being an East Prussian meant during a period of war. After discussing the "close personal

---

[45] Tätigkeitsbericht Kdo. 121. Inf.-Division (Fü-Abt.) vom 5.10.40 bis 14.2.41, BA-MA RH 26–121/2.

[46] See the series of reports 1. Inf.Regt.422 (1./I.R. 422) Erkennungsmarkenverzeichnis (Veränderungsmeldung), dated 7 July 1941 to 8 December 1941, WASt, 82026; 2. Inf. Regt.424 Veränderungsmeldung zur Liste der ausgegebenen Erkennungsmarken, 7 August 1941 through 10 December 1941, WASt, 82066.

[47] For the 1.1/415, see the series of reports beginning with Erkennungsmarken Nachweise der 1./IR 415 (ehem. 9. Inf. Regt. 9) to 1. Kompanie Infanterie-Regiment 415 Erkennungsmarkenverzeichnis /Veränderungsmeldung/ 10.6.1941, WASt, 80744. For the 1.1/416, see the initial 1. Kompanie Inf.Rgt.416 (Bisher 9./IR 67) report to the June 1941 memo: 1. Kompanie Inf.Rgt.416 1. Bataillon Erkennungsmarkenverzeichnis Veränderungsmeldung 7. Juni 1941.

[48] Rass, *Menschenmaterial*, p. 107.

[49] Walther Manoschek argues that the Wehrmacht deliberately placed units disproportionately composed of Austrians in occupied Serbia as Hitler and the High Command believed these men better understood the Serbian mentality than soldiers from Germany proper; see Manoschek, *Die Wehrmacht in Rassenkrieg*, pp. 142–67, here pp. 145–6. Ben Shepherd's recent examination of the German Army's anti-partisan policy in Yugoslavia develops this point much further; see his *Terror in the Balkans* (Cambridge, 2012). In his study of occupied Greece, Mark Mazower, *Inside Hitler's Greece*, pp. 158–9, also argues that the Germans deliberately used Austrian commanders in Greece due to their familiarity with the Balkans.

and social ties" between an East Prussian division and East Prussian society, he stated that

> the political border problem of the exclave East Prussia, the East Prussian lifestyle and character, the East Prussian joy of military service, the conservatism and persistence of this tribe were found in the spiritual foundations of its work as well as its expression, as the spiritual alertness of all of their essential components and the philosophical thoroughness of Immanuel Kant's *Heimat*.[50]

Such a belief in the uniqueness of their region's character typified the attitudes of many German soldiers. This cultural distinctiveness ensured a degree of cohesion between men native to the same area. During the initial meeting of the recently formed 121st ID's Communications Section, the soldiers from two different East Prussian units being merged into the new formation eyed each other warily. Over "beer and schnapps," however, they exchanged "impressions and experiences" and soon learned that the "others were also completely practical guys."[51] A member of the Rhenish-Westphalian 254th ID related a similar account of working with a unit also drawn from Wehrkreis VI.

> A good relationship existed between the two medical units, having arisen from the men's neighboring regions [*nachbarlicher Landsmannschaft*]. One driver ... was a Westphalian farmer, the other driver ... a mechanic out of the Ruhr area. The men paired Rhenish agility with Westphalian toughness and reliability. One drove well with this pairing.[52]

This feeling carried over to the battlefield, even between units. During the fighting in January 1944, a member of the East Prussian 21st ID commented that "the excellent I[nfantry] R[egiment] 405 of the 121st ID was our left neighbor. It was always a joy to work with the 121st ID. One never had the impression that they were strangers."[53]

The importance of maintaining regionally homogeneous units was therefore apparent to both the leadership and the men. It is certainly no accident that the postwar histories of the 121st and 126th IDs were titled *The History of the 121st East Prussian Infantry Division 1940–1945* and *The History of the Rhenish-Westphalian 126th Infantry Division 1940–1945* respectively; clearly the men identified with what they believed to be "their divisions."[54]

---

[50] Geschichte der 21. Inf. Div. Von Dieter Stein, BA-MA Msg 2/2779.
[51] Chronik der 2. Kompanie Nachrichten – Abteilung 121, BA-MA RH 44/381.
[52] Einsatz der 1/SanKp 254 in Nordrußland – Erinnerungsbericht von Oberfeldarzt d.R. a. D. Dr. Franz Eckstein, BA-MA Msg 2/4558.
[53] Erinnerungen von Dieter Stein, GR 45 Dec 1943-Apr 1944, BA-MA Msg 2/2777.
[54] Rass, *Menschenmaterial*, p. 103. He is referring to the 253rd D and the two postwar histories that both reference its home region, but the point is certainly valid for the 121st and 126th IDs; see Division Tradition Group (ed.), *Geschichte der 121.*

Such territorially based recruiting practices, however, did not always work as intended. The pre-invasion records of the 123rd ID indicate a unit that struggled to maintain the discipline and cohesion generally associated with the Wehrmacht. The division commander complained of rampant thievery throughout the unit in December 1940, while "Comradeship Evenings" also appeared to get out of hand, and he found it necessary to issue an order regarding proper conduct at such events.[55] Such ill-disciplined behavior also led to the commander issuing a blistering order forbidding the "the unmilitary and unsoldierly" use of *Sie* without the use of rank and *Herr*, with continued violators being subject to punishment.[56] Even more disturbingly from his perspective, practices within the division led him to "expressively forbid" an NCO club that functioned as an exclusive organization within one company, replete with a constitution and dues. He stated that this club "reminds one of the evilest times after 1918" and declared that all meetings required the presence of officers; such a reference to the breakdown of discipline within the *Kaiserheer* during the 1918 revolution and the subsequent implosion of the army signified both how disgusted he was with such developments and the importance he attached to them.[57] Worries about seemingly revolutionary practices, slack military discipline, and petty crime consumed a considerable amount of time for the 123rd ID during the lead-up to the invasion and the fact that the majority of the men originated in Berlin and its environs is not a coincidence. As previously discussed, "Red Berlin" proved the toughest nut for the Nazis to crack and the men who grew up and were socialized in left-leaning working-class milieus would necessarily be antagonistic to military discipline and to submitting themselves to the most militaristic pillar of the Nazi state. The 123rd ID's problems should be kept in mind as they highlight the rocky transition from civilian to barracks life experienced by both individuals and the Wehrmacht as an institution.[58]

When the first artillery shells were fired across the German–Soviet border in the early morning hours of 22 June 1941, these were the infantry divisions that began the march into northwest Russia. None of the three

---

Ostpreussische Infanterie-Division 1940–1945 (Münster, Frankfurt, and Berlin, 1970); and G. Lohse, *Geschichte der rheinisch-westfälischen 126 Infanterie-Division* (Bad Nauheim, 1957).

[55] 123 ID, 12.12.40, Divisionsbefehl, BA-MA RH 26–123/2; 123 ID Kommandeur, 5.3.1941, Betr.: Kompaniefeste, Kameradschaftsabends u. dergl., BA-MA RH 26–123/2.

[56] 123 ID, Kommandeur, 6.2.41, Betr.: Anrede des Vorgesetzten, BA-MA RH 26–123/2.

[57] 123 ID, Kommandeur, 26.11.1940, An die Herren Kommandeure, BA-MA RH 26–123/2.

[58] For a discussion of this issue, see Römer, "Volksgemeinschaft in der Wehrmacht? Milieus, Mentalitäften und militärische Moral in den Streitkräften des NS-Staates," p. 79.

divisions could be termed elite or even above average; suffering deficiencies in able, veteran leadership and matériel, the 121st, 123rd, and 126th IDs probably closely fit Christian Hartmann's description of the 296th ID – an eighth-wave formation – as "below average."[59] Unit cohesion, however, was deemed at least a partial salve for the matériel deficiencies that plagued the German Army even before the invasion opened. This focus on morale as well as the inner bearing of each individual soldier was not merely linked to battlefield performance, however. The planning for Operation Barbarossa encompassed far more than mere operations; this was a war between irreconcilable ideologies that from the Nazi perspective could only end with the destruction of one or the other. The German infantry needed to be prepared for this aspect of the conflict as well.

II. The economic and ideological framework for the *Vernichtungskrieg*

On 30 March 1941, Adolf Hitler lectured his leading military commanders for over two and a half hours concerning Germany's strategic situation.[60] After touching on affairs in the Mediterranean area, Hitler turned his focus to the upcoming clash with the Soviet Union. While couching the discussion in strategic terms, his description of the imminent conflict left no doubt in the minds of his audience that this would be a new type of war. According to Halder, he declared that this would be a "war between two ideologies." Since

> communism [is] an enormous danger for our future ... we need to move away from the idea of soldierly camaraderie. The communist is a comrade neither before nor after the battle. This is a war of extermination ... We are not fighting a war to preserve the enemy.

Hitler continued by stating that "Bolshevik Commissars" as well as the "Soviet intelligentsia" needed to be destroyed. Notions of normal military justice were dismissed as the troops needed "to defend themselves with the means" that the criminal Bolsheviks themselves would surely employ.[61] The commissars "devastated everywhere they went in an Asiatic manner. They had earned no mercy."[62] He concluded with the

---

[59] Hartmann, *Wehrmacht im Ostkrieg*, p. 55.
[60] For a concise yet informative discussion of this meeting, see Hürter, *Hitlers Heerführer*, pp. 1–13.
[61] Halder, *Kriegstagebuch*, vol. II, 30 March 1941, pp. 335–7.
[62] Colonel-General Hermann Hoth's notes from the meeting; quoted in Hürter, *Hitlers Heerführer*, p. 7.

statement that "this war will be very different from the war in the West," especially as this conflict was predicated on "colonial tasks."[63]

Working within the context offered by Hitler's speech, the Germans structured their invasion of the Soviet Union around both economic and ideological goals, with the former perhaps supplying the primary motivation in the German decision for war in 1941.[64] Determined to avoid the collapse of the home front experienced by imperial Germany, bureaucrats in Berlin transformed Hitler's desires for the ruthless exploitation of Europe's raw materials and food supplies for Germany's benefit into concrete policies that extended across the continent.[65] While occupied Poland served as the proving grounds for such a callous and exploitive course, it was in the Soviet Union that such technocratic fantasies reached their horrifying zenith.[66]

Perhaps the most important German planner with regard to the Soviet Union was Herbert Backe. As *Staatssekretär* in the Reich Ministry for Food and Agriculture, Backe was increasingly responsible for squaring the circle of keeping the German home front adequately nourished and feeding a large standing army while the continent was blockaded by the Royal Navy. The answer to this seemingly insoluble problem was found in the Soviet Union: here, the raw materials and even more important foodstuffs from the black-soil region of the Soviet Union necessary to both fuel the German war economy and feed the Wehrmacht and home front seemingly existed in a real abundance.[67]

---

[63] Halder, *Kriegstagebuch*, vol. II, 30 March 1941, p. 337.
[64] Rolf-Dieter Müller, "Das 'Unternehmen Barbarossa' als wirtschaftlicher Raubkrieg," in Ueberschär and Wette, *Der deutsche Überfall auf die Sowjetunion*, pp. 125–58; Adam Tooze, *The Wages of Destruction: The Making and Breaking of the German War Economy* (London, 2006), pp. 461–85. Alex J. Kay writes that "by the end of 1940, however, economic arguments assumed the key role in plans being developed for the invasion and occupation of the Soviet Union"; see his *Exploitation, Resettlement and Mass Murder*, p. 27; more provocatively, Gerlach, *Kalkulierte Morde*, p. 45, argues that "the racial-ideological war of extermination" was "the means rather than the goal of the war against the Soviet Union ... The primary German goal was either to avoid a long war of attrition from the start or to carry one on with the help of Soviet raw materials and agrarian production."
[65] For concise overviews of the food situation in occupied Europe, see Polymeris Voglis, "Surviving Hunger: Life in the Cities and Countryside during the Occupation," in Robert Gildea et al. (eds.), *Surviving Hitler and Mussolini: Daily Life in Occupied Europe* (New York, 2007), pp. 16–41; and Mark Mazower, *Hitler's Empire: How the Nazis Ruled Europe* (New York, 2008), pp. 274–90.
[66] Götz Aly and Susanne Heim, *Architects of Annihilation: Auschwitz and the Logic of Destruction* (Princeton, 2002).
[67] Müller, "Von der Wirtschaftsallianz zum kolonialen Ausbeutungskrieg," pp. 141–209; Hillgruber, *Hitlers Strategie*, pp. 516–21. A recent synthesis of this topic is found in Lizzie Collingham, *The Taste of War: World War II and the Battle for Food* (New York, 2012), pp. 18–48.

From Backe's perspective, the Russian Empire's function as *the* traditional grain exporter for Europe had been fundamentally changed by Soviet policies. The focus on rapid industrialization and its consequent urbanization meant that Soviet grain remained at home, forcing Europe's consumption to decline.[68] Therefore, one means of solving Germany's tenuous food situation was to secure Soviet surplus grain for German use, and this could only be accomplished by depriving Soviet urbanites of food.[69]

In order to fruitfully exploit the Soviet Union's resources, Hitler tasked Hermann Göring, head of the Four-Year Plan, in early 1941 with establishing an organization devoted to this project. Göring then turned to General Georg Thomas, chief of the War Economy and Armaments Office section of the OKW, who described the creation of a "war-economy apparatus" as the "most important task" of the War Economy and Armaments Office for the forthcoming campaign.[70] This new economic organization, code-named "Oldenburg," was finally established on 21 February 1941.[71] Subordinated to Göring's Four-Year Plan, by mid-March "not only ... the war economy, but now the entire economy," of the occupied Soviet territories would fall under the Economic Staff East's umbrella.[72] In addition to securing the industrial resources necessary for the Reich's war economy, it was now also to help "supply the troops off the land," greatly increasing the scope of the organization's responsibilities. Major-General Hans Nagel, one of the founding members of the Economic Staff East, later wrote about this shift in policy: "economic goals [now] needed to be differentiated between long-term economic polices and the use of the land for the *war economy*."[73] The latter became its primary function during Operation Barbarossa as its other tasks were seen as objectives that could be fulfilled once the blitz campaign had ended.[74]

---

[68] Kay, *Exploitation, Resettlement, Mass Murder*, p. 61.
[69] Rolf-Dieter Müller, "Das Scheitern der wirtschaftlichen 'Blitzkriegstrategie'," in Boog et al., *Der Angriff auf die Sowjetunion*, pp. 1168–1202. See also Gerlach, *Kalkulierte Morde*, pp. 50–1.
[70] "Grundlagen für eine Geschichte der deutschen Wehr- und Rüstungswirtschaft," *Trials of the Major War Criminals*, Doc. 2353-PS, vol. XXX, pp. 260–80.
[71] Ibid. This was the beginning of the Economic Staff East, though it did not receive such a designation until 9 June 1941; see Gerlach, *Kalkulierte Morde*, p. 143.
[72] "Besprechung mit den Wehrmachtteilen am Dienstag, den 29. April 1941," *Trials of the Major War Criminals*, Doc. 1157-PS, vol. XXVII, pp. 32–8.
[73] Rolf-Dieter Müller (ed.), *Die deutsche Wirtschaftspolitik in den besetzten sowjetischen Gebieten 1941–1943: Der Abschlußbericht des Wirtschaftsstabes Ost und Aufzeichnungen eines Angehörigen des Wirtschaftskommandos Kiew* (Boppard am Rhein, 1991), p. 24. Emphasis in the original.
[74] Gerlach, *Kalkulierte Morde*, p. 143.

During May 1941, Nazi food policies towards the Soviet Union crystallized around what has become known as the "Starvation Plan." A meeting of state secretaries, including Backe, on 2 May laid out the German approach to the upcoming war.[75] Beginning with the premise that the war could only be continued when the entirety of the Wehrmacht – including the 3-million-man force tasked with the invasion – were fed from Soviet stocks, it thus soberly, yet brutally, concluded that "as a result, x-million people will doubtlessly starve, if we extract from the land what is necessary for us." Such coldly bureaucratic formulations found further expression in the Economic–Political Guidelines for Economic Staff East, published on 23 May 1941.[76] After clearly stating that "the food-political goals of this campaign" were "to guarantee the [food] supply of the German Wehrmacht as well as the German population for years to come" and to "permanently include Russia's agricultural economy in the European framework," it then divided the Soviet Union into "surplus" and "deficit" areas based on their grain production and consumption. Deficit areas, or the forest zone, which included the majority of central and northern Russia and the two metropolises of Moscow and Leningrad, would no longer receive grain shipments from the black-earth surplus areas; these would be instead diverted to the Germans for their own use. As a result of these policies, German planners estimated that upwards of 30 million Soviet inhabitants would die during the war, with urban inhabitants paying the heaviest price. In addition to civilians, prisoners of war were similarly targeted with intentional neglect as little to no food was allocated for their nourishment.[77] By adopting such strategies, German decision-makers, including members of the German High Command,

---

[75] "Aktenotiz über eine Besprechung der Staatssekretäre vom 2.5.1941," Document 2718-PS, in *Trial of the Major War Criminals*, vol. XXXI, p. 84; for a discussion of this meeting, see Alex J. Kay, "Germany's Staatssekretäre, Mass Starvation and the Meeting of 2 May 1941," *Journal of Contemporary History* (41, 4) October 2006, pp. 685–700.

[76] Allgemeine wirtschaftspolitische Richtlinien für die Wirtschaftsorganisation Ost, Gruppe Landwirtschaft, vom 23.5.1941, printed in Ueberschär and Wette, *Der deutsche Überfall auf die Sowjetunion*, pp. 323–5, here p. 323.

[77] On Soviet prisoners of war, see Christian Streit's seminal work *Keine Kameraden: Die Wehrmacht und die sowjetischen Kriegsgefangene 1941–1945*, 3rd edn (Bonn, 1991); as well as Alfred Streim, *Die Behandlungen sowjetischer Kriegsgefangener im "Fall Barbarossa"* (Heidelberg, 1981). More recent contributions include Christian Hartmann, "Massensterben oder Massenvernichtung? Sowjetische Kriegsgefangene im 'Unternehmen Barbarossa.' Aus dem Tagebuch eines Lagerkommandanten," *Vierteljahresheft für Zeitgeschichte* (49) 2001, pp. 97–158; and two works by Christian Gerlach: *Krieg, Ernährung, Völkermord: Deutsche Vernichtungspolitik im Zweiten Weltkrieg* (Munich, 2001) and "Die Verantwortung der Wehrmachtführung: Vergleichende Betrachtungen am Beispiel der sowjetischen Kriegsgefangenen," in Hartmann, Hürter, and Jureit, *Verbrechen der Wehrmacht: Bilanz einer Debatte*, pp. 40–9. A chapter devoted to

created the conditions necessary for the "systematic starvation of millions of civilians" and captive Red Army men.[78]

These various strands were woven together into the "Green Folder," first distributed on 16 June 1941.[79] Designed to serve as "the official handbook for the economic territories of the occupied Soviet territories," the document was sent down the military hierarchy to the division level.[80] It ordered that "all necessary measures needed to be taken for the *immediate and highest possible exploitation of the occupied territories* that would lead to the benefit of Germany."[81] It continued by stating that "the first objective is, as far as possible, to *supply German troops completely* from the occupied territories."[82] Moscow and Leningrad – areas dependent on the surplus grain now targeted for confiscation – "constituted difficult problems in terms of dealing with the population [*Menschenbehandlung*] ... especially because these million-man cities required heavy food subsidies."[83] Thus while not spelling out the anticipated results of restricting food shipments to the Soviet metropolises to the north, the Green Folder clearly indicated the horrific direction of German planning.

These calculated yet terrifyingly ruthless food policies were predicated on the racism that characterized Nazi society; here the ideological precepts that animated the Reich's racial policies towards the Soviet Union received a bureaucratic sheen. Other aspects of German planning more starkly highlighted the war of *Weltanschauungen* desired by the Reich's leadership. Aptly described by the German historian Andreas Hillgruber as "Hitler's true war," the German invasion of the Soviet Union would allow for a final reckoning with the "Judeo-Bolshevik" clique that governed the Soviet Union, one which Hitler believed threatened Germany's existence.[84] The Wehrmacht's

---

the experiences of Ukrainian POWs is found in Karel Berkhoff, *Harvest of Despair: Life and Death in Ukraine under Nazi Rule* (Cambridge, 2004), pp. 89–113.

[78] Götz Aly and Susanne Heim, "Deutsche Herrschaft 'im Osten': Bevölkerungspolitik und Völkermord," in Rürup and Jahn, *Erobern und Vernichten*, pp. 84–105, here p. 98; Gerlach, *Kalkulierte Morde*, pp. 44–80; Aly and Heim, *Architects of Annihilation*, pp. 234–52.

[79] Richtlinien des Wirtschaftsführungsstabes Ost für die wirtschaftliche Ausplünderung der besetzten sowjetischen Gebiete (Grüne Mappe, Teil I: Aufbau und Organisation der Wirtschaft), Juni 1941, in Moritz, *Fall Barbarossa*, pp. 363–99.

[80] Kay, *Exploitation, Resettlement, Mass Murder*, p. 164.

[81] Richtlinien des Wirtschaftsführungsstabes Ost für die wirtschaftliche Ausplünderung der besetzten sowjetischen Gebiete, p. 365. Emphasis in orginal.

[82] Ibid., p. 366. Emphasis in original.   [83] Ibid., p. 387.

[84] Hillgruber, *Hitlers Strategie*, p. 519; Jürgen Förster, "Das Unternehmen 'Barbarossa' als Eroberungs- und Vernichtungskrieg," in Boog et al., *Der Angriff auf die Sowjetunion*, pp. 481–521.

complicity in this war of extermination and rapacious plunder manifested itself in a group of directives that historians have labeled the "criminal orders."[85] The first of these four orders concerned the relationship of the Wehrmacht to the SS *Einsatzgruppen* (mobile death squads) in the occupied Soviet Union.[86] During spring 1941, the Army High Command and the SS engaged in negotiations in an attempt to avoid the conflict that plagued relations between the two institutions during the occupation of Poland.[87] Following the establishment of a military occupation administration in that country, SS units roamed the countryside, murdering both members of the Polish intelligentsia and Jews. Such actions sparked widespread criticism by the army; in one case, a military tribunal imprisoned the perpetrators.[88] When this opposition reached Hitler, he lashed out at the "soft" army, claiming that "you can't wage war with Salvation Army methods."[89] The replacement of the most vociferous critics and the amnesty issued by Hitler for all crimes committed in Poland made it quite clear how the issue would be resolved.

For the forthcoming invasion of the Soviet Union, both institutions desired a clear delineation of roles and expectations. These talks culminated in an agreement on 28 April 1941 which established a division of labor between the army and the SS in securing the occupied territories. The German Army proved much more accepting of the SS units in the Soviet Union than it had for the Polish campaign for both military and ideological reasons. From a military perspective, it believed the *Einsatzgruppen* necessary to pacify the rear areas which the army feared it was unable to properly control, due to its lack of manpower. While the Wehrmacht focused on defeating the Red Army in the field, small,

---

[85] For an overview of these orders, see Gerlach, *Kalkulierte Morde*, pp. 81–94. All four orders are reproduced in Ueberschär and Wette, *Der deutsche Überfall auf die Sowjetunion*, pp. 248–59.

[86] The fundamental study of the *Einsatzgruppen* and their relationship with the Wehrmacht remains Helmut Krausnick and Hans-Heinrich Wilhelm, *Die Truppe des Weltanschauungskrieges: Die Einsatzgruppen der Sicherheitspolizei und des SD 1938–1942* (Stuttgart, 1981). See also Peter Klein (ed.), *Die Einsatzgruppen in der besetzten Sowjetunion 1941/42: Die Tätigkeits- und Lageberichte des Chefs der Sicherheitspolizei und des SD* (Berlin, 1997).

[87] On Poland, see Alexander B. Rossino, *Hitler Attacks Poland: Blitzkrieg, Ideology, and Atrocity* (Lawrence, KS, 2003); Klaus-Michael Mallmann and Bogdan Musial, *Genesis des Genozids: Polen 1939–1941* (Darmstadt, 2004); and Jochen Böhler, *Auftakt zum Vernichtungskrieg: Die Wehrmacht in Polen 1939* (Frankfurt, 2006).

[88] On this specific incident, see Krausnick and Wilhelm, *Die Truppe des Weltanschauungskrieges*, pp. 80–1. A more general examination of this issue is found in Hürter, *Hitlers Heerführer*, pp. 181–90.

[89] Quoted in Ian Kershaw, *Hitler, 1936–1945: Nemesis* (New York, 2000), pp. 247–8.

mobile SS squads were to follow in the wake of the German Army with the express intention of eliminating communist functionaries, members of the intelligentsia, and male Jews of military age. Of course, many of the potential resisters feared by the army were automatically identified as communist fanatics – here, ideological motivations blended seamlessly with the army's view.

The essence of the National Socialist war of extermination was encapsulated in the Guidelines for the Conduct of the Troops in Russia, the second criminal order.[90] Stating that "Bolshevism is the mortal enemy of the national socialist German *Volk*," it called for "ruthless and energetic measures against Bolshevik zealots, guerillas, saboteurs, and Jews and the complete elimination of all active or passive resistance." Following in this vein of destroying the foundation of communist rule, the third directive, the Commissar Order, called for the immediate separation of Soviet commissars, or political officers, from other soldiers following their capture.[91] They were then to be shipped to the *Einsatzgruppen* or other SS units for execution. If delivery was deemed impossible, officers were given the power to shoot the commissars on the spot. This license to murder dovetailed with the final criminal order, the Gerichtsbarkeitserlass (Curtailment of Military Jurisdiction Decree) which both effectively removed any legal constraints on German soldiers in their dealings with Soviet civilians as long as military effectiveness was not endangered and denied a trial to any Soviet individual suspected of committing a crime, with the officer on the spot deciding if immediate execution was necessary.[92]

In order to ensure that members of the 121st, 123rd, and 126th IDs fought the upcoming campaign as a brief, brutal, and ideologically driven war, the Nazi state and the German High Command disseminated these ideological themes and orders throughout the Wehrmacht. General Eduard Wagner, chief quartermaster of the German Army, explained the new face of war in the east to the quartermasters of II,

---

[90] "Richtlinien für die Verhalten des Truppen in Rußland," BA-MA RH 26–121/9.
[91] For a first-rate comprehensive examination of the Commissar Order, see Römer, *Der Kommissarbefehl*. Other discussions of the order include Hans-Adolf Jacobson, "The Commissar Order and the Mass Execution of Soviet Prisoners of War," in Hans Bucheim et al., *Anatomy of the SS State* (Cambridge, 1968), pp. 505–34; and Förster, "Die Sicherung des 'Lebensraumes,'" pp. 1258–65.
[92] Helmut Krausnick, "Kommissarbefehl und 'Gerichtsbarkeiterlass Barbarossa' in neuer Sicht," *Vierteljahrshefte für Zeitgeschichte* (25) 1977, pp. 684–737. For a more recent appraisal, see Felix Römer, "The Wehrmacht in the War of Ideologies: The Army and Hitler's Criminal Orders on the Eastern Front," in Kay, Rutherford, and Stahel, *Nazi Policy on the Eastern Front*, pp. 73–100.

XXVIII, and X Corps in Bartenstein, East Prussia, on 20 May.[93] Stating that the army group commander in chief would no longer have sole responsibility for the rear areas, Wagner informed his audience that the SS was "entrusted with special tasks" and would have primary responsibility in the "so-called political areas" in the rear.[94] He also explained that the idea of military jurisdiction towards the civilian population was "completely different than before. There is no military jurisdiction for the Russian population." Wagner then divided the Soviet population between the "good" who would continue working for the German authorities and the "bad" who were to be "treated as guerillas, ruthlessly without military jurisdiction": there was no middle ground. The various corps subsequently issued their own orders explaining the ideological nature of the war to their troops.

II Army Corps, the immediate superior to 121st ID, instructed its subordinate units that while the majority of the population would welcome the Wehrmacht as liberators, Jews living in urban areas would inevitably support the communist resistance in the German rear areas; already before the invasion, the construct of Jews as partisans was already quite prevalent.[95] XXVIII Army Corps also warned its soldiers to be prepared for "sabotage acts" by civilians or soldiers in civilian clothing and thereby created an atmosphere of distrust before such events occurred.[96] This inevitable resistance, "active or passive," was to be "nipped in the bud" through the use of "ruthless conduct towards the sections of the population hostile to Germany."[97] This emphasis on irregular warfare led the 121st ID to note that since partisans were forbidden by the Hague Convention, they were to be "eliminated in the field or in flight."[98] The 126th ID dedicated a portion of its training towards anti-partisan measures. It called for more exercises focused on "defense against attacks from ambushes and other uses of ruses (wounded playing dead, feigning breakdowns with combat vehicles with the

---

[93] Besprechung bei O. Qu. in Bartenstein 20.5, BA-MA RH 24–2/460. These three corps were the immediate superior formations to the 121st, 123rd, and 126th Infantry Divisions. The following is drawn from this document.

[94] The 123rd ID made contact with the Gestapo posts in Eydtkau and Schirwindt in early June, presumably to discuss the new division of responsibilities. See Tätigkeitsbericht Mai/Juni 1941, 14.6.41, BA-MA RH 26–123/143.

[95] General Kommando II A.K., Anlage 3 zu 0100/41 g. Kdos., 28.5.41, BA-MA RH 26–121/6.

[96] Anlage zu Gen.Kdo. XXVIII. A.K. Abt. 1a, Nr. 320/41 g. Kdos. v.14.5.41, BA-MA RH 26–123/11.

[97] Gen.Kdo. XXVIII AK, Nr. 320/41 g. Kdos. v. 14.5.41, Anordnungen für die Versorgung Anlage, BA-MA RH 26–123/11. Emphasis in original.

[98] 121 ID, Abt. Ia, Besondere Anordnungen zum Div.-Befehl für den Angriff, 20.6.41, BA-MA RH 26–121/6.

Economics and ideology in the *Vernichtungskrieg* 77

intention of shooting at the oncoming enemy at close range), letting weak units (infantry points, etc.) pass by in order to attack the main section."[99] Certainly military units should prepare for all eventualities during battle, but such training also hardened the belief that Red Army soldiers would fight a malicious and devious war and that German soldiers should reflexively resort to using the utmost force in any ambiguous situation. Here, the Prusso-German Army's traditional fear of "people's war" played an important role in radicalizing the Wehrmacht's approach towards the Soviet Union.

The army also made clear the importance of the seizing of Soviet goods and foodstuffs during the upcoming campaign. Since the army was utterly dependent on Soviet booty – in particular foodstuffs – the High Command explicitly forbade "senseless plundering" as well as a "desire for destruction." An additional reason for such an order was the realization that living off the land was going to antagonize the civilian population and the Wehrmacht wanted to limit as much resistance from this quarter as possible.[100] Any German soldiers who engaged in such acts on their own initiative were to be "punished with the heaviest penalties."[101] Unfortunately for the Soviet population, such orders generally served as mere window dressing during the first eight months of the war.

The troops also received orders on the handling of prisoners of war and commissars. Since German authorities claimed that members of the Red Army would invariably act in a dishonorable and cowardly way, "the utmost caution and sharpest attention must be shown towards all members of the Red Army. The Asiatic soldiers are particularly unpredictable, treacherous and callous."[102] Within the prisoner collection camps, officers and political commissars needed to be immediately separated from the enlisted men.[103] The ranking intelligence officer lectured the remainder of the 121st ID's officers about various aspects

---

[99] 126 Infanterie Division, 20.5.1941, Betr: Richtlinien für die Ausbildung, BA-MA 26–126/24.
[100] Besprechung Unterabschnitt Ostpreußen I am 26.5.41, BA-MA RH 26–121/6. Members of all three division staffs would have been present at this meeting.
[101] Generalkommando II Armeekorps, Studie Barbarossa, 8.6.41, BA-MA RH 24–2/460.
[102] Gen. Kdo. XXVIII AK Nr. 320/41 g. Kdos. v. 14.5.41, Anordnungen für die Versorgung Anlage, BA-MA RH 26–123/11. Emphasis in original. II Corps issued a similar order concerning resistance and treatment of prisoners of war to its subordinate divisions; Generalkommando II Armeekorps, Studie Barbarossa, 8.6.41, BA-MA RH 24–2/460.
[103] Gen. Kdo. XXVIII AK Nr. 320/41 g. Kdos. v. 14.5.41, Anordnungen für die Versorgung Anlage, BA-MA RH 26–123/11; 121 ID, Abt. Ia, Besondere Anordnungen zum Div.-Befehl für den Angriff, 20.6.41, BA-MA RH 26–121/6; 126 ID, Abt. I, Merkblatt über die Behandlung von Kriegsgefangenen bei der fechtenden Truppe, 7.6.41, BA-MA RH 26–126/114.

of the upcoming campaign on 18 June and he specifically mentioned "red commissars (political and military)" as individuals who required special attention.[104] Finally, the army–SS agreement of April first blossomed into real co-operation in early June when members of the 123rd ID contacted the Gestapo branches in Eydtkau and Schirwindt in East Prussia.[105]

The commanders of Eighteenth and Sixteenth Armies – Küchler and Busch – each met with their corps and division commanders in early June, with the former also participating in an additional meeting with rear-area leaders as well. According to Eighteenth Army's war diary, Küchler wanted to "make known the Führer's decree, with the additions of the Army's commander in chief, about the treatment of political commissars in the ranks of the Red Army, also behavior towards the population and plunderers."[106] Busch also took the opportunity offered by his conference to "make the Führer's intentions and fundamental guidelines known" to his subordinate officers.[107] The manner in which such orders reached the lower levels of the army – i.e. from the division down through the regimental levels – can best be traced by an examination of the files of one of Sixteenth Army's units, the 123rd ID.[108]

In late May, the division commander, quartermaster, and ranking intelligence officer all took part in war games run by Sixteenth Army. During these exercises, the participants determined that prisoners would be used for labor, a direct violation of the Geneva Convention.[109] Divisional headquarters then communicated the results to the regimental commanders two days later.[110] Approximately a week before the invasion started, the division finished drafting its order concerning the treatment of the civilian population and then communicated the ideological foundations of the invasion to its regimental officers, with the Commissar Order the primary focus of discussion.[111] The Guidelines for the Behavior of the Troops in Russia were also distributed at this meeting in sealed envelopes, to be opened only on the division commander's orders. On 20 June, the division commander met his regimental and

---

[104] 121 ID, KTB, 18.6.41, BA-MA RH 26–121/3.
[105] Tätigkeitsbericht Mai/Juni 1941; 14.6.41, BA-MA RH 26–123/143.
[106] Cited in Römer, *Der Kommissarbefehl*, p. 123.
[107] 123 ID, KTB, 15.6.41, BA-MA RH 26–123/8.
[108] Of the three divisions under investigation, detailed documentation exists only for the 123rd ID.
[109] 123 ID, KTB, 26.5.41, BA-MA RH 26–123/8.   [110] Ibid., 28.5.41.
[111] Ibid., 14.6.41, 15.6.41. Felix Römer also arrives at this conclusion; see Römer, *Der Kommissarbefehl*, p. 124.

battalion commanders for one last pre-invasion meeting. While the majority of the meeting centered on operational matters, the final item on the agenda concerned the Curtailment of Military Jurisdiction Decree. Though the commander certainly placed special emphasis on this particular order, it is impossible to determine why based on the division commander's handwritten notes.[112] The ideological buildup culminated with the reading of the Guidelines for the Conduct of the Troops in Russia and Hitler's "Soldaten der Ostfront" proclamation during the night of 21–2 June 1941.[113] Operating within the context of these directives and orders, as well as the Wehrmacht's institutional belief that partisan warfare was inevitable, the soldiers of the 121st, 123rd, and 126th Infantry Divisions invaded the Soviet Union.

The army, however, wanted to ensure that the rank and file understood not only why such orders were being issued but also why they were absolutely necessary. The traditional system of *geistige Betreuung* – the spiritual and moral care that an officer was expected to exercise over his men – had already begun to transform by 1938 as the army became increasingly concerned with "disseminating ideology" instead of "stressing character issues." The goal was to create the "'political soldier,' in whom professionalism and politics, weapon and *Weltanschauung*, would be identical."[114] Such efforts, however, coexisted alongside more conventional forms of *Truppenbetreuung* during the first two years of war as ideological fare mixed with leisure-time activities, such as popular films, sporting events, and trips.[115] In preparation for the invasion of the Soviet Union, however, the army increased its efforts to mold its soldiers into racial warriors.

At approximately the same time as the divisions of the eleventh wave were formed, the commander in chief of the army, Brauchitsch, called for a new program of "ideological education" that aimed to ensure that "a unified view about the foundation of National Socialism exists and it is the common heritage for all soldiers."[116] Brauchitsch organized this new type of spiritual care around four primary themes: "the German Volk," "the German Reich," "German Lebensraum," and "National

---

[112] The phrase was blocked off with pencil.
[113] Ibid., 21.6.41. The "Soldaten der Ostfront" order is printed in Ueberschär and Wette, *Der deutsche Überfall auf die Sowjetunion*, pp. 265–9.
[114] Jürgen Förster, "Motivation and Indoctrination in the Wehrmacht, 1933–1945," in Paul Addison and Angus Calder (eds.), *Time to Kill: The Soldier's Experience of War in the West, 1939–1945* (London, 1997), pp. 263–73, here p. 267.
[115] Rass, *Menschenmaterial*, p. 313. For a brief overview of the pre-Barbarossa period for three active units, see Bartov, *The Eastern Front*, pp. 68–73.
[116] Anlage 4 zu "Ob. d.H./Gen. St. d.H./O. Qu.I Nr. 500/40 g. v. 7.10.40," Weltanschauliche Erziehung, BA-MA RH 26–123/173.

Socialism."[117] Under the subject "the German Volk," soldiers were to be instructed on the main points of "a clean race, health and hearty women. Many children," with Hitler's *Mein Kampf* recommended as a text. "The German Reich" focused on subjects such as "the State as the Living-Form of the Volk" and "Party and Wehrmacht as Pillars of the State," while "German Lebensraum" made the case for the necessity of German autarky in the agricultural sphere. Finally, "National Socialism as Foundation" detailed the importance of the Nazi movement for a "healthy and united Volk," a "strong Reich," and the "securing of Lebensraum."

These "four core elements" were grafted onto previous *Truppenbetreuung* practices in the lead-up to Operation Barbarossa.[118] In February 1941, men of the 126th ID attended lectures that touched on various topics. Some, such as "Today's War in the Area of the Mediterranean Sea" or "Victory Opens the Door to the World for Germany," focused on current events. Others, such as "The Centuries-Old Struggle for the German West" and "Verdun 1916–1940," examined German history from a distinctively ultra-nationalist view. More blatantly ideological material was also featured, including "The Struggle for German Living Space" and "My Experiences as a Resettlement Commissar in Russia," which focused exclusively on the Soviet Union.[119] Members of the 123rd ID also attended similar programs on "historical" topics such as "Pre- and Early Modern History of East Prussia" and "Old German Cultural Autonomy," while the present war received a great deal of attention through lectures titled "The Political Situation in the Mediterranean" and "Can England Win the War?", among others. Ideological programs, however, predominated. Topics such as "Socialism against Plutocracy," "The Battle for Survival of the German Volk," and "The German East in the German Economy," among others, all helped hammer home the Nazi message.[120]

All of these lectures attempted to provide the Wehrmacht's soldiers with a broader context of the war that the Reich was presently waging and how this conflict fit into the larger arc of German history. The use of more blatantly ideological material that emphasized the Germans'

---

[117] Beilage 1 zu Anlage 4 zu "Ob.d.H./Gen.St.d.H./O.Qu.I Nr. 500/40 g. v.7.10.40," Richtlinien für die weltanschauliche Erziehung, BA-MA RH 26–123/173. Emphasis in original.
[118] Rass, *Menschenmaterial*, p. 314. Evidence of these programs exists only for the 123rd and 126th IDs.
[119] 126 Inf. Division, Abt. Ic, 5.2.1941; 126 Infanterie-Division, Abt. Ic, 20.3.1941: Tätigkeit für Kriegstagebuch Februar 1941, BA-MA RH 26–126/113.
[120] 123 Inf. Division, Abt. Ic/Az: B-VR, Betr.: Vortragsredner, 17.5.1941, BA-MA RH 26–123/132.

"special mission" in the east, as well as the life-and-death struggle facing Germany, was intended to prepare the soldiers for the upcoming war of *Weltanschauungen*. The cumulative effect of this concerted effort to indoctrinate the rank and file and of the criminal orders was to create an atmosphere in which German soldiers and policemen, as the unquestioned *Herrenmenschen*, were actively encouraged to murder specific groups of Soviet citizens and treat others as mere obstacles to final victory. The behavior generated by this ideological brew, however, was only exacerbated by the army's view of the upcoming campaign, as its notions of military necessity found much common ground with Nazi goals for the campaign.

Küchler's framing of the invasion for his subordinates highlights the interplay between internal army impulses and the external demands of the Reich's political leadership. In April 1941, Eighteenth Army's commander, a man best described as a traditional conservative, met with his senior leadership and division commanders to discuss Operation Barbarossa.[121] He opened by justifying the upcoming war:

a deep ideological and racist chasm separates us from Russia. Russia is an Asiatic state due to the majority of its territory [being located there]. But a stabilization of Europe is unthinkable without a quarrel between Germany and Russia. The present Russian state will never give up its goal of world revolution; a lasting peace with present-day Russia is ruled out. It will always strive for an expansion to the west. Even in times of peace, it will be a threatening black cloud over eastern Europe, that would always like to erupt over Germany whenever it liked ... If Germany wants to have peace for generations from the growing danger in the East, it cannot be a matter of pushing Russia – even if it were hundreds of kilometers – back, rather the goal must be the destruction of European Russia, the dissolution of the Russian European state.[122]

Küchler also noted "that we are fighting against racially foreign soldiers" who deserved "no mercy" if, as expected, they behaved in a duplicitous and nonprofessional manner.[123] This use of racist rhetoric, however, fit neatly within his military conception of the campaign: as previously noted, he instructed his division commanders that only a "blitz victory" could be considered a success, and therefore

---

[121] For more on Küchler, see Johannes Hürter, "Konservative Mentalität, militärischer Pragmatismus, ideologisierte Kriegführung: Das Beispiel des Generals Georg von Küchler," in Gerhard Hirschfeld and Tobias Jersak (eds.), *Karrieren im Nationalsozialismus: Funktionseliten zwischen Mitwirkung und Distanz* (Frankfurt, 2004), pp. 239–53.

[122] "Notizen des Oberbefehlshaber der 18. Armee, Generaloberst von Küchler, für eine Vortag vor seinen Divisionskommandeuren am 25. April 1941," in Wilhelm, *Rassenpolitik und Kriegsführung*, pp. 133–9, here pp. 135, 136.

[123] Römer, *Der Kommissarbefehl*, p. 87.

"Russian resistance needed to be broken quickly."[124] The need for an immediate victory thus legitimized any and all measures taken against an enemy whose racial composition would necessarily lead it to wage an unprofessional and irregular war, thus slowing the German advance.

Küchler then expounded upon his view of the Soviet civilian population, dividing it into three groupings.[125] Civilians unaffiliated with the Soviet state constituted the first group and he stated that they should be "treated well" unless they became involved in irregular warfare; in this case they were to be "treated as guerillas, and brought to justice with corresponding severity." The second group consisted of Red Army soldiers who, due to their "racially foreign" background, needed to be watched vigilantly at all times.

Küchler then moved on to a discussion of the third group – political commissars – and, as Felix Römer aptly notes, he "adopted Hitler's argument down to the last detail." Commissars were "criminals" who "enslaved the population." The murder of the commissars would "drive a wedge between the Soviet political leadership" and the "decent Russian soldier," which would "save ... us German blood and we will quickly advance"; here the ideological and military campaigns coalesced into one. From Küchler's perspective, the ideological components of the upcoming campaign smoothly elided into the army's traditional vision of military necessity.

The remaining three criminal orders neatly fit into the army's desire for a quick and decisive victory. General Wagner clearly elucidated this idea in February 1941 when he wrote, "on the principle that preservation of the army's mobility was the supreme law of warfare, security and ruthless utilization of the country were to have precedence initially over an orderly administration in the interest of the Soviet population."[126] The quest for victory thus provided one motivation for the army willingly ensnaring itself in the Nazi machinery of annihilation and extermination; however, the ideological congruence between the Wehrmacht and Nazi institutions (such as the SS) when it came to Bolshevism also played a key role in delineating their relationship in the East. In this case, military necessity and ideology worked in concert to create the preconditions for a brutal occupation policy.

---

[124] "Notizen des Oberbefehlshaber der 18. Armee, Generaloberst von Küchler, für eine Vortag vor seinen Divisionskommandeuren am 25. April 1941," in Wilhelm, *Rassenpolitik und Kriegsführung*, pp. 133–4.
[125] The following is based on Römer, *Der Kommissarbefehl*, pp. 161–2.
[126] Cited in Strachan, "Time, Space and Barbarisation," p. 81.

The Guidelines for the Conduct of the Troops in Russia explicitly encouraged German soldiers to participate in the destruction of any and all irregular resistance that could slow the German advance while the Curtailment of Military Jurisdiction freed German soldiers from any doubts regarding their spur-of-the-moment actions; as long as their activities could be construed as advancing the Wehrmacht's quest for final victory, they could utilize force in any circumstance. Jürgen Förster has persuasively written that these policies were designed "to disable not only the supports of the Bolshevik Stalinist system, but also the potential cells of an organized resistance against German power."[127] While Operation Barbarossa developed into a war of unimaginable brutality and violence primarily due to the regime's ideological and economic demands, the army's traditional view of military necessity – one radicalized by the challenges of time and space facing it – easily assimilated the ideological categories delineated by the Reich's political leadership into its own thought process. Military necessity and Nazi ideological precepts thus worked very closely and towards the same ends during 1941.

While the Wehrmacht clearly strove to inculcate the troops with the necessary motivation for the upcoming war, the results of this effort are difficult to gauge for the men of the 121st, 123rd, and 126th IDs. Senior officers certainly tried to motivate their men with ideologically tinged orders: Lieutenant-General Otto Lancelle, commander of the 121st ID, proclaimed in May 1941, "Do not believe that the friendship between here and there will exist forever. There is no permanent friendship between National Socialism and Bolshevism. The time is coming when you will man your posts! Then there will be no excuses, then the slate will be wiped clean."[128] Many German soldiers strung out along the entirety of the front certainly absorbed the language and ideas of this ideological indoctrination, as their letters and diaries utilize rhetoric nearly identical to that of the Nazi regime.[129] For the three divisions under examination, however, the minimal existing evidence is much more ambiguous. What is clear is that some soldiers felt both a strong pride and a heavy responsibility in taking part in such a massive operation for the "fate of Europe."[130]

---

[127] Förster, "Die Sicherung des 'Lebenraumes'," p. 1227.
[128] "Der Todesmarsch nach Leningrad: Ein Kampfbericht II Battaillon IR 407 im Rahmen der 121. Infanterie-Division aufgezeichnet an Hand des Kriegstagebuches vom 22. Juni bis zum 15. September 1941. Geschrieben im Ortslazarett Modlin im März-April 1942," p. 18, BA-MA Msg 2/2580.
[129] See Buchbender and Sterz, *Das andere Gesicht des Krieges*, pp. 68–107; Fritz, *Frontsoldaten*, pp. 195–218; Bartov, *Hitler's Army*, pp. 106–78.
[130] "Der Todesmarsch nach Leningrad," p. 18, BA-MA MSg 2/2580.

3 "Attack with a ruthless offensive spirit and ... a firestorm of destruction"
The opening phase of Operation Barbarossa

I. Drive through Lithuania

At 3:05 in the morning on 22 June 1941, members of the 121st ID crossed the border into the Soviet Union alongside their peers.[1] By the conclusion of the first day of the operation, Leeb noted that the "troops have not yet pushed into any serious resistance."[2] Such a perspective might have been justified by focusing on the armored groups as German mechanized forces plunged deep into the Soviet Union.[3] For the infantry, however, it was clear that the opening days of the invasion were indeed some of the bloodiest of the first six months of war.

The 121st ID reported that once the initial surprise of the assault passed, Soviet troops defended "stubbornly" in settlements.[4] This proved especially true for II/405th Infantry Regiment, which fought a "very tough battle against numerous small nests and individual soldiers, who, in small bunkers, houses, cellars, barns, etc., often sacrificed themselves [*Selbstaufopferung*]."[5] An NCO in the engineer battalion admiringly noted that "the Russian is a master in constructing positions," while another German soldier noted the disquieting fact that "Red Army men defended their positions until the last breath."[6] Plunging into an area ringed by skillfully defended hedges, the 123rd ID also suffered

---

[1] 121 ID KTB, 22.6.41, BA-MA RH 26–121/8.
[2] Wilhelm Ritter von Leeb (ed. Georg Meyer), *Tagebuchaufzeichnungen und Lagebeurteilungen aus zwei Weltkriegen* (hereafter *Tagebuchaufzeichnungen*) (Stuttgart, 1976), 22 June 1941, p. 275.
[3] Halder's entry for the first day of war focuses overwhelmingly on the armored groups; see his *Kriegstagebuch*, vol. III, 22.6.41, pp. 5–6. In Army Group North's area of operations, Panzer Group 4 did indeed make good progress on the first day of war; see Walter Chales de Beaulieu, *Der Vorstoß der Panzergruppe 4 auf Leningrad 1941* (Neckargemünd, 1961), pp. 16–23; Manstein, *Lost Victories*, pp. 182–3; and David Glantz (ed.), *The Initial Period of War on the Eastern Front, June 22–August 1941* (London, 1993), pp. 78–154.
[4] 121 ID KTB, 22.6.41, BA-MA RH 26–121/8.
[5] Ergänzungen für die Zeit vom 22. Juni bis 5. Juli 1941, BA-MA Msg 2/3146.
[6] Uffz. Schneider 1./Pi. 121, Einsatz unseres Zuges bei Kybarti am 22.6.41, BA-MA RH 46/716; "Der Todesmarsch nach Leningrad," p. 36, BA-MA Msg 2/2580.

"relatively high casualties" during the first day of fighting.[7] Such reports of this intense combat eventually bubbled up to the higher echelons of the army, leading Leeb to note four days into the campaign that

> the overall impression of the enemy won in the past few days is that he fights very stubbornly, doggedly and, at times, underhandedly, and better than he did in the World War. He is very skilled at camouflage. He gives nothing away, but would rather fight in hopeless situations to the end.[8]

Battlefield reports and Leeb's diary highlight two important points. First, the popularly held notion that the German Army simply pushed aside a disorganized and ill-prepared Soviet border defense system needs to be revised. While German units, particularly panzer and motorized divisions, did make significant advances during the opening days of the campaign, these were not victories on the cheap. During the first nine days of fighting, the German Army suffered an astounding total of some 95,000 casualties; to put this into context, during the three-month war in western Europe, army casualties totaled 158,412.[9] Two of the three divisions under examination here suffered extremely high losses during the month of June alone. The East Prussians had lost 669 men by 30 June; that these breakthrough battles were particularly costly is evidenced by the division's losing an additional 416 soldiers during the next *three weeks*.[10] Thus within the first month of action, nearly 1,100 men were struck from the 121st ID ranks for varying lengths of time. The 123rd ID's 760 casualties up through mid-July demonstrated the fierceness of its fighting.[11] Only the Rhinelanders of the 126th ID fared comparatively well during the first three weeks of the campaign, recording only 173 losses by 10 July.[12] The experiences of the 121st and 123rd IDs thus fall squarely into the collective experience of the Wehrmacht during June and July 1941.[13]

---

[7] 123 ID KTB, 22.6.41, BA-MA RH 26–123/8.
[8] Leeb, *Tagebuchaufzeichnungen*, 25 June 1941, p. 280. On the same day, the OKW described Soviet resistance opposite Army Group North as "tough and dogged." Schramm, *KTB OKW*, vol. II, 25 June 1941, p. 420. On the growing German respect for the Red Army and its defensive tenacity, see Hürter, *Hitlers Heerführer*, pp. 370–1.
[9] For Operation Barbarossa casualty numbers, see Kroener, "The Manpower Resources of the Third Reich," p. 1020. This includes killed, wounded, missing, and sick. As Kroener, ibid., p. 1010, notes, already by the end of July, the Wehrmacht had suffered more casualties in the Soviet Union than they had during the entirety of the western campaign. On casualties during the fighting in the Low Countries and France, see Hans Umbreit, "The Battle for Hegemony in Western Europe," in Klaus A. Maier et al., *Germany and the Second World War*, vol. II, *Germany's Initial Conquests in Europe* (Oxford, 2000), pp. 229–326, here p. 304.
[10] Verlustlisten, 24.6.41–15.9.41, BA-MA RH 24–2/379.
[11] Tätigkeitsbericht der Abt. IIa vom 15.7.41, BA-MA RH 26–123/161.
[12] 126 Inf. Div. Meldung vom 20.7, BA-MA RH 26–126/23.
[13] Hartmann reaches similar conclusions regarding the breakthrough efforts in June and July 1941; see his discussion of casualties in *Wehrmacht im Ostkrieg*, pp. 201–30, here

Second, while Soviet defenders took a heavy toll of the Germans, they had not always fought in a manner consistent with the laws of war, at least from the perspective of the Wehrmacht. Both Leeb and the 126th ID described Soviet combat methods as "underhanded" and the three divisions repeatedly mentioned this theme during the opening phase of combat. The 126th ID's war diary recorded that "the underhanded combat methods of the enemy, for the most part from Asia (Kalmycks), are already unpleasant for the troops."[14] The engineer battalion's first company came under fire from "guerillas" identified as "primarily Asiatic types."[15] The 123rd ID also complained of the Soviets employing "devious and treacherous methods of war" during the first day of war.[16]

During the first weeks of the campaign, these actions of Soviet soldiers seemed to meld seamlessly with the German propaganda construction of a savage enemy fighting outside the parameters of civilized war; this in turn only further radicalized German behavior towards perceived guerillas. Prewar German directives, such as the Guidelines for the Conduct of the Troops in Russia, explicitly singled out "the Asiatic soldiers of the Red Army [as] devious, unpredictable, underhanded and callous," while the Regulations for Prisoners of War stated that prisoners of "Asiatic origin" were particularly prone to "treacherous behavior."[17] Fortified by these racist pronouncements, German troops conflated what they considered treachery with the allegedly primitive nature of the Red Army's rank and file and generally responded with violence whenever confronted with an ambiguous situation.[18] Wilhelm von Heesch, an NCO in the 121st ID's 408th Infantry Regiment, related the following incident:

A few meters from my severely wounded comrade, several Russians are lying in shallow ditches alongside the road. Their faces are turned to the ground. Are they dead? No blood anywhere. No traces of battle. Are the Soviet soldiers playing dead? I kick one of the Soviet soldiers in the side with my boot.

---

p. 212. See also Rass, "Das Sozialprofil von Kampfverbänden des deutschen Heeres 1939 bis 1945," p. 667.

[14] 126 ID, Abt. Ia, 22.6.41, BA-MA RH 26–126/5; 126 ID KTB, 22.6.41, BA-MA RH 26–126/4.

[15] Pionier Btl. 126, Kriegstagebuch Ostfeldzug 21.6.1941–30.12.1941, 22.6.41, BA-MA RH 46/414.

[16] IR 418, Tagesmeldung 22.6.41, BA-MA RH 26–123/36.

[17] "Richtlinien für das Verhalten der Truppe in Rußland," BA-MA RH 26–121/9; "Bestimmungen über das Kriegsgefangenenwesen im Fall Barbarossa vom 16.6.1941," printed in Ueberschär and Wette, *Der deutsche Überfall auf die Sowjetunion*, p. 261.

[18] An excellent analysis of the spiraling of violence during the opening months of the war is found in Römer, *Der Kommissarbefehl*, pp. 226–75.

He doesn't move. I see, however, how his eyes blink. Aha, so this is the situation, I thought. I shouted out to my comrades "Be careful" and then we cleared up the situation.[19]

In such cases, ideology – the racist pronouncements and orders that depicted the Red Army as a collection of deceitful and racially inferior soldiers – and military necessity – the German Army's desire to smash all resistance as quickly as possible in pursuit of final victory – combined to encourage violent behavior by German soldiers.

It is clear that no organized partisan activity confronted Army Group North during the opening weeks of the invasion. Rather, the speed of the German advance dislocated Soviet resistance, and bypassed Red Army stragglers who continued the fight proved troublesome to the growing German lines of communication and supply.[20] XXVIII Corps observed that due to the infantry regiments ranging far to the front, rear-area troops, such as artillery, supply, and communications units, found themselves tasked with "cleaning out ... scattered Russians" who were shooting from houses, cornfields, and forests "sometimes far behind the front."[21] The 123rd ID confirmed that such actions continually took place, reporting "resistance from scattered Russians, who fight to the last man and who constitute a permanent threat to our march columns."[22]

The combination of combat-weary troops, irregular resistance, and traditional German anti-partisan policy should have culminated in an outburst of violence on 24 June in the Lithuanian village of Kazlai. As members of the 121st ID marched through the community, several random shots were fired at them. According to doctrine, the division was well within its rights to carry out a collective action against the village and its inhabitants. Instead, the division commander, General Lancelle, ordered the collection of all male inhabitants and then had them put under armed guard. The action stopped here, though; the 121st ID did

---

[19] Wilhelm von Heesch, *Meine 13. Infanterie-Geschütz-Kompanie Grenadier-Regiment 408* (n.p., 1962), p. 66. Other soldiers also found Red Army men pretending to be dead but drew different conclusions. One believed that they feared immediate execution following their surrender and therefore hoped to escape by lying motionless. "Der Todesmarsch nach Leningrad," p. 36, BA-MA Msg 2/2580.

[20] For more on this topic, see Hürter, *Hitlers Heerführer*, pp. 367–70; Gerlach, *Kalkulierte Morde*, pp. 860–1; Shepherd, *War in the Wild East*, p. 62.

[21] Gen. Kdo. XXVIII. A.K., Abt. Ia, 23. Juni 1941, Hinweise vom AOK (Barbarossa Studie), BA-MA RH 24-28/15. Such concerns worked their way all up to Halder, who noted on 28 June that "numerous scattered groups, sometimes armed with tanks, are causing worries in the area of Army Group North, by wandering around the forests and plundering and burning down villages." Halder, *Kriegstagebuch*, vol. III, 28 June 1941, p. 23.

[22] Tätigkeitsbericht der Abteilung Ic, 23.6.41, BA-MA RH 26-123/143. For similar actions undertaken by the 253rd ID, see Rass, *Menschenmaterial*, pp. 335–6.

not execute any civilians in retaliation.[23] Such an incident fits into a larger pattern of behavior displayed by the Wehrmacht during the opening months of the invasion as murderous collective measures proved more the exception than the rule.[24] Despite the restraint demonstrated at Kazlai, a landscape of burning dwellings marked the passage of the 121st ID through Lithuania as the war in the east increasingly diverted from the *Normalkrieg* generally waged by the Wehrmacht in western Europe.[25]

Following the initial breakthrough, all three divisions began forced marches in attempts to close up to the rapidly advancing German armor (see Map 3.1). The 123rd ID's advance quickly "took on the character of a pursuit," with some units pushing up to twenty kilometers on the second day of war, while the 121st ID covered up to thirty-five kilometers per day during the last days of June.[26] The 126th ID already felt the strain of trying to keep pace with Panzer Group 4 a mere five days into the campaign.[27] Entering a vacuum created by Hoepner's armor in which there was little to no organized Red Army resistance, the division's primary military task centered on rounding up those Soviet soldiers scattered by the panzer group.[28] The 126th ID busied itself nearly exclusively with this activity until mid-July, seeing no combat at all between 1 and 10 July.[29] Further to the south, the 123rd ID faced even less resistance, fighting only two major engagements during the period stretching from 30 June to 25 July, with the remainder of the period devoted to clearing forests and swamps of scattered Soviet troops.[30] Only the 121st ID's advance

---

[23] 121 ID KTB, 24.6.41, BA-MA RH 26–121/8. Interestingly, Lancelle's restraint here is in marked contrast to his inflammatory order of 21 June 1941.

[24] Hartmann, *Wehrmacht im Ostkrieg*, p. 714, concludes his analysis of German anti-partisan policies by stating that "in the war of movement phase, outbreaks of force remained the exception."

[25] Tagebuchartige Aufzeichnungen des Lt. Schmidt, 23.6.41, BA-MA RH 37/3095. The question who set these fires remains open. It is clear that the Red Army did utilize "scorched-earth" tactics during the early stages of Operation Barbarossa, especially in the territories outside the Great Russian areas, and another unit within the 121st ID claims that the Soviets were responsible for numerous burning buildings; see "Chronik der 2.Kompanie Nachrichten-Abteilung 121," BA-MA RH 44/381. Another example is found in "Schicksalkämpfe des II.Gren.Rgt.454 (254 ID) 1939–1945," BA-MA RH 37/3098. The author relates that according to Estonian civilians, "the majority of houses [were] totally plundered and burned down" by withdrawing Red Army troops.

[26] 123 ID KTB, 23.6.41, BA-MA RH 26–123/8; 121 ID KTB, Abt. Ib, 24.6.41, BA-MA RH 26–121/65.

[27] 126 ID KTB, 23.6.41, BA-MA RH 26–126/4.

[28] 126 Infanterie-Division, Abteilung Ia, Gefechtsberichte Noworscheff (10.–20.7.1941), 24.6.41, BA-MA RH 46/415.

[29] 126 ID KTB, 28.6.41, 10.7.41, BA-MA RH 26–126/4; Tätigkeitsbericht Ic, 10.7.41, BA-MA RH 26–126/115.

[30] Fernspruch 19.7, 01.40 an 416 Infanterie-Regiment, BA-MA RH 26–126/15.

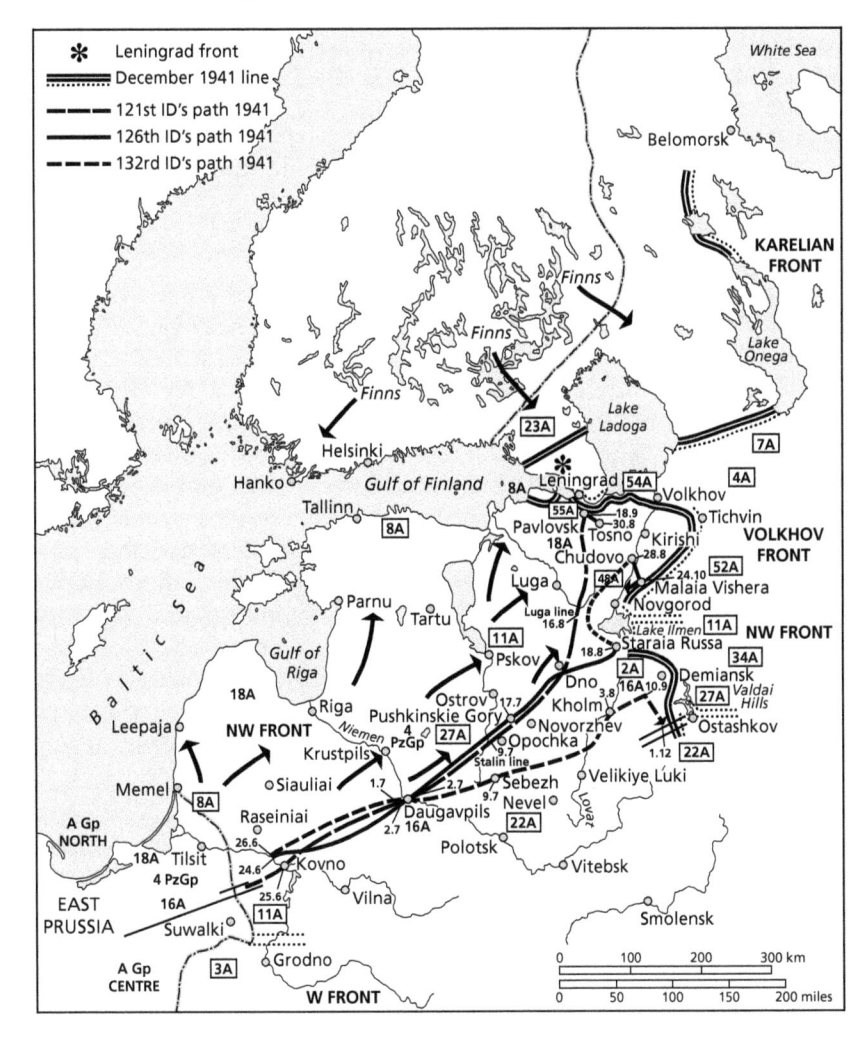

Map 3.1 The drive on Leningrad

slowed as it approached the important road junction of Dvinsk.[31] After a delay of several days due to frantic Soviet resistance, the division finally crossed the Dvina river and headed for the vaunted Stalin Line.[32]

---

[31] 121 ID KTB, Abt. Ib, 24.6.41, BA-MA RH 26–121/65.
[32] Leeb, *Tagebuchaufzeichnungen*, 3 July 1941, p. 286; Halder, *Kriegstagebuch*, vol. III, 29 June 1941, p. 27.

These fortifications provided serious resistance to Panzer Group 4 in early July and only the closing of German infantry permitted a comprehensive breaching of the line.[33] Between 9 July and 11 July, the three divisions battered through the fortified position and entered Russia proper for the first time in the campaign.[34] While each division underwent its first sustained combat since the opening days of the campaign, the 123rd ID engaged in the heaviest fighting, suffering "considerable casualties" before finally cracking the Soviet position.[35]

Once this line was breached, the experiences of the three divisions began to diverge. After eight days of relatively uninterrupted advance, the 121st ID suffered its first considerable losses in approximately a month while assaulting fortified bunker positions. Noting that the Red Army "fiercely defended" the position, the ranking intelligence officer cryptically noted that "no prisoners [were] taken," following the Germans' seizure of the position.[36] The division also captured and executed its first commissar on 1 July.[37] Heavy combat continued as the 121st ID participated in the destruction of four Soviet divisions and then proceeded to sweep the area for prisoners, bagging a total of 4,000 POWs between 24 and 26 July, including another commissar who was then presumably shot.[38]

The tasks of the 123rd ID mirrored its earlier activities: with the exception of one episode of major combat, the division continued to advance into a vacuum, marching over 800 kilometers by 2 August, with

---

[33] On Panzer Group 4's assault on the Stalin Line, see Charles Sydnor, *Soldiers of Destruction: The SS Death's Head Division, 1933–1945* (Princeton, 1990), pp. 161–8; Manstein, *Lost Victories*, pp. 187–8, 192–4.

[34] On the 121st ID, see Der Kommandierende General des II. Armeekorps 10.7.41, BA-MA RH 26–121/10; for the 126th ID, see 126 Infanterie-Division Abteilung Ia, Gefechtsberichte Noworscheff (10.–20.7.1941), 9.7.41, BA-MA RH 46/415; and for the 123rd ID, see 123 ID KTB, 10.7.41, BA-MA RH 26–123/8.

[35] AK XXVIII KTB, 10.7.41, BA-MA RH 24–28/14; 123 ID KTB, 10.7.41, BA-MA RH 26–123/8; Generalkommando XXVIII AK, Abt. Ia, 11.7.1941, Korpsbefehl Nr. 15, BA-MA RH 26–123/4.

[36] 121 ID KTB, 19.7.41, BA-MA RH 26–121/8. The division lost thirty dead and 124 wounded – this was the first battle in which German casualties were recorded; for the intelligence officer's comments, see 121 ID KTB Ic, Anlagen, vol. I, 19.7.4, BA-MA RH 26–121/55. Such a formulation usually indicated that any prisoners taken were then immediately executed. On this phenomenon, see Hartmann's extended discussion in *Wehrmacht im Ostkrieg*, pp. 516–67; Gerlach, *Kalkulierte Morde*, p. 775; Rass, *Menschenmaterial*, pp. 335, 337–8; and Hans-Joachim Schröder, "German Soldiers' Experiences during the Initial Phase of the Russian Campaign," in Bernd Wegner (ed.), *From Peace to War: Germany, Soviet Russia, and the World, 1939–1941* (Providence and Oxford, 1997), pp. 309–24.

[37] 121 ID, Abt. Ic, 1.7.41, BA-MA RH 26–121/55.

[38] 121 ID KTB, 26.7.41, BA-MA RH 26–121/8. The capture of the commissar is noted in 121 ID KTB Ic, 24.7.41, BA-MA RH 26–121/55.

at least one unit covering up to forty-four kilometers on a single day.[39] While the battlefield crisis was short-lived, it did foreshadow a serious problem that would increasingly plague the Wehrmacht during the eastern war. On 22 July, one of the 418th Infantry Regiment's battalions found itself in "serious trouble" as a strong Soviet counterattack supported by tanks threatened to overrun it. In what was to become a recurring theme for the German Army, XXVIII Corps dismissed the division's cries for assistance and ordered it to use its own forces – specifically its supply battalion and artillery formations – to rectify the situation.[40] The integration of divisional rear-area units into its combat section became a routine matter during the 1941–2 winter crisis for the majority of the Wehrmacht; for the 123rd ID, this process had already begun in July 1941.

The continual advance caused one member of the 418th Infantry Regiment to complain about "the enormous strains of the march caused by hunger and thirst, heat and dust and impassable roads."[41] Another Berlin-area soldier wrote,

we entered a city today and will stay here for a day. Thank God that we can get some proper sleep for once. I really felt sorry for the poor lads as they ran 80 kilometers in 28 hours yesterday [sic] and are accordingly *kaputt*.[42]

The division commander futilely protested the relentless pace of the march to XXVIII Corps, which, despite recognizing that the men were "quite exhausted due to the fighting and exertions of the march," merely stated that Sixteenth Army's urgent demands for the "quickest advance" needed to be met.[43] The army deemed a speedy advance necessary to maintain contact with Army Group Center, a role fulfilled by the 123rd ID until the January 1942 Soviet counteroffensive in this region.[44] By the end of July, however, Red Army resistance had intensified as the fighting neared the city of Kholm and it was here that the 123rd ID's relatively fluid advance sputtered to a halt.

---

[39] 121 ID KTB, 2.8.41, BA-MA RH 26–123/9.
[40] XXVIII AK KTB, 22.7.41, BA-MA RH 24–28/14.
[41] Lt. Wilhelm Berg, 418th Infantry Regiment, 17.7.41, BfZ, Sammlung Sterz.
[42] Corporal Fritz Lieb, 68th Infantry Regiment, 3.7.41, BfZ, Sammlung Sterz.
[43] XXVIII AK KTB, 13.7.41, BA-MA RH 24–28/14.
[44] 123 ID KTB, 11.7.41, BA-MA RH 26–123/8. On 29.7.41, Army Group North agreed to transfer L Corps to Army Group Center in order to instill a unity of command in the German forces fighting near Velikie-Luki; see Halder, *Kriegstagebuch*, vol. III, 29 July 1941, p. 131. Leeb was furious at a further dissipation of his force, as II AK would now have to swing further to the south, "meaning that instead of the 9th Army covering our flank, we need to help them! This is already the third time [in the campaign]"; see Leeb, *Tagebuchaufzeichnungen*, 30 July 1941, p. 313.

While the 121st and 123rd IDs participated in brief periods of combat, the 126th ID received its first real baptism of fire during the second week of July.[45] Beginning on 15 July, the 126th ID participated in the encirclement of Soviet forces.[46] While terming the battle a "very tough fight," the division also complained that "similarly to the border battle, the Russian has fought on 15 and 16 July not as a soldier but as a partisan."[47] Their "underhanded methods" included "playing dead," and this ruse led to a machine gun company being attacked from the rear with the subsequent loss of ninety men. The Soviets then committed "beastly atrocities" against wounded and prisoners, killing them with "numerous bayonet stabs."[48] For the next four days, the 126th ID engaged in mopping-up operations, a process that made "tough demands" on the troops and which resulted in "severe casualties." Though division command maintained that the troops remained in good spirits despite the preceding trials, an outburst of violence on 21 July highlights the tension, weariness, and frustration felt by members of the 126th ID as well as the institutional legacy pulsing within Wehrmacht units.[49]

As it moved through the small village of Dorochova, the fourth battalion of the division's artillery regiment was ambushed as several shots were fired at it. A lieutenant, instructed to proceed "ruthlessly" in identifying the perpetrators, led a small group of soldiers attached to the medical unit and combed through the village and surrounding area. After interrogating village inhabitants and finding only two young women rather vaguely described as "suspiciously hanging around," regimental leadership decided that "villagers had obviously supported the Bolsheviks or participated themselves in the sniper attack." Despite the fact that only one soldier was wounded during the ambush, the Germans immediately gathered the seven draft-age men who lived in Dorochova, shot them and then burned the village down, hoping that such "sharp measures" would "stop a further spread

---

[45] Tätigkeitsbericht des Ev. Divisionspfarrers bei der 126 ID für die Zeit vom 22.6 bis 21.12.41, BA-MA RH 26–126/140.
[46] Leeb, *Tagebuchaufzeichnungen*, 15 July 1941, p. 296; 126 ID, Abt. Ia, 17.7.41, Divisionsbefehl für die Fortsetzung der Einschliessung der Feindteile um Puschkinskje-Gory, BA-MA RH 26–126/5.
[47] 126 ID KTB, 16.7.41, BA-MA RH 26–126/4.
[48] 126 ID, 16.7.41, Tagesmeldung dem Generalkommando X. AK, BA-MA RH 26–126/8. The "bestial cruelty" of the Russians in this instance is discussed in 126 Infanterie-Division Abteilung Ia, Gefechtsbericht Noworscheff (10.–20.7.1941), BA-MA RH 46/415.
[49] 126 ID KTB, 21.7.41, BA-MA RH 26–126/4. For a detailed description of the action, see Artillerie-Regiment 126, 24. Juli 1941, BA-MA RH 26–126/116. The following discussion is based on this report.

of the bandit war."[50] Due to the "behavior of the population, especially the increasingly frequent shootings [at members of the 126th ID] during the march," the troops felt a "considerable bitterness" towards civilians and were prepared to act against this "danger with the sharpest means."[51] Though it remained the division's only use of a collective measure during the first two months of the campaign, the contrast between this action of the 126th ID and that of the 121st ID one month earlier could not have been greater.[52]

This incident highlighted two important issues. First, the destruction of this small Russian village was not simply the result of Nazi ideology; military events also played an important role. Following a particularly costly battle, one which was the first real combat faced by the 126th ID in Operation Barbarossa, its troops then came upon the mutilated bodies of several of their comrades. Following this gruesome discovery, the men were then forced to undertake the dangerous work of flushing Red Army men out of hiding. This task required numerous small groups of soldiers to comb through isolated areas, and with the images of their slain comrades fresh in their mind, such a mission must have kept the tired and frustrated men on edge. A combustible situation like this required only a spark and the random shots within Dorochova served such a purpose.[53]

Second, the implementation of a collective measure also highlighted the growing radicalization of the Eastern Army's behavior and rhetoric, as the division utilized the ideologically laden phrase "bandit war" to describe irregular warfare.[54] Such language was inextricably tied to developments on the battlefield. In other words, military events cannot be separated from the ideological context of the war. The erasure of

[50] 126 ID KTB, 21.7.41, BA-MA RH 26–126/4; AR 126 Tagesmeldung, 22.7.41, BA-MA RH 26–126/9.
[51] 126 ID KTB, 21.7.41, BA-MA RH 26–126/4.
[52] Tätigkeitsbericht zum Kriegstagebuch, 31.7.41, BA-MA RH 26–126/115.
[53] For a similar response to the discovery of mutilated German corpses by the 4th Panzer Division, see Hartmann, *Wehrmacht im Ostkrieg*, p. 711. The mutilation of German prisoners and wounded was widely reported across the front and doubtlessly led to an increased radicalization of German behavior on the front. For more on this issue, see Römer, *Der Kommissarbefehl*, pp. 226–51; Hürter, *Hitlers Heerführer*, pp. 360–2; Rass, *Menschenmaterial*, pp. 334–5; and Förster, "Die Sicherung des 'Lebensraumes,'" pp. 1232–3.
[54] The first official use of the phrase "bandit war," which was used to delegitimize such resistance, was issued in Field Marshal Wilhelm Keitel's 16 September 1941 order that called for an increasingly brutal response to partisan activities; the 126th ID's formulation thus pre-dated the institutional use of this phrase by nearly two months. For Keitel's order, see "Befehl Keitels über die schonungslose Unterdrückung der Befreiungsbewegung in den besetzten Länden und Geiselerschießungen," in *Wehrmachtsverbrechen: Dokumente aus sowjetischen Archiven* (Cologne, 1997), Document #19, pp. 80–3.

Dorochova from the physical landscape and the murder of its male inhabitants resulted not merely from the toxic effect of Nazism on the Wehrmacht, but also from the development of the army's own antipartisan doctrine. Dorochova's fate surely would have surprised neither Moltke the Elder if it had occurred during the 1870–1 Franco-Prussian War nor his nephew if it had occurred in Belgium in 1914: such responses were hard-wired into the German Army's anti-partisan policy. What is unique about the event is that the 126th ID carried out such an order during the period of the advance; this served as both an anomaly for the summer of 1941 and an ominous indication of future developments.

II. The *Weltanschauungskrieg*

The night before the invasion, the 121st ID's commander, Lieutenant-General Otto Lancelle, issued an order to his men that relied heavily on Nazi imagery to justify the upcoming invasion.[55] Lancelle stated that

the war against Russia is a battle of National Socialism against Bolshevism, a continuation of the struggle victoriously ended within Germany on 31.1.33 by the Führer against the center of this movement, whose goal is the destruction of the world, the destruction of all cultural assets. It is the struggle of Europe against the Asiatic will to destroy. Europe will never live in peace if this dragon's head is not cut off.

He called upon his soldiers "to attack with a ruthless offensive spirit and to break the resistance, which will be strong initially, with a firestorm of destruction" in this "conflict of two *Weltanschauungen*." Lancelle directed his troops to prosecute the war in a "harsh and irresistible" manner to ensure a speedy victory and concluded that "as you are true National Socialists and brave soldiers of the 121st Division, glory, honor, and victory will be pinned to our banner." While the ideological content is unmistakable, Lancelle's language in the second part of the order also points to the German Army's institutional view of war. By emphasizing the need to fight with a "ruthless offensive spirit," Lancelle reinforced the army's traditional doctrine that emphasized quick offensives. The "firestorm of destruction" was necessary to defeat a numerically superior enemy rapidly, before the Soviet Union's advantage in manpower and resources could be brought to bear. The 121st ID commander's order thus encapsulated both Nazi ideological tenets and the army's institutional view of war.

---

[55] 121 Inf. Division Kommandeur, 21.6.41, BA-MA RH 26–121/70.

Lancelle was not the only commander in Army Group North to issue such an inflammatory order. While Leeb himself did not contribute to the criminal atmosphere surrounding the invasion, two other senior commanders in the army group – Küchler and Hoepner – did frame the conflict in an ideological manner. The armor commander instructed his subordinate units that

> the war against Russia is an essential component of the German *Volk*'s fight for survival. It is the old struggle of the German against the Slav, the defense of European culture against the Muscovy-Asiatic flood, the repulse of Jewish-Bolshevism.
>
> This war must have the goal of smashing present-day Russia and therefore needs to be conducted with unprecedented severity. All actions, in conception and execution, must be guided by an iron will that will lead to the merciless and total destruction of the enemy.[56]

In an order issued to Eighteenth Army on the day of the invasion, Küchler stated that the present conflict was "the continuation of the centuries-old war between Germandom and Slavdom." He considered the area through which his army would be advancing to be a "rough and hostile environment" whose only trace of culture could be found in the Romanovs' German-inspired palaces.[57] The fact that these two officers – both of whom should be viewed as conservative instead of radical – issued orders steeped in the racism that infused Nazism highlights how pervasive such attitudes were within German society.[58] With the exception of Busch, not one of the four senior leaders of Army Group North could be considered an advocate of National Socialism, yet the poisonous rhetoric synonymous with the Third Reich nonetheless permeated the upper echelons of the army group.

Various members of the 121st ID supported an ideological view of the war. A platoon leader in the 407th Infantry Regiment agreed that "there was no going back from this fundamental conflict between National Socialism and Bolshevism," while an officer in the division's communications section described the upcoming battle in much more dramatic fashion: "The most violent phase of this struggle of peoples

---

[56] Befehl des Befehlshaber der Panzergruppe 4, Generaloberst Hoepner, zur bevorstehenden Kampfführung im Osten vom 2.5.1941, in Ueberschär and Wette, *Der deutsche Überfall auf die Sowjetunion*, p. 251.

[57] Hürter, *Hitlers Heerführer*, p. 477.

[58] Ibid. Hürter describes Küchler in this way; such a characterization can also be fruitfully applied to Hoepner. For more on Küchler, see Hürter, "Konservative Mentalität, militärischer Pragmatismus, ideologisierte Kriegführung"; on Hoepner, see Heinrich Bücheler, *Hoepner: Ein deutsches Soldatenschicksal des Zwanzigsten Jahrhunderts* (Herford, 1980).

began – the fight against Bolshevism! – Not only for Germany – no – it is for culture and human rights in all of Europe, in the entire world!"[59] This, however, did not constitute a unanimous position within the division: the very same platoon commander in the 407th Infantry Regiment who supported the invasion recorded that several men in his unit "shook their heads, as by treaty, Hitler was allied to the Soviet Union."[60] So while many members of this division did indeed view the upcoming war with the Soviet Union as one that would save Western civilization, others viewed it from a more critical perspective.

The largest crime committed by the Third Reich was undoubtedly the murder of Europe's Jews. Army Group North's participation in the Holocaust was relatively limited in comparison with German units further to its south, despite the fact that Einsatzgruppe A, the SS detachment assigned to Army Group North, was one of the more terrifyingly effective formations in carrying out its murderous activities.[61] Due to the fact that the overwhelming majority of Jews in its area of operations lived in the Baltic states, the army's complicity was generally limited to the first few months of the invasion while it advanced towards Leningrad.[62]

---

[59] "Der Todesmarsch nach Leningrad," p. 5, BA-MA Msg 2/2580; "Chronik der 2. Kompanie Nachrichten-Abteilung 121," unpaginated, BA-MA RH 44/381.

[60] "Der Todesmarsch nach Leningrad," p. 5, BA-MA Msg 2/2580. The commander of the East Prussian 61st Infantry Division also believed that his troops needed to be convinced about the necessity of the invasion; see Walther Hubatsch, "Das Infanterie Regiment 151 1939–1942: 1944," BA-MA RH 37/2785.

[61] For Einsatzgruppe A, see Hans-Heinrich Wilhelm, *Die Einsatzgruppe A der Sicherheitspolizei und des SD 1941/42* (Frankfurt, 1996); and Kilian, *Wehrmacht und Besatzungsherrschaft*, pp. 481–503. On Army Group Center's participation in the murder of Jews in its area of operations, see Gerlach, *Kalkulierte Morde*, pp. 503–774; for Army Group South, see Wendy Lower, *Nazi Empire-Building and the Holocaust in Ukraine* (Chapel Hill, 2005), pp. 44–97; Oldenburg, *Ideologie und Militärisches Kalkül*, pp. 159–224, 297–306; *Verbrechen der Wehrmacht*, pp. 154–85; Dieter Pohl, "The Murder of Ukraine's Jews under German Military Administration and in the Reich Commissariat Ukraine," in Ray Brandon and Wendy Lower (eds.), *The Shoah in Ukraine* (Bloomington, 2008), pp. 23–76, especially pp. 25–40.

[62] On the Baltic states as a whole, see Sebastian Lehmann, Robert Bohn, and Uwe Danker (eds.), *Reichskommissariat Ostland: Tatort und Erinnerungsobjekt* (Paderborn, 2012). On Lithuania, see Christoph Dieckmann, *Deutsche Besatzungspolitik in Litauen, 1941–1944* (Göttingen, 2011); and his chapter "The War and the Killing of the Lithuanian Jews," in Ulrich Herbert (ed.), *National Socialist Extermination Policies: Contemporary German Perspectives and Controversies* (New York, 2000), pp. 240–75; Kim C. Primel, "Sommer 1941: Die Wehrmacht in Litauen," in Vincas Bartusevičius, Joachim Tauber, and Wolfram Wette (eds.), *Holocaust in Litauen: Krieg, Judenmorde und Kollaboration im Jahre 1941* (Cologne, 2003), pp. 26–39. For Latvia, see Sven Jüngerkes, *Deutsche Besatzungsverwaltung in Lettland 1941–1945: Eine Kommunikations- und Kulturgeschichte nationalsozialistischer Organisationen* (Constance, 2010); Margers Vestermanis, "Local Headquarters Liepaja: Two Months of German Occupation in the Summer of 1941," in Heer and Naumann, *War of Extermination*, pp. 191–236. For Estonia, see Anton Weiss-Wendt, *Murder without Hatred: Estonians and the Holocaust* (Syracuse, 2009), pp. 84–108.

In fact, the army controlled Lithuania and Latvia only until 25 July 1941, when these areas passed over to civilian control.[63] During this one month of conquest and occupation, however, Army Group North played a key role in Hitler's *Vernichtungskrieg* against Soviet Jews.

Of the three divisions under analysis, only the 121st ID appeared to have direct contact with Lithuanian Jews. This began almost immediately after the formation crossed the Soviet border as members of its 407th Infantry Regiment embarked on a campaign of looting and plundering that especially targeted Jews. As the unit passed through a Lithuanian village during the opening days of the invasion, it discovered several Jews hiding in a courtyard, as well as numerous goods. A platoon leader cryptically stated they were "taken care of" and the company continued the advance.[64] When the men stopped for the night, they commandeered a house inhabited by a Jew, who spoke fluent German. While he "understandably turned the house over" to the soldiers, the Germans permitted him to stay in the basement without any further harassment.[65] This markedly contrasted with the behavior of the men earlier in the day as well as on 24 June when they entered the town of Kazley-Ruda, described as "a nest of Lithuanian trader-Jews." As the soldiers were given some free time early in the morning,

> many simple [*biedere*] soldiers went off in search of items of food and clothing. Oh, that was not all that was claimed that day. Radios, cloth. Lemonade, seltzerwater, pickles, heaps of canned fish. Cigarettes, chocolate and many other things ... Someone brought me numerous photos autographed by actors. War booty according to the *Landser*'s way.[66]

The difference between the treatment accorded the Jew whose language skills gave the appearance of German culture and that meted out towards Lithuanian Jews in these examples is striking. It leads one to speculate that these particular soldiers differentiated between German and foreign Jews, to the detriment of the latter, indicating that the while some members of the 121st ID may have failed to completely absorb the Nazi notion of the "universal Jew," eastern Jews were quite likely to feel the wrath of German soldiers during their advance into the Soviet Union.

As the 121st ID continued its advance through Lithuania, it reached the capital, Kovno, on 25 June at 3:00 a.m.[67] Several of the division's soldiers spoke of the friendliness with which the population greeted them;

---

[63] Hürter, *Hitlers Heerführer*, p. 537.
[64] "Der Todesmarsch nach Leningrad," BA-MA Msg 2/2580, pp. 40–3.
[65] Ibid., p. 46. [66] Ibid.
[67] 121 ID KTB, BA-MA RH 26–121/4. Other Wehrmacht units had reached the city in the late afternoon of 24 June 1941. See Klaus-Michael Mallmann, Volker Rieß, and

one soldier wrote that "a clapping jubilant population greeted us as saviors from Bolshevism and threw flowers to us ... a strange war, alternating between flowers and bullets," while another recorded that "the population greeted [the troops] with cheers and flowers."[68] The men believed that such an outpouring of support demonstrated the hatred of the Soviet occupiers.[69] As the East Prussians settled into the city for a brief rest, they observed the gruesome events taking place around them. Following the withdrawal of the Red Army on 23 June, Lithuanian nationalists began persecuting the city's Jews, whom they associated with Soviet power. Kovno possessed one of the largest Jewish populations in eastern Europe, with nearly a quarter of its 200,000 inhabitants classified as Jews.[70] For four days, these Jews were humiliated, beaten, and murdered by Lithuanian gangs while Wehrmacht units stood by and watched.[71]

While numerous soldiers voyeuristically surveyed the nightmarish scene, no evidence exists that implicates members of the 121st ID in the massacre, though they were well aware of the pogrom.[72] One NCO in the 407th Infantry Regiment witnessed Lithuanian activists forcing "Bolsheviks out of their hiding spots and driving them all into one house." For this *Landser*, the logic behind this action was impeccable: "I thought this was the reckoning for 1940," i.e. the Soviet annexation of Lithuania.[73] Members of the 408th Infantry Regiment also observed "Lithuanian irregulars chas[ing] Bolsheviks and Jews out of their hiding spots."[74] Following a 24 June order issued by the OKH to both Eighteenth

---

Wolfram Pyta (eds.), *Deutscher Osten 1939–1945: Der Weltanschauungskrieg in Photos und Texten* (Darmstadt, 2003), p. 61.

[68] Tagebuchartige Aufzeichnungen des Lt. Schmidt, 25.6.41, BA-MA RH 37/3095; "Mein Regiment," 25.6.41, BA-MA RH 37/3096.

[69] Mazower, *Hitler's Empire*, pp. 174–5. For more on the identification of Jews with Bolsheviks in Lithuania and the Baltic states, see Hürter, *Hitlers Heerführer*, p. 537; Weiss-Wendt, *Murder without Hatred*, pp. 50–6; Joachim Tauber, "Vergangenheitsbewältigung in Litauen: Politik, Gesellschaft und der Holocaust nach 1945," in Lehmann, Bohn, and Danker, *Reichskommissariat Ostland*, pp. 331–48.

[70] Jürgen Matthäus, "Kaunas 1941–1944," in Gerd Ueberschär (ed.), *Orte des Grauens: Verbrechen im Zweiten Weltkrieg* (Darmstadt, 2003), pp. 83–91, here p. 83.

[71] Helmut Krausnick, *Hitlers Einsatzgruppen: Die Truppe des Weltanschauungskrieges 1938–1942* (Stuttgart, 1985), p. 179. The author cites one Army Group North staff officer saying that the events were the "most heinous" he had witnessed in two world wars; p. 179.

[72] No mention of the massacre can be found in the divisional files and neither of the two primary collections of eyewitness source material concerning the massacre makes any reference to members of the 121st ID. See Ernst Klee, Wille Dressen, and Volker Rieß (eds.), *"The Good Old Days": The Holocaust as Seen by Its Perpetrators and Bystanders* (New York, 1991), pp. 23–38; and Mallmann, Rieß, and Pyta, *Deutscher Osten 1939–1945*, pp. 61–7.

[73] "Der Todesmarsch nach Leningrad," p. 53, BA-MA Msg 2/2580.

[74] "Mein Regiment," 25.6.41, BA-MA RH 37/3096.

and Sixteenth Armies to allow for Lithuanian "cleansing actions" to take place, the 121st ID spent the remainder of 25 June resting and refitting in Kovno, taking no action to halt the massacre.[75] Members of the 121st ID renewed their advance during the night of 25–6 June, silhouetted by the flames leaping from the city's synagogues.[76]

How did the upper echelons of Army Group North react to such murderous events? Sixteenth Army established its headquarters in the city and was clearly aware of the large-scale atrocities being committed in the near vicinity. Busch, in response to protests from his staff, merely stated that it "was an internal Lithuanian matter that does not concern us as soldiers."[77] Sixteenth Army's only true concern about the massacres was that such disturbances could lead to a deterioration of the troops' discipline; moral or ethical issues were not considered and Busch simply stated that his troops would not become involved with an "internal political affair."[78] Following the entrance of sections of Einsatzgruppe A into the city, the mass murder became a much more organized process, with forts on the outskirts of the city now serving as the sites of execution. This corresponded with arrival of the army group's headquarters, forcing Leeb to confront the reality of the Nazi New Order. While he was personally repulsed by the continuing murder in Kovno, he failed to intervene. After meeting with the commander in chief of Army Group North's rear area, General Franz von Roques, and discussing the issue with him, Leeb confided to his diary that "we have no influence over these measures. All that remains for us is to keep our distance." He continued that "the Jewish question cannot be solved in this manner" and instead suggested that "all male Jews" be sterilized.[79] Leeb and his leadership coterie's relatively benign view of the mass murder in Kovno led the ranking intelligence officer of the Kommandostabes Reichsführer-SS

---

[75] Mallmann, Rieß, and Pyta, *Deutscher Osten 1939–1945*, p. 61. One member of Sixteenth Army's staff who witnessed the events stated "we German soldiers were silent spectators; [we] had no order to stop the bloodbath in any way"; quoted in Krausnick, *Hitlers Einsatzgruppen*, p. 179; "Beiträge zur Geschichte des Gren. Regts. 405 vom 22. Juni bis ende Dezember 1941," BA-MA Msg 2/3146; "Ergänzungen für die Zeit vom 22. Juni bis 5. Juli 1941," BA-MA Msg 2/3146.
[76] "Mein Regiment," 26.6.41, BA-MA RH 37/3096.
[77] Quoted in Hürter, *Hitlers Heerführer*, p. 539.
[78] Ibid.; Andrej Angrick, "Der Stellenwert von Terror und Mord im Konzept der deutschen Besatzungspolitik im Baltikum," in Lehmann, Bohn, and Danker, *Reichskommissariat Ostland*, pp. 69–87, here p. 74.
[79] Leeb, *Tagebuchaufzeichnungen*, 8 July 1941, p. 289. For an examination of this issue from Roques's perspective, see Jörn Hasenclever, *Wehrmacht und Besatzungspolitik in der Sowjetunion: Die Befehlshaber der rückwärtigen Heeresgebiete, 1941–1943* (Paderborn, 2010), pp. 542–5.

to inform his superiors in mid-July that "the co-operation between this Einsatzkommando and the Wehrmacht [Army Group North] continues to flow smoothly."[80] With such an approach taken by the highest ranks of the army group, German soldiers marching through Kovno, including the 121st ID, could only receive the impression that their superiors not only tolerated such actions but perhaps encouraged them as well.

While the Wehrmacht's participation in the Holocaust was perhaps the vilest stain on its mantle, its treatment of Soviet civilians constituted the largest war crime in terms of scale that it committed during the war. From the opening of the 1941 invasion to the last days of the 1944 scorched-earth retreat, the German Army was in continual contact with the Soviet population. Rear-area units charged with pacifying the huge stretches of occupied territory behind the front obviously had more dealings with civilians, but frontline combat units also became increasingly engaged with civilians during the war.

As the German infantry marched through the Soviet Union, it was struck by the relative primitiveness of life.[81] Members of the 121st ID possessed the most uniformly negative views of the Soviet Union. One soldier viewed the USSR as a "bleak area, a bleak country."[82] Another man described the countryside as "a few dirty straw cottages, in which people, who possessed neither the desire nor means for orderly fields, lived."[83] This notion coincided with the view of an NCO who saw the German invasion as an attempt to impose "order on chaos."[84] The wooden houses that dominated the Lithuanian countryside also struck East Prussian soldiers as less "cultivated" than their more sturdy German stone counterparts.[85]

Men serving in the 126th ID and other Rhenish divisions shared similar views on life across the German border. One soldier noted,

> The first look at the country on the other side of the border was unforgettable. The difference between East Prussia, with its paved roads, villages and cities, and Lithuania, with its poorly marked sandy paths and poor cottages, showed that another world began here.[86]

---

[80] Quoted in Mallmann, Rieß, and Pyta, *Deutscher Osten 1939–1945*, p. 62.
[81] More examples of these types of sentiment are found in Kilian, *Wehrmacht und Besatzungsherrschaft*, pp. 188–92.
[82] Tagebuchartige Aufzeichnungen des Lt. Schmidt, 23.6.41, BA-MA RH 37/3095.
[83] "Der Todesmarsch nach Leningrad," p. 88, BA-MA Msg 2/2580.
[84] Pi.Btl. 121, 3. Juli 1941, BA-MA RH 46/717. For a further discussion of this issue, see Lower, *Nazi Empire-Building and the Holocaust in Ukraine*, p. 21.
[85] Tagebuchaufzeichnungen aus dem Rußlandfeldzug des Kp. Chef. San Kp. 21. Dr. Michael Henze vom 18.6.1941–27.07.1943, 2/3.7.41, BA-MA Msg 2/2778.
[86] Lohse, *Geschichte der rheinisch-westfälischen 126. Inf. Div. 1940–1945*, p. 12.

Members of the Rhenish 254th ID concurred with this view of the Baltic states: "The cleanliness, the care for farmland and houses that we knew in East Prussia, disappeared after we crossed the border. Primitive living conditions, shabbily clothed women and girls, poorly cultivated fields."[87] The fact that more members of the 121st ID possessed the most contemptuous views of the Soviet Union should come as no surprise. As previously noted, East Prussia was at the forefront of the fight between the German Army and Freikorps units on the one hand and communist insurgents on the other during the immediate postwar period and, as a borderlands area, took immense pride in its position as an advanced outpost of Western civilization in the "barbaric east."[88]

Though soldiers regarded Lithuania as primitive in comparison to East Prussia, they viewed social conditions in Russia proper as absolutely primordial. Heesch, an NCO in the 121st ID, recounted his impressions of the Soviet Union:

The settlements which we march through are unkempt and the houses are without exception very primitive. The inhabitants are poorly dressed. The "natives" stand on the street, the men, without shoes, wearing pants that had been patched over several times and a dirty Russian shirt ... The youngsters, wearing makeshift clothes and with heads shaven bald, look at us. The clothing of the women is completely opposite of "feminine." One frequently sees women standing along the road who nurse their children completely uninhibited. The people here are very primitive [*Naturmensch*].[89]

Lt. Schmidt wrote,

we have been in Russia for two days. The moment that we crossed the border the countryside changed completely. Instead of individual farms only villages. Instead of small fields, large fields with up to 50% lying fallow for years. The small amounts of Lithuanian culture are completely gone, now only filth ... So we march in endless expanses and only hope to soon turn north, so that we will be back in a civilized area.[90]

---

[87] Einsätze des A.R. 254. im Rußlandfeldzug von Juni 1941 bis Juli 1942, pp. 2, 7, BA-MA Msg 2/3295.
[88] Robert Traba, *Ostpreußen – die Konstruktion einer deutschen Provinz: Eine Studie zur regionalen und nationalen Identität 1914–1933* (Osnabrück, 2010), pp. 213–88.
[89] Heesch, *Meine 13. Infanterie-Geschütz-Kompanie Grenadier-Regiment 408*, p. 68. Such an assessment of the area was quite similar to Hoepner's description in a letter he wrote to his wife: "Now I am in old Russia for the first time. It is quite wretched ... The ... living quarters are terribly neglected, dirty, not livable [*betretbar*]"; for this quote and other descriptions of the area by senior commanders of Army Group North, see Hürter, *Hitlers Heerführer*, p. 443.
[90] Tagebuchartige Aufzeichnungen des Lt. Schmidt, 11.7.41, BA-MA RH 37/3095.

Seven days later, he described the first Russian city that he traveled through as "something so miserable, you can't even imagine."[91] An NCO found Russian "villages to offer the same, extremely pathetic picture that we have lived with for four weeks," adding that the houses were "dirty, primitive, and unappetizing. We would rather sleep outside than use these homes." He described the inhabitants as "all poor. Poor like a church mouse!"[92] A member of the East Prussian 21st ID's medical unit provided this view of collective-farm life: "The people, unbelievably filthy and ragged, live in rooms thick with dirt, man and animal, old and young, together. The kolkhoz cattle stand in collapsing stalls, starving and emaciated, while dying baby calves lie in waterholes."[93] Living conditions in the Soviet Union also shocked men from the Berlin-Brandenburg area. A lieutenant in the 93rd ID, remarked that the "population was frightfully poor. For some salt or sugar, they offer us chickens and butter."[94] A member of the 123rd ID was far more scornful in his outlook: "I am disappointed by the primitive lifestyles of the inhabitants of this country. They are white niggers, nothing else."[95] A soldier from Wehrkreis VI noted,

when we crossed the border for the old Russian Empire, we found no "Paradise of Labor," no trace of culture, no charming girls, who the troops wanted so badly to see, only primitive living conditions, children with torn clothing, women with discontented faces and calloused hands, people who had learned to make no demands on life, villages in which frequently only ruins testified to their once being houses.[96]

These contemptuous views of the physical appearance of the Soviet Union and its inhabitants were easily transferred to the Red Army's soldiers and the racial threat so fervently proclaimed by the Third Reich's leadership soon found its way into the letters and diaries of its soldiers.

Members of the 121st, 123rd, and 126th IDs had blamed "Asiatics" as the cause of the "devious" and "underhanded" tactics utilized by the Red Army during the initial fighting, and such characterizations only increased as the Germans advanced into Russia proper. A member of

---

[91] Ibid., 18.7.41.
[92] "Der Todesmarsch nach Leningrad," pp. 96, 77, 85, BA-MA Msg 2/2580.
[93] Tagebuchaufzeichnungen aus dem Rußlandfeldzug Dr. Michael Henze vom 10.7.41, BA-MA Msg 2/2778.
[94] Privates Kriegstagebuch aus dem Osten des Ltn. Heinrich Müller, 14.7.41, BA-MA Msg 2/2488.
[95] Lt.Wilhelm Berg, 418 Infantry Regiment, 7.7.41, BfZ, Sammlung Sterz.
[96] Einsätze des A.R. 254. im Rußlandfeldzug von Juni 1941 bis Juli 1942, pp. 2, 7, BA-MA Msg 2/3295.

the 121st ID scornfully detailed the enemy soldiers found during house-to-house fighting: "Here and there they emerged: Kirghiz, Tartars, Chechens, a complete mix of races in animal forms" who "scattered ... like rats" when flushed out of their fortifications.[97] A medic in the East Prussian 21st ID, upon seeing a wounded "Mongolian" soldier who could only utter unintelligible sounds, exclaimed "we see for the first time what we have before us."[98] Lt. Schmidt also viewed the Asian soldiers in the Red Army as extremely dangerous and inhuman: "of course the soldiers out of the Caucasus ... are nasty in their grinning fanaticism. One fights against them as one would against animals, without the feeling of having anything in common with them."[99] The Communications Section concurred with this assessment, stating that "the first prisoners made such an animal and completely inhuman impression on us. Completely depraved forms! Or if [they were] men, their miserable existence, which they were forced to lead, could literally be read in their eyes."[100] The themes hammered home by Nazi propaganda, as well as those that existed within traditional German culture, certainly found fertile ground within Army Group North's infantry divisions.

Such negative views of the Soviet Union and its inhabitants influenced the treatment of enemy civilians. Irritation caused by sporadic irregular warfare elided with Nazi propaganda and the Prusso-German Army's traditional aversion to people's war to make each and every Soviet civilian a potential resister, and this led the 126th ID to act pre-emptively and arrest various civilians during the opening weeks of war.[101] Beliefs that "a pack of kolkhoz workers" were no more than "a pack of gorillas" certainly increased the hostility of German soldiers to the surrounding inhabitants and eased the implementation of such actions.[102] Confusion concerning the treatment of these individuals forced the division's ranking intelligence officer to issue an order stating that "civilians (communists, Jews) who have committed offenses against German soldiers, and suspicious elements, are <u>not</u> to be sent to the division. They are to be handled according to the guidelines given out at the commander meeting on 21.6."[103] The blatantly ideological formulation of this order in which

---

[97] Pi.Btl. 121, 3. Juli 1941, BA-MA RH 46/716.
[98] Tagebuchaufzeichnungen aus dem Rußlandfeldzug Dr. Michael Henze, 23.6.41, BA-MA Msg 2/2778.
[99] Tagebuchartige Aufzeichnungen des Lt. Schmidt, 15.7.41, BA-MA RH 37/3095.
[100] "Chronik der 2. Kompanie Nachrichten-Abteilung 121," BA-MA RH 44/381.
[101] Abt. Qu, Tagesmeldung 5.7.41, BA-MA RH 26–126/138. The division had arrested 322 civilians since the invasion began.
[102] Tagebuchaufzeichnungen aus dem Rußlandfeldzug Dr. Michael Henze, 10.7.41, BA-MA Msg 2/2778.
[103] 126 ID, Abt. Ic, 2.7.41, BA-MA RH 26–126/116; emphasis in original.

all suspicious elements were equated with "communists" and "Jews" left no doubt that these civilians faced immediate execution.

Distrust and overt hostility towards the Soviet population, however, were not universally held by all German soldiers. Some saw Russian civilians as victims of the communist regime and viewed their lot with varying degrees of pity. One soldier from the 121st ID wrote,

older people from the Tsarist period still live in poverty today. The new generation has not been made any richer by the Soviets. They live as best as one can in an apathy that was reflected in their faces. Joy and pleasure were dead, the belief in a better future taken away.[104]

Another member of the division believed that the Soviet "people had scarcely any feeling left after decades of suffering under Bolshevism." He also excused the Soviet population from conducting a "treacherous or even underhanded" war because Stalin had called for such a struggle and it was "led by the *politruks*, the political combatants," placing Soviet citizens in a "cauldron which we can't understand."[105] Others from Wehrkreis III also viewed the population, especially those who suffered from the effects of the fighting, in a sympathetic manner:

I no longer get worked up seeing all of the dead bodies, but, as in France, it is much more the various individual fates of the civilian population that preoccupy and burden me. The houses and barns burn, the horses are requisitioned by the troops, the man is shot, miscarriages, tears, worries, screams. So it goes all day.[106]

The racism that permeated the army failed to completely eradicate every soldier's compassion; one East Prussian NCO recognized that even the "Mongolian faces under shaven heads" were "sons of the Russian earth [who] had mothers at home" and these women "would cry for days." This individual's personal humanity, however, faded before the larger processes at play, a fact he was indeed well aware of: "but such is war!"[107]

This relative sympathy for civilians, however, was paralleled by a hatred of the Soviet state. One subunit of the 121st ID wholeheartedly agreed with "the words of the Führer ... that the victory of Bolshevism would mean the downfall of European culture."[108] This sentiment was shared by another divisional soldier, who, after entering a house filled

---

[104] "Mein Regiment," 21.9.41, BA-MA RH 37/3096.
[105] "Der Todesmarsch nach Leningrad," pp. 112, 104, BA-MA Msg 2/2580. Attached to lower-level units such as platoons and companies, *politruks* were political officers charged with giving political guidance to the men. For a brief discussion of *politruk* activities, see Reese, *Stalin's Reluctant Soldiers*, pp. 79–80.
[106] Corporal Fritz Lieb, 68 Infantry Regiment, 28.6.41, BfZ, Sammlung Sterz.
[107] "Der Todesmarsch nach Leningrad," p. 36, BA-MA Msg 2/2580.
[108] "Chronik der 2. Kompanie Nachrichten-Abteilung 121," BA-MA RH 44/381.

with Soviet propaganda materials, thanked God for saving him from this "culture and civilized progress," adding that "even the dumbest soldier soon understood what Bolshevism would have meant in every respect for Germany."[109] He suffered no illusion, however, that the Soviet people "would become happier through our 'liberation'":

> Though the field kitchens come on most evenings, the soldier must supply himself during the course of the day. He had no choice but to plunder the gardens during the day ... The poor population then had more items absolutely necessary for their livelihood taken by the baggage units. Behind us came other organizations who took up this cause and this did not contribute to any increase in trust in the German leadership.[110]

As noted by this soldier, the policy of living off the land not only seriously threatened available food stocks in the country, it also led to growing discontent on the part of civilians with the German Army.

III. A question of food

While the German infantry learned that the Red Army, however ineptly led and trained, was prepared to defend bitterly its country, armed resistance was just one issue afflicting the Wehrmacht during June and July 1941. Leeb believed that "the strains of the campaign up until this point have been caused by the relentlessness [of the advance], the poor conditions of the roads and the extremely hot weather ... Those troops dependent on horses are the most strained."[111] Leeb's concerns zeroed in on what was the Achilles heel of the Wehrmacht: logistics. Utterly focused on achieving decisive success on the battlefield, German planners neglected this aspect of the campaign. Prewar supply planning overwhelmingly focused on ensuring that the panzer groups were able to maintain the rate of their advance; this meant that the army's available trucks were concentrated for the use of the panzer and motorized divisions while the majority of the infantry remained dependent on slow-moving horses and carts.[112]

---

[109] Such a sentiment was quite pervasive throughout the *Ostheer*; for several examples of similar statements, see Bartov, *Hitler's Army*, pp. 155–7.
[110] Der Todesmarsch nach Leningrad," pp. 112, BA-MA Msg 2/2580.
[111] Leeb, *Tagebuchaufzeichnungen*, 12 July 1941, p. 293.
[112] Müller states that seventy-seven German infantry divisions were entirely dependent on horse-drawn supply; see Müller, "Das Scheitern der wirtschaftlichen 'Blitzkriegstrategie,'" pp. 1138–44, here p. 1140. For an interesting discussion of Army Group Center's horse-drawn transport challenges, see Stahel, *Operation Barbarossa*, pp. 184–5. On the logisitic problems facing the Wehrmacht during Operation Barbarossa, see Klaus Jochen Arnold, *Die Wehrmacht und die Besatzungspolitik in den besetzten Gebieten der Sowjetunion* (Berlin, 2005), pp. 214–25.

Illustration 3.1 German troops confidently advance towards Leningrad in the summer of 1941.

Despite this, Army Group North actually fared the best of the three invading army groups in terms of supply.[113] The more constricted theater of operation for Leeb's army group was partially responsible for this. Unlike Army Groups Center and South, whose advances created extremely large operational areas and consequently long supply routes, Army Group North advanced within a relatively more compact area. The northernmost army group also possessed other advantages. In comparison with the other theaters of war, the rail and road networks in the Baltic states were relatively well developed and once the Germans had seized the Estonian coast, its harbors also provided a means for goods to be shipped from Germany to Army Group North.[114] According to prewar planning, however, such supplies were to be limited primarily to ammunition and other military essentials and this worked to the disadvantage of German forces in the area. Despite the prewar belief that the region's agricultural surplus would provide little or no food for the Wehrmacht, the men of Army Group North were no different than the remainder of the *Ostheer* in that they were expected to live off the land.[115] Once again, the quest for decisive victory that served as the

---

[113] Müller, "Das Scheitern der wirtschaftlichen 'Blitzkriegstrategie'," p. 1145; Martin van Creveld, *Supplying War: Logistics from Wallenstein to Patton* (Cambridge, 1977), p. 162.
[114] Müller, "Das Scheitern der wirtschaftlichen 'Blitzkriegstrategie'," p. 1145.
[115] Hass, "Deutsche Besatzungspolitik im Leningrader Gebiet 1941–1944," pp. 66–7; Alexander Hill, *The War behind the Eastern Front: The Soviet Partisan Movement in North-West Russia 1941–44* (London, 2005), p. 26; de Goure, *The Siege of Leningrad*, p. 6.

foundation for military necessity intersected with the German state's racial hierarchies to the detriment of Soviet civilians.

The tension caused by Economic Staff East's conflicting aims – feeding the Eastern Army and ensuring that Soviet production was effectively exploited for the Reich – led to real conflict between German institutions in the East.[116] Initially, the upper echelons of the Wehrmacht tried to limit the "wild plundering" of the troops. II Corps, the 121st ID's superior formation, issued an order on 3 July stating that the confiscation of horses without payment "is plundering and will be treated as such."[117] The corps also complained of troops giving out receipts to farmers "with unrecognizable, very vague, or unreadable writing" in an attempt to escape payment.[118] Already during the first three weeks of war, the problem reached such proportions that Sixteenth Army demanded a halt to these practices, arguing that confiscations destroyed the relationship between the Wehrmacht and civilians. The army allowed the purchase of goods required for the war effort but the troops needed to follow the dictates of common sense: no soldier was to take the last cow or horse from a peasant.[119]

This initial restraint, however, was soon jettisoned. Christian Gerlach has observed that "only two to four weeks after the beginning of the invasion, the organized plundering of the occupied territories for food was declared a primary objective of German divisions," and this certainly rings true for the infantry divisions in Army Group North.[120] In a stunning reversal from its earlier position a mere three weeks earlier, II Corps, claiming that the supply situation was at a "breaking point," ordered its subordinate troops to "exhaust all means" to alleviate the situation.[121] From late July through the end of the 1941–2 winter crisis, the German Army plundered the Soviet Union and its inhabitants on a scale unprecedented in modern European history.

---

[116] For an examination of this clash of interests between the Wirtschaftsstab Ost and the 121st ID, see, Rutherford, "The Radicalization of German Occupation Policies," pp. 139–46.
[117] Der Kommandierende General des II. Armeekorps, Korpstagesbefehl, 3.7.41, BA-MA RH 24-2/83.
[118] Generalkommando II. Armeekorps, Abt. Qu., Besondere Anordnungen für die Versorgung des II A.K. Nr. 22, 18.7.41, BA-MA RH 24-2/462. One German official noted that peasants frequently were given receipts that stated "paid for by the love of God" or, less eloquently, "kiss my ass"; see Müller, *Die deutsche Wirtschaftspolitik*, p. 595.
[119] Armee Oberkommando 16, Armeetagesbefehl Nr. 17, 14.7.41, BA-MA RH 24-2/83. Further examples of these types of orders are found in Bartov, *Hitler's Army*, pp. 77–9.
[120] Gerlach, *Kalkulierte Morde*, p. 255.
[121] Generalkommando II. Armeekorps, Abt. Qu., Besondere Anordnungen für die Versorgung des II A.K. Nr. 30, 26.7.41, BA-MA RH 24-2/462.

Why the shift in policy? Halder noted in early July that Army Group North's supply situation was "satisfactory."[122] A closer look at this diary entry, however, reveals the fundamental weakness of Operation Barbarossa. While the Army Chief of Staff mentioned the "mass of the army," i.e. Sixteenth and Eighteenth Armies, his focus was on Panzer Group 4. Though Army Group North's supply system was never fully put at the disposal of Hoepner's unit, it was increasingly concentrated for his tanks and this meant that the infantry armies were given much less priority for resupply.[123] As 1941 continued on, the infantry units, especially those attached to Sixteenth Army, felt the shift in favor of the armor, and requisitioning became interwoven in the everyday activities of German infantry divisions.[124]

The supply situation of all three divisions roughly followed the evolution sketched above. "Living off the land assumed a great importance during the advance," claimed the 126th ID's quartermaster, and such an assessment applied to both the 121st and 123rd IDs as well.[125] While both of the latter divisions received regular shipments of food throughout the first two weeks of the invasion, the men from each unit requisitioned foodstuffs as they marched east.[126] One soldier noted that "our supply functions reasonably well so no one can complain even when, of course, we are missing fresh vegetables, butter, etc."[127] These missing vegetables and other items such as chickens were increasingly procured from the countryside, supplementing official supplies to a great extent.[128] One soldier wryly noted that "many hens found in hidden corners were forced to give up their lives for Germany's Wehrmacht." The commandeering of pigs and other animals became such an everyday occurrence that Russian peasants "watched these goings-on

---

[122] Halder, *Kriegstagebuch*, vol. III, 1 July 1941, p. 32.
[123] Müller, "Das Scheitern der wirtschaftlichen 'Blitzkriegstrategie'," p. 1145; Creveld, *Supplying War*, p. 159.
[124] Halder, *Kriegstagebuch*, vol. III, 23 July 1941, p. 106.
[125] 126 Infanterie-Division, Abt. IVa, 15.3.1942, Tätigkeitsbericht der Abt. IVa für die Zeit vom 22.6 bis 31.12.1941, BA-MA RH 26–126/140.
[126] For the 123rd ID, see 123 ID, Abt. IVa, 9.12.41, Tätigkeitsbericht für die Zeit vom 22.6–30.6.41; 123 ID, Abt. IVa, 16.12.1941, Tätigkeitsbericht für die Zeit vom 1.7–31.7.41, BA-MA RH 26–123/198; for the 121st ID, see KTB I, Abt. Ib, Divisionsintendant 121 Inf. Division 10.3.1942, Tätigkeitsbericht für die Zeit vom 20.6.41 bis 20.9.41, BA-MA RH 26–121/65.
[127] Tagebuchartige Aufzeichnungen des Lt. Schmidt, 13.7.41, BA-MA RH 37/3095. He also added that "where we have been marching, there are no chickens and only a few lean pigs – what will we do if the rations no longer come on schedule?" Ibid., 15.7.41.
[128] KTB, Abt. Ib, Divisionsintendant 121 Inf. Division, 10.3.1942, Tätigkeitsbericht für die Zeit vom 20.6.41 bis 20.9.41, BA-MA RH 26–121/65. The quartermaster excused these unlawful requisitions by arguing that the "considerable strains" on the troops in combat made them "essential."

with indifference."[129] Payment for these requisitions was quite haphazard; while the 121st ID's quartermaster claimed that every attempt was made to reimburse the collective farms or village mayors, this frequently proved impossible and the troops simply seized many cattle without payment.[130]

By late summer, the German supply system faced new strains. The summer heat spoiled meat deliveries from the rear, forcing the Germans to find such nourishment in the Soviet Union itself. In combination with these high temperatures, the increasing pace of the advance also wreaked havoc on the army's horses, causing many of them to "fall like flies."[131] Another cause of the horses' overexertion was the primitive Soviet road network.[132] Finally, those Red Army soldiers scattered by the initial German advance found themselves in a sparsely occupied rear area and they hit German supply columns with increasing frequency. While the 121st ID complained of its supply columns being "frequently attacked by partisans," the 123rd ID suffered several rather debilitating attacks. The most damaging took place on 19 July when superior Soviet forces destroyed the 418th Infantry Regiment's supply convoy, with the Germans suffering heavy casualties. This forced the division to utilize "all available troops" to keep supplies moving towards the front, a dissipation of strength it could ill afford.[133] Cumulatively, these developments led to a growing radicalization of the Wehrmacht's requisitioning policy.

The 123rd ID was the first unit to order its men to "cover" their own needs every second day in late June and, by early July, the combat troops were ordered to "cover their immediate needs."[134] The East Prussians

---

[129] "Der Todesmarsch nach Leningrad," pp. 74, 112, BA-MA Msg 2/2580. The author also noted (p. 94) that "many pigs, even when dead, took part on our march to Leningrad."

[130] KTB, Abt. Ib, Divisionsintendant 121 Inf. Division, 10.3.1942, Tätigkeitsbericht für die Zeit vom 20.6.41 bis 20.9.41, BA-MA RH 26–121/65; for similar statements from the 126th ID, see 126 Infanterie-Division, Abt. IVa, 15.3.1942, Tätigkeitsbericht der Abt. IVa für die Zeit vom 22.6 bis 31.12.1941, BA-MA RH 26–126/140.

[131] Lt. Wilhelm Berg, 418 Infantry Regiment, 6.7.41, BfZ, Sammlung Sterz.

[132] For the 121st ID, see KTB, Abt. Ib, Divisionsintendant 121 Inf. Division, 10.3.1942, Tätigkeitsbericht für die Zeit vom 20.6.41 bis 20.9.41, BA-MA RH 26–121/65; for the 123rd, see Kommandierende General des XXVIII AK, 21.7.41, Grundsätze für die weitere Durchführung des Vormarsches nach Nordosten, BA-MA RH 26–123/15.

[133] On this incident, see 19. Juli, 22:00 Uhr von Ib, BA-MA RH 26–123/15; 123 ID Abt. Ia/Az.IV/Op. Tagesmeldung, 19.7.41, BA-MA RH 26–123/36; and Quartiermeister Kriegstagebuch, 19.7.41, BA-MA RH 24–28/10.

[134] 123 ID, Abt. IVa, 9.12.41, Tätigkeitsbericht für die Zeit vom 22.6–30.6.41; 123 ID, Abt. IVa, 16.12.1941, Tätigkeitsbericht für die Zeit vom 1.7–31.7.41, BA-MA RH 26–123/198; Anlage zu den Besonderen Anordnungen für den Versorgung am 6.7.41, Erfassung vom Beute und Verräten, BA-MA RH 26–123/184.

were instructed to feed themselves and their horses every second day on 20 July. Lt. Schmidt vividly described the process:

> mounted troops swarm like the Huns to the right and left of the route of advance, searching for hay, pigs, calves, [and] chickens in villages kilometers away. There is, however, little there and when we are gone, there is nothing left.[135]

By "unleashing the locusts," the German Army encouraged the hitherto unorganized and minuscule resistance movement.[136] As one soldier noted, a *Landser* who slaughtered a farmer's last cow merely to satisfy his desire for a taste of liver added "another family to the partisans."[137]

Already in the summer of 1941, the army's practice of living off the land threatened the Soviet population with starvation. On 10 July, the 126th ID's ranking intelligence officer noted that the native inhabitants "literally were breadless, as they had no private stocks."[138] An officer in the 123rd ID corroborated this view, stating that "the system of Russian economic life has collapsed. The delivery and distribution of foodstuffs is tied up with this. The specter of famine threatens the civilian population!"[139] He continued by adding that "there is no organization available that can be made responsible for the continuation of the economy and for the feeding of the civilian population." While he recognized the results of the Wehrmacht's policy of confiscating foodstuffs, he was also clear that the army itself could not be responsible for the civilian population. The requirements of the army – the need to defeat the Soviet Union in a lightning victory – meant that the needs of civilians were simply ignored by the Wehrmacht. Military necessity trumped all.

IV. The radicalization of military necessity

On 3 July, a soldier attached to a Rhenish division in Army Group North noted "the cities and villages which we pass through are all destroyed and gutted by flames. Where have the many people gone? We don't see them.

---

[135] Tagebuchartige Aufzeichnungen des Lt. Schmidt, 20.7.41, BA-MA RH 37/3095.
[136] The phrase is Ben Shepherd's; see his *War in the Wild East*, p. 186.
[137] "Der Todesmarsch nach Leningrad," p. 117, BA-MA Msg 2/2580.
[138] 126 ID, Abt. Ic, Stimmungsbericht über die russische Bevölkerung aus Krasnoj am 10.7.41, BA-MA RH 26–126/116. Though this report blamed the Russians for "having burned the best buildings and destroyed all of the [food] stocks," German requisitions from the destitute population could only have catastrophic effects on their living standards.
[139] Anlage zu den besonderen Anordnungen für die Versorgung vom 24.7.41. Verhalten der Organe des Kdt. d. rückwartige Armee Gebiet und der Truppe bei Wiederingangsetzung der russischen Landwirtschaft, BA-MA RH 26–123/184.

They run around the ruins [and] live in the forests."[140] Such a sentiment expressed the devastating effects of the German invasion of the Soviet Union, an operation that not only targeted the Soviet state and Red Army but also directly affected the lives of noncombatants. While earlier German campaigns resulted in civilians taking to the roads in the millions trying to escape the onrushing Wehrmacht, the design of Operation Barbarossa ensured that the tenuous civil society that existed in Stalinist Russia simply crumbled in many places.[141] Individual soldiers at times reacted sympathetically to the plight of civilians, but for the army as an institution, such matters were of little to no concern. From the perspective of Army Group North's infantry divisions, the military struggle came before all else and this included both their role in the *Weltanschauungskrieg* and their responsibility for the civilian population.[142] This focus on defeating the Red Army in battle is perhaps best exemplified by Lt. Schmidt's musings on the topic. The regime's presentation of the conflict infuriated him, despite his racist view of Asian soldiers. He angrily wrote, "these PK [Propaganda Company] reports make one sick, even when they are well written, because they try to paint these serious, manly events theatrically. We speak of 'Russians' while the Prop [aganda] people only speak of the 'Reds'." He then provided a sample remark produced by the propaganda companies: "The soldiers excitedly call for the Red Panzer," noting contemptuously that "such a remark is unthinkable," coming from an actual soldier.[143] For Schmidt, the defeat of the Soviet Army required professionalism and grit, not slogans that cheapened the trials of combat. While he undoubtedly possessed a racist view of the Asian soldiers in the Red Army, Schmidt did not subscribe to Operation Barbarossa as a "crusade" against Bolshevism; rather it was a contest of arms.

This focus on the destruction of the Red Army in combat crystallized during the opening days of the invasion, when the German Army suffered significant casualties. Instead of meeting a shapeless and poorly led mass of *Untermenschen* on the battlefield, the Wehrmacht found itself locked in a hitherto unprecedented war of savagery. The brutality of this

[140] Corporal Fritz Lieb, 68th Infantry Regiment, 3.7.41, BfZ, Sammlung Sterz.
[141] An examination of French refugee movement during the summer of 1940 is found in Hanna Diamond, *Fleeing Hitler: France 1940* (Oxford, 2007); for a superb look at the breakdown of prewar Greek society under the strains of German occupation, see Mazower, *Inside Hitler's Greece*.
[142] Hartmann's description of the activities of the 296th ID – "similarly to most of the combat units, the 296th ID was also completely occupied with military happenings [during the opening months of the invasion]" – applies, with some qualification, to the 121st, 123rd, and 126th IDs. See Hartmann, *Wehrmacht im Ostkrieg*, p. 303.
[143] Tagebuchartige Aufzeichnungen des Lt. Schmidt, 11.7.41, BA-MA RH 37/3095.

war was due not merely to intense combat or ideological considerations but also to arbitrary violence on the battlefield as the mutilation and murder of German prisoners by Soviet soldiers and reciprocal actions carried out by the Germans on captured Red Army men led to a spiraling of violence on both sides.[144]

The Soviet use of "treacherous" and "underhanded" behavior on the battlefield also led German soldiers to respond with increased violence, though this was directed against civilians in many cases as the notion of total war animated the thinking of the Wehrmacht as an institution. Not all divisions, however, fought Hitler's intended *Vernichtungskrieg* against Soviet society at this stage of the war. While the 126th ID carried out a murderous collective action against the Russian village of Dorochova, the 121st ID had behaved in a much more restrained manner a month previously towards the inhabitants of the Lithuanian village of Karzai. While both divisions were heirs to the same institutional anti-partisan legacy and were subjected to the same ideological pressure from the Nazi state, they nonetheless reacted differently. Here, situational factors loom large in explaining their diverse reactions. Varied understandings of military necessity also played a role in determining the actions of the two divisions. During the summer of 1941, the 121st ID subscribed to a more nuanced version of military necessity, one in which not all civilians were viewed and treated as potential enemies. Certainly the threat of violence was present in the East Prussians' dealings with civilians, but during the first two months of the war, it failed to bubble to the surface.[145] The 126th ID, however, followed a more radicalized interpretation of military necessity and this led it to utilize force as the only means to achieve its military mission.

One area in which all three divisions acted uniformly concerned their forced requisitions of foodstuffs. With the pace of the advance playing havoc with their supply, the German infantry increasingly followed the dictates of Berlin in living off the land. Here, the Wehrmacht's focus on successfully completing their military objective meant that civilians and their fate were generally ignored. Even when it became clear that civilians were going to starve on a vast scale, the divisions continued with their

---

[144] For a perceptive discussion of the violence unleashed by the Soviet state and its Red Army, see Amir Weiner, "Something to Die for, a Lot to Kill for: The Soviet System and the Barbarization of Warfare, 1939–1945," in Kassimeris, *The Barbarization of Warfare*, pp. 101–25.
[145] 121 ID, Abt. Ic, 1.7.41, BA-MA RH 26–121/55. One NCO wrote that during searches for members of the Red Army in villages, the inhabitants were warned that in case of ambush, the Germans would be "forced to burn down all of the straw huts"; see "Der Todesmarsch nach Leningrad," pp. 61–2, BA-MA Msg 2/2580.

plundering of the countryside.[146] When one soldier lamented that "the good days are gone in the Soviet-paradise ... honey and wild strawberries are the only food available to supplement the hungry *Landser*'s rations," he failed to consider how the surrounding civilians who were not receiving "*Landser*'s rations" would survive on such meager nourishment.[147]

Racist views of the Soviet population undoubtedly played a role in easing the consciences of the German High Command, as did the communist political system that ruled the area. This did not mean, however, that every individual in field gray subscribed to such a uniformly negative view of the Soviet population. One soldier viewed civilians with a mixture of pity and shame:

> we ... came to what can really be described as a city ... and once again experienced the misery of refugees and other things which one cannot say a word about for many reasons and which are very difficult to think about.[148]

Such sympathetic views were also complemented by much more critical perspectives.

One soldier in the 121st ID questioned not only the idea of crusade against "Jewish Bolshevism," but that of the war itself. He discussed the legitimacy of the invasion with a close friend:

> In secret we thought about the war of Christendom against the atheistic *Untermenschen*! But since when was that a legitimate reason? One should first suffer an injustice before he commits one. One loses himself in endless debate! And then is one marked as a defeatist? ... Yes, yes, the Fatherland! I learned from my mother to sing, I am a Prussian, I learned my colors and the refrain that my Fatherland must be greater. Should Hitler's Reich stretch to Leningrad and Moscow?

His friend replied that one needed to trust in the Führer and "do our duty without any consideration of what may come. There is no longer any escape."[149] Instead of racial warriors determined to create a new Aryan empire in eastern Europe, this exchange reveals two soldiers who carried out their patriotic duty but nonetheless questioned the basis for such a duty. While this was in all likelihood a minority viewpoint within the *Ostheer*, it does highlight the wide spectrum of perspectives within the army's ranks during the summer of 1941.

---

[146] This was not a practice limited to Army Group North. Further to the south, 18th Panzer Division continued to confiscate foodstuffs on a large scale despite the knowledge that this would lead to serious problems for the native population; see Bartov, *The Eastern Front*, p. 131.
[147] Lt. Wilhelm Berg, 418 Infantry Regiment, 17.7.41, BfZ, Sammlung Sterz.
[148] Heinz Bucholz, Art. Regt. 227, 7.7.41, BfZ, Sammlung Sterz.
[149] "Der Todesmarsch nach Leningrad," pp. 107–8, BA-MA Msg 2/2580.

Despite working within the context of the criminal orders and the considerable racist sentiments that the men of the Wehrmacht carried with them, each division behaved in a relatively restrained manner during the first two months of the invasion. While the men of the 121st, 123rd, and 126th IDs plundered the civilian population for food and occasionally reacted with real violence towards the threat of irregular warfare, as called for by their ideologically driven superiors, they primarily focused on their military task: defeating the Red Army in battle. As their military situation worsened during the following months, however, the tenets of military necessity and ideology became increasingly blurred and the war in the east took on a new shade of brutality.

4 "Will the continuation of this attack be worth it?"
The drive on Leningrad

As Ernst Klink has remarked, the "basic problem confronting the Wehrmacht in the East [was] providing the necessary fighting forces in an expanding theater of operations from an unchanging and limited number of available soldiers."[1] While this proved to be an increasingly insurmountable problem for Army Groups Center and South due to their deployment in much more expansive areas, Leeb's army group also found that the factors of time and strength began to work against a successful campaign in the late summer and early fall of 1941. He noted that his front had grown from 200 kilometers at the beginning of the invasion to one that stretched over 650 kilometers by mid-July, while the strength of the army group had decreased with the loss of two divisions.[2] Leeb believed that he required thirty-five divisions to successfully complete his various missions, but he had only twenty-six at his disposal.[3] The transfer of these divisions to Army Group Center highlighted the increasing confusion within the German command over the operation's ultimate goals. The simmering conflict between Hitler and the OKH that existed from the very beginning of the campaign now began to boil over: was the focus of the operation to be Moscow, as favored by Halder, or the advance on the wings, as advocated by Hitler?[4]

Leeb, as commander of the formation charged with capturing the cradle of Bolshevism, certainly wanted to pin this honor to his mantle. The constant hemorrhaging of troops to Army Group Center, however, decreased the likelihood of such a triumph. Compounding this problem, the terrain lying across the most direct route to Leningrad was a swampy

---

[1] Klink, "Die Operationsführung," in Boog et al., *Der Angriff auf die Sowjetunion*, pp. 451–652, here p. 625.
[2] Leeb, *Tagebuchaufzeichnungen*, 17 July 1941, p. 298. The two divisions were sent to Army Group Center. Army Group North would later lose another two divisions to its southern neighbor; see his entry for 2 August 1941, p. 317.
[3] Klink, "Die Operationsführung," p. 628.
[4] For a persuasive and nuanced discussion of this "leadership crisis," see ibid., pp. 576–84; and Stahel, *Operation Barbarossa*, pp. 273–9.

morass, "thoroughly unsuitable as tank country."[5] As the situation developed up through mid-July, Leeb became increasingly convinced that "large [armor] raids need to be avoided" and he forced Panzer Group 4 to wait for the advancing infantry to close up and strengthen its forces for what he believed would be a much more traditional battle.[6] In order to compensate for the relative weakness of his army group, he also counted on Panzer Group 3 turning north in order to assist with the clearing of Sixteenth Army's right flank and to break the Moscow–Leningrad rail line. This coincided with Hitler's view and the Führer promised Leeb the use of the additional armor during a meeting at Army Group North headquarters on 21 July.[7]

Halder and the General Staff, however, continued to view Moscow as the operation's primary goal, and in a new directive released on 31 July, Panzer Group 3 remained under the command of Army Group Center. The directive also changed Army Group North's objectives: instead of capturing Leningrad, the city was now to be merely isolated from the remainder of the Soviet Union.[8] In addition to this task, Leeb also needed to construct a defensive front to the east of the Leningrad encirclement, a task he believed "impossible" as the proposed line measured 360 kilometers north to south and he simply did not have enough troops to man such a position.[9] Sixteenth Army, whose primary task in the new directive concerned the construction of the defensive line running from the boundary with Army Group Center to the besieging lines outside Leningrad, would now most certainly have to dedicate more units to encircling Leningrad, due to the heavy casualties suffered by Eighteenth Army and especially Panzer Group 4.[10] This new mission forced its subordinate corps to move in divergent directions in order to fulfill their

---

[5] Quoted text in Manstein, *Lost Victories*, p. 199; see also de Beaulieu, *Der Vorstoß der Panzergruppe 4*, p. 151; Hürter, *Hitlers Heerführer*, p. 287.
[6] Leeb, *Tagebuchaufzeichnungen*, 26 July 1941, p. 308.
[7] For Hitler's view on the situation, see Schramm, *KTB OKW*, vol. II, Führererwägung am 17. Juli 1941, p. 1029. On the meeting, see ibid., Besuch des Führers bei Heeres-Gruppe Nord am 21. Juli 1941, pp. 1029–30; Leeb, *Tagebuchaufzeichnungen*, 21 July 1941, p. 302. Hitler's 19 July war directive codified this view; see Weisung Nr. 33, Fortführung des Krieges im Osten, in Hubatsch, *Hitlers Weisungen*, pp. 163–5, here p. 164.
[8] Halder, *Kriegstagebuch*, vol. III, 15 July 1941, p. 80. For a detailed examination of the German decision-making process concerning Leningrad, see Jörg Ganzenmüller, "... die Stadt dem Erdboden gleichmachen": Zielsetzung und Motive der deutschen Blockade Leningrads," in Stefan Creuzberger et al. (eds.), *St. Petersburg – Leningrad – St. Petersburg: Eine Stadt im Spiegel der Zeit* (Stuttgart, 2000), pp. 179–95.
[9] Leeb, *Tagebuchaufzeichnungen*, 31 July 1941, p. 313.
[10] This proved especially true when the OKH ordered Army Group North to release Panzer Group 4 as well as VIII Air Corps to Army Group Center by 15 September for the assault on Moscow. See Klink, "Die Operationsführung," p. 632.

objectives. At the beginning of August, the 121st ID's parent, XXVIII Corps, drove on the eastern flank of Panzer Group 4 as it advanced in a northeasterly direction towards Leningrad while II Corps, which contained 123rd ID, marched to the east towards Kholm. 126th ID and its superior, X Corps, advanced between these two formations towards the Staraia Russa–Novgorod region.

Up through July, the 121st, 123rd, and 126th IDs fought relatively similar wars and intersected with Soviet civilians in a generally comparable manner, though the 126th ID certainly behaved more radically than its peer divisions. Beginning in August, however, as their missions changed, so did the circumstances that each division faced. Since circumstances frequently had some causative effect on their behavior, the divisions began to respond to their new situations in different ways. While this seems self-evident, it is nonetheless an important point: if these three divisions, operating in the most concentrated and homogeneous environment of any of the three army groups, reacted in different manners to their surroundings, the difficulty in ascribing a "model" behavior or attitude to the 139 German divisions that invaded the Soviet Union in June 1941 becomes clear.

I. From blitzkrieg to *Stellungskrieg*

During early August, all three divisions found themselves locked in increasingly heavy combat. Leeb's command charged XXVIII Corps, the 121st ID's superior formation, with the task of breaking the last known fortified Soviet position before Leningrad, the Luga Line, and then with shielding Panzer Group 4's right flank as it drove on Leningrad.[11] The cracking of this position was a methodical and bloody process that led to "extraordinarily heavy casualties" in the 405th Infantry Regiment. One cause of the division's difficulties was its deficiency in artillery: possessing less than half of the artillery normally allotted to an infantry division, the East Prussians were forced to turn to Stuka dive-bombers to blast through the bunker system.[12] After an advance that took four days instead of the originally scheduled two, the 121st ID finally reached the Luga river on 13 August and prepared to cross the river the next day. The heavy fighting

---

[11] Sydnor, *Soldiers of Destruction*, p. 171.
[12] 121 ID KTB, 11.8.41, BA-MA RH 26–121/8. The bunkers were constructed out of wood and covered with up to six feet of earth. See 121 ID, KTB, 12.8.41, BA-MA RH 26–121/8. On casualties as well as artillery strength, see XXVIII AK KTB, 10.8.41, 11.8.41, BA-MA RH 24–28/20. Members of the 121st ID viewed the strength of the Stuka dive-bombers as primarily "moral" as "it is well known that the Russian loses his head when a plane is in the air"; 121 ID KTB, 11.8.41, BA-MA RH 26–121/8. For more on the Luga Line, see Salisbury, *The 900 Days*, pp. 173–4; and Glantz, *The Battle for Leningrad*, pp. 60–1.

Illustration 4.1 German infantry units fight north of the Luga Line during the advance.

and hitherto unprecedented casualties suffered by the division, however, led one officer to comment, "Will the continuation of this attack be worth it?"[13]

While the East Prussians methodically battered through the Luga Line, their comrades in the 126th ID faced similar combat against a well-entrenched opponent in their attempt to seize Staraia Russa.[14] During the eight-day fight for the city, the division suffered an astounding 1,200 casualties. Such losses led the division commander to report that "all in all, the troops are near the end of their physical and material combat strength."[15] A promised period of rest and refitting failed to materialize, however, as the need for a quick and decisive victory

---

[13] 121 ID KTB, 11.8.41, BA-MA RH 26–121/8. One soldier noted that "this was the worst fighting with the most casualties since we had been in the East"; see "Der Todesmarsch nach Leningrad," BA-MA Msg 2/2580.

[14] 126 ID KTB, 6.8.41, BA-MA RH 26–126/4; 126 ID, 4.8.41, Divisionsbefehl für die Fortführung des Angriffs auf Staraja Russa am 5.8.41, BA-MA RH 26–126/5; Leeb, *Tagebuchaufzeichnungen*, 6 August 1941, p. 321.

[15] 126 Inf. Div. Meldung vom 22.8.41, BA-MA RH 26–126/23. The division's war diary noted that the "combat strength of the division has been considerably lowered during the recent fighting"; 126 ID KTB, 10.8.41, 12.8.41, BA-MA RH 26–126/4. See also Tätigkeitsbericht der Abt. IIa/b, Stand vom 30.9.41, BA-MA RH 26–126/131.

remained paramount and the division was thrown back into the fray in defensive fighting in the Novgorod region.[16] The Red Army's stubborn and repeated attacks again took a serious toll on the troops, with the 424th Infantry Regiment's commander reporting that "not only is the combat strength weakened," but also his troops were so exhausted that "sentries are increasingly caught sleeping at their posts."[17] Despite these strains, some Rhenish infantrymen maintained their belief in a speedy victory. One wrote, "from now on, we are entering into the final battle. In a few weeks, victory will certainly be ours. Difficult days stand before us *Frontsoldaten*, but we will conquer come what may."[18]

Further to the south, the 123rd ID also engaged in its first sustained combat of the campaign during the late summer of 1941. As the division approached Kholm, its advance precipitously slowed for the first time in three weeks: Soviet heavy artillery caused over 100 casualties in the 415th Infantry Regiment, forcing the division to call off the assault planned for the next day.[19] Two days later, the advance resumed and, though hampered by the Red Army's destruction and mining of bridges and roads, the 123rd ID reached Kholm on 3 August.[20] Even though German forces had successfully seized the western section of Kholm, the results of the recent fighting put a damper on any feelings of accomplishment:

since 25 July the battle took place almost exclusively in a scrub-filled, confusing terrain as well as in forests. The heavy casualties that the 415th and 416th Rgts. have suffered since 25 July confirm the intensity of the fighting and the difficulties of a type of combat that our own troops have yet to figure out but which the enemy masterfully owns.[21]

Already by early August, the heady days of quick advances and minimal resistance that had characterized much of July seemed to be a thing of the past; this, of course, augured ominously for an end to the campaign in 1941.

As Leeb surveyed his army group in August 1941, he grew increasingly concerned about Sixteenth Army's situation on his right flank. Eighteenth Army gradually secured Estonia and Panzer Group 4 continued to drive, albeit slowly, on Leningrad, but Busch's army faced a much more

---

[16] 126 ID, 28.8.41, Divisionsbefehl für die Verteidigung des Wolchow-Abschnitts, BA-MA RH 26–126/5; Leeb, *Tagebuchaufzeichnungen*, 11 August 1941, p. 326.
[17] Infanterie-Regiment 424, 13. Sept. 1941, BA-MA RH 26–126/13.
[18] Uffz. Peter Lahm, 474 Infantry Regiment, 8.10.1941, BfZ, Sammlung Sterz.
[19] 123 ID KTB, 31.7.41, BA-MA RH 26–123/8; 123 ID Abt. Ia/Az. IV/Op., Division Befehl Nr. 48, 30. Juli.1941, BA-MA RH 26–123/16. Leeb recorded that "the enemy is holding very tough in front of Kholm"; see Leeb, *Tagebuchaufzeichnungen*, 1 August 1941, p. 315.
[20] 123 ID KTB, 2.8.41; 3.8.41, BA-MA RH 26–123/9.
[21] Ibid., 4.8.41.

precarious situation. Leeb, rightly believing that Sixteenth Army's units remained too widely dispersed both to provide adequate flank protection for Panzer Group 4 and to maintain an effective link with Army Group Center, demanded the return of his units placed under the command of the latter from Brauchitsch. When the army commander in chief responded that the units would remain with Army Group Center, Leeb bitterly wrote,

> through the ruthless removal of divisions by Army Group Center, Army Group North is no longer in a state to continue the attack on the right wing ... The postponement of the attack south of Lake Ilmen, especially by II Corps, is very regrettable.[22]

Both Leeb and Busch wanted to pull the 123rd ID out of the Kholm area and move it north to fill the gap between II and X Corps in the area of Staraia Russa, as neither wanted it "to be roped into the defense."[23] Continuous Soviet activity, as well as the necessity of maintaining some sort of tenuous link with Army Group Center, however, ensured that the division remained near Kholm.[24] For the remainder of August, the 123rd ID defended the Kholm bridgehead against numerous attacks – including seven separate assaults on 12 August itself – while undertaking limited offensive action itself.[25] Determined Soviet assaults coupled with the increasingly weak condition of II Corps led both the division and corps to fear the possibility of a breakthrough and the Germans began making preparations for a second defensive line in the rear.[26] Not even two months into the invasion, the Wehrmacht's momentum had been seriously blunted in this isolated yet important section of the front.

The 123rd ID's striking power was significantly weakened by the removal of the 418th Infantry Regiment as it pushed north to fill the gap between X and II Corps.[27] This deployment highlighted the almost desperate situation facing the Wehrmacht in this area: the dispatching of an infantry regiment away from its home division signified how numerically

---

[22] Leeb, *Tagebuchaufzeichnungen*, 2 August 1941, 3.8.41, pp. 316–17. Several days later, Halder dismissively wrote of Leeb's "wild demands" for more men and matériel; Halder, *Kriegstagebuch*, vol. III, 15 August 1941, p. 180.
[23] Ibid., 11.8.41, p. 327; II AK KTB, 4.8.41, BA-MA RH 24–2/60.
[24] 123 ID KTB, 9.8.41, BA-MA RH 26–123/9.
[25] 123 ID KTB, 12.8.41, BA-MA RH 26–123/9.
[26] Both the 415th and 416th Infantry Regiments suffered extremely high casualties during the fighting around Kholm, with the latter reporting its companies at a strength of only sixty to seventy men; II AK KTB, 16.8.41, BA-MA RH 24–2/80.
[27] II AK KTB, 7.8.41, BA-MA RH 24–2/80. A Soviet attack isolated the 418th Infantry Regiment from the remainder of the division on 18 August and costly attacks by the 123rd ID to regain contact failed. The regiment was thus removed from the 123rd ID's order of battle by mid-August; see 123 ID KTB, 18.8.41, BA-MA RH 26–123/9.

weak the army actually was in this section of the front. It also bode ill for the 123rd ID as a whole as this siphoning away of its organic units would increase as the war dragged on. In summing up the division's activities for August, its war diarist noted,

> for over four weeks, the Rgts. lay in a very broad section of the line, almost exclusively on defense against nearly daily attacks by the enemy and without the possibility of replacing units for even a short period of time. Heavy rains, the most difficult conditions for movement, and at times primeval forest areas increased the not insignificant conditions under which the battle was conducted.

He concluded by stating that in a little over a month, the division suffered just short of 1,300 casualties. In this weakened state, the 123rd ID prepared to push on to its next objective: Demiansk.[28]

The 121st ID found itself in a far different situation than their comrades from Berlin. Instead of being forced onto the defensive in a remote location, the East Prussians were attached to the armored wedge pushing towards Leningrad. By 18 August, the 121st ID stood only 100 kilometers from the metropolis, making it the closest German infantry division to the city.[29] After securing Tosno, an important rail junction, the 121st ID dug in and for three days successfully fought off Soviet attempts to regain it.[30] Despite this victory, the division was unable to immediately resume the offensive due to the serious attrition of its striking power: its infantry regiments.[31] The nature of combat proved eerily reminiscent of the fighting on the Western Front in the First World War. Not only did the Soviet use of artillery approximate that of the British twenty-five years previously, but the advance degenerated into a series of pitched battles for

---

[28] 123 ID KTB, 7.9.41, BA-MA RH 26–123/9; II AK KTB, 6.9.41, BA-MA RH 24–2/80.
[29] 121 ID KTB, 18.8.41, BA-MA RH 26–121/8.
[30] Leeb, *Tagebuchaufzeichnungen*, 20 August 1941, p. 339; XXVIII AK KTB, 28.8.41, BA-MA RH 24–28/20; 121 ID, Abt. IIa/Ia Tagesbefehl 4.9.41, BA-MA RH 26–121/12; KTB, 2.9.41, BA-MA RH 26–121/8. It was during this fighting that the division encountered its first female combatants in uniform; Ic Meldung, 23.8.41, BA-MA RH 26–121/56. The use of uniformed female soldiers infuriated the Germans, who viewed it as yet another example of the Bolsheviks' unsoldierly behavior. As early as 29 June, Field Marshal Günther von Kluge, commander of Fourth Army in Army Group Center, issued an order calling for the execution of all women in uniform; see Geoffrey Megargee, *War of Annihilation: Combat and Genocide on the Eastern Front, 1941* (New York, 2006), p. 59. On the topic of women in the Red Army, see Reina Pennington, "Offensive Women: Women in Combat in the Red Army," in Addison and Calder, *Time to Kill*, pp. 249–62.
[31] The 405th Infantry Regiment suffered such serious losses that two of its battalions numbered only around ninety-five men while the third contained merely 131 men. The division's other two infantry regiments found themselves in a similar predicament; see XXVIII AK KTB, 3.9.41, BA-MA RH 24–28/20; Leeb, *Tagebuchaufzeichnungen*, 31 August 1941, p. 346.

fortified positions. The East Prussians described the area between the Izhora river and the outskirts of Leningrad as "an extensively subdivided defense system [that] the enemy tenaciously defended in numerous bunkers, reinforced by steel beams and arches and concrete blocks, behind mines and barbed wire." In just three days of fighting in mid-September 1941, XXVIII Corps suffered 2,320 casualties as "a tremendous amount of blood flowed" during this period of "long, bitter, hard and difficult" combat.[32]

The advance finally ended with the seizure of Slutsk/Pavlovsk on 18 September, following the defeat of a spirited Red Army defense of the town.[33] This proved important on two counts. First, it meant that the Germans now completely controlled the inner encirclement line around Leningrad.[34] Second, the 121st ID advanced no further than Pavlovsk: it settled into the besieging line to await the anticipated capitulation of Leningrad. While the war of movement had certainly slowed down for the 121st ID in August and early September, now it completely ended. The earlier instances of warfare similar to that of the First World War now became part of everyday life as "the '*Blitzkrieger*' of the Second World War was now damned to be like his father in the First World War, [with] a piece of trench 'to the last'."[35] Conditions in the trenches before Leningrad closely compared to those during the First World War: "de-lousing, ration commandos, increasing casualties, dugouts with howling grenades."[36] By early fall, the blitz campaign towards Leningrad had failed and the Wehrmacht settled into the kind of bloody, attrition-style positional warfare that Barbarossa had been consciously designed to avoid.

As the 121st ID settled into occupation duties in Pavlovsk, its sister divisions to the east and southeast faced far more critical situations.

---

[32] XXVIII AK KTB, 12.9.41, 15.9.41, BA-MA RH 24–28/20; Heesch, *Meine 13. Infanterie-Geschütz-Kompanie Grenadier-Regiment 408*, p. 93.
[33] XXVIII AK KTB, 18.9.41, BA-MA RH 24–28/20a. For more on the fighting in Pavlovsk, see Suzanne Massie, *Pavlovsk: The Life of a Russian Palace* (Boston, 1990), pp. 197–200.
[34] Leeb, *Tagebuchaufzeichnungen*, 18 September 1941, p. 359.
[35] *Geschichte der 121. Ostpreussische Infanterie-Division*, p. 60. Another soldier, Lt. Heinz E. of the 405th Infantry Regiment, wrote "we built our accommodation underground ... the old participants of the World War can use their proven methods of shelter construction." Leutenant Heinz E., Feldpostbrief, 26. Oktober 1941, in Jahn (ed.) *Blockade Leningrads*, p. 138.
[36] "Der Todesmarsch nach Leningrad," p. 212, BA-MA RH 2/2580. For more on the troops' constant battle with lice, see Hans-Joachim Schröder, *Die gestohlene Jahre. Erzählgeschichten und Gesichtserzählung im Interview: Der Zweite Weltkrieg aus der Sicht ehemaliger Mannschaftsoldaten* (Tübingen, 1991), pp. 433–6.

Sixteenth Army's commander in chief explained to his divisional and corps adjutants that

> despite the enormous expansion of the army and the numerous drafts of soldiers, Germany does not have the army required for the Eastern Campaign. We vastly underestimated the Russians in terms of personnel and matériel. In addition to the fact that 80 million are fighting against 160 million, the enemy [possesses] a fanaticism and psyche against which we, as a *Volk* of high moral standing [*sic*], are too decent.[37]

He then scolded his officers, telling them that "the div[ision] commanders need to see the big picture." Though he recognized that "their troops are tired and at the end of their strength," the wide disparity between the Wehrmacht and the Red Army – "200 German divisions and 400 Russian divisions" – meant that "no one is getting pulled out of the line." He ended the meeting with the demand, "the last man to the front!" Despite the fact that Busch painted such an eye-opening picture of Sixteenth Army's true condition, his men were soon on the offensive again.

After a month of defensive fighting, the 126th ID took part in the last major offensive launched by Army Group North in 1941. Hitler conceived of the operation both to destroy Soviet forces that faced the besieging German troops in the Šlissel'burg (Schlüsselburg)–Mga "bottleneck" area and to link up with Finnish troops northeast of Lake Ladoga.[38] Neither Leeb nor Halder believed the operation was feasible due to Sixteenth Army's weakness, but it nonetheless opened on 16 October.[39]

Despite switching over to the offensive for the first time in nine weeks, the 126th ID successfully seized and defended two important bridgeheads over the Volkhov river needed by XXXIX Panzer Corps.[40] The combination of tenacious Soviet defense and weather that alternated between rain and snow significantly slowed the Rhinelanders' advance, though they reached their first objective, the small town of Malaia Vischera, on 9 November, the same day that other elements of Army

---

[37] Niederschrift über die Adjutantenbesprechung beim AOK 16 am 6.10.41, BA-MA RH 26–126/23. The remainder of this discussion is based on this document unless otherwise noted.

[38] Weisung Nr. 33, Fortführung des Krieges im Osten, in Hubatsch, *Hitlers Weisungen*, pp. 174–7, here p. 176; Leeb, *Tagebuchaufzeichnungen*, 3 October 1941, p. 368; Generalkommando XXXIX AK, Korpsbefehl Nr. 33, 15.10.1941, BA-MA RH 26–126/6; Klink, "Die Operationsführung," p. 638.

[39] Leeb, *Tagebuchaufzeichnungen*, 2 October 1941, p. 368; 14.10.41, p. 375. Halder termed Hitler's idea a "phantasy." See *Kriegstagebuch*, vol. III, 1 October 41, p. 262.

[40] 126 ID KTB, 16.10.41, BA-MA RH 26–126/4; Klink, "Die Operationsführung," p. 639.

Group North seized the important rail junction of Tichvin.[41] Two days later, the division suffered its first major crisis of the war when counterattacking Soviets encircled its reconnaissance section in a small village to the south of Malaia Vischera. With no reserves available from either the corps or army level, the division rectified the situation using only its own resources.[42] A soldier from the Rhenish 227th ID who participated in the Tichvin offensive wrote, "I have been in a daze for the last four days. And I can only thank God, that I am still alive. I thought that hell had broken loose ... I can't write much as I am ready to collapse from exhaustion."[43]

The division then experienced a period of sustained battle and "crisis" that lasted until mid-December when, after several earlier tactical retreats, it finally pulled back behind the Volkhov river.[44] Leeb had ordered this on his own initiative as Hitler and the OKH, rightly focusing on the more threatening developments in front of Army Group Center, gave the field marshal some leeway and then retroactively sanctioned his decision.[45] Reports received by Leeb only confirmed his fears:

> the troops in the XXXIX Army Corps, just like those in the 126th ID, are so exhausted, less by the enemy's [actions] than due to the combined effects of their present shelter, insufficient winter equipment, relative combat strength, and the extremely cold weather of the past few days, that they no longer possess a large amount of defensive staying power, let alone offensive capabilities.[46]

---

[41] Leeb, *Tagebuchaufzeichnungen*, 20 October 1941, p. 378; 23 October 1941, p. 380; Klink, "Die Operationsführung," p. 639; Generalkommando XXXIX AK, Korpsbefehl für die Umgliederung der Südgruppe, 22.10.1941, BA-MA RH 26–126/6; Schramm, *KTB OKW*, vol. II, Tagesmeldung der Operations-Abteilung des GenStdH vom 22.6–6.12.1941, 9. November 1941, p. 749; Evan Mawdsley, *Thunder in the East: The Nazi–Soviet War, 1941–1945* (New York, 2005), p. 90. In the first ten days of the offensive, the 422nd and 426th Infantry Regiments suffered a combined total of 700 casualties; see 126 ID, Tagesmeldung, 25.10.41, BA-MA RH 26–126/17.
[42] Leeb, *Tagebuchaufzeichnungen*, 12 November 1941, p. 380.
[43] Corporal Alois Bracher, 366 Infantry Regiment, 25.11.41, BfZ, Sammlung Sterz.
[44] The war diary of the 126th ID labeled 15 and 16 November, as well as 4, 5, and 6 December, as "crisis" or "critical" days for the division, a characterization that Leeb agreed with. For the division, see KTB, 18.11.41, 4., 5., 6.12.41, BA-MA RH 26–126/4. For Leeb's views, see Leeb, *Tagebuchaufzeichnungen*, 16 November 1941, p. 380; 4 December 1941, 5 December 1941, pp. 403–4. Halder admitted to "serious worries" about the Tichvin offensive on 7 December; see Halder, *Kriegstagebuch*, vol. III, 7 December 1941, p. 331. Three days later, Halder wrote, "retreat to the Volkhov ordered." Ibid., 15 December 41, p. 349.
[45] While he approved of the already completed retreat behind the Volkhov river, Hitler categorically stated "other retrograde movements can only be carried out when an acute danger threatens the entire front." Schramm, *KTB OKW*, vol. II/2, Op. Abt. (IM), Nr. 1725/41 g. Kdos. Chefs., 16. December 1941, p. 1083.
[46] Leeb, *Tagebuchaufzeichnungen*, 10 December 1941, pp. 411–12.

The division commander shared this appreciation of his troops, as the extraordinarily high losses in the ranks of junior officers and NCOs had "noticeably diminished the inner stability as well as the previously excellent attitude of the troops."[47] Following the division's retreat west of the Volkhov river, the war diarist summed up the recent fighting:

> with [the retreat], an extraordinarily crisis-rich and painful section of the Eastern Campaign came to an end. While the division had achieved only successes in the offensive up to the seizure of Mal.[aia] Vischera, it was forced onto the defensive for the past eight weeks by an enemy who was numerically far superior and who was much better equipped for winter.[48]

Three months after the 121st ID's offensive ended in the relatively comfortable confines of Pavlovsk, the 126th ID, suffering significantly more casualties due to both enemy action and climate, settled into a defensive position along the Volkhov river. In comparison to the 123rd ID, however, the Rhinelanders' situation could almost be characterized as stable.

By late summer, the 123rd ID displayed the characteristics of a formation that had experienced a period "of very strenuous advance and ... difficult combat."[49] The division commander complained about a "considerable [display of] unmilitary conduct" within his unit. Soldiers displayed little march discipline, "going wherever they wanted," with "completely irregular uniforms" and "weapons hanging any which way." This loosening of military discipline was especially prevalent in the baggage and supply sections of the troops. On 1 September, the division commander issued a blistering order that demanded a more soldierly attitude in the rear area:

> The baggage troops need to be always prepared for battle. Security at every rest and at night. The individual soldier needs to know what to do in case of an attack. A true baggage section does not exist in Russia – here everyone belongs to the combat troops ... When the Rgt. fights a defensive battle on three fronts and the baggage troops are playing cards in their swimming trunks that is impudence [*Unverschämheit*]![50]

Clearly the issues that plagued the 123rd ID during its mustering continued to fester during the campaign and this was exacerbated by the heavy casualties suffered by the officer corps as well as by NCOs during the Kholm fighting; these weakened the bonds of discipline and

---

[47] 126 Inf. Div. Meldung vom 21.11.41, BA-MA RH 26–126/23.
[48] 126 ID KTB, 21.12.41, BA-MA RH 26–126/4.
[49] Divisions-Führer, 123 Inf. Division Nr. 1054/41 geh. Betr.: Mannszucht, 6. September 1941, BA-MA RH 26–123/19. The following discussion is based on this document.
[50] Divisions-Führer 123 ID, Nr. 1052/41 geh., Erfahrungen aus dem Russen-Feldzug, 1.9.41, BA-MA RH 26–123/19.

decreased the unit's combat efficiency.[51] Unlike the 121st and 126th IDs, both of which had suffered heavy casualties by September 1941 but which nonetheless maintained their combat effectiveness, the 123rd ID appeared to be cracking at the seams and, in this weakened state, it was forced to resume the offensive.

As part of II Corps, the division needed to push east towards the Valdai Hills and Ostashkov to secure a favorable line for the assault on Moscow. Thus, even during "the last decisive preparatory phase" of the assault on Leningrad, "elements of Sixteenth Army were assigned to co-operate with Ninth Army."[52] Leeb wondered "who was going to cover the 100-kilometer flank between Valdai and Lake Ilmen" as II Corps certainly lacked the necessary strength for the three tasks assigned to it: the maintenance of contact with Army Group Center, the seizure of the Valdai Hills, and the preservation of a common front with X Corps, which drove along a more northerly axis.[53] Here, the factor of space was ignored by the German leadership in Berlin as the factor of time assumed a decisive importance.

Within nine days of the opening of the offensive, II Corps had captured Demiansk and then continued towards the area between the Valdai Hills and the Lake Seliger region.[54] The 123rd ID, operating on the southern wing of the advance, plunged ahead into the swampland of the latter area, where the combination of nearly impassable terrain, inclement weather, and fierce Soviet resistance, supported by numerous tanks, slowed the 123rd ID's advance to a crawl. One soldier wrote that it rained for five days without interruption, with "the mud up to 30 cm high on the roads."[55] II Corps recognized the problems facing the division and cancelled an attack planned for 21 September because "the condition of the 123rd [ID] is such that one cannot trust them with protecting the southern flank"; since the 415th Infantry Regiment described its men as "looking like corpses," it appears that the corps made the correct decision.[56] The next day, the corps remarked that "the situation is made more difficult above all by the 123rd ID and all three of its regiments being no longer fully operational, completely unable to undertake

---

[51] Divisions-Führer 123 Inf. Division, Nr. 1054/41 geh. Betr.: Manneszucht, 6. September 1941, BA-MA RH 26–123/19.
[52] Klink, "Die Operationsführung," p. 631.
[53] Leeb, *Tagebuchaufzeichnungen*, 25 August 1941, p. 342.
[54] Generalkommando II AK, Korpsbefehl Nr. 60, 2.9.41, BA-MA RH 24–2/90; Leeb, *Tagebuchaufzeichnungen*, 7 September 1941, p. 351; II AK KTB, 8.9.41, BA-MA RH 24–2/80.
[55] Lt. Wilhelm Berg, 418 Infantry Regiment, 3.9.41, BfZ, Sammlung Sterz.
[56] II AK KTB, 21.9.41, BA-MA RH 24–2/80; 17.35 Uhr Von IR 415, 23. September 1941, BA-MA RH 26–123/32.

offensive operations and whose condition is only limited to defensive combat."[57] In what increasingly became the Wehrmacht's answer to shortages of men and matériel, II Corps's commander stressed the importance of the individual soldier's belief in final victory. Despite acknowledging the decimated state of his subordinate divisions, the commander explained that

the efforts and sacrifices of these weeks and days will give way to better conditions in the not so distant future. The fateful enormity of our assignment obligates every individual and every troop section to unconditional devotion ... A troop can only see this when the commander instructs and educates in this sense ... then the impossible will be possible.[58]

Despite exhorting the troops to continue the advance in confident hopes of victory, II Corps found the situation so worrisome that it convinced Sixteenth Army to ask Army Group Center for assistance. The Army High Command denied the request, however, and II Corps was forced to make do with what it had or, in other words, make the impossible possible.[59]

The 123rd ID remained on the defensive until 8 October when it received orders to continue its advance to the southeast. Due to the opening on 2 October of Operation Typhoon, Army Group Center's drive on Moscow, Red Army forces facing II Corps had begun to retreat and the southern wing of the corps filled the resultant vacuum.[60] For the next month, the 123rd ID thrust into a gap between Soviet formations, suffering relatively light casualties.[61] The lack of opposition led one of the division's soldiers to write home that "the *Red Front* is destroyed. All that remains is a Soviet opponent. A profound feeling of happiness has seized all of us. Victory is within reach."[62] Lacking enough strength to take and hold

---

[57] II AK KTB, 22.9.41, BA-MA RH 24–2/80. See also the division's report of 26 September in which the commander states that both the 415th and 416th Infantry Regiments are "no longer fully operational," being "able only to defend light attacks." He listed the following as causes of the present predicament: continual action since the beginning of the invasion, especially in the Kholm region, heavy losses of officers and NCOs, and "the privations caused by the terrain." See 123 ID, Divisionsführer, Meldung, 25. Sept. 1941, BA-MA RH 26–126/20.
[58] Generalkommando II Armeekorps, Abt. Ia, 26.9.1941, BA-MA RH 26–126/30.
[59] II AK, KTB, 22.9.41, BA-MA 24–2/80; Halder, *Kriegstagebuch*, vol. III, 23 September 1941, p. 246.
[60] 123 ID KTB, 7.10.41, BA-MA RH 26–123/9; An Alle Korps!, 7.10.1941, BA-MA RH 24–2/95; David Glantz and Jonathan House, *When Titans Clashed: How the Red Army Stopped Hitler* (Lawrence, KS, 1995), p. 79.
[61] II AK KTB, 4.11.41, BA-MA RH 24–2/80. Between 17 October and 2 November, the 123rd ID suffered only 199 casualties, while its sister divisions in II Corps, the 12th ID and the 32nd ID, had losses that totaled 969 and 1,802 men respectively.
[62] Leutnant K.S., Rgts. Stab/Inf. Rgt. 418, 123th ID, 10.10.41, in Buchbender and Sterz, *Das andere Gesicht des Krieges*, p. 83. Emphasis in original.

positions, however, the 123rd ID's advance soon degenerated into a series of raids on Soviet lines, in which the primary objectives were the burning down of houses and mining of roads.[63] The optimism present at the beginning of October had vanished and another member of the division commented that "presently, the situation does not appear too rosy."[64]

When the attack finally petered out, II Corps found itself in a position with "three divisions (which can only be valued as reinforced regiments) for 122 kilometers of front." Though well aware of the problem, Sixteenth Army could do nothing to rectify it: according to the army, "there is not one single man available."[65] Due to this manpower shortage, the 123rd ID proved unable to construct a solid defensive line; instead, it relied on a series of loosely connected strongpoints that contained "broad areas in which not a single German soldier stands."[66] With only fifty infantrymen for every kilometer of front, both the division and II Corps recognized that a determined Soviet attack would easily crack the Germans' positions due to "simple arithmetic" and that it could "not take responsibility for what happens."[67] One of the "two critical points of the Army Group" thusly prepared for the next stage of the campaign.[68]

II. "The partisans are to be publicly hanged and left hanging for some time": the radicalization of anti-partisan policy

As summer turned to fall, German anti-partisan policy increasingly radicalized as currents from above and below reinforced one another.[69]

---

[63] 123 ID KTB, 23.11.41, BA-MA RH 26–123/9. Both German and Soviet forces burned down houses to prevent the enemy from warding off the elements during the winter. According to the 123rd ID's war diary, the Red Army burned down a total of five villages between 23 November and 4 December; see the war diary's entries for 23.11.41 and 4.12.41. II Corps believed that the Red Army "apparently just wanted to burn down buildings to deprive German troops of shelter"; II AK KTB, 5.12.41, BA-MA RH 24–2/80. The 123rd ID ordered its men to "completely destroy" all villages following tactical retreats on the part of the Germans: "all villages, including barns and individual houses between the front and the new defensive line, are to be destroyed"; see 123 ID, Abt. Ia/Az. IV a Nr. 1216/41 geh., Div. Befehl Nr. 107, 12. Dezember 1941, BA-MA RH 26–123/23.
[64] Lt. Wilhelm Berg, Inf. Rgt. 418, 31.10.1941, BfZ, Sammlung Sterz.
[65] II AK KTB, 1.12.41, 10.12.41, BA-MA RH 24–2/80; Leeb, *Tagebuchaufzeichnungen*, 1 December 1941, pp. 399–400.
[66] Fernschreiben an Armee-Oberkommando 16, 21.11.41, BA-MA RH 26–123/22.
[67] II AK KTB, 20.11.41, 21.11.41, 4.12.41, 11.12.41, BA-MA RH 24–2/80; Generalkommando II Armeekorps, Abt. Ia Nr. 1564/41 geh. 2.12.1941, BA-MA RH 26–123/23.
[68] Leeb, *Tagebuchaufzeichnungen*, 18 December 1941, p. 420.
[69] For the evolution of German anti-partisan policy from July through October 1941, see Hartmann, *Wehrmacht im Ostkrieg*, pp. 720–33; Shepherd, *War in the Wild East*, pp. 84–108; Gerlach, *Kalkulierte Morde*, pp. 875–84; and Hürter, *Hitlers Heerführer*, pp. 411–20.

First, the violent rhetoric that permeated the upper echelons of the Third Reich's leadership now began to appear more regularly in Wehrmacht anti-partisan directives. Second, the realization that the campaign would indeed take more than eight to ten weeks led the army as an institution to demand a more radical approach to any and all resistance; from the perspective of the Wehrmacht, only in this way could the Soviet Union's military power finally be destroyed. Third, the men themselves began to act in a more arbitrary and barbaric way. Succumbing to the pressures, strains and frustrations of the advance, and finding themselves harangued by their leaders to eradicate any and all opposition to their mission, German divisions now began to fight a much more vicious war against Soviet partisans, both real and imagined.

The negative views towards the Soviet population began at the very top as Hitler believed that the Germans would be dealing with a "totally Bolshevik-incited population" that could only be subjugated through the use of terror.[70] Hitler's views of the simmering partisan war were perhaps best encapsulated in a meeting between himself and several of his highest-ranking subordinates on 16 July. The main topic of the meeting concerned how the Germans should rule their new eastern empire. In response to Stalin's call for Soviet society to rise up as a whole to "annihilate" the German invaders, Hitler declared that the development of such a "partisan war behind our front" gave the Germans an opportunity to "shoot anyone who even looks askance" at the occupiers.[71] Such a formulation certainly increased the scope of German extermination policies, especially with regard to the development of the "final solution of the Jewish question" in the Soviet Union and later Europe; for the purposes of this study, however, its most important effect was to legitimize a radicalization of existing anti-partisan doctrine and practices.

One week later, Hitler's belief that the merciless use of force should be utilized to pacify the occupied areas of the Soviet Union was distributed to the army as a whole. In the Supplement to War Directive 33, Keitel declared that juridical means no longer sufficed to secure the eastern territories. Rather, the troops needed to utilize "terror" in order to "take away the population's appetite for resistance."[72] Such thinking also animated the upper levels of the OKH as a directive written by General Eugen Müller emphasized the "severity" required for controlling those

---

[70] Quoted in Hürter, *Hitlers Heerführer*, p. 410.
[71] For Stalin's order, see Alexander Hill (ed.), *The Great Patriotic War of the Soviet Union, 1941–1945* (Abingdon, 2009), Document #29, pp. 49–50, here p. 49. For Hitler's response, see *The Trial of the Major War Criminals, 14 November 1945–1 October 1946*, vol. XXXVIII, Doc. 221-L, "Aktenvermerk," pp. 86–94, here p. 88.
[72] Ergänzung zur Weisung Nr. 33, in Hubatsch, *Hitlers Weisungen*, pp. 166–8, here p. 167.

areas under German occupation.[73] He continued by stating that "the necessary *speedy* liberation of the country can only be accomplished when every *threat* from the enemy civilian population is ruthlessly eliminated" (original emphasis). Müller demanded the use of collective measures when the perpetrators could not be found, not only for shootings and acts of sabotage but also for passive resistance. As Christian Hartmann has noted, the fact that the OKH now deemed "the *possibility* of civilian resistance as a crime" highlighted the general radicalization of German anti-partisan policy during the summer of 1941.[74]

This process culminated with Keitel issuing a directive on "Communist Insurgency Movements in the Occupied Territories" on 16 September 1941.[75] Claiming that German countermeasures for the insurgency had "proven insufficient," Keitel demanded that the "sharpest means" be utilized to destroy what he termed a "unified movement" led by Moscow. In order to impress upon the population the ruthlessness of the German response to such attacks, he ordered that fifty to one hundred communists be killed in "atonement" for the death of every German soldier at the hands of partisans. In summation, these orders elucidate general German policy towards the occupied areas: "the structural weakness of the German occupation authorities was to be compensated for by the use of terror."[76]

As these various directives and orders from the highest echelons of the Third Reich's political and military leadership indicate, the violence and aggression inherent in National Socialism became more and more entrenched in the army's already severe anti-partisan doctrine during the late summer and fall of 1941. Part of this was due to this being Hitler's "true war," one that needed to be fought along ideological lines. Part, however, was also due to an issue that Müller explicitly stated in his order: the need to defeat the Soviet Union as quickly as possible. Here, the idea of military necessity became increasingly important to German military planners.

---

[73] Behandlung feindlicher Zivilpersonen und russischer Kriegsgefangener, Oberkommando des Heeres General z. B. V. Beim Oberbefehlshaber des Heeres, Az. 453 Gr. R.Wes, Nr. 1332/41 geh., 25.7.41, in Ueberschär and Wette, *Der deutsche Überfall auf die Sowjetunion*, pp. 295–6, here p. 295. The following discussion is also based on this document. For more on Müller, see *Verbrechen der Wehrmacht: Dimensionen des Vernichtungskrieges 1941–1944* (Hamburg, 2002), p. 435.
[74] Hartmann, *Wehrmacht im Ostkrieg*, p. 719.
[75] "Befehl Keitels über die schonungslose Unterdrückung der Befreiungsbewegung in den besetzten Länden und Geiselerschießungen," *Wehrmachtsverbrechen*, Document #19, pp. 80–3.
[76] Hartmann, *Wehrmacht im Ostkrieg*, p. 719.

In mid-August, Hoepner wrote home to his wife that "the campaign *needs* to be *concluded* by the end of September on account of the entire supply situation and the cold."[77] Such a sentiment mirrored the thinking of the German High Command as a whole, and while some commanders remained irrationally optimistic during the summer of 1941, others began to realize that the Soviet state was not going to simply disintegrate due to the German invasion.[78] The largest issue concerned the combat efficiency of the panzer groups which depended largely on the supply situation. Already on 1 July, Halder noted that the rear areas caused him "serious worries" as the security divisions entrusted to secure the occupied east were simply too few in number to pacify such a large operational area.[79] Some three weeks later, Halder met with Hitler and one of the topics of discussion concerned the problem of the burgeoning partisan movement and its effect on the supply situation.[80] Here, the operational demands of the campaign neatly dovetailed with the German Army's institutional view of irregular warfare. If achieving victory meant reacting with violence and brutality against the civilian population to snuff out resistance, so be it: the need for victory overrode all ethical and moral considerations.[81]

In northwest Russia, Army Group North first reported problems with partisans in late summer and Leeb and his senior commanders soon institutionalized the response to this development.[82] Küchler ordered his Eighteenth Army to combat what he viewed as a centrally organized movement with "all energy and severity." Five days later, the army group issued its first directive regarding the partisan menace. It demanded that the troops needed to be "educated to a *state of mistrust* against the population." Instead of merely threatening collective measures, German units needed to carry them out, and this included publicly hanging partisans and leaving them hanging with signs attached to their dangling bodies, warning other insurgents of their fate. Hoepner, in response to a

---

[77] Quoted in Hürter, *Hitlers Heerführer*, p. 291. Hoepner's emphasis.
[78] Perhaps the most wildly optimistic was Halder himself; see Stahel, *Operation Barbarossa*, p. 377; Hürter, *Hitlers Heerführer*, pp. 304–5. On the realization already by late summer that the campaign would stretch into the following year, see Christian Gerlach, "Operative Planungen der Wehrmacht für den Krieg gegen die Sowjetunion und die deutsche Vernichtungspolitik," in Quinkert, *"Wir sind die Herren dieses Landes"*, pp. 55–63; and Geoffrey Megargee, *Inside Hitler's High Command* (Lawrence, KS, 2000), p. 133.
[79] Halder, *Kriegstagebuch*, vol. III, 1 July 1941, p. 32. Several weeks later, the 221st Security Division found itself responsible for 35,000 square kilometers; see Shepherd, *War in the Wild East*, p. 61.
[80] Halder, *Kriegstagebuch*, vol. III, 23 July 1941, p. 104.
[81] Hürter, *Hitlers Heerführer*, p. 408.
[82] Ibid., pp. 414–15. The following discussion is based on Hürter's examination. Emphasis in original.

partisan attack that killed five German soldiers, ordered a nearby village "razed to the ground" and insisted that this would now be standard operating procedure in his area of operations. Towards the end of the month, Leeb distributed another decree to his army group in which he stated that the partisan movement was becoming "an increasingly serious danger" that the troops needed to control with "drastic and draconian means." Once again, the Wehrmacht's institutional view – here, the necessity of ruthlessly destroying any and all irregular resistance – melded seamlessly with the ideological vision of war advocated by Germany's political leadership.

How did the infantry divisions of Army Group North respond to this radicalization of policy from June through December 1941?[83] Though one can detect both an increasingly brutal attitude and behavior in all three units as the year progressed, no uniformity of action existed. In other words, each division approached the issue of partisan warfare in a different way, even if they all operated within the same general context.

As Army Group North's front fanned out from Leningrad to the southeast, partisan activity correspondingly rose. Several factors caused this increase. First, Eighteenth Army controlled the Baltic states, whose population's genuine support for the Wehrmacht during the opening months of the campaign ensured that resistance was quite limited in this area.[84] Panzer Group 4, despite advancing towards Bolshevism's birthplace and therefore dealing with a theoretically more ideologically convinced section of the population, functioned as part of a large force relative to the size of its area of operations. Such density of force made the development of a large-scale partisan movement difficult; it simply did not possess the necessary room to breathe, much less prosper.

Sixteenth Army, however, faced a different set of issues. The area under Army Group Center's jurisdiction was home to the largest partisan movement in the occupied Soviet Union and II Corps functioned as the link between the two army groups.[85] The junction

---

[83] For a solid examination of anti-partisan measures in Army Group North's rear area, see Kilian, *Wehrmacht und Besatzungsherrschaft*, pp. 504–87.

[84] See Weiss-Wendt, *Murder without Hatred*, p. 77, on this point.

[85] Gerlach argues "that there certainly cannot be talk of a 'partisan struggle without partisans' at any time," as by mid-August 1941 there were 12,000 partisans active in Belarus and by the end of the year the number had ballooned to 30,000; see Gerlach, *Kalkulierte Morde*, p. 861. More generally, see Richter, "Die Wehrmacht und der Partisankrieg in den besetzten Gebieten der Sowjetunion," in Müller and Volkmann, *Die Wehrmacht*, pp. 837–57.

between II Corps and Ninth Army, its neighbor to the south, remained rather fluid and partisan groups took advantage of this to penetrate into the German rear.[86] II Corps's area of operations consisted of numerous forests and swamps, unlike the more populated urban areas to the northwest. This terrain afforded bands of partisans numerous opportunities to conceal their base of operations. Finally, Army Group North was stretched thinnest along the axis of advance for II Corps. While every division complained of a manpower crunch and believed *its* section of the line to be the most threatened, both II Corps and the 123rd ID could legitimately make this case. Enough troops simply did not exist in this area to man adequately the front, much less mount the necessary patrols and raids needed to crush the partisan movement in the rear.[87]

The 121st ID continued to behave in a much more subdued manner than its peers. On 18 July, elements of the 408th Infantry Regiment rested in Tschavino during their march. While they were in the village, partisans ignited a blaze, resulting in one German casualty. Retribution, however, was limited to the temporary arrest of the male population, as decreed by the regiment's commander.[88] The restraint displayed here is noteworthy: despite not only being given the option of responding in a ruthless manner to partisan attacks, but in fact being ordered to do so, and despite having just experienced heavy combat during the fight for the Luga Line, the East Prussians moved on without committing an atrocity. Their behavior here was very similar to their earlier actions at Kazlai. While it is possible that such crimes were deliberately omitted from its records, the 121st Infantry Division did record other instances in which it carried out collective measures and executions during its later occupation of Pavlovsk; it seems that during the opening months of the invasion when victory was ostensibly certain, the division made no attempts to conceal its actions. This leads one to conclude that despite being subjected to what it viewed as "devious" and unprofessional methods of fighting as well as to Wehrmacht directives that called for harsh retaliatory measures, the division did not automatically respond with calculated violence. Restraint characterized its actions in Lithuania

---

[86] Generalkommando II. Armeekorps, Abteilung Qu/Ia 461/43 g. Kdos, Betr.: Bandeneinwirkung an Armee-Oberkommando 16, 15. Mai 1943, BA-MA RH 24–2/210.

[87] As noted by II Corps, "the partisan danger in the rear area can be stopped to a certain degree by an increase in the occupation of villages"; see II AK KTB, 19.11.41, BA-MA RH 24–2/80.

[88] Ic Meldung, 17.8.41, BA-MA RH 26–121/56. No mention of executions is found in the division's files.

and Russia proper during the summer of 1941. The 121st ID's vision of military necessity did not completely subscribe to the radicalized, ideologically influenced vision of other German divisions.

With the exception of this event, the East Prussians faced very little irregular opposition during their advance in 1941. Despite this lack of enemy activity, XXVIII Corps reiterated army doctrine to the partisan threat: "the brutal and devious fighting methods of the partisans are to be met with ruthless action. All cases of sabotage, such as cutting through cables, are to be punished sharply."[89] The division issued its own order, stating that "the fight against Bolshevik agitators, guerillas, saboteurs, and partisans demands ruthless and energetic measures," and suggested that collective measures were the best means of discouraging such resistance. Such responses included compulsory labor service for the male population, the confiscation of cattle and vehicles, restrictions of civilian movement, the closing of stores, and the taking of hostages. Notably absent were demands for murderous collective actions. The order also defined the category of a partisan: "all armed civilians, who commit enemy actions or are suspected of allowing it, fall under the term partisan."[90]

By early September, "partisan activities reached their high-water mark" and the unit responded with violence, executing seventeen partisans in a ten-day period.[91] The 408th Infantry Regiment's commander believed that "the attitude of civilians is extremely hostile. One notices the influence of propaganda that had been more intensive in Petersburg and its surroundings than in the countryside."[92] An NCO, sensing the antagonism of the region's inhabitants, remarked that "one sensed dangers from all sides, especially from fanatical civilians." The combination of fear and a command structure that painted resistance as the manifestation of a racially inferior yet dangerous political system led even more measured soldiers to utilize the regime's language in describing the war behind the lines:

A patrol captured a partisan. He was wearing civilian clothes and had a belt of ammunition around his body and carried a rifle in his hand. As we confronted him, he looked at us with the face of a criminal and subhuman.[93]

---

[89] Generalkommando XXVIII. A.K., Abt. Ia, 6.8.1941, Korpsbefehl Nr. 3, BA-MA RH 26-121/11. The order's two cited sentences were underlined in the division's files.
[90] 121 Inf. Division, Abt. Ic, 6.8.41, BA-MA RH 26-121/11.
[91] Ic Meldung, 5.9.41, 11.9.41, 14.9.41, BA-MA RH 26-121/56. For the quoted phrase, see "Chronik der 2.Kompanie Nachrichten-Abteilung 121," BA-MA RH 44/381.
[92] "Mein Regiment," 30.8.41, BA-MA RH 37/3096.
[93] "Der Todesmarsch nach Leningrad," p. 177, BA-MA Msg 2/2580.

"The partisans are to be publicly hanged" 135

Despite approaching the partisan issue in a restrained manner at the divisional level, at the individual level the men became more prone to viewing partisans in the manner called for by the regime. As the unit marched towards Leningrad, this dichotomy became increasingly prominent.

The Rhinelanders of the 126th ID utilized a much more proactive strategy in combating partisans than did their East Prussian comrades. "Worried" about scattered Red Army men and partisans behind their positions, the division mounted anti-partisan operations in its rear area, an area inhabited by increasingly suspicious ethnic Russians instead of the friendly and compliant populations of the Baltic states.[94] The 126th ID's commander castigated his men for failing to recognize this difference:

> Large-scale apathy and naïveté of the troops towards the civilian population has already led to casualties. The troops, and above all, the members of the baggage train, are therefore once more advised to maintain a careful surveillance of civilian traffic, especially on the main road. All suspicious elements passing through, especially those of draft age, are to be arrested and sent to the Prisoner Collection area. The resident population is, in general, to be treated in an accommodating manner.[95]

Following this outburst, the 126th ID more actively patrolled its area and engaged in numerous firefights with guerillas. One assault on a "well-camouflaged and fortified camp" led to six partisans being killed in battle with a further two being captured along with two machine guns and thirty-two rifles, while other mounted patrols netted five officers and twenty-five Soviet soldiers who had escaped from the Luga pocket and had been wandering through the forests in an attempt to reach their lines.[96] The special mention of the 426th Infantry Regiment's mounted patrol leader for his "prudence and bravery" during the operations

---

[94] Tätigkeitsbericht des Ev. Divisionspfarrers bei der 126 I.D. für die Zeit vom 22.6 bis 21.12.1941, BA-MA RH 26–126/140. Some of these Soviet forces behind the lines had parachuted in with the express purpose of igniting resistance to the Germans. The 126th ID captured three such women and handed them over to the Geheime Feldpolizei (Secret Field Police, or GFP) on 3 October, which shot them four days later. See Tätigkeitsbericht Ic, 3.10.41, 7.10.41, BA-MA RH 26–126/115.

[95] For I Corps's order, see Generalkommando I. Armeekorps, Korpsbefehl Nr. 101, 1.9.41, BA-MA RH 26–126/6; for the division's response, see 126 ID, 2. Divisionsbefehl für die Verteidigung am Wolchow, 2.9.41, BA-MA RH 26–126/5.

[96] 126 ID KTB, 11.9.41; 16.9.41, BA-MA RH 26–126/4. These scattered Red Army men constituted at least a minor threat to German forces, as demonstrated by an attack of individual soldiers on an artillery company in which two Germans were killed; see 126 ID KTB, 17.9.41, BA-MA RH 26–126/4.

demonstrated how important a frontline combat division considered anti-partisan combat in fall 1941.[97]

Despite these "successes," civilians reported that large groups of both partisans and Soviet soldiers remained in the area, leading to three large-scale operations in September. The normal mounted squadrons were reinforced by men from the division's reconnaissance section as well as a shock infantry force from the 426th Infantry Regiment.[98] While the first operation netted ninety-three prisoners as well twenty dead Red Army men, the final two failed to achieve any significant results.[99] The last major anti-partisan operation undertaken by the 126th ID took place on 10 October when it destroyed a group of ninety-six soldiers.[100]

Frequent partisan activity led to an increasingly brutal response by the 126th ID. Earlier orders which merely called for the arrest and delivery to prison camps of all suspicious elements were now superseded by a policy of *Abschreckung* or terror; here the Rhinelanders began to act more in accordance with the general policy established both by the OKH and by Army Group North.[101] A new directive issued on 1 October stated that "where deterrent measures are required to terrorize the civilian population, the partisans are to be publicly hanged and left hanging for some time. The population is to be warned by a corresponding sign."[102] In one of the first expressions of this policy, the inhabitants of the village of Vitka witnessed the execution of several partisans on 13 October.[103] Further attempts to stamp out resistance led to all communists and former Soviet officials, as well as their dependents, being immediately arrested and sent to prisoner collection camps even when no evidence indicating opposition existed.[104]

---

[97] 126 ID, 3. Divisionsbefehl für die Verteidigung des Wolchow, 14.9.41, BA-MA RH 26–126/5.
[98] The 253rd ID formed a similar unit dedicated to anti-partisan operations at the beginning of September; see Rass, *Menschenmaterial*, pp. 351–2.
[99] 126 ID KTB, 23.9.41, 24.9.41, 27.9.41, BA-MA RH 26–126/4. Though I Corps recognized that many of these men wanted to "wait out the cold and hunger [and] hoped to return to their families," it still ordered its subordinate units to round them up. See Anlage zum Korpsbefehl Nr. 110 vom 19.9.41, BA-MA RH 26–126/6.
[100] Generalkommando I. Armeekorps, Korpsbefehl Nr. 117, 6.10.41, BA-MA RH 26–126/6.
[101] For a relatively mild directive concerning the supervision of the civilian population, see 126 Infanterie-Division, Abteilung Ic, Überwachung der Zivilbevölkerung, 9.9.41, BA-MA RH 26–126/116. It is clear that the rhetoric and behavior of other combat units also radicalized; the 296th ID ordered that all partisans "be destroyed without consideration or false humanity" on 20 August 1941; see Hartmann, *Wehrmacht im Ostkrieg*, pp. 730–1.
[102] 126 ID, Abt. Ic, Zusammensetzung der Partisanen und Hinweise für ihre Bekämpfung, 1.10.41, BA-MA RH 26–126/116.
[103] Tätigkeitsbericht Ic, 13.9.41, BA-MA RH 26–126/115.
[104] 126 ID, Abt. Ic, Zusammensetzung der Partisanen und Hinweise für ihre Bekämpfung, 1.10.41, BA-MA RH 26–126/116.

"The partisans are to be publicly hanged"

Illustration 4.2 The radicalization of German anti-partisan policy led to the increasing use of public hangings in the fall of 1941.

138   "Will the continuation of this attack be worth it?"

In addition to its attempts to pacify its area of operations, the 126th ID also tried to impose administrative order, partially in an effort to exploit the local population for its own purposes. On 14 September, the division commander divided his area of responsibility into three sections: the forward combat area, a street commandant section, and the rear area of the division. He also ordered the retention of a *Bürgermeister*, or mayor, for every village, who, functioning as the Germans' representative at the local level, implemented their wishes, including the securing of food supplies.[105] The local population collected the harvest and also functioned as a labor pool for construction jobs, the latter of which took on special significance as the winter approached.[106] The *Bürgermeister* was additionally given the task of supervising the male population, both with continual roll calls to ensure that no insurgents had infiltrated the villages and with the registration of the village's population with the *Ortskommandant*. This information was required for another feature of combat divisions' occupation practices: the evacuation of civilians from their zones of operation.[107]

In mid-September, division command ordered its subordinate units to report on the necessity of evacuating the civilian population from their area of responsibility. Such an eventuality was not favored by the division's subunits.[108] While the regimental commanders recognized the importance of evacuating civilians from the combat zone to ensure their physical safety, more practical concerns overrode these humanitarian motives: in other words, military necessity was the determining factor.[109] Russians provided important functions for the occupiers, including intelligence gathering, and their presence also provided

---

[105] 126 ID, 3. Divisionsbefehl für die Verteidigung des Wolchow, 14.9.41, BA-MA RH 26–126/5.
[106] Generalkommando I. Armeekorps, Korpsbefehl 101, 1.9.41, BA-MA RH 26–126/6. The 422nd Infantry Regiment stated that while the gathering of harvest for winter had already begun, there were not enough people in its area of responsibility to complete the task, and this foretold a lack of food for not only the soldiers, but also the civilian population; see Infanterie-Regiment 422, Abt. Ia/Allg. Stellungnahme des Regiments zur Frage der Evakuierung, 16.9.41, BA-MA RH 26–126/14.
[107] 126 ID, 3. Divisionsbefehl für die Verteidigung des Wolchow, 14.9.41, BA-MA RH 26–126/5; Infanterie-Regiment 422, Abt. Ia/Allg. Stellungnahme des Regiments zur Frage der Evakuierung, 16.9.41, BA-MA RH 26–126/14.
[108] Infanterie-Regiment 422, Abt. Ia/Allg. Stellungnahme des Regiments zur Frage der Evakuierung, 16.9.41, BA-MA RH 26–126/14; Aufklärungsabteilung 126, Abt. Ia, Evakuierung der Zivilbevölkerung, 18.9.41, BA-MA RH 26–126/14.
[109] 126 Infanterie-Division, Abteilung Ia, Evakuierung der Zivilbevölkerung, 18.9.41, BA-MA RH 26–126/14.

"The partisans are to be publicly hanged" 139

camouflage for the army and its movements.[110] Finally, and most importantly, without the work of the civilians, the harvest could not be collected and this issue became increasingly important to the troops as the winter approached.[111] Line officers viewed civilians merely in the context of their military mission and the occupying force's responsibility for the civilians under its control was strikingly absent; all that mattered was what the civilians could do for the army.[112]

In addition to their being locked in constant combat from mid-July through mid-October, frequent partisan activity continued to plague the Rhinelanders. On 29 October, the war diarist complained that "in the entire divisional area, there is lively and organized partisan activity [with a] systematic increase in attempts on rear-area connections."[113] The frequency of attacks in the rear area continued to multiply, as evidenced by an assault on the supply section of the division's artillery regiment on 30 October. Though the unit suffered only two casualties, seven horses were killed in addition to four being wounded and it was these types of small-scale attack that crippled the mobility of a significant portion of the Wehrmacht's supply units.[114] Following three attacks in ten days, the artillerymen responded by executing a female suspected of being a partisan and displaying the body at a crossroads "as a warning to the population."[115]

Anti-partisan measures continued throughout the remainder of 1941 as the division particularly focused on eliminating the traces of communism in its area of operations.[116] Relying on village elders as well as other informers, the division tracked the arrival of people not indigenous to local villages and, following their arrest, then "shipped them" with other "suspicious elements ... to civilian collection camps."[117] By 19

---

[110] Infanterie-Regiment 426, Abt. Ia, Stellungnahme des Rgt. zur Frage einer evtl. Evakuierung der Zivilbevölkerung aus dem Rgt.-Abschnitt, 17.9.41, BA-MA RH 26–126/14; 126 Infanterie-Division, Abteilung Ia, Evakuierung der Zivilbevölkerung, 18.9.41, BA-MA RH 26–126/14.

[111] Infanterie-Regiment 422, Abt. Ia/Allg. Stellungnahme des Regiments zur Frage der Evakuierung, 16.9.41, BA-MA RH 26–126/14. The civilians also supplied the troops with a "certain quantity of milk, eggs, and flour"; see Aufklärungsabteilung 126, Abt. Ia, Evakuierung der Zivilbevölkerung, 18.9.41, BA-MA RH 26–126/14.

[112] As this case demonstrates, however, military necessity was not always a negative for the civilian population. Staying in one's home was sometimes preferable to being evacuated to the rear.

[113] 126 ID KTB, 29.10.41, BA-MA RH 26–126/4.

[114] Artillerie-Regiment 126, Tagesmeldung, 30. Oktober 1941, BA-MA RH 26–126/17.

[115] Artillerie-Regiment 126, Tagesmeldung, 6. November 1941; 8. November 1941, BA-MA RH 26–126/18.

[116] Aufklärungs-Abteilung 126, Tagesmeldung, 11.11.1941, BA-MA RH 26–126/19 and Tätigkeitsbericht Ic, 17.11.41, BA-MA RH 26–126/117; Zwischenmeldung Infanterie-Regiment 426 vom 30.11.41, BA-MA RH 26–126/20.

[117] Tätigkeitsbericht Ic, 30.11.41, BA-MA RH 26–126/67.

November, the quartermaster noted that "seven partisans, or rather seven suspected partisans, have been shot."[118] Anti-partisan activities in 1941 culminated with a "cleaning-up" action in a settlement recently vacated by members of the 250th ID, the Spanish Blue Division.

The 424th Infantry Regiment "discovered that the civilian population, partly in German uniforms and with German weapons – left by the Spanish in the village during their retreat – was participating in the battle. Twenty-nine partisans were summarily shot."[119] This incident provides grounds for some speculation concerning the behavior of the 424th Infantry Regiment's soldiers. To begin with, there is no mention of how it was ascertained that these civilians were actually fighting the Wehrmacht and since there is no mention of German casualties, it is clear that no pitched firefight took place. It seems much more probable that as German soldiers passed through the village, they noticed German uniforms and weapons in the area and, having neither the time nor desire to get to the bottom of the issue, decided to solve the problem in a quick and brutal manner. The fact that Russians were wearing German uniforms does not necessarily indicate an allegiance to the partisans: when one takes into consideration the drastic winter temperatures as well as the fact that German troops had already passed through this area during the advance and had in all probability looted every piece of winter clothing they could find, it seems logical to conclude that civilians wore whatever clothing was available in an attempt to survive.

The execution of these twenty-nine civilians appears to be the culmination of several factors: the growing exhaustion of soldiers who had been locked in strenuous combat for two months, increasingly radical directives on the treatment of partisans issued by the High Command, and a ruthlessness that permeated the 126th ID's approach to partisan warfare. While the murder of twenty-nine Russians was certainly the largest individual outbreak of violence perpetrated by the 126th ID in 1941, it also conformed to the general pattern of how the division responded to such resistance. Divisional practices certainly fit into both the larger context of the Wehrmacht's escalating violence as Operation Barbarossa ground on through fall 1941 and traditional German anti-partisan policy. The concept of military necessity was also understood in a much more radical and violent manner by the 126th ID than by its sister division from East Prussia. From the Rhinelanders' perspective, civilians were an obstacle to victory and needed to be treated as

---

[118] 126 ID, Abt. Ib, Orientierung über der derzeitige Versorgungslage der Division, 19. November 1941, BA-MA RH 26–126/126/139.
[119] Infanterie-Regiment 424, Tagesmeldung, 11.12.41, BA-MA RH 26–126/21.

such. Nazi ideological tenets certainly complemented and perhaps even influenced the division's policies, but it was the division's interpretation of military necessity that proved the prime cause of its murderous activities.

To a much greater extent than either the 121st or 126th Infantry Divisions and their superior corps, both the 123rd ID and II Corps lacked the necessary manpower to secure their area of operations, covered by numerous swamps and forests.[120] Several raids on suspected partisan bases captured significant stores of food and ammunition as well as numerous weapons and this led to the troops' growing awareness of their relative weakness on the ground.[121] This feeling of vulnerability, exacerbated by the confirmed presence of civilians fighting alongside regular Red Army units, led the division to lash out at the local inhabitants.[122] In an attempt to halt the troops' practice of "shoot first, ask questions later," the division castigated its men for the "repeated" shooting of "important Russians" before they were interrogated. The order explicitly mentioned partisans and suspicious civilians as categories of prisoner who required questioning.[123]

Though this order indicates that members of the 123rd ID acted in a brutal manner towards individuals they perceived as threatening, an additional order issued by the division eight days later suggests that the majority of the Berliners possessed a very different view of most civilians. The division commander rebuked his troops for what he perceived as their lackadaisical attitude towards women and children. Citing security concerns, he ordered his men to halt all civilian traffic crossing from the German to the Soviet lines.[124] Juxtaposed next to one another, these two orders highlight the contradictory impulses that ran through the 123rd ID. On the one hand, when faced with a threatening position, the Berliners could react with arbitrary violence. On the other hand, the men could also act in such a casual manner towards civilians that their commander believed they were jeopardizing their own security.

---

[120] Generalkommando II AK, Abt. Ia, Korpsbefehl Nr. 44, 3. August 1941; Generalkommando II AK, Abt. Ia, Korpsbefehl Nr. 45, 4. August 1941, BA-MA RH 26-123/16.
[121] 123 ID KTB, 25.8.41, BA-MA RH 26-123/9.
[122] The 418th Infantry Regiment encountered armed civilians for the first time on 10 August; Tagesmeldung 10. August 1941, 7.35 Uhr von IR 418, BA-MA RH 26-123/17. This was considered so noteworthy that the incident is recorded in both the divisional and the corps's war diaries; 126 ID KTB, 10.8.1, BA-MA 26-123/9; II AK KTB, 10.8.41, BA-MA RH 24-2/80.
[123] 123 ID, Abt. Ia/Az. IV/Op., Division Befehl Nr. 62, 12. August 1941, BA-MA RH 26-123/17.
[124] 123 ID, Abt. Ia, 20. August 1941, BA-MA RH 26-123/17.

142 "Will the continuation of this attack be worth it?"

II Corps issued a further order one week later that, while congratulating the soldiers on the capture and execution of numerous civilians engaged in nefarious practices, also demanded the continuation of such "ruthless" measures to end the partisan threat.[125] The 123rd ID had certainly been vigilant in identifying civilians as partisans: from 15 to 25 August, the division arrested twenty-one alleged guerillas and shot a partisan commissar.[126] The division also utilized public hangings as a means to deter resistance, as evidenced by the hanging of three partisans on 21 August.[127] While impossible to conclusively prove that all of these arrested civilians were indeed partisans, the seizure of significant stores of food and ammunition, as well as weaponry, indicates that an irritating if not mortally threatening partisan movement existed in the 123rd ID's area of operations.[128]

In an attempt to stifle partisan activity, forced evacuations and deportations became part of the division's antiguerilla arsenal. The uprooting of civilians from their homes was made much easier by the troops' racist attitudes. One junior officer wrote (apparently without irony),

looking at my notepad reminded me of a typical example of the intellectual level of these white niggers. I showed my servants [*Quartiersleute*], who are kolkhoz peasants, your illustrations. They leafed through the pictures like apes, without comprehension, indifferent, without any kind of feeling that they are looking at pictures of another world. These Huns![129]

The division ordered the clearing of all civilians from the operational area in early October, except those "necessary for economic purposes." Various sections of the division, including the artillery regiment, the engineer company, and the 416th Infantry Regiment, carried out the evacuations.[130] Such actions, however, did little to halt the growth of partisan activity.

Constant reports of partisan groups, some numbering upwards of 1,500 men, continued to filter into the 123rd ID's headquarters, with

[125] Generalkommando II AK, Abt. Ic, Betr. Partisanen und Saboteure, 23. August 1941, BA-MA RH 26–123/18.
[126] See I/418, 6.30 Uhr, 15.8; AA 123, 14.15 Uhr, 18. August 1941; AA 123, 20.00 Uhr, 19. August 1941, BA-MA RH 26–123/29; Oberleutenant Keuntje, 19.45, 25. August 1941, BA-MA RH 26–123/30.
[127] Tätigkeitsbericht der Abteilung Ic, 21.8.41, BA-MA RH 26–123/143. This fit into the larger context of *Abschreckung* as practiced by II Corps in late August. An attack on a supply convoy in which four men were killed with an additional four wounded led to the burning down of three villages and the hanging of "several suspicious people"; see II AK KTB, 24.8.41, BA-MA RH 24–2/9.
[128] Tätigkeitsbericht der Abteilung Ic, 25.8.41, BA-MA RH 26–123/143.
[129] Lt. Wilhelm Berg, Inf. Rgt. 418, 10.10.1941, BfZ, Sammlung Sterz.
[130] Stabskompanie Inf. Rgt. 416 an dem Regiment, 2.10.41; 123 ID Abt. Ia/Az. IV/Op., 6. Oktober 1941; 123 ID Abt. Ia/Ag. IV/Op., 7. Oktober 1941, BA-MA RH 26–123/20.

"The partisans are to be publicly hanged" 143

the predictable result that units needed for combat were siphoned off to the rear in generally futile operations.[131] These tips led to a dissipation of strength from the front as security was strengthened at the village level and sentry posts received further reinforcements due to what the division commander described as the "completely unsatisfactory manner" of rear-area security that bordered on "irresponsible carelessness."[132] In an attempt to bring structure to the division's anti-partisan measures, the division commander entrusted the 123rd ID's reinforced antitank section with the area's pacification.[133] This unit had some success in locating and fighting partisan units but it proved unable to silence the "especially lively" activity.[134] The escalating war behind the front led the partisans to target civilians: collaborators, such as village elders, were assassinated within the 123rd ID's operational area while villages were now subjected to the depredations of not only cold and hungry German soldiers but also partisans in similar straits.[135] Following the establishment of the division's anti-partisan unit, the 123rd ID shot nineteen partisans during the next month, with even members of the workshop company killing two partisans.[136] That these were no innocent civilians caught up in the maelstrom of war is indicated by the weapon caches seized by Wehrmacht units, including machine guns, grenades, mines, and sizable quantities of ammunition.[137]

Due to the failure of military operations to quash the partisan movement, the 123rd ID again resorted to forced evacuations. All civilians, with the exception of the very sick and those needed by the troops, were gathered together by village elders working in conjunction with various sections of the combat troops. Following a march to the nearest rail line, the evacuees were shipped in closed trains to the rear, accompanied by

---

[131] 123 ID KTB, 7.11.41, 13.11.41, 21.11.41, BA-MA RH 26–123/9; II AK KTB, 19.11.41, BA-MA RH 24–2/80; 123 ID Abt. Ia/Az. IV/Op., Aufträge für 7. November, 6. November 1941, BA-MA RH 26–126/22; Meldung des Munitionskommando Dobroje, 15.20 Uhr, 7. November 1941, BA-MA RH 26–123/34. For the estimate of 1,500 partisans, see Tätigkeitsbericht der Abteilung Ic, 13.11.41, BA-MA RH 26–123/143.
[132] 123 ID KTB, 12.11.41, BA-MA RH 26–123/9. For the commander's views, see 123 Inf. Division Kommandeur, 7. November 1941, BA-MA RH 26–123/22.
[133] 123 ID KTB, 13.11.41, BA-MA RH 26–123/9.
[134] 123 ID KTB, 24.11.41, 29.11.41, BA-MA RH 26–123/9; II AK KTB, 25.11.41, BA-MA RH 26–123/9; Panzerjägerabteilung 123 Abt. Ia, Abteilungsbefehl zur Vernichtung von Partisanen durch verstärkte Pz. Jg. Abt. 123, 13.11.1941, BA-MA RH 26–123/34.
[135] Tätigkeitsbericht der Abteilung Ic, 28.11.41, BA-MA RH 26–123/143. On 6 December, a group of sixty partisans burned down a village in the division's area after stealing cattle and food. See the Ic's war diary entry for 6 December 1941.
[136] Tätigkeitsbericht der Abteilung Ic, 19.11.41, 24.11.41, 28.11.41, 30.11.41, 2.12.41, 14.12.41, BA-MA RH 26–123/143.
[137] Tätigkeitsbericht der Abteilung Ic, 19.11.41, 14.12.41, BA-MA RH 26–123/143.

rear-area troops. While the planning was straightforward enough, the actual execution of the evacuation proved problematic. In the 415th Infantry Regiment's sector, the commander reported that his men were unable to move the 1,700 people that required evacuation. The civilians needed to march approximately 120 kilometers to the nearest rail line and neither his men nor the region's inhabitants possessed enough vehicles to ensure their arrival. The commander was also concerned by what he perceived to be a lack of food and other supplies for the civilians along the march route.[138] Following the evacuation, German soldiers were now given "the right to shoot any non-German without first calling out to them," as any civilian in the area was automatically deemed a partisan.[139]

These deportations, however, did not bring a halt to partisan activity in the 123rd ID's operational area. Clashes between German patrols and groups of irregulars ranging from twenty to 200 individuals repeatedly occurred during late December 1941 and early January 1942.[140] The failure of the division to destroy the partisan movement led its superior formation, II Corps, to launch a "punishment expedition" in its rear that concluded on 16 December with eleven villages burned down and "85 Russians shot of which 12 were proven to be partisans."[141] II Corps also evacuated and burned down several other villages located near the primary supply road in the winter of 1941–2 in attempts to squash the partisan movement.[142] And as a report issued by Sixteenth Army makes clear, civilians frequently bore the brunt of Wehrmacht anti-partisan policies. During a seven-day period spanning the end of November and early December 1941, 387 partisans were shot and 124 Red Army men and thirty-five "suspicious" civilians were arrested. This was all achieved

---

[138] 17.45 Uhr von IR 415 (Kdr.), Meldung zum Evakuierungsbefehl, 1. Dezember 1941, BA-MA RH 26–123/35. The area's poverty is underscored by the fact that these 1,700 people had only twenty horses and carts between them.

[139] 123 ID Ib, Betr.: Evakuierung der Gefechtszone, 29.11.41; 123 ID Abt. Ib, Betr.: Evakuierung der Gefechtszone, 30.11.1941, BA-MA RH 26–123/22.

[140] 123 ID KTB, Überblick der Zeit 16.12.41–5.1.42, BA-MA RH 26–123/46; enemy fire destroyed the original war diary for this time period. See also Tätigkeitsbericht Ic, 20.12.41, 23.12.41, 1.1.42, BA-MA RH 26–123/147. Disturbed by reports of a group of 100 partisans active in the village of Gnutischtsche, the division assembled a commando consisting of members of the antitank unit, engineers, and combat troops from the 415th Infantry Regiment to "exterminate" the partisans. As no further mention of this particular partisan grouping is found in the division's files, it appears the operation failed.

[141] AK II KTB, 16.12.41, BA-MA RH 24–2/107.

[142] Generalkommando II. Armeekorps, Abteilung Qu/Ia 461/43 g. Kdos, Betr.: Bandeneinwirkung an Armee-Oberkommando 16, 15. Mai 1943, BA-MA RH 24–2/210.

at a cost of a mere ten Germans killed and eleven wounded.[143] While the 123rd ID could plausibly claim that it was fighting against an actual enemy, the actions of its superior formations are much, much harder to justify from a military standpoint. Rather, it seems that the pressure exerted by the German political and military leadership on the lower levels of the German field army to ruthlessly crush the nascent partisan movement combined with the army's increasing desperation to achieve victory and caused increasingly violent interactions between German units and Soviet citizens.

III. "We take pigs, chickens, geese, [and] cows from the poor civilians so that we have something to eat": the crisis of supply in late 1941

While anti-partisan operations constituted one aspect of the increasingly volatile relationship between civilians and soldiers, the food issue affected an even larger number of individuals on both the Soviet and German sides. Much like the cases of military operations and partisan activity, each division's logistic situation depended to a large extent on its particular location and circumstance. While the 121st ID certainly continued its practice of living off the land, normal supply reached the East Prussians much more regularly than either the 123rd or 126th IDs.[144] As previously noted, the 121st ID operated in an industrial area, crisscrossed by rail lines, while the 123rd and 126th IDs found themselves considerably further east and consequently much more reliant on delivery by motor vehicles and horse-drawn carts.[145] As Leeb noted in mid-December, the "supply situation has become very difficult because the railroad cannot meet the demands. The reasons for this are lack of locomotives and inadequate repair opportunities."[146] Furthermore, the East Prussians' location in an industrial area led to a real dependence on supplies brought up from the rear. In contrast, the 123rd and 126th IDs operated in a rural section of the Soviet Union and theoretically had access to its agricultural production by living off the land.

---

[143] O. Qu. (Qu 2), Partisanenbekämpfung in der Armee in der Zeit vom 29.11–5.12.41, 7.12.41, BA-MA RH 24-2/327.
[144] The supply situation of the 121st ID will be examined in much more detail in the following chapter.
[145] The shortage of locomotives plagued the *Ostheer* from the beginning of the campaign and the problem only increased as 1941 wound down. On this topic see Klaus Schüler, "The Eastern Campaign as a Transportation and Supply Problem," in Bernd Wegner (ed.), *From Peace to War: Germany, Soviet Russia and the World, 1939–1941* (Providence, 1997), pp. 205–22.
[146] Leeb, *Tagebuchaufzeichnungen*, 11 December 1941, pp. 412–13.

The sheer magnitude of forced requisitioning by the troops, however, threatened the long-term exploitation of the region so desperately required by the Germans.[147] This development led to repeated orders by superior formations to cease such practices. On 16 July, Leeb felt the need to instruct his army group that "the reconstruction by the economic department has been wrecked by the senseless 'organization' of the troops."[148] I Army Corps followed this line of thinking when it explained to its subordinate formations that "the maintenance of the Russian rural economy is vital for the continuation of the war" and that every head of cattle and every piece of fodder required fair payment.[149] The 126th ID itself stated that such requisitions could only occur following written permission from a battalion commander.[150] The quartermaster of the 123rd ID also ordered a ban on the collection of all goods in Kholm due to the local population's destitution.[151] At the institutional level, the apparent crises that emerged in the fall of 1941 led the army group's leadership to try to control the food requisition issue in a more structured way.

Despite the significant institutional power that the army exercised over the individuals in its ranks, "wild actions" continued unabated by the men.[152] As Omer Bartov has noted, the distinction between "legitimate" exploitation by the state and "senseless" plundering by individuals was perhaps too fine for many troops, and with combat operations remaining the focus of the military leadership, German soldiers on the ground only increased their forced requisitions from the surrounding population.[153] The approaching winter worried some divisional headquarters and they tried to impress upon the men the need for a much more organized requisitioning. Castigating the men for "not possessing any understanding of how important the collection of the harvest is," the 126th ID's quartermaster sought to accumulate stocks of potatoes, root crops, vegetables, and wheat. He ordered the troops to organize and supervise the collection of the harvest by civilians; when adequate numbers of Russians

---

[147] The clash between the short-terms needs of the army and the long-term plans of the Wirtschaftsstab Ost are made clear in Müller, *Die deutsche Wirtschaftspolitik*; and Rutherford, "The Radicalization of German Occupation Policies."
[148] Quoted in Hürter, *Hitlers Heerführer*, p. 492.
[149] Generalkommando I AK, Korpsbefehl 84 für den 9.8.41, 8.8.1941, BA-MA RH 26–126/11.
[150] Merkblatt über Beutegut. (Verpflegung) und dem Land entnommene Verpflegung, no date, BA-MA RH 26–126/139.
[151] 123 Inf. Division Ib, Betr.: Beitreibungen, 11.8.41, BA-MA RH 26–123/187.
[152] For a penetrating look at the army's institutional power, see Rass, *Menschenmaterial*, pp. 205–330.
[153] Bartov, *Hitler's Army*, pp. 77–8.

could not be located, the soldiers were to bring in the produce themselves. All of the gathered stocks, however, required payment as they were the property of the area's *Bürgermeister*. The quartermaster also wanted to ensure that at least a minimum of food was left over for the civilian population. This, however, was frequently ignored by the troops in the field.[154] One member of the Rhenish 69th ID wrote, "we need to feed ourselves so we take pigs, chickens, geese, [and] cows from the poor civilians so that we have something to eat."[155] Despite clear orders to the contrary, the Kholm commandant claimed that troops regularly exchanged bogus receipts for chickens and cows and physically abused civilians who tried to protect their property. In one particularly disturbing case, a seventy-five-year-old woman on her knees begging mounted troops not to take her last cow was punched repeatedly in her face. To add insult to injury, as she stood up, she witnessed the soldiers also steal a lamb and a chicken as they rode off.[156] It is therefore abundantly clear that the claim of the 126th ID's quartermaster that "food was never really a problem" for the division was only made possible by the troops' ravaging of the countryside.[157]

The same case could not be made by the quartermaster of the 123rd ID. Only two weeks after the division moved out of its positions near Kholm and renewed the offensive, it reported its supply situation as "extremely strained," leading the corps commander to cancel an attack in order to use all available roads to alleviate the supply situation.[158] A delay based on logistic considerations was striking in an army so focused on operations and it emphasized the problems facing the 123rd ID. Due to wet weather that aggravated the problems caused by the nearly non-existent road network, the troops were placed on emergency rations and instructed to live off the land as much as possible.[159] This, however, proved extremely difficult as the villages which the division passed through had simply nothing to offer. The lack of available food in the area was compounded by "no regular supply for days," leaving the men incapable of attack or of defending a strong enemy assault.[160] II Corps's commander believed that the most pressing issue facing the 123rd ID was "not a problem of the

---

[154] 126 Infanterie-Division, Abt. Ib, Einbringung der Ernte, 25.9.41, BA-MA RH 26–126/139. The following is drawn from this document.
[155] Gefr. Ernst Schneider, 4. Company/Grenadier Rgt. 157, 1.11.41, BfZ, Sammlung Sterz.
[156] Der Ortskommandant, Kholm, den 19.8.41, BA-MA RH 26–123/187.
[157] 126 Infanterie-Division, Abt. IVa, Tätigkeitsbericht der Abt. IVa für die Zeit vom 22.6 bis 31.12.1941, BA-MA RH 26–126/140.
[158] II AK KTB, 19.9.41, BA-MA RH 24–2/80.
[159] 123 ID Abt. IVa, Tätigkeitsbericht für die Zeit vom 1.9–30.9.41, 20.12.41, BA-MA RH 26–123/198.
[160] Gespräch Ia – Kdr./IR 415, 23.September 1941, BA-MA RH 26–123/32.

enemy, but rather a problem of supply."[161] In defending the conduct of the 123rd ID to Sixteenth Army, he argued that "one cannot in any way reproach the troops." Suffering from "continuous bombing and heavy artillery fire," as well as the results of a horribly flawed supply system, their "strength was at an end."[162] In the case of the 123rd ID, the division's combat effectiveness directly corresponded with its supply.

This "supply crisis" worsened throughout the month of October as a variety of factors, including the growing distance between supply depots and the front lines, deteriorating roads, shorter periods of daylight, and the worsening condition of all available vehicles, played havoc with the division's logistics.[163] The first snow, while transforming the landscape into a "*Heimat*-like Christmas scene," also exacerbated the "unimaginably difficult supply situation."[164] To an even greater extent than in previous months, the troops ravenously foraged the surrounding area for food. As the quartermaster admitted, however, since the region's civilians had very little to offer, both man and horse had a "very difficult" time meeting their needs. Village elders were ordered to deliver needed goods to the troops, but when this failed to meet the men's minimum requirements, the troops resorted to outright robbery. An *Ortskommandant* in the rear of the 123rd ID complained to the division staff that the Berliners were taking fur coats and boots from women as well as stealing the last remaining foodstuffs from villagers, both under threat of violence.[165] While he reminded the men that such actions were expressly forbidden, the complete breakdown of the supply situation on 22 October meant that such rebukes were ignored both by the troops and by their divisional and corps superiors, and Wehrmacht soldiers scoured the countryside in search of food.[166]

The scarcity of fodder for horses led to both a virtual "hay war" between German divisions and more concerted efforts by the 123rd ID to gather the harvest.[167] The division's requirements, however, needed to be balanced

---

[161] Gespräch zwischen Oberst i.G. Boekh und Kom. Gen., 19.9.41, BA-MA RH 24–2/93.
[162] Gespräch zwischen Generaloberst Busch und Kom. General, 23. September 1941, BA-MA RH 24–2/93.
[163] 123 ID Abt. IVa, Tätigkeitsbericht für die Zeit vom 1.10–31.10.1941, 21.12.41. BA-MA RH 26–123/198. The following discussion is based on this document.
[164] Lt. Wilhelm Berg, Inf. Rgt. 418, 10.10.41, BfZ, Sammlung Sterz.
[165] Der Ortskommandant in Schukovo, 24.10.41, BA-MA RH 26–123/33.
[166] II AK KTB, 29.10.41, BA-MA RH 24–2/80. During the last week of October, the men of the 123rd ID received only half of their usual rations and, since the area they were operating in was so desolate, they estimated that they could only live off the land until 2 November; see Tagesmeldung der 123 ID, 29. Oktober 1941, BA-MA RH 24–2/98.
[167] On the "hay war," see II AK KTB, 12.11.41, BA-MA RH 24–2/80; on the division's efforts, see 123 ID KTB Ib, 14.11.41, BA-MA RH 26–123/183.

with the Wehrmacht's long-term exploitation of the area and both economic experts and the corps command instructed the 123rd ID to ensure a minimum subsistence for civilians as it feared a "famine" in the coming months.[168] By December, the supply situation had begun to improve as a more regular delivery system developed. A lack of animal fodder for both civilian and Wehrmacht horses was settled in favor of the army, with 15 percent of all stocks left to the Soviets as an "existence minimum." Though German leaders foresaw a catastrophe for the region's inhabitants, the demands of the Wehrmacht needed to be met first.

As the temperature continued to fall, authorities realized that food was not the only thing in short supply. The extreme shortage of winter clothing constituted a major problem for the *Ostheer* as a whole and for both the 123rd and 126th IDs in particular. Already in September, members of the 123rd ID requested warm clothing from family members at home, while just over a month later, a member of the 93rd ID from Wehrkreis III complained that "it was already constantly cold ... we still haven't received our winter clothing. That should be: a pair of gloves, a warm hat, and an overcoat."[169] At the institutional level, the Rhinelanders reported a "catastrophic clothing condition" in early October, a sentiment echoed by the 123rd ID's superior formation, II Corps, which noted, "one certainly cannot talk about a proper organization of winter equipment ... the troops have suffered from this."[170] When the front finally received uniforms from the rear, however, they were merely replacements for worn-through summer clothing and failed to suffice for the Russian winter.[171] In an attempt to alleviate this shortage of winter clothing, both divisions ordered their troops to either purchase or requisition furs and other winter clothing from the civilian population, though the men were to ensure that each inhabitant kept at least one set for themselves.[172]

As the 126th ID's intendant noted, however, "the result was extraordinarily meager."[173] Lacking sufficient winter uniforms, numerous

---

[168] 123 ID KTB Ib, BA-MA RH 26–123/183, 21.11.41, 24.11.41. The 253rd ID, located on the right flank of 123rd ID, distributed over 15,000 loaves of bread to villagers in the area in a proactive attempt to avert large-scale starvation; ibid., 25.11.41.
[169] Lt. Wilhelm Berg, 418 Infantry Regiment, 3.9.41, BfZ, Sammlung Sterz; Private Konrad Weber, 272 Infantry Regiment, 13.10.41, BfZ, Sammlung Sterz.
[170] 126 Infanterie-Division, Dem Herrn Kommandierenden General des XXXIX Armeekorps, 3.11.41, BA-MA RH 26–126/23; II AK KTB I, 28.11.41, BA-MA RH 24–2/80.
[171] 126 Infanterie-Division, Dem Herrn Kommandierenden General des XXXIX Armeekorps, 3.11.41, BA-MA RH 26–126/23.
[172] Ibid.; 123 ID KTB Ib, 27.11.41, BA-MA RH 26–123/183.
[173] 126 Infanterie-Division, Abt. IVa, 15.3.1942, Tätigkeitsbericht der Abt. IVa für die Zeit vom 22.6. bis 31.12.1941, BA-MA RH 26–126/140.

soldiers in the 126th ID suffered frostbite. During the first seventeen days of December, the division reported that more than 600 men were incapacitated for a minimum of six weeks, with the majority being out of action for three months.[174] A member of the Rhenish 254th ID complained of the constant operations "without winter clothing. The extent of frostbite is shocking. The troops have gone completely mad about taking felt boots from the Russian dead."[175] Soldiers now increased the practice of stripping prisoners of their boots and clothing in an attempt to survive the cold.[176] The outbreak of frostbite during the last gasp of the German offensive ominously foreshadowed the events of the approaching winter crisis.

As Operation Barbarossa sputtered to an end near Lake Seliger and along the Volkhov river, the 123rd and 126th IDs, having advanced over 1,000 kilometers against increasingly stiffening opposition and at the end of an extremely tenuous supply line, settled into defensive positions. The Rhinelanders looked forward to a "period of time to refresh both numerically and spiritually, as they are at the end of their strength."[177] The war diary for the 123rd ID betrayed a considerably more bitter assessment of the situation:

After almost six months of uninterrupted combat, much of it under the harshest conditions, after enormous efforts by the heavily taxed troops with their considerable casualties (from 22.6.41–6.1.42, 1221 dead and 4564 wounded), the division stands on 5.1.42 with a front of around 90km, dispersed in strongpoints in small and smaller villages, in terrain with no visibility, without finished or wired positions, with all mobile strength on restricted roads for emergency use, without the necessary winter equipment or training, in the icy cold, prepared to carry out its assignment of "defense."[178]

The gamble of Barbarossa had failed and a weakened German infantry prepared for its first Russian winter.

---

[174] 126 Infanterie-Division, Tagesmeldung vom 17.12 an XXXVIII AK, 17.12.41, BA-MA RH 26–126/22. The 424th Infantry Regiment reported 127 cases of frostbite of which seventy-six required hospitalization on 16 and 17 December; see Ausfälle des Infanterie-Regiment 424 am 16. und 17.12.1941, BA-MA RH 26–126/22. The engineer battalion also complained that "frostbite has seriously lowered the battalion's strength"; Pionier Btl. 126 Kriegstagebuch Ostfeldzug 21.6.1941–30.12.1941, 7.12.41, BA-MA RH 46/414.
[175] Einsatz der 1/San. Kp 254 in Nordrußland – Errinerungsbericht von Oberfeldarzt d.R. a.D. Dr. Franz Eckstein, Wehsarg, BA-MA Msg 2/4558, p. 48.
[176] Corporal Ernst Schneider, 4. Company/Grenadier Regiment 157, 1.11.41, BfZ, Sammlung Sterz.
[177] 126 ID KTB, 21.12.42, BA-MA RH 26–126/4.
[178] 123 ID KTB, Band II, Überblick 16.12.41–5.1.42, BA-MA RH 26–123/46.

5 "It is only a question of where, not if, civilians will starve"
The 121st Infantry Division and the occupation of Pavlovsk

Following its arrival in Pavlovsk on 19 September 1941, the 121st ID settled into its position in the Leningrad siege line, a spot occupied by the East Prussians until 30 April 1942, when they deployed to the Volkhov region.[1] The division's occupation of Pavlovsk is instructive for several reasons. First, its experiences during this time period significantly differ from those of the 123rd and 126th IDs, highlighting the difficulty in ascribing one master narrative for all German units during Operation Barbarossa. Second, the fate of Pavlovsk fits into two larger and interconnected themes: general German policy towards Soviet urban centers and, more specifically, German objectives towards Leningrad as well as the Wehrmacht's complicity with the regime's planned war of annihilation. Up until this point in the war, the men of the 121st, 123rd, and 126th IDs generally fought their war only alongside other Wehrmacht units. With the ending of the advance, however, the nature of the war transformed and various German organizations, such as the Economic Staff East and the SS-Police, now began to work much more closely with Army Group North's combat infantry in occupying and securing Hitler's newly conquered eastern empire. The primary mission of frontline combat divisions certainly remained that of defeating the Red Army in battle. The end of the blitzkrieg, however, also meant that the German

---

[1] On the dates of occupation, see Divisionsintendant, 121 Inf. Division, 30.4.42, Tätigkeitsbericht für die Zeit vom 21.9.1941 bis 30.4.1942, BA MA RH 26-121/65; *Geschichte der 121. Ostpreussische Infanterie-Division*, p. 349; XXVIII AK KTB, 26.9.41, BA-MA RH 24–28/20a; and the Chrezvychainaia Gosudarstvennaia Komissiia po Ustanobleniiu i Rassledobaniiu Zlodeianii Nemetsko-Fashistskikh Zakhvatchikov i ikh Soiuznikov (hereafter Chrezvychainaia Gosudarstvennaia Komissiia), United States Holocaust Memorial Museum (hereafter USHMM), RG 22–002M, Reel 18, Pavlovsk, p. 2. For a critical examination of this source, see Marina Sorokina, "People and Procedures: Towards a History of the Investigation of Nazi Crimes in the USSR," *Kritika* (4) 2005, pp. 797–831; obviously care needs to be exercised in utilizing the findings of this organization. Soldiers of the 121st ID occupied the towns and villages of Pushkin, Finskie Lipizti, Tiarelvo, Putrolvolo, and Pavlovsk in their section of the line; see Lagekarten 24.9.41, BA-MA RH 26–121/15k.

infantry now had to assume tasks that it was simply unprepared for, and this led it into the larger exploitative web spun by other Nazi institutions in the East.

Third, the division's occupation of Pavlovsk highlighted the importance of military necessity – or, as expressed by the division commander, "the interests of the troops' security."[2] During the occupation, the 121st ID enacted policies which, though both influenced by and congruent with the ideological considerations and the actions of other Nazi institutions, were primarily based on the notion of ensuring the division's combat effectiveness. Finally, as will become clear in the examination of Pavlovsk, this co-operation amounted to complicity in the crime of genocide and the establishment of forced-labor programs. Perhaps most devastating to the local inhabitants, the division also helped to implement National Socialist starvation policies, and though individual soldiers did sometimes circumvent the barbarous orders they received from their superiors, this did little to arrest civilian suffering. Unfortunately for Pavlovsk's inhabitants, they failed to exist within the Wehrmacht's narrowly defined notion of military necessity and suffered a horrible fate during the 1941–2 winter.

I.   Pavlovsk under German rule

The dual nature of German strategy – the need for an operational blitzkrieg and the desire to smash the Soviet state and decimate its urban society – led to a paradox regarding Soviet cities.[3] With the operation's success predicated on speed, it was imperative for the Wehrmacht to exploit the road network, as the experiences of the French campaign demonstrated. In the Soviet Union, the very few roads that did exist frequently intersected cities and this forced the German Army to expend precious time and resources securing these areas. This clashed with the general tenets of the war of annihilation, however, according to which large Soviet cities needed to be isolated and their populations decimated. Instead of merely fencing in such communities or destroying them through aerial bombardment as planners in Berlin desired, the army needed to control them for its operations. Pavlovsk, despite being a smaller city as opposed to a major urban center, nonetheless fits into this context, as German troops

---

[2] Divisions-Befehl 24.9.1941 – Behandlung von Zivilpersonen, KTB, BA-MA RH 26-121/12. Seventeenth Army, operating in Ukraine, issued a similar order in August: "In the interest of the security of the German Wehrmacht, one should not shrink from severity against the civilian population"; quoted in Hürter, *Hitlers Heerführer*, p. 474.

[3] Wettstein, "Operation 'Barbarossa' und Stadtkampf," pp. 21–44.

conquered it during the drive on Leningrad and then, following the decision to besiege the metropolis on the Neva, found themselves responsible for securing and administering the area (see Map 5.1).

During the East Prussians' advance towards Pavlovsk in early September, the division became extremely cognizant of the perceived dangers posed by civilians passing through German lines into the rear areas. Interrogations revealed that civilians and Soviet soldiers in civilian attire passed back and forth across the front line and reported on German troop deployment to the Red Army. In order to halt to such occurrences, the highest-ranking officer in each village was given the rank of *Ortskommandant* and the power to take "the sharpest action" to stop the traffic between the front lines.[4] Such population movements between German and Soviet positions also increased the threat of partisan activity behind German lines, according to the corps command:

in his unscrupulous and treacherous way, the enemy wants to relieve the desperate food situation in Leningrad and the surrounding industrial suburbs by attempting to move the sections of the population that will not fight in both smaller and larger groups behind our lines.

Apart from other disadvantages, this would above all make things considerably more difficult for our conduct of the war and must be opposed with all means. All traffic by civilians between the two lines is therefore to be stopped, even through the use of weapons. Only soldiers are to be taken prisoner.[5]

Eighteenth Army, which initially controlled only the western section of the encirclement, ordered its subordinate units on 13 September to shoot women and children if they attempted to pass through the lines.[6] XXVIII Corps framed a similar directive in terms of partisan warfare, arguing that since many of these civilians carried arms, the troops should combat "this type of disgraceful guerilla behavior ... with the sharpest means."[7] Despite these numerous directives, the 121st ID felt the need to issue yet another order regarding civilians as the troops neared Pavlovsk. Stating that the "large waves of Russian civilians" who had passed through the German lines during the past few days were "undesirable ... on espionage and economic grounds," the order demanded that the front lines halt the movement of refugees, authorizing the use of weapons in extreme cases.[8] The division again re-emphasized this theme on 19 September,

---

[4] 121 Inf.-Division, Abt. Ia, 4.9.41, BA-MA RH 26–121/12.
[5] Generalkommando XXVIII AK, Abt. Ia/Ic., 11.9.1941, BA-MA RH 26–121/12.
[6] Hürter, "Die Wehrmacht vor Leningrad," p. 400.
[7] XXVIII AK, Tätigkeitsbericht Teil III, 17–19.9.41, BA-MA RH 24–28/109.
[8] 121 Inf.-Division, Abt. Ia – Div. Befehl für die Einahme von Ssluzk am 18.9.1941–19.9.1941, BA-MA RH 26–121/12.

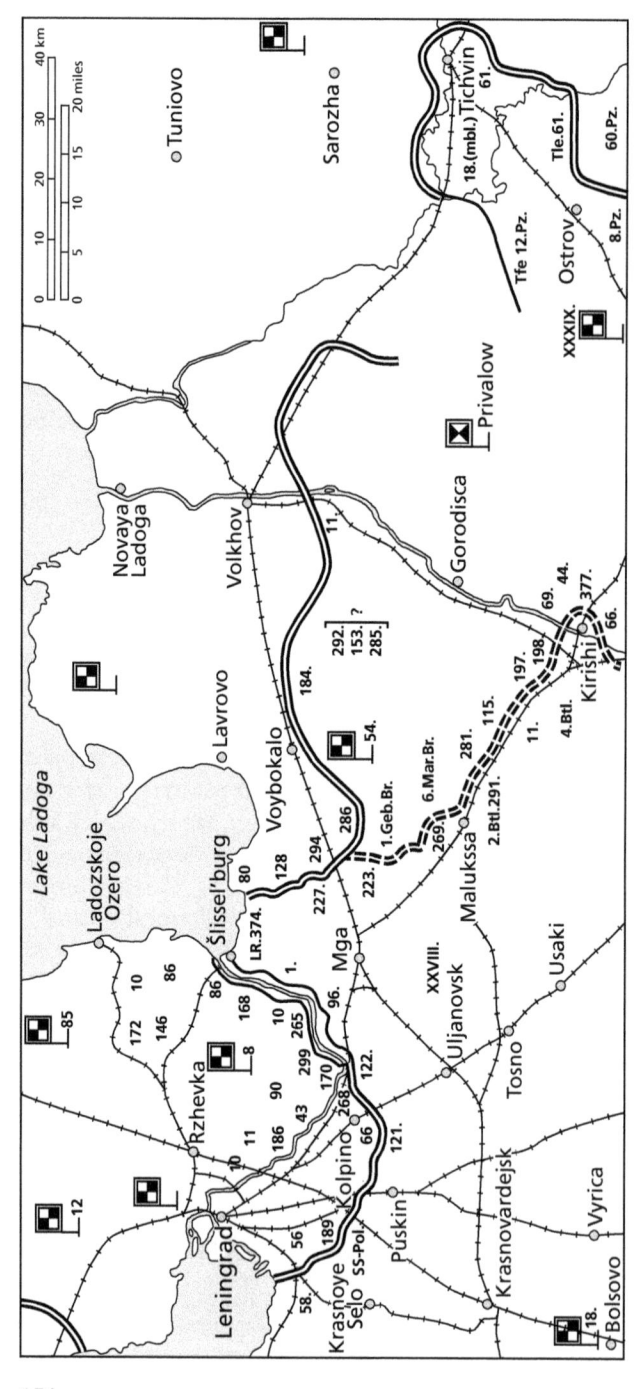

Map 5.1 The Leningrad siege line

emphatically stating that "all traffic of civilians through the front line is to be stopped by the use of brute force."[9] Such formulations received sanction at the highest levels of the military hierarchy as Jodl informed Brauchitsch that "whoever leaves the city and comes towards our lines is to be turned back by fire."[10] From the OKW down to the division, the German Army viewed any manifestation of popular resistance as a threat to its mission in northwest Russia and this institutional view certainly permeated the 121st ID during fall 1941.

Repeated orders demanding the halt of all civilian traffic through the front lines, however, also indicate that this movement continued unabated during the remainder of September, suggesting that despite the racist and anti-Bolshevik attitudes held by many members of the 121st ID and other German formations, this did not prevent them from showing mercy towards women and children, despite the possible threat these refugees represented for the troops. The commander of the 58th ID went so far as to claim that his men were more worried about shooting "women, children and defenseless old men" than they were with their own strained military situation.[11] While the siege of Leningrad and the subsequent starvation of the city certainly rank among the most heinous war crimes committed by the Wehrmacht, the actions and attitudes of individual soldiers involved in the siege, including members of the 121st ID, highlight the wide spectrum of behaviors and attitudes within the ranks of the Wehrmacht.

Once the 121st ID cleared Pavlovsk of Red Army troops, it immediately began to secure German control. Wehrmacht policy following the seizure of a town and or city called for the immediate registration of the population. As historian Dieter Pohl has noted,

the primary objective of this registration was not to determine the size of the population, but rather to create a classification of the inhabitants based on social

---

[9] 121 Inf.-Division, Ia – Div. Befehl für den Übergang zur Verteidigung 19.9.1941, BA-MA RH 26–121/12. L Corps, bordering the 121st ID on the right, distributed the following order to its subordinate units: "The pushing of the civilian population out of the encircled area is to be stopped through the use of weapons if necessary. In the combat area, the population is to be strictly controlled. The male population is to be brought together in several villages and guarded from the outbreak of darkness to daybreak. Whoever wanders around during the night makes himself a suspected partisan and will be shot. Civilians are also forbidden from leaving their home district during the day." L AK, Abt. Ic, Feindnachrichtenblatt, 21.9.41, NARA T-314, Roll 1234.
[10] Oberkommando der Wehrmacht, Nr. 44 1675/41 g. K. Chefs. WFSt/Abt. L (I Op.), 7.10.41, printed in Ueberschär and Wette, *Der deutsche Überfall auf die Sowjetunion*, pp. 280–1.
[11] KTB HGr. Nord, 24.10.41, printed in Ueberschär and Wette, *Der deutsche Überfall auf die Sowjetunion*, pp. 281–2. See also Hürter, "Die Wehrmacht vor Leningrad," p. 401; and Ganzenmüller, *Das belagerte Leningrad 1941–1944*, p. 70.

groups and to control the mobility [of civilians], especially as a means to hinder and combat resistance activities. The registration also served in the determination of possible laborers who could then be transported to the Reich.[12]

Two days after entering the city, the 121st ID's commander ordered all males between the ages of fourteen and seventy to report for registration in an attempt to identify both disguised soldiers and people not native to the city.[13] He justified the procedure as a response to several German cables being cut during the night; here, the link between registration, popular resistance, and the army's mania for total control is strikingly clear.[14]

The registration turned up 13,000 inhabitants, of whom approximately 3,000 were either refugees or Red Army soldiers.[15] Following the discovery of the latter, the commander of XXVIII Corps decided, after consultation with other corps-level officers, as well as members of the II SS-Brigade,[16] that those capable of labor should be transferred to a prisoner-of-war camp, to serve as an available pool of workers for the 121st ID.[17] Men deemed suspicious were placed into a separate camp under armed guard while those unable to work were issued identification cards and allowed to stay in the city.[18] The civilians subjected to this process viewed it as completely humiliating and dehumanizing: following physical examinations that made the inhabitants feel "like cattle, like working horses," each resident of Pavlovsk was given a number for identification.[19] After the conclusion of this identification process, the

---

[12] Pohl, *Die Herrschaft der Wehrmacht*, pp. 134–5. Gerlach, *Kalkulierte Morde*, p. 220, notes that the Germans – both army and SS formations – instituted such practices throughout Belarus.

[13] Divisions-Befehl 24.9.1941 – Behandlung von Zivilpersonen, BA-MA RH 26–121/12.

[14] According to the Corps's Intelligence Section, the mass arrests were due to an enemy air attack on the "completely camouflaged accommodations" of the 121st ID's headquarters. The Germans believed that only spies within the city could have passed such detailed information along to the Red Army. See XXVIII AK, Ic Tätigkeitsbericht Teil III, 21–23.9.41, BA-MA RH 24–28/109.

[15] Chrezvychainaia Gosudarstvennaia Komissiia, USHMM RG 22–002M, Reel 18, Pavlovsk, p. 4.

[16] The II SS-Brigade was utilized by XXVIII Corps as well as Sixteenth Army for anti-partisan sweeps and to dispense "special treatment" to different categories of prisoner.

[17] XXVIII AK KTB, 24.9.41, BA-MA RH 24–28/20a. The use of these prisoners for labor by the division itself differed from practices in larger cities such as Kiev or Feodosia where the civilian population was dispersed for labor purposes by army commands or shipped back to the Reich; see Berkhoff, *Harvest of Despair*, p. 144; and Oldenburg, *Ideologie und militärisches Kalkül*, p. 111.

[18] XXVIII AK KTB, 21.9.41, BA-MA RH 24–28/20a.

[19] Chrezvychainaia Gosudarstvennaia Komissiia, USHMM RG 22–002M, Reel 18, Pavlovsk, p. 1.

Illustration 5.1 In September 1941, the local population was forced to register with German authorities at Pavlovsk Palace.

German authorities deemed anyone who "surfaced" a "partisan to be treated correspondingly."[20]

Conditions within the labor camp mirrored those of other civilian collection centers established by the Germans.[21] Survivors told of backbreaking work lasting up to sixteen hours a day and arbitrary violence by guards that frequently resulted in the death of prisoners.[22] In addition to the initial deportation, the Germans organized three additional mass transports, totaling approximately 6,000 civilians, who were sent to various labor camps in northern Russia as well as to work in Germany itself. While the local branch of the Economic Staff East termed the recruitment of volunteers for labor in the Reich "successful," it also laconically noted, "it requires no special mention that the willingness to be shipped [to Germany] has been primarily

---

[20] XXVIII AK KTB, 21.9.41, BA-MA RH 24–28/20a; Divisions-Befehl 24.9.1941 – Behandlung von Zivilpersonen, BA-MA RH 26–121/12. Such a formulation also fit neatly into German practice in 1941; see Gerlach, *Kalkulierte Morde*, p. 220.

[21] An evocative portrayal of such camps in Minsk is found in Paul Kohl, *Der Krieg der deutschen Wehrmacht und der Polizei 1941–1944* (Frankfurt, 1995), pp. 90–1, 99–100.

[22] Chrezvychainaia Gosudarstvennaia Komissiia, USHMM RG 22–002M, Reel 18, Pavlovsk, pp. 1, 5, 6. The remainder of this discussion is based on this document.

caused by the food situation."[23] Of this number, some 3,500 perished, never to return to Pavlovsk.

The 121st ID also established three separate prisoner-of-war camps in the city and their conditions reflected those of other German POW camps in late 1941.[24] These prisoners were a mix of Red Army soldiers from the Leningrad front and civilians picked up from the smaller towns and villages outside Pavlovsk.[25] Numerous soldiers in these camps were wounded but received no medical care.[26] Similarly to their civilian counterparts, the captive soldiers were subjected to "daily beatings" as well as being forced to work long hours on extremely arduous tasks. Provided with a meager daily diet of twenty-eight grams of ersatz bread and a revolting gruel, these prisoners faced an extremely high mortality rate with over 1,000 dying during the course of the war. After three months of decimating a readily available labor force, the division quartermaster finally approved an increase in rations in the hope that this would lead to a corresponding rise in labor productivity.[27] The issue of Soviet prisoners' survival existed outside the moral universe of division command, reduced to a mere question of pragmatism.

As an occupying force, the 121st ID was responsible for providing order and care for both the population and prisoners of war under their control.[28] The German Army, however, was not responsible for

[23] Wi. Kdo. Krasnogwardeisk, Gru. Fü., Monatsbericht Februar 1942, 23.2.1942, BA-MA RW 31/948.
[24] Chrezvychainaia Gosudarstvennaia Komissiia, USHMM RG 22-002M, Reel 18, Pavlovsk, pp. 5–6. Unless otherwise noted, this discussion is based on this document. For more on conditions within German POW camps, see Streit, *Keine Kameraden*, pp. 171–9; and Hamburger Institut für Sozialforschung (ed.), *Verbrechen der Wehrmacht: Dimensionen des Vernichtungskrieges 1941–1944* (Hamburg, 2002), pp. 217–69.
[25] According to Russian sources, over 2,000 refugees fleeing the Germans had made the cellar of Pavlovsk Palace their new home during late August and early September; Massie, *Pavlovsk: The Life of a Russian Palace*, p. 197.
[26] This corresponded to a general order issued by the OKH categorically stating that only Soviet medical personnel were to attend to wounded Red Army soldiers. If none were available, then German medics could intervene, but this certainly was not encouraged; AK XXVIII KTB Abt. Qu., OKH Generalquartiermeister, Versorgung verwundeter Kriegsgefangener und Seuchenverhütung, 7.7.1941, BA-MA RH 24-28/192. For a further discussion of this policy, see Streit, *Keine Kameraden*, pp. 183–7.
[27] Besprechungspunkte für Kdr. Besprechung, 12.12.41, BA-MA RH 26-121/17. This decision was a direct consequence of the Reich leadership's decision to utilize Soviet prisoners of war as workers for Germany's increasingly overextended war economy. For a discussion of this radical shift in policy and the effects it had on Soviet POWs, see Streit, *Keine Kameraden*, pp. 201–8, 249–53.
[28] Hürter, "Die Wehrmacht vor Leningrad," pp. 385–6. On the Wehrmacht's responsibilities according to international law, see "Hague Convention (IV) Respecting the Law and Customs of War on Land, Annex to the Convention," in W. Michael Reisman and Chris T. Antoniou (eds.), *The Laws of War: A Comprehensive Collection of Primary Documents on International Laws Governing Armed Conflict* (New York, 1994), pp. 232–3.

eliminating "racial" enemies, even under the National Socialist system, as evidenced by the agreement giving Himmler's police units operational freedom to pursue their ideological tasks. Despite possessing the ability to remain outside the persecution and extermination mania, Eighteenth Army ordered the registration of all Jews and then forced them to wear distinguishing armbands.[29] This assisted SS personnel in Pavlovsk who carried out examinations of civilians and prisoners of war based on "racial characteristics – hair color, nose shape, accent and circumcision, etc., etc."[30] These degrading medical exams, however, served as only a precursor to a much worse fate.

According to a postwar Soviet report, "German soldiers burst into civilians' quarters, rounded up entire Jewish families, arrested them and then later shot them, sparing neither children nor the elderly."[31] A group of twenty-five Jews were driven into the park behind Pavlovsk Palace where they were shot and buried in mass graves. This was soon followed by a second group of sixteen Jews which included a twenty-five-year-old woman and her two-year-old son. A Russian witness testified that the "German barbarians wounded the child in front of the mother, then shot her and threw her body into the grave along with that of her still breathing son." The town's Jewish population was "destroyed to a man."[32] While no known documentation exists on the German side as to who perpetrated this massacre, it is clear that it occurred soon after the 121st ID began its occupation of Pavlovsk when the division exercised complete control over the city. Though it is unlikely that the East Prussians directly participated in the killings, the 121st ID certainly allowed the incident to take place in its area of responsibility.[33] This local incident of murder fits into a much larger mosaic of Wehrmacht

---

[29] Ereignismeldung Nr. 94, 25. Sept. 1941, NARA T 175, Roll 233. The decision to implement such a policy closely followed general Wehrmacht practice; generally, see Pohl, *Die Herrschaft der Wehrmacht*, p. 249. On the identification of Jews in Belarus, see Gerlach, *Kalkulierte Morde*, pp. 514–15; in Latvia, see Vestermanis, "Local Headquarters Liepaja," p. 228; in Ukraine, Lower, *Nazi Empire-Building*, p. 48.

[30] Pokazaniia bezhavshego iz nemetskogo plena bivshego voemmosluzhashchego Bobtseva Georgia Iakovlevicha (hereafter Pokazaniia bezhavshego iz nemetskogo plena), p. 5. I am indebted to Dr. Alexander Hill for providing me with a copy of this document.

[31] Chrezvychainaia Gosudarstvennaia Komissiia, USHMM RG 22–002M, Reel 18, Pavlovsk, pp. 2–3. The remainder of this discussion is based on this document.

[32] Pokazaniia bezhavshego iz nemetskogo plena, p. 5.

[33] Even though the report states that "German soldiers" carried out the roundup and shootings, this does not necessarily indicate the participation of members of the 121st ID. Soviet citizens frequently failed to distinguish between the different German organizations they came into contact with during the organization. For more on this topic, see Wolfram Wette, "Sowjetische Erinnerungen an den deutschen Vernichtungskrieg," in Kohl, *Der Krieg der deutschen Wehrmacht*, pp. 315–37, here p. 327.

complicity in the Holocaust, one in which the army, as the "most powerful organization by far in the occupied eastern territories ... accepted that [its] occupation area was the site of one of the largest genocides in the history of mankind."[34]

Inextricably linked to both the civilian roundups carried out immediately after the seizure of Pavlovsk and the murder of the town's Jews were the division's broader anti-partisan policies. During the last days of September, Sixteenth Army's quartermaster ordered the evacuation of all male civilians between the ages of fifteen and fifty from the battle zone, in an attempt to remove potential partisans from the area.[35] This followed several incidents of partisan activity in Pavlovsk. After an attack on a German soldier in the city, members of Sonderkommando 1B, a subunit of Einsatzgruppe A, shot nine Russian civilians on 24 September, six of whom were caught with explosives following curfew.[36] The 121st ID also actively participated in the campaign against saboteurs and espionage, arresting three civilians found in possession of a radio transmitter as well as two females described as "agents" on 2 October. The three civilians were handed over to the Secret Field Police attached to Eighteenth Army.[37]

Divisional troops executed five partisans found in possession of papers belonging to German soldiers on 5 October before carrying out its first murderous collective measure of the war the following day when it shot ten civilians after the repeated cutting of telephone wires. Prior to this incident, the division had warned the civilian population that drastic measures would be taken if sabotage continued.[38] Another ten civilians were shot four days later; the available source material does not allow for a precise identification of the perpetrators.[39] In any case, in just over two weeks, the 121st ID and the SS police units in Pavlovsk had executed thirty-four civilians for resistance activities.

---

[34] Hartmann, *Wehrmacht im Ostkrieg*, p. 653.
[35] XXVIII AK, Tätigkeitsbericht Teil III, 28–29.9.41, BA-MA RH 24–28/109. It appears that this order was not completely carried out, based on later discussions concerning further evacuations.
[36] Sicherheitspolizei und SD Sonderkommando 1B an XXVIII AK, 24.9.41, BA-MA RH 24–28/100.
[37] Ic Meldung, 2.10.41, BA-MA RH 26–121/57. On the Secret Field Police, which brutally enforced Wehrmacht security directives, see Klaus Geßner, *Geheime Feldpolizei: Zur Funktion und Organisation der faschistischen Wehrmacht* (Berlin, 1986); and, more recently, Pohl, *Die Herrschaft der Wehrmacht*, pp. 104–5.
[38] Ic Meldung, 7.10.41, BA-MA RH 26–121/57.
[39] Tätigkeitsbericht Teil III, 6–8.10.41, BA-MA RH 24–28/109. This incident is also mentioned in Chrezvychainaia Gosudarstvennaia Komissiia, USHMM RG 22–002M, Reel 18, Pavlovsk, p. 3.

Pavlovsk under German rule 161

These episodes highlight the institutional co-operation between the 121st ID and the SS in "the surveillance of the civilian population, the surveillance of partisan activity and the obtaining of intelligence about the situation in Leningrad."[40] Following the executions, SD headquarters in Pavlovsk publicized the actions and warned the population that in the future, such acts of sabotage would be punished by the shooting of twenty civilians.[41] Einsatzgruppe A described its relationship with the 121st ID as "so close, that discussions of locally important questions regularly took place in the headquarters of Einsatzgruppe A with the town commandants and other participating Wehrmacht authorities (for example in Pavlovsk)."[42] In the case of Pavlovsk, the 121st ID and SD murder squads worked hand in hand to secure German authority.

Further anti-partisan and other security activities continued through the fall and winter of 1941. In one instance, a Russian set the house lodging an NCO and his men afire. While the sergeant understood the man's reasoning for committing such an act, he nonetheless found the man's execution deserved:

he believed he was serving his country by making life difficult for us ... for the security of the troops, the struggle against the partisans allowed no mercy. Through appropriate measures against these people, it needed to be made clear that partisans were not soldiers and were to be treated in principle as guerillas. So it happened in this case.[43]

Such incidents led the East Prussians to follow more uniformly the regime's prescriptions for combating any and all irregular resistance. In late October, troops forced ten civilians, who were attempting to cross the lines in the direction of Leningrad, to turn back; it appears that the High Command's constant haranguing of the troops finally had begun to show effect.[44] Patrols in the no-man's-land between German and Soviet

[40] XXVIII AK, Tätigkeitsbericht Teil III, 10–11.9.41, BA-MA RH 24–28/109.
[41] Ereignismeldung Nr. 116, 17. Okt. 1941, T-175, Roll 234, NARA. See also Operational Situation Report USSR No 116, in Yitzhak Arad, Shmuel Krakowski, and Schmuel Spector (eds.), *The Einsatzgruppen Reports: Selections from the Dispatches of the Nazi Death Squads' Campaign against the Jews in Occupied Territories of the Soviet Union, July 1941– January 1943* (New York, 1989), pp. 191–3.
[42] Ereignismeldung Nr. 150, 2. Januar 1942, T-175, Roll 234, NARA.
[43] Heesch, *Meine 13. Infanterie-Geschütz-Kompanie Grenadier-Regiment 408*, p. 99. Division orders seem to support Heesch's statement; on 17 April 1942, the men were ordered not to "trust any civilians working for the army"; 121 Infanterie Division, Geheimhaltung, 17.4.42, BA-MA RH 26–121/20.
[44] 121 ID KTB, 31.10.41, BA-MA RH 26–121/16. The war diary states that they were "turned back by weapons." Though this formulation is rather vague, it appears likely that the Germans did not shoot anyone as no mention is made of any casualties or deaths.

162 "It is only a question of where, not if, civilians will starve"

lines also netted numerous civilians, with the division delivering those considered the most dangerous to the SD while the remainder were sent to the labor camp outside the city.[45]

While the 121st ID continued to actively hunt partisans into 1942, it reported that aside from one blown bridge and several cut wires, "partisan activity in the division's area can still be characterized as minimal."[46] The Economic Staff East agreed with this assessment, stating that most partisan actions during the first months of the new year did not take the form of "offensive activity against the Wehrmacht in the form of attacks and sabotage acts" but were directed rather as a general "terror against the civilian population" which pushed it into a "unproductive apathy and passivity."[47] Traces of partisan activity continued, however, throughout the division's occupation of Pavlovsk, as even during March 1942 telephone wires were found cut and sentries reported coming under sniper fire.[48] This caused the division to increase the number of patrols in the area as well as to enact a more stringent policy of identifying civilians and led to one civilian being shot as he attempted to cross the front line in the direction of Leningrad.[49] In addition to repressing any resistance within their operational area, the East Prussians enlisted the assistance of civilians by rewarding them for information with both money and, more importantly, foodstuffs.[50]

The 121st ID's response to partisan activity underwent a marked evolution during the first month or so of occupation in Pavlovsk.[51] During its advance on the town, the East Prussians reacted to irregular resistance in a very restrained manner, especially in comparison with other German divisions across the front; mass arrests constituted its most severe response. Once in Pavlovsk, however, the division either carried

In a discussion at the Eighteenth Army quartermaster's headquarters, however, the participants decided that "under all circumstances the civilian population trying to come to us from Leningrad and Oranienbaum are to be stopped through use of machine guns and artillery"; AOK 18, O. Qu., 21.11.41, Punkte für Chef-Besprechung, NARA T-312, Roll 766.

[45] XXVIII AK, Tätigkeitsbericht Teil III, 21–22.10.41, BA-MA RH 24–28/109.
[46] 121 ID Abt. Ic, 16.2.42, BA-MA RH 26–121/18.
[47] Wi. Kdo. Krasnogwardeisk, Gru. Fü., Monatsbericht März 1942, BA-MA RW 31/948.
[48] 121 ID KTB, 10.3.42, BA-MA RH 26–121/16.
[49] 121 Infanterie-Division, Abt. Ia, Betr.: Partisanentätigkeit, 10.3.1942; III Abteilung Artillerie-Regiment 121, Abt. Ia, Partisanentätigkeit, 6.3.42; both in BA-MA RH 26–121/19; 121 Infanterie-Division, Abt. Ic, 6.3.42, BA-MA RH 26–121/60.
[50] 121 Infanterie-Division, Abt. Ic, Feindlagen-Bericht Nr. 1, 16.2.42, BA-MA 26–121/18.
[51] An examination of the 121st ID's anti-partisan policies within the larger context of Wehrmacht practice during the summer and fall of 1941 is found in Jeff Rutherford, "'One Senses Danger from All Sides, Especially from Fanatical Civilians': The 121st Infantry Division and Partisan War, June 1941–April 1942," in Ben Shepherd and Juliette Pattinson (eds.), *War in the Twilight World* (Basingstoke, 2010), pp. 58–79.

out collective measures itself or supported those initiated by SS-Police units, with some thirty-four people executed within the three weeks of the occupation. What explains this shift in policy? First, as previously discussed, general Wehrmacht anti-partisan policy radicalized during September 1941; this occurred nearly simultaneously with the 121st ID's occupation of Pavlovsk. As the tenor of the army's directives became increasingly violent, this necessarily affected the division's behavior. Second, the East Prussians now found themselves working on a day-to-day basis with members of the *Einsatzgruppen* units; the attitudes and behaviors of these *Weltanschauung* warriors were bound to have an effect on how the men of the 121st viewed the civilian population around them. Finally, many Germans saw Leningrad as the birthplace of Bolshevism – a view that Hitler himself endorsed.[52] Due to Pavlovsk's proximity to Leningrad, its inhabitants were consequently seen as especially suspect in the eyes of the Germans.

Following this initial spasm of violence, however, the division settled into much more of a division-of-labor approach to securing the city. In October, East Prussian patrols turned up forty-two potential partisans; the 121st ID, however, did not pull the trigger. Though it is extremely likely that the overwhelming majority of these civilians and Red Army men perished – being sent to the SD, back into Leningrad, or to a labor camp in late 1941 were all probable death sentences – it is significant that the division's anti-partisan policies did not immediately lead to large-scale shootings. Here, its participation in fighting the partisan threat had not degenerated into a brutal dirty war; rather, it worked with other organizations, such as the SD or the Secret Field Police, who carried out the bulk of the anti-insurgency actions. The prewar agreement concerning the *Einsatzgruppen* between the SS and the army created a situation in which the 121st ID was able to pass on the actual executions to other units. This, of course, does not absolve the division of responsibility for the deaths of these civilians; the 121st ID was certainly complicit in their fate. Nevertheless, the division's approach to partisan warfare had not yet deteriorated into capricious violence.

This return to a relatively moderate approach to the surrounding civilian population highlighted the other side of the occupation coin. If the use of sticks formed one aspect of German occupation policy, the use of carrots became an increasingly valuable tool in the German arsenal, though certainly the former was the dominant response to civilians in 1941. The army hoped to build on the perception that it had

---

[52] Ueberschär, "Der Angriff auf Leningrad und die Blockade der Stadt," p. 94.

liberated the Soviet population from the Bolshevik yoke and that prosperity would soon return. In order to maintain this perceived goodwill, XXVIII Corps explicitly ordered its subordinate formations to assist homeless evacuees, to provide medical care to the native inhabitants, and to stop all types of forced requisitioning without any sort of compensation.[53]

These tangible policies were complemented by the renaming of the city. The original name of the settlement, constructed in the late eighteenth and early nineteenth centuries, was Pavlovsk. After the Bolshevik seizure of power, the town was renamed Slutsk in honor of a communist martyr to the cause. Delegates from the city approached the Germans after their conquest and requested that the city's name be returned to its Tsarist name.[54] Both division and corps command approved this request and the division commander instructed that the name change be part of a larger festivity during an upcoming church holiday. This celebration proved to be a "psychological success of great value." Taking place during the first religious service in more than a decade, the overflowing church celebrated the "true Christian Adolf Hitler" who had "freed the city from Satan and his helpers." According to a German officer sent to witness the event, the assembled citizens thanked him profusely for ending the Bolsheviks' atheist policies.[55] In combination, these steps generated some goodwill amongst the anti-Bolshevik section of the population, though how widespread it was is impossible to determine.

Complementing these tangible initiatives, the Wehrmacht as a whole orchestrated a much more intensive propaganda campaign designed to sway the Soviet people behind the occupiers.[56] In Pavlovsk, the division established a local newspaper, employing native Russians as the writers and editor, with the 121st ID maintaining final say over its content.[57] Entitled *Pravda* (Truth), the paper advocated "unifying the country in

---

[53] Gen. Kdo. XXVIII AK, Erfahrungsbericht über den Umgang mit der Zivilbevölkerung, 15.11.41, BA-MA RH 24-28/110.
[54] XXVIII AK, Tätigkeitsbericht Teil III, 13.10.41, BA-MA RH 24-28/109.
[55] Ortskommandantur Pavlovsk (Slutzk), 14.10.1941, BA-MA RH 26-121/70. For more on German policies towards religion in the occupied eastern territories, see Pohl, *Die Herrschaft der Wehrmacht*, pp. 139–41; on Ukraine, see Berkhoff, *Harvest of Despair*, pp. 232–52.
[56] Babette Quinkert, *Propaganda und Terror in Weißrussland 1941–1944: Die deutsche "geistige" Kriegführung gegen Zivilbevölkerung und Partisanen* (Paderborn, 2009), pp. 167–73, 183–9.
[57] XXVIII AK, Tätigkeitsbericht Teil III, 18–20.10.41, BA-MA RH 24-28/109. This initiative was approved with some trepidation by the OKW as it charged the division with "complete responsibility" for the newspaper's content; see the entry for 21-2 October 1941.

Pavlovsk under German rule 165

the fight against Bolshevism."[58] Following the line set forth by Berlin, *Pravda* emphasized the German liberation of Soviet civilians from "the blood terror of Bolshevism" and the need for civilians to be vigilant in the fight against "foreign elements" sent by Moscow to "destroy their property."[59] Economic activity returned to the city as the Wehrmacht attempted to reopen public facilities, though the earlier forced evacuations of able-bodied males caused a labor shortage.[60] The Economic Staff East also controlled various enterprises and their employees within the town, leading to frequent contact between the two organizations, with the division reporting that relations between it and the economic authorities were "close and profitable."[61]

For example, during one meeting with the commander of the local Economic Staff East branch at division headquarters, the 121st ID placed an order for twenty felt blankets needed for wounded soldiers. The economic officer agreed but stipulated that such work could only be completed if the soldiers provided sustenance for the workers. The division promised to deliver dead horses to the workshop and the matter was settled.[62] This example typified the relationship between the division and the Economic Staff East as the latter "continually provided labor" for the former.[63] In addition to establishing a factory in Pavlovsk to produce badly needed Russian felt boots for the troops, the division also opened a workshop to turn out sweaters.[64] The 121st ID also resurrected a mechanical repair shop in Pushkin which built three motors and performed numerous smaller repairs for the troops.[65] Pushkin additionally housed a knitting factory that produced upwards of forty sweaters and 450 pieces of warm winter headgear for the troops.[66] By late February 1942, over 1,300 civilians

---

[58] Pokazaniia bezhavshego iz nemetskogo plena, p. 4.
[59] Quoted in Quinkert, *Propaganda und Terror*, p. 169.
[60] XXVIII AK, Tätigkeitsbericht Teil III, 21–22.10.41, BA-MA RH 24–28/109.
[61] Wi. Kdo. Krasnogwardeisk, Gru. Fü., 23.2.42, Monatsbericht Januar 1942, 7.1.42, 14.1.42, BA-MA RW 31/948; Erfahrungsbericht Heeresversorgung, 7.12.1941, BA-MA RH 26–121/65.
[62] Wi. Kdo. Krasnogwardeisk, Gru. Fü., 23.2.42, Monatsbericht Januar 1942, 26.1.42, BA-MA RW 31/948.
[63] Wi. Kdo. Görlitz, Gef. St. Krasnogwardeisk, Lagebericht (Monat Dezember 1941), BA-MA RW 31/948.
[64] Pokazaniia bezhavshego iz nemetskogo plena, p. 5; Divisionsarzt 121 Division, Tätigkeitsbericht über den Einsatz der Sanitätsdienste bei der 121. Inf.-Division im Ostfeldzug vom 1. Oktober 1941–30. April 1942, 10.6.42, BA-MA RH 26–121/65; and Generalkommando L AK, Tätigkeitsbericht der Abt. IVa, Gen. Kdo. L AK für die Zeit vom 13.8.41–7.5.42, BA-MA RH 24–50/173.
[65] Wi. Kdo. Görlitz, Gef. St. Krasnogwardeisk, Lagebericht (Monat Dezember 1941), BA-MA RW 31/948.
[66] Lagebericht vom 10.1.42, BA-MA RW 31–498.

worked for the occupiers.[67] Many of these people were organized in labor companies designed to keep the streets clear of snow and for other construction purposes.[68] As these few examples demonstrate, the 121st ID and other organizations viewed the labor of Pavlovsk's inhabitants as necessary for German combat efficiency; this would become an increasingly important issue for the Wehrmacht as the war continued.

The occupation of towns and cities necessarily led to soldiers and civilians interacting on a daily basis. For the Wehrmacht, this situation was fraught with danger. As the historian Regina Mühlhäuser has pointed out, "from the outset of the German invasion of the Soviet Union, various Nazi authorities were deeply concerned with the control and regulation of rape, sexual enslavement, military and civil prostitution, sexual affairs and romantic relationships" as these threatened the power and standing of the German Army in the region.[69] In an attempt to ensure the security of the troops, many commanders issued orders similar to that of Eighteenth Army which demanded the "sharpest separation between the troops and the civilian population" in early November.[70] The 121st ID, however, did not follow suit until the following February, when it called for a "strict separation" from civilians.[71] This "strict separation," however, does not appear to have led to the creation of areas within Pavlovsk devoted exclusively to either Germans or Russians.[72] Instead, Russians lived in specific houses, prominently marked with an "R," which German soldiers were forbidden to enter.[73] Two further pieces of evidence indicate that a ghettoization of the remaining population did not occur. First, following a typhus

---

[67] Ortskommandantur I (V) 309 Abt. Ia, Pawlowsk 23.2.1942, Vorschläge der Ortskommandantur zur Bekämpfung von Flecktyphus, BA-MA RH 26–121/18.

[68] Strassenstützpunkt 8, Betr.: Einsatz der Arbeitskompanien an 121 ID, 16.3.1942, BA-MA RH 26–121/19; 121 Infanterie Division, Ausbau gefährdeter Strassenteile, 30.4.1942, BA-MA RH 26–121/20.

[69] Regina Mühlhäuser, "Between 'Racial Awareness' and Fantasies of Potency: Nazi Sexual Politics in the Occupied Territories of the Soviet Union, 1942–1945," in Dagmar Herzog (ed.), *Brutality and Desire: War and Sexuality in Europe's Twentieth Century* (Basingstoke, 2009), pp. 197–220, here p. 197.

[70] Cited in Kilian, *Wehrmacht und Besatzungsherrschaft*, p. 198.

[71] 121 Inf.-Division Abt. Ia, Ausbau der Ortsunterkünfte als Stützpunkte, 5.2.1942, BA-MA RH 26–121/18.

[72] Pohl, *Die Herrschaft der Wehrmacht*, p. 131, writes that "especially from fall 1941 on, commanders allowed for entire city districts to be emptied in order to prevent the mixing of soldiers and civilians, as this was held to be a great risk." Eleventh Army utilized such an approach in creating areas where only Germans lived in Simferopol and other cities in the Crimea; see Oldenburg, *Ideologie und Militärisches Kalkül*, p. 111.

[73] Divisionsarzt 121 Division, Tätigkeitsbericht über den Einsatz der Sanitätsdienste bei der 121. Inf.-Division im Ostfeldzug vom 1. Oktober 1941–30. April 1942, 10.6.42, BA-MA RH 26–121/65.

outbreak in late February 1942, the *Ortskommandant* argued against any attempt to quarantine the remaining civilians from the troops because not only would this result in their ultimate starvation, but it would also severely curtail any economic activity in the town.[74] Second, sixty-seven members of the 121st ID were infected by venereal disease during the occupation of Pavlovsk. Obviously, the separation of troops and the women who remained in the city was less than complete, a fact derisively noted by division command: "there doubtlessly exist forbidden relationships" between the troops and "the female section" of the civilian population.[75] Calls for such a separation were contradicted by the very use of Soviet women in Wehrmacht facilities; one former soldier in Army Group North who participated in the siege of Leningrad wrote of a girl who worked in a kitchen becoming "romantically involved with one of the German kitchen staff."[76] Finally, the division created contingency plans for a possible Red Army attack on the position; in the case of such an eventuality, German troops would "ruthlessly drive the entire population together into the smallest area, with the male population under especially strict watch. Weapons at the ready."[77] Such planning would have been unnecessary if all Soviet civilians had been already concentrated in ghettos.

The primary goals of the 121st ID during its occupation of Pavlovsk boiled down to security and productivity. In order to achieve the former, the division, in concert with the *Einsatzgruppen* troops stationed in the town, enacted repressive measures designed to strangle any nascent opposition movements in the cradle; these included several collective measures against civilians as well as the murder of the town's Jews, a group long identified with stoking resistance to German rule. For the latter, the Germans presented themselves as the harbingers of a prosperous future following the population's liberation from the yoke of Bolshevism and hoped that this would motivate the inhabitants to work

---

[74] Ortskommandantur I (V) 309 Abt. Ia, Pawlowsk, 23.2.1942, Vorschläge der Ortskommandantur zur Bekämpfung von Flecktyphus, BA-MA RH 26–121/18.
[75] Divisionsarzt 121 Division, Tätigkeitsbericht über den Einsatz der Sanitätsdienste bei der 121. Inf.-Division im Ostfeldzug vom 1. Oktober 1941–30. April 1942, 10.6.42, BA-MA RH 26–121/65. The division's doctor estimated that 2,500 people remained in the city, "the majority of whom are female." Women who tested positive for venereal disease were placed into special labor battalions; on the division's appraisal of the situation, see 121 Infanterie Division, Geheimhaltung, 17.4.42, BA-MA RH 26–121/20. For a further discussion of venereal disease and the Wehrmacht's response to it, see Neitzel and Welzer, *Soldaten*, pp. 220–1.
[76] William Lubbeck, *At Leningrad's Gates: The Story of a Soldier with Army Group North* (Philadelphia, 2006), p. 113.
[77] Besprechung des Div. Kdr. mit den Ortskommandanten am 5.2.1942, BA-MA RH 26–121/16.

for the Wehrmacht. Both the 121st ID and the Economic Staff East desperately needed such labor for their own purposes; already by fall 1941, the Germans felt the sting of an increasing manpower shortage. While the security and labor programs appeared to be at least somewhat fruitful from the Wehrmacht's perspective, a third German policy proved extremely counterproductive to these programs, eventually causing the failure of both. German food policy in northwest Russia not only worked at cross-purposes with these other plans, but its impact on the general civilian population of the area (including Pavlovsk) was far more devastating than either anti-partisan or anti-Jewish measures.

II. Soviet cities in the war of annihilation

In mid-1941, Nazi propaganda minister Joseph Goebbels complained of a "very bad" food situation in Berlin, while recognizing that "the position in the occupied territories is much worse. In some areas, there is real starvation."[78] The starvation noted by Goebbels occurred in Athens; another occurrence of this catastrophe broke out in the Netherlands in 1944.[79] While Athens, Salonica, Amsterdam, and The Hague all suffered from real food shortages at various points during the conflict, these horrifying incidents should not obscure the fact that "the struggle for survival" dominated the lives of the overwhelming majority of Europeans living under the Nazi boot.[80] Cities throughout the occupied territories of western and southeastern Europe, from Montpellier in Vichy France to Belgrade in Serbia, all felt the pangs of constant hunger.[81] The further east one traveled

---

[78] Joseph Goebbels, *The Goebbels Diaries, 1939–1941* (trans. and ed. Fred Taylor) (New York, 1983), 28 June 1941, p. 434. For overviews of the food situation in occupied Europe, see Collingham, *The Taste of War*, pp. 155–218; Voglis, "Surviving Hunger: Life in the Cities and Countryside during the Occupation"; and Mazower, *Hitler's Empire*, pp. 274–90. The effects of the Royal Navy's blockade of the continent should be mentioned regarding this topic; see Tooze, *The Wages of Destruction*, p. 397.

[79] On Athens, see Mazower, *Inside Hitler's Greece*, pp. 23–64. On the Netherlands, see Gerhard Hirschfeld, *Nazi Rule and Dutch Collaboration: The Netherlands under German Occupation* (New York, 1992); and Bob Moore, "The Netherlands," in Jeremy Noakes (ed.) *The Civilian in War: The Home Front in Europe, Japan and the USA in World War II* (Exeter, 1992), pp. 126–49.

[80] Julian Jackson, *France: The Dark Years, 1940–1944* (Oxford, 2001), p. 249.

[81] On Belgrade, see Stevan K. Pavlowitch, *Hitler's New Disorder: The Second World War in Yugoslavia* (New York, 2008), pp. 97, 100–1; on Montpellier, see Jackson, *France: The Dark Years*, p. 250. For more on hunger in France, see Richard Vinen, *The Unfree French: Life under the Occupation* (New Haven, 2006), pp. 215–46; and Robert Gildea, *Marianne in Chains: Daily Life in the Heart of France during the German Occupation* (New York, 2003), pp. 90–115.

through the German empire, however, the more one encountered increasingly desperate conditions as Nazi racism generated more violent and callous policies. Poland, whose Slavic population was deemed superfluous by Hitler and the Nazi leadership, suffered terribly under German occupation. Conditions in cities in the General Government bordered on starvation already in 1940 as civilians in Warsaw and Krakow received an average of only 660 calories per day; this situation was only exacerbated in 1942 when Germany demanded an eightfold increase in the amount of Polish grain sent to the Reich.[82] During the entirety of the war, Polish citizens received the lowest average caloric intake of any country under Nazi rule west of the Soviet Union.[83]

Certainly the Nazi *Weltanschauung* and its emphasis on caring for the "racially superior" German population played a major role in the hunger that swept across Europe; the Reich leadership was determined to feed its population at the expense of everyone else on the continent. Other factors, however, helped cause this situation. In the case of Greece, the transportation and distribution system broke down under the strains of war while the Dutch famine was an indirect result of German military strategy. In no case, with the partial exception of Poland, did the Germans actively implement a policy of starving the occupied populations. Such calculations dramatically shifted, however, when Hitler and his leadership considered the Soviet Union.

The German political and military leadership almost uniformly viewed Soviet cities as areas that the Germans neither wanted to nor could adequately supply and therefore their inhabitants should be forced to fend for themselves.[84] Such attitudes led to a situation in which even cities in the "surplus" zones suffered terribly from hunger and starvation during 1941.[85] The two largest cities in Ukraine – Kiev and Kharkov – both felt the sting of German food policies. German leaders frequently stated that "Kiev must starve" in order for Ukraine's agricultural bounty to be at the disposal of the Wehrmacht.[86] At the beginning of October 1941, Ukrainian auxiliaries established a corridor around Kiev, halting

---

[82] Martin Housden, *Hans Frank, Lebensraum and the Holocaust* (Basingstoke, 2003), pp. 93–4; Richard Lukas, *Forgotten Holocaust: The Poles under German Occupation, 1939–1944* (New York, 1997 [1986]), pp. 30–1. A brief overview of the food situation in Warsaw is provided by Stephan Lehnstaedt, *Okkupation im Osten: Besatzeralltag in Warschau und Minsk, 1939–1944* (Munich, 2010), pp. 258–61.
[83] Voglis, "Surviving Hunger: Life in Cities and the Countryside during the Occupation," p. 25.
[84] Kay, *Exploitation, Resettlement, Mass Murder*, p. 186.
[85] Müller, "Das Scheitern der wirtschaftlichen 'Blitzkriegstrategie'," p. 1189.
[86] Berkhoff, *Harvest of Despair*, p. 165.

the delivery of food into the city.[87] By December 1941, Kiev's nonworking citizens received a mere 200 grams of bread per week and though such rations were eventually increased, it was too late in the day for many of the city's inhabitants, leading its population to decrease from 850,000 in June 1941 to 295,600 two years later. While starvation was certainly not the exclusive cause of this drastic population decline, it surely played a decisive role.[88]

Kharkov, home to some 430,000 inhabitants at the beginning of the German occupation, was ruthlessly plundered, first by the German Sixth Army and then by the German military occupation administration.[89] As Sixth Army moved through the city, its commander, Field Marshal Walther von Reichenau, ordered his troops to "increasingly live off the land" as this conflict "was not only a war of weapons but also an economic war."[90] The occupation of the city during the fall and winter of 1941 led to a much more systematic exploitation involving both military units and sections of Wirtschaftsstab Ost in their quest to secure the Wehrmacht's food for the coming winter. During this period, German authorities decided that "those people not working in the interest of the Wehrmacht ... will starve" and, by December 1941, the first reported cases of starvation emerged from the city.[91] The need to supply German forces and thus spare the Reich from making such sacrifices led to nearly 12,000 starvation deaths in Kharkov; here the de-urbanization policies of Nazi Germany proved more consequential than the city's position in the "bread basket" of Europe.

Further to the south, the German Eleventh and Seventeenth Armies enacted similar policies towards urban residents.[92] In the Crimea, where some 150,000 to 200,000 people lived in cities, Erich von Manstein's Eleventh Army found itself at the end of a tenuous supply line. In an

---

[87] Ibid., p. 169. Müller, "Das Scheitern der wirtschaftlichen 'Blitzkriegstrategie'", p. 1189, notes that the population was "practically left to itself" concerning the collection of foodstuffs.

[88] Berkhoff, *Harvest of Despair*, pp. 169, 186.

[89] On Kharkov, see Andrej Angrick, "Das Beispiel Charkow: Massenmord unter deutscher Besatzung," in Hartmann, Hürter, and Jureit, *Verbrechen der Wehrmacht*, pp. 117–24; and Norbert Kunz, "Das Beispiel Charkow: Eine Stadtbevölkerung als Opfer der deutschen Hungerstrategie 1941/1942," in ibid., pp. 136–44. See also *Verbrechen der Wehrmacht: Dimensionen des Vernichtungskrieg*, pp. 328–46.

[90] Armee-Befehl des Oberbefehlshabers der 6. Armee, 28.9.41, reproduced in *Verbrechen der Wehrmacht: Dimensionen des Vernichtungskrieg*, p. 330.

[91] Quoted in Kunz, "Das Beispiel Charkow," p. 140. On the beginning of the starvation in December, see Müller, "Das Scheitern der wirtschaftlichen 'Blitzkriegstrategie'," p. 1191.

[92] The following section is based on Oldenburg, *Ideologie und militärisches Kalkül*, pp. 75–96, unless otherwise noted.

attempt to keep his men fed, Manstein ordered the army to "increasingly feed itself from the land" and, as a result of this, "especially in enemy cities, a large section of the population must starve."[93] While Eleventh Army provided some assistance for civilians, this amounted to less than the "existence minimum, especially [for] those who performed no 'useful' work [for the Germans]." By mid-December, starvation threatened some 100,000 civilians.[94]

Seventeenth Army, operating in the Donets basin, recognized that "starvation will break out in the foreseeable future," but nonetheless decided against providing the civilians with food from its stocks as "pity" was simply out of place in such a war.[95] This led one economic officer to suggest putting those civilians who did not work for the Wehrmacht into ghettos where they would simply starve![96] One cause of Seventeenth Army's decision not to assist civilians was the belief that urban workers were "politically infected" due to their relationship with the Bolshevik regime; here, the fate of Soviet cities was determined both by the German desire to live off captured Soviet stocks and the suspicion with which members of the German command viewed the urban population.[97]

Perhaps the region most affected by the Germans' rapacious economic policies was Belarus. Minsk, the largest city in the area, was already threatened by the specter of starvation a mere twenty days after the invasion.[98] By the beginning of August, police units reported that "it is not going too far to speak of a starvation emergency in the cities of this region that even exceeds that in Minsk."[99] Since the nourishment of the city was, according to one German, dependent on "the mercy of German troops," it was clear that Minsk and the surrounding area would suffer greatly in 1941–2.[100] As a result of such food shortages, diseases, such as typhus, dysentery, tuberculosis, and diphtheria, ravaged the region. By spring 1942, five of the largest cities in Belarus were reduced to receiving only rationed bread from the authorities.[101]

---

[93] Armeebefehl des Oberbefehlshabers der 11. Armee, Generaloberst von Manstein, vom 20.11.1941, printed in Ueberschär and Wette, *Der deutsche Überfall auf die Sowjetunion*, pp. 289–90, here p. 290.
[94] Oldenburg, *Ideologie und militärisches Kalkül*, p. 78.
[95] AOK 17, Ia B.Nr. 973/41 geh., 17.11.1941; AOK 17, O.Qu, KTB, 2.11.41, both quoted in ibid., p. 232.
[96] Quoted in ibid., pp. 232–3.   [97] Ibid., p. 234.
[98] An economic officer attached to the Fourth Panzer Army reported on 10 July 1941 that "the urban population suffers – now that Minsk is nearly completely destroyed – from hunger ... Hunger and thirst drive the people to desperate attempts to help themselves," quoted in Gerlach, *Kalkulierte Morde*, p. 266.
[99] Ibid.   [100] Lehnstaedt, *Okkupation im Osten*, p. 259.   [101] Ibid., pp. 290, 302.

As this brief discussion has indicated, while hunger and starvation threatened urban areas all across the continent during the war, it found its harshest expression in the occupied Soviet territories. Such a situation directly resulted from German prewar planning for the Soviet Union in which its urban populations needed to be sacrificed for the Reich's larger war effort. The Soviet city that suffered the largest numbers of deaths due to Germany's starvation policies was Leningrad. The intended fate of Leningrad reverberated throughout northwest Russia and Pavlovsk became ensnared in the desperate hunger that blanketed the region.

III. "This war will witness the greatest starvation since the Thirty Years War": German *Hungerpolitik* in northwest Russia

According to Johannes Hürter, "the decision over Leningrad's future fate was the kick-off for a ruthless occupation policy in [Eighteenth] Army's area."[102] The German siege of Leningrad was one of the most horrific events of the Second World War as some 1 to 1.5 million Soviet civilians died due to artillery fire and aerial bombardment, disease, and starvation.[103] The large-scale starvation of the city, while certainly envisaged by technocrats within the Reich leadership, did not figure into the initial military planning for the campaign as the Barbarossa Directive charged Army Group North with seizing the city.[104] By mid-July, however, Halder had decided that Leeb's Army Group was merely to "seal it off."[105] What led to this radical transformation of German goals in the region?

Several interrelated motivations seem to have intersected. First, Hitler's view of the war as a merciless struggle between ideologies necessitated the destruction of Leningrad, the birthplace of Bolshevism. A week before Halder instructed Eighteenth Army of its new mission regarding the city, Hitler had declared that "he wanted Moscow and Leningrad razed to the ground."[106] Second, the population politics that so strikingly characterized Nazi occupation policies east of the Oder reached their fullest fruition with regard to Leningrad. While the implementation of starvation plans

---

[102] Hürter, "Die Wehrmacht vor Leningrad," p. 438.
[103] See the careful discussions of Salisbury, *The 900 Days*, pp. 513–17; and Ganzenmüller, *Das belagerte Leningrad*, pp. 237–9, which both place the number somewhere between 1 and 1.5 million deaths.
[104] Weisung Nr. 21: Fall Barbarossa, in Hubatsch, *Hitlers Weisungen*, pp. 96–101, here pp. 98–9.
[105] Halder, *Kriegstagebuch*, vol. III, 15 July 1941, p. 80.
[106] Schramm, *KTB OKW*, vol. II, Sonderakte, 8. Juli 1941, p. 1021.

seemed shockingly simple to the technocrats in Berlin, the wholesale starvation of millions of people in the occupied areas proved not only difficult to carry out but counterproductive to German military goals in the Soviet Union.[107] Leningrad, however, seemed to offer the perfect marriage of ideological and ruthlessly pragmatic thinking. Hitler stated that both Leningrad and Moscow should be destroyed so that the Germans "did not have to feed them in the winter."[108] For an army whose transportation capabilities only worsened during late 1941, removing the burden of feeding some 3 million civilians certainly promised increased military efficiency for the besieging force: all the food that reached the front would feed German stomachs. The fact that these starving civilians would be outside German lines seemingly eliminated any of the problems related with disease, resistance, or labor that previously had proved detrimental to German rule. Finally, military considerations also influenced German strategy towards Leningrad. While Army Group North's commanders all believed that they possessed the necessary force to storm the city, the seizure of Leningrad rated as a secondary objective for the planners in Zossen.[109] For Halder and the OKH as a whole, Moscow remained the key to the campaign, and any forces that could be stripped from Leeb's forces to support the drive on Moscow would necessarily be sent south. The loss of Hoepner's Panzer Group 4 seriously diminished the striking power of Army Group North, making the siege strategy more palatable to a disappointed Leeb and Küchler; without the armor and motorized troops of Panzer Group 4, capturing the city seemed out of the question.[110] During September, these various ideas coalesced into a strategy that condemned Leningrad to widespread starvation.[111]

Though the decision to starve Leningrad into submission was only formally communicated to Army Group North towards the end of

---

[107] Gerlach, *Kalkulierte Morde*, pp. 266–7.
[108] Halder, *Kriegstagebuch*, vol. III, 8 July 1941, p. 53.
[109] Ganzenmüller, *Das belagerte Leningrad*, p. 15. In fact, Ganzenmüller argues (pp. 15–16) that "this fundamental operative decision was the genesis of a strategy that led to the genocide of Leningrad's civilian population." See also Hürter, *Hitlers Heerführer*, p. 501.
[110] Hürter, "Die Wehrmacht vor Leningrad," p. 394.
[111] Halder noted on 5 September that as regards Leningrad, "the goal was achieved ... Panzer (Corps Reinhardt) and Luftwaffe given up [to Army Group Center]"; Halder, *Kriegstagebuch*, vol. III, 5 September 1941, p. 215. Hitler's War Directive 35, issued on 6 September 1941, called for "all of the strength of the army and air force to be concentrated, including that which is expendable by the wings" of the operation, for the last push on Moscow; see Weisung Nr. 35, in Hubatsch, *Hitlers Weisungen*, pp. 174–7, here p. 174. On 20 September, Keitel informed Army Group North that "we will not enter the city and we cannot feed the city"; quoted in Hürter, *Hitlers Heerführer*, p. 499.

September, the German policy of living off the land had already wreaked havoc with northwest Russia's food situation.

As early as mid-August, SD units described conditions in northwest Russia as "economic anarchy," a situation that drastically worsened during the fall and winter of 1941.[112] A Soviet report dating from early October stated that "in the occupied districts, where there has been a German presence, all domestic poultry has been seized ... leaving very little livestock. The population eats in general only potatoes."[113] Six days after the 121st ID occupied Pavlovsk, Einsatzgruppe A described the situation:

> the entire Russia proper area that has been occupied by Army Group North presents a uniform picture of economic and cultural misery ...
>
> In several areas, for example near Luga and Lake Samra, nearly all cattle herds and horses have been carried off. German troops have requisitioned nearly the entire chicken population, so that the food situation is extraordinarily difficult for the civilian population.[114]

Nearly simultaneous with the 121st ID's capture of Pavlovsk, German authorities attempted to create uniform regulations concerning the feeding of Soviet civilians. This was first sparked by elements of the Economic Staff East which presciently observed that the simmering resistance in the rear areas was due to food shortages; thus, feeding the entire civilian population would ensure a much more manageable occupation.[115] Though this remained a pipe dream for a variety of pragmatic and ideological reasons, Wirtschaftsstab Ost did publish guidelines on 4 September which established rations for urban civilians.[116] These guidelines set the tone for the remainder of the occupation as only those working for the Germans would receive enough to survive; those whom the Germans viewed as nonessential received little to no aid from the occupiers.[117]

This division of civilians between those essential to German interests and those deemed "useless eaters" was further codified during a meeting on 16 September, between Göring, military officials attached to the general quartermaster's office, and Backe himself.[118] The *Reichsmarschall*

---

[112] Ereignismeldung Nr. 53, 15. August 1941, NARA T-175, Roll 233. For a discussion of this policy concentrating on the meat extracted from the region, see Kilian, *Wehrmacht und Besatzungsherrschaft*, pp. 378–88.
[113] Quoted in Hill, *The War behind the Eastern Front*, p. 54.
[114] Ereignismeldung Nr. 94, 25. September 1941, NARA T-175, Roll 233.
[115] Müller, "Das Scheitern der wirtschaftlichen 'Blitzkriegstrategie,'" p. 1184.
[116] Berkhoff, *Harvest of Despair*, p. 166; Gerlach, *Kalkulierte Morde*, pp. 269–70.
[117] Gerlach, *Kalkulierte Morde*, p. 270.
[118] On the meeting, see Streit, *Keine Kameraden*, p. 143. The following is based on Streit unless otherwise noted. Emphasis in original.

made the explicit connection between food stocks on the home front and the exploitation of the occupied territories. Beginning the meeting by adamantly declaring that "rations in the *Heimat* can under no circumstances be lowered in any way" for fear of damaging the German population's morale, he then explained that in order to raise rations, the occupied territories would have to pay. He concluded by detailing how the confiscated foodstuffs from the Soviet Union would be dispersed:

first come the *fighting* forces, then the remaining troops in *enemy countries* and then the *troops at home* ... Next the *German* nonmilitary population is supplied.

Only then comes the *population in the occupied territories*. Basically, in the occupied territories only those people who work for us should be assured of appropriate food supplies. Even if one *wished* to feed all the rest of the inhabitants, one *could not* do so in the newly occupied eastern territory.

This basic formula was reaffirmed by various authorities during late 1941 and the results of such thinking were clear to the Reich's political and military leadership. General Georg Thomas believed that foodstuffs should be distributed in the following manner: "1) needs of the troops, 2) transport to the *Heimat* [and] 3) needs of the population."[119] Such thinking animated the general quartermaster's office as well. In early October, XXXVIII Corps was already asking for instructions concerning the starving population in its area of operations. The response from Chief Quartermaster Wagner, via Eighteenth Army, was that "every supply train out of the *Heimat* cuts down on stocks in Germany. It is better if our people have something and the Russians starve."[120] As Göring himself stated, "the fate of the great cities, especially Leningrad, is of absolutely no importance ... This war will witness the greatest starvation since the Thirty Years War."[121]

The closer German troops came to Leningrad, the more desperate the situation appeared. In the city of Pushkin, L Corps notified Eighteenth Army in early October that "20,000 people, most of whom are factory workers, are without food. Starvation is expected." Eighteenth Army's quartermaster replied that "the provision of food by the troops for the civilian population is out of the question"; this attitude towards the

---

[119] Gerlach, *Kalkulierte Morde*, p. 274.
[120] Quoted in Hürter, "Die Wehrmacht vor Leningrad," p. 409. For more on Wagner and his responsibility in planning and carrying out the war in the east, see Christian Gerlach, "'Militärische Versorgungszwänge', Besatzungspolitik und Massenverbrechen: Die Rolle des Generalquartiermeisters des Heeres und seiner Dienststellen im Krieg gegen die Sowjetunion," in Norbert Frei et al. (eds.), *Ausbeutung, Vernichtung, Öffentlichkeit: Neue Studien zur nationalsozialistischen Lagerpolitik* (Munich, 2000), pp. 175–208.
[121] Aktennotiz, Besprechung beim Reichsmarschall am 8.11.1941 im Sitzungssaal des Reichsluftfahrtministeriums, printed in Ueberschär and Wette, *Der deutsche Überfall auf die Sowjetunion*, pp. 331–2, here p. 332.

civilian population mirrored that of other commands in Army Group North.[122] In a meeting between members of Sixteenth Army and XXVIII Corps on 29 October, the corps was told that "in no case is there a question of feeding the civilian population." Sixteenth Army then ordered the establishment of evacuated zones behind the front lines, with the civilians shipped to labor camps.[123] Eighteenth Army also began to view evacuation as a means to get around the problem of starving civilians in its midst: on 28 September, Küchler ordered the removal of all civilians from the forward area of operations in response to his corps commanders' fears of epidemics and the effects on the troops' discipline caused by watching starving women and children.[124] Less than two weeks later, 18,000 civilians had already been evacuated out of the forward combat area and a further 10,000 were scheduled to follow shortly thereafter.[125] More than 75,000 civilians were deported from the forward combat lines and sent to the army group's rear area by May 1942; this, however, did not lead to a satisfactory solution to the food issue.[126] It merely shifted the problem onto the shoulders of rear-area officers and led to a "ghetto-like refugee reservation."[127]

German transportation capacity, however, was insufficient to carry out a complete evacuation of the civilian population and those who remained in the cities and towns ringing Leningrad faced an increasingly desperate struggle for survival.[128] L Corps complained to Eighteenth Army that

the population's situation has deteriorated to such an extent that it is intolerable for the troops' morale to continually have to see such misery. For example, women and children come to the troops' local headquarters and beg for food. They suggest that they would rather be shot immediately than be abandoned to an excruciating death by starvation.[129]

---

[122] AOK 18, Kriegstagebuch Oberquartiermeister, 5.10.41, in Peter Jahn (ed.) *Blockade Leningrads*, p. 126.
[123] XXVIII AK KTB, 29.10.41, BA-MA RH 24–28/20a. At this time, there were approximately 40,000 civilians in XXVIII Corps's area of responsibility. See XXVIII AK, Tätigkeitsbericht Teil III, 23–24.10.41, BA-MA RH 24–28/109.
[124] See Hürter, "Die Wehrmacht vor Leningrad," p. 411; and Hürter, *Hitlers Heerführer*, p. 477. The local branch of the Economic Staff East also viewed these evacuations as positive measures due to the "increasingly worsening food situation"; Wi. Kdo. Görlitz, Gef. St. Krasnogwardeisk, Lagebericht (Monat Dezember 1941), BA-MA RW 31/948.
[125] Heeresgruppenkommando Nord, Ib, Nr. 7991/41 geheim., 21.10.41, Betr.: Behandlungen der Zivilbevölkerung aus den Vorstädten von Leningrad, NARA T-312, Roll 766.
[126] Ganzenmüller, *Das belagerte Leningrad 1941–1944*, p. 76.
[127] Hürter, "Die Wehrmacht vor Leningrad," p. 413.
[128] Eighteenth Army was forced to postpone the evacuation of 35,000 civilians as a result of "the extremely strained transportation situation"; Armeeoberkommando 18, Abt. O. Qu./Qu. 2 Betr.: Flüchtlinge 14.12.1941, NARA T-312, Roll 767.
[129] Generalkommando L AK, Abt. Qu. 29.11.41, Betr.: Flüchtlingsverkehr, NARA T-312, Roll 766.

The sight of "pitiful [civilians] feeding themselves on dead horses, potatoes and cabbage that are still found in the fields, or from food begged from the troops" led XXVIII Corps to request a new food policy for civilians.[130] Some field units began to question official directives after witnessing the plight of civilians in their areas of occupation.

The Wehrmacht's institutional response to the growing starvation was encapsulated in Reichenau's infamous order of 10 October 1941. Reichenau neatly summed up the ideological motivations behind the war, and Hitler, finding the order to mirror his own thinking, had it distributed to other *Ostheer* units. The 121st ID received the directive on 6 November. Addressing the food situation in the occupied territories of the Soviet Union, Reichenau stated that

> the feeding from troop kitchens of native inhabitants and prisoners of war who are not in the service of the Wehrmacht is the same misconstrued humanity as is the giving away of cigarettes and bread. What the *Heimat* has spared, what the command has brought to the front despite great difficulties, should not be given by the troops to the enemy, even when it comes from war booty. This is a necessary part of our supply.[131]

XXVIII Corps attached its own formulation to Reichenau's directive, before sending it to its subordinate divisions, including the 121st ID. Stating that the general situation required that "soldiers must be educated to be extremely tough," it then "stressed" that

> 1.) Every piece of bread that is given to the civilian population is one taken from the *Heimat*.
>
> 2.) Every civilian, including women and children, who wants to cross through our encirclement ring around Leningrad is to be shot. The fewer eaters there are in Leningrad increases the resistance there, and every refugee tends towards spying or being a partisan; all of this costs the lives of German soldiers.
>
> 3.) German soldiers are not to transport the Russian population.[132]

Küchler's thinking on the food issue converged with these orders. He ordered the strict separation of the Russian population from the

---

[130] Hürter, "Konservative Mentalität, militärischer Pragmatismus, ideologisierte Kriegführung," p. 245.

[131] Armeebefehl des Oberbefehlshabers der 6. Armee, Generalfeldmarschall von Reichenau, vom 10.10.1941, printed in Ueberschär and Wette, *Der deutsche Überfall auf die Sowjetunion*, pp. 285–6.

[132] Generalkommando XXVIII AK, Tätigkeitsbericht Teil II, 6.11.41, BA-MA RH 24-28/108. In its own order concerning the arrest of two Russian agents in Pavlovsk, L Corps stated that "all good-naturedness towards the population supports partisan and espionage activity"; Generalkommando L AK, 9.10.41, Zivilverkehr, BA-MA RH 24-50/145.

occupying forces, in part due to the danger of espionage and in part "so that the soldiers aren't continually tempted to give their food to the inhabitants." During a visit to the Waffen-SS-Polizei Division in late November, Küchler emphasized that "under no circumstances could food be given to the civilian population," utilizing the familiar slogan that such misplaced acts of charity were costing the German home front food.[133] The views of Eighteenth Army's commander on this question were certainly echoed by other members of the German High Command.[134]

On 4 November, Wagner distributed a directive to all army and panzer groups which stated that the Economic Staff East and not the Wehrmacht was responsible for feeding Soviet civilians.[135] He then categorically forbade the provisioning of foodstuffs to the surrounding population, ordering local commandants to merely supervise the distribution of food in villages and towns. A similar line was taken at the meeting of Halder and the commanders and quartermasters of the *Ostheer* at Orša on 13 November 1941. According to the notes of Eighteenth Army's chief of staff, Colonel Gerhart Hasse, "the food question is especially worrying."[136] Since winter deliveries could not be sufficiently sent to the front, "it [was] of especial importance that the troops do everything possible to live off the land for as long as possible." The plight of the civilian population was then considered:

> The question of feeding the civilian population is catastrophic. To reach some sort of solution, one needs to proceed towards a classification system. It is clear that within this classification, the troops and their needs stand at the highest level. The civilian population will only be allowed a minimum necessary for existence ... The question of feeding the large cities is unsolvable. There is no doubt that especially Leningrad will starve as it is impossible to feed this city. The commanders' only objective can be to keep the troops as far as possible away from this and its associated occurrences.

---

[133] Quoted in Hürter, "Konservative Mentalität, militärischer Pragmatismus, ideologisierte Kriegführung," p. 246.

[134] This is not to say that there were no critics of Eighteenth Army's occupation policies. Major-General Hans Knuth, commandant of the rear army area, wrote Küchler's headquarters that if "one gives the people something to eat, then every problem is solved"; ibid., p. 245.

[135] Oberkommando des Heeres, Gen St d H/Gen Qu, Abt. K.Verw., Nr. II/7732/41 geh., Betr. Ernährung der Zivilbevölkerung im Operationsgebiet, 4.11.41, reproduced in Hamburger Institut für Sozialforschung, *Verbrechen der Wehrmacht: Dimensionen des Vernichtungskrieges*, p. 301.

[136] Merkpunkte aus der Chefbesprechung in Orscha am 13.11.41, reproduced in Ueberschär and Wette, *Der deutsche Überfall auf die Sowjetunion*, pp. 308–9. See also Hürter, *Hitler's Heerführer*, p. 493.

"The greatest starvation since the Thirty Years War" 179

Such policies led Colonel Wolfgang Bucher, Eighteenth Army's chief quartermaster, to comment in mid-November that "it is only a question of where, not if, civilians will starve."[137] A further meeting between the corps quartermasters and Bucher in December neatly summed up the prevailing attitude: it was decided that when it came to the civilian population, "feeding was a crime."[138] With such agreement at the highest levels of the German Army, civilian deaths caused by starvation in Leningrad's occupied suburbs only increased during the winter of 1941–2.

Holstein, the code name of the Wirtschaftsstab Ost branch deployed in Army Group North's area of operations, found itself in an extremely difficult position. On the one hand, while it generally completed its original mission – that of supplying the advancing Wehrmacht as it drove through the Soviet Union – the army's competition for the region's scarce resources only increased the difficulty of this task.[139] On the other hand, its primary mission was now exacerbated by an additional task – feeding civilians in the occupied territories from the same limited resources. The former problem had festered since the early days of the campaign, forcing Leeb to proclaim in mid-August that the "senseless 'organization' of the troops was ruining the reconstructive work of the economic departments."[140] This relentless foraging by German units only increased during the fall and winter of 1941 due to the strained transportation situation. Holstein reported that

the transport situation of the railroad is so bad that Army Group North has discontinued all transport to and from the *Heimat* indefinitely [*bis auf weiteres*] ... Here as well there is a considerable deficit of fuel. Locomotives are frozen by the extreme cold as there aren't enough available garages for them.[141]

This general lack of transport capacity limited the Wehrmacht to deliveries of either ammunition or food; this created a situation where one or the other was invariably in short supply.[142]

---

[137] Quoted in Ganzenmüller, *Das belagerte Leningrad 1941–1944*, p. 72.
[138] Besprechung O. Qu. am 1.12.1941, BA-MA RH 24–50/175.
[139] One of the reserve economic commandos working in Army Group North's rear area reported in November that it had delivered, among other foodstuffs, a million kilograms of rye and over 3 million kilograms of potatoes to the army since the outbreak of war; see Monatserfassungbericht des Wi. Kdo. Görlitz, Aussenstelle Opotschka Gr. La für die Zeit vom 1.11–29.11.41, BA-MA RW 31/584.
[140] Quoted in Hürter, *Hitlers Heerführer*, p. 492.
[141] Wi In Nord Fp. Nr. 46376 Az.: Chefgr. Fü/Id, B. Nr. 1139541 geh., 31.12.41, Betr.: Lagebericht für die Zeit vom 16.–31.12.41, BA-MA RW 31/584.
[142] O. Qu. Tagesmeldung XXVIII AK für den 8.10.1941, NARA T-312, Roll 763.

Insufficient stores or stocks in the Russian interior aggravated these problems. One junior officer attached to the 121st ID reported that when such establishments were found, "they were either ransacked or burned down as is nearly every village" by either the retreating Soviet forces or the pursuing German units.[143] All of this contributed to the scourge of wild requisitioning which different organizations correctly saw as threatening to destroy the fragile relationship between the Wehrmacht and the civilian population in the occupied areas of northwest Russia. The Economic Staff East complained that

> the department finds itself ... in a difficult and just as hopeless defensive struggle against the "organizing" of the individual man as well as that of entire units and finds a thankful understanding for its tasks from only a few units. The guilt lies less with the men, and more with ... leadership ...[144]

Due to the Wehrmacht's ill-disciplined behavior, the Wirtschaftsstab Ost found it extremely difficult to carry out a systematic and organized exploitation of northwest Russia.

The addition of several hundred thousand civilians to their rolls by the army dramatically increased the problems facing Wirtschaftsstab Ost. Army units had been pressuring the Economic Staff East to pick up this burden at the local level since early August and the organization grudgingly acquiesced to Wehrmacht wishes following Wagner's announcement.[145] Wirtschaftsstab Ost made the caveat, however, that it would undertake this responsibility "so long as it was possible not to interfere with German interests."[146] Unfortunately for the economic authorities and, more importantly, Soviet civilians, no unified "German interests" existed in northwest Russia. While the Economic Staff East attempted to bring some type of ruthless structure to the economic exploitation of the region, it found itself continually frustrated by army policies. Perhaps most damaging to any chances of successfully feeding civilians was the Wehrmacht's evacuation program. The *Wirtschaftskommando* (Economic Commando) located at Krasnogvardeisk reported that the constant influx of bedraggled and hungry people into the area made the "food situation increasingly

---

[143] Tagebuchartige Aufzeichnungen des Lt. Schmidt, 2.8.41, BA-MA RH 37/3095. Catherine Merridale suggests that many of these stores were in fact looted by Soviet citizens after the Red Army had pulled out of an area; see her *Ivan's War: Life and Death in the Red Army, 1939–1945* (New York, 2006), p. 107.
[144] Wi. Kdo. Görlitz, Gef. St. Krasnogwardeisk, Lagebericht (Monat Dezember 1941), BA-MA RW 31/948.
[145] On Army pressure for the economic authorities to care for civilians, see Gerlach, *Kalkulierte Morde*, p. 268.
[146] Norbert Müller (ed.), *Die faschistische Okkupationspolitik in den zeitweilig besetzten Gebieten der Sowjetunion (1941–1944)* (Berlin, 1991), Nr. 53, p. 212.

difficult."[147] Similar concerns plagued the *Wirtschaftskommando* in Opotschka, where 11,550 refugees had been evacuated.[148] The command staff of Holstein estimated that an additional 40,000–45,000 refugees had been added to the already 3.5 million civilians under its responsibility. These refugees "constituted a noticeable burden in terms of the food situation" and the competition for scant resources led to increasing hostility on the part of the civilian population. Food was so scarce that "the majority of the population was starving and sections of it could not even leave their beds due to weakness."

From the perspective of the Economic Staff East, the army had created a humanitarian crisis through its misguided and mismanaged policies. Instead of an orderly evacuation, civilians simply wandered to the rear through forests and swamps, avoiding German sentries posted on the main roads. This made the process "simply uncontrollable."[149] Not only did the situation degenerate into near chaos, but it seemed that various levels of the army actually encouraged this:

> The urge to wander in the rear areas is consequently much more noticeable and this cannot be stopped as, on the one hand, the wanderers use back roads and, on the other, the commanders, especially of the frontline troops, have supported and encouraged this wandering through certain measures because they don't want the sight of civilians' starvation to be a strain on the nerves of the troops ...[150]

When Holstein reported that "the difficulties [in feeding the civilian population] were so considerable that immediate measures need to be taken," it did so knowing full well that only a concerted effort with the Wehrmacht could have any effect.[151]

The disastrous results of this policy for civilians were certainly well known to German authorities. The local branch of the Wirtschaftsstab Ost operating in northwest Russia reported the condition of civilians during the winter of 1941–2:

> The population's mood in the combat area has undergone fluctuations, but is increasingly pessimistic. This is due less to the accompanying effects of the

---

[147] Wi. Kdo. Krasnogwardeisk Gruppe La, Bericht (no date; presumably end of December 1941), BA-MA RW 31/948.
[148] Wi. In Nord, Fp. Nr. 46376 Az.: Chefgr. Fü/Id, B. Nr. 1133/41 geh., 18.12.41, Betr.: Lagebericht für die Zeit vom 1.–15.12.41, BA-MA RW 31/584. The remainder of this discussion is based on this document unless otherwise noted.
[149] Wi. Kdo. Krasnogwardeisk Gruppe La, Bericht (no date; presumably end of December 1941), BA-MA RW 31/948.
[150] Wirtschaftskommando Krasnogwardeisk, Monatsbericht vom 1.–31.1.1942, 5.2.42, BA-MA RW 31/948.
[151] Wi. In Nord, Fp. Nr. 46376 Az.: Chefgr. Fü/Id, B. Nr. 1133/41 geh., 18.12.41, Betr.: Lagebericht für die Zeit vom 1.–15.12.41, BA-MA RW 31/584.

fighting itself (shots, bombings, etc., etc.) and much more to the recently increasing incidence of death by starvation, along with typhus, which children, adolescents, and the elderly fall prey to ...

Due to hunger, a large section of the population has come to the troops for work. For the female population, this is not completely possible. The very low number of male workers has, in contrast, as good as completely dried up. There already exists an urgent need for them [workers] that cannot be satisfied from the surrounding area. The morale of the male workforce is, in so far as they have families, very depressed, because they can only survive themselves with their allocated rations and they cannot protect their family members from starvation. In addition, the insufficient food causes a constant decrease in worker capabilities.

The official continued by warning of a possible collapse of the agricultural economy due to the population's continual wanderings in search of food, forced evacuations, and, most importantly, starvation, which "brought the demise of hundreds every day."[152]

Police reports confirmed the economic authorities' findings. Einsatzgruppe A stated in January that

the question of food supply for the civilian population in the area around Leningrad is becoming increasingly problematic. Food or food stocks are not available. Recently the population is trying to find food in neighboring villages or by working for Wehrmacht units. The predicament has advanced to such a stage that even the skin of dead or slaughtered animals has found a use.[153]

The Economic Staff East reported in February that

due to the catastrophic fodder situation, there can be no talk of cattle or milk ... the minimal potato stocks that the peasants had are now at an end. Since there are as good as no potato stocks available, one cannot count on any potato deliveries in February 1942.[154]

By March, "the mood in the cities and the northeast sector was poor, determined by the increasingly desperate development of the food situation."[155] One month later, Einsatzgruppe A reported that the surviving civilian population was attempting to find the graves of horses buried the previous *summer* and eating the disinterred carcasses; as one member of the 121st ID who witnessed such acts noted, their "hunger led them to

---

[152] Wirtschaftskommando Krasnogwardeisk, Monatsbericht vom 1.–31.1.1942, 5.2.42, BA-MA RW 31/948.
[153] Ereignismeldung Nr. 162, 30. Jan.1942, NARA T-175, Roll 234.
[154] Wi. Kdo. Krasnogwardeisk Gruppe La., Monatsbericht Februar 1942, BA-MA RW 31/948.
[155] Ereignismeldung Nr. 186, 27. März 1942, NARA T-175, Roll 234.

"The greatest starvation since the Thirty Years War" 183

do something that was impossible for us."¹⁵⁶ In Liuban, infant calves were being slaughtered due to the "disastrous state of the food situation." While such short-term solutions would have devastating long-term effects on meat and milk supply in the area, the immediate emergency demanded such actions.¹⁵⁷ As the testimony of these two organizations shows, the situation for civilians in northwest Russia, especially in the towns and cities, had long since passed a crisis point by spring 1942.

Conditions within Pavlovsk fit into this general picture of famine and misery in occupied northwest Russia. They also highlight the logistical problems that afflicted the Wehrmacht in late 1941. Though the 121st ID's supply system functioned reasonably well during the drive on Pavlovsk, once the advance stopped, the supply of cattle dried up and the men were forced to rely on deliveries from the army's butcher station in Krasnogvardeisk or on their own foraging.¹⁵⁸ In response to the latter, XXVIII Corps declared that the following actions all contributed to an increasing bitterness of the civilian population towards the Wehrmacht: the forceful requisitioning of cattle without compensation, especially when children were present; the taking of a farmer's last grain or cow without payment; and rummaging through a house and confiscating items used daily by the inhabitants. It then ordered an outright ban on "wild requisitions."¹⁵⁹

Though "wild requisitions" were theoretically banned, the organized plunder of Pavlovsk received official sanction. Soon after their arrival in the town, German authorities confiscated all food stocks in warehouses and markets as well as those held in individuals' homes.¹⁶⁰ According to the Soviet Extraordinary Commission, this "created a situation of incredible hunger in the city, the result of which caused the intentional death of the population."¹⁶¹ Over 6,000 inhabitants of the town died due to starvation and the various diseases that accompany hunger.¹⁶² In the

---

[156] Ereignismeldung Nr. 190, 8. April 1942, NARA T-175, Roll 234. Heesch, *Meine 13. Infanterie-Geschütz-Kompanie Grenadier-Regiment 408*, p. 98. He, of course, failed to acknowledge the German responsibility for the population's predicament.
[157] Wirtschaftskommando Krasnogwardeisk, Befehlstelle Ljuban, Monatsbericht für April 1942, 18.4.42, BA-MA RW 31/948.
[158] Divisionsintendant 121. Inf. Division, Tätigkeitsbericht für die Zeit vom 21.9.1941 bis 30.4.1942, 30.4.42, BA-MA RH 26–121/65; Wirtschaftskommando Krasnogwardeisk, 5.2.42, BA-MA RW 31/948.
[159] Gen. Kdo. XXVIII, Erfahrungsbericht über den Umgang mit der Zivilbevölkerung, 15.11.41, BA-MA RH 24/28–110.
[160] Chrezvychainaia Gosudarstvennaia Komissiia, USHMM RG 22–002M, Reel 18, Pavlovsk, p. 1.
[161] Ibid.
[162] Ibid., p. 6. While this is the total number of starvation deaths during the entire occupation, it is clear from the context that the overwhelming majority of these deaths occurred during the first winter of the war.

most tragic case of organized starvation, 387 children between the ages of three and thirteen died during the winter of 1941–2 while staying in an orphanage established by the Germans. According to witnesses, the death of ten to fifteen children on a single day due to hunger occurred more than once.[163]

In an attempt to survive, many civilians resorted to crimes of desperation. In Pushkin, an ethnic German killed his aunt in order to trade her jewelry for food; he was arrested and shot.[164] The disappearance of a dozen children and adolescents in Pushkin led to the arrest of a man whose home contained various female body parts. He had been selling human flesh as pork at the local market.[165] In Pavlovsk, a married couple were hanged for cannibalism in February 1942. Apparently they had killed one of their grandfathers and, after consuming part of his remains at home, sold the rest at market as rabbit meat. The couple then murdered three children and disposed of their bodies in the same manner as that of the elderly man. They were finally apprehended while in the midst of dismembering a fifth victim – a nine-year-old girl.[166] An investigation into the disappearance of several children led German police units to the apartment of yet another woman in April. Finding human flesh there, they arrested her and brought her in for questioning. While admitting to having eaten five children, she claimed to have killed no one; rather she had disinterred them from the town's cemetery. Neither members of the Russian auxiliary police nor the German Security Police believed the woman and she was executed.[167] These cases, specifically those concerning cannibalism, seemed to provide vivid confirmation of Nazi propaganda in the eyes of some Germans in the region. The Communications Section of the 121st ID believed that

> these bestial acts in our immediate vicinity have confirmed for us that the rotten beasts are absolutely devoid of feeling and that when civilians from the circle of the so-called intelligentsia perpetrate this type of act, one cannot expect any better from the subhumans thrown together in the Red Army.[168]

In reality, however, such acts merely highlighted the desperation felt by Soviet citizens under the boot of German occupation.

---

[163] Ibid., p. 4.
[164] Ereignismeldung Nr. 169, 16. Februar 1942, NARA T-175, Roll 234.
[165] Wi. Kdo. Krasnogwardeisk, Gru. Fü., Monatsbericht Februar 1942, 23.2.1942, BA-MA RW 31/948.
[166] Chronik der 2. Kompanie Nachrichten-Abteilung 121, BA-MA 44/381; Ereignismeldung Nr. 169, 16. Februar 1942, NARA T-175, Roll 234.
[167] Sicherheitspolizei u. S.D., Außenstelle Pawlowsk, 3. April 1942, BA-MA RH 26–121/70.
[168] Chronik der 2. Kompanie Nachrichten-Abteilung 121, BA-MA 44/381.

"The greatest starvation since the Thirty Years War" 185

Members of the staffs of Army Group North and Eighteenth Army viewed these developments with resignation. After visiting Pavlovsk to check on the possibility of an outbreak of dysentery, the ranking medical officer in Eighteenth Army told Küchler that

> there is no epidemic ... the primary cause of all of the population's sickness is hunger and the general weakness caused by this. The population will be medically watched as far as this is possible. Medicine is in short supply, as are the materials needed for it. They just suffice for the needs of the troops ... Nothing can be done for the population.[169]

Some soldiers on the ground, however, viewed the bleak situation in more humane terms. Even men who had previously viewed the Soviet Union's inhabitants with a mixture of contempt and revulsion displayed varying degrees of compassion and pity for their plight during the winter of 1941–2. A medic in the East Prussian 21st ID described the situation in late December 1941:

> a man is lying on the street, a civilian or a prisoner of war. He is completely broken down by exhaustion in the freezing weather, and steam rises off his still warm head. In general, ragged and starving civilians. They stagger and drag themselves till then [death JR], in –40-degree weather. Their houses are destroyed, either by the Bolsheviks or by us. No one can help them. With weakened arms, they try to hack pieces out of frozen horse cadavers. Many children are dying in the villages, one sees many with prematurely aged faces and with bloated stomachs. Children and women look through the horse excrement on the street ... in hopes of finding something edible.

> Shortly before we left our last position in Myssalovo, a Russian family stood in their house in front of a warm oven, crying with faces pale from terror because they knew that their house would shortly be in flames. Finally an old woman tore herself away from the oven and put her last rags on a hand-pulled sled and moved out into the icy cold.[170]

Several members of the 121st ID attempted to alleviate the starvation they witnessed all around them despite the official directives forbidding such practices. The commander of the 408th Infantry Regiment noted that

> the question of sustenance [for civilians] is becoming increasingly burning. It can and will only be solved when thousands are evacuated from the occupied area. This process is developing very slowly. Until then hundreds of the hungry and

---

[169] KTB 18 AOK, Besprechung des Chefs mit Genst. Arzt Dr. Gunderloch, 26.10.41, NARA, T-312, Roll 782.
[170] Tagebuchaufzeichnungen aus dem Rußlandfeldzug Dr. Michael Henze, 26.12.41, BA-MA Msg 2/2778.

those without employment are drawn to German field kitchens for food or are given ad hoc support by the Russian mayors.[171]

Lt. Thomas Berdahl, writing home about the upcoming winter, also addressed the plight of the Russian inhabitants:

The civilian population will suffer a great deal as fuel and food are not available. Our field kitchens are already besieged. I see large-scale starvation coming. For one piece of bread, the women work the entire day for us.[172]

Heesch also commented on the soldiers' efforts to assist the starving civilians:

Because we had direct contact with the civilian population, we got to know their desperation. We learned of their supply difficulties and about their other worries. When one of our horses died and was given away, the population divided it amongst themselves. This divvying out consisted of a crowd of people – men, women, and children – with axes, knives, etc., pouncing on the horse, with everyone trying to get a piece of meat in this way. When the crowd left, there was not much more than the horse's tail left.

He also noted more proactive measures taken by the 121st ID:

When German troops were able to ease the starvation, they did. It was not only those who did something useful, for example potato peelers, woodcutters, laundry girls, etc., but also children who were always found in great numbers around the field kitchens.[173]

A member of the Rhenish 254th ID described his experiences in Liuban during January 1942:

due to the continual heavy bombing attacks, Liuban has been partially evacuated. We have dug in near the cemetery on the banks of the Tigoda. The civilian population that is still in Liuban suffers frightfully. Nothing to eat and no possibilities for fuel in the freezing weather. The death rate for the Russians is shockingly high. Day after day, those Russians who themselves are barely able to move, drag the bodies of those who died from starvation or cold to the cemetery. Our few field kitchens are constantly mobbed by hundreds of women and children when the food is distributed. When we try to help, it is always only a drop in the ocean. Our rations themselves are smaller and smaller every day and

---

[171] "Mein Regiment," 21.9.41, BA-MA RH 37/3096.
[172] Lt. Thomas Berdahl, Feldpostbriefe 30. Oktober 1941, in Jahn (ed.), *Blockade Leningrads*, p. 139.
[173] Heesch, *Meine 13. Infanterie-Geschütz-Kompanie Grenadier-Regiment 408*, pp. 98, 99. While Heesch provides some evidence of the army's endeavors to assist civilians, his more animated description of the "selfless actions" of German officials to ensure that "our brave horses" did not suffer a starvation "catastrophe" during the winter of 1941–2 emphasizes the relative worth he placed on the lives of Soviet civilians and German horses; see p. 97.

the soup is always thinner. The few transports bring scarcely enough munitions for the desperate fighting on the front.[174]

That such actions by individuals continued during the winter months is evidenced by yet another order in February forbidding German troops from providing civilians with food, tobacco, and even fuel.[175]

Soviet authorities also recognized that German troops generally acted sympathetically towards women and children: they instructed female agents to approach German field kitchens and beg, as "many German soldiers have children at home and can't stand to watch the misery of children in this country."[176] SD units also believed that soldiers played an important role in assisting numerous civilians in surviving the winter, reporting "it must be assumed, that the population was able to beg food from Wehrmacht units ... Wehrmacht camps have alleviated the worst of the emergency situation by making foodstuffs available to the civilian population." Einsatzgruppe A also noted that the troops slaughtered horses during the winter and gave at least some of the meat to civilians.[177] Other members of the Wehrmacht, however, exploited the suffering around them to satiate their carnal desires. One German soldier in the besieging line later related that

There were other troops in my regiment who exploited the dire Russian food situation for sexual gratification. Putting a loaf of bread under their arm, these men would head for a certain area a couple of miles behind the front where there were hungry Russian women or girls who would willingly exchange sexual

---

[174] Schicksalskämpfe des II. Gren. Rgt. 454 (254 ID) 1939–1945, BA-MA RH 37/3098. Wi. Kdo. Krasnogvardeisk, Gru. Fü., Monatsbericht April 1942, BA-MA RW 31/948. The Economic Staff East branch in the Krasnogvardeisk region concurred with this assessment, as it described the population of Liuban as "reserved, resigned and passive" due to the "increasingly catastrophic food situation"; Wi. Kdo. Krasnogvardeisk, Gru. Fü., Monatsbericht April 1942, BA-MA RW 31/948.

[175] Generalkommando L AK, Abt. Qu., Besondere Anordnungen für die Versorgung Nr. 170, 7.2.1942, BA-MA RH 24–50/176.

[176] Ereignismeldung Nr. 130, 7. Nov. 1941, NARA T-175, Roll 234.

[177] Ereignismeldung Nr. 190, 8. April 1942, NARA T-175, Roll 234. The men of the 121st ID were not the only soldiers who attempted to alleviate the suffering of Russians in their area of responsibility. Bernhard Chiari has written that "Eighteenth Army soldiers attempted to supply civilians in their area of responsibility with food and even to take their needs into consideration"; Chiari, "Grenzen deutscher Herrschaft: Voraussetzungen und Folgen der Besatzung in der Sowjetunion," in Jörg Echternkamp (ed.), *Das Deutsche Reich und der Zweite Weltkrieg*, vol. IX/II, *Die Deutsche Kriegsgesellschaft, 1939 bis 1945: Ausbeutung, Deutungen, Ausgrenzung* (Munich, 2005), pp. 877–976, here p. 885. Other units along the front also followed similar practices: in the spring of 1942, Third Panzer Army, operating southwest of Moscow, noted in its war diary that "although no provisions may be handed over to the civilian population, the civilian population is, for the most part, being fed by the Wehrmacht"; quoted in Müller, "Das Scheitern der wirtschaftlichen 'Blitzkriegstrategie,'" p. 1223, n. 355.

Illustration 5.2 The ravages of battle and German occupation policies doomed thousands of Soviet civilians to starvation.

favors for food ... Most German officers and troops disapproved of such behavior, but I knew of no one who was reprimanded or punished for engaging in this type of act.[178]

These varied responses highlight the different ways in which individual soldiers responded to the crisis in their midst. While some took advantage of the desperate circumstances that Wehrmacht policy created, others did what they could to ease the suffering in the region.[179] Few, if any, however, explicitly linked their service with the 121st ID to the utter hopelessness and despair of the surrounding civilian population.

In addition to the confiscation of foodstuffs, members of the 121st ID also turned to the civilian population for winter clothing; the largest problem from the individual soldier's point of view concerned the delivery of clothing and equipment. Once again the quartermaster's claim that "by and large the troops can't complain" was wishful thinking. Numerous items were in short supply, including coats, boots, and woolen underclothes, despite the fact that recently arrived replacements came with a full complement of winter gear.[180] By late November, only 50 percent of the gloves and 5 percent of the felt boots required by Eighteenth Army had been delivered to the men.[181] A lack of gloves proved especially problematic as the cold made it nearly impossible for the men to use their weapons effectively.[182] Soldiers were reduced to asking their relatives and friends at home for such items.[183] By early December, the division ordered its troops to purchase the necessary items from the civilian

---

[178] Lubbeck, *At Leningrad's Gates*, pp. 113–14.
[179] Oldenburg notes that German soldiers "were interested in the fate of civilians and that they did not close their eyes to their suffering"; see Oldenburg, *Ideologie und militärisches Kalkül*, p. 245. Regina Mühlhäuser has also noted that "soldiers tried to help native women and sometimes even their families" during the war; however, she also cites a report issued by the OKH's general quartermaster that noted food "frequently" was used as payment for prostitution. See her *Eroberungen: Sexuelle Gewalttaten und intime Beziehungen deutscher Soldaten in der Sowjetunion 1941–1945* (Hamburg, 2010), pp. 251, 163.
[180] 121 Inf. Division, Winterausstattung, 10.1.42, BA-MA RH 26–121/65. Despite the soldiers' procuring of needed items from Russian POWs and civilians, the division had, for example, 827 fur coats, 989 felt boots, and 2,519 pairs of woolen underwear for the 12,719 men in the division. While a significant number of these men undoubtedly were replacements who came equipped for the winter, the difference between the number of total soldiers and the number of coats, boots, and underwear is striking.
[181] Besprechungspunkte!, NARA, T-312, Roll 766. One example of the results of these shortages concerns a raiding party sent out for several hours on 24 January 1942. Upon its return, "90% of the men suffered light to medium frostbite"; 121 ID KTB, 24.1.42, BA-MA RH 26–121/16.
[182] O. Qu. Tagesmeldung XXVIII AK für den 28.9.1941, NARA T-312, Roll 763.
[183] Tagebuchartige Aufzeichnungen des Lt. Schmidt, 18.8.41, BA-MA RH 37/3095; Leutnant Thomas Berdahl, Feldpostbriefe, 4. September 1941 and 14. Oktober 1941, in Jahn, *Blockade Leningrads*, pp. 136–8.

population and if the native inhabitants refused to sell these items, his superiors empowered the *Landser* to force Russian communities to sell clothing and boots.[184] One member of the East Prussian 61st ID wrote that his comrades were so desperate for warm clothing that "with greedy eyes, the soldiers pounced on every dead or wounded Russian in order to snatch his felt boots and quilted winter uniform."[185] A slogan in the 121st ID was "prepare yourself in any way!" and this meant that German soldiers frequently looted fallen and wounded Soviet soldiers, not only for the prized waterproof boots, but also for any other clothing that could help them survive the dropping temperatures.[186] The felt-boot workshop in Pavlovsk turned out seven pairs of boots a week but this in no way sufficed for the needs of the division.[187] With their superior officers effectively giving the troops free rein to acquire clothing, it seems extremely likely that once ordered to collect these goods, forced requisitioning and outright robbery became standard practices.

IV. War of attrition: the 121st ID defends Pavlovsk

The ensnaring of Leningrad between the German and Finnish Armies did not end the combat in the region as the Soviets launched repeated and desperate attempts to regain contact with the city.[188] With the distance between German and Soviet front lines varying between twenty and 200 meters along the siege line, the 121st ID and other Wehrmacht units were forced to remain vigilant.[189] XXVIII Corps released a directive stating that the corps commander himself would issue orders down to the battalion level to ensure his troops maintained their tactical superiority over the Red Army in this no-man's-land. The order also added that the troops had maintained their "belief in victory and are far superior to the enemy in combat morale."[190]

---

[184] Abt. Ib KTB, 7.12.41, BA-MA RH 26–121/65; Generalkommando L AK, 18.8.42, Tätigkeitsbericht der Abt. IVa Gen. Kdo. L AK für die Zeit vom 13.8.31–7.5.42, BA-MA RH 24–50/173.
[185] Grenadier-Regiment 162, BA-MA Msg 2/5415.
[186] "Der Todesmarsch nach Leningrad," p. 63, BA-MA Msg 2/2580.
[187] Generalkommando L AK, Tätigkeitsbericht der Abt. IVa, Gen. Kdo. L AK für die Zeit vom 13.8.41–7.5.42, BA-MA RH 24–50/173.
[188] For an overview of these operations, see Glantz, *The Battle for Leningrad*, pp. 92–116. Even a cursory glance at the OKW war diary for fall 1941 illustrates the constant combat on this section of the front; see Schramm, *KTB OKW*, vol. II, pp. 670 ff.
[189] 3. (preuß) Inf-Regt., BA-MA Msg 2/249, p. 3. The 1st ID occupied the far eastern section of the line along Lake Ladoga and the Neva river.
[190] On the Corps's order, see 121 ID, Abt. Ib KTB I, 20.9.41, BA-MA RH 26–121/65; on morale, XXVIII AK KTB II, 24.9.41, BA-MA RH 24–28/20a.

This order suggests two interesting and interrelated points. First, such micromanagement of its subordinate units indicates that the corps feared that due to high casualties, individual units would take the opportunity to lick their wounds behind their fortifications, ceding the initiative to the Red Army. Second, the failure to capture the city proved to be a powerful psychological blow to Army Group North, from Leeb down to the enlisted men. The claim regarding the "superior combat morale" seems to be an attempt to convince junior officers and the rank and file that the German Army remained an effective combat force even if its formations were exhausted and seriously weakened after some three months of combat.

While XXVIII Corps professed to believe in the troops' staying power, it recognized the strained condition of the divisions, with their severely depleted infantry strength, dangerously low levels of artillery ammunition, and nearly complete absence of any air support. The corps informed Eighteenth Army that a strong Soviet push would in all probability punch through the corps's extremely thin line.[191] This fear is confirmed by evidence from lower levels of the 121st Infantry Division, which indicates that at least some units precariously teetered on the edge of mutiny. Several days before the seizure of Pavlovsk, the 407th Infantry Regiment ordered its troops to continue the attack shortly before the onset of darkness.[192] Members of the II Battalion, however, felt "too worn-out" and "had no desire" to attack at such a late hour. Though the battalion commander believed the troops were close to crumbling under the demands made of them, he believed an order was an order and must be carried out. This led to a "mutiny" by the company commanders, who refused to attack. An argument ensued between the battalion and company commanders, with the former threatening the latter with "immediate shooting" if they failed to launch the attack. Fortunately for both sides, the regiment then decided to cancel the assault. One NCO stated that this was quite providential as his men "would have flown into a rage and even would have assaulted their superiors." Even the 121st ID, a division characterized by strong morale and high combat efficiency during the opening months of the invasion, now found itself cracking under the pressure of war.

The 121st ID's break from heavy fighting ended on 11 November 1941 when the Red Army launched a major offensive aiming at breaking

---

[191] Kommandierender General des XXVIII AK, 28.9.41, BA-MA RH 24–28/26.
[192] The following is drawn from "Der Todesmarsch nach Leningrad," p. 200, BA-MA Msg 2/2580.

the encirclement.[193] Defensive fighting marked the remainder of the year, with especially heavy fighting occurring in late November.

Crippling shortages of artillery ammunition complicated German defensive efforts, an especially debilitating problem in positional warfare. Red Army guns fired without fear of reprisal from mid-December on as the 121st ID was ordered not to respond to Soviet barrages.[194] This also allowed the Red Army to deploy its forces for its winter counteroffensive without being disturbed by German shelling.[195] On 15 December 1941, Red Army units in the Leningrad region unleashed their part of the general Red Army counterattack. While the German position held at this time, the next major attempt to break the lines succeeded on 22 December, causing a "serious crisis" in the 121st ID. A weakened 407th Infantry Regiment proved unable to seal off the breakthrough and the division, denied help from either corps or army levels, was forced to plug the gap with baggage, supply, and veterinary troops.[196]

The division commander characterized 23 December as "the most serious day of the entire Eastern Campaign," with the combat reaching such proportions that "one walked through fields of corpses."[197] Red Army armor proved to be a major problem for the German infantry. Despite having destroyed numerous tanks in combat, the underequipped *Landser* frequently faltered in front of Soviet armor. In a letter to the OKH, the 121st ID's commander explained that while the "German infantryman feels himself to be 100 times superior to the Russian in all situations, he cannot stand up to the heavy tanks." It was the heavy Soviet armor that broke through the 407th Infantry Regiment's lines, and though the regiment was "East Prussian, which means you have men upon whose toughness you can always count," even they felt

---

[193] Ia Tagesmeldung an AOK 18, 11.11.41, BA-MA RH 24–28/108. The intense fighting even garnered a mention in the OKW war diary: "the enemy attacked in unexpected strength. The 121 I.D. defended all attacks, destroying 11 enemy tanks, including a 64 and six 52 tonners"; Schramm, *KTB OKW*, vol. II, 11 November 1941, p. 753.

[194] 121 ID KTB, 14.12.41, BA-MA RH 26–121/16.

[195] On the Soviet counteroffensive in December 1941, see Glantz and House, *When Titans Clashed*, pp. 87–94; John Erickson, *The Road to Stalingrad* (London, 1998), pp. 249–97; and more specifically on the Leningrad region, Glantz, *The Battle for Leningrad*, 103–19.

[196] 121 ID KTB, 22.12.41, BA-MA RH 26–121/16. L Corps informed its subordinate commands that no reserves existed at corps or army level in the sector and that it was incumbent on each division to solve its own problems; Generalkommando L AK an Divisionen-Kommandern, 21.12.41, BA-MA RH 26–121/17. This was echoed by Leeb, who wrote that while "the breakthrough requires especially close observation," he was in no position to help the 121st ID which "shows the weakness of the Army and Army Group as they have no strong reserves with which to intervene here"; see Leeb, *Tagebuchaufzeichnungen*, 23 December 1941, 24 December 1941, p. 422.

[197] Letter written by General Wrangel to General Brand in the OKH, 24.12.41, BA-MA RH 26–121/17.

overwhelmed by the tanks. According to the commander, the men urgently required a weapon to end the "tank fear."[198] Despite Red Army superiority in both armor and artillery, however, the 121st ID held its position as 1941 ended.[199]

V. Conclusion

What during the summer of 1941 had seemed like an inexorable drive on Leningrad – the Soviet Union's gateway to the west and the symbol of the Bolshevik state – degenerated into a war of attrition by early fall and increasingly became a war of matériel during the winter of 1941–2. While the 121st ID continued to fulfill its primary mission of fighting the Red Army, it found itself responsible for an entirely new task: the occupation of Pavlovsk. Unlike other Wehrmacht occupations earlier in the campaign, the frontline troops of the 121st ID simply could not turn over the administration of the town to rear-area formations due to its position in the front line. Home to approximately 15,000 citizens on the eve of the German invasion, the community suffered the loss of over 10,000 inhabitants during the war. This horrific death toll resulted from harsh security policies, the murder of the city's Jews, the deportation of civilians to labor camps in the army's rear area as well as in Germany, and the starvation of the city's population.[200]

Two interconnected ideas explain such a horrifying outcome in Pavlovsk. First, the division more ruthlessly carried out programs designed to maintain and even improve its military efficiency. Second, while in Pavlovsk, the East Prussians established a close working relationship with two other Reich institutions: Einsatzgruppe A and Wirtschaftsstab Ost. While both of these organizations had their own missions, in many ways the elimination of "enemies" and the exploitation of the local economy were both intended to secure German military power in the region. The goals of the occupation – as conceived by the SS, Economic Staff East, the 121st ID, and, by extension, Eighteenth Army, Army Group North, and the military leadership of both OKH and OKW – led to the civilian population in the Leningrad district being sacrificed on the altar of military necessity.[201]

---

[198] Ibid. The relative superiority of the Red Army in both quantity and quality of weaponry and its effect on the German soldier has been suggestively discussed by Bartov in his look at the "demodernization of the front" in *Hitler's Army*, pp. 12–28.
[199] 121 ID KTB, 24.12.41, BA-MA RH 26-121/16.
[200] Chrezvychainaia Gosudarstvennaia Komissiia, USHMM RG 22-002M, Reel 18, Pavlovsk, p. 6.
[201] Such thinking permeates Hürter, "Die Wehrmacht vor Leningrad."

From a security standpoint, the actions of the 121st ID clearly radicalized, if only temporarily, following the initial seizure of the town. Working within the context of increased calls for ruthlessness by Keitel and other superior commanders and formations and sharing such duties with SS units, the East Prussians executed far more alleged partisans during the first three weeks of the occupation than they had during the previous three months of the invasion. The division's acquiescence in the murder of Pavlovsk's Jews also betrays a distorted, but nonetheless real, desire for security: in an army in which a Jew was equated with a partisan, the eradication of Jews would seemingly mean a more peaceful occupation.

Economic matters could have complemented such ideological thinking. Both Christian Gerlach and Manfred Oldenburg have suggested that German authorities in Belarus as well as the Crimea and Donbas, respectively, murdered Jews as a means to free up more resources for German use. No direct evidence links the Holocaust in Pavlovsk to such a coldly pragmatic policy but the elimination of one group in an area bereft of agricultural production to ensure more resources for other groups certainly seems plausible when the largest crime committed by the 121st ID – the large-scale starvation of Pavlovsk's civilian population – is considered.

In order to ensure the troops' strength, the 121st ID entered Pavlovsk and immediately confiscated winter clothes and boots, commandeered dwellings, and requisitioned all of the food it could lay its hands on. Such actions had a twofold effect: for soldiers such as the East Prussian Heesch, they allowed him to claim that Pavlovsk was "not the worst position!" as the troops found the town relatively hospitable.[202] For civilians, however, these policies "amounted to nothing less than death sentences."[203] The behavior of the 121st ID in Pavlovsk fits neatly into the general starvation policies developed before the war. The question of intent, however, is more difficult. Did the 121st ID order or willingly create the conditions for the starvation of Soviet civilians simply so they would die? Or should the notion of military necessity also be applied to this situation? An examination of the division's records reveals no discussion of Soviet civilians, with the important exceptions of their potential for resistance and labor. In other words, civilians and their fate were generally ignored by the 121st ID as defeating the Red Army remained of primary importance. The 121st ID did not seize Pavlovsk with the intent of starving its inhabitants; however, the racist ideological foundation of

---

[202] Heesch, *Meine 13. Infanterie-Geschütz-Kompanie Grenadier-Regiment 408*, p. 103.
[203] Megargee, *War of Annihilation*, p. 143.

Conclusion 195

the Nazi state and the increasing absorption of Nazi precepts by the German High Command, the ever more tenuous supply situation, the onset of winter, and the downgrading of the northern theater of operations to a "secondary theater of war"[204] all conspired to create a situation in which the quest for military necessity had catastrophic results for those deemed superfluous to combat effectiveness.

While the division certainly bears a heavy burden for what transpired in the town, what about the men who filled its ranks? Should they be viewed as racial warriors who willingly starved women and children? Here again, conclusions are mixed. On the one hand, it is clear that racial bigotry accompanied the 121st ID as it advanced through the Soviet Union into Pavlovsk. Terms such as "subhuman," "beasts," and "rats," among others, were used by the division's soldiers to describe Soviet soldiers and civilians alike. On the other hand, the German High Command certainly recognized that mass starvation would cause morale problems for the troops and they made numerous attempts to convince the troops that such actions were indeed essential for the German war effort. The OKH believed that the German soldier

> would be inclined to give some of his rations to the population. But he must say to himself: every gram of bread or other food that I give to the population of the occupied territories out of the goodness of my heart, I am taking away from the German people and therefore my family ... Therefore the German soldier needs to remain hard in view of the starving women and children. If he doesn't do this, he endangers the food supply of our people. The enemy is now experiencing the fate he had intended for us. He alone bears the responsibility before the world and history.[205]

Orders such as Reichenau's, as well as previously cited army and corps orders, should be viewed in this light: attempts to convince the troops of the need for the starvation of large sections of the Soviet population. The increasing frequency with which they were released, however, highlights the troops' relative indifference and/or resistance to obeying their superiors. Even though the Wehrmacht's supply system suffered severe bottlenecks during the winter of 1941–2, members of the 121st ID continued to share their limited rations with Soviet civilians. This reached such proportions that L Corps, the 121st ID's superior formation, publicized the execution of two soldiers who worked at an army supply camp for selling food to Russian civilians.[206]

---

[204] Halder, *Kriegstagebuch*, vol. III, 6 September 1941, p. 215.
[205] Quoted in Streit, *Keine Kameraden*, p. 162.
[206] Generalkommando L AK, Abt. Qu., Besondere Anordnungen Nr. 207, 10.4.1942, BA-MA RH 24-50/179.

While the actions of individual soldiers clearly failed to halt the widespread starvation in the division's area of operations – a starvation that the army's actions precipitated in Pavlovsk – this does not change the fact that some men did try to alleviate the suffering in their midst. The daily horrors that occurred during the winter of 1941–2 were therefore the result of a coldly pragmatic and ruthless mind-set that focused on a narrowly defined military necessity. While some soldiers actively worked against the more inhumane and radical demands of the German political and military leadership, the combination of ideological hatred, situational factors, and the army's own strict understanding of military necessity ensured that scenes of apocalyptic misery and horror emerged daily during Pavlovsk's winter of 1941–2.

6 The failure of Operation Barbarossa
The fusion of ideology and military culture

On 3 July 1941, Halder famously noted, "it is thus probably no overstatement to say that the campaign against Russia has been won within fourteen days."[1] A little over five months later, Jodl made reference to Napoleon's disastrous 1812 retreat following the withdrawal of German forces involved in the Tichvin operation.[2] What caused this dramatic reversal of the Wehrmacht's initial success, specifically with regard to the 121st, 123rd, and 126th IDs? Three issues can be identified: a crippling manpower shortage, supply difficulties that increasingly limited the army's effectiveness, and a myopic focus on battlefield success that completely ignored the plight of civilians until they were driven to resistance. In combination, these problems highlighted the Prusso-German Army's traditional focus on battlefield operations. This belief in a generally, if not always, ruthless concept of military necessity not only stoked increasing resistance from the Soviet civilian population, but also paradoxically served as the basis for the Wehrmacht's failure to destroy the Soviet Union in one campaign. The combined effects of these three issues led to an exhausted and dramatically weakened Wehrmacht by the end of 1941, one that could not achieve any of its prewar objectives. Leeb's complaint about fighting a "poor man's war" referenced his army group's situation but it could readily be applied to the *Ostheer* as a whole.[3]

I. "The replacement situation is unfortunately proving to be catastrophic": the state of the infantry

At the most fundamental level, Army Group North simply did not possess enough men and machines to complete its ever-expanding mission: capture Leningrad, maintain a common front with Army Group Center, and construct a defensive front linking the wings of its advance. During

---
[1] Halder, *Kriegstagebuch*, vol. III, 3 July 1941, p. 38.
[2] Leeb, *Tagebuchaufzeichnungen*, 16 December 1941, p. 418.
[3] Ibid., 8 September 1941, p. 352.

the first month and a half of war, only 14,000 replacements entered the ranks of Army Group North in a futile attempt to replace its 42,000 casualties.[4] The resulting deficit in manpower wreaked havoc on the ability of the army group to function as a coherent whole. While Eighteenth Army concentrated its forces in the siege line around Leningrad, Sixteenth Army's mandate forced its units to advance in divergent directions, and this permitted very little mutual support between its corps.[5] The shifting of Panzer Group 4 in mid-September to Army Group Center for the final drive on Moscow only further strained the situation.[6] When Eighteenth Army's commander complained of this situation in late September, he was informed by Halder that "the numerical superiority of the Russians is a fact that we will continue to face, despite the lack of personnel on his side that is gradually becoming discernible. It will be balanced out through the high value of the German soldier."[7] In other words, Soviet superiority in quantity would have to be defeated by a German quality that was rapidly shrinking in numbers.

The results of such manpower shortages clearly arose in two meetings held between Busch and his Sixteenth Army corps and divisional officers during the last three months of 1941. In early October, Busch provided depressing details on the Wehrmacht's material resources to the assembled officers. He informed them that the 400,000-man reserve available at the outset of the campaign had already been "used up" and that they "cannot count on any reserves"; only convalescents would be returning to their units for the foreseeable future. He then exhorted them to scour the rear areas for all available men and ended the meeting with the demand "the last man to the front!"[8] Just over two months later, the situation had only worsened. His division commanders painted a grim picture of German weakness to Busch in mid-December 1941:

> continuous Russian activity, constant tactical patches, living from hand to mouth. Impossible to construct fortifications. Troops remain overextended. Everyone must be permanently ready for action ... Constant weakening of combat power. Daily average 30–40 [men lost] ... The situation is extraordinarily serious. Strength is not sufficient to hold this position for an extended period of time.[9]

---

[4] Halder, *Kriegstagebuch*, vol. III, 2 August 1941, p. 145.
[5] Even in its rather limited area of operations, Eighteenth Army complained of insufficient numbers of troops; see Hürter, "Die Wehrmacht vor Leningrad," p. 398.
[6] Seaton, *The Russo-German War, 1941–1945*, p. 152.
[7] Megargee, *Inside Hitler's High Command*, p. 181.
[8] Niederschrift über die Adjutantenbesprechung beim AOK 16 am 6.10.41, BA-MA RH 26–126/23.
[9] Vortrag des Divisionskommandeurs beim Oberbefehlshaber der Armee am 12.12.41, BA-MA RH 26–126/23.

"The replacement situation is proving to be catastrophic" 199

Illustration 6.1 German military cemeteries in northwest Russia testified to the intensity of combat in 1941.

The fact that such a bleak picture of the German Army was being discussed even before the Soviet counteroffensive of January 1942 tore gaping holes in Sixteenth Army's lines speaks volumes about the failure of Germany's June 1941 gamble.

From its very beginnings, the invasion was predicated on a very precarious manpower situation. At the outset of hostilities, the German Army possessed a pool of 475,000 trained reserves, of which 385,000 were intended for the army.[10] Some 90,000 were already placed into *Feldersatzbataillonen* and sent to the east, ready to supplement the attacking divisions. While such a number of replacements certainly would have sufficed for the invasion of France and the Low Countries, the German High Command understood this would not be the case in the eastern campaign. Colonel-General Friedrich Fromm, commander of the *Ersatzheer* (Replacement Army), informed Halder in May that casualties for the upcoming campaign were estimated at 275,000 for the border battles and an additional 200,000 for the month of September. Casualties at this rate would completely exhaust the reserves by October

[10] Halder, *Kriegstagebuch*, vol. II, 20 May 1941, p. 422. The remaining 90,000 were earmarked for the Luftwaffe.

200 The failure of Operation Barbarossa

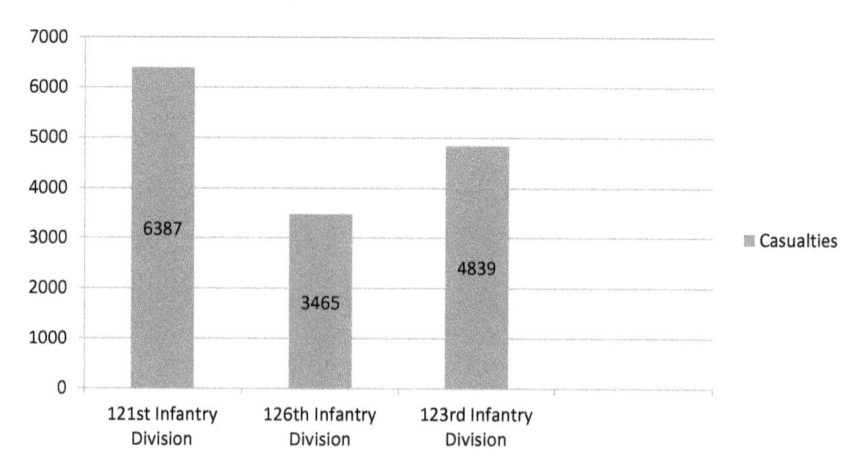

Figure 6.1 Casualty numbers for June–September 1941

- 121st Infantry Division: 6387
- 126th Infantry Division: 3465
- 123rd Infantry Division: 4839

unless the 1922 class was conscripted in August, several months before it was scheduled to be called to the colors. Halder believed that "the risk of having no trained reserves in October is one we can take."[11] Thus, Operation Barbarossa had to be fought in blitzkrieg style: if the Soviet Union still provided determined resistance in October 1941, the Wehrmacht's striking power would steadily decline until the next batch of reserves could be delivered to the front in early 1942.[12]

Within a mere three months of fighting, total casualties – 583,000 – dwarfed the prewar estimates.[13] As a result of both an insufficient number of trained reserves and a strained transportation system, eighty-four German divisions in the east already ran a deficit of a minimum of 2,000 soldiers by the end of August. Of these divisions, fourteen had suffered over 4,000 casualties and a further forty had losses totaling more than 3,000.[14] By the end of November, the Eastern Army ran short some 340,000 men.[15] The experiences of the 121st, 123rd, and 126th IDs all fit into this general bloodletting suffered by the Wehrmacht during the invasion. The 121st ID lost an astounding 6,387 men during this period; this equated to somewhere around 35 percent of the unit's initial strength.[16] The Rhinelanders

---

[11] For a succinct discussion of this issue, see Klink, "Die Landkriegführung," p. 320.
[12] The inability to reconcile manpower needs with operational demands is scathingly detailed by Kroener, "The Manpower Resources of the Third Reich," pp. 1009–10.
[13] Halder, *Kriegstagebuch*, vol. III, 28 September 1941, p. 257.
[14] Burkhart Mueller-Hillebrand, *Das Heer 1933–1945*, vol. III, *Der Zweifrontenkrieg: Das Heer vom Beginn des Feldzuges gegen die Sowjetunion bis zum Kriegsende* (Frankfurt am Main, 1969), p. 19.
[15] Ibid., p. 20.   [16] 121 ID KTB Qu., 6.10.41, BA-MA RH 26–121/65.

"The replacement situation is proving to be catastrophic"   201

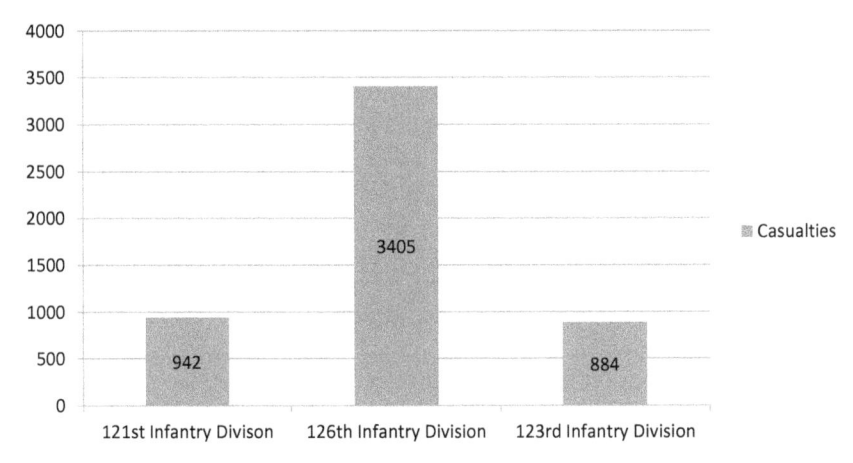

Figure 6.2 Casualty figures for October–December 1941

of the 126th ID suffered a total of 3,465 casualties during these operations, while the Berliners had lost 4,839 men by mid-October (see Figure 6.1).[17]

July, August, and September, however, proved to be the high point of casualties both for the Wehrmacht as a whole and for all three divisions; somewhat paradoxically, as the German Army entered the last desperate phase of Barbarossa, its losses actually decreased and the experiences of the 121st, 123rd, and 126th IDs all conformed to this pattern, though the Rhinelanders' participation in the Tichvin offensive ensured that their casualty numbers were only slightly lower (see Figure 6.2[18]).

Despite the decrease in casualty numbers during the last months of 1941, each division still suffered from a strained manpower situation as the replacement system failed to keep pace; Halder's exuberant belief that the war would be over by October ensured that the army's manpower situation teetered dangerously on the edge of catastrophe as the year concluded.

[17] For the 126th ID, see 126 Inf. Div. Meldung vom 22.8; 126 Inf. Div. Meldung vom 22.9, BA-MA RH 26–126/23; Tätigkeitsbericht der Abt. IIa/b Stand vom 30.9.41, BA-MA RH 26–126/131. For the 123rd ID, see Tätigkeitsbericht der Abt. IIa vom 15.7.41; Tätigkeitsbericht der Abt. IIa vom 15.7.-15.8.41; Tätigkeitsbericht der Abt. IIa v.16.8. bis 15.9.1941; Tätigkeitsbericht der Abt. IIa vom 16.9.41–15.10.41, BA-MA RH 26–123/161.
[18] 121 ID KTB Qu., 3.12.41, BA-MA RH 26–121/65; 126 Inf. Div. Meldung vom 25.10; 126 Inf. Div. Meldung vom 21.11; 126 Inf. Div. Meldung vom 23.12, BA-MA RH 26–126/23; 126 ID Meldung 23.1, BA-MA RH 26–126/47; Tätigkeitsbericht der Abt. IIa vom 16.10.41–15.11.41; Tätigkeitsbericht der Abt. IIa vom 16.11.41–15.12.41, BA-MA RH 26–123/161; Verlustliste 123 Inf. Division vom 16.12.41 bis 31.3.1942, BA-MA RH 26–123/164. Hartmann's examination of the 4th Panzer Division, the 45th Infantry Division, and the 296th Infantry Division all fall into this general pattern of casualty rates; see Table 19, "Verluste aller Divisionen pro Monat," in Hartmann, *Wehrmacht im Ostkrieg*, p. 212.

Prior to Operation Barbarossa, divisions would request replacements from their superior army formation, which would then contact the division's home military district for fresh recruits. As Bernard Kroener has noted, "this system had generally maintained a balanced age-range in the formations as well as their regional unity, a factor which was important for their mental resilience and internal cohesion."[19] The unprecedented number of casualties caused by the early fighting forced the Wehrmacht to adjust its replacement system and now troops were sometimes arbitrarily grouped in large field replacement battalions and sent to the front with no real provision for linking a recruit's military district with the appropriate division.[20]

Another innovation intended to maintain the division's cohesion concerned the establishment of convalescent units. These formations gathered a given division's officers, NCOs, and men who had sufficiently recovered from their wounds to return to the front into march companies numbering 150 men.[21] Not only did these help to maintain a unit's regional identity, but it also ensured that experienced veterans continued to be rotated into the line alongside green recruits. The army certainly recognized the importance of these convalescent companies in maintaining unit cohesion: in late November 1941, the 122nd ID came under attack outside Leningrad, with its 411th Infantry Regiment suffering especially heavy casualties. XXVIII Corps needed to reinforce the 411th Infantry Regiment but its parent division's convalescent company was too small to provide adequate support. While the idea of using other divisions' convalescent companies was discussed, in the end corps command decided that the importance of returning convalescents to their own units outweighed that of reinforcing the 411th Infantry Regiment, which was subsequently removed from the line.[22]

Reinforcements entered the 121st, 123rd, and 126th IDs in similar, if not identical, ways. Following the heavy fighting of June and July, the commander of the 121st ID had requested reinforcements for his depleted division on 1 August.[23] Between 31 July and 12 December, six march battalions from the rear, totaling 5,267 men, were integrated into the ranks of the 121st ID.[24] Despite the relatively impressive number of recruits sent to the front, Wehrmacht replacement practices in 1941 reflected the German Army's difficulty in keeping a trained force in the field in the face

---

[19] Kroener, "The Manpower Resources of the Third Reich," p. 1019.   [20] Ibid.
[21] Zur Kommandeur-Besprechung am 12.10.41, BA-MA RH 26–121/17.
[22] Gliederung des A.K. zur Verteidigung, 23.11.41, BA-MA RH 24–28/108.
[23] Notizen für die Kommandeurbesprechung (IIa/IIb), 1.8.41, BA-MA RH 26–121/11.
[24] Tätigkeitsbericht der Abt. IIa/IIb für die Zeit vom 31. Juli bis 30. Nov. 1941, BA-MA RH 24–28/157; L AK KTB, 18.12.41, BA-MA RH 24–50/15.

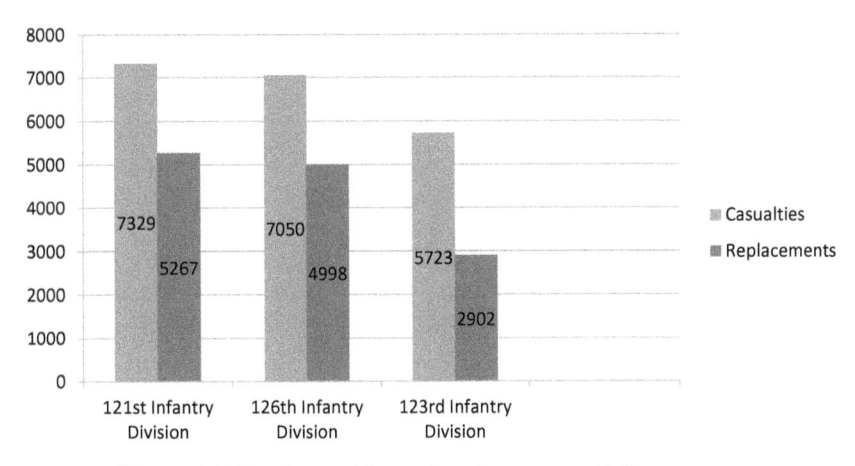

"The replacement situation is proving to be catastrophic" 203

[Bar chart showing casualties and replacements for three divisions:
- 121st Infantry Division: Casualties 7329, Replacements 5267
- 126th Infantry Division: Casualties 7050, Replacements 4998
- 123rd Infantry Division: Casualties 5723, Replacements 2902]

Figure 6.3 Total casualties and replacements, 1941

of ever-spiraling losses. The 408th Infantry Regiment reported in September that less than half of the NCO replacements it received were actually trained as infantrymen; the majority of these men were unprepared to lead offensive operations.[25] Division command reported "the main deficiency of the [December] march battalion as reported by all regiments: above all, an inadequate soldierly bearing, an inadequate feeling of duty and honor. Besides that, inadequate training in marksmanship and an unsuitable selection of specialists."[26] One platoon leader described the dozen men who arrived as replacements for his unit:

they are mostly older soldiers, from whom one can expect little in terms of combat experience. They impressed me as mere ghosts. So these men will be immediately sent into the battle. Today or tomorrow, they will already be dead or wounded ... the best have already fallen before the enemy. They rest in Poland, France, in the Balkans and now in the east. Or they have been turned into cripples.[27]

These problems were magnified by the fact that at least one of these march battalions came from the Chemnitz region, serving to dilute the regional cohesion of the division (see Figure 6.3).[28]

---

[25] General Kommando XXVIII AK, Ersatzlage (Uffz. und Mannschaften), 14.9.1941, BA-MA RH 24–28/25.
[26] 121. Inf.-Division, Abt. 1a, Ausbildungszustand der Marschbataillone, 3.1.42, BA-MA RH 26–121/17.
[27] "Der Todesmarsch nach Leningrad," p. 197, BA-MA Msg 2/2580.
[28] Ibid. This was not true of all of the march battalions received during this time period, however; see 1. Kompanie Infanterie-Regiment 405, 4. Jan. 1942, Betr.: Veränderungen zur Liste der Erkennungsmarkern, Deutsche Dienststelle (hereafter WASt), 80549.

By the end of the year, 4,998 men joined the 126th ID, leaving it with a deficit of approximately 2,050 men by the turn of the year.[29] Of these 4,998 *Ersatz*, 1,977 were active-duty soldiers who had completed the entire training program. The remaining reserve soldiers were divided into three different categories based on their training: 1,814 men who had completed an abbreviated program were classified as Reserve I, the 956 Reserve II soldiers had undertaken a minimum of two to three months' training, and the remaining 251 were grouped under the heading *Landwehr* due to their extremely short period of training and their relatively advanced age.[30] As these numbers indicate, the majority of troops who entered the 126th ID during Operation Barbarossa had completed a significant portion, but by no means all, of their training.

These replacements contributed to the regional cohesion in the ranks, as 898 previously wounded soldiers returned to the division. They were joined by an influx of a minimum of 2,043 recruits who originated from Wehrkreis VI.[31] Two sizable contingents of soldiers from outside the Rhineland-Westphalia area also joined the division; in one case, however, it was from the neighboring Wehrkreis XII, centered on Wiesbaden and including the Catholic areas of Saarland and the Palatinate. In any case, approximately 60 percent of the troops who entered the division between June 1941 and the turn of the year were either convalescents rejoining their comrades or Rhenish and Westphalian men.

Much like its two sister divisions, the 123rd ID failed to receive enough soldiers during Operation Barbarossa to compensate for the casualties suffered by the unit. 2,902 soldiers entered the division's rolls in 1941, a number substantially lower than the 5,700 men lost.[32] The regional composition of the troops that joined the 123rd ID also differed from the pattern set by the East Prussians and the Rhenish-Westphalian divisions, as the majority of its replacements failed to originate from Wehrkreis III. Initially, the division was content to wait for replacements

---

[29] 126 Inf. Div. Meldung vom 25.10; 126 Inf. Div. Meldung vom 21.11; 126 Inf. Div. Meldung vom 23.12, BA-MA RH 26–126/23; 126 ID Meldung 23.1, BA-MA RH 26–126/47.

[30] For an age breakdown of the various reserve groups, see the diagram in Kroener, "The Manpower Resources of the Third Reich," p. 833.

[31] Tätigkeitsbericht der Abt. IIa/b, Stand vom 30.9.41; Tätigkeitsbericht der Abt. IIa/b, Stand 31.12.41, BA-MA RH 26–126/131.

[32] Tätigkeitsbericht der Abt. IIa vom 15.7.41; Tätigkeitsbericht der Abt. IIa vom 15.7.–15.8.41; Tätigkeitsbericht der Abt. IIa vom 16.9.41–15.10.41; Tätigkeitsbericht der Abt. IIa vom 16.10.41–15.11.41; Tätigkeitsbericht der Abt. IIa vom 16.11.41–15.12.41, in BA-MA RH 26–123/161.

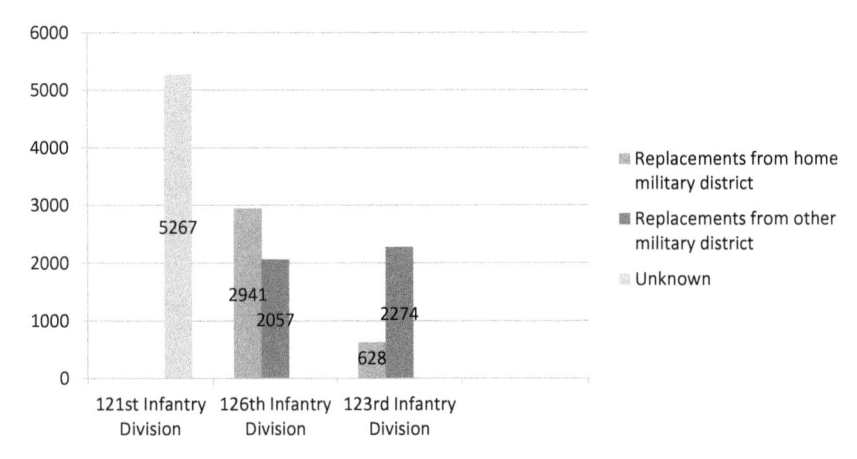

"The replacement situation is proving to be catastrophic" 205

Figure 6.4 Origin of replacements. Note: while specific numbers regarding the origin of the 121st ID's replacements are unknown, it is clear that the majority came from Military District I.

from the Berlin area, but when these were delayed, it was forced to turn to other sources of men.[33] Significant numbers of troops from Saxony, Hannover, Württemberg, Baden, and Rhineland-Westphalia entered the division's ranks. Of the 2,902 replacements received by the 123rd ID during 1941, only 628 men actually originated in Wehrkreis III (see Figure 6.4).

In addition to being generally drawn from areas outside the division's home region, the quality of the replacements in 1941 was also considered quite low by the 123rd ID. In late September, the 415th Infantry Regiment simply reported that the "*Ersatz* has no combat value."[34] Such complaints were echoed by the division's personnel officer.[35] He noted that many of the recruits not only possessed a "nonexistent" knowledge of machine guns but they also lacked "the necessary hardness against strains and hardship" needed by frontline soldiers. Fully 75 percent of the men from Württemberg were between the ages of thirty-five and forty and most were married and had children. Their "training is in every respect unsatisfactory" and, even worse, the men had "no real desire to be soldiers." The personnel officer concluded that "one can say from the start that the majority of the Württembergers will have no usefulness in

---

[33] Tätigkeitsbericht der Abt. IIa vom 15.7.41, BA-MA RH 26–123/161. The report noted that there were considerable gaps in the unit, but it was deemed important "to wait on sending men to the Feld-Ersatz Btl. by Stellv. Gen. Kdo. III AK."
[34] 23. September 1941, 9.00 Uhr, Von IR 415, BA-MA RH 26–123/32.
[35] Tätigkeitsbericht der Abt. IIa vom 16.9.41–15.10.41, BA-MA RH 26–123/161.

206   The failure of Operation Barbarossa

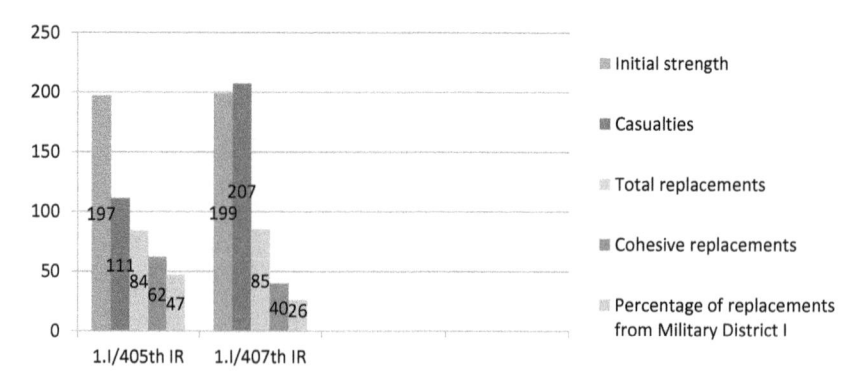

[Bar chart showing data for 1.I/405th IR and 1.I/407th IR with categories: Initial strength, Casualties, Total replacements, Cohesive replacements, Percentage of replacements from Military District I. Values shown: 1.I/405th IR: 197, 111, 84, 62, 47; 1.I/407th IR: 199, 207, 85, 40, 26]

Figure 6.5 Personnel changes in 1.I/405th Infantry Regiment and 1.I/407th Infantry Regiment, 121st Infantry Division, 1941

combat." Recognizing these training problems, division command placed the onus on junior officers for training the recruits: "the man should receive the basics for his conduct in battle in this campaign, with this enemy, in this terrain."[36] This proclamation foreshadowed what became a general practice for all the units within Army Group North, as frontline divisions became increasingly involved with the training of their own recruits as the war continued.

An examination of the company level allows for an even more detailed picture of the casualty and replacement process for the 121st, 126th, and 123rd IDs. The 1.I/405th and 1.I/407th of the 121st ID provide the first ground-level approach to Wehrmacht personnel policies (see Figure 6.5).

Though the companies' combat strength decreased, regional and unit cohesion were boosted by the reinforcements. Even with the Wehrmacht's replacement system creaking under the strains of the unprecedentedly costly fighting in the Soviet Union, 36 percent of the soldiers entering these companies originated in East Prussia. Cohesive replacements – consisting of men who were transferred from within the division and thus were well acquainted with its ethos, who entered the division through its field-training battalion or an infantry replacement battalion linked to the unit, or who were returning convalescents – totaled 102 men of 169 incoming recruits.

A similar situation existed within the ranks of the 126th ID. The 1.I/422 Infantry Regiment and 2.I/424 Infantry Regiment lost a total of 192 men during the first six months of war, with 153 entering their

[36] 123 Inf. Division Kommandeur, 18. Aug. 1941, Ausbildungsbefehl für das Marschbataillon, BA-MA RH 26–123/82. Emphasis in original.

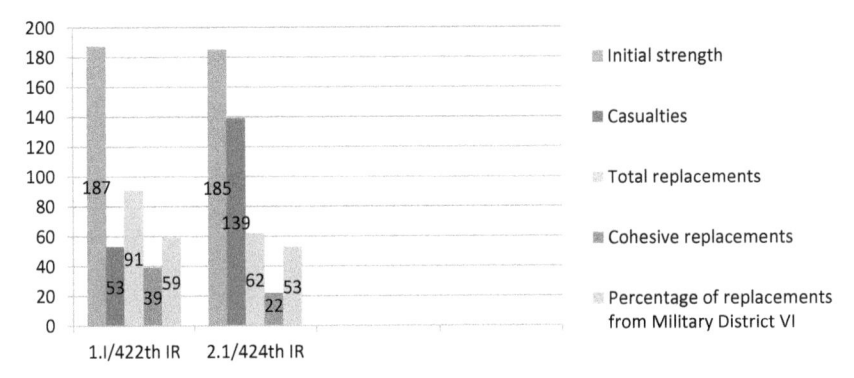

"The replacement situation is proving to be catastrophic" 207

[Bar chart showing:
- 1.I/422th IR: 187, 53, 91, 39, 59
- 2.I/424th IR: 185, 139, 62, 22, 53
Legend: Initial strength, Casualties, Total replacements, Cohesive replacements, Percentage of replacements from Military District VI]

Figure 6.6 Personnel changes in 1.I/422nd Infantry Regiment and 2.I/424th Infantry Regiment, 126th Infantry Division, 1941

ranks.[37] While only sixty-one of these recruits could be considered cohesive replacements, a total of eighty-seven men (57 percent of all recruits) did originate in Wehrkreis IV (see Figure 6.6).

Despite suffering a total of 258 casualties, the 123rd ID's 1st Company, 1.I/415th Infantry Regiment, and 1.I/416 Infantry Regiment received only 125 replacements and these served to dilute their regional cohesion.[38] While eighty-two of these men could be considered cohesive, a mere 17 percent came from the Berlin-Brandenburg area (see Figure 6.7).

The brief examinations of these rifle companies reveal several important points about Army Group North's infantry power in 1941. On the positive side, in two of the three divisions, regional cohesion

---

[37] See the 1. Inf. Regt. 422 (1./I.R.422) Erkennungsmarkenverzeichnis (Veränderungsmeldung), dated 7 July 1941 to 8 December 1941, WASt, 82026; 2. Inf. Regt. 424 Veränderungsmeldung zur Liste der ausgegebenen Erkennungsmarken, 7 August 1941 through 10 December 1941, WASt, 82066.

[38] 1. Kompanie Infanterie-Regiment 415 Erkennungsmarkenverzeichnis /Veränderungsmeldung, 7 July 1941 through 12 December 1941, WASt, 80744; 1. Kompanie Inf. Rgt. 416 1. Bataillon Erkennungsmarkenverzeichnis Veränderungsmeldung, 8 July 1941 to 22 December 1941, WASt, 80763. A word of caution regarding the reports from companies in the 123rd ID: following the encirclement of the 123rd ID in the Demiansk pocket in March 1942, company reports were neither as regular nor as accurate as they had been previously. To ensure accuracy, the various casualty reports submitted by the companies during the early period of the Demiansk encirclement have also been utilized. For the 415th Infantry Regiment, see Infanterie Regiment 415, Namentliche Verlustmeldungen Nr. 7: 7.12.1941–9.4.1942; and for the 416th Infantry Regiment, see Namentliche Verlustmeldung Nr. 8, Berichtszeitraum 16.10.41–20.12.41; Namentliche Verlustmeldung Nr. 3, Januar 1942; Nr. 4 Januar 1942; Nr. 5 Januar 1942; Nr. 6 Januar 1942; Nr. 7 Januar 1942; April 1942; Nr. 1, 1.–30. Mai 1942; Nr. 2, 1.–30. Mai 1942, and Nr. 3, 1.–30. Mai 1942, WASt; on the casualties and replacements for this company, see 1. Kompanie Infanterie-Regiment 415 Erkennungsmarkenverzeichnis /Veränderungsmeldung/, dated 12.7.1941 to 12.5.42, WASt, 80744.

208 The failure of Operation Barbarossa

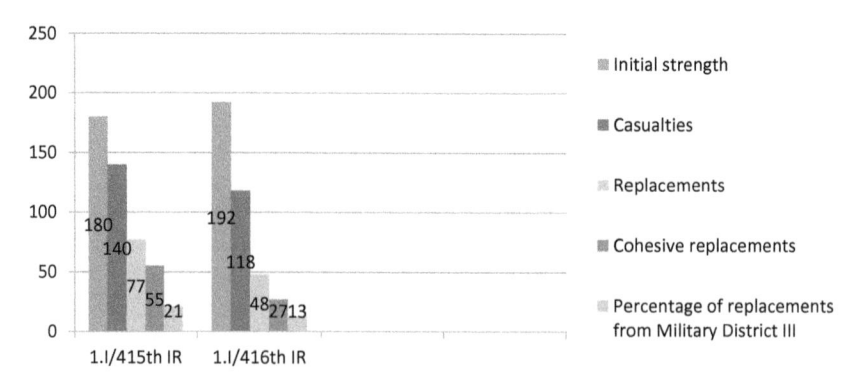

[Bar chart showing personnel data for 1.I/415th IR and 1.I/416th IR with values: 1.I/415th IR – 180, 140, 77, 55, 21; 1.I/416th IR – 192, 118, 48, 27, 13. Legend: Initial strength, Casualties, Replacements, Cohesive replacements, Percentage of replacements from Military District III]

Figure 6.7 Personnel changes in 1.I/415th Infantry Regiment and 1.I/416th Infantry Regiment, 123rd Infantry Division, 1941

was generally maintained with the addition of replacements. Only the 123rd ID failed to receive a majority of its replacements from its own *Wehrkreis*. The 121st ID also received a significant number of convalescent veterans, providing a welcome addition of experience and, perhaps even more importantly, reinvigorating old bonds between themselves and their comrades. In 1941, however, the negatives far outweighed the positives. The largest problem afflicting the replacement system was that it simply failed to provide enough men to make good the casualties of the eastern campaign. Companies that averaged 190 men at the outbreak of hostilities had decreased to a mere 133 by December, a loss of 30 percent of their original strength.[39] Exacerbating this problem of quantity, the recruits who entered these divisions were uniformly viewed as poor *Menschenmaterial* by divisional officers. Older married men who showed no interest in being soldiers provided little to no real value to infantry divisions that, in the case of the 123rd and 126th, faced continual combat. So not only did the quantity of replacements fail to meet requirements, the quality of such replacements was also substandard. The consequently weakened infantry – which constituted the majority of Army Group North's striking power until the end of September, at which time it became its *only* striking power – ensured that Leeb and his forces would be unable to fulfill their ever-expanding mission.

---

[39] If the 1.I/422 is removed from the equation – as its fifty-three casualties were by far the fewest and it received the third-highest number of replacements (seventy-two) – the average company strength drops to 117 soldiers.

II. "The supply situation is gradually taking on a catastrophic form": supply in Army Group North

The second major problem facing Army Group North was its supply situation. Arrogantly confident of victory by the fall of 1941, the German High Command completely underestimated the logistical requirements of the actual campaign. Reflecting the German military leadership's "attitudinal ... problem" towards questions of transport and supply, the topic simply failed to receive meaningful attention during the prewar planning period.[40] In a postwar interview, Halder declared that "the materiel has to serve the spiritual. Accordingly, our quartermaster service may never hamper the operational concept."[41] This dismissive attitude displayed by the former Chief of the German General Staff – especially noteworthy after the role supply played in the failure of Operation Barbarossa – was symptomatic of the general German view of logistics. The blind faith in a speedy victory that played such havoc with the manpower replacement system had similarly debilitating effects on the delivery of supplies to the front. As letters and diaries written by infantrymen in Army Group North clearly illustrate, some units were not receiving sufficient rations already as early as July and they consequently began to scour the countryside in hopes of supplementing their meager food.[42] Of the thirty-four daily trains requested by the army group, only eighteen were promised by the High Command and this number was reached on only a few occasions; on 19 December one single train actually reached Leeb's forces.[43] Once these limited trains reached the end of the rail lines, the army group faced more problems with its organic transport units, as these suffered a higher breakdown rate than those of any other army group, due primarily to the region's swampy terrain.[44] This issue, especially for

---

[40] Megargee, *Inside Hitler's High Command*, p. 122.   [41] Cited in ibid.
[42] Such practices were well known to the Red Army, which in turn utilized the hunger of German troops to its own benefit. War correspondent and novelist Vasily Grossman commented on this strategy: "A joke about how to catch a German. One simply needs to tie a goose by the leg and a German would come out for it. Real life: Red Army soldiers have tied chickens by the leg and let them come out into a clearing in the woods, and hid in the bushes. And Germans really did appear when they heard the chickens clucking. They fell right into the trap." Vasily Grossman, *A Writer at War: Vasily Grossman with the Red Army 1941–1945* (ed. and trans. Antony Beevor and Luba Vinogradova) (New York, 2005), p. 21.
[43] Schüler, "The Eastern Campaign as a Transportation and Supply Problem," p. 213, n. 6. According to the German Army's quartermaster, Army Group North's logistic situation was still the "the best by far" for the Eastern Army, even with such low numbers; see Creveld, *Supplying War*, p. 162. Leeb, *Tagebuchaufzeichnungen*, 19 December 1941, p. 420.
[44] Halder, *Kriegstagebuch*, vol. III, 3 August 1941, p. 149; Stahel, *Operation Barbarossa*, p. 349.

II Corps on the right flank of Sixteenth Army, was recognized by the highest levels of the German Army.[45] As the men advanced further east, the situation became even more strained. The onset of winter only exacerbated the system as both foodstuffs and clothing were increasingly needed by exhausted troops.[46] By mid-December, Leeb termed the situation "catastrophic," noting that "if a fundamental change doesn't take place here, a very difficult situation will arise."[47]

While each division had its own issues concerning supply, their specific experiences significantly differed from one another. Although the 121st ID failed to receive its requirements in both food and winter clothing, its relative situation compared very favorably to that of the 123rd and 126th IDs. These two divisions operated in an area described by Sixteenth Army as "an absolute desert without a hinterland" and were therefore unable to meet their needs by scouring the countryside; they also fell prey to a much more irregular delivery of supplies due to their distance from Army Group North's supply depots.[48] This proved especially true for the Rhinelanders during the Tichvin offensive and for the Berliners after advancing out of the Kholm bridgehead into the marshy Lake Seliger area. From a narrowly military perspective, an ill-equipped and poorly clad army's combat efficiency would obviously diminish. A broader overview, however, one that takes into account the army's interactions with the surrounding civilian population, highlights the deleterious effects of the Wehrmacht's supply problems on Soviet citizens.

III. "What matters is that Bolshevism must be exterminated": the Wehrmacht and the *Vernichtungskrieg*

The commander of the 121st ID's 407th Infantry Regiment presented his appreciation of the war in the Soviet Union in March 1942. In a report entitled "The Effects of the Soviet Peoples' Character on the Conduct of War," he wrote,

---

[45] Halder, *Kriegstagebuch*, vol. III, 23 July 1941, p. 106.
[46] For a discussion concerning the Wehrmacht's preparations for supplying winter clothing, see Müller, "Das Scheitern der wirtschaftlichen 'Blitzkriegstrategie,'" pp. 1161–3.
[47] Leeb, *Tagebuchaufzeichnungen*, 19 December 1941, p. 420. More generally, see Klaus A.F. Schüler, *Logistik im Russlandfeldzug: Die Rolle der Eisenbahn bei Planung, Vorbereitung und Durchführung des deutschen Angriffs auf die Sowjetunion bis zur Krise vor Moskau im Winter 1941/42* (Frankfurt, 1987).
[48] "Aus dem Protokoll einer Besprechung beim Chef des Wehrwirtschafts- und Rüstungsamtes des OKW über die Wirtschaftslage in den okkupierten sowjetischen Gebieten, 29. und 30. Dezember, in Müller (ed.), *Deutsche Besatzungspolitik in der UdSSR*, Document 84, p. 206.

the peculiarity and character of the Soviet people have determined the form and development of the fighting in Russia. The Soviet theater of war differs from all of the other European theaters in this war in that the enemy fights with almost animal-like doggedness and cruelty and therefore every single German soldier is forced to fight to the last with absolute severity. The legacy of middle-Asian blood [*Bluterbe*] and the Bolshevik teaching of crass materialism, which strips even life of its higher worth and sees it as useful, something functional, so that the failure to reach a goal set from the outside ... means he has no legitimate reason to exist and merits being wiped out, is reinforced by the political and military leaders of all ranks and is also absorbed by numerous simple soldiers of the Red Army to perfection. We must not forget the spiritual dullness and weak character training of primitive, soulless Russians.

He added that while part of the Red Army's tenacity was due to "the Russian instinct," "the influence of the Judeo-Bolshevik terror methods" certainly contributed to Soviet staying power.[49]

While traditional German stereotypes of the Russian mentality are present in this remarkable document – the description of the "primitive, soulless Russians" and "simple soldiers" could certainly be drawn straight from the Wilhelmine era – more radical Nazi-type rhetoric permeates its entirety.[50] Discussions of "Asian blood," the "crass materialism" advocated by Marxism, the "animal-like doggedness" of the Red Army man, and the "Judeo-Bolshevik terror methods" all betray the influence of National Socialist thought. The fact that this report originated in the least arbitrarily violent division points to how pervasive such thinking was in the Wehrmacht. And this is an extremely important point: while claims that the overwhelming majority of the German Army fought Hitler's war as convinced racial warriors reek of exaggeration, it is nonetheless clear that the Nazi *Weltanschauung* complemented – and at times radicalized – the army's institutional approach to the war and that soldiers themselves absorbed various pieces of it during the war in the east. This ideological component to the war only exacerbated the problems caused by the manpower shortage and the supply difficulties, radicalizing the army's conception of military necessity.

The planning of the war as a blitzkrieg – the only campaign actually envisioned as such by the German High Command during the years of German victories – necessitated a quick decision, as neither the manpower nor the supply situation was sufficient for a long, drawn-out

---

[49] Infanterie-Regiment 407, Abt. Ia, Nr. 89/42 geh., 1.3.42, BA-MA RH 26–121/18.
[50] On traditional views of Russia and the Soviet Union, see Peter Jahn, "Russenfurcht und Antibolschwismus: Zur Entstehung und Wirkung von Feindbildern," in Rürup and Jahn, *Erobern und Vernichten*, pp. 47–62, especially pp. 52–9; Wette, *Die Wehrmacht*, pp. 14–25.

struggle. The immensity of the task before the Wehrmacht meant that any and all means would be employed to ensure victory. Mindful of the weakness of the invading army relative to the physical size of the Soviet Union, the army opted for the use of terror to ensure a submissive Soviet population.[51] The criminal orders should be collectively viewed not only as an expression of the ideological congruence between the military and political wings of the Third Reich but also as the logical evolution of the army's military culture and doctrine. The absolute need for speedy, offensive action lay at the heart of Operation Barbarossa. Even when decimated by casualties and exhaustion, the divisions were continually prodded along; rest would have to wait until after the final victory. In this quest for decisive victory, the army paid nearly no attention to the well-being of civilians. Traditional German stereotypes about Slavs and Russians, as well as Nazi ideological precepts, all played a role in this thinking, but the army's narrow focus on achieving victory no matter the cost ensured that civilians would have been caught in the cross fire regardless of ideology. Such a clash for survival between the two groups necessarily led to violence and brutality: here, Nazi ideology acted as an accelerant and not as the primary cause.

The Commissar Order provides the best example of the fusion of ideological and operational goals. Each division executed somewhere between five and ten commissars and *politruks*; in this respect their actions closely corresponded to those of the remainder of the *Ostheer*.[52] The motivation behind these murders, however, was a mix of military pragmatism and ideological stereotyping. The frequent references to commissars in war diaries, prisoner-of-war interrogations, and intelligence reports indicate that the Wehrmacht had elevated the commissar to a position of near mythic powers. Many German soldiers viewed commissars as the only reason the Red Army remained in the field; if these commissars were eliminated, then Red Army resistance would end that much quicker.[53] Here, ideology and pragmatism blended seamlessly together.

---

[51] Hürter, *Hitlers Heerführer*, p. 466.
[52] For the 121st ID, see 121 ID, Abt. Ic, 1.7.41, BA-MA RH 26–121/55; Ic Meldung, 3.9.41, BA-MA RH 26–121/56; *Geschichte der 121. Ostpreussische Infanterie-Division*, p. 43. For the 126th ID, see Aufklärungs-Abteilung 126, Tagesmeldung, 11.11.1941, BA-MA RH 26–126/19; Tätigkeitsbericht Ic, 17.11.41, BA-MA RH 26–126/117; Zwischenmeldung Infanterie-Regiment 426 vom 30.11.41, BA-MA RH 26–126/20. Römer notes that "the overwhelming majority of the German frontline units willingly put the Commissar Order into practice"; see Römer, *Der Kommissarbefehl*, p. 551; Förster, "Die Sicherung des 'Lebensraumes'," pp. 1258–65; Hartmann, *Wehrmacht im Ostkrieg*, pp. 477–515.
[53] Papers found on a dead commissar elucidated the primary tasks of such political officers: "education of the men in a spirit of unshakeable love and devotion to the Fatherland, to

The co-operation between the German Army and the SS-Police units in the latter's ideological war of genocide also highlights the importance of military necessity to the Wehrmacht. Army commanders viewed Himmler's police as a valuable resource in securing the spacious tracts of land behind the front lines as well as in liquidating ideological enemies who would inevitably oppose the Germans. The *Einsatzgruppen* in particular complemented the functions of the Wehrmacht during the initial drive to the east: while the army grappled with its Soviet counterpart, the *Einsatzgruppen* eliminated what were perceived as potential carriers of resistance. This "co-operation" between the two institutions functioned "exceedingly well" in Army Group North.[54] The majority of this co-operation took place in the rear areas, however. Only in mid-August did the army's pace slacken enough to allow for the police units to catch up to the front line, and even here it seems that Panzer Group 4 was the most receptive of Army Group North's subordinate units to working with the *Einsatzgruppen*.[55] Despite this slowing of operations, there is no evidence in the divisions' files of any co-operation during the invasion between the 121st, the 123rd, and the 126th IDs and SS-Police units. The experience of the 121st ID during its occupation of Pavlovsk, however, does suggest that even units which previously fought a clean and professional war could easily be caught up in the gears of genocide depending on the shifting circumstances. In all probability, the low number of Jews living

---

the Party, and to Soviet power, to drum into them a bitter hatred against the fascist villains, to consolidate a belief in victory, educate them in heroism, bravery, and sacrifice, and lasting willingness to fight to the last drop of blood"; 121. Inf. Division Abt. Ic, 21.12.41 to Generalkommando L. A.K., BA-MA RH 26–121/58. Transcripts of prisoner-of-war interrogations show that many captured Red Army soldiers confirmed this belief, even if they may have had entirely different motivations for doing so.

[54] Ereignismeldung UdSSR Nr. 12, 12. Juli 1941, NARA, RG 242, T-175, Roll 233.
[55] In a summary of Einsatzgruppe A's activities during the opening months of Operation Barbarossa, its commander Walther Stahlecker wrote "it must be stressed from the beginning that co-operation with the armed forces was generally good, in some cases, for instance with Panzer Group 4 under General Hoepner, it was very close, almost cordial. Misunderstandings which cropped up ... in the first days were cleaned up mainly through personal discussions"; *The High Command Case*, p. 332. Such a characterization has been vehemently challenged by former officers who served in Panzer Group 4; see Peter Steinkamp, "Die Haltung der Hitlergegner Generalfeldmarschall Wilhelm Ritter von Leeb und Generaloberst Erich Hoepner zur verbrecherischen Kriegführung bei der Heeresgruppe Nord in der Sowjetunion 1941," in Gerd Uberschär (ed.), *NS-Verbrechen und der militärische Widerstand gegen Hitler* (Darmstadt, 2000), pp. 47–61, here pp. 57–8. Only one explicit mention of co-operation with specific formations in Army Group North – in this case, Sixteenth Army – was found in an examination of the *Einsatzgruppen* situation reports and it was limited to the observation that "EK 1b, assigned to 16 Army, is moving with units spearheading the advance." See Ereignismeldung UdSSR Nr. 53, 15. August 1941, NARA, RG 242, T-175, Roll 233.

in this section of the Soviet Union proved more decisive in limiting co-operation between these infantry divisions and the police than any moral qualms. Nonetheless, the experiences of these three units illustrate that not every German infantry division in the *Ostheer* was inextricably entwined with the SS-Police units and their murderous tasks during Operation Barbarossa.

Perhaps the most revealing perspective concerning the importance of military necessity is that of Wehrmacht–civilian interaction. For all three divisions, civilians remained on the periphery of their existence in the Soviet Union, emerging out of the shadows only when irregular resistance appeared. The Germans' response to such partisan activity highlighted the extremely narrow vision of the army; instead of taking a broader approach to the civilian population, one that tried to solve potential problems and defuse opposition, the Germans resorted to brutality and terror in an attempt to physically eradicate any resisters and deter any potential hostility. No attempt to win hearts and minds existed during the advance. Only during the occupation of Pavlovsk did the behavior of the 121st ID begin to point towards a different understanding of military–civilian relations and this was only after several collective measures had been implemented by the division and SD units within the city.

Despite working within the same context, the three divisions did differ in their implementation of anti-partisan policies. Of the three units, the East Prussian 121st ID distinguished itself as the most humane and professional in its dealings with Soviet civilians during the advance of 1941. Despite coming under fire that it identified as originating from irregular troops on the first day of war, the division recorded the execution of "only" twenty-three partisans during its drive to Pavlovsk. Even more noteworthy was the division's reluctance to implement collective measures. On two separate occasions, the 121st ID would have been more than justified in implementing a collective measure against a village, according to traditional German antiguerilla doctrine that dated back some seventy years. In each case, the East Prussians arrested the males of a village and kept them under guard as the division passed through. This was the extent of the punishment, however: there were no mass executions and no burning down of the communities. On the whole, the 121st ID's mobile campaign in 1941 would be difficult to distinguish from those undertaken by German troops in the First World War, though such behavior certainly changed once the division settled into the occupation of Pavlovsk. Here the close working relationships it established with both the Economic Staff East and SS-Police forces heralded a descent into Nazi-style war, though its adherence to the idea of military necessity did allow for the implementation of more conciliatory policies.

The 123rd and 126th IDs, however, engaged in a more brutal war than their East Prussian comrades, with the Rhinelanders behaving in the most vicious fashion. Each division executed over fifty partisans or suspected partisans, with the Rhinelanders shooting well over 100. Each also resorted to public hangings and both kept corpses on display to terrorize the surrounding population, though here again the 126th ID utilized such practices more frequently. The Rhinelanders also carried out the only collective measure by the three divisions during the advance.[56] How does one explain the differences in behavior between the 121st, on the one hand, and the 123rd and 126th IDs, on the other?

Clearly, situational factors loom large here. Approximately 20,000 partisans were active in Army Group North's area of operations in 1941, with the vast majority operating in the Lake Ilmen sector; thus, both the 126th and especially the 123rd IDs faced a much larger and more active partisan movement than did the 121st ID.[57] Since the map of partisan strength corresponded to that of German weakness, overtaxed and exhausted German units increasingly resorted to terror as a means both to intimidate the population and to eradicate irregular resistance. Of the three divisions, the 121st ID was part of a larger force deployed in a relatively more constricted area than was the 123rd ID, which was undermanned for the numerous tasks it was charged with; the 126th ID fell somewhere in between the two extremes. Here the notion of military necessity has real explanatory power: both the 123rd and 126th IDs believed that the only way for them to carry out their military missions at the front was to utilize whatever means necessary to pacify their respective areas of operation. Since the divisions were constantly harangued by their superiors to maintain a breakneck pace, resistance demanded a quick and decisive response, or, in other words, terror. The fact that the units directed this policy against civilians deemed racial and political enemies by the state and High Command only eased the implementation of such brutal tactics.

German food policy in 1941 also starkly highlights the intersection of racial ideology and military necessity. Sent into the Soviet Union with limited rations, the troops needed to find their own sustenance along their invasion route. Such a situation presupposed an adversarial

---

[56] Sixteenth Army carried out a minimum of fifteen such collective measures between 7 September 1941 and 15 January 1942; see Steinkamp, "Die Haltung der Hitlergegner," p. 53.
[57] Leonid D. Grenkevich, *The Soviet Partisan Movement, 1941–1944: A Critical Historiographical Analysis* (London, 1999), p. 162. Hill conclusively shows that the partisan movement in the Leningrad area itself was numerically weak at this stage in the war; Hill, *The War Behind the Eastern Front*, pp. 76–9.

relationship between the soldiers and civilians as the question of food was necessarily a zero-sum game in northwest Russia in 1941. Constant requisitioning as well as the near-complete breakdown of economic activity in the region led to widespread starvation beginning in the fall of 1941 and continuing on into the spring of 1942. While this result corresponded with the wishes of German planners in Berlin, it caused several difficulties for soldiers at the local level. First, even though the military leadership peppered the troops with propaganda emphasizing the necessity of starving the Soviet populace, individual soldiers found the misery surrounding them increasingly divorced from abstract slogans and some offered assistance to civilians. Second, the Economic Staff East, charged with systematically exploiting the Soviet economy for Germany's needs, found the army's similarly predatory, yet much more arbitrary, policies completely disruptive and counterproductive to its mission. So instead of an orderly program of foodstuff collection and distribution that increased the army's combat efficiency, the arbitrary actions of the Wehrmacht – at both the institutional and individual levels – only increased the chaos and uncertainty in the communities of northwest Russia.

Third, and most importantly from the German perspective, the desperate conditions created by German food policies led to a growing resistance by the civilian population. In other words, the demands of military necessity – in this case living off the land – sparked another component of the same philosophy – ruthless reactions to any opposition. German policies thus kindled an ever-spiraling cycle of violence as Soviet civilians – viewed as nothing more than potential resisters by the Germans – had nothing to lose in opposing Wehrmacht rule.

7 The Soviet winter offensive, 1942
Demiansk and the Volkhov river

I. The Soviet counteroffensive, winter 1942

By the end of December 1941, Leeb believed that a "certain stabilization of the entire front [had] taken place" and that the "primary worry" facing his command was to "protect the troops to some extent from the tremendous cold."[1] Such an appraisal differed dramatically further to the south along the German front. Two days after Leeb's sanguine assessment of his army group, Halder wrote "*a very difficult day!*" as the southern and central sectors of the front faced very threatening developments.[2] Matters appeared especially ominous for Army Group Center as the primary Soviet counterattack targeted the increasingly exhausted and weary troops charged with seizing Moscow. Within four days of launching the operation, three separate German armies faced encirclement or isolation and the entire front threatened to crack.[3] While the 1941–2 winter crisis was most pronounced in the center of the front, Leeb's forces did not remain immune from such threats. By the end of 1941, Army Group North had settled into a tenuous defensive line that began on the Finnish Sea, wrapped around the outskirts of Oranienbaum and Leningrad, stretched eastwards to the Volkhov river, and followed the river south until it bulged out around the village of Demiansk. Such a defensive position directly resulted from both the Soviet counterattack at Tichvin, which forced the 126th ID, among other units, to retreat behind the Volkhov river, and the determined resistance of Leningrad. The Rhinelanders and the 121st ID each felt the sting of a surprisingly resurgent Red Army during December; unfortunately for Leeb and his men, this December fighting served as mere preliminary to the main event. After exceeding its initial expectations,

---

[1] Leeb, *Tagebuchaufzeichnungen*, 27 December 1941, p. 419; 2 January 1942, p. 428.
[2] Halder, *Kriegstagebuch*, vol. III, 29 December 1941, p. 369. Emphasis in original.
[3] For discussions of the Soviet Moscow offensive and the German reaction, see Klink, "Die Operationsführung," pp. 689–704; Hürter, *Hitlers Heerführer*, pp. 318–40.

Stavka (the Soviet High Command) expanded the Moscow counter-offensive to include the entirety of Army Group North.

In contrast to Leeb's quiet confidence, local commanders viewed the situation with more apprehension. Such a perspective clearly emerges from a meeting between the 126th ID's officer corps and its division commander.[4] Lieutenant General Paul Laux opened by recognizing the Soviets' seemingly unlimited ability to mobilize new formations: "despite the supposed destruction of x-hundred of divisions, tanks, etc., etc., enough reserves were available to launch a counterattack across the entire front." He considered the quality and efficiency of these newly raised units to be extremely low, however, arguing that the Red Army "is in the crisis of the war," forcing it to "get every guy who can carry a gun, no matter his age, even through terrorist measures ... he needs to put it all on one last card or he has lost." In comparison, the German soldier proved his "moral and material superiority" over the Red Army in December 1941 by holding the line despite being "prepared neither clothing- nor equipment-wise for the winter." He continued by declaring that the Rhinelanders' "superhuman achievements" in the face of "incredibly difficult terrain, the [Soviet] offensive, the outbreak of winter and the exhaustion of the troops" constituted a "glorious chapter in German military history."

Finally, he placed Germany's current predicament into historical context. The Red Army planned a similar fate for the Wehrmacht as the Russian Imperial Army had for Napoleon's Grande Armée. In order to avoid the catastrophe that befell the French, the commander painted a picture that called for grim and determined resistance to the final soldier: "behind us is nothing more than further Russian expanses, extremely deficient in roads, covered in snow, and frozen. There are no established positions or reserves!" Therefore, retreat simply was not an option: "through the use of the last man and the last weapon," the present "crisis" for the German Army could also be overcome as long as all soldiers, both frontline and rear-area, displayed "fanatical decisiveness." Such an attitude would enable soldiers "to hold every village to the last bullet, even when encircled." Only after the exhaustion of all ammunition could the troops break out to the next village. Upon leaving, though, the soldiers needed to destroy everything: "no village that fell into their hands would be useful to the Russians."

He continued by arguing that the winter actually helped the Germans since the deep snow limited the Red Army to small patrols armed only

---

[4] Kommandeur Besprechung am 12.1.42, BA-MA RH 26–126/47.

with light weaponry and the Rhinelanders "really had no need to have any fear of these." This implied, of course, that massed infantry attacks supported by armor and artillery had caused a great amount of anxiety, if not panic, in the ranks of the 126th ID in the fighting in December 1941. In fact, the commander of the 126th ID implicitly recognized both the quantitative superiority of the Red Army and its qualitative superiority in weaponry and equipment. The increasingly utilized trope of the supremacy of the individual German soldier vis-à-vis his Soviet counterpart remained the only advantage for the Wehrmacht in northwest Russia, and even here the commander acknowledged the men's fear and anxieties concerning large-scale Red Army attacks. In perhaps his most revealing comment on the state of the 126th ID in January 1942, he argued that the freezing temperatures and constant snow *helped* the Rhinelanders: if soldiers who possessed only minimal winter clothing and suffered from severe shortages of food needed to be thankful for the onset of winter because it limited the offensive ability of Soviet troops, then the Germans indeed faced an increasingly dangerous military situation. Such a detailed appreciation of the 126th ID's situation highlights both the various problems facing the division and the relative disconnect between the various levels of the Wehrmacht hierarchy during the winter of 1941–2.

A mere week after writing that his main fears for his men concerned their winter clothing, Leeb's appreciation of the situation dramatically changed. As part of "Stalin's first strategic offensive" designed to destroy Army Groups North and Center, the three Soviet *fronts* facing Army Group North – the Leningrad, Volkhov, and Northwestern – launched a major attack on German positions north and south of Lake Ilmen during the second week of January 1942.[5] Designed to smash the "bottleneck," i.e. the German-controlled corridor separating Leningrad from the Red Army, and thereby break the siege, as well as to destroy German troop concentrations in the Leningrad, Demiansk, and Staraia Russa areas, Army Group North faced complete destruction if the offensive evolved as imagined by Stalin and *Stavka*. Despite the fact that the offensive's objectives in the Leningrad area far outstripped the Red Army's capabilities and therefore possessed little chance of complete success, the size and timing of the offensive nonetheless led to numerous crises for the Wehrmacht, including the 123rd and 126th IDs (see Map 7.1).[6]

---

[5] Erickson, *The Road to Stalingrad*, p. 297; Glantz, *The Battle for Leningrad*, pp. 149–50.
[6] Glantz, *The Battle for Leningrad*, p. 153; Erickson, *The Road to Stalingrad*, p. 297. For a more recent appraisal, see Mawdsley, *Thunder in the East*, pp. 127–9.

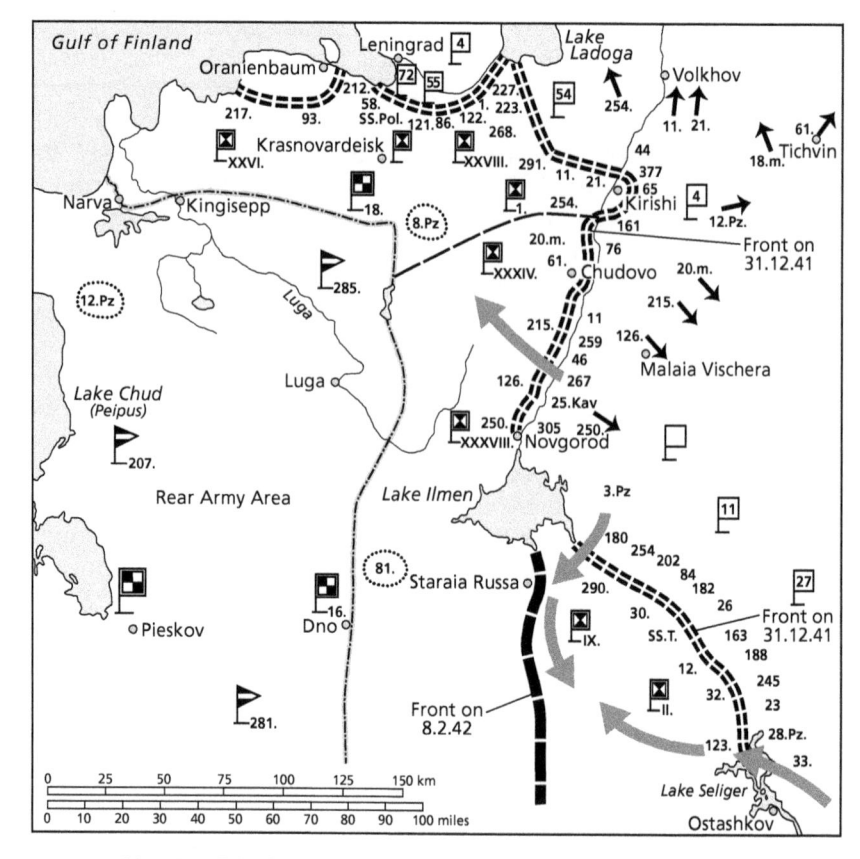

Map 7.1 The Soviet winter offensive, January 1942

II. The 123rd Infantry Division and the formation of the Demiansk pocket

South of Lake Ilmen, the Soviet Northwest *Front* launched its part of the offensive on 7 January with its northern wing given the task of seizing Staraia Russa and its southern wing charged with capturing Demiansk, a small village whose name would soon become synonymous with the life-and-death struggle of the Eastern Front.[7] The second stage of the offensive called for the combined forces of the Northwest *Front* to drive

---

[7] Mawdsley notes that Demiansk had a population of only 2,500 in 1926; see his *Thunder in the East*, p. 125.

The 123rd ID and the formation of the Demiansk pocket 221

to the northwest to cut off the retreat of German troops from the Volkhov area.[8] While the initial assault on Staraia Russa made excellent progress and Red Army units reached the outskirts of the city on 8 January, German resistance had stiffened by the third day of the attack and the Wehrmacht maintained its possession of the important supply and transportation hub.[9] In the Demiansk area, however, the Red Army's offensive threatened the destruction of Sixteenth Army's southern front as well as the tenuous link that remained between Army Groups North and Center.

As early as 20 December, the highest echelons of the German leadership recognized that Army Group North and especially the exposed Demiansk position were targeted by the Red Army.[10] The entire German military hierarchy in the region – from the army group to the division level – viewed a Soviet attack on the Berliners' position as inevitable, but no steps were taken to reinforce the line.[11] Here, the strained manpower situation of the Reich proved extremely detrimental to German interests. The division, already stretched exceedingly thin, needed to allocate significant numbers of men to patrol the rear area for partisans as well as to secure its supply lines. Anticipating the arrival of another division to help it hold the front, it instead received a security regiment, an inadequate response to the situation.[12] In other words, the multiplicity of tasks facing an exhausted combat division ensured that it could not successfully fulfill its primary task: combat. Since no substantial reserves existed to strengthen the line, the 123rd ID faced the onslaught of five enemy divisions by itself and its front predictably broke on 10 January.[13]

The events of January demonstrated the advantages and disadvantages of being a secondary theater of operations. While Army Group Center received the lion's share of reinforcements, it also received the undivided attention of Hitler and the OKH. Such supervision resulted in the field commanders possessing very little freedom of action as Hitler became

---

[8] Glantz, *The Battle for Leningrad*, p. 150.
[9] Ibid., p. 184; Klink, "Die Operationsführung," p. 713.
[10] Hitler himself declared that "large attacks will start against Army Group North in ten to fourteen days"; Halder, *Kriegstagebuch*, vol. III, 20 December 1941, p. 360. Halder also noted that such events increasingly pointed to such an attack during the last days of December; for example, see his entries for 27 December 1941, p. 367, and 28 December 1941, p. 368.
[11] 123 ID KTB, 6.1.42, BA-MA RH 26–123/46. Leeb, *Tagebuchaufzeichnungen*, 9 January 1942, p. 431; Sydnor, *Soldiers of Destruction*, p. 211.
[12] 123 ID KTB, Überblick von 16.12.41–5.1.42, BA-MA RH 26–123/46.
[13] On the breakthrough, see 123 ID KTB, 10.1.42, BA-MA RH 26–123/46; Leeb, *Tagebuchaufzeichnungen*, 10 January 1942, p. 432.

overly involved in the decision-making process down to the tactical level. In contrast, Army Group North, though generally starved of tangible support, retained a more pronounced freedom of action than its counterparts to the south.[14] Leeb had already exploited this situation in December by ordering the retreat from Tichvin first and receiving permission second, and he attempted a similar tactic after the Soviets tore open the 123rd ID's positions.[15] By the evening of 10 January, Soviet troops had penetrated the German defensive line to such an extent that Leeb feared the "useless sacrifice" of the division's infantry regiments if they were not allowed to withdraw.[16] Hitler, however, emboldened by the success of the "No Step Back" order of 21 December in staunching the bleeding on the central sector of the front, was determined to replicate the feat in the Demiansk region.[17] Despite the "Führer's strict order" to the 123rd ID instructing them "stay where they were," events at the tactical level forced both corps and division command to permit various withdrawals, though not before ten strongpoints "fell after heroic defense to the last bullet."[18] Such a description meant the fighting had degenerated into "bloody hand-to-hand combat ... with axes, hatchets, spades and rifle-butts."[19] The commander of the 416th Infantry Regiment described the retreat:

the physical and psychological condition as well as the combat strength of the troops were already weakened following the first difficult night march through meter-high snow, by the freezing cold, and by the fighting at Lake Stersh. This situation worsened daily. No supply, constantly increasing numbers of sick, wounded,

---

[14] Hürter, *Hitlers Heerführer*, p. 340. An examination of Halder's diary in late December and early January strikingly illustrates the very different levels of attention given to each front. While Leeb eventually resigned due to disagreements with Hitler over operational matters, it is certainly noteworthy that he was only high-ranking officer in the northernmost army group reassigned as opposed to the hemorrhaging of commanding officers in Army Group Center.

[15] For a detailed examination of the decision-making process behind Army Group North's retreat, see Megargee, *Inside Hitler's High Command*, pp. 143–9.

[16] Leeb, *Tagebuchaufzeichnungen*, 10 January 1942, p. 432; Halder, *Kriegstagebuch*, vol. III, 12 January 1942, pp. 381–2.

[17] For the order, see Fernschreiben, FHQu, den 21. Dezember 1941, in Schramm, *KTB OKW*, vol. II, pp. 1085–6. Such sentiments were amplified in a further order issued on 26 December – see ibid., pp. 1086–7 – and one promulgated two days before the attack. See Führerbefehl vom 8. Januar 1942, betr. Verteidigung aller Stellung, in Schramm, *KTB OKW*, vol. II, pp. 1264–5.

[18] Leeb, *Tagebuchaufzeichnungen*, 12 January 1942, p. 432; 123 ID KTB, 11.1.42, BA-MA RH 26–123/46. On the defense of the strongpoints, see 123 ID KTB, 15.1.42, BA-MA RH 26–123/46.

[19] Bericht über die Kampfhandlungen im Abschnitt des verst. I. R. 418 während des sowj.-russ. Angriffs nördl. Ostaschkow in der Zeit vom 9.1.1942 bis 27.1.1942, BA-MA RH 26–123/85.

The 123rd ID and the formation of the Demiansk pocket   223

and frostbite made both combat and retreat much more difficult ... The attitude of all officers, NCOs, and men was, in view of the tremendously difficult conditions – continual combat against a superior enemy, no supply, a lack of ammunition, icy cold between –30° and –40° [Celsius], no special clothing or equipment for winter, day-long marches through meter-high snow – admirable.[20]

For the first time during Army Group North's war, a Soviet offensive threatened the destruction of a German division as well as the encirclement of its parent corps.

The superior mobility of the Red Army allowed it frequently to capture sections of planned lines in the German rear before Wehrmacht combat units could completely occupy them, while the chaos accompanying the German retreat led to a complete breakdown of the supply situation, leading to the majority of the 123rd ID's men having neither food nor blankets during a period when temperatures reached –40° Celsius.[21] A lack of such essential winter equipment had catastrophic effects on the division's combat effectiveness. The veterinary company, forced into a combat role, reported 108 cases of frostbite (in comparison to thirty-three casualties) during a two-week period, while the 418th Infantry Regiment recorded 148 men sick or with frostbite and forty-eight casualties. The Reconnaissance Section reported 160 cases of frostbite in addition to a further 169 sick soldiers.[22] Despite such desperate conditions, Hitler proved unwilling to sanction a retreat, and instead ordered on 13 January that "the position is to be defended to the last man." The division commander issued his own order the following day threatening "a drumhead court-martial for any soldier who leaves his position without permission" and, "in urgent cases," immediate execution without court-martial.[23] While Hitler's order prevented any type of planned large-scale retreat, Soviet pressure forced

---

[20] Bericht des Kommandeurs des verst. IR 416 über den Verlauf des Rückmarsches vom 11.–26.1.1942, BA-MA RH 26–123/87.
[21] 123 ID KTB, 15.1.42, BA-MA RH 26–123/46; Artillerie-Regiment 123, Abteilung Ia, Betr.: Gefechtsbericht, 21.2.42, BA-MA RH 26–123/86.
[22] For the veterinary company, see Abschnitt Schroeder, Abteilung IIa, 29.1.1942; for the 418th Infantry Regiment, see Bericht über die Kampfhandlungen im Abschnitt des verst. I. R. 418 während des sowj.-russ. Angriffs nördl. Ostaschkow in der Zeit vom 9.1.1942 bis 27.1.1942; and on the Reconnaissance Section, see Aufklärungs-Abt. 123, Gefechtsbericht für die Zeit vom 8.1 bis 30.1.1942. All three reports are in BA-MA RH 26–123/85. The 123rd ID's frostbite casualties fall into the larger pattern experienced by the Wehrmacht during the winter 1941–2 as 228,000 German soldiers suffered from frostbite; see Mueller-Hillebrand, *Das Heer 1933–1945*, vol. III, *Der Zweifrontenkrieg*, p. 28.
[23] For Hitler's order, see Korpsbefehl, 13. Januar 1942, BA-MA RH 26–123/50; on the division's order, see 123 ID Kommandeur, Erfahrungen der Abwehrkämpfe, 14. Januar 1942, BA-MA RH 26–123/48.

the Germans into haphazard and hasty tactical withdrawals that eventually opened up the right flank of II Corps.[24] Differing appreciations of the situation led to a contentious discussion between Leeb and Hitler on 13 January. The field marshal, utterly disgusted by Hitler's obstinate refusal to countenance the withdrawal of II Corps, submitted his resignation on 15 January, with Eighteenth Army's commander Georg von Küchler taking control of Army Group North on 18 January.[25] The reshuffling of the army group's leadership, however, did nothing to stop the outlines of the Demiansk pocket, in which the 123rd ID occupied the southeastern-most position, becoming visible a mere week after the attack commenced.

On 19 January, division command characterized the motley collection of units that survived the retreat as "physically and spiritually no longer capable of action" following a "ten-day march through cold and snow and in constant fear of being cornered by the enemy." Of the 8,000–9,000 men available, over three-quarters suffered from severe frostbite, including over 90 percent of the II/416th Infantry Regiment.[26] In a report to II Corps, the division commander

points out the seriousness of the situation, especially the high number of cases of frostbite, that have consequently led to a rapid sinking of combat strength, as well as the enormous strain on the nerves of the men in the forward lines, that has led to many crying fits in the line. The Ia emphatically stresses that the men are at the end of their strength.[27]

The divisional doctor reinforced this point by noting that "the troops are, through the many week-long strains, partially undernourished and the majority of them are overtired and exhausted."[28] Another officer pointed out that "the severe cold and demands placed on every man through fortification construction and sentry duty are decisively weakening the combat ability of the companies." He added that shoddy equipment,

---

[24] AK II KTB, 17.1.42, BA-MA RH 24–2/107. Klink argues that this order, much like Hitler's earlier "No Step Back" order, saved much heavy equipment and artillery. He also places the crisis in Army Group North within the context of the much more desperate situation facing Army Group Center. Both Hitler and Halder felt that the withdrawal of II Corps would unhinge the entire northern flank of Army Group Center; see Klink, "Die Operationsführung," pp. 714–15.

[25] Leeb, *Tagebuchaufzeichnungen*, 13 January 1942, 15.1.42, 18 January 1942, pp. 433–44; Halder, *Kriegstagebuch*, vol. III, 13 January 1942, p. 383.

[26] AK II KTB, 19.1.42, 21.1.42, BA-MA RH 24–2/107.

[27] 10.30 Uhr an II A.K., BA-MA RH 26–123/50.

[28] Divisionsarzt 123 Infanterie Division, Betr.: Gesundheitsbericht, 31. Januar 1942, BA-MA RH 26–123/50; Bataillonsarzt II./Infanterie-Rgt. 415, 6.2.42, BA-MA RH 26–123/83.

especially boots, led to frostbite which only further taxed the men.[29] The divisional troops in the worst condition were those encircled in the Kholm pocket, located southwest of the main body of the 123rd ID. The artillery regiment's doctor described the condition of the men following the retreat as "completely shocking," with some of them in "an unbelievably dilapidated condition." He saw soldiers with "bare feet, half-naked and on all fours crawling through the high snow [and] those who were wounded, painstakingly forging ahead, without any help." A company commander wrote, "since the middle of January, the men have had no clean underwear, and what is more, have not had any time to wash the underwear they have been wearing due to operations. It is dreadful when one sees the completely filthy and lousy things."[30] Bludgeoned by the Soviet offensive, the 123rd ID desperately tried to survive a struggle against the Red Army and the unforgiving climate.

In early February, the division stabilized its line, though it highlighted the precariousness of the position in a report to II Corps: "the manning of the position has become so thin, that the line is no longer an HKL [*Hauptkampflinie* or main combat line] but rather a security line."[31] The 123rd ID began to comb through its rear-area units in hopes of strengthening its combat units and defending its tenuous position.[32] While the use of such troops for combat had severely disrupted the division's supply earlier in the war, this became a moot point by 8 February.[33] On this day, "the last truck from the rear area reached II AK at 7 p.m." as Soviet troops completely closed the pocket by late evening, encircling the entire II Corps as well as units from X Corps.[34] Formations had been receiving a considerable amount of their supplies

---

[29] Infanterie-Regiment 415, Abteilung Ia, Betr.: Gefechtsberichte für die Zeit vom 8.–30.1.42, BA-MA RH 26–123/86.

[30] Stabsarzt u. Regts.-Arzt A.R. 123, Kurzer Bericht über die sanitären Verhältnisse während des Rückmarsches der Stabsbattr. IV./-, 11./-, u. 4./- A.R. 123 und der Verteidigung in Cholm vom 11.1.42 bis 5.5.1942, BA-MA RH 26–123/87; Auszug aus einem Brief des Lt.d.R. Hannemann, Kp.-Führer der Reste II./IR 416 u. Teile 13. u-14. IR 416, v. 13.3.42, BA-MA RH 26–123/87.

[31] Tagesmeldung 9. Februar 1942, BA-MA RH 26–123/203.

[32] 123 ID KTB, 7.2.42, BA-MA RH 26–123/46. Already in mid-January, one of the division's combat groups had over 200 men from the veterinary company and sixty-seven men from the medic company in the front line; Kämpfstärke und Waffenbesetzung der Gruppe Schröder, no date, BA-MA RH 26–123/48.

[33] Halder, *Kriegstagebuch*, vol. III, 10 February 1942, p. 397.

[34] AK II KTB, 8.2.42, BA-MA RH 24–2/107. The units trapped in the pocket included elements of X Corps's Waffen-SS Totenkopf Division, the 290th and 30th IDs as well as II Corps's 12th, 32nd, and 123rd IDs; Abschlussmeldung. Die Verteidigung der "Festung Demjansk" vom 8.2–21.4.42 durch das II AK im Rahmen der vom 8.1.–21.4.42 dauernden Abwehrschlacht im Höhengelände des Waldaj und südostw. des Ilmensees, BA-MA RH 26–123/220.

Illustration 7.1 After the establishment of the Demiansk pocket, supplies could only be delivered to the encircled German troops by air.

from air-drops for approximately one week by this point; now, this was the only manner in which food, ammunition, and other necessities could get through.[35] The first two days of exclusive air-drops did not bode well for the future: while II Corps estimated that 300 tons would fulfill the daily minimum requirements for the approximately 100,000 men in the pocket, a mere sixteen tons were dropped on 9 February and only twenty-seven tons on the following day, leading it to caustically note that "the corps cannot survive with this type of supply."[36]

The paucity of air-drops certainly contributed to the appallingly high number of cases of frostbite in the division: between December 1941 and March 1942, some 2,488 men suffered from exposure to the severe cold in the 123rd ID.[37] The majority of the 123rd ID still lacked winter clothing and with temperatures reaching thirty degrees below zero and snow at "chest-deep" levels, the failures of the Wehrmacht's supply system only increased the difficulties of holding the line.[38]

[35] IVa, Tätigkeitsbericht für die Zeit vom 1.2.–28.2.42, 1.4.1942, BA-MA RH 26–123/226.
[36] Ibid., 10.2.42.
[37] Tätigkeitsbericht der Abteilung IIa vom 16.2.42–15.3.42, BA-MA RH 26–123/163.
[38] Sydnor, *Soldiers of Destruction*, p. 217.

Once the pocket was closed, Red Army forces hammered at the encircled German troops and members of the 123rd ID counted over 3,500 dead in front of its positions between 16 January and 15 March.[39] In addition to fending off numerous infantry assaults, massive artillery bombardments pounded the Berliners, which, according to the Germans, specifically targeted dwellings. This became part of general Soviet strategy towards the pocket as the SS-Totenkopf Division also complained of the destruction of all shelters.[40] The continual loss of lodging during the winter contributed to what one officer viewed as an "alarming ... sinking of the men's physical and moral powers of resistance."[41] Casualties and the inability to send any more than a trickle of replacements into the pocket forced 688 rear-area soldiers into frontline combat roles – 512 of which manned front positions for approximately one month without break.[42] Within two weeks, this number had nearly doubled to 1,268 rear-area soldiers in the main battle line, including forty-five from the medic company and 168 from the veterinary company.[43] These troops were much less prepared for winter fighting than even the regular infantry forces. The veterinary company acerbically noted that the 109 men under its command lacked sixty-five pairs of boots, 100 pairs of socks, eighty pairs of gloves, 100 pairs of underwear, and 130 wool blankets. Lacking these necessary articles for winter survival as well as basic combat items such as thirty-two steel helmets, the company commander unsurprisingly reported that "the morale of the troops is depressed."[44] The lowering of rations by a third at the end of January also had a negative effect on the men's spirits.[45] By this point, the primary meal for troops within the pocket consisted of thirty-six grams of dried vegetables and sixty grams of horse meat replete with bones; reports from prisoners taken by the Soviets indicate that food was in such short supply that Germans had been tried for eating oats

---

[39] 18.2.42, 18.3.42, BA-MA RH 26–123/46.
[40] Sydnor, *Soldiers of Destruction*, p. 219, n. 10.
[41] Tagesmeldung 5. Februar 1942, BA-MA RH 26–123/52.
[42] Tagesmeldung 7. Februar 1942, BA-MA RH 26–123/52. The crisis facing the division clearly emerges from the company-level personnel records. Between the months of January and May 1942, only one company tallied a monthly casualty total and it did so only once. The 1.I/415th IR reported fifty-seven casualties for January to February 1942; this from a total of 113 men available to the company highlights the manpower crises facing the division. See 1. Kompanie Infanterie-Regiment 415 Erkennungsmarkenverzeichnis /Veränderungsmeldung/, WASt, 80744.
[43] Gruppe Rauch, no date [presumably 20.2.42 or 21.2.42], BA-MA RH 26–123/88.
[44] Veterinärkompanie 123, Betr.: Zustandsbericht der Vet. Kp. 123, 27. Februar 1942, BA-MA RH 26–123/203.
[45] Kommandierende General des II Armeekorps, Qu. Nr. 80/42 geh., 18.1.1942, BA-MA RH 26–123/219.

designated for horses.[46] When II Corps issued yet another directive calling on its subordinate units to fill the gaps in the line with rear-area troops, the 123rd ID's commander could truthfully reply that no superfluous troops remained in the rear; it was stripped bare.[47] Short of supplies and men, the 123rd ID dug in and hoped to survive the encirclement.

III. Crisis on the Volkhov: the 126th Infantry Division and the Volkhov pocket

While the Soviet offensive south of Lake Ilmen threatened to split the link between Army Group North and Center as well as annihilate II Corps, the main thrust of the Red Army's winter offensive was designed to advance across the Volkhov river, destroy German troop concentrations in the Liuban–Tosno–Mga area, and subsequently break the siege of Leningrad.[48] Though skirmishing on the Volkhov flared on and off following the German withdrawal in late December, the full brunt of a five-army Soviet offensive fell on German troops, including the 126th ID, on 8 January 1942.[49] Though his men initially held the line, Leeb had no illusions regarding the ability of his forces to withstand the Soviet offensive and this led him to contact Küchler on 11 January and tell him to prepare contingency plans for the withdrawal of troops from the siege line in case they were needed on the Volkhov.[50] Soviet pressure continued to increase until a breakthrough of the German lines at the junction of the 126th ID and the 215th ID occurred on 14 January; from this point on the Rhinelanders faced an unremitting war of attrition.[51]

Complaining of heavy fighting along its entire front, the division made a frantic request for both replacements and Luftwaffe support; without such assistance, it "appeared to be impossible" to carry out its orders.[52] A mere two days after the Red Army's breakthrough, heavy fighting rendered several of the division's infantry battalions "no longer capable

---

[46] Bartov, *The Barbarization of Warfare*, p. 25.
[47] For II Corps order, see Fernschreiben von Gen. d. Inf. Graf Brockendorff, 7.3.42, BA-MA RH 26–123/53. For the division's reply, see Gruppe Rauch Kommandeur, Nr. 191/42. geh., 17. März 1942, BA-MA RH 26–123/54.
[48] Glantz, *The Battle for Leningrad*, p. 150.
[49] Halder, *Kriegstagebuch*, vol. III, 8 January 1942, p. 377. It should be noted that a Soviet *front* was roughly equivalent in size to a German corps.
[50] Leeb, *Tagebuchaufzeichnungen*, 12 January 1942; Klink, "Die Operationsführung," p. 714.
[51] Leeb, *Tagebuchaufzeichnungen*, 14 January 1942, p. 437; Glantz, *The Battle for Leningrad*, pp. 157–67.
[52] 126 ID KTB, 15.1.42, BA-MA RH 26–126/34.

of combat."⁵³ On what has been described as a "black day for Army Group North," the Soviet offensive disintegrated a portion of the 126th ID's front, tearing a six-mile gap between it and the 215th ID and, in the process, severing the junction between Sixteenth and Eighteenth Armies.⁵⁴ The Second Shock Army poured through the gap, pounding away at the 126th ID while simultaneously driving into the German rear and fanning out in an attempt both to sow chaos in the rear of Sixteenth Army and to seize the important rail junction of Liuban.⁵⁵ The division certainly recognized the precariousness of its situation:

> our own situation has been basically determined by the high number of combat casualties and losses from frostbite which the division has suffered in the now ten days of continual fighting in the Volkhov position. The powers of resistance of the troops, who have been fighting with the utmost courageousness, have been considerably reduced as a result of the relentless pressure of an enemy considerably superior in numbers and heavy weapons as well as the terrific strains caused by the weather and equipment unsuitable for the weather. The division awaits the enemy's mass attacks with great concern.⁵⁶

During the first three weeks of fighting after the Red Army penetrated the Volkhov front, the 126th ID suffered nearly 2,500 casualties; approximately a thousand of these were due to frostbite.⁵⁷ The 426th Infantry Regiment bore the lion's share of these casualties and division command considered it "practically shattered," with its combat power reduced to that of a "weak battalion."⁵⁸ Despite these heavy casualties, the 126th ID regrouped and, after utilizing baggage troops, artillerymen, and engineers as infantry, held the German position just south of the narrow corridor that linked the mass of the Second Shock Army with the Red Army units east of the Volkhov river.⁵⁹

---

[53] 126 Infanterie-Division, Tagesmeldung vom 16.1.42 an XXXVIII A.K., BA-MA RH 26-126/38. Leeb, however, considered the situation not as serious as that in the Demiansk area due to the imminent arrival of reinforcements; see Leeb, *Tagebuchaufzeichnungen*, 16 January 1942, p. 439.

[54] Gerald R. Kleinfeld and Lewis A. Tambs, *Hitler's Spanish Legion: The Blue Division in Russia* (Carbondale, 1979), p. 165; Werner Haupt, *Heeresgruppe Nord, 1941–1945* (Bad Nauheim, 1967), p. 119.

[55] Erickson, *The Road to Stalingrad*, p. 319.

[56] 126 ID KTB, 22.1.42, BA-MA RH 26-126/34.

[57] 126 ID KTB, 28.1.42, BA-MA RH 26-126/34; Generalkommando XXXVIII A.K., Tagesmeldung vom 26.1.42, BA-MA RH 26-126/38.

[58] Verband 126 Infanterie-Division, Meldung 23.1.42, BA-MA RH 26-126/47. The crisis facing the army group at this point was clear to the OKH; Halder noted that there existed "a very tense situation for Army Group North on the Volkhov"; Halder, *Kriegstagebuch*, vol. III, 30 January 1942, p. 393.

[59] Verband 126 Infanterie-Division, Meldung, 21.2.42, BA-MA RH 26-126/47.

While the 126th ID manned strongpoints south of the breakthrough, the Soviets continued to force troops through the bottleneck into the German rear, reaching a total of approximately 100,000–130,000 in early February.[60] Due to the familiar problems of command and control, poor tactics, and insufficient supply, as well as improvised German defenses, Second Shock Army failed to seize Liuban and remained somewhat immobilized in the German rear.[61] Though this force obviously constituted a serious threat to Army Group North, it also presented the Germans with an opportunity to destroy a significant number of Red Army troops. While the Soviets continued their attempts to break out to the northwest, Hitler ordered Army Group North to prepare an offensive designed to choke off the Second Shock Army from its supplies and effectively encircle the Soviet army.[62] Two German assault groups, one each on both the northern and southern sides of the Soviet corridor, made preparations to seal the Soviet penetration. Combat elements of the 126th ID, formed into Kampfgruppe Laux (Battle Group Laux – named for the commander of the formation), took part in this offensive on its southern wing while the 121st Division's III/408th Infantry Regiment, foreshadowing the later deployment of the entire division, was shifted to the northern combat group and participated in the operation to seal the pocket.[63]

Launched on 15 March, Operation Raubtier (Beast of Prey) made "satisfactory" progress on its northern wing but only "minimal" progress on the southern wing during the first day of the operation.[64] This was, in part, due to the weakened condition of the units involved in the attack. During the previous month, members of the 126th ID suffered from a lack of sleep, insufficient supplies, poor hygienic conditions, and constant attrition through battle and sickness. The 424th Infantry Regiment complained that due to low combat strength, its men were able to get only two hours of sleep a night before having to retake their posts. It also informed division that the men were rife with lice and lacked even minimal food.[65] These circumstances, exacerbated by the men having

---

[60] Glantz, *The Battle for Leningrad*, p. 167. Seaton estimates the number of Red Army troops at 130,000; see Seaton, *The Russo-German War*, p. 243.
[61] Glantz, *The Battle for Leningrad*, pp. 168–9.
[62] Halder, *Kriegstagebuch*, vol. III, 2 March 1942, p. 412. What is notable about Hitler's intentions, as well as Halder's tacit approval of the Führer's directive, is that the men of the surrounded Second Shock Army were not to be taken prisoner; rather, they were "to be allowed to starve ... in the swamps."
[63] "Mein Regiment," BA-MA RH 37/3096.
[64] Halder, *Kriegstagebuch*, vol. III, 15 March 1942, p. 414.
[65] Tagesmeldung IR 424 v. 1.2.42, BA-MA RH 26–126/39; Tagesmeldung vom 31.1.42, BA-MA RH 26–126/39.

no "hope of being pulled out of the line," led morale to be "characterized as sinking to an alarming level."[66] The need to plug rear-area troops into the front line aggravated the supply situation as it left too few men to distribute the available food and ammunition.[67] Winter clothing did begin to trickle to the front, but the process was so slow that when a soldier received a pair of boots or a jacket, it was cause for celebration.[68] According to the 422nd Infantry Regiment, there were "too few bunkers and not enough tents [which] means the battalions are for the most part lying in the open with no protection from the cold," which reached lows of forty-two degrees below zero; these conditions led to a corresponding increase in illness, including bronchitis.[69] Soviet air attacks targeted dwellings, contributing to the scarcity of shelter.[70] The end result of inadequate shelter and clothing was the striking number of cases of frostbite reported by the division in January 1942: 1,212 soldiers were diagnosed with various degrees of frostbite and 870 had to be sent to hospitals in the rear to recover.[71] This constituted over 11 percent of the division's entire strength and nearly 16 percent of its combat strength.[72]

IV. War behind the front: radicalization during a time of crisis

During the crisis caused by the Soviet 1941–2 winter offensive, the behavior of the 123rd ID, much like that of the Wehrmacht as a whole, radicalized. With victory not only no longer assured but the very survival of the *Ostheer* now in doubt, the army ruthlessly implemented any and all measures that it deemed necessary for its combat effectiveness. Civilians, largely ignored as irrelevant to the military operation during the advance of 1941 (with the significant exception of those deemed resistant to German rule), now became both targets and tools of the Wehrmacht. Perhaps the most noteworthy manifestation of this strict interpretation of military necessity was the practice of scorched

---

[66] Tagesmeldung vom 6.2.42, BA-MA RH 26–126/39.
[67] Infanterie Regiment, Betr.: Nochmaliges Auskämmen der Trosse, 10.2.1942; Infanterie Regiment 422, Abt. Ia/Allg. Betr.: Bericht, 6.2.1942, BA-MA RH 26–126/40.
[68] Corporal Alois Bracher, 366 Infantry Regiment, 18.1.42, BfZ, Sammlung Sterz.
[69] Tagesmeldung vom 8.3.42, BA-MA RH 26–126/42; for the temperature, see Generalkommando XXXVIII AK, Tagesmeldung am AOK 16, 2.1.42, BA-MA RH 26–126/34; on the rise in bronchitis, see Tagesmeldung 11.3.42, BA-MA RH 26–126/42.
[70] 126 Infanterie Division, Zwischenmeldung an XXXVIII AK, 20.3.42, BA-MA RH 26–126/42.
[71] Tätigkeitsbericht der Abt. IIa/b, Stand: 31.1.1942, BA-MA RH 26–126/132.
[72] Stärken und Waffen für KTB Januar–Juni 1942, BA-MA RH 26–126/47.

earth.[73] During the Wehrmacht's frantic retreat on the center section of the front in mid-December, the destruction of shelters became part of the army's "daily routine" even before Hitler demanded that all "farms given up [by the Wehrmacht in retreat] are to be burned."[74] Both the 123rd and 126th IDs carried out such a callous, yet arguably pragmatic, policy. Two days after the main Soviet offensive smashed into Army Group North, II Corps instructed its subordinate formations that "all villages and buildings lying before the front are to be burned and destroyed."[75] When questions arose as to whether some villages should remain standing, the 123rd ID's commander emphatically responded "*Führerbefehl*! All houses without German soldiers are to be burned."[76] Corps and divisional command anticipated the army group's thinking on this matter; at the end of January, it stated that

the recent revival of partisan activity in the rear area ... demands that action be taken ... with the greatest ruthlessness. Partisans should be destroyed wherever they appear as should their hiding places [i.e. villages], if they are not needed by our troops for accommodation.[77]

Various subordinate units carried out this order during the retreat: numerous "quarters, cellars, and dugouts [were] burned," while one unit reported that it left a town "in bright flames" for the advancing Red Army.[78] That this would expose numerous civilians to the harsh winter was not lost on German authorities; a directive issued by the division one week later again ordered the destruction of all dwellings "without consideration for the civilian population."[79] In fact, civilians became targets of German troops as the division instructed its men that "all felt boots are to be taken <u>immediately</u> from the population without consideration of age or sex," an order that condemned numerous women and children to

---

[73] For more on the context of this policy during the winter crisis, see Hartmann, *Wehrmacht im Ostkrieg*, pp. 765–88.

[74] For the "daily routine," see ibid., p. 777. The 253rd ID received an order from XXIII Corps on 10 December calling for the "creation of a complete desert" in which "the Russian will find neither fortifications, nor a house, barn, a bale of straw, a cow, or a potato"; see Rass, *Menschenmaterial*, p. 380. For Hitler's declaration, see Halder, *Kriegstagebuch*, vol. III, 20 December 1941, p. 360.

[75] Generalkommando II Armeekorps, Ia Nr. 53/42 geh., Korpsbefehl Nr. 89, 11. Januar 1942, BA-MA RH 26–123/50.

[76] 12. Januar 1942, BA-MA RH 26–123/48.

[77] Cited in Bartov, *Hitler's Army*, p. 91.

[78] Gefechtsbericht über die Zeit vom 8.–30.1.1942, I/415; III Bataillon Infanterie-Regiment 415, Bericht über die Ereignisse bei IR 415 (ohne II./415) seit dem 11.1.42, 2.II.42. See also Bericht über den Einsatz der 2./Ar 123 vom 8.1.1942 bis 12.1.1942, BA-MA RH 26–123/85.

[79] Gruppe Rauch, Abt. Ia/Az. IVa, Div. Befehl Nr. 121, 18. Januar 1942, BA-MA RH 26–123/50.

Illustration 7.2 During the 1941–2 winter crisis, the German Army increasingly utilized civilians for labor.

severe frostbite and, in all likelihood, death.[80] While Hitler himself ordered that "prisoners and civilians were to be ruthlessly stripped of winter clothing" in late December, German units had been operating in this manner for weeks before the directive; once again, radicalizing impulses from below anticipated those from above.[81] The division also began to "mobilize ruthlessly [all] <u>inhabitants of villages, including women and children</u>," for the construction of fortifications; any resistance would be answered with execution.[82]

While other Wehrmacht formations had been utilizing forced civilian labor since the opening days of the invasion, this practice became part of the everyday experience of combat units as they struggled for their very

---

[80] 123 Infanterie-Division, Abt. Ia/Straßenkommandant, Betr.: Walinkis-Filzstiefel, 19.1.42, BA-MA RH 26–123/50. Emphasis in original. The division recorded that it was able to procure thirty-four pairs of boots in this "action"; see Filzstiefelaktion, 19.1.42, BA-MA RH 26–123/48. The 12th ID, also caught in the rapidly forming pocket, similarly ordered that "felt boots be ruthlessly taken off the civilian population" in January 1942; see Bartov, *The Barbarization of War*, p. 132.

[81] Abt. LIH Op., Geheime Kommandosache, 21. Dezember 1941, in Schramm, *KTB OKW*, vol. II, p. 1085.

[82] Gruppe Rauch, Abt. Ia/Az. IVa, Befehl für die Verteidigung der Nachschubstraße, 30. Januar 1942, BA-MA RH 26–123/50. Emphasis in original.

existence during the winter crisis; the 123rd ID merely followed the general trend within the army.[83]

The issue of food supply also became an extremely important question during the tumultuous days of January and February 1942. The 123rd ID was poorly supplied in its forward position in the Demiansk sector even before Soviet forces encircled II Corps and the situation obviously worsened as the battle dragged on. Immediately after the Red Army offensive began, the division confiscated whatever foodstuffs it could extract from the surrounding countryside:

All stocks from the land are to be seized for the feeding of the troops. Confiscations are to be ordered and supervised by officers. Unauthorized requisitioning is to be avoided in all cases. Cattle are to be seized and kept for use in special emergency situations. All of the countryside's hay is to be seized for the feeding of the troops' horses, *panje* horses, and the available cattle.[84]

While air-drops sufficed to maintain a minimum level of activity, they were in no way adequate for all of the division's needs. II Corps accordingly ordered the "ruthless exploitation of the countryside." This order, however, failed to correspond with reality. As the divisional quartermaster noted, there simply were "no supply goods left in the area." All that remained were several cows and even after the return of several requisition commandos, the quartermaster counted a mere twenty head of cattle.[85] While the division attempted to square its own circle of supply problems, the surrounding civilian population was left with little or no possibility of sustenance. Relentless foraging by the men meant that "despite the most difficult of conditions, the division was able to extract the necessary fresh meat from the countryside."[86] Civilians, however, generally remained outside the division's food calculations during the crisis of early 1942.

One possible solution to the civilian food issue employed by the German Army in increasing frequency as the war progressed was the forced evacuation of a region's inhabitants. Such orders to evacuate the population were ignored by the division in late January as it did not possess the necessary manpower for such an undertaking during a period of desperate

---

[83] On the use of civilian labor by the 253rd ID, see Rass, *Menschenmaterial*, p. 361.
[84] Gruppe Rauch, Ib, Besondere Anordnungen für die Versorgung für den 19.1.42, BA-MA RH 26–123/217. *Panje* horses were horses native to the USSR that the Germans found to be better suited to the climate and terrain of the Soviet Union than German breeds.
[85] 123 ID KTB Qu., 12.2.42, 13.2.42, BA-MA RH 26–123/200. A report from the supply company indicated twenty-five cattle were seized; Stab Dinafü 123, 15. Februar 1942, BA-MA RH 26–123/203.
[86] Tätigkeitsbericht für die Zeit vom 1.2.–28.2.42, IVa, 1.4.1942, BA-MA RH 26–123/226.

fighting and retreat.[87] By mid-February, however, fears of a revolt in the town of Molvotitsy led to the forced evacuation of the town's 1,130 inhabitants, the majority of whom were women and children. A mere one day after the idea was first broached, members of the division forced civilians out of their homes and then jettisoned them into the neighboring 12th ID's area of responsibility.[88] In all probability, a significant number of these uprooted individuals perished. Molvotitsy was merely the tip of the iceberg; evacuations of countless smaller villages such as Sodki, in which all thirty inhabitants were forcibly driven to the rear, took place on a large scale during February and March 1942.[89] Focused on halting the Soviet offensive, the division took no chances with possibly rebellious civilians in the rear area: it drove them from their homes in the midst of winter into the chaotic rear areas of other German units. In the calculations of division command, the welfare of women and children received no attention.

While the 123rd ID began ruthlessly securing and even mobilizing its rear area as it attempted to survive the Soviet attack, the 126th ID dealt with increasingly worrisome partisan activity in its rear even before the Soviet offensive surged across the Volkhov. Frequent hit-and-run attacks on supply sleds and small patrols forced the division to task men to the rear in hopes of providing at least minimal security despite their urgent need at the front.[90] On 6 January 1942, the division released a new directive to the men on the partisan threat that warned the men about civilians in their midst:

every responsible leader and soldier needs to be continually clear that we stand in the enemy's territory and are involved with an enemy whose character is marked above all by treachery and deceit. Again and again, the Russian [partisan] finds support, voluntary or forced, from the population. The all-too trusting nature [*Vertrauensseligkeit*] of the German soldier is all too often exploited to his disadvantage. Caution and suspicion should therefore be shown towards the Russian population.[91]

---

[87] 123 ID KTB Qu., 22.1.42, 12.2.42, BA-MA RH 26–123/200.

[88] Ibid., 14.2.42, 15.2.42, 16.2.42, BA-MA RH 26–123/200. On the 12th ID and its condition during the fighting, see Bartov, *The Eastern Front, 1941–1945*, p. 25.

[89] Chrezvychainaia Gosudarstvennaia Komissiia, USHMM, RG 22–002M, Reel 18, 174. Oldenburg notes similar, though much larger-scale, programs undertaken by Eleventh Army during the spring of 1942 that produced comparable results; see his *Ideologie und militärisches Kalkül*, pp. 90–2.

[90] For examples of these incidents, see 126 Infanterie Division, Tagesmeldung vom 12.1.42 an XXXVIII A.K. and General Kommando XXXVIII AK, Tagesmeldung am AOK 16, 2.1.42, both in BA-MA RH 26–126/37.

[91] 126 Infanterie Division, Abt. Ic., Betr.: Wach.-u. Sicherheitsdienst gegenüber Partisanen, Anlage 254, BA-MA RH 26–126/118.

Once again, a Wehrmacht command castigated its men for the perceived civility and good-naturedness they displayed towards the civilians in their midst. This rebuke of the men for their allegedly moderate behavior was reinforced by an order issued by the division's ranking intelligence officer following a partisan attack on a member of the artillery regiment.[92] Although the incident resulted in only the wounding of a German lieutenant, the division ordered the establishment of a "combat-strength commando" to investigate the crime, demanding that "the attack is to be punished by the sharpest measures." The division strictly defined the preferred outcome: either "the eventual shooting of numerous male inhabitants or the burning down of the entire village" – the local commander was given no choice in the matter. While no documentation exists on how this case eventually unfolded, the division's stated policy towards partisans and, by extension, civilians became clear with the shooting of seven alleged partisans in mid-January.[93]

The men of the 126th ID, which had already established itself as a brutal unit during 1941, became increasingly radicalized in the fighting of early 1942. One Rhenish infantryman spoke of his "murderous rage towards these damned Russians" and feelings such as these translated into ruthless treatment of captured Red Army men.[94] The intelligence officer reported that "the fighting in the last few days has been conducted with extraordinary bitterness, which has experienced a sharpening with the discovery of murdered German prisoners."[95] Members of the division found several mutilated Germans, including one man who was shot twice in the leg, had his head smashed in by a rifle butt, and whose chest was ripped open and his heart cut out.[96] On the same day as these bodies were found, the 422nd Infantry Regiment reported taking one officer and fifteen men prisoner, noting that "the rest were shot" following a small engagement.[97] As a report on the battle makes clear, "the rest"

---

[92] 126 Infanterie Division, Abteilung Ic, Betr.: Überfall auf Leutnant Parthom, 10.1.42, BA-MA RH 26–126/118; 126 ID KTB Ic, 10.1.42, BA-MA RH 26–126/118.
[93] 126 ID KTB Ic, 14.1.42, 16.1.42, BA-MA RH 26–126/118. While it is impossible to verify if those shot were indeed partisans, there is no doubt that partisans were active in the division's area of responsibility. For example, see the division's report on a partisan attack on a village in an attempt to procure foodstuffs; 126 Infanterie Division, Abt. Ic, 18.1.1942, Betr.: Partisanen-Bekämpfung, BA-MA RH 26–126/118.
[94] Corporal Alois Bracher, 366 Infantry Regiment, 6.3.42, BfZ, Sammlung Sterz.
[95] 126 ID KTB Ic., 20.1.42, BA-MA RH 26–126/118.
[96] 126 Infanterie Division, Betr.: Verstümmelung von deutschen Soldaten, 23.1.42; Schuld, Uffz., 1./Nachtrichten Abt. 126, Tatsachenbericht, 19. Januar 1942; both in BA-MA RH 26–126/118.
[97] Tagesmeldung Infanterie Regiment 422 vom 19.1.42, BA-MA RH 26–126/38.

numbered 100 men who, though originally taken prisoner, "were not brought back"; instead, they were executed on the spot. The fifteen men recorded as taken prisoner were later shot as they allegedly attempted to attack the guards detailed to bring them to the rear.[98]

This incident proved to be the first of several such massacres:

After the abuse and murder of German prisoners on 17.1, the bitterness of the fighting troops towards the enemy has considerably increased. During three prisoner transports on the 22nd, 25th and 31st of January, prisoners were shot by some members of the division, and especially by members of the SS units subordinate to the division.[99]

The division concluded that

in general, it is reported that as a result of the bestial murder of German prisoners and wounded such a great bitterness prevails among the fighting troops, that the repeatedly given order to take prisoners away is no longer obeyed.[100]

These two war diary entries prove interesting on several levels. First, subordinate units of both the 126th ID and the II SS-Brigade each found themselves under the command of the other formation; for example, the 424th Infantry Regiment controlled the SS Anti-Aircraft Section for a period of time while the SS unit temporarily commanded both the I and III Battalions of the 126th ID's artillery regiment and the division's armored reconnaissance battalion.[101] As previously noted, Army Group North utilized the II SS-Brigade as an anti-partisan unit and it fulfilled this role in the brutal manner befitting a Waffen-SS unit.[102] In addition to its anti-partisan sweeps, this was neither the first nor the last time that members of this SS unit shot regular military prisoners: in August 1942, the commander in chief of Eighteenth Army, Colonel General Georg Lindemann, complained to Himmler about the II SS-Infantry Brigade's propensity for committing such murders.[103] Forced into the line due to Germany's manpower crisis in the winter

---

[98] Ic Fernschreiben, Betr.: Gefangene vom 19.1, 20.1.1942, BA-MA RH 26–126/118.
[99] Tätigkeitsbericht zum Kriegstagebuch, Ic, 4.2.42, BA-MA RH 26–126/119.
[100] Ic Fernschreiben, Betr.: Gefangene vom 19.1, 20.1.1942, BA-MA RH 26–126/118.
[101] On the SS-Flak unit, see Obltn. v. Wolffersdorf an die 126 Infanterie-Div., Abt. Ia, 17.5.1942, BA-MA RH 26–126/45; on the artillery battalions, see 126 ID KTB, 1.7.42, BA-MA RH 26–126/57; on the reconaissance unit, see 2. SS-Inf. Brigade (mot), Der Kommandeur 5. Juni 1942, BA-MA RH 26–126/45.
[102] On its activities, see Fritz Baade (ed.), *Unsere Ehre heisst treue: Kriegstagebuch des Kommandostabes Reichsführer SS, Tätigkeitsberichte der 1. und 2. SS-Inf. Brigade, der 1. SS Kav.-Brigade und von Sonderkommandos der SS* (Vienna, 1965), pp. 32–91.
[103] George H. Stein, *The Waffen SS: Hitler's Elite Guard at War* (Ithaca, 1994), p. 273, n. 63.

of 1941–2, the practices of the highly indoctrinated *Weltanschauung* warriors were likely to influence the conduct of their comrades in the army.[104]

Second, as the latter entry notes, the men blatantly ignored orders issued by division command regarding the taking of prisoners. In contrast to the directives concerning treatment of partisans and civilians, division command called for a proper and correct treatment of regular prisoners; despite this direct order, the men wantonly murdered the captured Red Army men. Clearly, the division experienced a loss of control of its own soldiers during the last two weeks of January as the violence emanating from the men themselves overrode any institutional authority possessed by divisional headquarters. The fear of senior Wehrmacht officers that the "criminal orders" would curtail their ability to control the troops seems at least partially confirmed by these incidents.[105]

Third, of the three divisions under analysis, only the 126th ID reacted to the discovery of bodies of tortured and mutilated comrades in such a vicious manner. Both the 121st and 123rd IDs found German soldiers mistreated in this way, yet there is no record of them taking out their frustrations on defenseless prisoners.[106] This outburst by the 126th ID fits into the general pattern of its behavior since the opening days of the invasion. It consistently utilized the most ruthless and brutal methods of the three divisions in their dealings with civilians and prisoners. And as the above discussion of the repeated massacres of Soviet prisoners

---

[104] On the employment of the II SS-Infantry Brigade as a combat unit, see ibid., p. 156. Even Himmler, who was dead set against the employment of the unit for frontline duties, was forced to face the reality of Germany's manpower crisis in the winter of 1941–2. For Himmler's view, see the diary entry for 15 September 1941 in Baade (ed.), *Unsere Ehre heisst treue*, p. 33. A recent look at the ideological indoctrination of the Waffen-SS is Jürgen Förster, "Die Weltanschauliche Erziehung in der Waffen-SS," in Jürgen Matthäus et al., *Ausbildungsziel Judenmord? "Weltanschauliche Erziehung" von SS, Polizei und Waffen-SS im Rahmen der "Endlösung"* (Frankfurt am Main, 2003), pp. 87–114.

[105] For the most important manifestation of this thinking, see "Behandlung feindlicher Zivilpersonen und Straftaten Wehrmachtsangehöriger gegen feindliche Zivilpersonen" issued by Brauchitsch on 24 May 1941, printed in Ueberschär and Wette, *Der deutsche Überfall auf die Sowjetunion 1941*, pp. 253–4. Brauchitsch feared that such orders would lead to a "brutalization of the troops," a concern shared by Army Group Center's commander in chief, Field Marshal Fedor von Bock, who wrote in his diary that the military jurisdiction order "was unacceptable and incompatible with discipline." See Fedor von Bock (ed. Klaus Gerbert), *Generalfeldmarschall Fedor von Bock: The War Diary, 1939–1945* (Atglen, 2000), 4 June 1941, p. 218. For further discussion, see Förster, "Das Unternehmen 'Barbarossa' als Eroberungs- und Vernichtungskrieg," pp. 517–20; and Römer, *Der Kommissarbefehl*, pp. 71–2.

[106] Obviously, this could merely be the result of gaps in the record. Without the appearance of any further documentation, however, this is the only viable conclusion.

indicates, the troops themselves precipitated such actions on their own initiative. Even a Rhenish soldier whose letters distinguish him as a thoughtful man who desired nothing more than to be home with his family viewed the Soviets through blinkered eyes:

I see the day when I can finally turn my back on Russia. If there are no opportunities for a decent man in peace, there are far fewer now in war. But it is still better than if the Russians were in Germany shooting everything to pieces. I am continually amazed by the toughness of these devils. They run day after day into our lines and have bloody casualties every time ...[107]

The belief that the war between Germany and the Soviet Union was inevitable comes through in this letter, as does the Nazi view that the Bolshevik "devils" would certainly destroy Germany if the fight took place in the Reich. Such attitudes certainly influenced the conduct of war by Rhinelanders in the east. While circumstances – heavy fighting by a weakened and demoralized force and the close proximity of a Waffen-SS unit – need to be taken into account, the past practices of the 126th ID make clear that this was not an isolated incident. The Rhinelanders practiced a more ideologically tinged version of military necessity, resulting in a more blatantly murderous treatment of Soviet citizens, than either the 121st or 123rd IDs.

---

[107] Corporal Alois Bracher, Inf. Rgt. 366, 24.3.42, BfZ, Sammlung Sterz.

8 "The population ... shouted out to the interpreter that one would rather be shot instead of being left to starve"
The evolution of military necessity

I. The destruction of the Volkhov pocket: the 121st and 126th Infantry Divisions

While the 123rd and 126th IDs experienced real crisis in early 1942, the 121st ID experienced a relatively tranquil beginning to the year. For the most part, continual Red Army patrols and raids, complemented by steady artillery fire, confronted the East Prussians.[1] Both of these activities forced the 121st ID to maintain constant vigilance with decreasing numbers of men, which in turn led to a declining morale and effectiveness.[2] The Red Army's crushing superiority in artillery caused heavy casualties in the infantry regiments manning the forward lines and led to frantic calls for reinforcements as well as demands for a break from the fighting.[3] Though replacements trickled in from the rear, the constant attrition forced the establishment of two combat companies from supply and administrative troops.[4] Despite these issues, the Leningrad front remained relatively tranquil, especially during the spring of 1942. In a letter sent home, a member of the East Prussian 1st ID wrote, "the front on the Narva has become quiet. The days of up to four attacks have died down like a stormy wave on the sea. Our dam has stood firm, even though many holes have been torn in it."[5]

During this break from heavy fighting, the soldiers took stock of their situation. Frustrated at their inability to seize Leningrad when it stood so close to their positions, they nonetheless took pride in their ability to repulse every Red Army attack.[6] One East Prussian in the 21st ID commented,

---

[1] See, for example, Schramm, *KTB OKW*, vol. III, 29. Januar 1942, p. 270. On the number of attacks, see the undated and unsigned document in BA-MA RH 26–121/60.
[2] 121 ID KTB, 3.1.42, 22.2.42, BA-MA RH 26–121/16.
[3] Aktenvermerk für KTB, 28.2.42, BA-MA RH 26–121/16.
[4] 121 Inf.-Division, Abt. Ib, Br. B. Nr. 342/42 g., 10.2.1942, BA-MA RH 26–121/18.
[5] Corporal Andres Zimmerman, Infanterie-Regiment 43, 13.3.42, BfZ, Sammlung Sterz.
[6] "Mein Regiment," BA-MA RH 37/3096. For more on this general sense of disappointment that permeated all of Eighteenth Army, including Küchler, see Hürter, *Hitlers Heerführer*, p. 296.

The destruction of the Volkhov pocket 241

the Russian comes through the swamp and primeval forest, where no one believes possible. His tanks know no obstacles ... His equipment is very good ... his tactical leadership is also good ... his weapons are good. And yet he fails against the German infantryman.[7]

This tribute to the German soldier carried more than an implicit admission of admiration for his opponent: the respect earned by the Red Army during the opening weeks of the invasion only continued to grow during the war, especially in those theaters in which movement had all but disappeared from the front.[8] The division's respite, however, proved short-lived: in mid-February, Army Group North began shifting units from the Leningrad front to deal with the threatening situation on the Volkhov river, and the 121st ID deployed to this region in late April 1942.[9]

German units first temporarily sealed the Volkhov pocket on 20 March (see Map 8.4).[10] Fierce Soviet resistance and the climate, however, claimed a large number of German casualties. This proved especially true for the 126th ID's 426th Infantry Regiment, which reported 427 losses (of which 343 were frostbite and forty-eight cases of sickness) in the first two days of the attack, leaving its three infantry battalions with only 185 combat effectives.[11] While the Red Army launched numerous assaults to reopen the artery and eventually succeeded in doing so, the beginning of the rainy season set in before the Soviets could increase the size of the narrow path. Paralyzed by flooded roads and accurate German artillery fire, only Red Army men on foot could successfully navigate the corridor.[12] With the Second Shock Army effectively encircled by the Wehrmacht, the initiative on the Volkhov river passed over to Army Group North.

The battle to reduce the Volkhov pocket lasted until 28 June 1942 when the final Red Army formations surrendered.[13] Both the 121st and 126th IDs bore heavy burdens in the fighting, with the mass of the East

---

[7] Tagebuchaufzeichnungen aus dem Rußlandfeldzug des Kp. Chef. San Kp. 21. Dr. Michael Henze, 30.1.42, BA-MA Msg 2/2778. The feeling of superiority that the German political and military leadership attempted to inculcate in each and every soldier certainly shines through here. For more on this topic, see Edele and Geyer, "States of Exception," pp. 357–8, 393.
[8] Based on their analysis of prisoner transcripts, Neitzel and Welzer conclude that "Wehrmacht soldiers had great respect, however, for their Russian opponents. They respected and feared their sacrificial courage and their brutality"; see Neitzel and Welzer, *Soldaten*, p. 335.
[9] Klink, "Die Operationsführung," p. 721; 121 Infanterie-Division, Geheimhaltung, 17.4.42, BA-MA RH 26–121/20.
[10] Halder, *Kriegstagebuch*, vol. III, 20 March 1942, p. 416.
[11] 126 Infanterie Division, Tagesmeldung an XXXVIII AK, 16.3.43, BA-MA RH 26–126/42.
[12] Glantz, *The Battle for Leningrad*, p. 182.
[13] 121 ID KTB, 28.6.42, BA-MA RH 26–121/24.

Illustration 8.1 A German soldier navigates the swampy terrain during the battle for the Volkhov pocket.

Prussians being thrown into the battle in early May.[14] Despite extremely heavy casualties, the 121st ID continued to drive south to close the corridor and Wehrmacht forces finally sealed the pocket for good on 31 May 1942.[15] Desperate Soviet attempts both to rescue the encircled army and to break out to the east generally proved futile as the men of the 121st ID steadfastly followed their instructions: "there is no retreat from a position or a resistance point. They will be held until the last cartridge."[16] The destruction of Second Shock Army degenerated into a series of smaller, pitched battles in which both sides suffered frightful losses: one of these relatively minor engagements between the 121st ID and elements of one Soviet armored and three infantry divisions caused the former over 850 casualties while the latter lost 3,500 men with a further 1,000 taken prisoner.[17] The intensity of the fighting led one member of the 121st ID to lament that the "Bolsheviks ... always fight with an animal-like

[14] Ibid., 2.5.42, 4.5.42.   [15] Glantz, *The Battle for Leningrad*, p. 203.
[16] 121 Infanterie Division, Auszug aus bisher ergangenen Befehlen, 28.4.1942, BA-MA RH 26–121/20.
[17] 121 ID KTB, 13.5.42, BA-MA RH 26–121/24.

The destruction of the Volkhov pocket

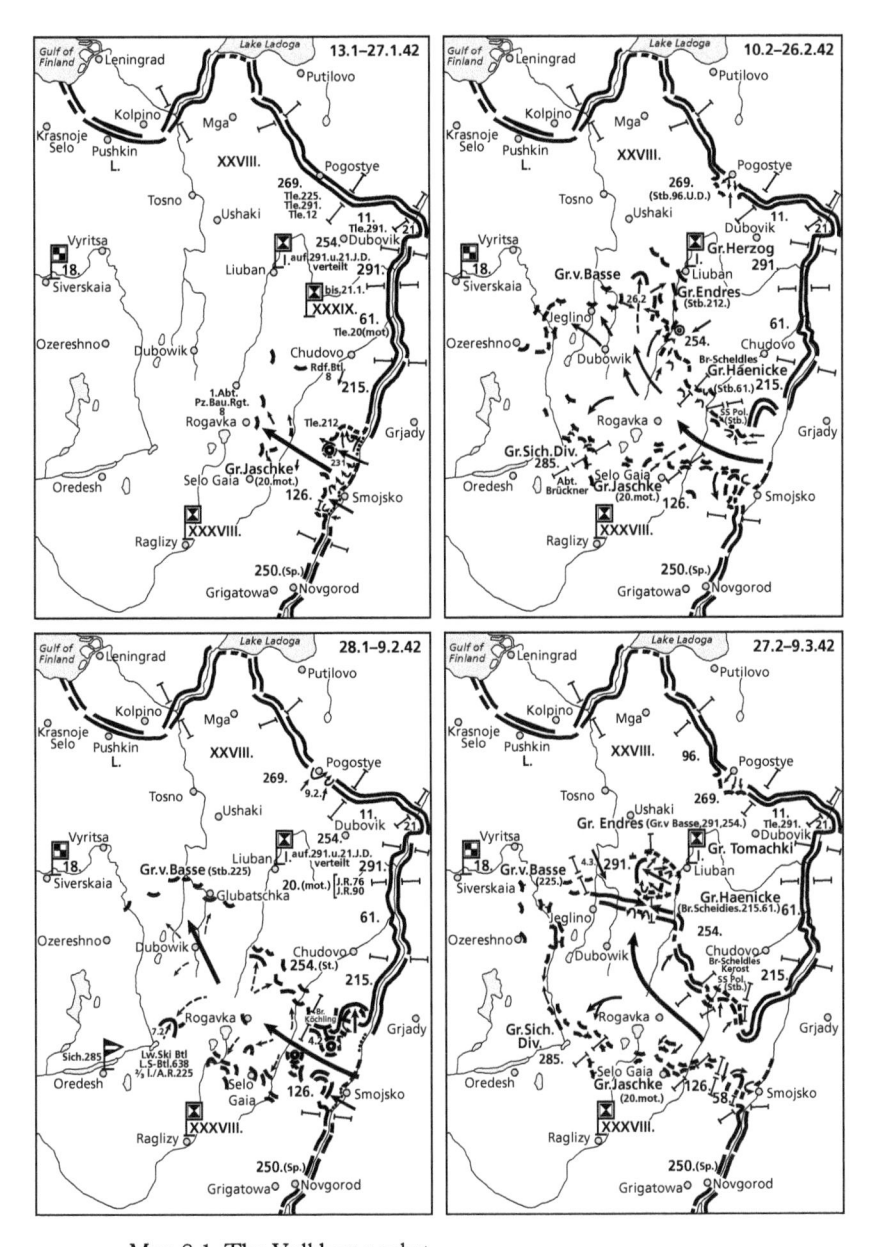

Map 8.1 The Volkhov pocket

244   The evolution of military necessity

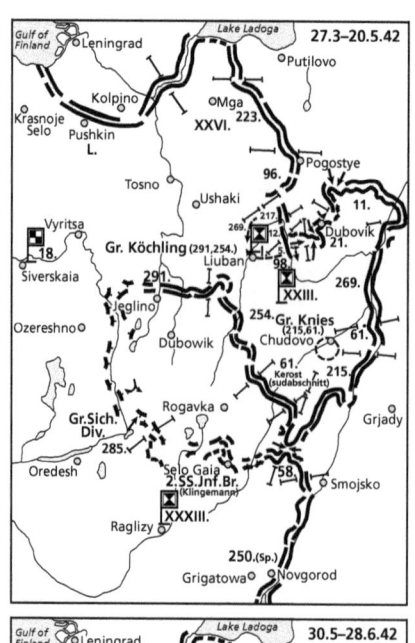

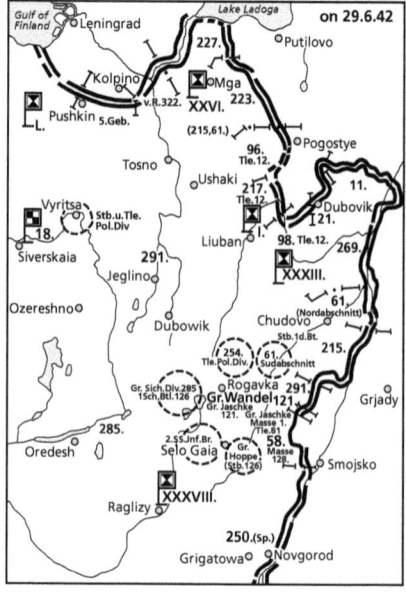

Map 8.1 (cont.)

ferociousness."[18] The desperate resistance of the Red Army, especially its officers and commissars, led to the fighting being "characterized by great bitterness and extraordinary severity by both sides"; as already noted, such a formulation leads one to speculate that the Germans frequently murdered surrendering Red Army men out of hand.[19] When the battle finally ended, the 121st ID had only been involved in operations on the Volkhov river for approximately seven weeks but in this short period of sustained combat, the division suffered 598 battle deaths, 4,122 wounded, and 120 missing.[20]

A similar situation existed on the southern edge of the pocket. The 126th ID reported that its recent replacements were already "fought out" in heavy fighting mere weeks after arriving and that they additionally suffered from sickness as their equipment "corresponded in no way to the present weather or the constant demands" placed on the troops.[21] The constant fighting – in a six-week period stretching from mid-January to the end of February, the division faced over 150 enemy attacks by twenty-nine different enemy regiments – and no foreseeable chance to visit loved ones at home also led to a decline in the morale of the division.[22] The division's evangelical chaplain noted that "the men are in good spirits, though in individual conversations many domestic worries come through."[23] Many of these misgivings focused on the increased bombing of cities in Rhineland-Westphalia by the RAF.[24] Morale became such an issue that the corps commander felt obligated to address it. While acknowledging the various causes of the troops' low morale, he claimed that letters sent from the front that focused on themes such as hopelessness or contained "illegitimate criticisms of the leadership" did not accurately portray the general morale of the troops and caused unrest at home.[25] It seems clear, however, that morale within the 126th ID did suffer during the battle for the Volkhov pocket in early 1942. This was primarily due to the shockingly high number of casualties suffered by the

---

[18] 121 Infanterie Division, Gruppe Wandel Tagesbefehl, 14.5.1942, BA-MA RH 26–121/25.
[19] Das I. Armeekorps in der Schlacht am Wolchow vom 8. Jan.–28. Juni 1942, no date, BA-MA RH 24–1/62.
[20] 121 ID KTB, 28.6.42, BA-MA RH 26–121/24. Glantz, *The Battle for Leningrad*, p. 208, gives Soviet casualties as over 410,000.
[21] Gruppe Hoppe, Ia, Tagesmeldung, 11.4.42, BA-MA RH 26–126/44.
[22] Verband 126 Infanterie-Division, Meldung, 23.3.42, BA-MA RH 26–126/47; XXXVIII AK, Ic Tätigkeitsbericht, NARA T-314, Roll 900.
[23] Tätigkeitsbericht des Ev. Divisionspfarrers bei der 126 Infanterie Division für die Zeit vom 1.1.1942 bis 20.6.42, BA-MA RH 26–126/145.
[24] Corporal Alois Bracher, 366 Infantry Regiment, 6.3.42, BfZ, Sammlung Sterz.
[25] Generalkommando XXXVIII AK, Abt. Ic, Nr. 439/42 geheim, Betr.: Aufklärung und Belehrung der Truppe, 23.2.1942, NARA T-314, Roll 900.

Rhinelanders from January through May 1942: 1,214 dead, 3,907 wounded, 341 missing, and 1,545 cases of frostbite.[26] The first strategic Soviet offensive in northern Russia had been defeated but at an extremely high cost to Army Group North's infantry.

II. Transitions

The onset of the rainy season in early April only worsened the already primordial terrain in the Volkhov sector. One soldier in the Rhenish 254th ID described it as

> only marshes, only primeval forest! The thickest leafy forest ... with plentiful undergrowth and lush, almost tropical plant growth that places extreme limits on visibility, hiding and concealment are very easy, the ability to surprise is readily available. In the forests, no culture, no attempts to tame the woods [*Forstwirtschaft*] are recognizable. The majority of the paths and lanes, the clearings and open areas cleared out years or even decades ago, have become overgrown, so that they are only recognizable from the lower tree stands. When one thinks one has found a lane, one needs to look up. When one can see a broad strip of the sky (and not a canopy of overgrown trees), then it is a path! In the forest, the following lie all over the place: dead branches, brushwood, tree stumps of every size, sometimes fresh, sometimes already decayed. The trees lie where the wind or disease has thrown them. Trees and tree stumps tower above in various sizes. Roots curl all around the terrain, sometimes above ground, making for nature's own traps. Entire trees have been ripped from the earth with all of their roots by storms, forming large craters. And in between all of this, are hidden marshy areas of dark water, which reach from men's ankles to their knees and sometimes to their chest. The only islands in this swampy area, tree stumps – more or less decayed – frayed roots – and tree trunks.[27]

Such a portrayal not only describes the actual condition of the landscape but also betrays the imperialist gaze of the author. The primitive appearance of this region – and the Soviet Union, by extension – where disease, death, decay, and darkness predominate, literally screamed for German order and modernization; such a view corresponded to the general trope of German cultural and racial superiority vis-à-vis the "wild East." In a rather less eloquent manner, a sign posted at the end of the paved road that marked the 121st ID's boundary simply stated, "The world's asshole begins here!"[28]

---

[26] See the Tätigkeitsbericht der Abt. IIa/b from 31.1.42, 28.2.42, 31.3.42, 30.4.42, 31.5.1942 in BA-MA RH 26–126/132. Unfortunately, the report for June 1942 contains incomplete information on the unit's casualty figures.

[27] Erfahrungen im Angriff durch das sumpfige, urwaldähnliche Gelände des Wolchowkessels Juni 1942, BA-MA RH 37/3105. Emphasis in original.

[28] Einsatz der Veterinärdienste der 121. Inf.-Division unter besonders erschwerten Verhältnissen in den Monaten Mai und Juni 1942, BA-MA RH 26–121/67.

Illustration 8.2 The 121st Infantry Division's commander stated, "the world's asshole begins here," when describing the muck and mud in the Volkhov theater.

These descriptions, however, did point to the difficulties caused by the terrain. For soldiers operating in the mud and the muck, nature became as deadly an enemy as the Red Army. One member of the 121st ID stated that "when someone is wounded [in the mud], he can rarely be saved. If his comrades are unable, with all of their might, to rescue him, he will remain there and die."[29]

Rains and melting snow only exacerbated the difficulties facing German troops in negotiating this terrain. As rising temperatures melted the winter snow, numerous corpses, both human and horse, emerged; in order to avoid the outbreak of disease, soldiers and civilians were constantly burying the remains of the winter's fighting.[30] The combination of the melting snow and spring rain also flooded German fortifications and roads and paths. The German High Command's order issued on 12 February 1942 concerning combat operations recognized the army

[29] "Mein Regiment," BA-MA RH 37/3096.
[30] Verstärktes Inf. Rgt. 424, I A, Tagesmeldung, 30.4.1942, BA-MA RH 26–126/44.

group's problems.[31] Noting that the "muddy period" had led to a "limited securing" of the front, it ordered Küchler's men to "again construct a closed and continuously manned defensive line," one that would be "constantly improved and deepened," once the terrain had sufficiently dried out. This order emphasized the transformation in Army Group North's mission: instead of continuing the advance towards Murmansk, it now was to dig in and defend its gains.[32] While such an order only officially confirmed what had transpired on the ground during the previous fall and winter – an exhausted and armor-depleted command no longer possessed the necessary striking power to fulfill its initial objectives – it also augured an evolution in the relationship between German soldiers and Soviet civilians.

Up to this point, the army had generally ignored the majority of civilians during its seemingly triumphal days of advance and then ruthlessly turned against them as a potential fifth column during the winter crisis. Now, however, the course of the war demanded a new occupation policy. While Soviet citizens were certainly viewed with suspicion, one based on both racism and experience, frontline divisions, lacking the necessary manpower needed for combat tasks, construction programs, and rear-area security, adopted a more conciliatory attitude towards those in their midst. Recognizing that the war in the north had transformed into one that increasingly resembled the battles of matériel that had characterized the First World War, German units looked to harness the labor of civilians and perhaps even their support for the Reich's war effort. The guiding principle of military necessity overcame the brutal dictates of racial war and civilians now were to be exploited and even conciliated as opposed to ignored or exterminated.

All along the front, Wehrmacht practice transformed from the pitiless character of 1941 to a more "constructive occupation policy" towards the Soviet population.[33] While some sections of the army leadership recognized the need for such a change in course in late 1941, only following the winter crisis did it become increasingly discussed and practiced.[34]

---

[31] Weisung für die Kampfführung im Osten nach Abschluß des Winters, in Schramm, *KTB OKW*, vol. II, 12. Februar 1942, pp. 1093–6, here p. 1095.
[32] The one exception to this general defensive trend concerned an offensive designed to break the Demiansk encirclement.
[33] Hürter, *Hitlers Heerführer*, p. 457. For the general shift towards a more conciliatory policy among the field commanders of the Eastern Army, see ibid., pp. 456–65. The remainder of this discussion is based on Hürter unless otherwise noted.
[34] Brauchitsch called for a more "positive" propaganda line in October 1941, emphasizing the need to impress upon the Soviet population that German rule would restore their land and their right to practice religion, and create better living conditions; see Quinkert, *Propaganda und Terror*, p. 202.

Perhaps the most surprising manifestation of this conceptual shift was a document written by Reichenau (now commander in chief of Army Group South) in January 1942 before his fatal heart attack later that month. Discovered in his personal papers by his successor Field Marshal Fedor von Bock following his death, the memorandum revealed a radical change in perspective by the author of the October 1941 order that demanded a highly ideological war against the Soviet state and its people.[35] Cognizant that "a quick decision in the east could no longer be counted on," he then complained of policy errors that had led to a Ukraine which believed it had "meaning only as a colonial area to be exploited, in which no consideration for the existence of the population would be taken and in which the German conqueror took no notice of the starvation or annihilation of millions of Ukrainians." In order to arrest this development and harness the Ukrainian population to the German cause, he implored the use of propaganda, promises of future limited autonomy, food deliveries to civilians, and the use of armed Ukrainians to help combat the Red Army. Bock noted that he agreed with its contents and forwarded it on to the Army High Command in hopes of bringing it to Hitler's attention and thereby fundamentally altering the German approach to the east.[36] This shared vision of how the Wehrmacht should administer the occupied territories, one that both an older conservative and a much more radical ideologue believed to be necessary for final victory, emphasizes the shift in the field commanders' thinking that emerged after the winter crisis: for the army, victory on the battlefield was the overriding goal and any and all means would be exploited to achieve it.

The OKH also attempted to convince frontline troops to modify their practices in the east. On 10 May, the Army High Command issued "Guidelines for the Treatment of the Native Population."[37] While the German soldier "should feel as master in the east ... mastery should never degenerate into contempt towards the vanquished that are defenseless. The Russian is compliant and willing when he is strictly but correctly treated." Clearly, even Zossen realized that the army's policies needed to be reformulated and this order highlighted the relative agreement between the High Command and the field armies. Such convergent thinking led to more nuanced policies in 1942 than had existed in 1941.[38] In the Crimea,

---

[35] On the discovery and the document itself, see Bock, *Generalfeldmarschall Fedor von Bock*, p. 410.
[36] Ibid., p. 410.   [37] Cited in Pohl, *Die Herrschaft der Wehrmacht*, p. 298.
[38] For an opposing take on this development, see Edele and Geyer, "States of Exception," pp. 377–81.

for example, Eleventh Army called for more considerate occupation policies towards those sections of population deemed both anticommunist and willing to collaborate.[39] This "friendly and courteous treatment," however, was complemented by "immediate ruthlessness" against those deemed threatening to German goals in the region.[40]

Such pragmatism appeared even earlier within Seventeenth Army's area of operations. On 6 February 1942, in response to urgent pleas for help by one of its subordinate corps on behalf of the starving population of Slaviansk, Seventeenth Army sent bread grain from its own stocks to the city for the population's use on the *same* day.[41] Such an action during 1941 was all but unthinkable as, according to the notion of military necessity, civilians were inconsequential to final victory. By 1942, however, the Wehrmacht had modified its view of civilians. Seventeenth Army fed the city not out of any humanitarian impulse but rather as means to secure the rear area and hence the army's security: "the army leadership saw the feeding of Slaviansk's entire population as a military necessity."[42]

This more conciliatory approach towards the civilian population culminated with First Panzer Army's efforts in the North Caucasus in late 1942. The German need for oil from this area, coupled with a Nazi racial hierarchy that viewed the Caucasus peoples as having higher "value" than Russians or Ukrainians, led to a much more conciliatory occupation.[43] In this region, "the considerations of the bureaucrats, economic specialists and racial ideologues all corresponded with the military situation: already in the summer of 1942, it was apparent that Germany could not win the war without the support of the occupied peoples."[44] In an attempt to create goodwill and co-operation in the region, Field Marshal Ewald von Kleist's formation abolished collectivization, allowed for the freedom of religion, and even recognized several local administrations as legal governments.[45]

This more constructive policy filtered down to the army rear areas as "the efforts of the commanders in chief to bring about a substantial

---

[39] Oldenburg, *Militärisches Kalkül*, p. 108.   [40] Quoted in ibid., pp. 109, 136.
[41] Ibid., pp. 236–7.
[42] Ibid. Dieter Pohl has also emphasized that the new occupation course was enacted in part to "curtail the resistance threat"; *Die Herrschaft der Wehrmacht*, p. 298.
[43] Chiari, "Grenzen deutscher Herrschaft," p. 957.   [44] Ibid., p. 958.
[45] Timothy Mulligan, *The Politics of Illusion and Empire: German Occupation Policy in the Soviet Union, 1942–1943* (New York, 1988), p. 128; Pohl, *Die Herrschaft der Wehrmacht*, pp. 299–303. Such conciliatory developments, however, should not overshadow German policies of economic exploitation and racial extermination; see Chiari, "Grenzen deutscher Herrschaft," pp. 958–62.

change in occupation policy gained intensity in spring 1942."[46] This transformation in policy was most clearly realized by the security divisions charged with pacifying the rear areas. The 221st Security Division, which had killed more than 1,100 "partisans" in a mere four weeks in October–November 1941, now began a concerted "hearts-and-minds effort" that utilized both propaganda and less arbitrary anti-partisan sweeps that attempted to spare innocent civilians' lives.[47] The division recognized "the need to rein in the brutality of its troops, and to combine military force targeted at the partisans specifically with a sustained effort to cultivate both the population and potential partisan deserters."[48] A catalyst similar to that which motivated the Eleventh and Seventeenth Armies' evolution in policy existed in the rear area as well. Facing an increasingly large, well-armed, and well-trained partisan movement, the comparatively weak 221st Security Division realized that its only hope of achieving its military mission lay in cleaving the civilian population away from the partisans and drawing them into the German war effort.[49]

Other German institutions also realized that victory required a change in course. Major-General Nagel of Wirtschaftsstab Ost argued for the following as a means of gaining civilian support:[50]

(a) more attention to food supplies for the civilian population, which cannot be "simply allowed to starve to death";
(b) decent behavior by the troops towards well-disposed civilians, no confiscation of animals or chattels without payment, no beatings or similar measures . . .;
(c) no coercion in the recruitment of labor; . . .
(g) help by troops with agricultural work;
(h) no confiscation of the last cow;
(i) allocation of land.

Foreign Armies East also called for a fundamental transformation of German policy. In November 1942, it noted that "the attitude of the Russian individual to the German power" was the key to war and the only way in which the occupiers could favorably manipulate this attitude was by dispensing with the belief that "the Russian . . . is objectively inferior" who existed merely "as an object of exploitation possessing no rights."

---

[46] Hasenclever, *Wehrmacht und Besatzungspolitik in der Sowjetunion*, pp. 247–54, quote on p. 247.
[47] Shepherd, *War in the Wild East*, pp. 103, 135–.   [48] Ibid., p. 129.   [49] Ibid., p. 142.
[50] Quoted in Bernd Wegner, "The War against the Soviet Union, 1942–43," in Horst Boog et al., *Germany and the Second World War*, vol. VI, *The Global War: Widening of the Conflict and the Shift of the Initiative 1941–1943*, pp. 842–1215, here p. 1015.

Its commander, Major-General Reinhard Gehlen, suggested that the Germans make gestures towards political autonomy, while instituting more concrete educational, economic, and religious concessions towards the civilian population.[51]

Army Group North was not immune to these changes in the Wehrmacht's appreciation of the war. Küchler emphasized this reverse in course on 6 February, stating in an order that "fear alone could never" secure the flanks or rear-area lines of communication. While "fear and terror" would continue to be used, the Germans needed to "tie together" the "material interests of the remaining population, especially the peasants, with German interests."[52] As this general tone filtered down the hierarchy of the army group, men on the local level gradually began to utilize civilians in an attempt to improve their own military situation, though the stick certainly received more use than the carrot in certain units. The 121st ID first recruited and – when this failed – then forcibly impressed local inhabitants to assist with road maintenance.[53] The division also increasingly mobilized civilian manpower for construction purposes as I Corps ordered that all rear fortifications needed "to be built first and foremost by civilians," while the 126th ID employed over 275 civilians in March and April 1942 for the construction of bunkers and shelters as well as for road work.[54] This number failed to suffice, however, as "rain, in combination with the melting snow," made it "very difficult to build fortifications and shelters" or to "maintain the supply road," and the division pleaded for more civilian laborers.[55]

Non-German labor was required to tame the particular climate and terrain of northwest Russia; these same issues also played havoc with supply. While the Wehrmacht's supply system had at least partially regained its equilibrium in March–April 1942, the delivery of materials and foodstuffs in the Volkhov river area proved extremely difficult. The dirt roads of northwest Russia quickly turned into muddy quagmires, placing strict limits on the amount of food, ammunition and other equipment that could reach the front.[56]

---

[51] Ibid., pp. 1015–16.   [52] Quoted in Hürter, *Hitlers Heerführer*, p. 457.
[53] General Kommando L AK, Voraussichtlicher zeitlicher Ablauf der Schneeschmelze und Schlammzeit, 12.3.1942; General Kommando L AK, Straßeninstandhaltung im Frühjahr, 16.2.42, BA-MA RH 26–121/21.
[54] On the 121st ID, see Generalkommando I AK, Korpsbefehl Nr. 187 für den Stellungsbau, 5.6.42, BA-MA RH 24–1/69; on the 126th ID, see Pionierbataillon 126, Wochenmeldung, 24. März 1942; Pionierbataillon 126 Wochenmeldung, 30. März 1942; Pionierbataillon 126, Wochenmeldung, 8. April 1942, BA-MA RH 26–126/43.
[55] Tagesmeldung vom 15.4.42, BA-MA RH 26–126/44.
[56] 121 Infanterie Division, Merkblatt: Gründsätze für das Heranziehen der Truppe in der "Schlauch," 4.5.1942, BA-MA RH 26–121/25.

Illustration 8.3 German troops deployed in the devastated Volkhov region.

One of the 126th ID's regiments reported that "the old supply road is impassable for soldiers of medium or smaller size as men sinking up to their arms in mud and waterholes has occurred."[57] Mobility in the rear areas was confined to corduroy roads.[58] While the 121st ID attempted to use trucks to bring supplies forward, they frequently became paralyzed in the mud, and horses became the predominant means of both bringing food and ammunition to the front as well as transporting the wounded back to the rear.[59] This system, however, proved insufficient to keep the troops adequately fed in relation to the high demands placed upon them.[60] Despite (or perhaps due to) the scarcity of food in the area of operations, some German soldiers continued to share their minimal rations with civilians, causing I Corps to declare that the feeding of Soviet

---

[57] Infanterie-Regiment 422, Abt. Ia/Allg., Tagesmeldung, 21.4.42, BA-MA RH 26–126/44.
[58] Haupt, *Heeresgruppe Nord*, p. 128. Corduroy roads were roads covered with logs and other pieces of wood; the wood would sink into the mud giving the "road" some firmness.
[59] Divisionsintendant 121 Inf.-Division, Tätigkeitsbericht für die Zeit vom 1.5.42 bis 5.7.1942; Einsatz der Veterinärdienste der 121. Inf.-Division unter besonders erschwerten Verhältnissen in den Monaten Mai und Juni 1942, BA-MA RH 26–121/67.
[60] 121 ID KTB Abt. Ib, 7.5.42, BA-MA RH 26–121/66.

citizens remained the responsibility of the Economic Staff East and that German rations were in no way to be shared with civilians. Only food stocks captured in the Soviet Union could be shared with the surrounding population and this only in an "extraordinary emergency."[61]

For the 126th ID, whose supply had been problematic even before the Red Army's attack in January, the Soviet advance across the Volkhov river disrupted both the highway and the rail line that linked the division with its rear-area supply dumps.[62] This resulted in frequent shortages of food and, more importantly, winter clothing, which "had an especially negative effect on winter operations." Even after the terrain dried out during the summer of 1942, the Rhinelanders continued to complain that they failed to receive adequate rations of such basic staples as potatoes and bread.[63] Unlike their experiences in the summer and autumn of 1941, however, the area of operations in early 1942 offered the soldiers extremely minimal opportunities to live off the land.

The battle to eliminate the Volkhov pocket offered partisans various opportunities to operate. In addition to the terrain, which provided partisans with numerous places for concealment, German forces were too thinly stretched to keep small groups of Red Army men from escaping the encirclement into the forests and swamps, where many joined partisan units, providing a marked increase in their firepower. In an attempt to limit partisan numbers, the 121st ID ordered that all men between the ages of sixteen and sixty were to be treated as prisoners of war as long as they were not partisans; the latter, obviously, were to be shot out of hand. All other civilians were to be kept under guard until their identity had been cleared by security organs attached to the corps or army.[64]

During this time period, the practices of the 121st ID became increasingly brutal despite an ideological retreat by the highest levels of political and military leadership. On 6 May, Hitler, after being convinced by his military leadership that Soviet resistance would lessen if commissars were no longer shot out of hand, rescinded the Commissar Order.[65] This was

---

[61] Generalkommando I AK, Besondere Anordnungen für die Versorgung der Truppe, Nr. 355, 20.6.1942, BA-MA RH 24–1/327.
[62] Tätigkeitsbericht vom 1.1. bis 30.6.1942, Abt. IVa, BA-MA RH 26–126/145. The remainder of this discussion is based on this document unless otherwise noted.
[63] Verband 126 Infanterie Division, 21.6.42, BA-MA RH 26–126/47.
[64] Kampfgruppe Wandel, 20.6.42, BA-MA RH 26–121/25; Fernschreiben, 19.6.42, BA-MA RH 24–1/71.
[65] Schramm, *KTB OKW*, vol. III, 6. Mai 1942, p. 341. For a comprehensive discussion of the reversal of the Commissar Order, see Römer, *Der Kommissarbefehl*, pp. 526–50. This decision also fits into the general trend of transitioning to a more total war effort, one that recognized that violence needed to be leavened with a more thoughtful approach to winning the war.

conveyed to the troops, and I Corps, the 121st ID's superior formation, ordered leaflets dropped in the pocket guaranteeing commissars and *politruks* that "they would be treated as any other soldier or officer."[66] It appears that units operating under the command of the 121st ID followed this new order: while a commissar was shot after capture on 13 May, one taken prisoner on 30 June was not executed.[67] Of course, being treated as a regular prisoner certainly did not ensure survival. While the horrendous mortality rates of 1941 had begun to subside, prisoners were now utilized for construction tasks as well as for mortally threatening tasks. The 121st ID requested 100 POWs from I Corps in order to clear minefields in the Volkhov area.[68] Here, a lower-level formation began to radicalize its conduct while the upper echelons of the Reich's political and military leadership made a concession, albeit small, to pragmatism.

On the southern side of the pocket, the 126th ID attempted to stamp out any attempts at espionage by the civilian population. Due to what it termed "irresponsible behavior" of local *Ortskommandanten*, the division instituted a much more stringent pass system in hopes of halting the movement of civilians between the lines.[69] By 1 May, this increased surveillance program culminated in the introduction of a "unified system of identification passes" as well as a comprehensive registration of all civilians in the division's area of operations.[70] Though the division recognized that partisan activity in its area now amounted to practically nil, it viewed the new identification system as the means to "nip in the bud" any potential resistance.[71] It also noted, however, that the "existing famine, which can hardly be prevented," only exacerbated the partisan threat.

For both the 121st and 126th IDs, the destruction of the Volkhov pocket allowed them a period of refitting and rest. While problems with supply and with partisans certainly remained, these were minor nuisances in comparison with the experiences of the 123rd ID during its period in the Demiansk pocket. Despite, or perhaps precisely because

---

[66] AK I, 31.5.42, BA-MA RH 26–121/25.
[67] Zwischenmeldung vom 13.5.1942; Tagesmeldung vom 30.6.1942; both in BA-MA RH 26–121/26.
[68] 121 ID KTB Ib, 12.6.42, BA-MA RH 26–121/66. This followed an order by I Corps to utilize Soviet prisoners for this task; Generalkommando I A.K., Betr.: Minenräumen durch russische Gefangene, 9. Juni 1942, BA-MA RH 24–1/71. At approximately the same time, the 253rd ID established a construction company manned by prisoners of war; see Rass, *Menschenmaterial*, p. 362.
[69] 126 Infanterie Division, Abteilung Ic, Betr.: Bewegungsfreiheit der Zivilpersonen und Spionageabwehr, 2.3.42, BA-MA RH 26–126s/120.
[70] Ibid., 29.4.42.
[71] 126 Infanterie Division, Abt. Ic, Betr.: Bekämpfung feindlicher Agenten und Partisanen, 29.4.42, BA-MA RH 26–126/121. The following discussion is based on this document unless otherwise noted.

256   The evolution of military necessity

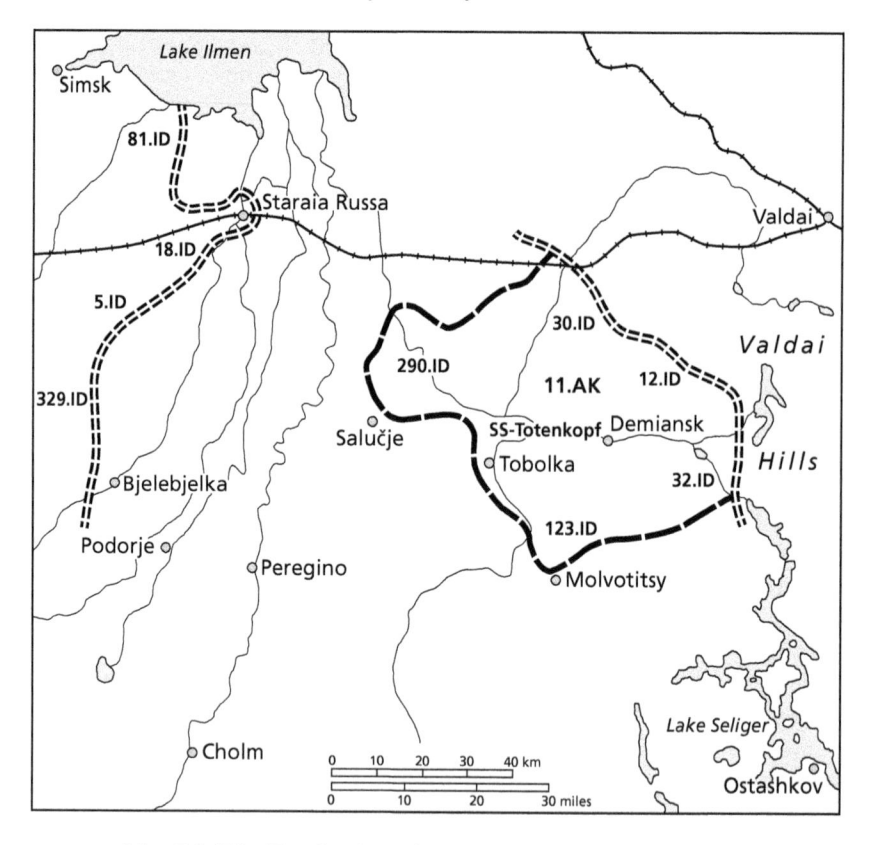

Map 8.2 The Demiansk pocket

of, its immediate circumstances, the 123rd ID actually carried out the most conciliatory program of these three divisions.

III. Life and death in the Demiansk pocket

During the opening months of 1942, the 123rd ID desperately tried to hold the line in the Demiansk pocket (see Map 8.2). With retreat ruled out by Hitler in hopes that the grandiloquently named "Fortress Demiansk" would serve as the jump-off position for a later attack on Moscow, the troops were instructed to "prepare for a long siege period."[72] They did this through the remainder of February and into early March,

---

[72] Halder, *Kriegstagebuch*, vol. III, 22 February 1942, p. 405. On Hitler's strategic justification for holding the Demiansk position, see Gerhard Weinberg, *A World at*

Life and death in the Demiansk pocket 257

alternating between brief periods of brutal fighting and scorched-earth retreats that finally ended with the reaching of the Pola river line on 6 March.[73] The commander of the formation (now reclassified as a battle group due to the chaos of the retreat) addressed his troops, stating that "the Pola position is the last position for Group Rauch in the defensive battle for Fortress Demiansk. It needs to be held until an attack from the outside brings relief. There is no other way."[74] In addition to holding the front, the 123rd ID also faced elements of the Red Army's 1st and the 204th Soviet parachute brigades dropped into the pocket in hopes of weakening German resistance from the inside.[75] Troops operating under the command of the 123rd ID finally eliminated the remnants of the paratroopers in early April, placing yet another burden onto the shoulders of the division.[76] The onset of wet weather complicated these combat missions. One soldier wrote home, "the cold has now broken and we have wet weather. You can imagine how one lives in bunkers in this weather."[77] The problem reached such proportions that the men were ordered to purchase both galoshes and rubber boots from the civilian population.[78] In addition to failing to supply the troops with adequate clothing, Sixteenth Army also proved unable to keep the men properly fed. Rations were reduced again by another third with only combat troops receiving full bread rations.[79] Constant enemy pressure, muddy spring weather, and inadequate supply were the burdens faced by the 123rd ID in the spring of 1942.

But who did the 123rd ID actually command? Unlike the 121st and 126th IDs, whose subordinate units generally remained together as a cohesive whole, the organic infantry and artillery battalions of the 123rd ID remained scattered throughout the Demiansk pocket, fighting under different commands, with one unit deployed at Kholm, completely outside

Arms: A Global History of World War II (Cambridge, 1994), p. 426; Generalkommando II Armeekorps, Abt. Ia, Nr. 333/42 geh., Korpsbefehl Nr. 109, 22. Februar 1942.
[73] One example of these scorched-earth tactics is found in the directive to retreat from the Molvotitsy Hedgehog position in which "all buildings [are] to be destroyed"; Gruppe Rauch, Abt. Ia/Az. IVa, Nr. 139/42 geh., 17. März 1942, BA-MA RH 26–123/53. For more on the brutal combat around the pocket, see Sydnor, *Soldiers of Destruction*, pp. 217–21.
[74] Gruppe Rauch, Abt. Ia/Az. IVa, Nr. 151/42 geh., Gruppenbefehl für den Ausbau der Polastellung, 6. März 1942, BA-MA RH 26–123/53.
[75] Generalkommando II Armeekorps, Abt. Ia, Nr. 803/42 geh., Korpsbefehl Nr. 119, 29. März 1942, BA-MA RH 26–123/55; Glantz, *The Battle for Leningrad*, p. 185.
[76] 123 ID KTB, 8.4.42, BA-MA RH 26–123/24.
[77] Private Konrad Weber, 272 Infantry Regiment, 26.3.42, BfZ, Sammlung Sterz.
[78] Gruppe Rauch, Ib, Besondere Anordnung für die Versorgung für den 27.3.1942, BA-MA RH 26–123/217.
[79] 123 ID IVa, Tätigkeitsbericht für die Zeit vom 1.–31.3.42, 6.4.1942, BA-MA RH 26–123/226.

Table 8.1 *415th Infantry Regiment's deployment, January–July 1942*

Dates of Deployment	Unit	Sections of 415th Infantry Regiment
13.1–1.3.42	32nd ID	I, III, 14th and Staff Company
13.1–5.3.42	32nd ID	I
6.3–12.3.42	30th ID	I
From 12.3.42	290th ID	I, III
2.3–11.3.42	Arko 105	III
1.2–31.5.42	Gruppe Eicke	Parts of 5th and 8th companies
1.6–10.7.42	Gruppe Eicke/SSTK Division	Parts of 5th and 8th companies

Table 8.2 *418th Infantry Regiment's deployment, August 1941–June 1942*

Dates of Deployment	Unit	Sections of 418th Infantry Regiment
28.8.41	3rd ID (mot)	IR 418th
14.9–12.10.41	12th ID	IR 418th
13.10–18.11.41	32nd ID	IR 418th
19.11–10.1.42	123rd ID	IR 418th
11.1–11.3.42	32nd ID	IR 418th
Since 12.3.42	290th ID	Rgts-Staff and Staff Company
Since 24.2.42	Gruppe Rauch	I
28.2–20.6.42	290th ID (Kampfgruppe Heckel)	II
21.6–23.6.42	II AK	II
Since 24.6.42	30th ID	II
4.3–14.6.42	290th ID	III
Since 15.6.42	SST-Div (Rgt. Brauer)	III

the pocket. Both the 415th and 416th Infantry Regiments were split up between different units in the pocket, while only one of the infantry battalions of the 418th Infantry Regiment remained under the command of the 123rd ID.[80] As Figures 8.1 and 8.2 indicate, subunits of the 415th and 418th Infantry Regiments fought the majority of 1941 and 1942 under command of other units instead of the 123rd ID.[81]

The division found itself commanding a motley group of units that one way or another had ended up in its area of operations during the

---

[80] Fernschreiben von 123 Infanterie Division an II A.K., Betr.: Einsatz der Btle., BA-MA RH 26–123/56.
[81] Unterstellungsverhältnisse IR 415, BA-MA RH 26–123/92; Unterstellungsverhältnisse IR 418, BA-MA RH 26–123/92.

Life and death in the Demiansk pocket 259

initial Soviet offensive and the subsequent chaotic German retreat.[82] The mixing of such units wreaked havoc on the division's regional cohesion as the amalgamation of these numerous "outsiders" severely weakened its combat efficiency.[83] Omer Bartov has suggested that as the Wehrmacht's replacement system broke down during the winter crisis, it reverted to a murderous military justice system along with a program of continual Nazi ideological indoctrination of the troops to keep them in the field; this had the secondary effect of converting individual soldiers into willing racial warriors for Hitler.[84] The experiences of the 123rd ID, however, seem to contradict this conclusion, as instead of morphing into an extremely violent, ruthless, and brutal unit, it followed an increasingly pragmatic course that differed from the tenets of *Vernichtungskrieg*.

While the various units of the 123rd ID battled against Red Army attempts to collapse the pocket, Army Group North prepared an offensive to break the encirclement. On 13 February 1942, Hitler demanded an attack from Staraia Russa to create a "land bridge" with the westernmost section of the pocket.[85] Only after German troops had regained the initiative on the Volkhov river could enough resources, particularly air assets, be assembled for Operation Brückenschlag (Bridging).[86] After several postponements, the attack was finally launched on 21 March and Gruppe Seydlitz initially made good progress.[87] A combat group inside the pocket, under the command of the Waffen-SS-Totenkopf Division and including elements of the 416th Infantry Regiment, prepared to meet the rescue forces.[88] Strong Soviet defenses on the banks of the Lovat river, however, soon

---

[82] While division command maintained control over the majority of its units (with the important exceptions of the infantry and artillery battalions), it also found itself commanding the following units: the 12th ID's reconnaissance unit, the 960th *Landschützen* Battalion, the 89th Infantry Regiment, Pionier Battaillon 671, Wachbataillon 707, a company of the 12th ID's anti-tank section, pieces of the 526th Artillery *Abteilung*, the 619th Motorcycle Battalion, and parts of 27th Infantry Regiment; see Kräfteverteilung 16. Januar 1942, BA-MA RH 26–123/224.
[83] Rass, "Das Sozialprofil von Kampfverbänden des deutschen Heeres 1939 bis 1945," pp. 680–2, here p. 681.
[84] Bartov, *Hitler's Army, passim*.
[85] Halder, *Kriegstagebuch*, vol. III, 13 February 1942, p. 399.
[86] See Klink's detailed discussion of the wrangling between Hitler, the OKH, Army Group North, and Sixteenth Army concerning the offensive; Klink, "Die Operationsführung," pp. 720–4.
[87] Halder, *Kriegstagebuch*, vol. III, 21 March 1942, p. 417. For one participant's view of the operation, see Gustav Höhne, "In Snow and Mud: 31 Days of Attack under Seydlitz during the Early Spring of 1942," in Steven Newton (ed.), *German Battle Tactics on the Russian Front, 1941–1945* (Atglen, 1994), pp. 109–35.
[88] SS-Totenkopfdivision Kampfstärken am 13.7.1942, BA-MA RH 26–123/92.

frustrated Seydlitz's assault, forcing II Corps's attack to be postponed yet again.[89] When the operation recommenced on 14 April, the Germans fell "upon the weakened Soviet units opposite them with frenzied vengeance."[90] Despite wet weather which not only flooded the German defensive system of bunkers and fortifications but also played havoc with the SS assault, the two combat groups met on 22 April, effectively ending the encirclement of II Corps.[91] For the 123rd ID, however, as well as for the rest of II Corps, the Demiansk saga had not yet concluded.

On 4 May, Army Group North called for a withdrawal of II Corps from their exposed position in the Demiansk area to the eastern banks of the Lovat river, but Hitler, maintaining his belief that the Demiansk position was necessary for any future operations against Moscow, vetoed such an operation.[92] His decision was reflected in a II Corps order of 19 May, which after congratulating the troops for holding their lines against superior enemy forces, emphasized the troops' mission: "The basic principle is as it was previously: no territory is to be surrendered to the enemy. Everyone holds his position until the last man and the last bullet!"[93] While II Corps no longer faced a struggle for survival, it still occupied a tenuous bulge in the enemy's line and this circumstance led to a large-scale program of fortification construction.[94]

The Demiansk bulge existed until late February 1943 when II Corps finally withdrew behind the Lovat river.[95] In the intervening nine months, the war in the Demiansk sector degenerated into wholesale positional combat. During 1942, engineers attached to the 123rd ID planted over 22,000 mines of various types while stringing out more than 400 rolls of barbed wire in front of the division's lines.[96] German

---

[89] Sydnor, *Soldiers of Destruction*, pp. 224–5. [90] Ibid., p. 225.
[91] On the effects of the Russian thaw, see II AK KTB, 10.4.42, 17.4.42, BA-MA RH 24–2/108; on the linkup between II Corps and Group Seydlitz, see 123 ID KTB, 22.4.42, BA-MA RH 26–123/46.
[92] Klink, "Die Operationsführung," p. 726.
[93] Generalkommando II Armeekorps, Abt. Ia, Nr. 1422/42 geh., Korpsbefehl Nr. 124, 19.5.1942, BA-MA RH 26–123/57. Emphasis in original. Five days after the encirclement was broken, II Corps issued an order stating that the troops were to "maintain defensive positions"; Generalkommando II. Armeekorps, Nr. 1177/42 geh., Korpsbefehl Nr. 120, 27.4.1942, BA-MA RH 26–123/56.
[94] See the six-page instructional pamphlet concerning fortifications: Gruppe Rauch, Abt. Ia/Az. IVa, Nr. 314/42 geh., Betr.: Ausbau der Pola-Stellung, 28. April 1942, BA-MA RH 26–123/56.
[95] Wegner, "The War against the Soviet Union 1942–1943," p. 1205.
[96] Anlage 2 zu Gruppe Rauch, Abt. Ia/Az. IVe 1 Nr. 1965/42 geh. vom 18.12.42, Anzahl verlegter Minen, Stand vom 17.12.1942, BA-MA RH 26–123/106; 123 ID Abt. Ia/Az. IVe 1 an Generalkommando II AK, 3. September 1942, BA-MA RH 26–123/106.

offensive action was limited to sniping while the Red Army kept pressure on German positions with frequent raids, shelling, and platoon-sized attacks.[97] Though no single engagement caused an inordinate number of casualties, in summation these firefights imposed the bloody logic of attrition on German formations, including the 123rd ID.[98] The transformation of the war into one of positions forced the 123rd ID to mobilize all possible resources to hold the line. While the fate of civilians scarcely registered with German authorities during the months of desperate fighting, men of the 123rd ID now began to recognize both the potential and the suffering of the civilian population in their area of operations.

The division's construction program relied on almost entirely civilian labor as the front line was unable to spare the men needed for this work. II Corps ordered "the ruthless use of all male and female members of the population" to improve defensive positions.[99] The engineer battalion immediately began utilizing numerous civilians as well as prisoners of war for these purposes, continuing this practice throughout summer 1942.[100] The fabrication of dwellings was especially important due to Soviet shelling of villages and towns in an attempt to deny German soldiers shelter.[101] Complicating the situation, heavy rains and thaws caused sudden floods that made many shelters unusable in the generally marshy area occupied by the 123rd ID.[102] The division also used civilians to maintain the roads, especially during fall when yet another muddy period set in. In one eleven-day period, for example, sixty men, 145 women, and seventy-three children worked under German supervision in repairing roads.[103] As had become

---

[97] Typical examples include the sixty-one claimed hits for the month of September and the forty-three for the month of October; see 123 ID KTB, 1.10.42, 1.11.42, BA-MA RH 26–123/46.
[98] II Corps complained that it had suffered over 4,000 casualties during the month of June despite the lack of any major combat.
[99] Generalkommando II Armeekorps, Abt. Ia, Nr. 1253/42 geh., Zusatz zum Korpsbefehl Nr. 123, 6. Mai 1942, BA-MA RH 26–123/56. Here again, a frontline unit – II Corps – anticipated orders from higher up the chain of command. In September, the OKH issued a directive which stated that "after hearing about how the Russians ruthlessly employ civilians in fortification construction, the Führer hoped that we were just as ruthless towards civilians in terms of constructing winter positions and especially tank ditches"; Oberkommando des Heeres, Gen St d H/Gen d Pi u Fest b Ob d H (L II O) Az. 39 OR, Nr. 5250/42 geh., 8.9.42, BA-MA RH 26–123/59.
[100] 123 ID KTB, 4.5.42, 7.5.42, BA-MA RH 26–123/46; Pionier Bataillon 123 Abt. Ia/M, Betr.: Riegelstellung "M," 31. Juli 1942, BA-MA RH 26–123/66.
[101] Gruppe Rauch, Abt. Ia/Az. Iva, 1. Mai 1942, BA-MA RH 26–123/56.
[102] Abschnitt Koßmala, Abt. Ia, Betr.: Kampfunterstände, 29.6.42, BA-MA RH 26–123/65. The I/418 reported that while thirty-three dugouts were finished, twelve of them were flooded.
[103] Fernspruch Nr. 17, Gruppe Rauch Ia an Gen Kdo II AK, Betr.: Einsatz russischer Zivilkräfte zum Straßenbau, 11.10.42, BA-MA RH 26–123/96.

Illustration 8.4 The food situation in the Demiansk pocket led civilians to find sustenance wherever possible.

the norm for German divisions operating in northwest Russia, civilians were also used to clear roads of snow during the winter months; in one particular case "the entire population" of two towns, including the elderly, women, and children, were ordered to take part in this work.[104]

Once a land connection was re-established to Sixteenth Army and the 123rd ID's situation became correspondingly more secure, it also focused more attention on the civilian population's food supply. Despite a continual increase in the division's rations until they reached their normal levels for the first time in three months in early May, the troops still scoured the landscape in search of food.[105] By mid-summer, numerous vegetables, including cabbage, turnips, and potatoes, were being cultivated in the pocket.[106] This summer harvest, however, came several months too late for many Soviet civilians. In late April, the veterinary company detailed that "civilians in Tobolka are on the point of starvation" and that "disease had broken out" as a result of malnourishment.[107]

[104] 123 Infanterie Division, Abt. Ia/Az. IV e 1, 18. December 1942, BA-MA RH 26–123/105.
[105] The opening of the land bridge connecting the pocket to Sixteenth Army allowed for rations to be raised; AK II KTB, 3.5.42, BA-MA RH 24–2/108; 123 ID IVa, Tätigkeitsbericht für die Zeit vom 1.-31.5.42, BA-MA RH 26–123/226.
[106] Lt. Wilhelm Berg, Inf. Rgt. 418, 31.7.42, BfZ, Sammlung Sterz.
[107] 123 ID KTB Qu., 25.4.42, BA-MA RH 26–123/201.

Nearly simultaneously, another divisional formation reported that starvation threatened a group of 192 refugees in a small village in its sector: "the food situation is so bad for the rest of the population, that there is nothing to give the refugees from their smallholdings."[108] Unrest had bubbled up in Pogorelizy, where "the population already has been rebellious and shouted out to the interpreter that one would rather be shot instead of being left to starve." As the quartermaster noted, "the supply situation for the civilian population is such that a decision needs to be made."[109]

Fearful of epidemics and possible revolts, the division contacted II Corps about the "emergency."[110] Though the two commands considered pushing the population across the front lines and making the civilians the responsibility of the Red Army, this idea was quickly dismissed as impracticable.[111] They finally decided to establish communal kitchens, under the supervision of the German-appointed civilian leader, in both Tobolka and Pogorelizy, where the inhabitants would receive a daily serving of thick soup.[112] The root of the problem in both villages appeared to be a number of refugees from the previously evacuated Molvotitsy. The survivors of that hastily carried-out evacuation, starving and wandering throughout the area, were refused any assistance by the poverty-stricken natives of the two towns and this clash created the volatile situation. The Molvotitsy evacuation and its results highlight the evolution of Wehrmacht policies towards civilians during the first half of 1942 as the division moved from an extremely ruthless and callous attitude towards Soviet civilians to one that demonstrated a more nuanced and conciliatory approach.

In an attempt to "improve" the "hopeless food situation for evacuated Russian civilians," the division issued a directive concerning the feeding of native inhabitants.[113] First, the division commander made the frontline commanders, as well as the German medics in each sector, responsible for implementing "emergency measures" in those villages that

---

[108] Abschnitt Noack Abteilung Ib, Betr.: Flüchtlinge in Gl.-Demidovo, 30.4.1942, BA-MA RH 26–123/204.
[109] Ibid., 30.4.1942.
[110] Ibid. The remainder of this discussion is based on this entry unless otherwise noted.
[111] The idea of forcing civilians across the line into Soviet-controlled territory was one that first surfaced in discussions concerning the fate of civilians in the Leningrad region and was finally put into practice on a horrifyingly large scale by Ninth Army in March 1944. On Leningrad, see Ganzenmüller, *Das belagerte Leningrad, 1941–1944*, pp. 37–8; for Ninth Army's actions, see Rass, *Menschenmaterial*, pp. 386–402.
[112] 123 ID KTB Qu., 1.5.42, BA-MA RH 26–123/201.
[113] Gruppe Rauch, Abt. Ib, Nr. 194/42 geh., Betr.: Ernährung der Zivilbevölkerung, 2. Mai 1942, BA-MA RH 26–123/205. The following discussion is based on this document unless otherwise noted.

required immediate help. In these especially affected communities, the troops were ordered to establish communal kitchens which, following the examples set in Tobolka and Pogorelizy, would be run by village leaders under the supervision of German units. The entire community would not receive sustenance from these kitchens; the distribution of a warm soup was to be limited to refugees only.

The section commanders were also to set aside a portion of the food intended for civilians already working for the army in order to supplement the soup. In order to qualify for this assistance, however, the refugees needed to provide labor for the Germans, be it construction or agricultural work. Though such a policy ensured that those civilians physically unable to work for the Wehrmacht still faced a struggle for survival, the commander pointed out that the division was unable to provide for everyone. He then stated that these communal kitchens and the supply of the "additional food strained the ... entire transport system etc., etc." and that the commanders needed to ensure that food was not wasted. Obviously, pragmatism and not humanitarianism constituted the bedrock of this initiative.[114]

Finally, the commander called for an "as intensive as possible cultivation of the land" as well as a close watch on all available seed in order to provide food and hay for both the troops and civilians during the upcoming months. In comparison with the previous summer, the division carried out the collection of food and hay in a much more organized manner. The division commander charged the *Ortskommandanten* and local economic officers with establishing hay commandos consisting of thirty civilians and soldiers to "ruthlessly bring in" all hay found in the area.[115] While "everything [needed] to be done to ensure a one hundred percent collection and securing of all animal food found in the divisional area," the responsible officers also had to make certain that villages received both payment for their hay and one ton of hay for each cow and horse within the village.[116] The division emphasized even more

---

[114] Similar motives guided the policy of Seventeenth Army as fear of unrest in its rear area led its commander, Colonel-General Hermann Hoth, to announce that "assisting [civilians] with food lies in the interests of the Wehrmacht and is an issue of extraordinary importance for the Army." The Seventeenth Army then began supplying civilians with food from its own stocks; see Oldenburg, *Ideologie und militärisches Kalkül*, p. 238.

[115] 123 Inf. Division, Ib/Wi., Betrifft.: Heuaufbringung im Div.-Bereich, 25. Juni 1942, BA-MA RH 26–123/206. One officer estimated that "thousands" of prisoners of war were used to gather the harvest; Lt. Wilhelm Berg, Inf. Rgt. 418, 31.7.42, BfZ, Sammlung Sterz.

[116] 123 Inf. Division, Ib/Wi. Betr.: Heuaufbringung im Div.-Bereich, 16. Juni 1942, BA-MA RH 26–123/206. A cynic, however, might ask how many such animals were still in the possession of civilians following the experiences of the winter fighting.

strongly that the fate of civilians was closely tied to that of the rye harvest, stating that "it is important that we bring in 100 percent of the harvest so the troops are not responsible for feeding the civilian pop[ulation] this winter."[117]

Such policies enacted by the 123rd ID led to an evolution of the relationship between soldiers and civilians in the operational area. A report issued by Sixteenth Army's intelligence section on 20 June characterized the attitude of the civilian population towards the Germans as "good."[118] While the overly optimistic tone of the report stretches credulity, the establishment of communal kitchens combined with German promises to eradicate the hated collective-farm system made at least some of the population more amenable to the invaders. The report also called for the "proper treatment" of civilians and prisoners of war in order to maintain this reservoir of goodwill. Other manifestations of this newfound attitude towards the Soviet population included the offering of medical services to civilians. In an order issued in November 1942, the division instructed its subordinate units that only those civilians whose injury or sickness "would be a burden on the troops" were to be sent to the primary civilian hospital located in Demiansk. The "closest troop doctor" needed to provide services for the remainder of civilians who required medical care and even appointments for "eyes, nose, ears, and throat . . . specialists" were made available to the population.[119]

Other orders issued by division command also indicated that the relationship between German soldiers and Soviet civilians, particularly women, had evolved to one far removed from a pitiless racial war. These were not isolated occurrences; various scholars have noted that the overwhelmingly male Wehrmacht showed real interest in the overwhelmingly female occupied areas, in both criminal and more personal ways; in other words, women were "a central aspect of their [German soldiers'] war experience."[120] The development of the division's situation played

---

[117] 123 Inf. Division, Ib/Wi., Betr.: Roggenernte, 12. August 1942, BA-MA RH 26–123/208.
[118] Armeeoberkommando 16 O. Qu/Qu.2, Verordnung zur Regelung des Arbeiteinsatzes, 18.7.1942, BA-MA RH 26–123/220.
[119] 123 ID Ib, 6.11.42, Besondere Anordnungen für die Versorgung zum Div.-Befehl Nr. 171, BA-MA RH 26–123/218.
[120] Neitzel and Welzer, *Soldaten*, p. 224. Rolf-Dieter Müller reaches a similar conclusion based on photo collections in the Russian–German Museum in Karlshorst, Berlin. While German soldiers took numerous pictures of their various experiences in the east, including those of dead enemy combatants, Müller states "that photos of encounters with native women were much more frequent"; Rolf-Dieter Müller, "Liebe im Vernichtungskrieg: Geschlechtergeschichtliche Aspekte des Einsatzes deutscher Soldaten im Rußlandkrieg 1941–1944," in F. Becker et al. (eds.), *Politische Gewalt in der Moderne* (Münster, 2003), pp. 239–67, here p. 239.

an important role in the growing interactions between the troops and the native population. With the transformation of the war from one of movement to one of positional warfare, the two populations were now living in the same areas and since the entire region could certainly be described as a "hinterland" that required closer relationships between soldiers and civilians for their mutual existence, it is not surprising that the Berliners became more involved with Russian women.[121]

Such developments were viewed with real consternation by Berlin and they resulted in Keitel issuing a statement on 9 September 1942 condemning these relationships:

> According to the existing reports, the lodgings [of German men] next to the civil population in the occupied Eastern territories led to closer contact and to partly steady relationships between German soldiers and local women. Apart from a significant increase of venereal diseases, this situation abets enemy spy activities and leads to a complete blurring of the necessary distance to the people of the occupied Eastern territories.[122]

Within three weeks, II Corps attempted to end the fraternization between women and soldiers by banning all long-term employment of Soviet females – as this led to co-habitation – and approved short-term work only during the day.[123] The troops' sexual desires and frustrations certainly played a part in causing such relationships, though this fails to tell the whole story. Members of the Eleventh and Seventeenth Armies also engaged in "very close relationships" with native women that were based on more than carnal appetites.[124] While acknowledging the importance of "satisfy[ying] sexual needs" as one component in the relationships between German soldiers and Soviet women, Regina Mühlhäuser also points to other causes, such as "the desire for normalcy and distraction, the wish for comfort or disentanglement from the family."[125] The continual attempts by the army to impress upon the soldiers that fraternization with Soviet civilians "threaten[ed] the respect for the power and strength of the German Army" illustrated the powerful attachments formed between the occupiers and the occupied.[126] While such developments certainly did not indicate that German soldiers had shed their racially tinged feelings of superiority towards the Soviets in

---

[121] Müller, "Liebe im Vernichtungskrieg," pp. 246–7.
[122] Cited in Mühlhäuser, "Between 'Racial Awareness' and Fantasies of Potency," p. 208.
[123] Generalkommando II AK, Korpstagesbefehl, 26.9.1942, BA-MA RH 26–123/97.
[124] Oldenburg, *Ideologie und militärisches Kalkül*, p. 316. See his further discussion of this issue on pp. 117–19, 245.
[125] Mühlhäuser, *Eroberungen*, p. 243.
[126] Armee-Oberkommando 16 Abt.: Ic/A. O. Nr. 463/42 geh., 20. Juni 1942, Betr.: Lagebericht Abwehr, BA-MA RH 26–123/220.

Life and death in the Demiansk pocket 267

general, it does point to a more nuanced relationship between occupiers and occupied than generally emerges in the literature.[127]

By attempting to halt the practice of arbitrary requisitioning, by proactively assisting starving civilians, and by striking up significant relationships with Soviet women, the actions of the 123rd ID and its men significantly departed from the planned war of annihilation. It is especially noteworthy that this modification of the division's earlier behavior took place while the division itself was undergoing supply problems as a result of the encirclement. Instead of radicalizing its behavior and ruthlessly exploiting the civilian population as the siege progressed, the 123rd ID implemented more conciliatory occupation policies designed to placate its rear area. Within the division's area of operations, pragmatism overrode ideological imperatives.[128]

These local initiatives, however, were sharply criticized by the Army High Command. On 23 August 1942, the OKH issued a directive to its forces in the Soviet Union entitled "Feeding of the Civilian Population in the Occupied Eastern Territories."[129] While the OKH recognized the difficulties facing civilians and their procurement of foodstuffs, it deemed "untenable" the "increasing number of commanders' petitions to make food drawn from army stocks available to civilians in both army and rear areas." The "serious food situation in the *Heimat*" meant that the civilians in the occupied areas should receive only a "minimum of food" and that these meager rations were in no way to be supplied by the German Army itself. The familiar refrain of how such assistance constituted a crippling burden on an already overstrained supply system was employed to justify a policy that "fundamentally prohibited" feeding civilians from the Wehrmacht's stores. Finally, the OKH asserted that "the supply of the civilian population is the exclusive task of the economic offices." Here, the center snuffed out policies on the periphery that, despite their obvious limitations, certainly presented civilians with increased chances of survival.

---

[127] As Mühlhäuser, "Between 'Racial Awareness' and Fantasies of Potency," p. 212, notes, "indeed, a German man could justify a romance with an 'ethnically alien woman' without questioning his racist ideas."

[128] Such opposition to the regime's goals also took place at much higher levels of the military hierarchy. The resistance of Field Marshal Erich von Manstein, commander in chief of Eleventh Army, to the plans to evacuate some 700,000 inhabitants of the Crimea to allow for the "Germanization" of the area, has been convincingly interpreted by Oldenburg as a triumph of pragmatism over ideology. See Oldenburg, *Ideologie und militärisches Kalkül*, p. 132.

[129] Generalkommando II Armeekorps, Qu. Nr. 987/42 geh., Besondere Anordnung für die Versorgung des II AK, Nr. 214, 23.8.42, BA-MA RH 26–123/220. The remainder of this section is based on this document unless otherwise noted.

While the available documentation gives no indication of the effects of this order on the 123rd ID's policies, it seems safe to assume that large-scale projects requiring noticeable amounts of food were shut down, while smaller, less-conspicuous programs continued. This, however, forced the division to find another solution to the problem of starving civilians in its midst. Evacuating civilians from the front area now dovetailed with the Reich's new program of labor procurement and this became the primary component of the division's relationship with civilians. The implementation of this forced-labor program, however, highlighted the contradictions inherent within military necessity. While the German Army required a quiescent and co-operative rear area in order to achieve victory on the battlefield, the voracious need for labor in the Reich led to the Wehrmacht's complicity in a program which roused more resentment and open resistance than any other during its occupation of the Soviet Union.[130]

The labor shortage that had plagued the Third Reich as far back as the late 1930s only intensified with the onset of global war in late 1941.[131] Ideological beliefs that militated against bringing "Bolshevik" laborers into Germany slowly faded with the realization that Operation Barbarossa had failed to destroy the Soviet state.[132] On 21 March 1942, Hitler appointed the *Gauleiter* of Thuringia, Fritz Sauckel, plenipotentiary for the mobilization of labor and charged him with gathering the necessary bodies to work in the factories, mines, and farms of the Reich.[133] In order to fulfill his duties, Sauckel and his 800 men employed in the occupied eastern territories were dependent on the Wehrmacht for support and assistance.[134] The German Army recognized this as a "task of decisive importance for the war" and its support of the program led to almost 3 million Soviet citizens being shipped to the Reich.[135]

---

[130] Berkhoff, *Harvest of Despair*, p. 274.
[131] For overviews of this problem, see Kroener, "The Manpower Resources of the Third Reich," pp. 846–940; Ulrich Herbert, *Hitler's Foreign Workers: Enforced Foreign Labor in Germany under the Third Reich* (Cambridge, 1997), pp. 27–137; and Tooze, *The Wages of Destruction*, pp. 260–4, 513–38.
[132] Ulrich Herbert, "Zwangsarbeit in Deutschland: Sowjetische Zivilarbeiter und Kriegsgefangene 1941–1945," in Rürup and Jahn, *Erobern und Vernichten*, pp. 106–30, here pp. 110–13; Herbert, *Hitler's Foreign Workers*, pp. 137–71, provides an excellent account of the decision-making process that resulted in the employment of Soviet laborers in the Reich.
[133] Peter W. Becker, "Fritz Sauckel: Plenipotentiary for the Mobilization of Labor," in Ronald Smelser and Rainer Zitelmann (eds.), *The Nazi Elite* (New York, 1993), pp. 194–201.
[134] Rolf-Dieter Müller, "Menschenjagd: Die Rekrutierung von Zwangsarbeitern in der besetzten Sowjetunion," in Hannes Heer and Klaus Naumann (eds.), *Vernichtungskrieg: Verbrechen der Wehrmacht, 1941–1944* (Hamburg, 1995), pp. 92–103, here p. 94.
[135] On the Wehrmacht's view, see ibid.; on the total numbers involved, see Herbert, "Zwangsarbeit in Deutschland," p. 107.

On 26 May, II Corps issued the order "The Recruitment and Deportation of Russian Workers for the Reich."[136] The corps presented this new policy as having "special meaning ... due to the poor food situation of the civilian population inside the pocket." Local *Ortskommandanten* were given the responsibility of working alongside village leaders in selecting workers. At this point, the search for labor focused only on volunteers, though some additional criteria existed: all workers aged sixteen to fifty years old were eligible, as were parents capable of work who had children under fourteen years of age. The troops were instructed that "politically and criminally unreliable" elements would not be brought to Germany, with "Asians and Jews" explicitly excluded. Various benefits were promised to the workers, including "preference in the parceling out of land [in the Soviet Union] after returning from the Reich, the rations of a German worker, appropriate shelter, and cash." After one week of recruitment in the 123rd ID's area of operations, 774 people reported for work in Germany; by 23 June, seven separate transports had evacuated 911 civilians out of the division's area.[137]

Since the numbers of volunteers were too low to solve the food issue in the pocket, the division turned to forced evacuations.[138] On 9 June, II Corps instructed its units to categorize the remaining civilians in their areas. The first category consisted of people whose work was indispensable either to the army or to the local economy and whose nourishment was secured, while the second category comprised productive workers with a precarious food supply. Inhabitants deemed "worthless for the corps or the economy" constituted the final group.[139] The division thus distinguished between "productive" and "non-productive" civilians, evacuating the latter to the rear. During the remainder of 1942, the division evacuated somewhere between 2,300 and 2,800 civilians from

---

[136] Gruppe Rauch, Ib, Betrifft: Anwerbung und Abschub russischer Arbeiter für das Reich, 26. Mai. 1942, BA-MA RH 26–123/205.

[137] 123 ID KTB Qu., 3.6.42, BA-MA RH 26–123/201; Gruppe Rauch, Ib/IV Wi., Betr.: Anwerbung und Abschub russischer Arbeiter für das Reich, 6. Juni 1942; 123 Inf. Division, Ib/Wi., Betr.: Anwerbung und Abschub russ. Arbeiter für das Reich, 16.6.42; Abteilung Ib, 23.6.42, BA-MA RH 26–123/205. The focus of recruitment subtly shifted in November 1942 when the division looked for "Russian women 15–35, healthy, no foreign/alien types, to go to Germany as household servants." Again, this was designed as a voluntary program; 123 Inf. Division, Abt. IV/Wi, 18.11.1942, BA-MA RH 26–123/211.

[138] As early as 5 May, II Corps contacted Sixteenth Army and argued for the "necessity of evacuating the civilian population out of the pocket" due to the difficulties in feeding civilians in the front areas and the destroyed villages who "crowded together in the middle of the pocket"; AK II KTB, 18.5.42, BA-MA RH 24–2–108.

[139] Generalkommando II. Armeekorps, Qu./IV Wi., Betr.: Abschub und Ernährung russischer Zivilbevölkerung, 9.6.1942, BA-MA RH 26–123/206.

its area of operations.[140] While the 123rd ID framed many of these evacuations in terms of the combat situation, the inability to feed these civilians also figured prominently in the decision-making process.[141] Though this process was much more organized than the earlier evacuation of Molvotitsy, similar problems afflicted the Germans. The 123rd ID complained that the "overflowing of villages with refugees and troops" in the rear area of the division held up the entire evacuation process.[142] Despite attempting to provide the evacuees with some sort of nourishment for the several-day march to Staraia Russa, the 123rd ID was able to allot only one piece of bread for every three people and hot soup at resting points during the trek.[143]

In addition to improving the food supply and creating a pool of available labor for the Reich, the evacuations in the summer of 1942 also were designed to reduce the partisan threat. Such measures had already been introduced by the 123rd ID during the previous fall, when they removed civilians in hopes of destroying the social networks that nourished partisan units. In contrast to the preceding fall and winter, however, partisan activity in 1942 was nearly nonexistent in the 123rd ID's area of operations. The division arrested several women and children on the ground of espionage but recorded the deaths of only two partisans between February and December.[144] One soldier wrote with relief that "it is a stroke of luck that the population has not followed Stalin's slogan to attack us in the rear."[145] Several reasons account for this decrease in activity. First, the concentration of German troops in the Demiansk pocket significantly increased the dangers for partisans of being discovered. Second, the German position was ringed by a fortification system that was much harder to penetrate than the more fluid front line

---

[140] See the entries in the 123 ID's quartermaster's war diary for 9.8.42, 11.8.42, 18.8.42, 22.8.42, 4.10.42, 4.11.42, BA-MA RH 26–123/201; Fernspruch 8.6.42, Betr.: Abschub russischer Arbeiter in das Reich, Fernspruch 16.6.42, II AK Qu, an alle Divisionen; Fernspruch, 21.7.42, an Ib, BA-MA RH 26–123/214; Fernspruch 123 ID, 16.11.42, BA-MA RH 26–123/216.

[141] 123 ID KTB Qu., BA-MA RH 26–123/201, 21.7.42; 1.8.42; 22.12.42. In October, the division requested the further evacuation of approximately 1,750 people as the "harvest yields would suffice for the civilian population until the end of the year." This food would last longer for those working for the Germans if the unproductive were deported; see Gruppe Rauch, Ib/Ia, Betr.: Evakuierung der Zivilbevölkerung, 23. October 1942, BA-MA RH 26–123/102.

[142] 123 Inf. Division, Abt. Ic, Betr.: Überwachung der Zivilbevölkerung, 28.9.1942, BA-MA RH 26–123/209.

[143] 123 ID KTB Qu., 9.8.42, BA-MA RH 26–123/201.

[144] Tätigkeitsbericht Ic mit Anlagen 21.6.–10.11.42, 14.8.42, BA-MA RH 26–123/155; Tätigkeitsbericht der 123 Inf. Division, Abt. Ic, für die Zeit vom 21.–30. November 1942, BA-MA RH 26–123/156.

[145] Lt. Wilhelm Berg, Inf. Rgt. 418, 31.7.42, BfZ, Sammlung Sterz.

of late 1941 and early 1942. Third, the foodstuffs required by partisans to survive simply did not exist in the Demiansk pocket as soldiers and civilians had stripped the area bare. Fourth, and perhaps most importantly, the division's more conciliatory occupation policies had helped ease the plight of the surrounding population; armed resistance accordingly lost some of its appeal with the change in circumstances. Nonetheless, the division ordered its men to remain vigilant of the partisan threat: "any weakness from our side will be seen by the Russian population as military weakness. It further undermines its obedience and trustworthiness towards the troops."[146]

IV. The crisis of the German replacement system?

The winter crisis of 1941–2 resulted from a suddenly resurgent Red Army putting immense pressure on an increasingly exhausted, underequipped, and, perhaps most importantly, undermanned German field army. According to the historian Bernhard Kroener, the winter crisis led to "the final collapse of a regular replacement system."[147] On the basis of his examination of three German combat divisions, Omer Bartov argues that the manpower pinch that faced the Wehrmacht in the fall and early winter of 1941 led the army to revamp its replacement system. Instead of ensuring that recruits from a specific military district were shipped to divisions originating from the same *Wehrkreis*, the army was forced to send its limited trained recruits to whatever units needed them, regardless of where they had been mustered. He continued, "the replacements which did arrive were too heterogeneous to make possible the formation of new 'primary groups,' and too few to make these veteran divisions once more militarily effective."[148] While Bartov concedes that the replacement system more or less staggered along during the first five months of Operation Barbarossa, the "Red Army's December counteroffensive ... finally destroyed whatever 'primary groups' may have remained intact."[149] Summing up his findings, he states,

one cannot avoid the conclusion that throughout the war in Russia the "primary groups" of the *Ostheer's* combat units could not have survived more than a few weeks at a time under battle conditions, and could thus not have played a significant role in the cohesion and motivation of the main bulk of the Wehrmacht's land forces.[150]

---

[146] 123. Inf. Division, Abt. Ic, Betr.: Überwachung der Zivilbevölkerung, 6.10.1942, BA-MA RH 26–123/98.
[147] Kroener, "The Manpower Resources of the Third Reich," p. 1025.
[148] Bartov, *Hitler's Army*, p. 38.   [149] Ibid., p. 41.   [150] Ibid., pp. 57–8.

On the surface, these contentions appear quite plausible. The unexpectedly high number of losses forced the German High Command to scramble in order to fill the gaping holes in the ranks. By mid-October, no trained reserves existed in Germany that could be sent to the front. Fromm ordered the creation of five new divisions, created around the cadre of men drawn from the staff of the Replacement Army. Raising these divisions was the last expedient of an Army High Command that had already shifted both numerous units from occupation duties in France and older soldiers, previously considered unfit for combat, to the Eastern Front.[151] All told, in addition to the 385,000 men available at the outbreak of hostilities, the Army High Command scraped together another 430,000 men, and sent nearly 815,000 replacements east. This, however, still left a shortage of nearly 836,000 soldiers.[152] Obviously, such a growing deficit placed severe strains on the tempo and success of German operations in the east. With the onset of the Soviet counterattack and subsequent winter crisis, the problem only increased in magnitude as, between December 1941 and March 1942, the *Ostheer* found itself short an additional 336,000 soldiers.[153] The question, however, is whether this should be seen as a general manpower crisis affecting the entirety of the *Ostheer* or if it was concentrated in specific areas around the front.[154]

Leeb's complaint of fighting a "poor man's war" in the fall of 1941 would only worsen during the winter crisis, though his army group was affected unevenly by the Soviet offensive.[155] On one end of the spectrum, the 121st ID lost 2,208 men between January and May 1942; while this certainly seems a high number, it nonetheless constituted a noticeable decrease from August and September when the division averaged 2,646 casualties per month.[156] Their comrades in the 126th ID suffered heavier casualties, due to the Soviet Volkhov offensive: during the course of the battle, 3,721 dead, wounded, and missing, as well as 1,636 men incapacitated by illness, were forced from the unit's ranks.[157]

---

[151] For an extended discussion of this process, see Kroener, "The Manpower Resources of the Third Reich," pp. 1018–23.
[152] Ibid., p. 1020.
[153] Mueller-Hillebrand, *Das Heer 1933–1945: Der Zweifrontenkrieg*, vol. III, p. 206.
[154] As Mueller-Hillebrand, ibid., p. 28, clearly illustrates, 76 percent of this soldier deficit was located within the ranks of Army Group Center (256,500 of the 336,300 missing spots).
[155] Leeb, *Tagebuchaufzeichnungen*, 8 September 1941, p. 352.
[156] Korpsarzt L. Armeekorps 10.7.42, Tätigkeitsbericht über die Zeit vom 15.8.41–7.5.42 – Personelle Verluste vom 1.12.41–28.2.42; Personelle Verluste vom 1.3–10.5.42, BA-MA RH 24–50/173.
[157] Tätigkeitsbericht der Abt. IIa/b Stand 31.12.41, BA-MA RH 26–126/131; Verband 126 ID Meldung 21.2.42; Verband 126 ID Meldung 20.3.1942; Verband 126 ID Meldung

Further to the south, the 123rd ID also saw its casualties temporarily fall during December, but then spike during the fighting for the Demiansk pocket. Between January and April 1942, the division suffered 4,239 casualties.[158] As illustrated by these numbers, the casualties inflicted by the Soviets on these three divisions considerably varied from one another. While each unit clearly felt the sting of the winter crisis in terms of its manpower situation, it is also clear that one master narrative cannot be applied to all three divisions. For some, the winter crisis actually served as a respite from the heavier fighting of the summer and fall of 1941, while for others a struggle for survival characterized the same time period.

Casualty numbers, however, are only one piece of the larger manpower mosaic. The numbers and types of replacements that entered Wehrmacht divisions are important on two accounts: first, did a reasonable number of young recruits from Germany stream to the front? Second, did these men originate from the home recruiting regions of each division? Understanding both of these issues is imperative in getting a grip on why German infantry divisions remained viable combat formations despite the numerous obstacles facing them (see Figure 8.1).

Following the severe manpower drain caused by the winter crisis of 1941–2, Wehrmacht replacement policy regained its equilibrium and began a more regular delivery of troops to the front.[159] In February 1942, 1,359 men joined the 121st ID, including 1,097 men from its designated training unit.[160] The largest contingent of men in this particular battalion was East Prussian, maintaining the division's internal cohesion.[161] Though the flow of recruits severely dwindled during the

vom 20.4.1942; Verband 126 ID Meldung 20.5.1942; Verband 126 ID Meldung 21.6.42, BA-MA RH 26–126/47.
[158] Verlustliste 123 Inf. Division vom 16.12.41 bis 31.3.1942, BA-MA RH 26–123/164; Tätigkeitsbericht der Abteilung IIa vom 16.1.–15.2.42, BA-MA RH 26–123/162; Tätigkeitsbericht der Abteilung IIa vom 16.2.42–15.3.42, BA-MA RH 26–123/163; Tätigkeitsbericht der Abteilung IIa v. 16.3. bis 15.4.42, BA-MA RH 26–123/165; Zustandsbericht 123 ID (o. IR 416, 4./ u.8/IR 418), Nr. 225/42 geh., 10.5.1942, BA-MA RH 26–123/230.
[159] According to Mueller-Hillebrand, *Das Heer 1933–1945: Der Zweifrontenkrieg*, vol. III, p. 206, Army Group North's manpower situation, while more strained than that of the southernmost army group, compared quite favorably to that of Army Group Center. In December 1941, the formation suffered 8,400 more losses than reinforcements. This number spiked to 26,400 in January 1942 before decreasing to 15,200 and 12,400 in February and March 1942 respectively. So while the crisis certainly had not been completely mastered by the German Army, its severity was trending towards a more manageable situation.
[160] L AK KTB, 10.2, 11.2, 28.2.42, BA-MA RH 24–50/15.
[161] 1./Inf. Regt. 407 (1. I.R. 407) [bisher 9. I.R. 3] Erkennungsmarken-Verzeichnis 2. April 1942, WASt, 80588; 1. Kompanie Infanterie-Regiment 405, 4. März 1942, Betr.: Veränderungen zur Liste der Erkennungsmarkern, WASt, 80549.

[Figure 8.1: Bar chart showing casualties and replacements for three divisions:
- 121st Infantry Division: Casualties 2208, Replacements 1412
- 126th Infantry Division: Casualties 5357, Replacements 5103
- 123rd Infantry Division: Casualties 4694, Replacements 1765]

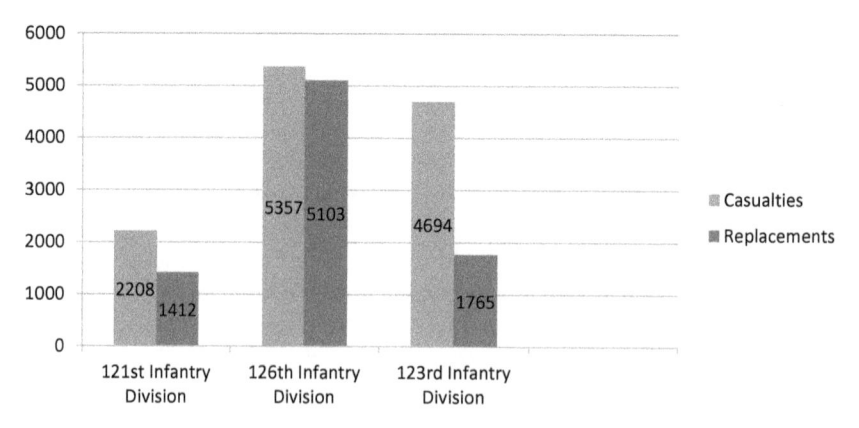

Figure 8.1 Divisional casualties and replacements during the winter crisis, mid-December 1941–April 1942

months of March and April, some 1,400 men entered the division's ranks, replacing approximately 65 percent of the division's casualties during the winter crisis.

The 126th Infantry Division also received a much larger stream of replacements during the winter crisis as 5,103 men joined its ranks by mid-April 1942.[162] Some 10 percent of this number were convalescents.[163] In addition to these veterans, five major shipments of men entered the division. Of these, three went through the unit's own *Feldersatzbataillon*, with another march company coming directly from the home military district. Only 132 men who originated in the Hamburg military district served to dilute the formation's homogeneity, but since these men were "mostly long-serving men who had been recently working in arms factories," division command decided such a dilution was worth the increase in combat-proven soldiers.[164]

These veteran soldiers were especially desirable due to the poor training that many of the new recruits had received before joining the division. They were variously described as having "large gaps in their training," being "inadequate" for combat and being prey to illness.[165]

---

[162] 126 ID Meldung 21.2.42; 126 ID Meldung 20.3.1942; 126 ID Meldung vom 20.4.1942, BA-MA RH 26-126/47.

[163] Tätigkeitsbericht der Abt. IIa/b, Stand: 28.2.1942; Tätigkeitsbericht der Abt. IIa/b, Stand: 31.3.1942; Tätigkeitsbericht der Abt. IIa/b, Stand: 30.4.1942, BA-MA RH 26-126/132.

[164] Tätigkeitsbericht der Abt. IIa/b, Stand: 28.2.1942, BA-MA RH 26-126/132.

[165] Tagesmeldungen vom 25.2.42; Tagesmeldungen vom 3.3.42; Tagesmeldungen vom 28.2.42, BA-MA RH 26-126/41.

The crisis of the German replacement system? 275

Negative judgments of incoming recruits were not unique to the 126th ID; such complaints echoed throughout the Eastern Army and were the result of the frantic attempts to send any and all men to the front, including "the least suitable members of their year-group."[166] While the superficial nature of training was universally derided within the division, the overall assessment of the incoming recruits was much more positive: "for the majority, the attitude towards military tasks is clear and firm. A youthful spiritedness and a confident mood generally exist. Discipline and external behavior are for the most part good."[167] So not only did the division's replacements add more than 1,000 additional men to the unit's rolls than had left between December 1941 and April 1942, they overwhelmingly originated in Wehrkreis VI and seemed to be made of solid, if unevenly trained, *Menschenmaterial*. Perhaps the Wehrmacht's replacement system had not been gutted by spring 1942.

The encircled German troops at Demiansk provided the system with its greatest challenge in the northern sector of the front. During the first month after the Soviet assault, it appeared the system had indeed collapsed as a mere 161 men reinforced the beleaguered unit.[168] The division did not receive its first significant *Feldersatzbataillon* delivery until late February/early March 1942, though another followed in short succession. Within the first three and a half months of 1942, 1,765 men joined the division's ranks, though such a number only filled less than half of the 4,233 spots opened during the fighting in early 1942.[169]

Company-level data supports these conclusions for all three divisions. The 121st ID's 1.I/405th and 1.I/407th suffered sixty-one and ninety-five casualties respectively from January to April 1942.[170] This average of just

---

[166] General Erich Fromm, commander of the Home Army and increasingly responsible for the replenishing of the Eastern Army, described the replacements in this way; quoted in Kroener, "The Manpower Resources of the Third Reich," p. 1063.
[167] 126 ID, 24.8.42, Betr.: Erfahrungsbericht über Ersatz, BA-MA RH 26–126/69.
[168] 123 ID, Tätigkeitsbericht der Abteilung IIa vom 16.1.-15.2.42, BA-MA RH 26–123/162.
[169] Tätigkeitsbericht der Abteilung IIa vom 16.1.-15.2.42, BA-MA RH 26–123/162; Tätigkeitsbericht der Abteilung IIa vom 16.2.42–15.3.42, BA-MA RH 26–123/163; Tätigkeitsbericht der Abteilung IIa v. 16.3. bis 15.4.42 BA-MA RH 26–123/165.
[170] For the 1.I/405th, see 1. Kompanie Infanterie-Regiment 405 4. Febr. 1942 Betr.: Veränderungen zur Liste der Erkennungsmarkern dem Bataillon; 1. Kompanie Infanterie-Regiment 405 4. März 1942 Betr.: Veränderungen zur Liste der Erkennungsmarkern dem Bataillon;1. Kompanie Infanterie-Regiment 405 4. April 1942 Betr.: Veränderungen zur Liste der Erkennungsmarkern dem Bataillon; 1. Kompanie Infanterie-Regiment 405 4. Mai 1942 Betr.: Veränderungen zur Liste der Erkennungsmarkern dem Bataillon; and 1. Kompanie Infanterie-Regiment 405 4.6 1942 Betr.: Veränderungen zur Liste der Erkennungsmarkern dem Bataillon, WASt, 80549. For the 1.I/407th, see 1./Inf. Regt. 407 (1. I.R. 407) [bisher 9. I.R. 3]

over thirty-five monthly combined casualties compares favorably to the more than forty-seven average losses each month during the advance in 1941. Incoming recruits actually exceeded losses for the first time in the war, with ninety-nine men joining the 1.I/405th Infantry Regiment and 147 soldiers entering the 1.I/407th Infantry Regiment; for the former, ninety-two were cohesive recruits, with 46 percent originating in East Prussia, while the latter took in 129 cohesive men and had a total of 30 percent of its intake call Wehrkreis I home.

For the men of the 126th Infantry Division's regiments – the 1.I/422nd and 2.I/424th – the fighting during the winter crisis led to 135 and 129 casualties respectively.[171] As a testament to the intensity of the fighting on the Volkhov river, this averaged out to nearly forty-one casualties per month or nearly seventeen more than during the advance in 1941. In the case of the 1.I/422nd and 2.I/424th Infantry Regiments, replacements nearly compensated for the losses suffered during the winter crisis. The former received 133 replacements – 71 percent of which came from Rhineland-Westphalia – 117 of whom were cohesive. The latter took in ninety-six men; 57 percent of this company's men were drawn from Wehrkreis VI and twenty-nine were cohesive replacements.[172]

While the 126th ID faced desperate fighting during the winter crisis, this paled beside the near existential struggle for survival waged by the 123rd ID, a fact reflected by the existing company-level documentation. Only the 1.I/415th Infantry Regiment reported casualties during the winter crisis but its reports were too sporadic to determine the company's number of losses.[173] The only existing documents are for April 1942, and during this month the 1.I/415th Infantry Regiment received sixty-eight reinforcements while its sister regiment, the 1.I/416th, saw 135 men enter its ranks. Of these 203 men, 44 percent originated in Wehrkreis III, but only forty were cohesive. The cases of these two companies suggest that the Germans struggled to get troops

---

Erkennungsmarken-Verzeichnis, dated 5. Feb. 1942; 1. März. 1942; 2. April. 1942; and 7. Mai. 1942, WASt 80588.

[171] For the 1.I/422nd, see 1. Inf. Regt. 422 (1./I.R. 422) Erkennungsmarkenverzeichnis (Veränderungsmeldung), dated 8.2.1942; 8.3.1942; 8. April. 1942; and 8. Mai. 1942, WASt, 82026. For the 2.I/424th, see the monthly reports 2. Inf. Regt. 424 Veränderungsmeldung zur Liste der ausgegebenen Erkennungsmarken 10.2.42 through 10.6.42, WASt, 82066.

[172] See the reports cited in n. 171.

[173] For the 1.I/415th, see 1. Kompanie Infanterie-Regiment 415 Erkennungsmarkenverzeichnis /Veränderungsmeldung/ 18.II.1942 and 1. Kompanie Infanterie-Regiment 415 Erkennungsmarken-Verzeichnis (Veränderungsanzeige) 12.5.1942, WASt, 80744.

The crisis of the German replacement system? 277

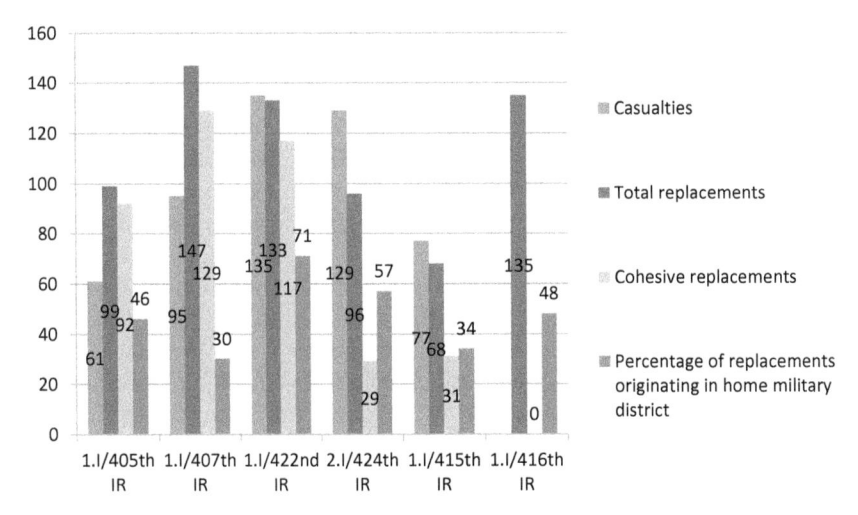

Figure 8.2 Company casualties and replacements during the winter crisis, January–April 1942. Note that records for the 1.I/415th are available only for January and April 1942 and that the 1.I/416th only has documentation for replacements from April 1942.

into the pocket during the initial, chaotic fighting and that while they made a concerted effort to shuttle men to the 123rd when the situation began to stabilize, they were unable to deliver troops specifically drawn from Berlin-Brandenburg. Nonetheless, even in the case of a division on a precarious section of the front, the German replacement system appears to have functioned relatively adequately (see Figure 8.2).

What do the personnel situations of the 121st, 123rd, and 126th IDs tell us about the German replacement system during the winter crisis? Certainly the German gamble to invade the Soviet Union resulted in a situation in which all three units were starved of replacements during the last few months of 1941. As the situation deteriorated at the front during the winter crisis, the replacement system paradoxically began to function in a more regular manner. Not only did more troops enter the ranks of the three divisions during the crisis period than in the opening months of invasion, but both the 121st and 126th IDs actually received more men than they lost during this period. Surely the experiences of these three divisions cannot be simply generalized to the rest of the *Ostheer* but they do suggest that the much maligned replacement system was perhaps not as ramshackle as previously thought.

V. From crisis to stability

The period stretching between January and May 1942 clearly illustrates the importance of military necessity to the combat units of Army Group North. While the virulent racism that riddled Nazi state and society certainly influenced the actions of both the army as an institution and the men themselves, the evolution of German policy towards Soviet civilians and prisoners demonstrates that the Wehrmacht was more concerned with defeating the Red Army in combat than in waging a merciless war against the Soviet population.

During the initial period of crisis in January and February 1942, German policy towards civilians quickly radicalized. Plunged into a true crisis by the Soviet offensive, the Wehrmacht ruthlessly carried out any and all programs designed to increase or, at the very least, maintain its combat efficiency while simultaneously lowering that of the advancing Red Army. Such a shift in German policy towards civilians neatly fits into the notion of military necessity: the hitherto ignored civilian population became an important tool or target (depending on the particular policy) once the fortunes of war shifted. This appears, however, as more of a desperate attempt to mobilize every available body in an effort to hold the line than part of an ideological war against the civilian population, though it certainly dovetailed with Nazi conceptions of the war. While the end result of these German policies likely resulted in the deaths of numerous civilians – malnourished women and children performing hard physical labor in the winter without proper clothing had little or no chance of surviving – these were not ideologically motivated deaths per se: rather, they were a result of the German Army's utilization of every and all means, no matter the collateral cost, to secure victory.

Once the army had mastered the crisis, however, it again shifted gears. Instead of waging an increasingly violent and arbitrary campaign against the Soviet people, the Germans attempted to construct a more stable relationship with civilians. This certainly did not mean that the German units treated civilians or prisoners with a newfound respect, as the practices of the 121st ID demonstrate. It did indicate, however, that the terror which characterized the frequently one-sided relationship between soldiers and civilians no longer operated as the sole means of interaction; this new dynamic was most clearly illustrated by the experiences of the 123rd ID in the Demiansk pocket.

The Berliners of the 123rd ID enacted by far the most conciliatory policies of the three divisions under analysis. Humanitarian concerns in all likelihood provided little of the impetus behind these programs, however; instead, the division realized its survival in the pocket depended on a quiescent rear area and it therefore attempted to neutralize preemptively any discontent before it could flare into open resistance. This break with the interpretation of military necessity that emphasized terror was even more noteworthy due to the division's situation. Insufficiently supplied, woefully undermanned, and lacking the internal cohesion of either the 121st or the 126th IDs, the 123rd ID's actions never degenerated into an all-encompassing war against the surrounding population. Rather, it provided specialized medical care for civilians trapped within the pocket and instituted a program designed to feed neighboring civilians. These were not the actions of "Hitler's Army." They were, however, the actions of a combat division that understood that its battlefield mission could only be completed if it modified its approach to Soviet civilians; here pragmatism, or military necessity, trumped ideology.

While these policies proved at least partially successful in creating the preconditions necessary for a successful defense of its positions, this same doctrine of military necessity also led to the establishment of the forced-labor program, one that worked at odds with more conciliatory policies. The 123rd ID, therefore, found it extremely difficult to, in the words of Küchler, "tie together ... the material interests of ... the peasantry with German interests" as the Germans failed to develop a coherent occupation policy that systematically took the problems of the civilian population into consideration.

9 "From one mess to another"
War of attrition in northwest Russia

I. Combat in late 1942: the 126th and 121st Infantry Divisions

During the remainder of 1942, Red Army pressure on the exterior of the pocket continued. Between July and September, the Northwest *Front* launched three major assaults on German positions.[1] Though none of these operations affected the 123rd ID in any significant way, the grim logic of attrition led to a general decrease in available German manpower within the Demiansk position, forcing Army Group North to transfer more units into the pocket.[2] One of these units was the 126th ID, which took up a position on the southern side of the land bridge, next to the 123rd ID.

After bearing the full brunt of the Soviet attack on the Volkhov river in January and then participating in the prolonged struggle to destroy the trapped Red Army forces during the spring, the 126th ID was pulled out of the line in early July for what it believed was a long and hard-earned period of rest and refitting.[3] Following a little more than two-week break, however, the division was ordered to deploy in the Demiansk land bridge. The division found this "completely surprising" and complained that "the full combat strength of the division was in no way restored [and] the combat value of the division was accordingly limited."[4] Army Group North's manpower crunch, however, was such that even mauled divisions were needed in the lines. One soldier wrote,

---

[1] Erickson, *The Road to Stalingrad*, p. 381.
[2] Wegner, "The War against the Soviet Union 1942–1943," p. 997. For the deleterious effects on German units engaged in this combat, see Sydnor, *Soldiers of Destruction*, pp. 238–50.
[3] 126 ID KTB, 3.7.42, BA-MA RH 26–126/57. Army group commander in chief Küchler visited divisional headquarters on 17 July and "promised" the division a long rest; 17.7.42, 19.7.42.
[4] Ibid., 19.7.42.

unfortunately the war still isn't over. But we are hoping for the best, that it will soon be over ... we will be moved out from here in the next few days and deployed somewhere else. From one mess to another.[5]

Following the shift, the division focused on training programs as well as other activities typical of all German divisions in northwest Russia: road building, the construction of fortifications, and maintaining rail lines.[6] This period of relative inactivity, however, soon ended with the advent of Operation Michael.[7]

Hitler and Army Group North wanted to enlarge the size of the land bridge to the Demiansk pocket to increase supplies delivered by truck. On 27 September, the offensive opened near the southern shoulder and the 126th ID and the 5th Light Division advanced several kilometers to the west (see Map 9.1).[8]

While historian Bernd Wegner has described the operation as "rapidly successful against an evidently surprised enemy," for the men on the ground, the reality appeared quite different.[9] The war diarist of the 126th ID noted that the first day of the operation "was one of the toughest days of battle during the Eastern Campaign that the division has gone through up until now."[10]

Operation Michael ended on 10 October after a ten-kilometer expansion of the land bridge.[11] The battle was especially costly to the division, as it suffered an astounding 1,830 casualties during the thirteen-day battle.[12] Once again, the bulk of the casualties were shouldered by the infantry regiments, with the 422nd Infantry Regiment losing over 50 percent of its combat strength and the other infantry regiments nearing this casualty rate.[13] Operation Michael was the last offensive in which any of the three divisions under investigation took part. For the remainder of

---

[5] Private Karl Hartmann, Inf. Rgt. 422, 5.7.42, BfZ, Sammlung Sterz.
[6] Ibid.; 126 Infanterie Division, Betr.: Weiterbildung des Ersatzes der Gruppe v. Knobelsdorff, 15.8.42, BA-MA RH 26–126/69; 126 Infanterie Division, Tagesmeldung an Gruppe v. Knobelsdorff, 17.8.42, BA-MA RH 26–126/60.
[7] In the 126th ID's records, the operation is called Operation Michael; in the war diary of the OKW, it is termed Operation Winkelried. Following my sources, I will use the former designation.
[8] Schramm, *KTB OKW*, vol. III, 28 September 1942, p. 773.
[9] Wegner, "The War against the Soviet Union 1942–1943," p. 907.
[10] 126 ID KTB, 27.9.42, BA-MA RH 26–126/57.
[11] 126 ID KTB, 9.10.42, BA-MA RH 26–126/57; Schramm, *KTB OKW*, vol. IV, 11. Oktober 1942, p. 819; Wegner, "The War against the Soviet Union 1942–1943," p. 907.
[12] 126 Infanterie Division, Tagesmeldung an Gruppe v. Knobelsdorff, 30.9.42, BA-MA RH 26–126/62; Generalkommando II. Armeekorps, Abschlußmeldung über die Kämpfe im Robja-Lowat-Winkel, BA-MA RH 26–126/63.
[13] Tagesmeldung vom 5.10.42, BA-MA RH 26–126/63.

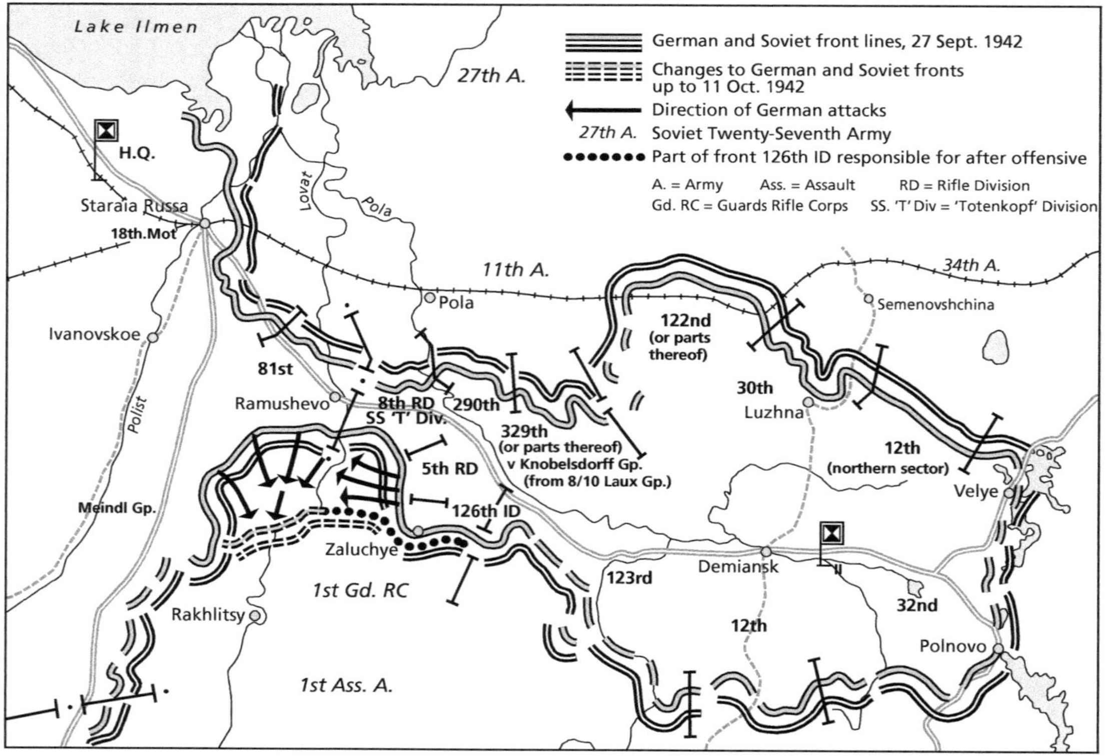

Map 9.1 Operation Michael

the war in northwest Russia, the Red Army held the initiative and Army Group North merely reacted to the enemy's operations.

Unlike the Rhinelanders, who were thrown back into battle almost immediately after the conclusion of the Volkhov pocket battle, the East Prussians of the 121st ID were ordered to return to their old positions outside Leningrad – Pavlovsk and Pushkin – for refreshing.[14] Division commander General Wandel, while certainly cognizant of the severity of the fighting on the Volkhov and the effects this had on his unit, nevertheless characterized the condition of the 121st ID as "quite satisfactory."[15] Refitting would be necessary, however, as the East Prussians were earmarked to participate in the 1942 offensive designed to seize Leningrad. German planning for Operation Nordlicht (Northern Light) commenced after the issuing of Hitler's War Directive No 41 on 5 April 1942.[16] While the primary focus of the Wehrmacht's 1942 summer offensive would be the oil fields of the Caucasus region, Hitler also charged Army Group North with three objectives: the seizure of Leningrad, the establishment of a common front with the Finns, and the capture of the Arctic ports through which the Allies delivered Lend–Lease materials to the Soviet Union.[17] Since he recognized that Army Group North lacked the necessary resources to fulfill these tasks, Hitler ordered the transfer of newly minted Field Marshal Erich von Manstein and his Eleventh Army to northern Russia in late August.[18] Fresh off its siege and subsequent capture of Sevastopol, Eleventh Army possessed both the necessary experience and what the German High Command described as artillery on the scale of "Verdun in the First World War" to finally crush Leningrad's defenses.[19] The 121st ID was placed under the command of Eleventh Army and prepared to take part in the general assault on the city, scheduled for 14 September 1942.[20]

Red Army activity, however, increased during late July 1942 both in an attempt to forestall any German offensives in the region and to relieve the

---

[14] 121 ID KTB, 30.6.42, BA-MA RH 26–121/24; "Mein Regiment," BA-MA RH 37/3096.
[15] Halder, *Kriegstagebuch*, vol. III, 7 July 1942, p. 476.
[16] Weisung 41, in Hubatsch, *Hitlers Weisungen*, pp. 213–19.
[17] The most comprehensive look at German planning for Operation Nordlicht remains Andreas Hillgruber, "'Nordlicht': Die deutschen Pläne zur Eroberung Leningrads im Jahre 1942," in Peter Classen and Peter Scheibert (eds.), *Festschrift Percy Ernst Schramm*, vol. II (Wiesbaden, 1964), pp. 269–87. See also Wegner, "The War against the Soviet Union 1942–1943," pp. 991–1001; and Schramm, *KTB OKW*, vol. IV, 23. August 1942, pp. 627–9, n. 1.
[18] Manstein, *Lost Victories*, pp. 259–60; Wegner, "The War against the Soviet Union 1942–1943," pp. 991, 993; Halder, *Kriegstagebuch*, vol. III, 23 August 1942, p. 509.
[19] Schramm, *KTB OKW*, vol. IV, 8. August 1942, p. 558, n. 2.
[20] Haupt, *Heeresgruppe Nord*, p. 134. For a detailed look at the actual deployment for the operation, see Kleinfeld and Tambs, *Hitler's Spanish Legion*, pp. 211–12.

pressure faced by Red Army units operating in southern Russia.[21] Though these assaults failed to influence decisively German operations, they did cause several units, including the 121st ID, some anxious moments. Soviet forces pushed the East Prussians out of their forward positions and these could only be retaken after savage hand-to-hand combat in a series of bunkers.[22] The Red Army finally canceled the operation on 4 August, by which point the 121st ID had recovered their former lines at a cost of over 110 casualties in the 405th Infantry Regiment alone.[23]

On the heels of these engagements, the Soviets launched a major offensive on 27 August designed to break through the German "bottleneck" that separated Leningrad from Red Army forces east of the city.[24] While German troops initially held the attack, by the second day the situation had deteriorated into a "truly unpleasant breakthrough."[25] Within four days, Soviet troops had penetrated a depth of nearly ten kilometers, nearing the high ground outside the strategically important town of Siniavino, but at this point the advance lost its momentum.[26] As a result, Army Group North deployed units earmarked for Operation Nordlicht in an attempt to seal off the Soviet penetration, effectively canceling any German offensive.[27] Hitler, infuriated at what he termed "irresolute leadership" on the part of Eighteenth Army, ordered Manstein to take command of German troops in this area on 4 September.[28] Two days later, the commander of LIV Corps informed the 121st ID that it was to deploy behind the battered Waffen-SS-Polizei Division, northwest of the breakthrough.[29] The East Prussians prepared for their part in the first Ladoga battle (see Map 9.2).

After several days of indecisive fighting, Eleventh Army launched an operation from the north and south of the bulge in an attempt to tie it off, with the former spearheaded by the East Prussians.[30] Three days into the attack, the division complained that "the continual melting away of combat strength" necessitated the delivery of further troops as it faced

---

[21] 121 ID KTB, 20.7.42, BA-MA RH 26–121/28; Glantz, *The Battle for Leningrad*, p. 215.
[22] 121 ID KTB, 25.7.42, BA-MA RH 26–121/28.
[23] Glantz, *The Battle for Leningrad*, p. 216; Tagesmeldung, 28.7.42, BA-MA RH 26–121/31.
[24] Erickson, *The Road to Stalingrad*, p. 381; Halder, *Kriegstagebuch*, vol. III, 27 August 1942, p. 511.
[25] Halder, *Kriegstagebuch*, vol. III, 27 August 1942, 28 August 1942, pp. 511–12.
[26] Glantz, *The Battle for Leningrad*, pp. 219–22.
[27] Halder, *Kriegstagebuch*, vol. III, 30 August 1942; Manstein, *Lost Victories*, pp. 264–6.
[28] Schramm, *KTB OKW*, vol. III, 4. September 1942, p. 678.
[29] 121 ID KTB, 6.9.42, BA-MA RH 26–121/28; Kleinfeld and Tambs, *Hitler's Spanish Legion*, p. 216.
[30] 121 ID KTB, 19.9.42, BA-MA RH 26–121/28; Schramm, *KTB OKW*, vol. III, 9. September 1942, p. 703; Wegner, "The War against the Soviet Union 1942–1943," p. 1000.

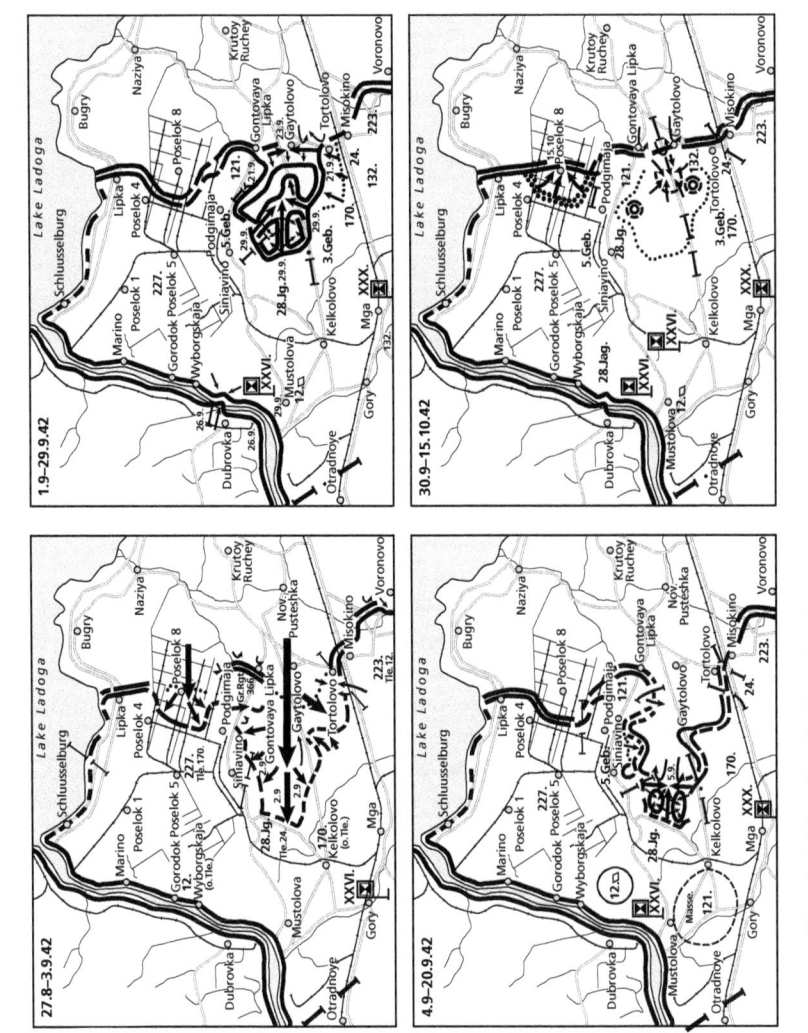

Map 9.2 The first Ladoga battle

Illustration 9.1 Fighting in the Ladoga region resembled that of the Western Front during the First World War.

constant Soviet counterattacks.[31] By 2 October, the numbers of dead testified to the intensity of the fighting: while the 121st ID took over 2,060 prisoners and counted another 1,000 dead in front of their positions, they suffered heavy casualties of their own, with 591 dead, 2,395 wounded, and ninety-seven missing.[32] That combat also exacted a toll on the division's matériel was evidenced by an order from XXVI Corps calling for the use of prisoners of war to scour the battlefield for clothing and equipment even before the fighting had ended.[33] Following the conclusion of the battle, the 121st ID was shipped to the Tosno area where, outside its duties of securing rail lines, it was given the opportunity to rest and refit.[34]

---

[31] 121 ID KTB, 22.9.42, BA-MA RH 26–121/28; Halder, *Kriegstagebuch*, vol. III, 22 September 1942, p. 527; Schramm, *KTB OKW*, vol. III, 24. September 1942, pp. 762, 775.
[32] 121 ID KTB, 1.10.42, BA-MA RH 26–121/28; 121 Infanterie Division, Zustandsbericht, 7.10.42, BA-MA RH 26–121/42.
[33] 121 ID KTB Qu., 30.9.42, BA-MA RH 26–121/66.
[34] Fernspruch, no date, BA-MA RH 26–121/44.

After its efforts in the first Ladoga battle, the commander of the 121st ID described his unit as "not ready for action."[35] While the division's continued success on the battlefield ensured "confidence and firmness" in the men, "the high physical demands, exhaustion, being covered in lice and susceptibility to health problems" had dramatically lowered their combat effectiveness. Since leaving Pavlovsk and Pushkin, the men had been forced to live in the field without any shelter and this had contributed to their exhausted state. All three infantry regiments required an extended period of convalescence both to integrate and to train newly arrived replacements as well as to provide the veterans with a period of much-needed rest. For the next three months, the 121st ID was given the opportunity to refit without serious combat.

II. The evolution of occupation policy in northwest Russia

While the 123rd ID developed more conciliatory occupation policies in an ad hoc manner due to its circumstances during 1942, both the 126th and 121st IDs did so in more systematic and considered manners. In the case of the Demiansk pocket, local conditions led to a reappraisal of policy; for the 121st ID in Pavlovsk and its surrounding region, high-level decisions played a much more important role. The leadership of Wirtschaftsstab Ost called for a program designed to boost the production of goods needed by the Wehrmacht in the occupied territories.[36] Focusing on the manufacture of materials that Soviet civilians had already been producing for the 121st ID since the previous winter – warm clothing, shelter, and repair shops for vehicles – the so-called *Generalquartiermeister-Programms* merely codified pre-existing local practices of putting the Soviet economy to work for the German cause.

In Pavlovsk, economic issues increasingly determined the fate of the civilian population. Home to scenes of unimaginable desperation and suffering during the winter of 1941–2, the communities of northwest Russia haltingly began to breathe again by summer. This was primarily due to more available food, a result of both a much smaller population (following the mass starvation and deportations of the preceding months) and a more efficient occupation administration. German authorities introduced ration cards on 1 July in Pushkin, Pavlovsk, Liuban, and other towns in northwest Russia, and these cards "brought noticeable

---

[35] 121 Infanterie Division, Zustandsbericht, 7.10.42, BA-MA RH 26–121/41.
[36] Gerlach, *Kalkulierte Morde*, pp. 428–9.

relief" to the civilian population.[37] The simple fact that a ration system was finally instituted signified a major shift in German attitudes; such measures had been consciously rejected during the first year of war because they could be interpreted as constituting a formal responsibility on behalf of the Wehrmacht to feed civilians.[38]

These improvements, however, were soon canceled out by other German policies as the 121st ID received an order from L Corps on 29 July calling for the complete evacuation of the Pavlovsk–Pushkin area on "defensive grounds."[39] This evacuation had been in the planning process for at least a month and it was motivated by both economic and military reasoning. Within four days, German troops began dividing the civilian population into categories based on their potential for productive labor.[40] On 6 August, L Corps ordered the beginning of the evacuation and specified how many civilians were to be transported to various camps. 1,200 people deemed unable to work were to be shipped to a refugee camp in Krasnogvardeisk, Eighteenth Army's engineer section was to receive 1,500 civilians believed capable of work, and a further 500 were designated for shipment to the Economic Staff East branch stationed in Krasnogvardeisk.[41] Placed in charge of the entire evacuation plan, the 121st ID had deported a total of 1,410 civilians from Pavlovsk and a further 1,810 from Pushkin by 9 August.[42] Further evacuations resulted in an additional 1,638 inhabitants from Pushkin and 991 from Pavlovsk being shipped to refugee camps as well as for labor with the Todt Organization and other German groups.[43]

Those civilians who remained in the area due to their economic indispensability, such as the 100 workers at the Pushkin Mechanical Works and skilled workers at the felt and cotton factories, had until 30 August to move into the ghettos established for them.[44] Doctors and nurses were also kept within the cities in order to attend to the remaining civilians and keep them healthy enough to work. A mere eight days after the operation began, the number of civilians had been pared down to 869 inhabitants in Pushkin and 1,329 in Pavlovsk, including

[37] KTB des Wirtschaftskommandos Krasnogvardeisk für die Zeit vom 1. Juli–15. Aug. 1942, 1.7.42, BA-MA RW 31/949; Wi. Kdo. Krasnogwardeisk, Az. Gr. Fü/HA./Mö Br. B. Nr. 42, Monatsbericht für die Zeit vom 20.6. bis 20.7.1942, BA-MA RW 31/949.
[38] Pohl, *Die Herrschaft der Wehrmacht*, p. 196.
[39] 121 ID KTB Abt. Ib, 29.7.42, BA-MA RH 26–121/66; II AK KTB Qu., 30.6.42, BA-MA RH 24–50/179.
[40] 121 ID KTB Abt. Ib, 31.7.42, BA-MA RH 26–121/66.   [41] Ibid., 6.8.42.
[42] Ibid., 9.8.42; II AK KTB Qu., 10.8.42, 13.8.42, BA-MA RH 24–50/179.
[43] 121 ID KTB Abt. Ib, 11.8.42, 12.8.42, 13.8.42, 14.8.42, BA-MA RH 26–121/66.
[44] Ibid., 17.8.42.

102 women and 418 children deemed incapable of labor. Women also constituted the overwhelming majority of workers – 1,258.[45]

As this discussion of the evacuations of Pavlovsk and Pushkin makes clear, frontline combat units in the Wehrmacht were not only complicit in rounding up labor for German use but actually played the leading role in the process. While the Germans legitimized the initial deportations from Pavlovsk in September and October 1941 under the mantle of security, it is clear that the evacuations of July and August 1942 were part of a larger program to create labor for the army and the Reich. The shipment of 674 civilians to the *Wirtschaftskommando* Group at Krasnogvardeisk, as well as the delivery of 613 people to the Todt Organization, confirms the economic reasoning behind the evacuations: these organizations needed labor and the 121st ID provided it.[46] Just as the actions of the 121st ID in Pavlovsk in 1941 emphasize the tight connections between ideological and security policies, so too do its actions in 1942 highlight the false dichotomy sometimes offered between military and economic goals: during the war against the Soviet Union, the tasks of combat, economic exploitation, and ideological purification became the joint responsibility of all German institutions and individuals in the east.

Christian Hartmann's claim that the procurement of labor fell outside combat divisions' primary tasks is simply wrong and Christoph Rass's contention that "while security aspects as well as the protection of the infrastructure counted as the primary motives [for evacuations] in 1942, economic interest played an important role by 1943 at the latest" also requires some modification.[47] The 121st ID organized and carried out the evacuations of Pavlovsk and Pushkin in the summer of 1942 primarily due to economic demands, with the majority of these men, women, and children being sent to work for one or another German organization in the occupied eastern territories. Those deemed unable to work faced a far grimmer fate. "Useless eaters" clearly fell extremely low on the Wehrmacht's list of priorities and, in all probability, disease and starvation claimed numerous victims. Once again, the dictates of military necessity led to Wehrmacht policies that contradicted one another. On the one hand, the 121st ID became much more involved in the feeding of the population in the ring around Leningrad because it needed

---

[45] Ibid., 16.8.42. The total number included 417 men who could work and three deemed unable to provide labor.
[46] 121 ID KTB Abt. Ib, 13.8.42, 15.8.42, BA-MA RH 26–121/66.
[47] Hartmann, "Verbrecherischer Krieg – verbrecherische Wehrmacht?", pp. 43–7; Rass, *Menschenmaterial*, p. 354.

its labor for the war effort. On the other hand, the Reich and the army's continual need for workers led to deportations, forced labor, and a classification of the population in which those deemed unable to work simply existed beyond the purview of military necessity. So instead of creating a pliant and supportive group of civilians, the army's policy merely antagonized them, resulting in open resistance to German rule.

Even the most brutal of the three divisions under examination – the 126th ID – modified its occupation policies during the summer of 1942. Following its transfer to II Corps in the Demiansk pocket, its occupation policy began to resemble the 123rd ID's but the violence which marred its advance in 1941 never strayed far from the surface. Since the Rhinelanders faced nothing like the crisis confronting the 123rd ID, its understanding of military necessity never demanded conciliatory occupation policies on the level of those of the Berliners. While security for the troops remained the primary issue concerning division command – much as it did for the 123rd ID – the 126th ID approached it from a different angle. Division command called for good relations with the civilian population as it believed this would stunt any partisan activity. This was to be achieved through a strict supervision of the population; such firmness, however, could also elide into terror: "whoever does not report the presence of partisans or supports them will be shot."[48]

In early September, the division scaled back its responsibilities by ordering its troops to stay out of the fray of village affairs. Crimes between individual civilians were to be punished by the local, native administration and not by the troops.[49] Only those actions which disrupted the division's ability to fight or threatened the hierarchical relationship between the occupiers and civilians received German attention. An attempt to soften the response of the troops to civilians and their actions also emerged from the same order. No longer should the men severely punish civilians for simple ignorance; for example, failure to report for work or traveling without a valid pass was not be punished severely. Instead a "light punishment," such as a warning or additional labor, was to be utilized and only in "difficult cases" would more severe penalties, including shipment to a prisoner-of-war camp or the death sentence, be employed.

---

[48] 126 Infanterie Division, Abt. Ia Nr. 735/42 geheim, 18.7.42, BA-MA RH 26–126/69.
[49] 126 ID, Abt. Ic – Nr. 303/42 geh., Betr.: Erfahrungen über durchgeführte Befehlsmaßnahmen gegen Fälle von Auflehnung oder Straftaten der Zivilbevölkerung sowie Vorschläge auf diesem Gebiet, 8.9.1942, BA-MA RH 26–126/124. The following discussion is based upon this document unless otherwise noted.

Perhaps even more noteworthy, the division also attempted to break the men of their habit of shooting partisans and suspected partisans out of hand as "immediate shooting closes the possibility of further disclosure." This type of order would only be needed if a unit engaged in violent and arbitrary behavior; as the earlier experiences of the 126th ID indicate, this was indeed such a unit. From the very beginning of Operation Barbarossa, it resorted to the use of terror in its dealings with alleged partisans and its massacre of prisoners during the Volkhov fighting further distinguished it from both the 121st and the 123rd IDs. Such an order indicates that many soldiers in the division simply resorted to on-the-spot executions without determining that such suspects were indeed partisans; these arbitrary applications of terror only worked against the grain of the new occupation order that was gradually and fitfully being forged in northwest Russia.

"Political expedience" became the foundation of this new system in the 126th ID's area of occupation. Recognizing the "privations" that all Russians lived with, the division tried to remove some of the challenges facing civilians in order to minimize the "hate and desperation" of the surrounding population. Division command also acknowledged that its "ruthless execution of the death penalty" during the fighting between January and March had lost its validity during a time of relative inaction and the division now implemented more lenient policies in an early manifestation of a hearts-and-minds campaign.

The Rhinelanders, however, did not completely discard their terror policies. Public shootings and hangings were still to be utilized in cases of serious offenses and the latter were to remain on display for up to two days as a warning to the remainder of the population. There was also a more concerted effort to involve the SD and the GFP in carrying out criminal investigations and in enforcing occupation policy. An example of this occurred in December 1942. Sixty civilians, suspected of supporting partisan activity, were arrested by members of the 126th ID.[50] Instead of executing the civilians out of hand, the division shipped the civilians to the local branch of the GFP in Staraia Russa. While such actions can be viewed as an attempt to focus the division's activities on combat duties, they also indicate the submerging of the 126th ID into the larger network of Nazi criminality that permeated the occupied territories of the Soviet Union.

Finally, and most interestingly, the division ordered the establishment of uniform guidelines for its rear area. While the lack of standardization

---

[50] Tätigkeitsbericht Ic, 1.10.1942–31.12.1942, 31.12.1942, BA-MA RH 26–126/125.

among German military and civilian agencies in occupying the eastern territories has long been recognized by historians, astoundingly no standardization existed during the first year of war even within the 126th ID's area of responsibility: as the division commander noted, a Russian employed as a supply column driver who pilfered a few sausages for himself could be publicly hanged by one officer while another would have merely jailed him for a few days.[51] In an attempt both to combat the partisan movement and to control the movements of refugees in its area of operations, the division introduced a unified pass system for civilians. Local collaborators also became increasingly utilized by the division in maintaining German rule.[52] German-appointed mayors were responsible for registering all inhabitants and dividing them into different categories: those indigenous to the village and outsiders who arrived after 22 June 1941. The latter, termed "aliens," had their passes marked "A," while Jews carried identification stamped with a "J"; here again, the army involved itself in the regime's genocidal policies, even if its soldiers were not personally pulling the trigger.

The 126th ID also endeavored to pacify the population by respecting its places of worship. Division command forbade the men from using Orthodox Churches as shelters or for any other military purpose.[53] These measures, designed to reduce friction between soldiers and civilians, showed real progress in at least one area: relationships between German soldiers and Soviet women. As the policies towards civilians relaxed, contact between soldiers and native females increased. This led the division to forbid "all social contact with Russians" as well as "going arm in arm with female Russians in public." The problem reached such proportions that numerous other activities were also prohibited, including giving photographs as presents, dancing, regular visits by Soviet women to German homes, and the cohabitation of Soviets and Germans.[54] Just like their comrades in the 123rd ID, numerous

---

[51] See, for example, Hans Umbreit, "Towards Continental Dominion," in Kroener et al., *Organization and Mobilization of the German Sphere of Power*, pp. 11–383, especially pp. 99–120; and Mazower, *Hitler's Empire*, pp. 223–56; Befehl über die Ausgabe von Ausweisen an die Zivilbevölkerung im Operationsgebiet, no date, BA-MA RH 26–126/124.

[52] On the need for native manpower to administer and police the occupied territories, see Kilian, *Wehrmacht und Besatzungsherrschaft*, pp. 162–85, especially pp. 163–70; Frank Golczewski, "Die Kollaboration in der Ukraine," in Dieckmann, Quinkert, and Tönsmeyer, *Kooperation und Verbrechen: Formen der "Kollaboration" im östlichen Europa, 1939–1945, Beiträge zur Geschichte des Nationalsozialismus*, pp. 151–82, here pp. 171–5; Gerlach, *Kalkulierte Morde*, pp. 196–214.

[53] 126 Infanterie Division, Abteilung Ic, Beitrag zur Dienstanweisung für Ortskommandanten, 20.9.1942, BA-MA RH 26–126/124.

[54] For very similar orders issued by the Economic Staff East and Rear Army Area 585 in early 1942, see Mühlhäuser, *Eroberungen*, pp. 261–3.

men within the 126th ID attempted to find "a small sliver of the feeling of home [*Heimatgefühl*] in the war."[55] In an attempt to escape at least momentarily from the "bleak and oppressive daily life" that faced them, soldiers looked to "create a 'parallel world' to theirs at home that would, however, remain carefully separated from it."[56]

The clear contradictions within the 126th ID highlight the difficulty in positing one master narrative for the German–Soviet war. Despite being members of a division that quickly resorted to arbitrary violence, it is apparent that many of the Rhinelanders viewed the surrounding population not merely as the *Untermenschen* of Nazi ideological lore but rather as people who shared at least some similarity to themselves; as Mühlhäuser has noted, if men from units such as the 126th ID could engage in such relationships, the army faced "a serious military problem" in its attempts to insulate its troops from the civilian population.[57]

Military necessity also led to a fundamental break in the army's previous practices. Following a decision made by the OKH, the 126th ID announced on 5 September 1942 that Soviet civilians and prisoners of war would be allowed to join the German Army in a limited capacity, thus freeing up German soldiers employed in the rear for combat duty; this decision was "especially" approved by the division leadership.[58] By the end of the month, the division already employed 237 prisoners and fourteen civilians and had set aside a further 210 slots for the *Hiwis* (*Hilfswilligen*, or volunteer helpers).[59] The use of Soviet prisoners of war and other civilians had two possible outcomes. First was that the troops' hierarchical ascension within the army would lead them to treat the auxiliaries with casual brutality and indifference. That this type of behavior did occur was reflected in a memorandum that spelled out the reasons for the rather high rate of desertion by these auxiliaries. According to the division's intelligence section, prisoners increasingly deserted due to "high labor demands with insufficient food; complete exhaustion without adequate medical care; poor shelter and clothing that in no way protects them from cold or wet; mistreated on the march or at

---

[55] Bernhard Chiari, "Zwischen Hoffnung und Hunger: Die sowjetische Zivilbevölkerung unter deutscher Besatzung," in Hartmann, Hürter, and Jureit, *Verbrechen der Wehrmacht*, pp. 145–54, here p. 149.
[56] Mühlhäuser, *Eroberungen*, pp. 248, 249. The more coercive aspects of the relationships between German soldiers and Soviet women should not be overlooked; see ibid., pp. 214–39, on the brothels established by the German Army.
[57] Ibid., p. 262.
[58] 126 Infanterie Division Abteilung Ia/Ic, Betr.: Landeseigene Hilfskräfte im Osten, 5.9.42, BA-MA RH 26–126/124; Tätigkeitsbericht Ic, 5.9.42, BA-MA RH 26–126/124.
[59] 126 Infanterie Division, Abt. Ic, Betr.: Landeseigene Hilfskräfte im Osten. Übersicht über die Hilfswilligen, 30.9.42, BA-MA RH 26–126/124.

294   "From one mess to another"

work (beatings)."⁶⁰ Second, continual contact between Germans and Russians had the possibility of decreasing animosity between the two. This was recognized as a possibility by the Soviet resistance, which targeted *Hiwis* not merely out of feelings of betrayal but also out of recognition that successful collaboration could lessen German violence and mortally wound the resistance movement.⁶¹

The East Prussians also took advantage of the OKH's decision to allow the use of *Hiwis*. Even before the fighting south of Lake Ladoga, the division began to use "released" prisoners of war and civilians to take over rear-area duties as part of a determined program to raise the unit's combat strength.⁶² While the troops were instructed to keep a close eye on the auxiliaries to ensure their loyalty, division command also wanted its men to view the Soviets as human beings and not through the prism of National Socialist ideology. It called for "good treatment, sufficient food, and accommodations suitable for a man" as these were "the means to create trust and to train the *Hilfswilligen* for voluntary and industrious work."⁶³ Further orders, however, contained traditional German views of the East. One that examined the training of *Hiwis* focused on "habituation to personal order and cleanliness"; here, the German Army strove to construct a more orderly and Germanized east one individual at a time.⁶⁴ But, as these orders indicate, the German Army was now forced to look at Soviet citizens in a far different light than it did during the heady days of advance in 1941 when they simply failed to register in the Wehrmacht's mission-oriented outlook.

III. The state of the infantry, late 1942: replacements and training

As the German military leadership planned its offensive operations for 1942, questions of manpower again came to the fore. With the class of 1921 already haphazardly sent to the front to staunch the bleeding of the

---

[60] 126 Infanterie Division, Abt. Ic – Nr. 417/42 geh., Betr.: Entlaufen von Kriegsgefangenen, 5.11.1942, BA-MA RH 26–126/125. Six days later, seventy civilians escaped from a labor camp due to the poor working conditions; Tätigkeitsbericht Ic, 1.10.1942–31.12.1942, 30.11.42, BA-MA RH 26–126/125.
[61] 126 Infanterie Division, Abteilung Ic, 19.9.42, BA-MA RH 26–126/124. For discussions of partisan attitudes towards collaborators, see Kenneth Slepyan, *Stalin's Guerillas: Soviet Partisans in World War II* (Lawrence, KS, 2006), pp. 79–84; and Weiner, "Something to Die for, a Lot to Kill for," pp. 118–19.
[62] 121 ID KTB Qu., 28.8.42, BA-MA RH 26–121/66; 121 Infanterie Division, Erhöhung der Kampfstärken, 27.10.1942, BA-MA RH 26–121/36.
[63] 121 Infanterie Division, Einstellung und Behandlung von "Hilfswilligen," 9.12.42, BA-MA RH 26–121/37.
[64] 121 Infanterie Division, Ausbildung von Hilfswilligen, 28.12.42, BA-MA RH 26–121/37.

winter crisis, that of 1922 began its training in early spring in the expectation that its 270,000 men would be available as replacements for the field army by fall.[65] Other measures, such as the creation of an organization of women to assume staff positions in both Germany and the occupied territories, as well as another combing through of western Europe for younger soldiers, also led to additional troops being sent east. Resistance from the new minster of armaments, Albert Speer, however, frustrated army attempts to outfit large numbers of industrial workers in field gray, as did the regime's fear of excessively straining the home front.[66] Despite these measures, the army as a whole had received only 350,000 replacements – including returning convalescents – by September 1942: such a number failed to balance out the 600,000 casualties suffered during the same period.

As a result both of the impossibility of completely filling all of the empty ranks and of Hitler's refusal to dissolve decimated units due to possible morale issues at home, the army underwent a dramatic restructuring. Beginning in summer 1942, the German Army was divided into four classifications. Only forty of the total 156 infantry divisions operating in the eastern theater of war received first-order classification, meaning that they would be replenished and equipped for offensive operations for the following summer. A further fifty-four divisions were classified as second-order units, meaning that either one of their infantry regiments or three battalions were dissolved, decreasing the formation's striking power by a third. An additional fifty-four divisions were now referred to as *Stellungsdivisionen*, intended for stationary defense. Finally, eight divisions possessed only one infantry regiment, though they were to be equipped with weapons designed specifically for defense.[67]

The 121st ID began this process on 15 July 1942, dropping from three to two battalions per infantry regiment, and it was joined by the 123rd and 126th IDs in being downgraded to a second-order division.[68]

---

[65] Mueller-Hillebrand, *Das Heer 1933–1945: Der Zweifrontenkrieg*, vol. III, pp. 50–2. The following discussion is based on his discussion unless otherwise noted.

[66] Bernhard Kroener, "'Menschenbewirtschaftung,' Bevölkerungsverteilung und personelle Rüstung in der zweiten Kriegshälfte (1942–1944)," in Bernhard Kroener et al., *Das Deutsche Reich und der Zweite Weltkrieg*, vol. V/II, *Organisation und Mobilisierung des deutschen Machtbereichs* (Stuttgart, 1999), pp. 777–1001, here pp. 821–4.

[67] Ibid., p. 828.

[68] Tessin, *Verbände und Truppen der deutschen Wehrmacht*, pp. 286–7. This process did stretch for a longer period of time in the case of some units such as the 123rd ID's 418th Infantry Regiment, whose II Battalion was not dissolved until 20 March 1943 due to the combat situation. See II AK KTB, 20.3.1943, BA-MA RH 24-2/110; Mueller-Hillebrand, *Das Heer 1933–1945: Der Zweifrontenkrieg*, vol. III, pp. 62–3.

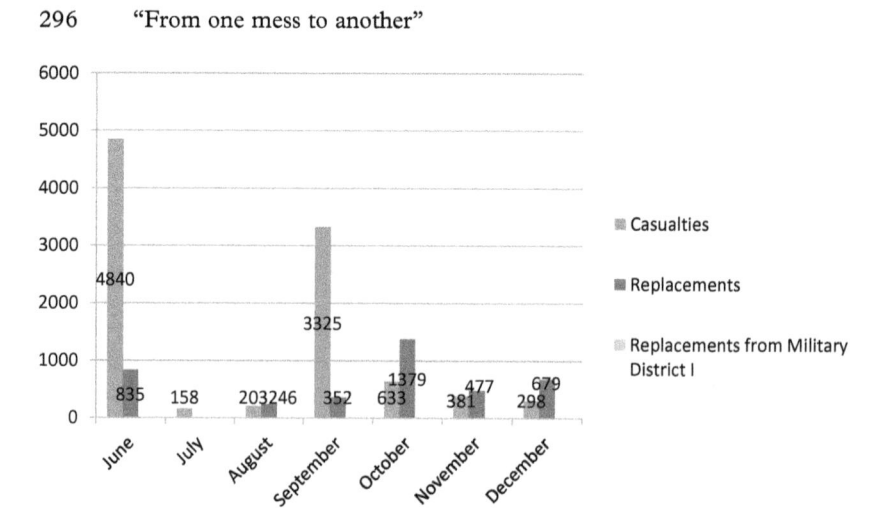

Figure 9.1 121st Infantry Division manpower, May/June–December 1942

Restructuring the divisions had real effects on their manpower situations. On the one hand, each unit now required fewer men to fill its ranks and this resulted in a situation in which its remaining infantry battalions more regularly approached the full-strength complement decreed by the High Command. In other words, each division could fill the gaps in its ranks with far fewer replacements. On the other hand, each division's combat power was significantly cut and while the army made real attempts to balance this loss of manpower through the use of more powerful and plentiful weapons, none of the divisions under examination here reached the levels of strength they had possessed in June 1941. So while the number of recruits entering the rifle companies generally compensated for the losses they suffered during mid-1942, they failed to increase the power and strength of the division as a whole.

As previously noted, heavy combat flared up twice for the 121st ID during the second half of 1942: the final reduction of the Volkhov pocket in June and the first Ladoga battle in September. Outside these two episodes of sustained combat, replacements outnumbered casualties during the remainder of the year (see Figure 9.1[69]). Though the front calmed in northwest Russia during the summer, fighting on other sections of the front and the consequent casualties forced training in the rear areas to be condensed to two months. In an attempt to alleviate the effects of this decision, the OKH ordered that the next shipment of

---

[69] 121 ID KTB, 26.5.42, 28.6.42, BA-MA RH 26–121/24;

The state of the infantry, late 1942   297

troops expected to arrive in July were to receive an additional four weeks of training behind the lines. Experienced members of the 407th and 408th Infantry Regiments needed to "educate them [the recruits] on the difficulties and strains of the *Ostkrieg*."[70] Earlier ad hoc measures now became official policy as the manpower situation continued to worsen and front units devoted increasing amounts of time to training incoming green recruits. Convalescent companies also began regularly returning to the division beginning in August. The division's ranking personnel officer commented that the "morale and training of those with the convalescence company ... were good" and that "the men made a good impression in every respect, showed great interest in the fighting of the division during their time away and were obviously happy to return to action in their old circle of comrades."[71] Eighty-seven officers and 897 men rejoined the division during the last five months of the year, providing a link between the division's new recruits and the front veterans.[72] In addition to these reinforcements, the 121st ID also received forty-eight replacement officers as well as an additional 1,358 soldiers as the year wound down.

Unlike their East Prussian counterparts, who underwent two periods of intense yet brief combat and then rested for longer periods of time, the men of the 126th ID found 1942 to be a year of rather consistent combat at the front. After being taken out of the front line during the battle for the Volkhov pocket in early spring 1942, the division entered a short-lived quiet period before becoming involved in the fight to widen and then hold the land bridge to the Demiansk pocket, where it remained locked in combat for the remainder of the year (see Figure 9.2[73]).

The most noteworthy development for the 126th ID's replacement situation during the second half of 1942 was the return of 2,412 convalescent troops, who were "immediately integrated into the units."[74] So even in the case of a division which had taken part in bitter fighting

---

[70] 121 ID, Ausbildung der Feld-Ersatz-Btl 121, 9.5.1942, BA-MA RH 26–121/25.
[71] Bericht über den eingetroffenen Ersatz mit Anlage "Eingetroffener Ersatz," BA-MA RH 26–121/63. The following section is based on this document unless otherwise noted.
[72] 121 ID KTB, 5.8.42, BA-MA RH 26–121/28. See source in note 71 above.
[73] 126 ID, Meldung 20.5.1942; 126 ID, Meldung 21.6.42, BA-MA RH 26–126/47; 126 Infanterie-Division Meldung vom 8.8.42; 126 ID, Meldung vom 8. Oktober 1942; 126 ID, Meldung vom 8. November 1942; 126 ID, Meldung vom 7. Dezember 1942, BA-MA RH 26–126/69; 126 ID, Meldung vom 7. Januar 1943 Zustandsbericht, BA-MA RH 26–126/91; Tätigkeitsbericht der Abt. IIa/b, Stand: 31.8.1942, BA-MA RH 26–126/133.
[74] Tätigkeitsbericht der Abt. IIa/b, Stand: 31.5.1942; Tätigkeitsbericht der Abt. IIa/b, Stand: 30.6.1942, BA-MA RH 26–126/132; Tätigkeitsbericht der Abt. IIa/b, Stand: 31.7.1942; Tätigkeitsbericht der Abt. IIa/b, Stand: 31.8.1942, BA-MA RH 26–126/133. The cited phrase comes from this document.

298 "From one mess to another"

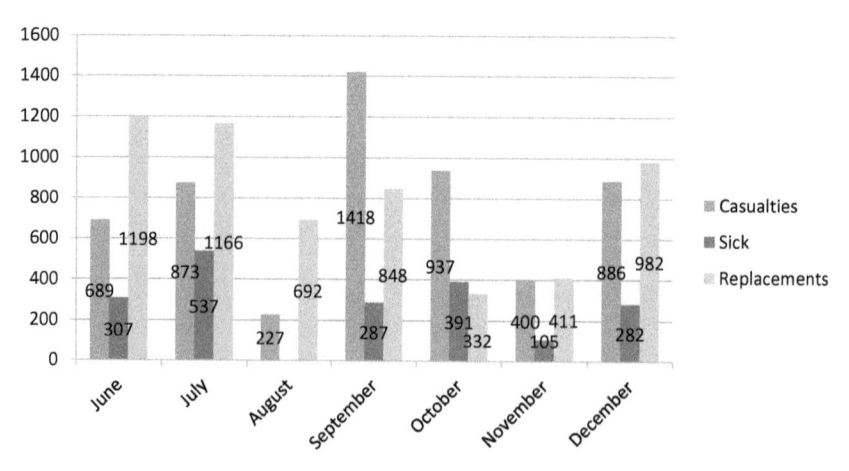

Figure 9.2 126th Infantry Division manpower, June–December 1942

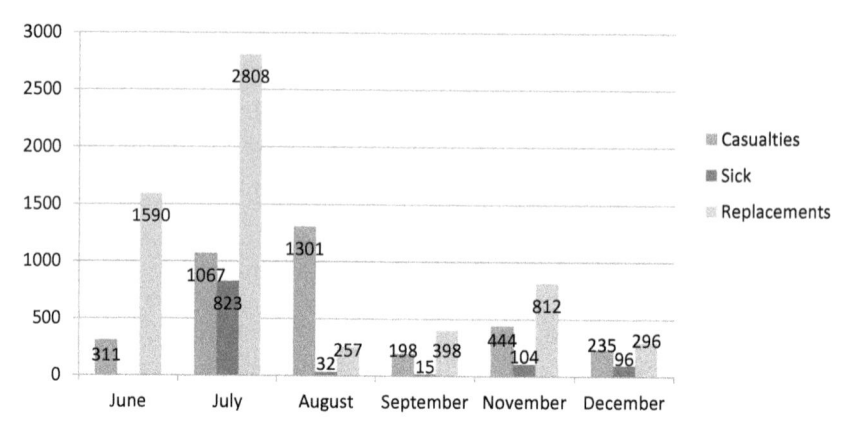

Figure 9.3 123rd Infantry Division manpower, June–December 1942

between May and December 1942, the German replacement system not only delivered a relatively robust number of men, but it also maintained the unit's cohesion.

The ebb and flow of battle during 1942 was also reflected in the casualty numbers of the 123rd Infantry Division. Relatively low losses in June and the last four months of the year, respectively, bookended dramatic increases in July and August (see Figure 9.3).[75] Set against

---

[75] Casualty numbers for the 123rd ID are difficult to ascertain due to the chaotic situation in the Demiansk pocket as well as the mixing of combat units and different commands.

these losses, the division received one extremely large shipment of men – over 2,800 men – in July,[76] and then integrated a constant stream of soldiers during the last five months of the year, as an additional 2,761 men joined the division, of whom 1,517 were convalescents returning to the unit.[77]

Unlike the previous year, when an overwhelming number of troops originated from outside Wehrkreis III, evidence suggests that troops from Berlin and Brandenburg constituted the bulk of replacements in 1942. The 415th Infantry Regiment stated that the "majority [of its additions] came out of Greater Berlin" while the 418th Infantry Regiment counted ninety-seven out of 169 recruits in one transport from the Brandenburg region.[78] Both the engineer battalion and the 415th Infantry Regiment reported similar findings, with each stating approximately 60 percent of its replacements hailed from Wehrkreis III.[79] The utility of the replacements, however, still occasioned complaints. One unit reported that "the Ersatz is deficiently educated and so superficially trained" that only a long period of intense training could make them into effective soldiers, while another angrily protested that one of its replacements was nearly blind.[80] In general, however, the value of the *Ersatz* was praised: "the *Menschenmaterial* is altogether good" and "made a fresh, lively impression and, with only a few exceptions, are healthy."[81]

See the Tätigkeitsbericht der Abteilung IIa v. 16.3. bis 15.4.42, BA-MA RH 26–123/165; Zustandsbericht 123 ID (o. IR 416, 4./ u. 8/IR 418) Nr. 225/42 geh., 10.5.1942; Zustandsbericht 123 ID (o. IR 416, 4./- u. 8/IR 418 und kleins Spliterrgruplen [*sic*]), 10.6.1942 Nr. 320/42 geh.; Zustandsbericht 123 ID, Nr. 436/42 geh, 1. August 1942, BA-MA RH 26–123/230; Zustandsbericht 123 ID, 1. September 1942; Zustandsbericht 123 ID, 1.10.1942; Zustandsbericht 123 ID, 1.11.1942; Zustandsbericht 123 ID, 1.12.1942; Zustandsbericht 123 ID, 1. Januar 1943, BA-MA RH 26–123/230.

[76] Zustandsbericht 123 ID, Nr. 436/42 geh., 1. August 1942, BA-MA RH 26–123/230.

[77] Zustandsbericht 123 ID, 1. September 1942; Zustandsbericht 123 ID, 1.10.1942; Zustandsbericht 123 ID, 1.11.1942; Zustandsbericht 123 ID, 1.12.1942; Zustandsbericht 123 ID, 1. Januar 1943, BA-MA RH 26–123/230.

[78] Infanterie-Regiment 415, Abt. Ia, 1. Juli 1942, Betr.: Erfahrungsberichte über den jungen Ersatz, der in der Feldersatzkp. 1 weitergebildet wurde; Infanterie-Regiment 418, Abt. Ia, Nr. 284/42 geh., 30.7.42, Betr.: Verteilung und Weiterbildung des Feldersatzbtls. 123/6, BA-MA RH 26–123/82.

[79] Pionierbataillon 123 Abt. Ia Br. B. Nr. 409/42 g., 1. Aug. 1942, Betr.: Verteidigung und Weiderbildung des Felders. Btls. 123/6; Infanterie-Regiment 415, Abt. Ia, 3. August 1942, Betr.: Beurteilung des Ersatzes Felders. Btl. 123/6, BA-MA RH 26–123/82.

[80] Infanterie-Regiment 418 Abteilung Ia Betr.: Einsatz des II. Btl., 4.7.42, BA-MA RH 26–123/58; Artillerie-Regiment 123 Abt. Ia, 25. Juni 1942, Betr.: Ausbildungsstand des Ersatzes, BA-MA RH 26–123/82.

[81] Artillerie-Regiment 123 Abt. Ia, 25. Juni 1942, Betr.: Ausbildungsstand des Ersatzes, BA-MA RH 26–123/82; Panzerjäger-Aufklärungs-Abteilung 123, Abt. Ia/IIb, 28.6.1942, Betr.: Ausbildungsstand und Eignung d. Ersatzes aus den Marsch-Batl. 123/4 u. -/5, BA-MA RH 26–123/82.

300 "From one mess to another"

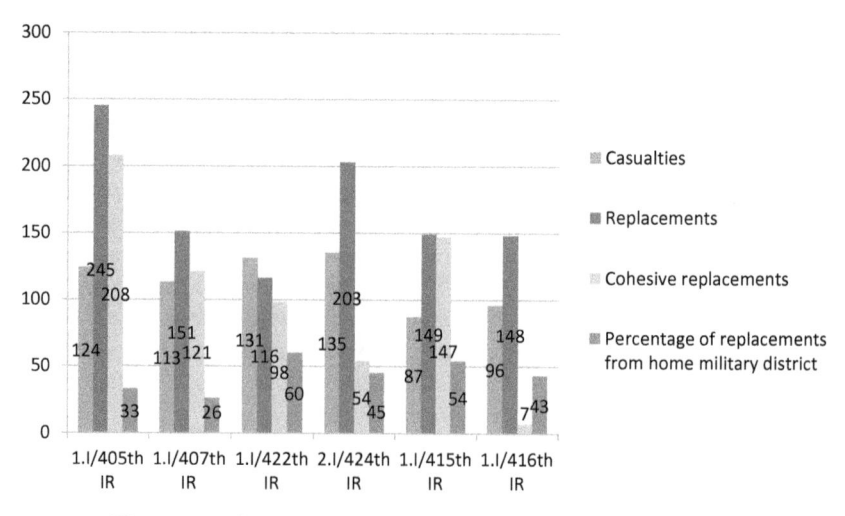

Figure 9.4 Company manpower, June–December 1942

Company-level documentation (Figure 9.4[82]) provides a more detailed look at the Wehrmacht replacement system in the months following the winter crisis.

Several points arise from this data. First, casualty rates per month were lower than during either the advance of 1941 or the winter crisis. Second, in five of the six companies, replacements outnumbered casualties during this time. Third, four of the six companies managed to ensure their cohesion, with significant numbers of recruits who either came from the company's home division or field training unit. Finally, with between 26 and 60 percent of incoming replacements originating from their home military district, a broader notion of regional consistency was generally maintained.

In the instances of the 2.I/424th and 1.I/416th Infantry Regiments, however, the number of cohesive replacements was low, especially for the

---

[82] For the 1.I/405, see Veränderungen zur Liste der Erkennungsmarkern dem Bataillon from 5 February 1942 to 5 January 1943 in WASt, 80549. On the 1.I/407, see the Veränderungen zur Liste der Erkennungsmarkern dem Bataillon from 5 February 1942 to 1 January 1943, WASt, 80588. For the 126th ID's companies, see 1. Inf. Regt. 422 (1./I.R. 422) Erkennungsmarkenverzeichnis (Veränderungsmeldung), 6. Juni. 1942 through 8.1.1943, WASt, 82026 and 2. Inf. Regt. 424 Veränderungsmeldung zur Liste der ausgegebenen Erkennungsmarken, 10.6.42 through 10.1.43, WASt, 80266. For the 123rd ID's companies, 1. Kompanie Infanterie-Regiment 415 Erkennungsmarken-Verzeichnis (Veränderungsanzeige), 12.6.1942 through 15.1.1943, WASt, 80744; 1/416 Veränderung zur Erkennungsmarkenliste der Dienststelle 10324B, 18.5.42 through 21.1.43, WASt, 80763.

latter. In its case, this meant that 141 men from more than fourteen different Wehrmacht formations joined the company during the course of 1942. What explains this anomaly? The most plausible explanation centers on the difficulty of funneling troops into the Demiansk pocket. Since neither the division itself nor the divisional field-training battalion transferred or sent a single soldier to the company during 1942, the division, faced with a pressing manpower situation, scraped together all available men and sent them to the company. While the pure numbers and therefore combat strength of the company were maintained, the amalgamation of men from so many units would lessen the hoped-for cohesion on the ground level.

Such a seemingly positive ratio from the German perspective needs to be qualified, however. First, the decision to dissolve an infantry battalion per division meant that many of these men were transferred to the companies under examination here; this was a case of reshuffling troops as opposed to green recruits. Second, these units received the lion's share of replacements as the Germans continued their practice begun during the winter crisis of reinforcing the fighting tip of their infantry divisions at the expense of their rear. This did not mean, however, that the logistical "tail" simply failed to exist; rather, as perceptively noted by Mark Edele and Michael Geyer, the tail was an "invisible one" because it consisted of "'Slavic' auxiliaries"; as noted above, the division increasingly utilized such men during the course of 1942.[83] The mobilization of the population therefore allowed the Wehrmacht to increase its combat power.

What is the importance of these numbers at both the divisional and company levels? First, while German infantry divisions certainly possessed less manpower in 1942 than they had at the opening of the invasion in June 1941 (due in no small part to the dissolution of at least one regiment), they continued to receive adequate numbers of replacements for their structure. Second, the system rather successfully shipped men from each division's home region to the front. Claims that a system that "had generally maintained a balanced age-range in the formations as well as their regional unity, a factor which was important for their mental resilience and internal cohesion," had broken down are too strongly worded.[84] It also appears self-evident based on these numbers that an increasing reliance on Nazi propaganda was not absolutely necessary as the more traditional use of regional bonds survived and kept units together in the face of hardship. Finally, the ever-increasing numbers of returning convalescents – the "old hares," in Rüdiger Overmans's

---

[83] Edele and Geyer, "States of Exception," p. 378, n. 154.
[84] Kroener, "The Manpower Resources of the Third Reich," p. 1019.

formulation – ensured that the smaller primary groups so important for combat effectiveness continued to be refreshed.[85] In sum, the German replacement system more than adequately functioned for the type of war waged by Army Group North in 1942 and the 121st, 123rd, and 126th IDs maintained their combat efficiency throughout the year.

The steady stream of troops to the front not only allowed each division to survive the year, but also served as the foundation for the development of occupation policy. Unlike outgunned and outmanned units that utilized terror as a means to compensate for their own weakness, these three divisions operated, if not from a position of absolute strength, then surely from one of confidence, and this allowed them to implement new, more conciliatory policies in the field.

IV. A successful transition?

On 20 October 1942, the newly appointed commander of the 126th ID, Colonel Harry Hoppe, issued a proclamation to his troops. He shared his expectations for the upcoming months:

> despite heavy casualties, we have beaten the Russians and conquered a new position. Now the position needs to be quickly fortified before the winter comes and freezing weather makes the work more difficult.
>
> I demand much from you, namely work and more work. Sweat saves blood!
>
> We need to have 5–6 rows of strong barbed-wire fence before our front lines, we need to have scattered pillboxes, strong and camouflaged, and we need bunkers with 2–3 levels, above ground or underground. We need to build these so that we can repulse any attack by the Russians. Then, following the construction of the position, we will attack the Russians with large-scale artillery fire and continually fire away until he is destroyed.
>
> In any case, no Russian will enjoy his life opposite the front of the 126th Division![86]

As this directive makes abundantly clear, Army Group North's formations no longer viewed the offensive as a viable option. After weathering the winter crisis of 1941–2, positional warfare was viewed as the norm. German units found themselves remaining in the same areas for a considerable amount of time, in stark contrast to their experiences during the first six months of combat. From September 1941 through September 1942, the 121st ID occupied the Russian towns of Pavlovsk and Pushkin,

---

[85] Rüdiger Overmans, *Deutsche militärische Verluste im Zweiten Weltkrieg* (Munich, 1999), p. 298.
[86] 126 Infanterie Division, Kommandeur, 20.10.42, BA-MA RH 26–126/70.

with the exception of a two-month hiatus during the Volkhov pocket battle. The 123rd ID remained in the southwest section of the Demiansk pocket from November 1941 through February 1943. Men in the 126th ID led a bit more varied existence, starting on the banks of the Volkhov river and ending the year in the neck of the Demiansk pocket, but nonetheless found themselves deployed in an area for several months at a time. The development of occupation policies thus became an important issue facing the army.

When examining the occupation policies of each division, the larger context of that division's experiences in the war needs to be examined. While the phrase "winter crisis" accurately describes the situations faced by the 126th and, especially, the 123rd IDs, nothing of the sort existed for the 121st ID. Simultaneous to their comrades' literal struggle for existence in January 1942, the East Prussians enjoyed a relatively peaceful occupation of Pavlovsk and the surrounding area. Such different experiences had two possible and contradictory effects on occupation policy. On the one hand, by avoiding the desperate combat of January 1942, the men of the 121st ID were not further brutalized by what degenerated into a slugging contest, devoid of humanity. This ferocious fighting certainly played a role in the 126th ID's repeated massacres of prisoners of war and it in all likelihood colored their views of the Soviet Union in general. On the other hand, the East Prussians never faced the existential crisis facing the 123rd ID and therefore never felt the need to radically modify their dealings with the Soviet population; in many ways, the 121st ID, the most restrained of the three divisions during 1941's advance, maintained a steady course through 1942 with the significant exception of its behavior in Pavlovsk during the 1941–2 winter. In contrast, the Berliners, realizing the precariousness of their situation, attempted to construct a more conciliatory occupation policy, one that would, if not harness the civilian population to their war effort, at least defuse any possibility of unrest or open resistance in their rear. Therefore, while the type, duration, and nature of combat affected the institutional mind-set of each division, it did not do so in a uniform way.

In the cases of both the 121st and the 126th IDs, attempts were made to construct a more rational occupation order by curbing the dispensing of arbitrary violent punishments and mitigating the worst Wehrmacht occupation practices in hopes of winning the population to the German cause. Facing the prospect of a lengthy war of attrition, each division viewed the creation of a quiet, stable, and productive rear area as a military imperative. In the case of the former, the distribution of ration cards proved extremely beneficial to those who had survived the previous catastrophic winter, while the latter attempted to impose a uniform occupation on its area of responsibility, one which took "political expediency" into consideration instead of merely relying on naked terror. The 126th ID made a real effort to rein in the worst and most violent impulses of its men, explicitly ordering them to refrain from reflex-like violence against alleged partisan actions or minor infractions committed by civilians. The attempt to "tie" German and Soviet interests together ordered by Küchler in February 1942 certainly had some impact on the policies of the 121st and 126th IDs.

Unfortunately, from the perspective of the German Army (and from those civilians who felt the brunt of German policy), military necessity was a two-sided coin. While one side called for a correct and even conciliatory approach towards civilians as a means of improving the army's chances of victory, the other demanded exploitation of civilians and the smashing of all popular resistance in pursuit of the *Endsieg*. This led the 126th ID to continue its horrifying practice of dangling the bodies of executed partisans for days at a time as well as to it becoming increasingly involved with the SS, the GFP, and other highly ideological agencies in policing the rear area. Finally, as the case of the 121st ID illustrates, all of the goodwill generated by a less rapacious occupation policy went for naught as German authorities viewed the population merely as a tool to be exploited and consequently deported large chunks of it to labor either in the Reich or in the rear areas; those not deemed able to work suffered a far more severe fate in camps that dotted the army's rear area. The need for labor, both for construction purposes at the divisional level and for war production work in the Reich, became an increasingly large issue for Germany during the war; military effectiveness in the age of machine warfare demanded a large pool of workers and frontline combat units carried out the rounding up of such workers regularly from 1942 on. These two sides to the coin of military necessity competed with one another into 1943 and beyond and, in the process, ensured that the Wehrmacht never implemented a uniform and rational occupation policy for the occupied territories.

10 "We need to fight to the end, *so oder so*"
Combat and the reconstruction of Army Group North

Nineteen forty-three has been variously described as both the "forgotten year" and the "culmination year" of the Second World War. While the latter description certainly applies to the dramatic and decisive events that took place on the southern and center sections of the Eastern Front, the former could be aptly applied to Army Group North and its area of operations.[1] Even more so than in the preceding year, the significance of the northwestern Russian theater paled in comparison to that of the remainder of the east. In the far south, Soviet forces smashed the German Sixth Army at Stalingrad and threatened to destroy all of Army Group South, the most powerful German field formation. While the Wehrmacht temporarily regained the initiative with Manstein's counter-attack and seizure of Kharkov in March 1943, the situation in southern Russia remained exceptionally threatening to German forces.[2] Soviet forces also launched a large-scale attack on the Rzhev salient in the center of the front that, while ultimately ending in failure for the Red Army, nonetheless increased the pressure on the Wehrmacht in late 1942 and early 1943.[3]

---

[1] "Der Ruckschlag des Pendels," in Karl-Heinz Frieser (ed.), *Das Deutsche Reich und der Zweite Weltkrieg*, vol. VIII, *Die Ostfront 1943/44: Der Krieg im Osten und an den Nebenfronten* (Stuttgart, 2007), p. 277; Walther Hubatsch, "Die deutsche Wehrmachtführung im Kulminationsjahr des Krieges," in Schramm, *KTB OKW*, vol. VI, pp. 1487–1634. Robert Citino's excellent operational study of the Wehrmacht in 1943, *The Wehrmacht Retreats: Fighting a Lost War, 1943* (Lawrence, KS, 2012), for example, simply omits any and all discussion of Army Group North.
[2] Literature on the battle of Stalingrad has reached epic proportions; some of the more important include Bernd Wegner, "The War against the Soviet Union 1942–1943," pp. 843–990, 1022–1184; Wolfram Wette and Gerd Ueberschär (eds.), *Stalingrad: Mythos und Wirklichkeit einer Schlacht* (Frankfurt, 1992); Manfred Kehrig, *Stalingrad: Analyse und Dokumentation einer Schlacht* (Stuttgart, 1974); Antony Beevor, *Stalingrad: The Fateful Siege* (New York, 1998); and the two published volumes of David Glantz's Stalingrad trilogy *To the Gates of Stalingrad: Soviet–German Combat Operations, April–August 1942* (Lawrence, KS, 2009) and *Armageddon in Stalingrad: September–November 1942* (Lawrence, KS, 2009).
[3] David Glantz, *Zhukov's Greatest Defeat: The Red Army's Disaster in Operation Mars, 1942* (Lawrence, KS, 1999).

The 1943 German summer offensive was designed to eliminate the bulge centered on Kursk created by the Rzhev and Kharkov fighting. Powerful Wehrmacht formations from Army Groups Center and South launched Operation Zitadelle on 5 July. Culminating in an unprecedented clash of armor, Red Army defenses blunted the German advance, allowing the Soviets to open up their first successful summer offensive, one that ended with Red Army troops reoccupying most Soviet territory.[4]

For the majority of Army Group North, however, its positions on 1 January 1944 remained strikingly similar to those it had held since February 1942, with the significant exception of the withdrawal from the Demiansk pocket. Hitler and the German High Command envisioned this front remaining stable during the first half of 1943 as the army group's *Schwerpunkt* remained "completely focused on the defensive."[5] The OKW's operational order additionally demanded that "the entire front needs to be brought to the highest possible readiness for the defensive."[6] Following the conclusion of the Zitadelle offensive, a third attempt to capture Leningrad had been originally envisioned.[7] The defeat at Kursk and the subsequent Soviet offensives forced its cancellation, however, and Army Group North merely continued to man its positions. That the Germans had ceded the initiative was made clear by Jodl, who stated that "the sole intention and the sole plan of the High Command is to hold our lines in the summer/fall 1943."[8] In fact, after the conclusion of the retreat from the Demiansk position in March, the 121st, 123rd, and 126th IDs engaged in only three brief, yet sharp, periods of battle during the remainder of the year. Instead of experiencing sustained combat, these units became increasingly involved with anti-partisan warfare and the subsequent deportations that became the foundation of German responses to the growing popular resistance; the claim that German frontline divisions were not inextricably entwined with the criminal nature of the war of annihilation certainly has no validity by 1943.

---

[4] On Kursk, see David Glantz and Jonathan House, *The Battle of Kursk* (Lawrence, KS, 1999); John Erickson, *The Road to Berlin* (London, 1996), pp. 87–137; and Karl-Heinz Frieser, "Die Schlacht im Kursker Bogen," in Frieser, *Die Ostfront 1943/44*, pp. 83–208.
[5] Operationsbefehl Nr. 5 (Weisung für die Kampfführung der nächsten Monate), 13.3.43, in Schramm, *KTB OKW*, vol. VI, p. 1421.
[6] Ibid.
[7] Ibid. For further discussion of this operation, see Ganzenmüller, *Das belagerte Leningrad 1941–1944*, pp. 80–1.
[8] Quoted in Bernd Wegner, "Die Aporie des Krieges," in Frieser, *Die Ostfront 1943/44*, pp. 246–74, here p. 246. For a concise examination of the larger context of German "strategy" in 1943, see Bernd Wegner, "Defensive ohne Strategie: Die Wehrmacht und das Jahr 1943," in Müller and Volkmann, *Die Wehrmacht: Mythos und Realität*, pp. 197–209.

While not chasing partisans, each division took advantage of the pauses in combat to institute rigorous training programs for their incoming recruits. Such programs that focused on the professional aspects of soldiering were complemented by ones that targeted the men's psyches; by the third year of war in the Soviet Union, doubts about final victory – doubts increasingly tied to the methodical destruction of their homes by American and British bombers – had become conspicuous within some units stationed in northwest Russia. The most noteworthy development in Army Group North, however, concerned Wehrmacht policy during tactical and operational withdrawals. As the German Army retreated, it implemented a methodical and destructive scorched-earth policy that laid waste to thousands of square miles of the Soviet Union.[9] The 121st, 123rd, and 126th IDs all created virtual deserts during their retreat, participating in the most devastating and comprehensive of all war crimes directly committed by the Wehrmacht on the Eastern Front.

I. The 1942–1943 Soviet winter offensives and the clearing of the Demiansk pocket

One major change in Army Group North's situation concerned the re-establishment of a tenuous land link between Leningrad and unoccupied Soviet territory. On 12 January 1943, Soviet forces unleashed Operation Spark, yet another attempt to crush the "bottleneck" in the Siniavino region.[10] Within five days, German troops had evacuated Šlissel'burg and elements of the Soviet Leningrad and Volkhov *Fronts* finally met; the siege had been broken. Subsequent attempts to increase the size of the land bridge, however, faltered with the heights of Siniavino remaining in German hands; from this commanding position, German artillery repeatedly shelled the narrow alley, severely diminishing its utility.

---

[9] On the general nature of German scorched-earth policy in the Soviet Union, see Wegner, "Die Aporie des Krieges," pp. 256–68; and Armin Nolzen, "'Verbrannte Erde': Der Rückzug der Wehrmacht aus den besetzten sowjetischen Gebieten, 1941/42–1944/45," in Günter Kronenbitter, Markus Pöhlmann, and Dierk Walter (eds.), *Besatzung: Funktion und Gestalt militärischer Fremdherrschaft von der Antike bis zum 20. Jahrhundert* (Paderborn, 2006), pp. 161–75. For case studies that focus on Army Group Center's area of operations, see Gerlach, *Kalkulierte Morde*, pp. 1.092–1104; Rass, *Menschenmaterial*, pp. 378–85; and Hamburger Institut für Sozialforschung, *Verbrechen der Wehrmacht*, pp. 421–8. See also Rass's discussion of a particularly vicious large-scale measure that combined evacuation as well as the stranding of the sick and weak in the spring of 1944, at pp. 386–402.

[10] For the most detailed description of the battle, see Glantz, *The Battle for Leningrad*, pp. 274–87. See also Wegner, "The War against the Soviet Union 1942–1943," pp. 1200–3; Erickson, *The Road to Berlin*, pp. 60–1.

Building on the successes and failures of Operation Spark, *Stavka* prepared a much more ambitious plan, Operation Polar Star, designed to destroy Army Group North as a whole. The Leningrad and Volkhov *Fronts* were once again to attack south and capture Siniavino as well drive into the German rear and seize the important rail junction of Tosno. These, however, were diversionary operations, with the Northwest *Front*, which surrounded the Demiansk pocket, tasked with the main thrust of the offensive. Red Army troops here were supposed to destroy the Demiansk land bridge and then drive west on Dno and northwest on Luga. Following the seizures of these cities, Soviet forces were then to continue their advance on Narva and Pskov, deep in the rear of Army Group North.[11] If successful, this operation would leave German forces battered, encircled, and on the edge of defeat.

Even before this major operation began in early February, the Red Army maintained unabated pressure on the southern front of the pocket during early 1943.[12] The 123rd ID reported that, after several days of constant combat, its men were "severely overtired and no longer [had] inner reserves [of strength] at their disposal."[13] While the southern front never collapsed, primarily due to the use of reserves from Eighteenth Army, this merely highlighted the manpower shortages plaguing the army group: such men were simultaneously needed to staunch Soviet attacks in the Leningrad area.[14] Finally, on 30 January 1943, after contentious debate between Hitler and the new Chief of the General Staff, General Kurt Zeitler, the latter convinced the Führer to allow Sixteenth Army to abandon the position.[15] The withdrawal reinforced the army group's defensive orientation and simultaneously increased its capability of actually carrying this mission out as it shortened the front by some 150 kilometers.[16]

The timing of the withdrawal coincided with the news of Sixth Army's capitulation at Stalingrad. One soldier from the 23rd ID out of Berlin commented on his unit's reaction to the news:

the news about the destruction of the Sixth Army has reached us. We are in no way pessimistic but are making an effort to be sober and objective ... we say in

---

[11] Glantz, *The Battle of Leningrad*, pp. 288–93.
[12] Schramm, *KTB OKW*, vol. V, 1. Januar 1943, p. 10.
[13] 123 ID KTB, 3.1.43, BA-MA RH 26–123/117.
[14] Küchler made this exact point; see Wegner, "The War against the Soviet Union 1942–1943," p. 1205, n. 129.
[15] On Hitler's view, see the comments of Greiner and Warlimont in Schramm, *KTB OKW*, vol. V, 30. Januar 1943, p. 86.
[16] Karl-Heinz Frieser, "Ausweichen der Heeresgruppe Nord von Leningrad ins Baltikum," in Frieser, *Die Ostfront 1943/44*, pp. 278–93, here p. 278.

somewhat cocky gallows humor as well as in complete seriousness that we will one day fight as partisans in the Grunewald [a large forest on the southwest fringes of Berlin]. In any case, we need to fight to the end, one way or another [*so oder so*], and we all know that we will do so.[17]

Another added, "now Sixth Army has fulfilled its fate. It has shaken us up. We grind our teeth together. That could have been us! It only makes us more determined and tougher."[18] As these two soldiers make clear, the defeat at Stalingrad solidified a last-stand mentality in the minds of many soldiers. Simultaneously, however, it also made the idea of a last stand very tangible as the catastrophe on the Volga signified the beginning of the end for the Third Reich.[19] To counter this obvious switch in the initiative across the entirety of the front, both the Wehrmacht as an institution and the individual soldier prepared to fight a war that increasingly diverged from the more conciliatory polices that had emerged during 1942. While the crisis that struck German forces on the southern sector of the front never came close to being replicated in the northern theater of operations, Army Group North's behavior during its retreats mirrored that of its counterparts as it now increasingly followed a radicalized version of military necessity, one determined to deny the advancing Red Army anything of even spurious military value, resulting in wholesale destruction.

The withdrawal began almost immediately as II Corps ordered the removal of all nonessential equipment and supplies from the pocket on 2 February.[20] Eleven days later, II Corps alerted the troops that due to the "development of the situation across the entire front," they would soon be retreating from the "fortress," though not before reassuring them that they had "fulfilled their task of defending the Demiansk combat area ... in glorious and successful combat."[21] The 123rd ID was charged

---

[17] Tagebuchnotizen als Beitrag zur Geschichte des IR 68, 28.1.43, BA-MA Msg 2/2519.
[18] Sergeant Helmut Römer, Grenadier Regt. 406, 30.1.43, BfZ, Sammlung Sterz.
[19] Mark Edele and Michael Geyer's claim that the fighting "generated a kind of solidarity that over time would make the Wehrmacht into a people's army – a fighting body unified by their experience of a war of survival," one predicated on "the sheer terror of survival," seems much more applicable here, to the post-Stalingrad era, than it does to the fall and winter of 1941 where they locate it; see Edele and Geyer, "States of Exception," p. 374.
[20] Generalkommando II. Armeekorps, Abteilung Ia, Nr. 117/43 g. Kdos, Betr.: Entrümpelungsaktion, 2. Febr. 1943, BA-MA RH 26–123/118; Generalkommando II. Armeekorps, Abt. Ia, Nr. 132/43 g. Kdos, Betr.: Studie "Frontverkürzung," 4. Febr. 1943, BA-MA RH 26–123/118.
[21] Generalkommando II Armeekorps, Abt. Ia, Nr. 192/43 g. Kdos, Betr.: Unternehmen "Ziethen," 13. Febr. 1943, BA-MA RH 26–123/118. Regimental commanders in the 123rd ID learned of the evacuation during a meeting at divisional headquarters on 8 February; 123 ID KTB, 8.2.43, BA-MA RH 26–123/118.

with holding its section of the line to allow the 12th and 30th IDs to leapfrog it as they withdrew from their positions (see Map 10.1).[22]

Unlike previous withdrawals in Army Group North, which were accompanied by destruction but fell far short of anything approximating total devastation, the evacuation of the Demiansk pocket marked the passage to an extraordinarily detailed policy of "scorched earth." On 13 February, the same day that the troops were alerted to the impending evacuation of the position, Hitler issued *Führerbefehl* No 4, which established the general guidelines for German retreats for the remainder of the war.[23] Arguing that retreat without any accompanying destruction "brought the enemy incalculable advantages," he then listed the numerous missions that needed to be fulfilled before Wehrmacht units pulled out of the line. In addition to the demolition of all military equipment and ammunition that could not be transported to the rear, everything that could be worthwhile to the enemy needed to be destroyed or burned, including all dwellings. The entire civilian population was to be deported with the troops; if not possible, all men between the ages of fifteen and sixty-five years were to accompany the Germans as they moved west. This order served as the basis for the Wehrmacht's scorched-earth policy in the east for the next two years.[24]

Despite having "only a few days for [their] extensive blocking and destruction tasks," the troops were very successful in devastating the pocket, according to a glowing report produced by II Corps, turning the region into "dead territory."[25] An order distributed by the 126th ID made clear the extent of the destruction.[26] All "military structures and dwellings," as well anything else that would make the construction of a forward line by the enemy "easier," needed to be ruined. Larger sections of forest, individual trees, and even bushes were to be destroyed to deny their use to the enemy for either construction or tactical purposes. Accompanying the order was a detailed list of over twenty separate planned demolitions and minings.

---

[22] 123 Inf. Division, Abt. Ia/Az. IVa E., Nr. 477/43 g. Kdos, Divisionsbefehl Nr. 1 für die Durchführung des Unternehmens "Ziethen," BA-MA RH 26–123/118.

[23] Norbert Müller, *Die faschistische Okkupationspolitik in den zeitweilig besetzten Gebieten der Sowjetunion (1941–1944)* (Berlin, 1991), Document 157, p. 390.

[24] For more on Ninth Army's nearly simultaneous scorched-earth retreat, see Rass, *Menschenmaterial*, pp. 381–2; and Müller, *Die faschistische Okkupationspolitik*, Document 154, p. 385.

[25] Anlage 3 zu Gen. Kdo. II. A. K. Ia Nr. 192/43 g. Kdos. vom 13.2.1943, BA-MA RH 26–123/118; Haupt, *Heeresgruppe Nord*, pp. 153–4.

[26] 126 Infanterie Division, Abt. Ia/Pi., 1.3.43, Richtlinien für die Zerstörungs- und Sperrung im Abschnitt der Division, BA-MA RH 26–126/89.

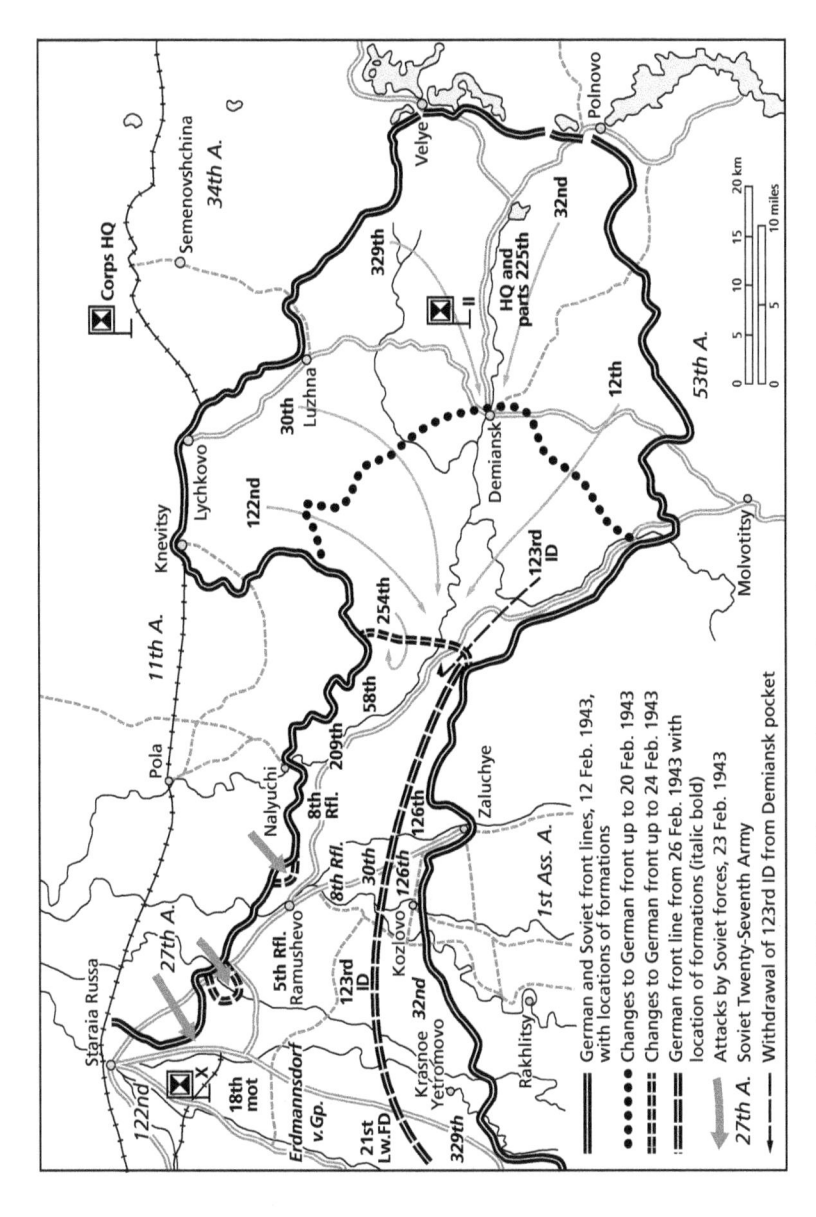

Map 10.1 Withdrawal from the Demiansk pocket

The retreating troops methodically carried out these tasks as they trudged west, destroying all shelters, bunkers, bridges, and roads while some attempts were made to "contaminate" the ground, leaving it useless for the advancing Red Army.[27] All available foodstuffs, from flour and oats to animal feed and cattle, as well as all clothing and other loosely defined "goods," were evacuated with the troops.[28] In addition to seizing all material goods in the area, the Wehrmacht also initiated the large-scale deportation of every single individual residing within German lines, as called for by Hitler. Earlier German practice usually consisted of the evacuation of draft-age men; here, the army resorted to a much more comprehensive effort. As the historian Bernd Wegner has noted, "the plundering, exploitation, evacuation, and deportation of the civilian population was an integral component of the scorched-earth concept" as not only materials but also labor were denied to the enemy.[29] Not only did the Wehrmacht ensure that these evacuees would not increase the military capabilities of the Soviet state and its army, but it also exploited these very same individuals for the German war effort. The *Ortskommandanten* registered and seized all men aged from sixteen to sixty-five while allowing women who had "proven themselves loyal" to the Germans to accompany the retreating army as a type of privileged refugee; the rest were to be driven to the German rear.[30]

Even the majority of the sick were loaded on *panje* sleds and evacuated, though some were diverted to the *Ortskommandanten*, where they faced a much grimmer fate. Despite the short notice, II Corps's units evacuated the civilian population in a more efficient, if not more humane, manner than similar earlier actions. The 126th ID's engineer battalion, for example, constructed a temporary camp for refugees to stay the night

---

[27] 126 Infanterie Division, Abt. Ia, Nr. 255/43, geheim, Divisionsbefehl für das Ausweichen in die Lowatj-Brückenkopfstellung (Nr. 126), 25.2.43, BA-MA RH 26–126/75; 123 Infanterie Division, Abt. Ia/Az IVa/R Nr. 544/43 geh., 21. Februar 1943, BA-MA RH 26–123/240; Gruppe Höhne, Ia 320/43 geh., Gruppenbefehl für Absetzen von Linie "F" auf Linie "C," 23.2.43, BA-MA RH 26–126/88; Gruppe Höhne Ia, 118/43 g. KdosHh., Betr.: Unternehmen "Ziethen," 19.2.43, BA-MA RH 26–126/89; 123 ID KTB Qu., 22.2.43, BA-MA RH 26–123/233.

[28] Fernschreiben 142, 16.2.43 von Chef des Generalstabes an 123 Infanterie Division, BA-MA RH 26–123/240. II Corps quartermaster ordered the removal of all cattle both to secure the German supply and to deny them to the oncoming Soviets; 123 ID KTB Qu., 16.2.43, BA-MA RH 26–123/233.

[29] Wegner, "Die Aporie des Krieges," p. 262.

[30] 123 Infanterie Division, Ib, Nr. 278/43 geh., Befehl für das Zurückführen der Zivilbevölkerung in den Abstellraum der Division, 16.2.43, BA-MA RH 26–123/240. The following discussion is based on this document unless otherwise noted; see also 126 ID KTB Qu., 12.2.43, 18.2.43, BA-MA RH 26–126/151. Such a formulation provides more evidence that serious relationships had developed between some German soldiers and Soviet women during the period of occupation.

Illustration 10.1 The 123rd Infantry Division's withdrawal from the Demiansk pocket included the evacuation of the civilian population.

and provided them with food.[31] This, of course, merely indicated that forced evacuations were now part and parcel of the Wehrmacht's everyday activities. By the conclusion of the retreat, the 123rd ID had evacuated 168 men of military age and an additional 1,114 civilians to the western bank of the Lovat river.[32]

As the evacuees trudged west, German authorities soon began to plug them into the gaping holes that dotted the ranks of their workforce. Just as the East Prussians deported workers from Pavlovsk, so the 123rd ID now participated in the Third Reich's forced-labor program. The branch of Economic Staff East attached to Army Group North reported that it faced a deficit of some 93,000 workers in January 1943 and this rose to over 98,000 workers the following month.[33] Such shortages were blamed on Germany's deteriorating military situation, the increasing activity of the partisan movement, the ineffectiveness of German

---

[31] Pionier Btl. 126, Kriegstagebuch Nr. 4, 1.1–30.6.1943, 20.2.43, BA-MA RH 46/416.
[32] 123 ID KTB Qu., 22.2.43, BA-MA RH 26–123/233. For a look at the 12th ID's activities in the withdrawal, see Bartov, *The Eastern Front*, p. 140.
[33] KTB, 1.Vierteljahr 1943, 31.1.43, 28.2.43, BA-MA RW 31/588.

counterpropaganda, and the general conditions of privation that had followed the German advance: as one officer pithily noted, "films and photos cannot overcome shortages and desperation."[34]

Stab Holstein painted a depressing picture of the areas into which the new evacuees were shepherded.[35] Due to a shortage of workers and beasts of burden, agricultural production continued to decrease. Partisan kidnappings and assassinations of local collaborators and agricultural specialists created a vacuum in the political and economic arena as no adequate replacements existed.[36] The population lived in dreadful poverty: economic authorities noted that small gestures such as the "distribution of clothes in the Ordesh district caused great joy."[37] The arrival of evacuees from the Demiansk pocket only exacerbated the population's destitution as these "streams of refugees terribly burdened the available food stocks."[38] Evacuees forced west overwhelmed the already precarious food-supply systems in villages, causing "restlessness and uncertainty" in the affected communities.[39] By adding an additional 30,000 people incapable of labor to the rolls of Economic Staff East, the evacuation of Demiansk further tipped the balance between civilians who could work – 628,500 – and those who could "make no contribution to their housing, food supply, or clothing" – 647,000 – in favor of the latter.[40] This was confirmed by the local Economic Staff East branch, which noted that "the evacuees out of the Demiansk pocket thought to be replacement [workers] have been proven overwhelmingly unable to work."[41] Four months later, this same branch still complained that feeding these evacuees proved extremely difficult as the majority of them possessed no food stocks of their own.[42] The actions of the frontline 123rd ID simply cannot be isolated from events in the rear; while the evacuation of the population certainly had some military benefit, the more than 1,200 hundred civilians unceremoniously dumped in an area already suffocating from poverty and desperation demonstrated the callous and single-minded nature of German military necessity as it evolved on the Eastern Front.

While the 126th and 123rd IDs' occupation policies shifted between conciliatory and ruthless practices in 1942 and 1943, the Economic Staff

---

[34] Ibid., 31.1.43.
[35] KTB des leitenden Wirtschaftskommandos Dno, p. 39, BA-MA RW 31/935.
[36] KTB, 28.2.43, BA-MA RW 31/588.   [37] Ibid., 11.3.43.
[38] Ibid., 28.2.43.   [39] KTB 1.Vierteljahr 1943, pp. 146, 165, BA-MA RW 31/937.
[40] For the numbers of evacuees from the Demiansk pocket, see Stabsbesprechung am 28.3.1943 in Sitzungssaal, BA-MA RW 31/588; on the numbers of civilians in the Army Group area, see KTB, 31.3.43, BA-MA RW 31/588. The phrase comes from the war diary entry for 30 March 1943.
[41] KTB des leitenden Wirtschaftskommandos Dno, p. 59, BA-MA RW 31/595.
[42] KTB 3.Vierteljahre, Woche v. 1.-10.7.43, BA-MA RW 31/939.

East released new guidelines in February 1943 based on the assumption that the "Russian of today cannot be compared with the one from 1914–1916."[43] This directive declared that "respectable and correct treatment [and] sufficient food" led to "industrious workers" and also "reduced the [population's] inclination towards the partisan bands."[44] In attempts to improve the daily lives of Soviet civilians, measures ranging from the introduction of bread rationing to the distribution of clothing and goods were implemented.[45] Of course, such positive policies were complemented by negative actions, including what amounted to the arrest of all males between the ages of sixteen and forty-five in Army Group North's area, as well as the seizure of all horses.[46] While the aim of this operation was to put an end to partisan recruiting, it backfired as numerous men fled to the forests to escape German imprisonment, simultaneously increasing the number of partisans and aggravating the labor shortage in the region.[47]

The German withdrawal from the Demiansk pocket began just as the Soviet Northwest *Front* made its final preparations for attack. Though poor weather disrupted the Red Army's timetable, Zhukov nonetheless ordered the attack to proceed once the Soviets detected the German movement.[48] While the operation as a whole predictably failed, Soviet assaults on the southern section of the land bridge did achieve minimal penetrations that caused worry in German headquarters.[49] Thus, while II Corps pulled back to the west, the Rhinelanders engaged in a tough defensive battle to keep the pocket open. The men of the 126th ID were some of the last soldiers to leave their positions, not withdrawing behind the Lovat river until 7 March. The war diarist summed up the retreat:

the separation from the battleground was difficult for the division. It had considerably widened the connection to the former "Fortress Demiansk" with heavy sacrifice and then successfully defended this area that it had captured against enemy attacks. Although weapons and equipment had been saved, an extraordinarily large number of their dead comrades' graves fell into enemy hands. This was the most painful part of the entire retreat.[50]

After thirteen months of combat in an "operationally pointless" position that cost the lives of approximately 110,000 men, Army Group North finally abandoned Fortress Demiansk.[51]

---

[43] Stabsbesprechung am 28.3.1943 in Sitzungssaal, BA-MA RW 31/588.
[44] KTB, 17.2.43, BA-MA RW 31/588.   [45] Ibid., 11.3.43.   [46] Ibid., 7.3.43.
[47] Rückblick des Wirtschaftsinspekteurs auf das vierte Viertaljahr 1943, BA-MA RW 31/594.
[48] Glantz, *The Battle of Leningrad*, p. 297.
[49] Schramm, *KTB OKW*, vol. V, 16. Februar 1943, p. 135, 17. Februar 1943, p. 136, 22. Februar 1943, p. 163.
[50] 126 ID KTB, 7.3.43, BA-MA RH 26–126/74.
[51] Wegner, "The War against the Soviet Union 1942–1943," p. 1205.

II. "One of the division's bloodiest battles of the war": combat in 1943

Following the evacuation of the Demiansk pocket, the infantry divisions of Army Group North settled into routines far different to those of 1941 or 1942. Unlike the near continuous fighting of Operation Barbarossa or the desperate and lengthy struggles for the Demiansk pocket or along the Volkhov river in 1942, these three infantry divisions participated in only three engagements during the seven months after the retreat concluded. The 121st ID witnessed the most combat as it gained a reputation as the "firemen" of Army Group North, sent to wherever the German line needed strengthening. The first occasion for this type of use occurred in early February when elements of the Volkhov *Front*, operating within the context of Operation Polar Star, attacked German troops in the Smerdynia region on 10 February 1943.[52] Viewed from Berlin, this portion of the offensive was a mere sideshow.[53] It proved serious enough, however, for the 121st ID to be deployed from its army-reserve position on 22 February in an attempt to shore up the line and halt the Red Army offensive.[54] Though the German front held, success was bought at a steep price. The 121st ID reported nearly 3,000 casualties in the month-and-a-half-long battle, with losses falling especially hard on officers and NCOs.[55]

After spending the next three months recuperating in the rear, the East Prussians once again deployed into the thick of the fighting. This was in response to the beginning of the fifth Soviet assault designed to seize Siniavino on 22 July (see Map 10.2).[56] Combat degenerated into savage hand-to-hand fighting and notwithstanding Soviet air and armor superiority, the German line again held.[57] The fighting caused over 1,900 divisional casualties up through 5 August when the Soviet offensive finally stalled, leading the 121st ID to state that it was "one of the

---

[52] Glantz, *The Battle for Leningrad*, p. 294.
[53] The OKW war diary fails to mention this area in any of its daily reports for the month of February; see Schramm, *KTB OKW*, vol. V, 11.–28. Februar 1943, pp. 117–76.
[54] Tätigkeitsbericht des Evangelical Pfarrers, 22.2.43 bis 5.8.1943, BA-MA RH 26–121/67.
[55] Verlust-Aufstellung, 16.2.43–1.4.43, BA-MA RH 26–121/39; Zustandsbericht, 121 Infanterie Division, 9.3.43, BA-MA RH 26–121/41.
[56] Glantz, *The Battle for Leningrad*, p. 309; 121 ID KTB, 23.7.43, BA-MA RH 26–121/47; Haupt, *Heeresgruppe Nord*, p. 161. A total of nine additional German divisions were needed to assist the corps's original seven divisions in breaking the Soviet offensive; see Generalkommando XXVI AK, Abt. Ia, Nr. 573/44 geh., An den Chef der Heeresarchiv Potsdam Zweigstelle Liegnitz, 7.2.1944, BA-MA RH 24–26/26.
[57] See the war diary entries for 23 July, 25 July, 26 July, 27 July, 28 July, 29 July, 30 July 1943, 121 ID KTB, BA-MA RH 26–121/47.

"One of the division's bloodiest battles of the war" 317

Illustration 10.2 Fighting in the Ladoga region often pitted Soviet armor against German infantry.

division's bloodiest battles" of the war.[58] The fighting took such a toll on the unit that XXVIII Corps still downgraded the division's combat efficiency *four* months after the battle concluded.[59]

In an attempt to halt this particular Soviet offensive, the 126th ID was also shifted to the front. Since their withdrawal from the Demiansk position, the Rhinelanders' military activities had been limited to sniping and regular shelling, though, due to the ten to twenty casualties suffered a day from this exchange, the division commander decided to cut back his unit's artillery fire in hopes of the Red Army following suit.[60]

---

[58] 121 Infanterie Division, Erfahrungsbericht beim Einsatz der 121. Inf.-Division während der 3. Abwehrschlacht südlich des Ladoga-Sees im Einsatzraum an der Newa in der Zeit vom 22.7.–5.8.1943, BA-MA RH 26–121/52; Bericht über die Verluste in der Berichtzeit mit Anlage "Tägliche Verlustmeldungen," BA-MA RH 26–121/64.

[59] Generalkommando XXVIII AK, Abt. Ia, Nr. 774/43 g. Kdos. Chefs, 4.11.1943, BA-MA RH 20–18/675.

[60] On sniper activity, see Tagesmeldung vom 30.4.43, BA-MA RH 26–126/83 in which the division claims twenty-nine kills for the month of April. On the artillery duel, see 126 ID KTB, 29.5.43, BA-MA RH 26–126/74 and X AK KTB, 24.5.43, BA-MA RH

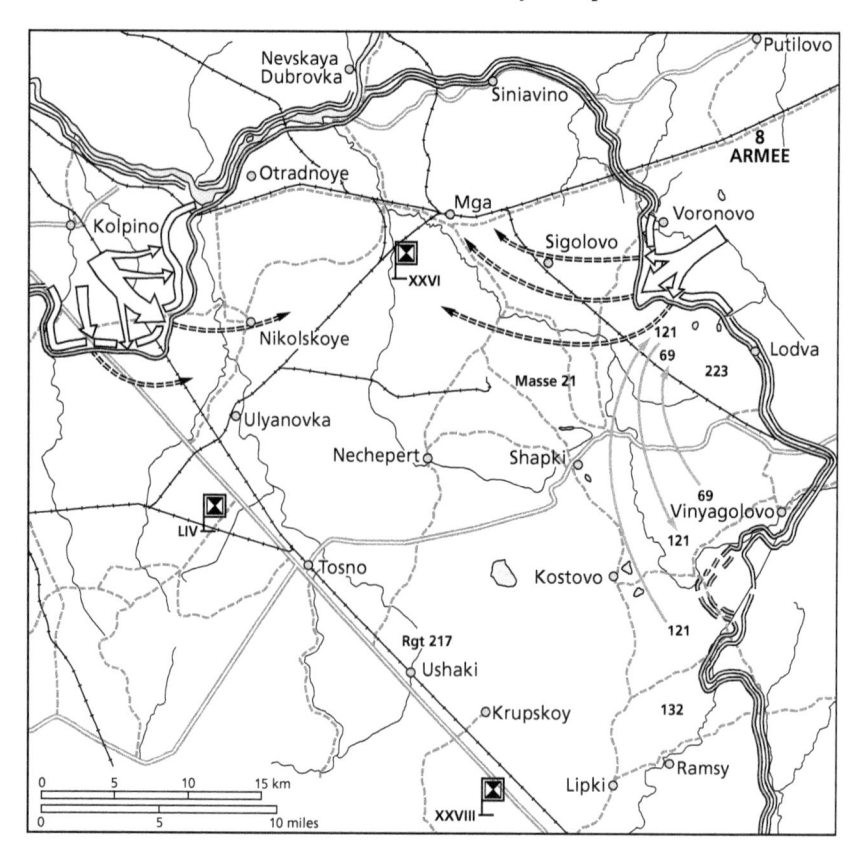

318   Combat and the reconstruction of Army Group North

Map 10.2 The second Ladoga battle

This "live-and-let-live" attitude quickly evaporated following the division's deployment to the line between the Red Army-occupied Oranienbaum and Leningrad positions. The troops complained that the positions they inherited were "unusually bad" as they were frequently forced to lie in the open where they suffered the ravages of repeated artillery attacks.[61] Weak or non-existent fortifications became a much more serious problem after a major Soviet attack that opened on 8 August – one day after the troops arrived in the line – and lasted for a

24–10/170. For more on this topic, though in a different context, see Tony Ashworth, *Live and Let Live: Trench Warfare on the Western Front* (Basingstoke, 2000).
[61] 126 ID KTB, BA-MA RH 26–126/74, 7.8.43. According to its superior formation, XXVI Corps, there were too many units in the area to provide shelter for them all; XXVI AK KTB Qu., 31.7.43, BA-MA RH 24–26/259.

week. While division command later described the combat as "a successful defensive battle" in which the unit maintained a "high level of morale," it hoped during the fight that "the next several days bring fewer heavy enemy attacks." Desperate hand-to-hand combat led to an increasing number of casualties, and divisional casualties for the month of August were in fact higher than the total number suffered during the remainder of 1943.[62]

Following this period of brief, yet intense, fighting, operations in the Leningrad area settled into combat typical of northwestern Russia: positional warfare marked by artillery fire and sniper activity. Mindful of the Soviets' superiority in mobile formations, Army Group North and its subordinate units spent much time buttressing its lines and creating some sort of reserve to deal with any Red Army breakthroughs.[63] The 126th ID contributed to this process by stepping up raids and patrols, in hopes of detecting any preparations for a large-scale attack.[64] The short distance between the opposing front lines made such operations brief, yet terrifyingly intense, as the diminutive no-man's-land provided little or no opportunity for maneuver or cover. In some places, the lines were so close that the Rhinelanders witnessed intoxicated Soviet soldiers firing weapons at each other. On another occasion, a drunken Red Army man, using his best German, shouted out plainly discernible curses towards the German lines and then followed these up with stones.[65] Such moments of levity, however, did not disguise the fact that trench warfare was a serious business in which carelessness cost many soldiers their lives.[66]

Though combat decreased in regularity by 1943, the battles became increasingly ferocious and concentrated. This shift in the nature of the war had important ramifications for German infantry divisions. First, while sustained combat – like that faced by both the 121st and 126th IDs – could severely weaken a unit's combat strength, the long periods of relative quiet gave these maimed units the opportunity to lick

---

[62] In August, the division suffered 1,851 killed, wounded, missing, and sick. For the months of July, September, October, November, and December, the division suffered a total of 1,651 casualties. See the monthly Zustandsberichte in BA-MA RH 26–126/107.
[63] For example, Der Oberbefehlshaber der 18. Armee, Ia Nr. 15717/43 geh., Kampferfahrungen und Lehren aus dem Durchbruch bei Newel, 28.10.43, BA-MA RH 26–126/100.
[64] Two examples include 6./Gre. Rgt. 422, Meldung über Ablauf des Stoß-Trupp-Unternehmens in der Nacht vom 10. zum 11. November 43, BA-MA RH 26–126/103 and Grenadier Reg. 426, Abt. Ia, Verlauf des Stoßtruppunternehmens des II./G.R. am 14.12.43, BA-MA RH 26–126/100.
[65] Zwischenmeldung, 7.12.43, BA-MA RH 26–126/104.
[66] 126 Infanterie Division, Abt. Ia, Tagesmeldung an L AK, 30.9.43, BA-MA RH 26–126/101; Durch Scharfschützen abgeschossene Russen, Monat Oktober, BA-MA RH 26–126/103; Tagesmeldung vom 17.11.43, BA-MA RH 26–126/103.

their wounds. Such a period of rest and refitting also allowed German formations to effectively integrate new recruits into their ranks by providing them with a rigorous and realistic training program designed for the static war in northwest Russia. Second, even more so than in 1942, frontline units became increasingly responsible for large sections of the occupied territories. This meant that the tasks facing such units only multiplied. In addition to their primary task of defeating the Red Army in battle, combat units devoted additional time and effort to trying to administer effectively their areas of operations. While elements of the more conciliatory policies of 1942 certainly remained in the Germans' continually evolving occupation policy, the Wehrmacht's approach to partisan activity and its complicity in the forced-labor program ensured that whatever goodwill was generated by its more humane policies was completely negated by the competing demands of military necessity.

III. The reconstitution of the infantry: replenishment and training in the 121st and 126th Infantry Divisions

The 121st Infantry Division's combat experiences resulted in a rollercoaster pattern of sharp peaks and drastic declines in the unit's casualty trends for 1943, though replacements arrived on a relatively consistent basis (see Figure 10.1[67]). Similarly to their comrades in the 121st Infantry Division, the men of the 126th Infantry Division also took part in two distinct periods of pitched and savage battles – the defense of the Demiansk shoulder during the evacuation and the third Ladoga battle – that alternated with periods of minimal activity (see Figure 10.2[68]).

---

[67] 121 Infanterie Division, Zustandsbericht 8.2.43; 121 Infanterie Division, Zustandsbericht 9.3.43; 121 Infanterie Division, Zustandsbericht 9.4.43, BA-MA RH 26–121/41; 121 Infanterie Division, Meldung 1.5.43; 121 Infanterie Division, Meldung 1.6.43; BA-MA RH 26–121/51; Meldung – 1. Juli. 1943, BA-MA RH 26–121/52; Tägliche Verlustmeldungen vom 1.7.1943 bis 31.12.1943, BA-MA RH 20–18/1167.

[68] 126 ID, Meldung vom 8. Februar 1943; 126 ID, Meldung vom 7. März; 126 ID, Meldung vom 7. April 1943, BA-MA RH 26–126/91; 126 ID, Meldung vom 7. Mai 1943; 126 ID, Meldung vom 7. Juni 1943; Zustandsbericht 126 ID, Meldung 7. Juli. 1943, BA-MA RH 26–126/90; Zustandsbericht 126 ID, Meldung 10.8.43, BA-MA RH 26–126/107; 126 ID, Meldung vom 8. Februar 1943; 126 ID, Meldung vom 7. März 1943; 126 ID, Meldung vom 7. April 1943; 126 ID, Meldung vom 7. Mai 1943; 126 ID, Meldung vom 7. Juni 1943; Zustandsbericht 126 ID, Meldung 7. Juli. 1943, BA-MA RH 26–126/90; Zustandsbericht 126 ID, Meldung 10.8.43; Zustandsbericht 126 ID, Meldung 8. September 1943; Zustandsbericht 126 ID, Meldung 1. Oktober 1943; Zustandsbericht 126 ID, Meldung 1. November 1943; Zustandsbericht 126 ID, Meldung 1. Dezember 1943, BA-MA RH 26–126/107; Zustandsbericht 126 ID, Meldung 1. January 1944, BA-MA RH 24–50/78.

The reconstitution of the infantry 321

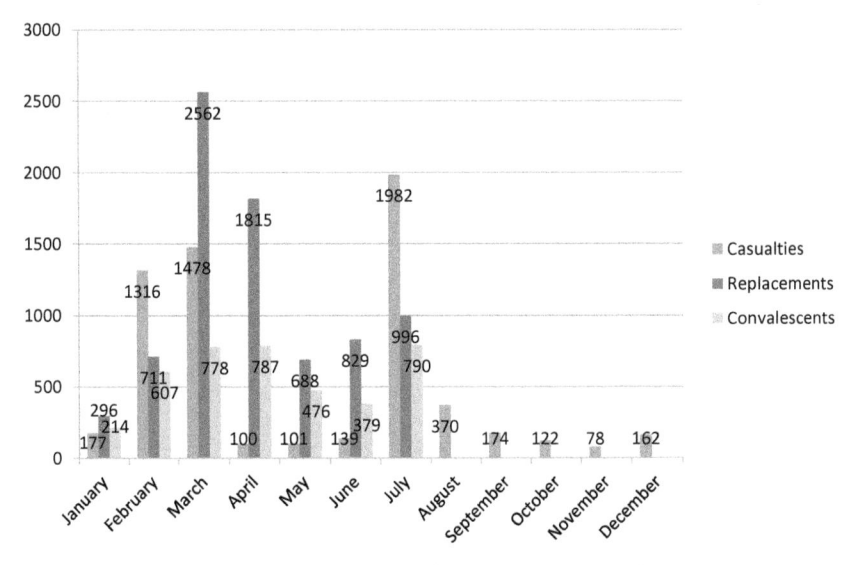

Figure 10.1 121st Infantry Division manpower, 1943

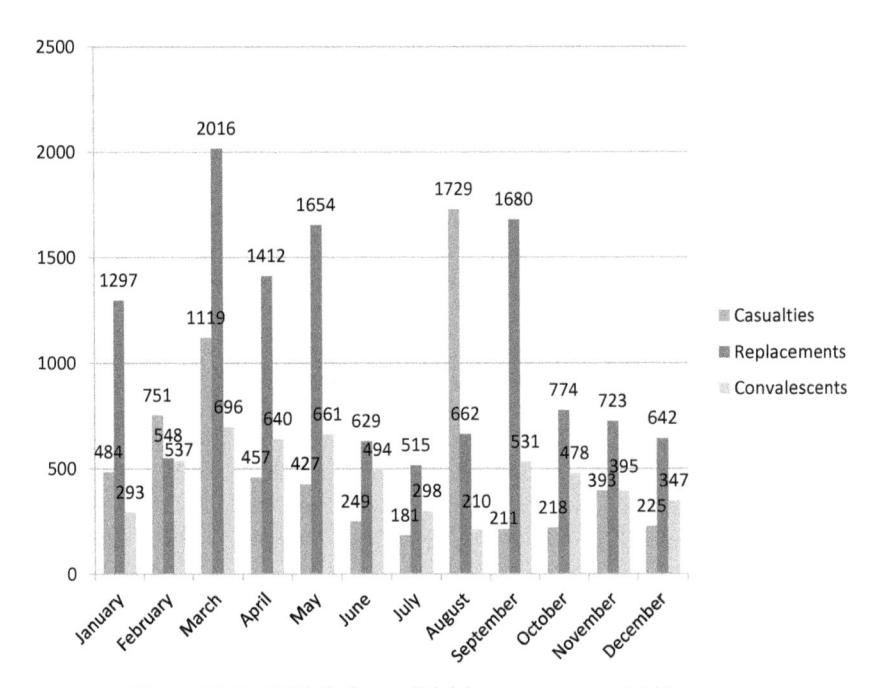

Figure 10.2 126th Infantry Division manpower, 1943

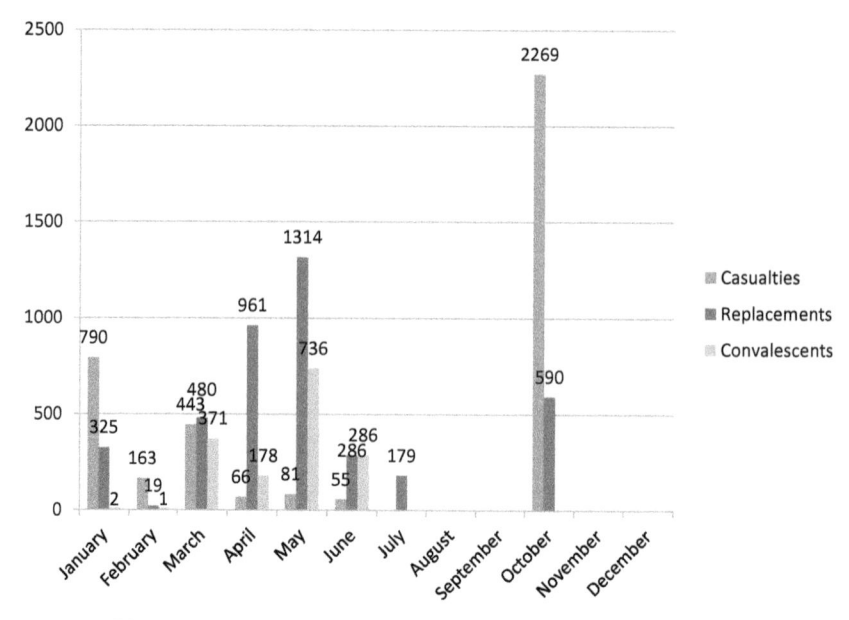

Figure 10.3 123rd Infantry Division manpower, 1943

The 123rd ID's casualty rate during the first eight months of 1943 (see Figure 10.3) proved to be extremely low before it was transferred to Army Group South in September and took part in the heavy fighting there.

Each division had similar experiences with their incoming recruits. The 121st ID complained that some of the replacements were "not uniform in their training or morale," displayed little "passion" for being soldiers, or were too old, and it shipped eight of the twelve officers and 217 of the 273 men from one march battalion back to I Corps's training battalion for further instruction.[69] The 126th ID also redirected a group of incoming recruits to another unit, though for different reasons. On 8 January 1943, 904 men from Field Training Regiment 639 entered the division's ranks.[70] These men originated in the Breslau Military District, however, and division command decided that instead of being integrated into the lines, they should be sent to the Breslau-based 81st Infantry Division. Divisional leadership recognized that "although

---

[69] Bericht über die Entwicklung der personellen Lage der Division während der Berichtzeit mit Anlage "Fehlstellen," BA-MA RH 26–121/63. The remainder of this discussion is based on this document.
[70] Tätigkeitsbericht der Abt. IIa/b, Stand 31.1.43, BA-MA RH 26–126/134.

this exchange is a heavy burden on the troops, the division hopes to serve the regional composition of the troop companies through this action."[71] The actions by both divisions seem counterproductive in an army that faced such a manpower crisis. Taken in concert, however, these events suggest that both the 121st and 126th IDs felt their own manpower situation was secure and stable; in other words, the much-maligned German replacement system continued to function adequately for infantry divisions in Army Group North during the third year of war in the Soviet Union.[72]

The emphasis on regional cohesion was also generally upheld in 1943. The 123rd ID received only one march battalion that originated outside Wehrkreis III and the 121st ID characterized its recruits as having "strongly reinforced the make-up of the division" with some three-quarters of the men originating in East and West Prussia. Perhaps even more important in upholding the internal cohesion of each unit was the influx of returning convalescents during 1943. The 126th ID received nearly 6,000 of these men while the 123rd ID welcomed some 2,170 veterans. The 121st ID noted that the returning troops made a "good impression in every way" as they were "glad to be back with their comrades."[73]

The crushing casualties suffered by the Wehrmacht on other sections of the front, however, meant that even units in Army Group North were forced to integrate large numbers of recruits from outside their home recruiting regions. Troops drawn from regions that fell outside the *Altreich* – Luxembourg for the 121st ID and, for the 126th ID, Eupen-Malmedy, Alsace and Lorraine, Vienna, the Sudetenland, and sections of Poland – were viewed with suspicion. The Luxembourgers initially made a "good impression," but the division soon deemed them unreliable, after several cases of desertion.[74] Such sentiments were shared by the commander of the 126th ID. In April 1943, he sent out a directive concerning the integration of "foreign" soldiers.[75] After praising their contributions to the recent fighting, he argued that they "need to feel trusted and part of the unit." Recognizing that the different backgrounds, values, and practices of these men would be viewed by the remainder of the division as somewhat

---

[71] 126 ID KTB, 8.1.43, BA-MA RH 26–126/74.
[72] For a brief overview of the German manpower situation in 1943, see Bernd Wegner, "Von Stalingrad nach Kursk," in Frieser, *Die Ostfront 1943/44*, pp. 3–79, especially pp. 8–18.
[73] Tätigkeitsbericht der Abt. IIa für die Zeit vom 16.3.43–15.5.1943, BA-MA RH 26–123/167; Bericht über die Entwicklung der personellen Lage der Division während der Berichtzeit mit Anlage "Fehlstellen," BA-MA RH 26–121/64.
[74] Bericht über die Entwicklung der personellen Lage der Division während der Berichtzeit mit Anlage "Fehlstellen," BA-MA RH 26–121/63.
[75] 126 ID Kommandeur, 620/45 g., 27.4.43, BA-MA RH 26–126/90.

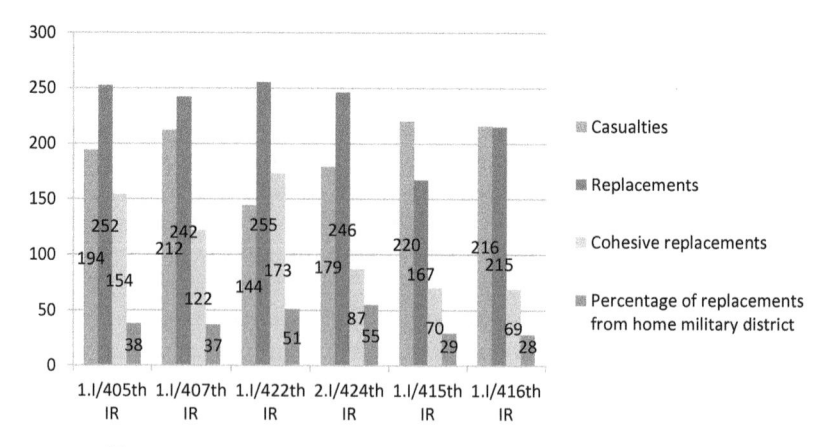

Figure 10.4 Company manpower, 1943

foreign, he tried to ensure that such distinctions would not damage the cohesiveness of the 126th ID. His own words, however, illustrated the exact attitude he was warning against as he instructed his officers to report to him directly on the "character, attitude, and combat value" of these troops. It seems that the Wehrmacht replacement system had continued to function smoothly up through 1943 or such orders to be vigilant of outsiders to the division would no longer be necessary; they would have become part of the division's everyday practices.

In sum, however, each division could note that the majority of recruits consisted of "good *Menschenmaterial*," who, after four to five months' training, "made a fresh and strong impression."[76] Fortified by thousands of returning veterans and continuing to receive men from their home recruiting regions, infantry divisions in Army Group North were able to maintain the cohesion needed to stay in the field against the Red Army. While each division suffered high casualties at various times during the year, the nature of war in northwest Russia meant such periods of bloodletting were generally confined to one month; the following period of relative calm allowed them to integrate fresh recruits and convalescents into combat-ready, cohesive units before once again entering the fray.

Company-level documentation confirms many of these trends (see Figure 10.4).[77] Five of the six companies saw their casualties more than

---

[76] Bericht über die Entwicklung der personellen Lage der Division während der Berichtzeit mit Anlage "Fehlstellen," BA-MA RH 26–121/63.
[77] 1.I/405 I.R., Veränderungen zur Liste der Erkennungsmarkern dem Bataillon, from 5. Februar 1943 to 4. Januar 1944 in WASt, 80549; 1.I/407, Veränderungen zur Liste der Erkennungsmarkern dem Bataillon, from 5. Februar 1943 to 5. Januar 1944,

compensated for by replacements and cohesive replacements predominated in three of the companies. Four of the six units also had the majority of their incoming men originate in their home military district, though the 123rd ID's two companies had less than 30 percent of their men call the Berlin-Brandenburg region home. Set against these successes, however, more men who were foreign to the 121st, 126th, and 123rd IDs entered these companies in 1943 than they had previously during the war and this spoke to the strains afflicting the German Army's manpower by this stage.

Despite the bouts of ferocious combat that periodically erupted across Army Group North's front, the balance of casualties and replacements fell in favor of the latter. In fact, the German replacement system adequately maintained the power of the 121st, 123rd, and 126th IDs, certainly in comparison to other Wehrmacht divisions along the southern sections of the front. Situational factors thus played an important role in the relative strength of these formations; Stephen Fritz has written that the divisions of Army Group North, "having been spared the brunt of battle in 1942 and 1943, had a level of primary group cohesion and combat effectiveness rare in German units at this point in the war"; such a claim seems to be confirmed by an analysis of these three units.[78]

As this discussion of replacements in 1943 indicates, the German Army continued to funnel adequate numbers of troops to the front of Army Group North, even if their initial training was not deemed satisfactory. Perhaps an underemphasized cause of the German Army's battle effectiveness during the Second World War was its focus on training the green recruits shipped to the front. While the Germans could never approach the standards of their 1941 army in terms of training and skill, they nonetheless diligently strove to ensure that their soldiers received the highest possible level of instruction available under the circumstances. More importantly, the Wehrmacht emphasized the importance of the mental aspect to warfare; as Hew Strachan has observed, the "essence [of German training] lay in its psychological effects."[79] In attempts to create a realistic combat environment for its

---

WASt, 80588; 1. Inf. Regt. 422 (1./I.R. 422) Erkennungsmarkenverzeichnis (Veränderungsmeldung), 8.2.1943 through 10. Januar 1944, WASt, 82026; 2. Inf. Regt. 424 Veränderungsmeldung zur Liste der ausgegebenen Erkennungsmarken, 10.2.43 through 7.1.44, WASt, 80266; 1. Kompanie Infanterie-Regiment 415 Erkennungsmarken-Verzeichnis (Veränderungsanzeige), 15.4.1943 through 15.1.1944, WASt, 80744; 1/416 Veränderung zur Erkennungsmarkenliste der Dienststelle 10324B, 8.4.43 through 20.1.44, WASt, 80763.

[78] Fritz, *Ostkrieg*, p. 432.
[79] Hew Strachan, "Ausbildung, Kampfgeist und die zwei Weltkriege," in Bruno Thoß and Hans-Erich Volkmann (eds.), *Erster Weltkrieg, Zweiter Weltkrieg*, pp. 265–86, here p. 283.

Illustration 10.3 Trenches in the Volkhov theater highlight the shift to attritional warfare in northwest Russia.

recruits, men underwent live fire exercises in inclement weather and experienced the exhaustion and desperation common to combat soldiers. The army also attempted to reconstruct each man's values by emphasizing its own martial virtues. Variously described as "bravery, obedience, and fulfilling one's duty" and "perseverance, staying power, [and] courage," the inculcation of these values certainly played a role in the Wehrmacht's ability to remain in the field, and one scholar has argued that the army's cohesion was due to the individual soldier's loyalty to the Wehrmacht as an institution.[80] Each division utilized the long periods of calm offered by the positional warfare on this front to carry out such important programs.

Such a process began for the 121st ID during its time in the rear area of Eighteenth Army. The men underwent a thorough training program while simultaneously integrating numerous replacements into the division. One soldier described the process as an attempt to "close the gaps of the short

[80] Neitzel and Welzer, *Soldaten*, p. 305; Strachan, "Ausbildung, Kampfgeist und die zwei Weltkriege," p. 284; Römer, "Volksgemeinschaft in der Wehrmacht?", p. 68.

period of training" the replacements received prior to reaching the unit "through continual work, instruction, and exercises." He then stressed that this "work can mean possibly their life or the holding or reaching of a ... position in a battle sector."[81] By January 1943, the division commander even hinted that his men would soon be prepared for offensive action – a somewhat startling admission for a unit in Army Group North at this stage of the war.[82] This training took place in a period of relative tranquility; not only did the 121st ID avoid combat, but there was "very little partisan activity" in its area.[83] In order to spare the East Prussians the task of combating enemy agents and partisans, the SD branch at Liuban transferred a commando to Chudovo for this very purpose.[84] Routine patrols, however, did turn up irregular resistance in the area:

These have been two strenuous days, patrols on both days. Not easy through the wet, deep snow. But both today and yesterday we found five stores of grain and we also found two forest camps on both days, unfortunately they were empty ... we arrested 50 civilians – bandit family members. War and fire – the villages were burned to the ground after everything of value was removed; the bandits will have neither hiding places, shelter, nor reconnaissance assistance from their family members.[85]

Following the conclusion of the fifth battle for Siniavino, the East Prussians again undertook a period of extensive training. The arrival of the wet season, while forcing the men to participate in the unpleasant tasks of removing corpses and garbage buried by the winter's snow and ice in order to avoid the "rat plague," also ensured that the Red Army remained relatively quiescent.[86] The recently arrived replacements were collected into a specially designated training battalion, where they received four weeks of instruction.[87] An entire battalion of the 408th Infantry Regiment was pulled out of the line for two weeks and participated in an intensive training program while the division sent a number of its NCOs to the Army NCO School at Jamburg for a five-week course.[88] Finally, during

---

[81] Seargent Helmut Römer, Gren. Rgt. 406, 30.1.43.
[82] Zustandsbericht, 121 Infanterie Division, 9.1.1943, BA-MA RH 26–121/41. The commander of I Corps, however, was not completely convinced by this appraisal; see his conversation with Küchler, O.B.-Besuch am 4.2.1943 auf Korpsgef.-Stand, BA-MA RH 24–1/124.
[83] Tätigkeitsbericht für die Zeit vom 1.1–31.3.1943, Gen. Kdo. A. K. I., Abt. Ic, BA-MA RH 24–1/277.
[84] Generalkommando I. Armeekorps, Personenkontrolle in Ortschaften, 8.1.1943, BA-MA RH 24–1/117.
[85] Sergeant Helmut Römer, Gren Regt. 406, 25.2.43, BfZ, Sammlung Sterz.
[86] Ibid., 1.5.43.   [87] 121 ID KTB, 25.4.43, BA-MA RH 26–121/47.
[88] Ibid., 26.4.43, 10.5.43.

the first three weeks of July, the entire division underwent an instructional course that focused on tactics, from squad to regiment levels.[89]

The 126th ID also began a similar training program in spring 1943. For the replacements who arrived in March, a three-week training course was implemented, led by officers and NCOs who had "experienced war in the East."[90] The division's *Feldausbildung* (field-training) battalion trained a second batch of green troops who arrived in the spring. This training unit put the new arrivals through an intense six-week program deemed so effective that the normal three-week training course given by the division at the front was viewed as unnecessary.[91] This period of instruction concluded with the establishment of a month-long combat school designed to train leaders of platoons, squads, and groups in the tactical lessons of the war.[92]

The completion of these replacements' training, as well as the more specialized programs for NCOs, had, by 1943, become the responsibility of German infantry divisions and this was a task that the Wehrmacht approached with utmost seriousness.[93] These practices not only improved the tactical efficiency of the infantry, but, perhaps, just as importantly, created a real sense of cohesion between the recruits and the officers and NCOs tasked to train them.[94] Historians have long recognized how significant the German Army's professional attitude towards the importance of training was in maintaining its battlefield efficiency and this certainly proved to be the case for both the 121st and 126th IDs in mid-1943.[95] This emphasis on preparing the newly arrived replacements for the rigors of war in the east favorably contrasts, for example, with the approach used by the American Army and the integration and training of its recruits, and it allowed regular Wehrmacht units to remain tactically effective during the later stages of the war.[96]

---

[89] Ibid., 20.6.43, 21.7.43.
[90] 126 Infanterie Division, Abt. Ia, Nr. 445/43 geheim, Betr.: Weiterbildung des Ersatzes, 30.3.43, BA-MA RH 26–126/90.
[91] 126 ID KTB, 22.5.43, BA-MA RH 26–126/74.
[92] 126 Infanterie Division, Abt. Ia/IIa, Nr. 882/43 geheim, Betr.: Aufstellung der Divisions-Kampfschule, 6.6.43, BA-MA RH 26–126/90.
[93] Creveld, *Fighting Power*, pp. 72–3.
[94] Strachan, "Ausbildung, Kampfgeist und die zwei Weltkriege," p. 271.
[95] Fritz, *Frontsoldaten*, pp. 11–30; Williamson Murray, "German Response to Victory in Poland: A Case Study in Professionalism," in Murray (ed.), *German Military Effectiveness* (Baltimore, 1992), pp. 229–39; Kevin W. Farrell, "'Culture of Confidence': The Tactical Excellence of the German Army of the Second World War," in Christopher Kolenda (ed.), *Leadership: The Warrior's Art* (Mechanicsburg, 2001), pp. 177–203, especially pp. 186–7.
[96] Critical views of American training include Creveld, *Fighting Power*, pp. 73–9; Stephen Ambrose, *Citizen Soldiers* (New York, 1997), pp. 273–89; Rick Atkinson, *An Army at*

More relevant for Army Group North's infantry was its opponent across the line: the Red Army. Soviet infantry divisions paid a heavy cost for their repeated offensives against German positions in 1943 and this resulted in numerous replacements being sent to the front.[97] According to the historian Walter Dunn, many of these newly recruited soldiers "were of inferior quality."[98] In fact, utilizing Soviet sources, the Germans estimated that "between July and December 1943, 40.9 percent of Soviet recruits were untrained and 26.7 percent had received less than a month of training."[99] David Glantz has corroborated this view of the diminishing power of Red Army infantry units in the later stages of the war:

> through 1943, the NKO [People's Commissariat of Defense] steadily eased the age restrictions on combat and noncombat military service in the Red Army to include younger, older, and less fit reservists and conscripts, ultimately conscripting men well under the age of 18 years and exceeding the age of 55 years into the Red Army's operating forces. Despite the new legal age limits on service, many soldiers exceeded these limits by the end of 1943.[100]

Thus, while the Wehrmacht's infantry certainly existed at a diminished level in comparison to 1941, much the same could be said about the units facing it. And while the Red Army became an increasingly well-armed force, relying heavily on weaponry to cover its infantry weaknesses, its forces in northwest Russia were of secondary importance to those engaged in the massive offensives in the central and southern regions of the Soviet Union and therefore failed to receive such weaponry in abundance. The German replacement system and its ability to send trained men to the front may have failed to meet the Red Army's challenge along the entirety of the front, but it did so adequately in Army Group North's operational area.

Dawn: The War in North Africa, 1942–1943 (New York, 2002), p. 404. Two studies which generally present the United States Army in a favorable light but nonetheless are critical of its training policies are Michael Doubler, *Closing with the Enemy: How GIs Fought the War in Europe, 1944–1945* (Lawrence, KS, 1995), pp. 29–30, 277–9; and Peter Mansoor, *The GI Offensive in Europe: The Triumph of American Infantry Divisions, 1941–1945* (Lawrence, KS, 2002), pp. 29–31, 43–5, 193–4. The British Army suffered from similar problems. Niall Barr has noted that "unfortunately, the British Army never seemed able to ensure that inexperienced units would not be flung into battle without proper preparation"; see his *Pendulum of War: The Three Battles of El Alamein* (London, 2005), p. 412.

[97] Walter S. Dunn Jr., *Hitler's Nemesis: The Red Army, 1930–1945* (London, 1994), p. 70.
[98] Ibid.   [99] Ibid., p. 97.
[100] David M. Glantz, *Colossus Reborn: The Red Army at War, 1941–1945* (Lawrence, KS, 2005), pp. 540–1.

11 A more rational occupation?
The contradictions of military necessity

Two days before the 123rd ID completed its withdrawal from the Demiansk position behind the Lovat river, Army Group North issued twenty-five pages of occupation guidelines for its area of operations.[1] This major policy initiative proves noteworthy in two ways. First, while the directive attempted to lay the foundation for a more conciliatory occupation policy, the fact that it was issued before elements of Sixteenth Army had finished with their destruction of the Demiansk position suggests that the rampant contradictions within German military policy remained irreconcilable. Second, the simple notion that the command felt the need to issue such a directive during the *third* year of war highlights the relative confusion that plagued German military occupation authorities in the Soviet Union. The conflicts inherent in their competing versions of military necessity ensured that this occupation policy would prove no more successful than previous ones in harnessing the civilian population to the German war effort.

Army Group North stated that it had the "task of re-establishing and maintaining public life and public order in the area, as this served the interests of the German Wehrmacht."[2] The division of labor between the army, SS-Police forces, and the Economic Staff East received further confirmation as the Wehrmacht was "not responsible" for economic matters or propaganda; it nonetheless "worked closely together" with Economic Staff East and the higher SS and police leader (HSSPF) for northwest Russia.[3]

The directive betrayed the military's traditional desire for "ordering" the area, in this case through a comprehensive registration system of all civilian inhabitants of northwest Russia and series of measures designed to lock them into one community. The army group called for the establishment of a unified pass system as well as the creation of lists

---

[1] Anordnungen für die Militärverwaltung, Oberkommando der Heeresgruppe Nord, 5.3.1943, USHMM RG-18.003.
[2] Ibid., p. 1.   [3] Ibid., p. 2.

for each community that noted age and place of origin, as well as possible association with the organs of Soviet power.[4] Everyone over the age of fourteen needed to carry this documentation with them at all times; the combination of the pass system and the community lists would hopefully allow for a more precise appraisal of the region's labor potential as well as limit partisan activity. Complementing these more repressive measures, the army group also called for more appealing policies. Schooling for children between the ages of eight and twelve was to be established while civilians would be able to buy and sell goods from newly opened markets and practice their religion.[5] The Germans exploited the latter with a major holiday celebration on 22 June 1943 – the second anniversary of the German invasion – by encouraging church services as well as other events designed to impress upon the Soviet population the benefits and perks of German rule; these included public dances with Soviet women and German soldiers, movies, and parades.[6] While none of these measures were undertaken due to humanitarian motives or even a real interest in the lives of Soviet civilians, they do nonetheless indicate the German Army's evolving attitude towards the population in its midst.

I. Military necessity: between conciliation and ruthlessness

Army Group North's attempt to impose some sort of uniformity onto its occupation practices in northwest Russia, as well as to create a quiet and stable theater of operations, depended on the actions of its subordinate units. In an attempt to transform his division's occupation, the commander of the 126th ID lectured his men on treating civilians in a more personable manner. In an order issued on 2 April 1943, he argued that a "mental adjustment of the entire German occupation system towards the Russian people is necessary."[7] Noting that the Soviets who worked for the Germans, as well as the armed auxiliaries, were not a "mass of humanity [*Menschenmass*] who should be led to the slaughterhouse," the directive called for a more humane and thoughtful treatment of Soviet citizens: "always keep in mind that the Russian is a man, who

---

[4] Ibid., p. 5.
[5] Ibid., p. 23; Mulligan, *The Politics of Illusion and Empire*, p. 125.
[6] Sicherheitspolizei und SD, Einsatzkommando 1, Einsatzgruppe A, 29.6.1943, Lage- und Tätigkeitsbericht – Ingermanland – (Berichtszeit vom 29.5 bis 28.6.1943), p. 9, BA-MA RH 24–1/281; Mulligan, *The Politics of Illusion and Empire*, p. 124. A similar event took place on the same day in Minsk; see Quinkert, *Propaganda und Terror*, p. 299.
[7] Gedanken zum totalen Arbeitseinsatz der russischen Zivilbevölkerung, 2.4.1943, BA-MA RH 26–126/128. Emphasis in original.

on the whole willingly works when he is treated in a correct manner, but who also possesses a marked sensitivity." By treating individuals as "people," civilians would not only work more industriously for the German cause, they would also convince their friends and relatives to support the Wehrmacht.[8] This document proves interesting on several different levels. First, it provides strong evidence against charges that the German Army as a whole "wage[d] war against an entire people with a goal of annihilation" by 1943.[9] Clearly, the 126th ID was attempting to bridge the gap between the occupier and the occupied, even if only for its own goals. The motivation for this change in course was obviously tactical, but the adjustment was made nonetheless. Second, the fact that such an order required dissemination shows how a combination of the dictates of military necessity, brutalization through combat, and Nazi ideology had forged soldiers who placed little or no value on the lives of civilians in their midst. That this order was found in the files of the 126th ID, clearly the most violent of these three divisions, is certainly not a coincidence.

From the very beginning of the year, German infantry divisions continued to forcibly uproot civilians from their homes and drive them to the rear. During 1943 such actions became both extremely commonplace and extremely detailed and systematic operations that involved various levels of the German military hierarchy. On 1 April, Eighteenth Army ordered the four-stage evacuation of a twenty-kilometer strip behind the main combat line as both a defensive measure and to create labor reserves for the Wehrmacht.[10] Every able-bodied individual over the age of fourteen without younger dependents was to be plugged into labor sections for the army's various corps and housed in designated villages under guard. Families with children under fourteen were to be kept immediately behind the evacuated area while everyone incapable of work was destined to be shipped further west. XXVIII Corps also instructed its subordinate units that those families whose nourishment was not secured also needed to be removed from the corps's area of

---

[8] Since the division employed 729 *Hiwis* by mid-summer, such a formulation possessed some validity; 126 Infanterie Division, Abt. Ic, Betr.: Meldung der beschäftigten Hilfswilligen, 22.6.43, BA-MA RH 26–126/128.
[9] Hamburger Institut für Sozialforschung, *Vernichtungskrieg: Verbrechen der Wehrmacht 1941–1944*, p. 152.
[10] Armee-Oberkommando, Abt. Ia/O. Qu., Nr. 1495/43, g. Kdos., Betr.: Bildung einer Evakuierungszone, 1.4.1943, BA-MA RH 24–28/240. The following discussion is based on this document unless otherwise noted. KTB AK XXVIII Qu., 7.4.43, BA-MA RH 24–28/236.

responsibility.[11] Some 620 people were evacuated out of Zone A, with approximately half being kept for labor purposes in the corps's area.[12]

Deployed behind the front line, the 121st ID did not participate in the action until the evacuation of Zone B. Two villages, Kostovo and Belevo, were located in this sector, with the latter primarily inhabited by Finns. The division quartermaster explained to the corps that the division did not want these villagers evacuated because they were "dependable and industrious" and provided much-needed services for the division.[13] While such a statement undoubtedly contained much truth and also reflected the quasi-alliance between Germany and Finland, racist thinking also surely played a role.[14] Out of the 1,545 people to be evacuated from I Corps's area, the 121st ID was responsible for 149 Finns and 269 Russians in the villages.[15] Eighteenth Army ordered the evacuation of Zone B beginning on 15 June. While it was anticipated that a total of 6,825 people would be removed from this area, XXVIII Corps itself was responsible for only 254 inhabitants.[16] This drastic lowering of the total number of individuals involved was due to indecision reflecting the Finns and fears that such a large-scale action would only exacerbate the already strained labor situation at the front.[17] The 121st ID, in the end, removed 143 ethnic Russians from the villages.[18]

At roughly the same time, the 126th ID also carried out its own forced evacuation. On 24 March, the divisional quartermaster announced that all civilians located within twenty kilometers of the front line were to be evacuated to the rear.[19] In preparation for the operation, the division's infantry regiments, as well as its troop of *Feldgendarme*, were to compile lists of inhabitants. Civilians were to be divided between those able and those unable to work, with a section of

---

[11] Gen. Kdo. XXVIII A. K., Ia/Qu., Nr. 85/43, g. Kdos., Betr.: Bildung einer Evakuierungszone, 3.4.1943, BA-MA RH 24–28/240.
[12] Gen. Kdo. XXVIII A. K., Abt. Ia/Qu., Nr. 85, g. Kdos., Betr.: Bildung einer Evakuierungszone, 19.4.43, BA-MA RH 24–28/241.
[13] KTB AK XXVIII Qu., 12.5.43, BA-MA RH 24–28/236.
[14] For more on ethnic Finns in this area, see Pohl, *Die Herrschaft der Wehrmacht*, pp. 189–90; and Kilian, *Werhmacht und Besatzungsherrschaft*, p. 283.
[15] Anlage zu Gen. Kdo. XXVIII A. K., Ia/Ic/Qu., Nr. 126/43, g. Kdos., 15.5.43, BA-MA RH 24–28/242.
[16] Armeeoberkommando 18, Abt. O. Qu./Qu., 2, 8.6.1943, Betr.: Fortsetzung der Evakuierung (Zone B), BA-MA RH 24–28/244.
[17] Gen. Kdo. XXVIII A. K., Ia/Ic/Qu., Nr. 126/43, g. Kdos., 14.5.43, Betr.: Evakuierungszone B, BA-MA RH 24–28/242.
[18] Gen. Kdo. XXVIII. A. K., Qu., Nr. 163/43, g. Kdos., 16.6.1943, Betr.: Evakuierung der Zone B, BA-MA RH 24–28/244.
[19] 126 ID KTB Qu., 24.3.43, BA-MA RH 26–126/151.

334 A more rational occupation?

Illustration 11.1 German anti-partisan and labor policies in 1943 were characterized by the forcible evacuations of entire villages.

the former being attached to the division for its own needs.[20] On 19 April, officers met with village elders to prepare them for the upcoming action.[21] Rather implausibly placing the retreat into the context of the total mobilization of all European resources to defeat Bolshevism, divisional personnel then provided assurances to the local leaders that no one would be shipped to Germany and that villages would remain as cohesive units.[22] The operation also seems to be an attempt by the division to rid itself of all Soviet civilians, outside those already inducted into *Hiwi* units, who had attached themselves to the division. With the exception of sixty-seven women who worked with the divisional laundry service, all employment of civilians outside the formal labor columns was expressly forbidden.[23]

---

[20] 126 Infanterie Division, Abt. Ib, Betr.: Evakuierung, 23. März 1943, BA-MA RH 26–126/152; 126 ID KTB Qu., 26.3.43, BA-MA RH 26–126/151.
[21] Tätigkeitsbericht zum Kriegstagebuch, Abteilung Ic, 19.4.43, BA-MA RH 26–126/127.
[22] Kurzer Inhalt des Vortrages an die Starosten am 19.4.43, BA-MA RH 26–126/128.
[23] 126 ID KTB Qu., 27.4.43, 30.4.43, BA-MA RH 26–126/151; 126 Infanterie Division, Abt. Ib, Nr. 207/43 geh., Betr: Evakuierung des Gefechtsgebietes, 27. April 1943.

The removal from the corps's rear area began on 1 May and the final evacuation of the combat area ended one month later.[24] This operation was ostensibly undertaken on defensive grounds; the evacuation of all civilians would hopefully end partisan activity in the division's area. In what reflected a lack of co-ordination between German military authorities, however, civilians continued to move freely throughout the division's area, including the evacuated area. Orders from the division instructed the men to post signs throughout the divisional sector threatening civilians with arrest and shooting if they continued to ignore German regulations.[25] Division command also castigated the men for their lackluster approach to security as well as a lackadaisical attitude towards regulations concerning civilian movement: *Ortskommandanten* had provided civilians with passes to re-enter the evacuated area even though this was a direct violation of German policy. During one week, twenty-six civilians, armed with German-issued passes, were arrested for traveling through the recently evacuated area.[26] Theoretically, all of these civilians should have been shot; however, only seven were subsequently sent to a civilian labor camp, with the rest being released after arrest.[27] The reflex-like brutality that accompanied the 126th ID into the Soviet Union in 1941 had somewhat tempered by the third year of war.

While the Germans ordered these evacuations of areas near the front based on security concerns, they resulted in a deteriorating security system in the rear areas as numerous civilians fled their villages before the deportations began and joined the ever-increasing ranks of the partisan movement. By 1943, popular resistance, which had generally proved an irritant during the first two years of war, had blossomed into a real military threat for the Wehrmacht.[28] As the general military situation noticeably turned against the Reich and it became increasing probable that Bolshevik power would be returning to areas presently under German occupation, partisan groups became more daring and found higher levels of support from the surrounding civilian population. This, combined with the German leadership's increasingly radical approach to exploiting the Soviet Union and its population, led to a more vibrant and,

---

[24] Fernspruch, 126 I.D., Abt. Ib, Betr.: Evakuierung, 30.4, 09,00 Uhr, BA-MA RH 26–126/152; 126 ID KTB Qu., 27.5.43, 2.6.43, BA-MA RH 26–126/151.
[25] 126 Infanterie-Division, Abteilung IIa/Ic, Betr.: Überwachung der Regimentsbereiche, 27.5.1943, BA-MA RH 26–126/128; 126 Infanterie-Division, Abteilung Ic, Betr.: Abwehrmaßnahmen gegenüber Landeseinwohnern, 17.6.43, BA-MA RH 26–126/128.
[26] 126 Infanterie-Division, Abteilung Ic, Rückkehr von evakuierten russ. Zivilpersonen in das evakuierte Gebiet, 24.6.1943, BA-MA RH 26–126/128.
[27] Tätigkeitsbericht zum Kriegstagebuch, Abteilung Ic, 30.6.43, BA-MA RH 26–126/127.
[28] Pohl, *Die Herrschaft der Wehrmacht*, p. 291.

from the German view, more dangerous partisan movement.[29] In Belarus and sections of Russia proper under occupation, the Germans responded with growing brutality and the practice of creating "dead zones" became a significant element of German anti-partisan policy. Sharing many goals with the scorched-earth policy implemented during tactical and strategic retreats, dead zones were cleared of anything and anyone which could conceivably aid partisans in any way. While rear-area units such as security divisions were certainly involved in carrying out such tasks, "large operations," ones that included SS-Police units as well as frontline combat divisions (including panzer units) became an integral part of the German campaign to destroy the partisan menace.[30]

Partisan activity also became increasingly threatening in Army Group North's area of operations throughout the course of 1943.[31] While events in northwest Russia failed to turn into the indiscriminate "orgies of violence" that erupted throughout the center of the front, popular resistance did become a growing concern for all three divisions during 1943.[32] Not only did they continue their previous practice of dealing with irregulars at the front, but two of the divisions actually provided troops specifically for anti-partisan operations in the rear.

The 121st ID became much more intensely involved in anti-partisan warfare than in previous years. Small partisan groups sporadically engaged in firefights with members of the division, and one wooded area became so notorious for being rife with partisans that the troops nicknamed it "Bandit Forest."[33] In an attempt to stamp out such activity, the unit increased patrols and established bulked-up sentry detachments to protect vital bridges and roads.[34] As part of this policy, even men of the workshop company were detailed to watch the area's primary rail line.[35]

---

[29] Shepherd, *War in the Wild East*, pp. 166–8.
[30] For a detailed look at such operations, see Gerlach, *Kalkulierte Morde*, pp. 884–918; for an examination of a frontline combat unit's participation in such an action, see Bartov, *The Eastern Front*, pp. 123–4.
[31] Hill, *War behind the Eastern Front*, pp. 156–61; Kilian, *Wehrmacht und Besatzungsherrschaft*, pp. 561–82.
[32] The phrase belongs to Rolf-Dieter Müller; see his "Die Wehrmacht: Historische Last und Verantwortung," p. 12. Examples of the growing partisan threat in Army Group North's area of operations are found in a February 1943 report from the commandant of Sixteenth Army's rear area; see Müller, *Die faschistische Okkupationspolitik*, Document 161, pp. 394–7.
[33] 121 ID KTB, 18.5.43, 24.5.43, BA-MA RH 26–121/47; Tagesmeldung 121 Inf.-Div., an Gen. Kdo. XXVIII A. K., 24.5.43, Morgenmeldung Gren. Regt. 405, 15.6.43, BA-MA RH 26–121/50; 121 Infanterie Division, Tagesmeldung, 25.4.43, BA-MA RH 26–121/50.
[34] 121 ID KTB, 25.5.43, BA-MA RH 26–121/47.
[35] 121 ID KTB Qu., 18.6.43, BA-MA RH 26–121/66.

Partisan activity proved much more disruptive in the rear area, however, and following the example of other German combat units (especially those operating in the center of the front), elements of the 121st ID were sent to the rear.[36] On 31 May, Eighteenth Army ordered the division to ship its *Jagd-Kommando* (mobile anti-partisan unit) to the rear to assist in the pacification of the army rear area.[37] During the unit's six-week stay behind the lines, Korück 583 launched no major anti-partisan operations. While approximately thirty partisans were shot and another twenty-five civilians were executed for providing support to the partisan movement during this time, the 121st ID's task force played no role in these deaths.[38] Members of the division did engage a group of twenty partisans in a quick firefight, but the guerillas escaped after inflicting two German casualties.[39] Outside this brief encounter, the 121st ID's units had little contact with partisans or civilians until their commitment ended on 27 June and they returned to their home unit.[40]

The Rhinelanders of the 126th ID also faced irregular resistance that it viewed as a real threat to its military effectiveness. Soon after moving into the Leningrad area in August 1943, the intelligence officer noted that "the sharpest measures are required in supervising the civilian population."[41] The division commander characterized Leningrad as "a center of agent and bandit headquarters that deploys these plagues throughout our present divisional area, and which need to be eradicated root and branch."[42] Firefights between members of the 126th ID and partisans confirmed these misgivings about the danger of irregular resistance and the division implemented a stricter occupation policy.[43] In an order issued on 11 September, the division's ranking intelligence officer established several *Sperrzonen* (restricted areas) in which no civilians could pass.[44] Those being evacuated out of these areas, however, were not to be manhandled. Since "a good word was easier to bear than

---

[36] For a succinct discussion of partisan activity in Army Group North's rear area in 1943, see Hasenclever, *Wehrmacht und Besatzungspolitik in der Sowjetunion*, pp. 448–53.
[37] 121 ID KTB Qu., 31.5.43, BA-MA RH 26–121/66; 121 ID KTB, 2.6.43, BA-MA RH 26–121/47.
[38] KTB Korück 583, 1.6.–30.6.43, BA-MA RH 23–277.
[39] Ibid., 14.6.43.
[40] 121 ID KTB Qu., 31.5.43, BA-MA RH 26–121/66.
[41] Tätigkeitsbericht Ic, 31.8.43, BA-MA RH 26–126/129.
[42] 126 Infanterie Division, Kommandeur, Ic, Nr. 480/43 geh., Betr.: Überwachung des Divisionsbereiches durch Streifen und Posten, 7.9.1943, BA-MA RH 26–126/129. The remainder of this discussion is based on this document unless otherwise noted.
[43] Tätigkeitsbericht Ic, 8.9.43, BA-MA RH 26–126/129.
[44] Anlage zu 126 Inf. Div. Ic/Ib vom 11.9.43, Betr.: Abwehrmaßnahmen gegenüber der Zivilbevölkerung im Divisionsbereich, BA-MA RH 26–126/129.

a severe measure," the troops were instructed to present civilians with a rationale for the evacuation that would appeal to their interests. The order continued by declaring, "improper treatment, inadequate care (food, goods), treatment as a forced laborer (fencing in the camp with barbed wire and other such things) drives those who up until now have lived here voluntarily into the arms of the bandits." The carrying out of the evacuation, however, failed to live up to these guidelines. Families were "torn apart" as the soldiers needed some civilians to fill labor columns while other civilians, worried that they would starve following the evacuation, resisted.[45] By 18 September, the evacuations had been completed but not without further cost to the Wehrmacht's reputation; here, the contradictory impulses that animated the German conception of military necessity only further antagonized the civilian population.[46]

Part of the new arsenal employed by the Wehrmacht in trying to convince Soviet civilians of the necessity of such actions included the use of propagandists.[47] The 126th ID employed two such ethnic Russian propagandists who traveled to villages and towns throughout the divisional area and attempted to drum up support for the German cause. Painting the conflict as one between Bolshevism and the combined might of Nazi Germany and Nationalist Russia, the duo tried to convince their audiences that Germany would indeed triumph.[48] The effects of such an attempt, however, can only have been meager: as SD reports from the region noted, "the unfulfilled expectations about the German summer offensive, the evacuation measures in the front area, and the massive conscription for the labor action led to a worrying effect" on the population and these all proved much more significant in determining the population's mood than the efforts of Wehrmacht propagandists.[49]

---

[45] 126 Infanterie Division, Abt. Ic, Nr. 583/43 geheim, Betr.: Stimmung bei Hilfswilligen und Zivilbevölkerung und Auswirkung getroffener Propagandamaßnahmen, 14.10.1943, BA-MA RH 26–126/130.

[46] 126 Infanterie Division, Abt. Ic – Nr. 502/43 geh., Betr.: Stimmung bei Hilfswilligen und Zivilbevölkerung und Auswirkung getroffener Propagandamaßnahmen, 14.9.43, BA-MA RH 26–126/129.

[47] For a persuasive examination of the growing importance of propaganda to the German war effort on the Eastern Front in 1943, see Quinkert, *Propaganda und Terror*, pp. 312–53.

[48] 126 Infanterie Division, Abt. Ic – Nr. 502/43 geh., Betr.: Stimmung bei Hilfswilligen und Zivilbevölkerung und Auswirkung getroffener Propagandamaßnahmen, 14.9.43, BA-MA RH 26–126/129.

[49] Sicherheitspolizei und SD, Einsatzkommando 1, Einsatzgruppe A, 29.6.1943, Lage- und Tätigkeitsbericht – Ingermanland – (Berichtszeit vom 29.5. bis 28.6.1943), p. 10, BA-MA RH 24–1/281.

Military necessity: between conciliation and ruthlessness   339

While the 121st and 126th IDs both found their construction of a more rational occupation order derailed by the internal contradictions of military necessity, the 123rd ID faced the largest partisan threat to its activities in 1943, primarily due its area of operations bordering on the partisan movement's largest concentration on the Eastern Front. The Berliners faced little threat from guerilla forces within the Demiansk pocket, but, following its withdrawal to the western bank of the Lovat river, clashes between the 123rd ID and partisan groups significantly spiked.

Within one week of establishing new positions, the combating of partisan activity had become the division's primary task. During the month of March, the unit reported the shooting of six partisans and the arrest of a further eighteen individuals. The majority of these partisans were not the disorganized individuals of the first months of war but members of the 21st Partisan Brigade.[50] The 123rd ID responded by enacting a stricter "supervisory" system in which infantry battalions were placed in control of designated areas, in hopes of suffocating the partisan movement.[51] Despite a lull in partisan activity in early April 1943, the Berliners became increasingly fixated with eliminating guerilla bands; the Prusso-German Army's traditional aversion to irregular warfare certainly reached its apex during the war in the east. This attention to insurgents worked itself up to the highest levels of Army Group North. During a visit to the division on 3 April, Küchler stated that "the present time is particularly favorable for partisan combat" and he suggested several measures designed to diminish partisan activity.[52] Two weeks later, the division established a "partisan-hunter" company to mount seek-and-destroy missions in its rear area, with its approximately 115 men drawn from various divisional units. The company then received one week's worth of instruction in anti-partisan combat before being sent into the field.[53] Before it had completed its training, however,

---

[50] II AK KTB, 14.3.43, BA-MA RH 24–2/110; 123 ID KTB, 14.3.43, BA-MA RH 26–123/119.
[51] 123 Infanterie Division, Abt. Ia/Az. IVa, Nr. 630/43 geh., Befehl für die Einteilung des Divisionsabschnitt in Wirtschafts- und Überwachungsgebiete, 7. März, 1943, BA-MA RH 26–123/119.
[52] Küchler wanted the division to vigorously patrol all roads and paths to deny their use to the partisans as well as use wires with numerous bells attached to them and "frightcharges" (*Schreckladungen*) to alert German sentries to the movements of partisans; Besprechungspunkte anläßlich der Anwesenheit des Herrn Oberbefehlshabers der Heeresgruppe, 3.4.1943, BA-MA RH 26–123/120.
[53] 123 ID KTB, 17.4.43, BA-MA RH 26–123/120; 123 Infanterie Division, Abt. Ia/Az. IVa, Nr. 1113/43 geh., Befehl für das Zusammenstellen einer Partisanjäger-Kompanie, 17.4.43, BA-MA RH 26–123/120.

the 123rd ID launched a major "cleansing action" (*Säuberungsaktion*) on 25 April.[54] A group of 120 partisans attempted to cross the division's front as it moved to the east. After repulsing the attempt, the 123rd ID encircled and hammered away at the trapped guerillas while also fighting off attacks launched by three different partisan brigades.[55] The operation concluded on 9 May with the division reporting 144 "bandits taken prisoner" and an additional 177 shot.[56]

How does this operation fit into the large-scale anti-partisan sweeps that occurred all across the front in 1943? On the one hand, the Germans clearly directed this operation at actual armed partisans and not at defenseless civilians caught up in the maelstrom of war. The amount and the types of equipment and arms seized by the Germans support such a contention.[57] On the other hand, though Wehrmacht casualty figures for the operation remain unknown, the monthly figures for the 123rd ID indicate that it suffered relatively few losses during the encounter.[58] The disproportionate numbers of casualties, however, appear axiomatic of clashes between armed civilians and soldiers; training and firepower usually triumph in the end. Thus while one can safely argue that this example highlights the fundamental problem with slogans such as "partisan warfare without any partisans," it also provides evidence of a frontline combat unit's extensive participation in the effort to defeat the insurgency.

This success led to a dramatic decrease in partisan activity in II Corps's area in June. In a report sent to Sixteenth Army, the corps concluded that "altogether, one has the impression that continual supervision of the rear area has forced the partisans to withdraw west of the

---

[54] II AK KTB, 25.4.43, BA-MA RH 24–2/110.
[55] 123 ID KTB, 25.4.43, BA-MA RH 26–123/120; II AK KTB, 26.4.43, BA-MA RH 24–2/110.
[56] 123 ID Abt. Ia/Az IVc, Tagesmeldung, 9.5.43, BA-MA RH 26–123/121; II AK KTB, 9.5.43, BA-MA RH 24–2/110.
[57] The Germans catalogued numerous weapons including grenade launchers, machine guns, anti-aircraft machine guns, rifles, machine pistols, and explosives. See 123 Infanterie Division, Abt. Ia/Az IVc, Tagesmeldung, 26. April 1943, 123 Infanterie Division, Abt. Ia/Az IVc, Tagesmeldung, 28. April 1943, 123 Infanterie Division, Abt. Ia/Az IVc, Tagesmeldung, 29. April 1943, BA-MA RH 26–123/120.
[58] For the entire months of May and June, the division suffered thirty-eight killed, 102 wounded, and seven missing. When the small-scale tactical offensives of late May and the constant "wastage" suffered by a frontline unit are taken into account, it is clear that the division suffered a very small number of casualties during the anti-partisan operation. For the casualty figures, see 123 Infanterie Division, Zustandsbericht, 1. Mai 1943, BA-MA RH 26–123/121; and 123 Infanterie Division, Zustandsbericht, 1. Juni 1943, BA-MA RH 26–123/122.

corps's area."[59] The local Economic Staff East branch supported this view, stating, "it appears that the activity of the bandits has decreased due to military counteroperations."[60] The 123rd ID's contribution to increased surveillance in the rear consisted of three mounted platoons, drawn from various divisional formations.[61] These units were expected to develop close, working relationships with village elders in hopes of enlisting their co-operation in strangling the partisan movement at the local level while also demonstrating the strength and ubiquity of the German Army to the local population. While these units may have accomplished the latter task, in reality they merely served to prove the weakness of the German Army. Unable to police its rear areas through the use of security divisions, police, and auxiliary units, the Wehrmacht's rear-area vulnerability forced it to draw desperately needed combat units from the front for deployment behind the lines.[62] The recognition of this weakness forced the division to once again consider forced evacuations as a way of destroying the partisan menace.

Following the pattern established by the 121st and 126th IDs, the 123rd ID also became much more intimately involved in the daily lives of civilians. Immediately after withdrawing from the Demiansk pocket across the Lovat river, the 123rd ID began to systematically organize and administer its rear area. In an attempt to provide food for both the troops and civilians, division headquarters charged its quartermaster with increasing the agricultural production of the area, effectively removing the Economic Staff East from having any say over the distribution of goods.[63] Though civilians were only allowed enough "food necessary for their livelihood," they did receive some protection from the arbitrary predations of marauding soldiers. Anyone caught stealing food from civilians was threatened with judicial proceedings while all one-on-one deals between Germans and Soviets – which more often than not benefited the person carrying the rifle – were also forbidden, as these only

---

[59] Generalkommando II. Armeekorps, Abteilung Ia, Nr. 2469/43 geh., Betr.: Bandentätigkeit im Juni 1943, 28. Juni 1943, BA-MA RH 24-2/216.
[60] KTB 2.Vierteljahre, Übersicht über den 5. Einsatzmonat, BA-MA RW 31/938.
[61] 123 ID, Abt. Ia/Az IVa, Nr. 1278/43 geh., Befehl für Überwachung des Gebiets und der Ortschaften in den Überwachungsabschnitten durch Reiterzüge, 6.5.43, BA-MA RH 26-123/121.
[62] Generalkommando II. Armeekorps, Abteilung Qu/Ia 461/43 g. Kdos., Betr.: Bandeneinwirkung an Armee-Oberkommando 16, 15. Mai 1943, BA-MA RH 24-2/210.
[63] 123 ID KTB Qu., 3.5.43, BA-MA RH 26-123/233; 123 Inf. Division, Ib, Befehl für die wirtschaftliche Ausnutzung des Divisionbereiches, 20.3.1943, BA-MA RH 26-123/235; KTB 2. Vierteljahre 1943, 18. April 1943, BA-MA RW 31/938. The Economic Staff East reported that due to the influx of evacuees into this area, it was for all intents and purposes washing its hands of administering it, leaving it to the 123rd ID; see p. 229 of the above KTB.

Table 11.1 *123rd Infantry Division's expected agricultural production, summer 1943*

Type	Evacuated area (in acres)	Non-evacuated area (in acres)	Statefarm Krestilovo (in acres)	Total area (in acres)	Expected yield (in pounds)
Rye	1,356	830	54	2,240	907,000
Wheat	15	15	40	70	28,000
Potatoes	637	118	74	830	1,580,000
Oats	447	240	99	786	159,000
Barley	59	59	74	192	39,000
Peas	37	151	12	200	40,500
Turnips for animals	0	0	25	25	200,000
Flax	0	37	5	42	5,100
Vegetables	81	0	20	101	----------
Meadows	2,791	4,125	988	7,904	3,200,000 (of hay)

increased the peasants' difficulties in meeting their delivery quotas. This is an important point: while the division tried to restrain its men in hopes of increasing agricultural production in the rear, this increase in food was to primarily benefit the troops themselves. While the dictates of military necessity called for better treatment of the civilians, humane considerations did not serve as the basis for the division's calculations.

Since it now wielded complete control over the area's agricultural production, the division extracted a large amount of food. Between 11 May and 10 June 1943 alone, it collected 24,601 liters of whole milk and 6,816 eggs.[64] The division's expectations for the summer harvest in its area of deployment were quite high (see Table 11.1).[65]

While the division's more focused agricultural production program did pay dividends for both civilians and soldiers, its success was somewhat blunted by two other programs that worked at cross-purposes with increasing food supplies: the evacuation of civilians from the combat zone and the implementation of a "labor action."[66] As the quartermaster pointedly noted, the evacuation of the civilian population meant that "there was no one left to take care of the fields." Due to a lack of manpower, the division was unable to spare enough troops to properly

---

[64] 123 ID, Ib, Nr. 844/43 geh., kurze Übersicht über die Versorgungslage, 16.6.1943, BA-MA RH 26–123/235.
[65] Ibid.   [66] 123 ID KTB Qu., 18.3.43, 19.3.43, BA-MA RH 26–123/233.

harvest the crops and this resulted in many rotting in the field.[67] Neither for the first nor for the last time did Wehrmacht food and security policies contradict one another.

On 17 March, Sixteenth Army's order concerning the evacuation of civilians from the combat zone reached the 123rd ID.[68] In May and June, the division organized twenty separate transports, emptying over thirty-five villages.[69] While the precise number of those evacuated remains unknown, one of the four sectors charged with carrying out the operation reported that it shipped 179 men, 582 women, and 731 children – a total of 1,492 people – to the rear.[70] The process proceeded smoothly, merely providing another piece of evidence that such evacuations now figured into the everyday activities of German combat units in northwestern Russia.

In addition to being evacuated from their homes, the civilian population was also targeted for labor roundups. In order to complete construction and other tasks required by the 123rd ID, the divisional quartermaster ordered the creation of five labor columns – two male and three female – consisting of one hundred workers apiece.[71] Though some allowances were made for children under fourteen who suffered from illness and were therefore excused from labor, the implementation of this policy was generally marked by callousness and cruelty.[72] Mounted platoons swooped throughout the rear areas, looking to "seize" enough able-bodied people to meet divisional deadlines; operating under such pressure, it can be assumed that niceties were dispensed with by the Berliners.[73] The men were instructed "that women with children up until the eighth year are to be evacuated when there are no other female members of the family. Women with older children are always to be put into labor columns."[74] Such actions did nothing to increase the morale or usefulness of the auxiliary Soviets attached to the division; many worried that family members sent to the rear were merely being abandoned to starve during the coming months.[75] More importantly,

---

[67] 123 ID, Ib, Nr. 844/43 geh., kurze Übersicht über die Versorgungslage, 16.6.1943, BA-MA RH 26–123/235; 123 Infanterie Division, Ib, Besondere Anordnungen für die Versorgung die Truppe, Nr. 70, 4.6.43, BA-MA RH 26–123/234.
[68] 123 ID KTB Qu., 17.3.43, BA-MA RH 26–123/233.
[69] See the 123 ID KTB Qu. entries for 19.5.43, 25.5.43, 2.6.43, and 14.6.43, BA-MA RH 26–123/233.
[70] Ibid., 2.5.43.
[71] 123 ID KTB Qu., 19.5.43, BA-MA RH 26–123/233. For the implementation of a similar policy by the 253rd ID, see Rass, *Menschenmaterial*, pp. 367–8.
[72] 123 ID KTB Qu., 1.5.43, BA-MA RH 26–123/233.
[73] Ibid., 25.5.43, 30.5.43, 28.6.43.   [74] Ibid., 13.5.43.
[75] Bericht an II AK, 123 ID KTB Qu., 23.7.41, BA-MA RH 26–123/233.

numerous civilians simply fled into the surrounding forests and swamps to avoid being pressed into service. Here, they joined partisan units, either out of conviction or as a means of survival. Either way, German policies continued to create partisans, and while the army was well aware of this, it either could not or would not modify these policies.[76]

The continual evacuations that marked the German occupation of northwest Russia culminated in October 1943 when Eighteenth Army announced its intention to deport all civilians from its area of operations: unlike the regimental actions which entailed the removal of several hundred civilians, the army planned to move a minimum of 150,000 people into the rear area of Army Group North.[77] This was part of Army Group North's larger goal of evacuating the staggering number of 900,000 civilians from both its combat and rear areas when it pulled back to the Panther Position, a fortified line on the old imperial Russian border.[78] Collection camps in Luga and Jamburg were established to receive the civilians, some 150 kilometers to the rear, before they were shipped to Estonia and Lithuania. That these evacuations were viewed with real distaste by the population was well known to the Germans. One police report noted,

the evacuation measures have led in some places to sheer panic. The ... population here made their bitterness clear in some cases with the destruction of household items ... the property left behind should not benefit the Germans. In Krasnoie Selo, the native police expressed doubts regarding possible uncooperative behavior in the carrying out of the evacuation. Bitter and crying faces were frequently seen. Absurd rumors circulated; the evacuated would never see the promised destination; the elderly would be simply killed; the rest would be left to their own means in some area. Negative experiences from the poorly organized refugee transport of the winter of 1941/42 had an excessively large impact on rumors.[79]

The army recognized that many citizens "would rather die here than evacuate" as they "assumed, with justification, that an evacuation means

---

[76] Generalkommando II. Armeekorps, Abteilung Qu/Ia 461/43 g. Kdos., Betr.: Bandeneinwirkung an Armee-Oberkommando 16, 15. Mai 1943, BA-MA RH 24–2/210.
[77] Armee-Oberkommando 18, Abt. A. H. Qu., O. Qu./Ic-Ao., Nr. 650/43 g. Kdos., Betr.: Evakuierung im Landmarsch, den 7.10.1943, BA-MA RH 20–18/1628. The remainder of this discussion is based on this document unless otherwise noted.
[78] Müller, *Die faschistische Okkupationspolitik*, Document 210, p. 480. The number of civilians was lowered to 250,000 when the army was unable to provide shelter for any additional evacuees.
[79] Sicherheitspolizei und SD, Einsatzkommando 1, Einsatzgruppe A, 29.6.1943, Lage- und Tätigkeitsbericht – Ingermanland – (Berichtszeit vom 29.5 bis 28.6.1943), BA-MA RH 24–1/281. Emphasis in original.

a land march of unimaginable misery and would cost numerous people their health or their lives."[80] Many civilians feared that they would not be able to bring any food with them; one German authority noted that "for many, the evacuation question is a potato question." There was also a fear of living in the Baltic states as this area was rightly perceived as being "not only non-Bolshevik but also hostile to Russians"; letters from civilians previously evacuated to these areas reinforced this belief.[81] Finally, "separation of family members" and a preference "for uncertainty of the future in their old homeland" over "the uncertainty of experience in *Ostland*" led many to resist the evacuation.[82]

While preparations for the deportations, including the establishment of rest places with shelters and the gathering of foodstuffs, had occurred, the army acknowledged that many people would flee into the woods at the first opportunity and subsequently join the partisan movement, especially since each trek of civilians would be accompanied by a mere five field gendarmes. German authorities also understood that the partisans would take advantage of the resulting chaos to steal food and other supplies both from the civilian columns and from the houses left behind.[83] Despite these misgivings, the Germans began extracting both civilians and animals at an accelerated rate: between 30 September and 16 October, "40,484 people, 987 horses, 2,545 bulls, 1,197 cows, 190 calves, and 1,220 goats and sheep" were evacuated from the rear areas of Eighteenth and Sixteenth Armies.[84] By February 1944, a total of 295,110 civilians took part in 343 separate marches out of northwest Russia.[85] The immensity and thoroughness of this operation demonstrated the

---

[80] That these Russian civilians were already in dire straits is made clear by a report from the SS-Police commander in Libau, who noted that the arrival of nearly 1,000 evacuees in July 1943 made "a profound impression" on the local population who were shocked by the "Russian poverty and misery" embodied by the refugees; Der SS- und Polizeistandortführer – Libau – 27. Juli 1943, Betr.: Lagebericht, Bundesarchiv-Berlin, R 70 Sowjetunion/20.

[81] Anlage 1 zu Armee-Oberkommando 18, Abt. A. H. Qu., O. Qu./Ic-Ao., Nr. 650/43 g. Kdos., 7.10.1943, Propaganda Staffel Gatschina, Stimmungsbericht für den Monat September 1943, 30. Sept. 1943, BA-MA RH 20–18/1628; Sicherheitspolizei und SD, Einsatzkommando 1, Einsatzgruppe A, 29.7.1943, Lage- und Tätigkeitsbericht – Ingermanland – (Berichtszeit vom 29.6 bis 28.7.1943), BA-MA RH 24–1/281.

[82] Wochenbericht zum KTB (10.–17.10.1943), BA-MA RW 31/594.

[83] 126 Infanterie Division, Abt. Ic, Nr. 615/43 geheim, Betr.: Haltung der Bevölkerung und Bandentätigkeit, 4.11.43, BA-MA RH 26–126/133. For a detailed examination of the link between forced evacuations and the burgeoning partisan movement in northwest Russia, see Hill, *The War behind the Eastern Front*, pp. 151–3.

[84] Beiträge zum KTB für die Zeit vom 1.10.–20.10.1943, BA-MA RW 31/594.

[85] He. Gr. WiFü. Nord, Abt. Arbeit, Az. 5006/5205.5L/wo. 1.2.44, Gesamtzahl der aus dem Bereich der Wi In Nord bis 1.2.44 evakuierten Personen, BA-MA RW 31/596.

346   A more rational occupation?

importance of scorched-earth retreats for the Wehrmacht as nothing was left for the advancing Red Army.

II.   A question of morale

During the course of 1943 the issue of morale became increasingly important to the German Army as a whole as well as to the infantry divisions of Army Group North. The most immediate cause of this "leadership and confidence crisis" within the German political and military leadership was the debacle at Stalingrad.[86] With the destruction of Sixth Army and the tearing open of the southern front, the political and military leadership in Berlin worried that the military catastrophe would influence the morale of the remainder of the Wehrmacht.

In addition to the shift in the initiative on the Eastern Front following the capitulation of Paulus's army, two other issues contributed to the apparent decline in German morale. First, the increasing intensity of fighting at the front was not complemented by a corresponding belief in imminent victory. While casualty numbers failed to reach the heights attained during the summer of 1941, the war's circumstances had dramatically changed since then as well. Expecting a quick victory during Operation Barbarossa, German troops accepted astoundingly high casualties; by 1943, as victory continued to slip ever further from their grasp, these same soldiers viewed the war in a much more realistic and even pessimistic manner. These increasingly cynical views of the war, combined with the grinding and inconclusive nature of attritional warfare, both more frequently exhausted units and led to more frequent requests for rest in the rear area. In early July, for example, the 126th ID asked to be removed from the front lines so that it could carry out its training and refitting in relative peace.[87] Following a visit by Sixteenth Army's commander in chief, as well as officers from X Corps, the measure was approved and the division received a promise of a four- to six-week period of quiet behind the front.[88] One day after arriving in its new quarters, however, X Corps informed the 126th ID that events in the Leningrad area necessitated it being transferred there in one week. Frustrated, tired, and angry, the Rhinelanders sourly boarded trains that deposited them in the Leningrad area in early August: the period of rest

---

[86] Jürgen Förster, "Geistige Kriegsführung in Deutschland 1919 bis 1945," in Echternkamp, *Die deutsche Kriegsgesellschaft, 1939–1945: Politisierung, Vernichtung, Überleben*, pp. 469–640, here p. 560.
[87] 126 ID KTB, 2.7.43, BA-MA RH 26–126/98.
[88] Ibid., 10.7.43.

had been quite short-lived.[89] Such occurrences became increasingly frequent as circumstances forced the manpower-depleted Wehrmacht to shift tired units from hot spot to hot spot. Battlefield events, however, proved to be of only secondary importance to the declining morale of German combat units.

As historian Ralf Blank has noted, "scarcely any other event confronted the German population so directly and continually with war and destruction as the bombing campaign from 1939 to 1945."[90] While British Bomber Command began raiding German cities in 1940, 1943 emerged as the turning point in the air war. Now fortified by the American Eighth Air Force and possessing more technologically advanced planes, the British waged a concentrated campaign designed to break German morale and destroy its war economy.[91] Civilian deaths from bombing, which averaged 750 per month in the summer of 1942, mushroomed to over 7,000 per month in 1943, before declining to a monthly total of approximately 5,500 in 1944: clearly, the intensity of the strategic bombing campaign peaked in 1943.[92] The intensified bombing constituted a real "physical and psychological strain" for German civilians in the *Heimat* and their fears, tales of destruction, and depression led both to a fracturing of the mythical *Schicksalgemeinschaft* (community of fate) and to a weakening of morale at the front.[93] The link between the home front and the military front once again assumed an importance for German military effectiveness during the Second World War, though in this case it had the opposite effect to what the German military leadership intended.

The opening round of Operation Pointblank – the combined Allied air offensive against Germany in 1943 – targeted the Ruhr industrial region

---

[89] Ibid., 25.7.43, 26.7.43, 2.-3.8.43.
[90] Ralf Blank, "Kriegsalltag und Luftkrieg an der 'Heimatfront,'" in Echternkamp, *Die deutsche Kriegsgesellschaft, 1939–1945: Politisierung, Vernichtung, Überleben*, pp. 357–461, here p. 357.
[91] For more on the strategic bombing campaign, see the official British history of the war, Charles Webster and Noble Frankland, *Strategic Air Offensive Against Germany*, vol. II, *Endeavour*, and vol. III, *Victory* (London, 1961); Max Hastings, *Bomber Command* (London, 2010); and Horst Boog, "The Strategic Air War in Europe and Air Defence of the Reich, 1943–1944," in Horst Boog et al., *Germany and the Second World War*, vol. VII, *The Strategic Air War in Europe and the War in the West and East Asia 1943–1944/5* (Oxford, 2006), pp. 9–458.
[92] Jeremy Noakes, "Germany," in Noakes, *The Civilian in War*, pp. 35–61, here p. 55.
[93] Blank, "Kriegsalltag und Luftkrieg an der 'Heimatfront,'" p. 357. For a perceptive examination of the effects of the bombing on the mentalities of Nuremberg's citizens, see Neil Gregor, "A Schicksalsgemeinschaft? Allied Bombing, Civilian Morale, and Social Dissolution in Nuremberg, 1942–1945," *Historical Journal* (43) Dec. 2000, pp. 1051–70.

and other cities located in the Rhineland and Westphalia.[94] While earlier bombing of the area led to German intelligence reports warning of "growing worry" and "fear" of Allied power, these initial raids paled in comparison to what became known as the "First Battle of the Ruhr."[95] During the five-month sustained campaign against the Ruhr, large cities such as Düsseldorf, Krefeld, Remscheid, and Wuppertal burned while others, such as Essen – after Berlin the most heavily bombed German city during the war – and Dortmund suffered extensive damage.[96] Goebbels, after touring Essen in June 1943, noted that the city

> suffered an exceptionally severe raid. The city of the Krupps has been hit hard. The number of dead, too, is considerable. If the English continue their raids on this scale, they will make things exceedingly difficult for us. The dangerous thing about this matter, looking at it psychologically, is the fact that the population can see no way of doing anything about it.[97]

Word of these attacks and their consequent destruction soon worked its way across the continent to the men from Military District VI serving at the front. Letters from home passed on wild rumors about the utter "ruined cities in the Ruhr basin," as well as death tolls that allegedly reached the tens of thousands for Dortmund and Düsseldorf and an astounding 27,000 killed in Wuppertal.[98]

Such rumors stretched credulity, but the reality of being bombed was no less horrific. One woman from Dortmund wrote,

> I want to leave here in any case, I do not want to take a risk with my children for any reason. It is absolutely dreadful here, every evening at 7:00, morning at 6:00 and a few times during the day. It was very damned dangerous again this week, the entire surroundings of Dortmund were bombed again, especially Essen and Bochum. I ask myself often, is this fate? Why are women and children killed in this way?[99]

And it was about Dortmund that Goebbels confided to his diary, "one can only repeat about air warfare: we are in an almost helpless inferiority and must grin and bear it as we take blows from the English and Americans."[100] It was this helplessness in the face of Allied airpower in

---

[94] Boog, "The Strategic Air War in Europe," p. 22.
[95] Quoted in Blank, "Kriegsalltag und Luftkrieg an der 'Heimatfront,'" p. 365.
[96] Jörg Friedrich, *The Fire: The Bombing of Germany, 1940–1945* (New York, 2006), p. 80; on Essen, see Boog, "The Strategic Air War in Europe," p. 25; on Dortmund, see Blank, "Kriegsalltag und Luftkrieg an der 'Heimatfront,'" p. 367.
[97] Joseph Goebbels, *The Goebbels Diaries 1942–1943* (ed., trans. and with an Introduction by Louis P. Lochner) (New York, 1948), 7 March 1943, p. 277.
[98] Quoted in Friedrich, *The Fire*, p. 423. On the rumors regarding casualty figures, see Earl Beck, *Under the Bombs: The German Home Front, 1942–1945* (Lexington, 1999), p. 59.
[99] Uta Brandt, Dortmund-Wambel, 16.1.43, BfZ, Sammlung Sterz.
[100] Goebbels, *The Goebbels Diaries 1942–1943*, 25 May 1943, p. 393.

A question of morale 349

the spring and summer of 1943 that weighed heavily upon the minds of the men of the 126th ID.[101] One soldier wrote that "one is always hearing frightful things out of the Ruhr area ... There are already numerous men in our company [whose homes] are completely destroyed."[102] This same soldier later noted that "almost all of my comrades from Cologne, and there are many of them, have had [their houses] damaged by the bombing."[103] A member of the Rhenish 254th ID stated that "it is terrible, that people at home have to endure more than soldiers at the front. Hopefully this war will end soon because if it continues on, they will make our entire homeland *kaputt*."[104] Another soldier from this same division wrote to his wife that "in general, we await the daily report that England has now attacked us again."[105] Clearly, the situation facing their families under Allied bombs weighed heavily on the minds of soldiers deployed a thousand miles away; one historian has even suggested that such worries led many men to wonder about the war and its aims.[106]

The consistent bombing of Germany resulted in the continual plummeting of the 126th ID's morale even during the relatively quiet months of late 1943. The division reported two deserters in November, the first recorded occurrence of this phenomenon for all three divisions under investigation.[107] While these particular cases were attributed to the soldiers originating from outside the *Altreich*, they nonetheless served as the most noteworthy manifestations of a larger problem.[108] In the monthly reports sent by the division to corps command during the second half of

---

[101] 126 Infanterie Division, Meldung vom 7. Mai 1943; 126 Infanterie Division, Meldung vom 7. Juni 1943, BA-MA RH 26–126/91.
[102] Corporal Fritz Lieb, 68 Infantry Regiment, 24.5.43, BfZ, Sammlung Sterz.
[103] Ibid., 8.7.43.
[104] Corporal Gerd Busch, Reconniassance Unit 254 ID, 18.6.43, BfZ, Sammlung Sterz.
[105] Oliver Seidel, 6.6.43, Museum für Kommunikation (hereafter MfK), Feldpostarchiv, 3.2002.0827.
[106] Michael Burleigh has stated that "of course the impact of bombing was not confined to the home front, but began to affect military morale. For if the troops on leave from the Eastern Front sowed despondency about the fighting qualities of the Red Army, so they themselves wondered what they were fighting for when they found their homes in ruins." See his *The Third Reich: A New History* (New York, 2000), p. 766.
[107] 126 Infanterie Division, Abt. Ia, Tagesmeldung an L AK, 12.11.43; 126 Infanterie Division, Abt. Ia, Tagesmeldung am L AK, 10.11.43, BA-MA RH 26–126/103. For discussions of this neglected aspect of the German Army's experience during the Second World War, see Wolfram Wette (ed.), *Deserteure der Wehrmacht: Feiglinge – Opfer – Hoffnungsträger? Dokumentation eines Meinungswandel* (Essen, 1995); and Magnus Koch, *Fahnenfluchten: Deserteure der Wehrmacht im Zweiten Weltkrieg. Lebenswege und Entscheidungen* (Paderborn, 2008).
[108] Kommandeurbesprechung auf dem Divisionsgefechtstand am 13.12.43, BA-MA RH 26–126/107.

1943, the division repeatedly noted that the bombings of western Germany depressed the men's morale.[109] Civilians in western Germany believed that "the English and Americans had decided to 'eradicate' one city after another" and such fears soon spread to the troops via correspondence from home.[110] Despite attempts by the state to stamp out the sending of such letters from home, sentiments such as the following continued to reach the front, exacerbating soldiers' feelings of helplessness and anger: "presently we are all such nervous wrecks that we run around the entire day like corpses, for 14 days we have slept in our clothes. Yes, who would have thought that we would have to live through such times."[111]

The division's welfare officer also commented on the troops' concern for their loved ones; worries about home resonated more strongly with the men than did continual reports about the army's constant retreats on the southern portion of the front.[112] Rumors concerning the "terrible destruction of the German cities and the tremendous casualties suffered by the civilian population" were so prevalent among the troops that they began to affect the attitudes of Soviet auxiliaries and the surrounding civilian population. This problem reached such proportions that the division's ranking intelligence officer instructed the Rhinelanders to keep their conversations about home out of earshot of Soviet *Hiwis* and citizens alike.[113] Elements of defeatism even appeared in the writings of some soldiers from Wehrkreis VI:

for the time being, things don't appear too rosy. Apparently the Duce ... has become sick and has resigned. Who knows what that is good for, perhaps it will help us end this war as soon as possible. But one can't realize that and therefore I don't want to try to do so. We have such good weather here today, the sun shines regularly from the sky, and if there wasn't the thunder of the guns, one could think one was sitting in peace.[114]

Another soldier in the same division, after hearing of the Allied landings in Sicily, wrote home, "well, you will see that the entire war won't last so much longer and then we can be together again, then we will come to life

---

[109] See the *Zustandsberichte* for the months of August, September, and October 1943, BA-MA RH 26–126/107.
[110] *Meldungen aus dem Reich*, vol. XV, Nr. 366, 11. März 1943.
[111] Uta Brandt, Dortmund-Wambel, 17.3.43, BfZ, Sammlung Sterz. On the June 1943 attempt by Martin Bormann to insulate the military front from the home front's worries, see Friedrich, *The Fire*, p. 421.
[112] 126 Infanterie Division, Abt. Ic, Arbeitsbericht des Divisions-Betreuungs-Offiziers, Berichtzeit: 15.9.–14.10.43, BA-MA RH 26–126/30.
[113] 126 Infanterie Division, Abt. Ic, Nr. 459/43 geh., 8.9.1943, BA-MA RH 26–126/129.
[114] Corporal Karl Weiss, GR 328, 17.4.43, BfZ, Sammlung Sterz.

A question of morale   351

again."[115] Such sentiments indicate a war-weariness that left some soldiers desiring an end to the war, with or without victory.

Following the conclusion of the First Battle of the Ruhr, the Allies then targeted Hamburg during the summer, with the campaign finally culminating in the five-month-long "Battle of Berlin." Between November 1943 and March 1944, Bomber Command launched nineteen heavy raids on the city, leaving more than 9,000 dead and missing and nearly 813,000 homeless.[116] Just as news of western Germany's destruction reached the front, so did that of Berlin, and it had a similar impact on the troops. For the men in 123rd ID, worries about home increasingly overshadowed their own problems. Civilians in Berlin wrote to the front, "you have no idea of the damage caused by the two attacks of the 22nd and 23rd [November]. And yesterday there was another."[117] Letters described sections of the city as "severely devastated."[118] After reading mail from his wife, who complained of "the frequent bombings," one soldier wrote that the Americans and British "certainly didn't fight fair" and that he was of the opinion that the Reich should strike a deal with the Soviets so that the two of them could fight together against the Anglo-Saxon powers; after all, "socialism [was] the only possible way for people to live together in the future."[119] It seems that the war against "Judeo-Bolshevism" had done little to change the attitude of this soldier from "Red Berlin." Other Berlin-area soldiers presented much more subdued musings: "today was more longing for the *Heimat*, for the love that burns the strongest within me, and the best would be running until I was with you."[120]

In recognition of the morale problems that spread throughout elements of Army Group North in 1943, officers began falling back on ideological indoctrination as a means of keeping the troops both motivated and militarily effective. Already in January 1943, the 126th ID's commander issued a proclamation on the tenth anniversary of Hitler's *Machtergreifung*.[121] After discussing the Führer's accomplishments in ending "hunger and unemployment," as well as recovering the German

---

[115] Private Heinrich Beck, GR 328, 10.7.43, BfZ, Sammlung Sterz.
[116] Boog, "The Strategic Air War in Europe," pp. 22 and 94.
[117] Helmut Schulz, Berlin-Wilmersdorf, 27.11.43, BfZ, Sammlung Sterz.
[118] Lt. Joachim Möller, Berlin-Tegel, 28.11.43, BfZ, Sammlung Sterz.
[119] Oliver Seidel, 13.6.43, 7.8.43, MfK, Feldpostarchiv, 3.2002.0827. Such a sentiment was not isolated among the German population; as Allied bombers rained down their payloads from the skies over Germany, significant sections of the German population saw them as the primary enemy who needed to be defeated. Such sentiments would certainly have reached the troops fighting in the Soviet Union. See Friedrich, *The Fire*, p. 427.
[120] Private Konrad Weber, IR 272, 23.12.43, BfZ, Sammlung Sterz.
[121] 126 Infanterie Division, Kommandeur, Soldaten und Kameraden der 126. Inf.-Division, 30. Januar, 1943, BA-MA RH 26–126/94.

lands lost to the "small robber-states" following the First World War, he then turned to the present conflict. Terming the war one of "existence or extinction" [*Sein oder Nichtsein*], he then examined the importance of this "final struggle" for Germany's future against "international Jewry [and] the war-machine of Bolshevism." He emphasized that the German Army possessed "better weapons, and was better supplied and clothed than the enemy"; all of these claims were debatable at best, outright falsities at worst. Since the Wehrmacht's growing material inferiority could not be addressed in any meaningful way, the army resorted to focusing on the will and psyche of the individual soldier in hopes of winning the war and remaining a great power.

The morale crisis that reverberated throughout the German Army in the post-Stalingrad phase led to the development of a much more concerted and focused propaganda program directed at the troops, one that even the more conservative members of the armed forces believed necessary to stave off final defeat. Even before this catastrophe, however, the conventional *Truppenbetreuung* that had marked the first three years of war began to radicalize. On 15 July 1942, Keitel issued a directive that demanded the introduction of a *wehrgeistige Führung* into the Wehrmacht.[122] The chief of the OKW called for a more focused political indoctrination, one that would lead to a "firm attitude in all political-*weltanschaulichen* questions."[123] That such a stance found resonance within the continuously hard-pressed field army is evidenced by Army Group Center initiating a similar program on its own accord nearly one month before Keitel's directive. Ninth Army described the program as one that would move beyond simple "propaganda imaginings" to one that provided "answers for the serious questions he [the German soldier] is confronting."[124] While earlier types of "care" focused on the material as well as spiritual health of a soldier, *wehrgeistige Führung* "aimed at the indoctrination and manipulation of the soldiers."[125]

The primary proponent of this more ideological spiritual care was Major Wilhelm Freiherr von Lersner, a member of Army Group Center's Ic section.[126] Lersner advocated a much closer relationship between

---

[122] *Wehrgeistige Führung* was a program designed by Germany's political and military leadership to provide soldiers with a firmer ideologically based understanding of the war. See Volker Berghahn, "NSDAP und 'Geistige Führung der Wehrmacht,'" in *Vierteljahresheft für Zeitgeschichte* 17 (1969), pp. 17–71, here p. 37. See also Förster, "Motivation and Indoctrination in the Wehrmacht," in Addison and Calder, *Time to Kill*, pp. 263–73, here p. 271.
[123] Quoted in Berghahn, "NSDAP und 'Geistige Führung der Wehrmacht,'" p. 38.
[124] Rass, *Menschenmaterial*, pp. 315–16.   [125] Ibid., 316.
[126] For more on Lersner, see Berghahn, "NSDAP und 'Geistige Führung der Wehrmacht,'" p. 35.

officers and the rank-and-file based on "bringing the war into an inseparable relationship with the [Nazi] *Weltanschauung*," placing the war into the context of "the history of the German *Volk*," and linking the conflict to "the German people, to the *Volksgemeinschaft* and to the *Heimat*."[127] Such a message appealed to Küchler, who invited Lersner to visit Army Group North in January 1943. Following a meeting between the two, Army Group North's commander in chief implemented this more ideological vision of spiritual care for his men.[128]

This new emphasis on *wehrgeistige Führung* led to an increased reliance on films, written materials, and instructional courses to strengthen the 126th ID's morale.[129] During the month of April, over 7,200 members of the division watched fifty-three films, while 692 books and 1,600 leaflets were disseminated throughout the division.[130] All of these materials were used to inspire the troops through a mixture of military and, increasingly, Nazi themes, and this program only became more important as the war stretched on.[131]

Perhaps the most noteworthy manifestation of this newfound emphasis on ideology and military performance was a lecture given by the 126th ID's commander to his officers. He began by commenting on the close relationship between the army and the NSDAP:

Come what may, they are connected. No criticism of each other. The Party fulfills important tasks (collections, NSV, care for vacationers, pre-military training in SA and HJ) in the *Heimat*. Numerous tasks that were incumbent on the representatives of the military districts during the First World War have been taken over by the Party, including numerous tasks that make the person in charge especially unloved. The soldier therefore is seen by the German people as merely a warrior who is paid respect.

He concluded by noting that "a firm belief in victory, which all officers need to exude, is the guarantee of final victory."[132] L Corps, the 126th ID's superior formation, attempted to persuade its men that victory would result in the realization of the long-hoped-for *Volksgemeinschaft*:

---

[127] Quoted in Rass, *Menschenmaterial*, p. 316.
[128] Berghahn, "NSDAP und 'Geistige Führung der Wehrmacht,'" p. 39.
[129] Tätigkeitsbericht zum Kriegstagebuch, Abteilung Ic, 31.1.43, 28.2.43, 31.3.43, BA-MA RH 26–126/126.
[130] Tätigkeitsbericht zum Kriegstagebuch, 30.4.43, BA-MA RH 26–126/127.
[131] For a discussion of this issue, see Bartov, *Hitler's Army*, pp. 117–27.
[132] Kommandeurbesprechung auf dem Divisionsgefechtstand am 18.7.43, BA-MA RH 26–126/107. The SA, or Sturm Abteilung ("Storm Section"), was the first Nazi mass organization, though it lost its position in the state following the Night of Long Knives in 1934. The HJ, or Hitler Jugend (Hitler Youth), served as the first organization for boys to be socialized in Nazi ideological concepts.

"We are fighting for a new, great German Reich in which every one of character and achievement will be given a place, regardless of class or background!"[133]

The division continually increased the *geistige Betreuung* of the troops during the year, as thousands of books and leaflets were distributed among the men while nearly 8,700 men attended films in the early fall.[134] In addition to these items, more mundane goods such as cigarettes, cigars, skat playing cards, short novels, and even piano accordions were parceled out to the troops. While ideological means were certainly utilized to rebuild the men's morale and sense of mission, their requests for more musical instruments, table tennis sets, and radios indicate that they were also interested in other forms of entertainment and distraction.

The general war situation served as both cause and accelerant of this indoctrination process. While the deteriorating position of the Reich and its armed forces led to an increased emphasis on propaganda to keep the men in the field, the predominance of positional warfare on the center and northern sectors of the front allowed for longer periods of more intensive propaganda. Rass notes that following its withdrawal behind the Buffalo Line in mid-1943, the 253rd ID underwent intensified training, of which "political indoctrination was normally, if not a central, certainly a regular piece of the lesson."[135] It stands to reason that the situation was similar for the 121st, 123rd, and 126th IDs. All three divisions witnessed a steep decline in the number of days in which they were engaged in combat and a dramatic rise in the amount of time dedicated to integrating new recruits into their ranks.

III. "War and fire": the development of German policy in northwest Russia, 1943

From one perspective, 1943 was indeed the "forgotten year" of the war for the infantry divisions of Army Group North. Unlike the previous two years, in which German formations engaged in long, if not continuous, periods of advance and combat, the third year inside the Soviet Union was relatively devoid of such events. With the significant exception of the clearing of the Demiansk pocket in February, the 121st, 123rd, and 126th IDs all experienced a war that generally lacked the most

---

[133] Der Kommandierende General des L. Armeekorps, 22.11.43, BA-MA RH 26–126/100.
[134] 126 Infanterie Division, Abt. Ic, Arbeitsbericht des Divisions-Betreuungs-Offiziers, Berichtzeit: 15.9.–14.10.43, BA-MA RH 26–126/30. The remainder of this discussion is based on this document unless otherwise noted.
[135] Rass, *Menschenmaterial*, p. 318.

fundamental aspect of armed conflict: battle. In comparison to the war-changing events further to the south, Army Group North's decidedly unromantic war of attrition paled in significance.

From another perspective, however, 1943 did serve as the "culmination year" of the eastern war. As German occupation policy developed during the first two years of war, it moved in divergent directions. The complete and callous disregard of non-Jewish and noncommunist civilians during the period of anticipated victory in 1941 transformed during the winter crisis into a targeting of all civilians as either potential enemies or objects to be exploited ruthlessly. Following the mastery of this period of real worry for the Germans, occupation policy during the remainder of 1942 evolved in a more conciliatory direction, one that attempted to harness the energies of the occupied Soviet population to the German war effort. As German infantry divisions surveyed the situation in mid- to late 1942, they realized that only through the mobilization of all available resources could the Wehrmacht defeat a qualitatively and quantitatively superior Red Army.

As the new year dawned, the question of German occupation policy remained: would it continue to move towards a more humane, though unquestionably utilitarian, program or would it treat civilians as objects to be exploited or neutralized? The rhetoric of the division commanders, as well as of other German authorities in the area, illustrated the realization among field commanders that at the very least the Germans required a quiescent population in order to achieve victory. Here, the notion of military necessity led sections of the German leadership to understand that victory in a conflict that had mushroomed into total war demanded a much more thorough mobilization of all available resources for victory. The lessons learned during the second part of 1942 seemed to be prodding German policy along a more pragmatic course.

The contradictions inherent within military necessity, however, proved impossible to reconcile during 1943. The desire of some commanders and soldiers to work with the local population was completely overridden by other segments of the German leadership and their demands to wage a ruthless and pitiless war that it believed necessary to achieve final victory. The army's traditional responses to problems, such as the burgeoning partisan movement or the growing need for labor both in the theater and in the Reich itself, led it to utilize coercion. Instead of trying to win over the hearts and minds of Soviet civilians – and this was a tactic attempted by various sections of the army and even Economic Staff East leadership across the front in late 1942 and early 1943 – the Wehrmacht increasingly tried to "solve" all problems through the application of force. Anti-partisan sweeps which devastated villages and towns, large-scale roundups of entire communities for forced labor, and the methodical and systematic use of scorched earth during German retreats all but ensured that the Soviet population would turn against the occupiers. This shift towards a more violent policy was not lost on the Soviet population; one partisan brigade noted that "in comparison to 1942, German attitudes towards the civilian population changed for the worse. The regime became harsher."[136]

This growing tendency to fall back on violence as a means to win the war was not only a result of the German Army's focus on military necessity, but also a result of the increasingly tight relationship between the military and the Nazi state and its ideological tenets. German soldiers, facing a seemingly intractable war at the front and agonizing over the utter ruin of their homes and, more importantly, their families, faced a real crisis of morale in 1943. In an effort to reverse this process, the Wehrmacht instituted a much more concerted ideological indoctrination to provide the troops with a greater legitimization for their efforts in the field. This overt propaganda of men socialized for years in the Nazi state combined with the army's strict interpretation of military necessity to unleash a destructive energy in 1943 and early 1944 that far surpassed that of 1942 or even 1941. While specific groups of the Soviet population – Jews, communist functionaries, urban inhabitants, and prisoners of war – had been targeted by the Germans in the earlier years of the war, the shift to an all-encompassing scorched-earth policy now brought an exponentially higher number of civilians into German sights as the entirety of the Soviet Union – its people, buildings, and even landscape – were now viewed as objects that could be not only acceptably but also necessarily either destroyed or otherwise denied to the enemy. Certainly ideology served as the fundamental basis to this utterly destructive policy, but the dictates of army doctrine itself provided the Wehrmacht with the necessary justification for the "war and fire" that devastated northwest Russia during the last years of war, literally turning it into a "desert zone."[137]

---

[136] Quoted in Hill, *The War behind the Eastern Front*, p. 151.
[137] The Economic Staff East's war diary entry for 31 October 1943 states that "Staff Panther takes over planning for the creation of the desert zone"; Wochenbericht zum KTB (10.–17.10.1943), BA-MA RW 31/594.

12 "As miserable representatives of the miserable twentieth century, we burned all of the villages"
The scorched-earth retreat to the Panther Line

The respite from major operations that occurred in late 1943 allowed Army Group North to prepare for an evacuation of Russia proper to the Panther Line, a fortified line that stretched along the old imperial Russian border with the Baltic states.[1] Beginning in October 1943, German authorities focused on two issues: the withdrawal of troops in a smooth manner and the necessity of carrying out a systematic scorched-earth retreat.[2] From the perspective of the army group, pulling back to a shortened, more defensible position was the only sensible option at this stage of the war. In terms of manpower and matériel, the Red Army completely surpassed Army Group North. By July 1943, Küchler commanded 710,000 troops, only half of which the Germans considered to be frontline soldiers. In support of the infantry, the Germans possessed roughly 2,400 guns and a mere forty tanks and other mechanized assault guns.[3] According to *Fremde Heere Ost*, the Soviet forces opposing Army Group North numbered 734,000 men, supported by nearly 2,800 guns and over 200 tanks; an additional 491,000 soldiers, 1,800 guns, and 209 tanks lay in reserve.[4] The shifting of German troops on the Eastern Front only exacerbated this problem as Army Group North functioned as a manpower reservoir for other German formations.

---

[1] Howard Grier, *Hitler, Dönitz, and the Baltic Sea: The Third Reich's Last Hope, 1944–1945* (Annapolis, MD, 2007), p. 3.
[2] On the general planning for the retreat, see Generalkommando XXVIII AK, Abt. Ia, Nr. 617/43 g. Kdos./Chefs., II. Ang., 11.10.43, BA-MA RH 24-28/72, in which the Panther Line is mentioned as a possible fall-back position. Stab Holstein noted on 1 October that preparations were being made to destroy everything between the present front line and the Panther Line; Wochenbericht zum KTB (1.–9.10.1943), BA-MA RW 31/594. For specifics on what the Germans hoped to extract from the area, see Earl Ziemke, *Stalingrad to Berlin: The German Defeat in the East* (Washington, DC, 1968), p. 249. The army group estimated that some 4,000 trainloads would be needed to extract the "million tons of grain and potatoes, half a million cattle and sheep," and other necessary military materials.
[3] Frieser, "Das Ausweichen der Heeresgruppe Nord," p. 279.
[4] Glantz, *The Battle for Leningrad*, p. 306.

Much like the 1941 campaign in which Leeb constantly complained of hemorrhaging units to Army Group Center, Küchler's command lost a total of eighteen divisions – some 40 percent of its total strength – to its southernmost neighbor during the second half of 1943.[5] This decrease in available manpower was aggravated by an increase in the section of the front that was his army group's responsibility. Following the withdrawal of Army Group Center to its section of the Panther Line in September 1943, Sixteenth Army was forced to lengthen its front to the south, giving Army Group North a front that extended for more than 1,000 kilometers. A Soviet attack on the now tenuous junction between the two army groups in October proved especially threatening to Sixteenth Army, and while Soviet attention remained focused on Army Group Center, Küchler certainly understood the mortal danger facing his command. Possessing not one single panzer or panzergrenadier division, his forces lacked the mobility required to ward off a Soviet offensive. A retreat to the Panther Line would be the simplest operational solution to these problems as it would not only shrink his front some 600 kilometers to a much more manageable length of 400 kilometers – freeing up eight divisions for use as an urgently needed reserve – but 180 kilometers would be covered by Lake Chud (Peipus). Finally, his largely immobile forces could be plugged into a prepared position and meet the Soviets on something approaching even ground.

Küchler wanted to begin the withdrawal in early January but Hitler refused on several grounds. First, he argued that any withdrawal would cause Finland to leave the war, and, as Germany's strategic position continued to deteriorate, the Reich needed to hold on to whatever allies it could.[6] Second, the Führer believed that because Eighteenth Army had engaged in relatively limited combat during the past year, it was "the elite army – the show-off army for the whole Eastern Army" – and that, as such, withdrawal was unwarranted.[7] Since Berlin demanded that other, much harder-pressed German units remain in the field, Hitler simply could not justify any sort of retreat for Küchler's men. Third, Hitler assumed that the Red Army had exhausted itself during its offensive in Ukraine and therefore lacked the necessary forces for

---

[5] Frieser, "Das Ausweichen der Heeresgruppe Nord," pp. 283–5. The remainder of this section is based on Frieser's discussion unless otherwise noted.
[6] Seaton, *The Russo-German War*, p. 409; Schramm, *KTB OKW*, vol. VI, 28. September 1943, p. 1148.
[7] See "Meeting of the Führer with Field Marshal von Küchler, December 30, 1943 at the Wolfsschanze," in Helmut Heiber and David Glantz (eds.), *Hitler and His Generals: Military Conferences, 1942–1945* (New York, 2003), pp. 375–84. The quoted passage is from p. 384. See also Fritz, *Ostkrieg*, p. 432.

another attack.[8] Finally, the German Navy vehemently protested against any withdrawal from the Leningrad region as this would allow the Soviets access to the Baltic Sea and, to all intents and purposes, end the German U-boat training program.[9] As a result of this meeting, what was left of Army Group North remained in its exposed positions. One unit, however, that would not be completing its war in northwest Russia was the 123rd ID, as it joined the First Panzer Army operating under Army Group South in September 1943.[10]

I. The 123rd Infantry Division and mobile warfare

Following its transfer, the 123rd ID was placed into the Zaporozhye bridgehead where it faced immediate action.[11] Regarded by both Hitler and the S*tavka* as the key position on the eastern bank of the Dnieper, the area soon became a focal point for military operations.[12] The division repulsed over 130 battalion-strength patrols during the next three weeks before it found itself defending against a major Soviet attack, beginning on 11 October.[13] Deep Soviet penetrations into the Zaporozhye position finally forced the Germans to begin disengaging from the bridgehead on 13 October.[14] For the remainder of the month, ferocious combat cost the Berliners nearly 2,300 casualties.[15] By the end of October, the 123rd ID reported that the "continuous and eventful combat" of the past few days had had a "heavily negative effect" on the unit's morale and combat strength. It concluded by stating that a further assault would in all likelihood break the division.[16] Fortunately for the 123rd ID, the Soviet offensive temporarily halted and the front stabilized for the remainder of the year.[17]

---

[8] Ziemke, *Stalingrad to Berlin*, pp. 250–1; Heiber and Glantz, *Hitler and His Generals*, p. 383.
[9] Grier, *Hitler, Dönitz, and the Baltic Sea*, pp. 10–13.
[10] Tessin, *Verbände und Truppen der Deutschen Wehrmacht*, p. 298.
[11] Aktennotiz über die 123. Infanteriedivision, 15. November 1943, BA-MA RH 24–17/114. The bridgehead had been under attack since the opening of a major offensive on 26 September; Schramm, *KTB OKW*, vol. VI, 26. September 1943, p. 1143.
[12] Ziemke, *Stalingrad to Berlin*, p. 175.
[13] Ibid.; XVII AK KTB, 11.10.43, BA-MA RH 24–17/111. Schramm, *KTB OKW*, vol. VI, 11. Oktober 1943, p. 1192.
[14] Ziemke, *Stalingrad to Berlin*, p. 177. The withdrawal from the city was completed two days later; Schramm, *KTB OKW*, vol. VI, 15. Oktober 1943, p. 1200.
[15] Verluste für die Zeit vom 1.–29.10.1943, BA-MA RH 24–17/113.
[16] 123 Infanterie Division, Nachtrag zur Tagesmeldung, 30.10, BA-MA RH 24–17/113.
[17] Ziemke, *Stalingrad to Berlin*, p. 189. For Manstein's view of the battle, see his *Lost Victories*, pp. 477–86.

In the midst of this heavy fighting, preparations for further evacuations in the rear took place. While no available documentation links the 123rd to forced evacuations in Ukraine, it seems entirely probable that during the lull in the fighting in the late fall and winter of 1943, the division once again became involved in driving Soviet civilians to the west. A Berliner in the 93rd ID stationed in Ukraine vividly described the deportation process for one community in a series of letters sent to his family. During the initial evacuation's preparations, he wrote,

> I feel sorry only for the civilian population, who will then be evacuated from here. They are already whimpering and packing their things. In general it is a complete mess [*Schweineschlachten*]. It is probable that perishable food and chickens will soon be very cheap.[18]

The next day, "everyone was nervous due to the massive movement that was presently taking place." He continued,

> It [the evacuation process] is generally working out perfectly. Everything that has any value will be taken with us. Machines will be dismantled, entire train stations with all of their fittings and barns will be brought back and what one cannot bring with one will be destroyed. The Russian will conquer only a pile of rubble. Everything will burn. They will find no shelter for the winter, no traffic installations functioning, and none which will be up and running in a short period of time, and no food will stay behind. Even the fields have been thoroughly destroyed.

Though he believed "such tactics are needed to keep the Russians out of the homeland," Junger felt sympathy for the uprooted civilians:[19]

> It is absolutely dreadful to watch. The cattle that won't be transported are slaughtered. The household goods are bundled together and other things are packed. But since there is such a shortage of horses and carts, they can only bring along a little. In many cases, what they can carry and their cow. The moaning is naturally very pronounced. The people know well that everything they leave behind is lost. It is well known that everything is burned during the retreat. Even from far away, one sees the enormous glow of the fire from the burning cities and villages. It is unbelievable what is destroyed here. Yes, one sees only distress and misery.[20]

Though individual soldiers regarded scorched earth as causing dramatic upheavals in the lives of ordinary Ukrainians, this had no effect on the implementation of the policy: the "distress and misery" this soldier described remained part of everyday life for Soviet civilians in 1943 and 1944 as the Wehrmacht retreated west.

---

[18] Heinz Junger, 1.9.43, MfK, Feldpostarchiv, 3.2002.0827.
[19] Ibid., 2.9.43.   [20] Ibid., 6.9.43.

Documents concerning the fate of the 123rd ID become extremely difficult to locate for the period following the fighting around the Zaporozhye bridgehead. What can be pieced together, however, is that as part of the XXX Corps, the 123rd ID came under attack by a large-scale Soviet offensive that opened on 30 January 1944.[21] Virtually destroyed in this offensive, the division was officially dissolved on 1 March 1944, with the surviving members of the unit integrated into another formation.[22]

II. The 121st and 126th Infantry Divisions and the Soviet winter offensive, January 1944

On the eve of the Soviet offensive targeting Army Group North in mid-January 1944, the Red Army enjoyed an overwhelming superiority in manpower and machines. Against its 1.25 million men, 20,183 guns, 1,580 tanks, and 1,386 planes, the Germans could only muster 397,763 soldiers, sixteen tanks, 109 self-propelled assault guns, and seventy-one aircraft.[23] In lieu of numbers, the Germans hoped that their units – and by extension their individual soldiers – would prove superior to their Soviet counterparts. During the generally quiet last months of 1943, several units in Army Group North, including the 121st and 126th IDs, were seemingly rejuvenated. XXVIII Corps rated both divisions as extremely capable units. Corps command termed the Rhinelanders "tough and tenacious" with "high combat morale and experienced and agile" leadership, while it viewed the East Prussians as constituting one of the two best divisions within the corps.[24] Notably, it was neither the physical prowess nor material strength of the divisions that received praise; rather, more intangible factors such as will, toughness, and leadership were singled out. While such factors certainly proved important on the battlefield, the crushing material superiority enjoyed by the Red Army led even highly rated Wehrmacht divisions to struggle to maintain combat effectiveness at this stage of the war.

---

[21] Ic Tätigkeitsbericht, XXX AK, 30.1.44, BA-MA RH 24–30/143. For a recapitulation of this operation, see Glantz and House, *When Titans Clashed*, p. 187; Erickson, *The Road to Berlin*, pp. 176–82.
[22] Tessin, *Verbände und Truppen der Deutschen Wehrmacht*, p. 298.
[23] Frieser, "Das Ausweichen der Heeresgruppe Nord," pp. 286–7.
[24] On the 126th ID, see Generalkommando L AK, Abt. Ia, Nr. 34/43 g. Kdos. Chefs, Betr.: Beurteilung des inneren Kampfwertes der Divn., 24.12.43; on the 121st ID, see Generalkommando XXVIII AK, Abt. Ia, Nr. 989/43 g. Kdos. Chefs, 24.12.1943, BA-MA RH 20–18/675.

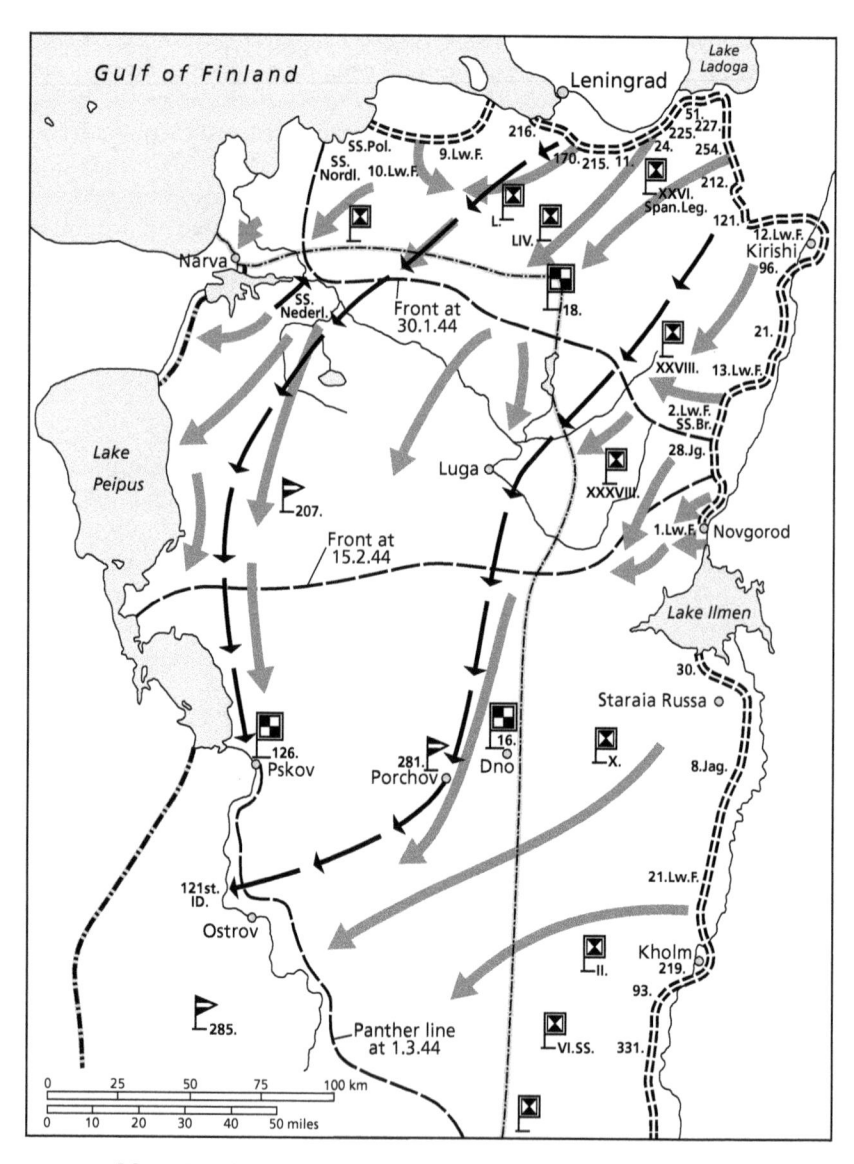

Map 12.1 Army Group North's retreat to the Panther Line, 1944

On the night of 13–14 January, the long-imminent Soviet offensive began (see Map 12.1).[25] The 126th ID, still deployed between the Oranienbaum and Leningrad positions, came under assault on 15 January.[26] While the Rhinelanders stubbornly defended their position, corps command shifted some of their potential combat strength to secure its connection to the neighboring 170th ID – here, the weakness of one formation wormed its way through the entire order of battle as the German Army cannibalized itself to plug threatening gaps.[27] Unlike previous German defensive operations in the Leningrad theater, in which just enough reserves existed to stave off the Red Army's assault, by the beginning of 1944 Army Group North disposed of a mere four weakened infantry divisions and three security divisions behind the lines, the majority of which were engaged in anti-partisan operations.[28] The Soviets had amassed enough troops and weapons to overcome the use of these paltry reserves and Eighteenth Army was gradually forced to yield ground despite Hitler constantly prohibiting such retreats.[29] Simultaneously with the Red Army offensive, partisan activity erupted in the rear area, forcing the Germans to fight an increasingly threatening two-front war. In a matter of five months, the partisan movement in just the Leningrad *oblast* increased from a mere 4,203 individuals to nearly 24,000 by the opening of 1944 and, in combination with other partisan detachments in Army Group North's area of responsibility, totaled some 40,000 partisans who operated with growing impunity in the rear area.[30] These insurgents, now organized into centralized brigades, wreaked havoc behind the German lines, burning some 58,000 barns, sabotaging 300 bridges, and destroying 133 transport trains.[31]

A strong push by Soviet armored units around the right wing of the 126th ID threatened the unit with encirclement four days after the offensive opened, and the Rhinelanders, along with 9th Luftwaffe Field Division, hastily retreated to avoid certain destruction.[32] Soviet pressure on his troops soon led the corps commander to lament "the considerably dissipated ... combat power" of both the 9th Luftwaffe FD and the 126th ID, with the former "having lost all combat worth," integrated into the

---

[25] Glantz, *The Battle for Leningrad*, p. 338.
[26] KTB AK L, 15.1.44, BA-MA RH 24-50/75.
[27] Ibid., 15.1.44, 16.1.44.
[28] Frieser, "Das Ausweichen der Heeresgruppe Nord," p. 283.
[29] A concise account of the bickering between the army group and Führer Headquarters is provided by Ziemke, *Stalingrad to Berlin*, pp. 250–7.
[30] On the Leningrad *oblast*, see Hill, *The War behind the Eastern Front*, pp. 156–7.
[31] Frieser, "Das Ausweichen der Heeresgruppe Nord," p. 289.
[32] Abschrift der Tagesmeldung an die Armee vom 17.1.44, BA-MA RH 24-50/82; KTB AK L, 18.1.44, BA-MA RH 24-50/75.

latter in an attempt to salvage the situation.[33] The same fate befell the 126th ID on 28 January when the 12th Panzer Division assumed control over both it and the 11th ID.[34] Both these command arrangements and L Corps's observation that "during the period of heavy fighting, the morale of the troops markedly deteriorated, with the number of scattered troops considerably increasing," indicate that Eighteenth Army faced a serious crisis in January 1944.[35]

During the "very confused" January battle in which no "clear front lines" existed, Eighteenth Army suffered crippling casualties: of the nearly 58,000 combat troops available on 10 January, some 49,000 were wounded and killed during the next three weeks, leaving the army with a total of 17,000 combat soldiers.[36] The fact that L Corps considered the 126th ID to be "easily the most combat-fit" of its subordinate formations, even though the division reported that its battle strength of 2,874 men on 15 January had declined to a mere 673 just one week later, demonstrated the weakness of German forces in the region.[37]

Entirely cognizant of the catastrophe facing his army group, Küchler continually pressed Hitler for permission to retreat during late January but the Führer stubbornly denied this request. When informed by Zeitler that Küchler wanted to retreat towards the Panther Line, Hitler derisively responded that

> the whole thing here is pure wordplay – the pulling back here. (The thing in front here can't be held), but he wants to hold this thing at all cost. It's all wordplay. It was shown again: if we go out of an installation ... that's the experience of three years – a shorter line without solid fortifications and ripped-out troops ... can't be held. Experience has shown that again and again.[38]

Finally, on 29 January, Küchler ordered a general retreat towards the Panther position, justifying the decision by stating that "Eighteenth Army has been split into three pieces. It is no longer in the position to

---

[33] KTB AK L, 21.1.44, 23.1.44, BA-MA RH 24–50/75.
[34] Fernspruch [number illegible] Ia, Morgenmeldung an AOK 18, 29.1.44, BA-MA RH 24–50/82.
[35] KTB AK L, 1.2.44, BA-MA RH 24–50/75.
[36] For the characterization of the battle, see Mawdsley, *Thunder in the East*, p. 289. On casualty figures, see Ziemke, *Stalingrad to Berlin*, p. 258. This number includes reinforcements the army received during the month.
[37] 126 Infanterie Division, Abt. Ia, Nr. 530/44 geheim, Gefechtsbericht: Abwehrschlacht Nördlich Pleskau (1.–10.3.44), 13.4.44, BA-MA RH 24–28/88. Even after receiving some reinforcements, the division still contained only 1,800 effectives, of which some 810 suffered from frostbite or were unable to walk two weeks after the assault opened; see Fernspruch Nr. 2720, Nachtrag zur Tagesmeldung, 30.1.44, BA-MA RH 24–50/82.
[38] Heiber and Glantz, *Hitler and His Generals*, Military Situation Report, 28 January 1944, p. 406.

Illustration 12.1 Exhausted German troops retreat to the Panther Line.

construct a continuous front along the present line. This would only be possible for the mass of the army in a general move to the Luga position."[39] From a purely military perspective, such a withdrawal was the only logical choice; Hitler recognized this and made no attempt to countermand the order, but nonetheless replaced Küchler as commander in chief of Eighteenth Army with Field Marshal Walter Model.[40]

On 2 February, L Corps began its headlong retreat to the intermediate position of the Luga Line.[41] Unfortunately for the Germans, Soviet forces moved more quickly and pierced elements of this defensive line before the Wehrmacht could arrive in force.[42] Following its withdrawal from the Luga Line, the 126th ID was diverted to the eastern shore of Lake Chud (Lake Peipus).[43] Here, in concert with 12th Panzer Division (and its thirty-six operational tanks) and the 12th Luftwaffe Field Division, the 126th ID prepared to launch a counterattack against the advancing Soviet forces. Soviet operations, however, pre-empted any concerted assault and the attack degenerated into numerous savage piecemeal engagements.[44] Despite Model's determination to rid the army group of "Panther psychosis," he realized that only a retreat to the Panther position could avoid complete catastrophe and he finally convinced Hitler on 17 February to order the general withdrawal.[45] For the 126th ID, this order merely officially approved a retrograde movement that had been under way since the first week of February.[46] One soldier who participated in the retreat provided a vivid description of the process, capturing the "misery, distress, and death" of the withdrawal:

it looks exactly like the retreat of 1918 ... The roads used for the retreat are constantly overflowing with cars, horse carts, civilians, herds of cattle. Everything, but everything, is going back, and far behind us one sees the empty villages burning at night. A dreadful picture ... The troops who have come directly from the front are so sad, that you have to see them. They are mostly scattered soldiers who have lost almost everything. One has only his helmet, the other has not even that, no rifle or even things like his field pack, underclothes, shaving kit ... The withdrawal from here began yesterday. The city will soon be only a heap of rubble, because as soon as the last German soldiers leave the city,

---

[39] Quoted in Frieser, "Das Ausweichen der Heeresgruppe Nord," p. 291.
[40] Ziemke, *Stalingrad to Berlin*, p. 257.
[41] KTB AK L, 2.2.44, BA-MA RH 24–50/75.
[42] Frieser, "Das Ausweichen der Heeresgruppe Nord," p. 292.
[43] KTB AK XXVIII, 10.2.44, BA-MA RH 24–28/85.
[44] Glantz, *The Battle for Leningrad*, pp. 378–80.
[45] Frieser, "Das Ausweichen der Heeresgruppe Nord," p. 293.
[46] KTB AK XXVIII, 7.2.44, BA-MA RH 24–28/84.

everything will be blown up. Civilians and all of their goods are going back with us. Yes, my love, when one sees such things, prisoners, a retreating army, fire, and destruction, then one says to oneself, how much longer will our God watch this? Misery, distress, and death are the winnings ...[47]

Recalling scenes of the 1941–2 winter crisis, but now including the wholesale movement of civilians as well, Eighteenth Army began a harried retreat back to the old imperial Russian border.

In addition to the Soviet offensives designed to clear the area south of Leningrad of German troops, the Red Army also attacked the eastern section of Eighteenth Army's line in the direction of Novgorod on 14–15 January.[48] The attack hit the 121st ID and the Waffen-SS-Polizei Division and while their front held, other sections of the line caved, forcing the division to march two days later in an attempt to halt the offensive north of Novgorod.[49] Despite a spirited defense that destroyed several Red Army breakthroughs, it became increasingly clear to XXVIII Corps command that the position was untenable.[50] While the corps bickered with Eighteenth Army about the necessity for a withdrawal, it also began to evacuate all remaining civilians within the area.[51] Heavy fighting in the Liuban region finally convinced Eighteenth Army that retreat was necessary and the 121st ID was chosen to serve as the rear guard for the withdrawal to the intermediate Luga position.[52] The East Prussians suffered similarly to the remainder of Army Group North during the months of January and February as they reported over 2,200 losses during the heavy fighting and consequent retreat.[53]

Following Hitler's decision to authorize the move to the Panther Line, German units began a fighting retreat as they raced back towards the position, hoping to reach it before the more mobile Red Army. The Rhinelanders engaged in desperate fighting north of Pskov (Pleskau) in early March, before entering the city itself and taking their position in the

---

[47] Private Thomas Becker, Pi.Btl. 505, 29.1.44, BfZ, Sammlung Sterz.
[48] Glantz, *The Battle for Leningrad*, p. 345.
[49] KTB XXVIII AK, 14.1.44, BA-MA RH 24–28/84; Heesch, *Meine 13. Infanterie-Geschütz-Kompanie Grenadier-Regiment 408*, p. 219.
[50] KTB XXVIII AK, 19.1.44, BA-MA RH 24–26/84.
[51] The corps complained that Eighteenth Army was operating under "false assumptions" concerning the balance of forces in the area; KTB XXVIII AK, 24.1.44, BA-MA RH 24–26/84; Ziemke, *Stalingrad to Berlin*, p. 256. On the evacuations, see KTB XXVIII AK Qu., 20.1, 23.1.44, BA-MA RH 24–28/283.
[52] KTB XXVIII, 27.1, 30.1.44, BA-MA RH 24–28/84.
[53] 126 Infanterie Division, Abt. Ia, Nr. 530/44 geheim, Gefechtsbericht: Abwehrschlacht Nördlich Pleskau (1.–10.3.44), 13.4.44, BA-MA RH 24–28/88; for the 121st ID, see Tätigkeitsbericht Januar/Februar 1944, RH 24–28/162.

Panther Line.[54] One soldier described this action as "tremendously difficult work, day and night without interruption."[55] The fighting of the previous three months had nearly wrecked the 126th ID. At the end of March, Eighteenth Army rated the 126th ID its weakest of all regular German infantry divisions, noting that this "former good division is completely burned out ... with considerably weakened combat power and is at this time temporarily unable to endure any large test."[56]

On 1 March, the 126th ID assumed administrative control as well as responsibility for security in the battle-ravaged city of Pskov.[57] While the division continued to resist Soviet attempts to break through the Panther Line, it also implemented a wholesale evacuation of the population in the Pskov area. The first two groups of civilians to be sent to collection camps in the rear were people whose homes were needed by the troops for shelter and all Soviet citizens who were working for the divisions.[58] This was followed by an Eighteenth Army order that called for the evacuation of all civilians in any old imperial Russian territory controlled by the Germans, with a focus on rounding up potential laborers.[59] These individuals were to be sent to the rear in columns numbering up to 3,000 people and the troops were instructed to "avoid severity" during the march.[60] By 5 March, the corps as a whole had deported 13,351 individuals, with the 126th ID contributing 2,517 souls (of whom 2,038 were women and children).[61] These were the final gasps of a labor

---

[54] KTB AK XXVIII, 3.3.44, BA-MA RH 24–28/85; 126 Infanterie Division, Abt. Ia, Nr. 530/44 geheim, Gefechtsbericht: Abwehrschlacht Nördlich Pleskau (1.–10.3.44), 13.4.44, BA-MA RH 24–28/88; Lohse, *Geschichte der rheinisch-westfälischen 126. Inf. Div. 1940–1945*, p. 182.

[55] Sergeant Christian Ziemann, 1. San. Kp. 126, 23.3.44, BfZ, Sammlung Sterz.

[56] Armee-Oberkommando 18, Abt. Ia, Nr. 028/44 g. K. Chefs, Betr.: Beurteilung des inneren Kampfwertes der Divisionen, 30.3.44, BA-MA RH 20–18/1575. The 126th ID was rated as more effective than only the notoriously ineffectual Luftwaffe field divisions and recently raised Estonian units.

[57] Generalkommando XXVIII AK, Abt. Ia, Nr. 387/44 g. Kdos., Korpsbefehl Nr. 73, 1.3.44, BA-MA RH 24–28/88. One soldier wrote that "the city in front of us has died out and one sees the Pleskau cathedral standing out among the glowing fires of the burning houses"; Sergeant Christian Ziemann, 1. San. Kp. 126, 23.3.44, BfZ, Sammlung Sterz.

[58] Fernschreiben Nr. 23, 29.2.44; Gen. Kdo. XXVIII AK, Betr.: Erfassung russischer Arbeitskräfte der Gruppe B, die von der Truppe nach Estland zurückgeführt wurden, 29.2.44, BA-MA RH 24–28/287.

[59] KTB Qu., 5.3.44, BA-MA RH 24–28/283; Fernschreiben Nr. 54, 5.3.44, BA-MA RH 24–28/287.

[60] Generalkommando XXVIII AK, Abt. Qu., Nr. 115/44 g. Kdos., Betr.: Evakuierung, 2.3.44, BA-MA RH 24–28/287.

[61] Evakuierung Zusammenstellung Stand: 5.3.44; Fernmündliche Vorausmeldung, 126 Infanterie Division/IB, Betr.: Evakuierung der Zivilbevölkerung, 11/12.3.44, BA-MA RH 24–28/287.

procurement policy that shipped 404,230 civilians from the greater Leningrad region to work for the Germans.[62]

Despite earlier preparations, numerous problems marred the evacuations, from a lack of transport to shortages of shelter for the civilians.[63] In an attempt to streamline the process, XXVIII Corps gave the 126th ID control over events in the entire Pskov area, and by the end of March over 16,500 civilians had been shipped to the rear.[64] The deportations continued throughout the months of April and May as increasing food shortages sparked fears of starvation throughout the area.[65] In addition to creating labor reserves for the Reich, the primary motivation for the evacuations was to deny the advancing Red Army anything that could be used to support its war effort.[66] By this point, German policy towards civilians had completely repudiated earlier conciliatory trends; now the Wehrmacht saw all civilians as potential threats that needed to be neutralized. The ideological indoctrination that the Wehrmacht increasingly resorted to from 1943 on now seamlessly worked with a radicalized interpretation of military necessity that viewed the Soviet state, its people, and its very physical existence as mortal enemies.

While the Rhinelanders fought delaying actions as they trudged back to Pskov, the 121st ID moved in the direction of Porchov along an axis that would eventually bring them into the Panther Line south of Pskov.[67] During the retreat, the East Prussians not only battled pursuing Red Army units, but also had to negotiate roadblocks constructed by partisans as well as engage in firefights with guerilla bands.[68] By March, the division had recovered to such an extent that it was characterized as having "outstanding combat-morale! Insuperable toughness!" and this reputation led XXXVIII Corps to count upon the "East Prussian, very good regiments" of the division.[69] One NCO described the division's view of the fighting:

---

[62] Hass, "Deutsche Besatzungspolitik im Leningrader Gebiet," p. 76.
[63] KTB Qu., 6.3.44, BA-MA RH 24–28/283.
[64] Fernschreiben Nr. 211, 22.3.44, BA-MA RH 24–28/88.
[65] Generalkommando XXVIII AK, Betr.: Evakuierung im altrussischen Gebiet, 11.4.44, BA-MA RH 24–28/289; KTB Qu., 1.5.44, BA-MA RH 24–28/284; Gen. Kdo. XXVIII AK Qu., Nr. 713/44 geh., Betr.: Ernährung der im Korpsbereich befindlichen arbeitsschwachen Landeseinwohner (Evakuierte) 7.5.1944, BA-MA RH 24–28/289.
[66] One order explicitly stated that "no men capable of military service or labor should be allowed to fall into the hands of the enemy"; Fernschreiben Nr. 317, Betr.: Evakuierung, 1.4.44, BA-MA RH 24–28/289.
[67] Heesch, *Meine 13. Infanterie-Geschütz-Kompanie Grenadier-Regiment 408*, p. 230.
[68] Ibid., p. 233; Mawdsley, *Thunder in the East*, p. 289.
[69] Generalkommando XXXVIII AK, Abt. Ia Nr. 017/44 g. Kdos. Chefs, BA-MA RH 20–18/1575; KTB XXXVIII AK, 5.3.44, BA-MA RH 24–38/112.

since 16.1, we have been in a heavy defensive battle east of Liuban in which every officer, NCO, and man must give his utmost. None of us know if we will once more come out of this hell. But it is precisely in this time that the camaraderie of German soldiers has proven itself.[70]

As this letter showed, morale in the division remained high, due in no small part to the feelings of a *Frontgemeinschaft* within the unit. The many soldiers who had been wounded in the fighting, however, viewed the situation in a much different fashion. According to reports from military hospitals in East Prussia, many of the casualties were "depressed" and their "joy" at being once again in their *Heimat* was overshadowed by the predicament facing both themselves and the Reich.[71]

Soviet attacks picked up in intensity during the month of March and despite holding its ground against the heavy armor assaults of three armored regiments and five additional divisions, the division frantically informed corps command that such superiority could not be blunted forever.[72] The line did hold, however, and the East Prussians soon found themselves employed in a myriad other operations that inevitably took a heavy toll on the division and Eighteenth Army pulled it out of the line before it "burned out."[73] Due to other crises on the front, however, this order was soon rescinded and the division remained in position along the Panther Line until the general retreat of July.

The 121st ID also participated in the forced evacuations that characterized the German retreat in northwest Russia. XXXVIII Corps ordered the rounding up of all men between the ages of sixteen and twenty-two deemed capable of work for shipment either back to the Reich or for the army's own use at the front.[74] The East Prussians received instructions to collect all inhabitants from its area of responsibility and to divide them into workers and nonworkers, with the former sent to labor organizations in the front area, and the latter simply shipped to the Baltic states.[75] These practices culminated in the evacuation of all civilians east of the Ostrov rail line immediately before the Panther Line itself was abandoned.[76]

As the soldiers retreated towards the Panther Line in February 1944, they passed through a landscape already ravaged by scorched-earth

---

[70] Sergeant Stefan Mann, Gren. Rgt. 408, 5.4.1944, BfZ, Sammlung Sterz.
[71] See the reports from 13.2.44 Lazarettzug 606; 24.2.44 Lazarettzug 655; and 20.3.44 Lazarettzug 502, GStA, XX. HA, Rep. 240, Nr. 31a–31g.
[72] KTB XXXVIII AK, 11.3.44, 12.3.44, BA-MA RH 24–38/112.
[73] Ibid., 26.6.44.
[74] KTB Qu., XXXVIII AK, 15.3.44, BA-MA RH 24–38/381.
[75] Generalkommando XXXVIII AK, Abteilung Qu., Evakuierung im Bereich des Gen. Kdo. XXXVIII AK, 13.3.1944, BA-MA RH 24–38/281.
[76] XXXVIII AK KTB Qu., 7.7.44, BA-MA RH 24–38/381.

tactics. The economic inspector for northwest Russia described a policy in which "the burning down of villages and dwellings" would "leave no shelter" for the oncoming Red Army, "forcing them to bivouac in the snow and ice."[77] This planned devastation of Soviet territory was complemented by increasingly violent anti-partisan measures. One East Prussian soldier of the 21st ID noted that

> the villages were deserted. In quite a few villages, one saw only the chimneys rising up out of the snow. Here the Commandant of Pleskau [Pskov] burned down the villages as revenge for partisan operations and the population of the villages still standing fled into the forest out of fear of further reprisals. This was all new to us. If there had been many *Franktireurs* here before, these measures will make the entire population into guerillas.[78]

Heesch of the 121st ID also described passing through "wide, empty plains [in which] all villages ... were burned down during combat with partisans or during retaliatory actions against partisan villages."[79] These very same soldiers, however, also participated in the destruction of Soviet territory as they moved west.

Heesch proudly recorded leaving "a smoking pile of rubble ... behind" so "the enemy would find no protection against the biting winter cold here."[80] The East Prussian of the 21st ID left behind a much more interesting rumination over German policy that deserves to be quoted in full:

> A word on setting houses on fire. There is nothing better for children and soldiers than to start a fire. Without doubt, it is also a wonderful experience to witness a fire, either of a house or even better an entire street-front, a village, or even a city. Many people, I believe almost everyone, feel a perverse pleasure in the act of destruction, especially when they themselves are the creator of the destruction. In present times, the era of movies and the "conforming person" [*nachgemachten Menschen*], in which one holds a picture of Napoleon in front of one's face and thinks one is looking in the mirror, in today's time, one loves cheap sensations. One doesn't burn down Rome and sing about it. No. Quite innocently, one burns down an unoccupied village, is pleased with the heat that singes the skin, rejoices in the thatched roofs flying through the sky, that then come down as a shower of sparks; one is happy with colorful images of the flames in the darkness and with the lighting effects on the sheets of snow. I have never burned down a house in which people were living. Not from a sense of decency or kindheartedness, but rather out of weakness. Thoughts of the poor people would leave me weak. I also do not want to hear the screams of the people ... But here was a cheap

---

[77] Rückblick des Wirtschaftsinspekteurs auf das 1. Vierteljahr 1944, BA-MA RW 31/596.
[78] Erinnerungen von Dieter Stein, GR 45, Dec 1943–Apr 1944, BA-MA RH MSg 2/2777.
[79] Heesch, *Meine 13. Infanterie-Geschütz-Kompanie Grenadier-Regiment 408*, p. 234.
[80] Ibid.

Illustration 12.2 The German scorched-earth retreat to the Panther Line left numerous villages burning in its wake.

pleasure – as already stated – for me and similar chaps and we had the order in our heads that read that the enemy should find nothing in his country. This order was admittedly surpassed by others as it was forbidden to burn down villages in order to cover our retreat. But the term "scorched earth" eased our consciences that repeatedly revolted against this brutality. And so, as miserable representatives of the miserable twentieth century, we burned all of the villages.

I would like to bring attention to the following, though: No person has the right to reproach us. Humans are all in the same moral situation. They are just as miserable or even more so than us. During their retreat, the Russians themselves burned many, many [villages]. But we don't need to justify such things. They have happened.[81]

Destruction for destruction's sake is celebrated in this passage; its nihilism certainly parallels many similar notions embedded within National Socialist ideology. The soldier also acknowledged the rush of adrenaline he felt by exercising his power to destroy. He stopped short, however, of admitting that he directly killed innocent civilians. The grenadier also described himself as "a miserable representative of the miserable twentieth century," which, while surely acting as a type of salve on his wounded conscience, also indicated that he perceived the Nazi Eden of a racial

---

[81] Erinnerungen von Dieter Stein, GR 45, Dec 1943–Apr 1944, BA-MA RH MSg 2/2777.

Volksgemeinschaft as just another belch of his "miserable" era. Ideology certainly played a role in each man's decision to wantonly destroy during the retreat in northwest Russia; it is quite debatable, however, if it acted as the primary motivator of such behavior. Instead, the institutional pressure exerted by the army – an organization prepared in early 1944 to do whatever it deemed necessary not to lose the war – created an atmosphere that not only permitted but demanded that soldiers leave a trail of destruction behind them as they moved west.

These acts committed by individuals and small groups of soldiers were dwarfed by the destruction committed in Pskov under the auspices of the 126th ID. As the Panther Line became increasingly untenable, the Rhinelanders systematically destroyed the city and all installations that could have some conceivable military value. Between 24 June and 5 July, the troops disabled, burned, and ruined nearly all of the city's manufacturing capacity and made plans to destroy the electrical plant, water works, and water tower.[82] The ravaging of Pskov fit into a much larger tale of willful destruction in the Leningrad region. According to Soviet sources, twenty cities and 3,135 villages in northwest Russia were severely damaged by the Germans during their retreat. Ninety percent of all industrial installations, 70 percent of all agricultural equipment, 60 percent of all collective farm barns and sheds, and 43 percent of the cattle population was either destroyed or plundered by the Germans.[83] When the Rhinelanders finally pulled out of Pskov on 14 July and retreated into the Baltic states, it too was a smoking pile of rubble, a final testament to the Wehrmacht's occupation of northwest Russia.[84]

---

[82] Included in this vast demolition program were the marmalade factory, the main generator plant, the metalworks, the thread factory, the city mill and saw mill, the felt factory, and the army bakery, as well as several other workshops dedicated to keeping the city running; Fernschreiben Nr. 1789, 126 Infanterie Division, Nr. 1102/44 geh., 13.7.44, BA-MA RH 24–28/292.

[83] Hass, "Deutsche Besatzungspolitik im Leningrader Gebiet," p. 76.

[84] Lohse, *Geschichte der rheinisch-westfälischen 126. Inf. Div. 1940–1945*, p. 182.

Conclusion

I. The primacy of military necessity

Sometime near the midpoint of its occupation, Army Group North compiled a list of several cities in its area of operations and compared their present populations with those of 1934.[1] The decline was eye-opening, if not altogether unexpected. Smaller communities such as Chudovo and Liuban, which numbered 12,000 and 11,800 respectively in 1934, dropped to 4,500 and 7,000 during the German occupation. The larger cities experienced a more drastic depopulation: Pavlovsk fell from 24,000 inhabitants to 1,200; Staraia Russa from 26,700 to 1,500; and, most shockingly, Pushkin from 51,000 to a mere 700. Policies of other German organizations such as the SS and the Economic Staff East actively contributed to this decimation of the Soviet population, but it was the Wehrmacht that exercised real power and authority over these areas and it therefore shoulders the overwhelming responsibility for the events that transpired in the swamps, forests, villages, and cities of northwest Russia.

Unlike the Baltic states, chunks of Belarus, and the majority of Ukraine, northwest Russia proper never passed over to civilian administration: the Wehrmacht controlled this region from fall 1941 to early 1944 without any serious challenge to its sovereignty.[2] Such a situation existed due to the simple fact that the military confrontation with the Soviet Union was never settled. This obvious, yet at times overlooked, reality needs to be kept firmly in mind during any discussion of the German Army's occupation policy in the Soviet Union. Combat in Army Group North's area

---

[1] Untitled and undated (presumably late 1942–early 1943), BA-MA RH 23–281. It is not clear where the figures for 1934 came from; due to this uncertainty, these numbers should be viewed only as approximations.

[2] Gert C. Lübbers's claim that the establishment and deployment of the Economic Staff East meant that "the sovereignty of the military in its very own occupation area was decisively limited" has no application to events in Army Group North's area of responsibility. Clearly the army maintained ultimate power in this region. See Lübbers, "Die 6. Armee und die Zivilbevölkerung von Stalingrad," *Vierteljahreshefte für Zeitgeschichte* (1) 2006, pp. 87–123, here p. 91.

of operations certainly paled in comparison to that on the central and southern sectors of the front, but to the army group and its soldiers battle remained the pre-eminent duty. During 1941 all three divisions fought pitched battles during the advance and the subsequent Soviet counterattacks during the winter. The year 1942 witnessed fierce fighting around the Volkhov river, the Demiansk pocket, and Lake Ladoga, while German troops continued to defend their positions in the Ladoga and Volkhov regions in 1943. And, of course, 1944 saw the major Soviet offensive that finally pushed the German Army out of Russia proper. Despite relatively long pauses in the fighting beginning in late 1942 and continuing through early 1944, the nature of war in northwest Russia – sniping, artillery fire, and constant raids – ensured that "wastage" ran high. Neitzel and Welzer have persuasively argued that "the war constituted the world that the men lived in. The men viewed prisoners of war, the civilian population, partisans and forced laborers from the perspective of this world: in short, everything that appeared before them." In other words, combat was and remained the primary duty of the German soldier and all other activities took place within this context.[3]

While waging this war against the Red Army, however, the German Army also willingly participated in Hitler's war of annihilation against Soviet society, as historical research over the past thirty years has amply demonstrated. The study of these three combat divisions in the hitherto neglected region of northwest Russia has certainly buttressed this claim as the crimes committed by the 121st, 123rd, and 126th Infantry Divisions ran the gamut of atrocities associated with the German war against the Soviet Union. Men from at least one of these divisions carried out or were at least complicit in the following offenses: the murder of Soviet Jews, the plundering of foodstuffs and the resulting starvation of Soviet civilians, a ruthless anti-partisan policy that resulted in the deaths of large number of "alleged" guerillas, the large-scale rounding up of civilians for forced labor, and finally the systematic devastation of Soviet territory during the lengthy retreats of 1943–4.

What explains the unprecedented savagery unleashed by the German Army against Soviet state and society during this war of annihilation? The predominant cause identified by historians has centered on ideology. Omer Bartov has described this ideology as one in which "God was with the Führer, and the German people were God's instrument, whose goal was to save the West from Asiatic barbarism and Jewish revenge."[4] Traditional German tropes of superiority vis-à-vis the uncivilized

---

[3] Neitzel and Welzer, *Soldaten*, p. 392.   [4] Bartov, *Hitler's Army*, p. 169.

and dirty east were now radicalized by Nazi racism that posited German superiority as not merely a cultural but also a biological truth. Fortified by the belief that they deserved the bounty of the east, German administrators, policemen, and soldiers, among others, utilized violence in an attempt to create their own bastardized Garden of Eden on the plains of the Soviet Union.

There is much to recommend this perspective when examining the activities of the 121st, 123rd, and 126th IDs. Racism certainly permeated the command structure of Army Group North, from its highest echelons down to the divisional level. Working within the context created by the criminal orders that demanded a war of ideologies, directives, and pronouncements filtered down the army group's hierarchy, both calling for and justifying a callous treatment of civilians, the ruthless suppression of any *perceived* resistance, and the necessity of eliminating especially threatening and devious groups, such as Jews or Red Army commissars, as a means to destroy the mortal enemy, Judeo-Bolshevism. Nazi rhetoric also appeared within the ranks as junior officers and enlisted men spoke of *Untermenschen* or "white niggers" who existed only as possible threats to German safety.

Nazi ideological tenets therefore served as an essential foundation to the German "mission" in the east. At the same time, however, as the war dragged on, ideological thinking became less pronounced throughout the hierarchy of Army Group North as pragmatic issues focusing on defeating the Red Army became more prevalent. The overwhelming majority of divisional orders were concerned with the latter, and while several utilized ideologically laden rhetoric, they constituted a distinct minority. Traditional stereotypes about Russians were more frequently used than the more hostile National Socialist descriptions. Overlap clearly existed between these two types of vocabulary and Nazi ideological beliefs certainly complemented and radicalized the army's various understandings of military necessity during the war, but the merging of these world views was frequently a case of the German Army's own internal development meeting Nazi ideology on common ground and not of the army simply adopting Nazi ideals in their entirety.

Letters and diaries compiled by the men also betray a noticeable lack of ideological content as the majority of such documents were concerned with more mundane matters: food, clothing, shelter, the weather at the front, and familial issues at home. While the surrounding landscape struck soldiers as primitive and dirty, this was not exclusively due to the effects of Nazi thought, as these descriptions of the eastern landscape proved very similar to those made by German soldiers during the First

World War.[5] The enemy himself, however, was usually, though not always, discussed with a tone of grudging respect. If German troops did enter the war believing that their Soviet counterparts were inferior soldiers, they were quickly disabused of such notions, as their own writings attest. An exclusive emphasis on ideology, therefore, is insufficient in explaining the twists and turns of the German Army's policies in northwest Russia.

In contrast to this ideological approach, military historians have emphasized the importance of situation in elucidating a unit's behavior. This approach is also quite useful in explaining the actions of the three divisions under examination here; it is particularly helpful in understanding the actions of the 123rd ID from fall 1941 through winter 1942. As its initial advance petered out and the weakened and exhausted division found its responsibilities to be far too much for its diminished capabilities, it turned to violence in hopes of stabilizing its position. Such a policy only radicalized during the winter crisis as the division battled for its survival. Once the crisis was mastered, however, and the 123rd ID believed itself secure, it changed course and began a more constructive engagement with civilians; clearly the situation served as an impetus to behavior modifications on the part of German units. The fact that all three divisions underwent similar changes in their occupation policies at roughly the same time, however, suggests that there was more at play than a mere reaction to events; rather, it seems likely that each unit was operating within a broader concept that drove army policy as a whole.

Thus, even though both ideology and situation provide useful, if imperfect, paradigms for understanding the German Army's actions during the Second World War, each tends to emphasize short-term trends or developments and this tends in turn to obscure longer-term processes at work. While the Wehrmacht's behavior and actions during the Second World War were unprecedented in terms of violence and scale, they nonetheless do fit onto a continuum of German practice that stretched back to the foundation of the German nation-state. The Prusso-German Army had traditionally subscribed to a radicalized notion of military necessity in which the institution focused on defeating the opposing army without regard for normal ethical or moral considerations. Attitudes towards civilians were inextricably entwined with the army's traditional view of operations. Perceiving itself (not entirely incorrectly) as possessing a weaker military potential than its constellation of possible enemies, the Prusso-German military leadership adopted an increasingly rigid

---

[5] Liulevicius, *War Land on the Eastern Front*, pp. 27–30.

mind-set that focused on achieving decisive victory through the use of maximum speed and power in the opening stages of war.

During the age of "people's war," however, military conflict was no longer limited to professional armies; now, the masses were intimately involved and this had two effects on the army's actions and thought. From a personnel perspective, the conscripts who entered the Wehrmacht all originated in a violent society. To such men, violence, sometimes driven by ideology, sometimes driven by more pragmatic causes, was a natural and everyday response to obstacles and this led to a tight fit with the army's institutional practices. These very same institutional practices became increasingly radical during the era of the unified German state. The realization of such policies led to brutal treatment of *francs-tireurs*, both real and perceived, during the Franco-Prussian War and the First World War, as well as genocidal policies in southwest Africa. This is not to say that other understandings of military necessity, ones that took a more nuanced approach to popular resistance and discontent, failed to exist during the army's history.[6] For the most part, though, real continuities existed between the Prusso-German Army's treatment of civilians and that of the Wehrmacht; as MacGregor Knox has noted, the various incarnations of the German Army were "unique among advanced nations in [their] ruthless contempt for the 'sentimentality and pathetic emotion-mongering [*weichlicher Gefühlsschwärmerei*]' of international humanitarian law."[7]

The evolution of war from the cabinet affairs of the eighteenth century to the people's war of the twentieth century also meant that a state's resources – including those under occupation – needed to be mobilized in the service of the war effort if victory was to be achieved. While Germany utilized labor particularly in occupied Belgium during the First World War, the example of Ober Ost in Lithuania provides the strongest example of the army's growing attempts to control absolutely the territories it conquered. Labor roundups, requisitioning of food and other resources, the confiscation of shelter: all of these point to a ruthless policy of exploitation designed to feed the German military in its quest for final victory.

The idea of military necessity, which threaded its way through the Prusso-German Army's existence from 1870 up through the Second World War, best explains the development of the Wehrmacht's occupation

---

[6] Lieb, "Aufstandsbekämpfung im strategischen Dilemma"; Liulevicius, *War Land on the Eastern Front*, pp. 183–6.
[7] MacGregor Knox, "Reading the Wehrmacht's Mind?" *Sehepunkt* (12) 2012, available at www.sehepunkte.de/2012/03/19936.html.

policies in the Soviet Union. Certainly, the imposition of the Nazi world view during the Third Reich made such a value-free approach to victory easier, but it was impulses generated within the institution of the Wehrmacht itself that both decisively contributed to the brutal war it waged in the east and motivated the much more conciliatory policies it implemented in 1942 and 1943.

Operation Barbarossa marked the first stage in this war. Germany's political and military leadership, realizing its quantitative inferiority versus the Red Army and the precarious economic position of the Reich, staked everything on one quick and decisive campaign. This emphasis on achieving a crushing and speedy victory was accompanied by a brutality designed to destroy any resistance to its operations and cow the remaining population into submission. During the invasion, men of the 121st, 123rd, and 126th IDs viewed the majority of the Soviet civilian population as a faceless and amorphous mass that nonetheless possessed the potential for treachery. Their primary interaction with Soviet civilians, however, occurred in barns and fields due to the army's policy of living off the land. The longer the operation lasted, the more dependent the Germans became on foodstuffs from the surrounding areas; this was especially true for the 123rd and 126th IDs, who found themselves at the end of an overextended, irregular supply line. The ideological framework of the campaign certainly helped radicalize the behavior of cold and hungry troops towards civilians, but the dire straits that the divisions found themselves in would have in all likelihood necessitated a ravaging of the local population in any case, regardless of its position in the Nazi *Weltanschauung*.

Following the Soviet counteroffensive of January 1942, significant segments of Army Group North – including the 123rd and 126th IDs – faced extremely threatening situations. During the 1941–2 winter crisis, German behavior towards Soviet civilians radicalized as the surrounding population was not only seen as potentially hostile but was now directly targeted by German troops for clothing and labor. Lacking appropriate winter gear, these same civilians were then forced to construct defensive positions for the Wehrmacht with predictable results. During this period, relations between the army and the civilian population reached their nadir as desperation, greased by the ideological demands of Germany's political and military leadership, led soldiers to ignore the needs of the surrounding population as they desperately strove not merely for victory, but also for survival. The army's interpretation of a strict and brutal military necessity – one that worked hand in glove with the Nazi state's ideological tenets – ensured that only the needs of the troops were recognized while civilians were viewed as mere impediments to victory.

Widespread starvation and suffering resulted from these ad hoc measures enacted by Sixteenth and Eighteenth Armies on the grounds of military necessity during the first ten months of war.

In the immediate period after the winter crisis had been mastered, various German field commanders in the east called for a policy that mobilized the civilian population behind the German war effort, diverging from the war of annihilation; here the continuities with Ober Ost from the First World War were striking. On the ground, such thinking led the 123rd ID, still encircled within the Demiansk pocket, to establish soup kitchens for starving civilians. To be sure, this did not occur until after the Germans had overcome the immediate military crisis in the pocket, but even with their strained supply situation, they assisted the surrounding population. An army driven solely by ideological considerations would find it extremely difficult to reverse course and attempt to improve relations with a group that had no future in a Nazi-dominated Soviet Union. Rather, the Wehrmacht viewed its professional duty of defeating the Red Army as more vital than its ideological mission of waging war against civilians and accordingly adjusted its view of the surrounding Soviet population.

Such institutional efforts were also undertaken by other smaller units and individual soldiers. During the worst period of starvation in Leningrad's industrial suburbs, some soldiers and field kitchens in the 121st ID, among others, provided at least a minimal amount of sustenance for starving civilians. Unlike larger-scale assistance programs, such as that of the 123rd ID, these actions were not based on pragmatism. Individual soldiers, while certainly cognizant that malnourished civilians could eventually find their way to partisan units, shared their precious stocks of food based on a common humanity with Soviet civilians. Despite the increasingly radical strictures of an Army High Command that prohibited such "misguided acts of charity" and despite their own participation in policies that resulted in such starvation, a not insignificant number of soldiers worked at ideological cross-purposes with their own leadership.

The recognition that Operation Barbarossa had failed forced frontline units to modify their previous practices. Instead of reacting in an even more ruthless manner towards the civilian population – a development that would seemingly follow the internal logic of both Nazi ideological tenets and one understanding of total war – the field commands realized that war needed to be waged with the *support*, or at least acquiescence, of the local population and *not against* them, and this was slowly absorbed by German field units during 1942 and 1943. This hesitant and haphazard evolution of German policy gradually moved towards a more unified system of occupation, though even by mid-1943 the efforts of the German Army to create a rational system of occupation had failed. The divisions enacted measures to ensure that civilians possessed sufficient stocks of food to survive – including more stringent orders to end wild requisitioning and more centralized planning for the planting and harvesting of the crops – and also became less involved in the day-to-day governance of the occupied areas, delegating authority to local, native administrations. The use of auxiliary Soviet troops also points towards a more pragmatic policy of occupation. While German soldiers certainly failed to welcome these men as equals, the fact that they were even included within the ranks of the Wehrmacht indicates the army's recognition that victory required the co-opting of the native population.

The "conflict between dogma and usefulness" that characterized general German occupation policy during the war also became apparent in Army Group North's attitudes towards civilians.[8] While elements of a more conciliatory occupation policy became visible, the competing visions of military necessity that existed within the Wehrmacht's institutional thinking cut across their policies. This was never more apparent than with the army group's policy of evacuating hundreds of thousands of the Soviet civilians during the war, the primary goal being the mobilization of labor for both the army and Germany. It is clear that this was one of the largest war crimes committed by these three divisions, both objectively in terms of numbers and more subjectively in terms of the tremendous amounts of misery it caused.

Evacuations of civilians from the front lines began in 1941 in Pavlovsk and the Demiansk region due to the catastrophic food situation as well as the need for shelter for the troops, while the need to create labor reserves both for the Economic Staff East and for the divisions themselves sparked such efforts in the summer of 1942. This only foreshadowed much more comprehensive efforts to depopulate Army Group North's area of operations with notable actions including the removal of the Demiansk pocket's entire population in early 1943 and the fantastically ambitious plan to send 900,000 Soviet citizens to the Baltic states and Germany in 1944. All three divisions participated in these larger actions by evacuating numerous small villages and towns at the local level. While Pavlovsk was the largest community emptied by the three divisions, examples abound in their records of smaller communities that ceased to exist following the appearance of German troops. In fact, one can convincingly argue that

---

[8] Hans Umbreit, "Die deutsche Herrschaft in den besetzten Gebieten 1942–1945," in Kroener et al., *Organisation und Mobilisierung des deutschen Machtbereichs 1942–1944/5*, p. 56.

outside combat, the evacuation of Soviet civilians, especially in the later stages of the war, constituted the single most important activity of these three divisions. Dieter Pohl has estimated that beginning in spring 1943, the *Ostheer* as a whole evacuated approximately 2.3 million people, though this does not include any "unauthorized expulsions" carried out by the troops.[9] Clearly, Army Group North's infantry divisions were important tools in executing this policy and, just as clearly, any and all attempts to gain the support of the civilian population foundered on the near continual displacement of Soviet individuals and their families.

The second major obstacle to the construction of a rational German occupation policy in northwest Russia was the frequent recourse to violence by German troops in the area. Though the three divisions committed only one large-scale massacre between them – the brutal murder of approximately 200 Soviet prisoners of war in late January 1942 – the sight of bodies dangling from gallows symbolized the terror that accompanied German troops. When the three divisions implemented a more conciliatory approach to Soviet citizens, their repeated orders to their men, especially in the case of the 126th ID, highlighted the difficulty they faced in transforming the attitudes of some soldiers towards the Soviet population. Repeated injunctions to treat civilians and later *Hiwis* correctly indicate that the troops' attitudes were much more difficult to change than the policies of the divisions themselves, and here the importance of ideology interacting with and reinforcing the more radical understandings of military necessity emerges quite clearly.

The inability to wipe away the vestiges of earlier policies predicated on an all-encompassing violence was rendered moot by the decision to fall back to the Panther Line in early 1944. Once again, the German Army modified its occupation policy, reverting to one based on terror and destruction. In order to deny the advancing Red Army anything with a possible application for military purposes, Army Group North engaged in a systematic and comprehensive program of scorched earth that devastated northwest Russia, rendering it a virtual desert. This was now viewed as the only means to achieve victory or at least a stalemate against the Soviets. German occupation policy had now swung full circle. Attempts to win over the population during late 1942 and in 1943 were discarded in favor of the application of force, resembling those practices that had occurred during Operation Barbarossa. As the Wehrmacht pulled out of Russia proper in mid-1944, it finally waged the all-encompassing and destructive war envisioned by Hitler in 1941.

---

[9] Pohl, *Die Herrschaft der Wehrmacht*, p. 327.

II. Splintering of the narrative

Criminality during the war of annihilation is generally applicable to the army as a whole; the concept, however, requires modification when examining the actions and behaviors of the units individually. Not each division engaged in each component of the *Vernichtungskrieg* and each division approached these issues with varying degrees of professional comportment, ideological intensity, and situational awareness. In other words, the master narrative that views the Wehrmacht as a willing tool in the Nazi attempt to destroy Soviet state and society in preparation for German colonization that certainly holds true on the macro level needs to be looked at more closely at the micro level.

The divergent experiences of the three divisions are most apparent regarding their relation to the Holocaust. Of the three units, existing evidence links only one of the formations to genocide. The 121st ID first witnessed the true nature of Hitler's war during its stay in Kovno in June 1941. As Lithuanian nationalist mobs celebrated the hasty retreat of Soviet power by brutally and publicly massacring Jews, the 121st ID failed to lift a finger to stop the violence. Here, military necessity intersected with ideological considerations: the importance of continuing the advance and the emphasis by the Reich's political and military leaderships on destroying the "Judeo-Bolshevik" state meant that such pogroms would be, at least, tolerated. The East Prussians' behavior during the occupation of Pavlovsk proved even more odious. SD murder squads exterminated the city's Jewish population in one evening while the 121st ID controlled the city. Though the men of the 121st ID did not pull the triggers, they were certainly complicit in Pavlovsk's own Holocaust.

Outside several other incidents in which individuals or small numbers of soldiers hassled or abused Jews during the initial advance in 1941, however, the Holocaust is strikingly absent from the army's war in northwest Russia. Dieter Pohl has estimated that German forces had murdered around 2,000 Jews in Sixteenth and Eighteenth Armies' area of responsibility by spring 1942; while scale is irrelevant in discussing the nature of a crime, the comparative numbers of Jews murdered in other army areas were much higher.[10] Several factors are at play here. First, commanders of Army Group North and its subordinate field armies themselves were not notoriously anti-Semitic. Though several of their orders during summer 1941 were certainly couched in ideological terms, these focused on the "Asiatic" and "Bolshevik" nature of the opponent,

---

[10] Ibid., p. 262.

with only secondary reference to Jews. In comparison to German field commanders on the southern section of the front, those in Army Group North appeared much less radically oriented towards the "Jewish Question."[11]

Perhaps the most important reason in explaining Army Group North's relative lack of participation in the Holocaust was the small Jewish population in its area of operations. Once the Wehrmacht advanced out of the Baltic states – where the machinery of the Holocaust soon functioned in a horrifyingly efficient manner – and into Russia proper, the possibility for the persecution of Jews dramatically decreased. Very few Jews lived in this region, with the majority of this small population residing in Leningrad itself.[12] It is certainly a possibility, if not a probability, that these Wehrmacht units would have taken a much more active role in murdering Jews if given the opportunity – as evidenced by the 121st ID's actions in Pavlovsk – but such a counterfactual obviously cannot be proven.

While the divisions' relationships with the surrounding population fell within a circumscribed range of behavior, they nonetheless varied in certain ways. The issue of food proved the most important issue in marking out the relationship between the two groups. All three divisions lived off the land during the 1941 advance and each recognized the likely results of such policies. It was only during the 121st ID's occupation of Pavlovsk that the horrifying, if logical, culmination of prewar planning and the rapacious nature of the campaign occurred. German seizure of the town's foodstuffs led to scenes of unimaginable desperation and horror, including the starvation of several thousand civilians. Neither the 123rd nor the 126th ID's food confiscation policies played such an important role in starving sizable communities such as Pavlovsk, but their records are replete with evidence of starvation in their areas of deployment.

The divisions' approaches to partisan warfare also proved to be more varied than uniform, at least during the opening stages of the conflict. During the initial invasion, the 126th ID reacted much more ruthlessly towards the partisan threat than either of its peer divisions, while the 121st ID responded in the most humane and professional manner. Once the latter division settled into the occupation of Pavlovsk, however,

---

[11] For a concise overview of the various attitudes of the *Ostheer*'s commanding officers to Soviet Jews, see Hürter, *Hitlers Heerführer*, pp. 536–95.
[12] Using 1939 Soviet census materials, Hill states that only 0.5 percent of the Leningrad *oblast* was Jewish – a total of 17,711 people of whom 12,994 lived in Leningrad's suburbs; see Hill, *The War behind the Eastern Front*, p. 33.

its recourse to collective actions and preventative deportations fit neatly into general German practice. As the war progressed, however, it was the 123rd ID that devoted more resources to combating partisans than either of the other two divisions, with this task receiving the bulk of the division's attention during early 1943. Unlike the 121st or the 126th IDs, the Berliners were tasked with destroying centrally controlled and organized partisan formations. During several major operations designed to destroy these partisan brigades, the Berliners' approach never degenerated into simple brutality by lashing out at civilians. This differed from their counterparts in the 121st and 126th IDs who waged an increasingly savage war behind Army Group North's front, especially during the scorched-earth retreats of 1943–4 when anti-partisan operations were simply rolled into the larger program of systematic devastation that accompanied the Wehrmacht's withdrawal.

What explains the different experiences of these three divisions during their war in northwest Russia? Several issues intersect in answering this question. First, despite all serving in the same theater, under the same army group (and, at times, army and corps) command, facing the same opponent, situational factors proved important in determining a unit's behavior at any given time. The 121st ID's behavior during the occupation of Pavlovsk was the most abhorrent of the three during the first three years of war. Presiding over the execution of the town's Jews and the starvation of the remaining population, the 121st ID had transformed into a willing cog in Hitler's war of extermination due to its close interaction with other Nazi agencies. Pavlovsk served as local headquarters for the *Einsatzgruppen* subunit in the area and members of the Economic Staff East were also quite active within the Leningrad siege line. Working within this larger web of murderous and exploitative institutions, the behavior of the division radicalized and it played a vital role in turning Pavlovsk into hell on earth.

Situational factors also led to the different types of occupation policy developed by each division. While the 121st and 126th IDs saw no reason to modify their approaches in 1941–2, the 123rd ID, faced with a near-fatal situation, realized that only a fundamental change in its practices could salvage the division's precarious position. In contrast to the more orthodox argument that weakness only served to radicalize German behavior, in the case of the 123rd ID a sense of its weakened state led it to implement more conciliatory policies.

A more suggestive, yet certainly far from conclusive, approach would be one that examines the unit's original *Wehrkreis*. The regions of East Prussia, Berlin-Brandenburg, and Rhineland-Westphalia, despite sharing some general similarities, were all very different places that produced different men. The evidence seems stronger in the cases of the 121st and 123rd IDs. Hailing from East Prussia, the 121st ID was viewed throughout the entirety of the war as one of the most able infantry divisions in Army Group North; such a claim is based both on assessments given by corps and army headquarters and on the numerous difficult assignments the division was assigned during the conflict. Its soldiers proved the most disciplined and moderate during the advance in 1941, leading one to speculate that the culture of East Prussia – a conservative, pious, and hierarchical one – stayed with the men during the initial fighting in the Soviet Union. The division's East Prussian ethos remained secure during the war as it not only continued to receive the majority of its replacements from Wehrkreis I but also reintegrated wounded veterans on a regular basis; it seems logical to conclude that its military effectiveness and behavior directly correlated to the cohesion afforded by these circumstances.

Of the three divisions examined in this study, only the 123rd ID failed to survive the war and it consistently proved the least militarily effective. Two reasons seem pertinent in explaining this low combat efficiency. First, the majority of the men who served in the division's ranks during the war originated in the socialist and communist stronghold of Berlin.[13] Years of socialization in such a milieu were not immediately wiped away by the Third Reich, a fact reflected in the division commander's scathing order abolishing a noncommissioned officers' club as it "remind[ed] one of the evil times after 1918" and the rather indifferent attitude to military discipline found within the division during the duration of the conflict.[14] Additionally, the 123rd ID was the only division of the three that received substantial numbers from replacements outside its home recruiting district. Such a dilution of the unit's cohesion played a role in the division's battlefield performance; when the Wehrmacht's replacement system failed to maintain a regional identity in a division, the effects could be disastrous.[15] It is certainly no coincidence that this division was the only one of the three units not to have a divisional history published in the postwar period, suggesting that the

---

[13] Neitzel and Welzer, *Soldaten*, p. 419, note that the "hard core of the former socialist... milieu" proved relatively resistant to military values.
[14] 123 ID Kommandeur, An die Herren Kommandeure, 26.11.1940, BA-MA RH 26–123/2.
[15] For an examination of divisions lacking any type of regional cohesion and their experiences during the fighting, see Robert Sterling Rush, "A Different Perspective: Cohesion, Morale, and Operational Effectiveness in the German Army, Fall 1944," *Armed Forces & Society* (25) 1999, pp. 477–508; and his larger study *Hell in Hürtgen Forest: The Ordeal and Triumph of an American Infantry Regiment* (Lawrence, KS, 2001), pp. 48–57.

123rd ID never became the "home away from home" for its men that either the 121st or 126th IDs did.

The behavior of the 126th ID is the most difficult to explain. This division surpassed its peers in viciousness during the entirety of the war as it proved the most likely unit to resort to violence in its dealings with civilians. Such attitudes in 1943 could be linked to the systematic destruction of their homes by Allied bombers; frustrated at their inability to protect their families, they lashed out at those in reach. Such an explanation, however, fails to clarify why the division acted as it did in 1941–2. One speculates that unlike the rigid conservative culture of East Prussia or the radical leftist milieu of Berlin, the dominant cultural ethos of Rhineland-Westphalia – Catholicism – proved more amenable to Nazi policies, especially in the east. The sociologist Michael Mann has suggested that the drive to carve out a new empire, one much more focused on the east, appealed to Reich Catholics as it logically "flowed from their ethnic *grossdeutsch* imperialism."[16] This emphasis on a German state that included all ethnic Germans proved especially tantalizing to men from the Rhineland who had spent sixteen years separated from Germany. The desire to create a greater Germany was also tied to the gradual demise of Catholicism as a means of identity. Recent research has indicated that Catholic soldiers viewed the Nazi regime with the same levels of support and identification as their Protestant counterparts and this highlighted the gradual weakening of the Center Party's mandate; only a residual Catholicism kept voters in the fold before Hitler's seizure of power.[17] Finally, the 126th ID also received the most reinforcements from its home district and, as Richard Evans has remarked, the constant flow of homogeneous replacements into a division led to the creation of an "organic national community, the *Volksgemeinschaft*, in miniature; and correspondingly, all the soldiers' aggressive masculinity was directed outwards, towards the enemy, and towards a population that, in the east at least, they regarded as racially inferior, indeed as barely human."[18] Such a conclusion certainly helps explain the behavior of both the 121st and 126th IDs during the latter years of the war and it perhaps offers some insight into the Rhenish-Westphalian troops' actions in the early years of the war. The striking homogeneity of the unit – one centered on men who viewed the creation of an eastern

---

[16] Michael Mann, *The Dark Side of Democracy: Explaining Ethnic Cleansing* (Cambridge, 2005), p. 232.

[17] Römer, "Volksgemeinschaft in der Wehrmacht," p. 64; Oded Heilbronner, *Catholicism, Political Culture, and the Countryside: A Social History of the Nazi Party in South Germany* (Ann Arbor, 1998), p. 198.

[18] Richard Evans, *The Third Reich at War* (New York, 2009), p. 501.

empire through the prism of a Catholic, *grossdeutsch* outlook – produced a more divisive "us-versus-them" mentality that manifested itself in ruthless behavior towards Soviet civilians during the advance in 1941. While ideology worked to varying degrees in motivating the troops of each division, the men of the 126th ID behaved in a manner more in ideological tune with the regime than did their peers in either the 121st or the 123rd IDs. Clearly, this is an area that requires more research, but hopefully this study has made some links between a division's home military district and its behavior in the field.

Ernst Nolte's characterization of the German–Soviet war as "the most monstrous war of conquest, enslavement, and annihilation" has stood the test of time.[19] While ideology certainly played a role in the army's waging of a savage war, it affected various divisions in different ways, and, at least in the case of these three divisions, never functioned as the primary cause of its behavior. Instead, the army's single-minded focus on achieving victory on the battlefield proved the primary impulse for its behavior. Michael Geyer has recently summed up the prevailing "worldview [that] established the ground rules for the German conduct of war in the East. Its key was an ideology of unadulterated, unrestrained violence, limited only by expediency, in a world of conquered people without rights"; this statement captures the essence of military necessity.[20] Increasingly radicalized by both the advent of total war and the onset of the National Socialist dictatorship, the German Army viewed the campaign against the Soviet Union as one that demanded violence on an unprecedented scale. While such a focus on achieving *Endsieg* paradoxically could and did lead to more conciliatory measures based on political expediency, the Wehrmacht's legacy in the war in the east was one of violence and destruction on a massive scale. Nazi ideological beliefs both created a context in which military necessity was encouraged to radicalize into open warfare against large segments of the civilian population and played a large role in convincing soldiers of the correctness and necessity of this ruthlessness. It was, however, the army's own appreciation of its position within a changing constellation of factors such as strength, space, and security that determined its final descent into barbarism.

---

[19] Ernst Nolte, *Der Faschismus in seiner Epoche* (Munich, 1963), p. 436.
[20] Geyer, "War, Genocide, Extermination: The War against the Jews in an Era of World Wars," pp. 139–40.

Bibliography

ARCHIVAL SOURCES

I. BUNDESARCHIV-MILITÄRARCHIV (BA-MA), FREIBURG IM BREISGAU

Division files
121st Infantry Division:
RH 26–121/1–70
RH 37/3095, RH 37/3096, RH 39/402, RH 44/381, RH 46/716
123rd Infantry Division:
RH 26–123/1–242
RH 37/7088, RH 37/7089
126th Infantry Division
RH 26–126/1–157
RH 37/6830, RH 46/414
Other divisional records:
RH 37/940, 2785, 6405, 3105, 3098
Corps files
I Army Corps:
RH 24–1/62, 66–7, 69, 71–2, 78–9, 86, 112, 114, 117, 120, 124, 130, 266–8, 270–1, 277–8, 281–2, 325–8, 335–8
II Army Corps:
RH 24–2/80, 87–102, 107–10, 303, 327–8, 373, 378–80, 383, 388, 390, 396, 458–65
X Army Corps:
RH 24–10/169–79, 361–3, 389, 529–35
XVII Army Corps:
RH 24–17/111–18, 121, 215–16
XXVI Army Corps:
RH 24–26/80–9, 121, 141, 180–2, 238–40, 259–61
XXVII Army Corps:
RH 24–27/10, 14, 15, 18, 19, 84–97, 151–7, 162, 181–3, 283–92
XXVIII Army Corps:
RH 24–28/20–7, 60, 69–74, 108–10, 157–60, 187, 236, 239–47
XXX Army Corps:
RH 24–30/103–4, 143–4
XXXVIII Army Corps:
RH 24–38/112, 119–20, 137, 147, 221, 280–5

L Army Corps:
RH 24–50/15, 20–9, 34, 39–42, 75–8, 80–2, 97–100, 127, 131–2, 145–7, 152, 157–8, 162–3, 176–81, 195–9, 207–9
Rear-area files
Korück 583:
RH 23–277, 281, 283, 287
Army files
Sixteenth Army:
RH 20–16/45
Eighteenth Army:
RH 20–18/675, 823, 824, 912, 913, 928, 933, 1167, 1575, 1628
Other German organizations:
Economic Staff East:
RW 31/584–5, 588, 590–9, 934–42, 948–9
Militärgeschichtliche Sammlung (MSg 2)
MSg 2/2580, 3146, 2429, 2779, 5415, 2777, 2488, 2519, 4558, 3295

II. BIBLIOTHEK FÜR ZEITGESCHICHTE (BFZ), STUTTGART

Sammlung Sterz
William D., Art. Regt. 227, 7.7.41
Corporal Heinz B., Infantry Regiment 68, 28.6.41, 3.7.41, 24.5.43
Corporal Fritz S., 366 Infantry Regiment, 25.11.41, 18.1.42, 6.3.42, 24.3.42
Corporal Alois W., 4. Company/Grenadier Regiment 157, 1.11.41
Private Ernst A., Infantry Regiment 272, 13.10.41, 26.3.42, 23.12.43
Corporal Konrad F., Infanterie-Regiment 43, 13.3.42
Private Andres V., Inf. Rgt. 422, 5.7.42
Sergeant Karl B., Grenadier Regt. 406, 30.1.43, 25.2.43
H.A.K., Berlin-Wilmersdorf, 27.11.43
Lt. Helmut H., Berlin-Tegel, 28.11.43
Corporal Joachim S., Communications Section 218, 16.8.43
Anneliese E., Dortmund-Wambel, 16.1.43, 17.3.43
Corporal Willi L., Reconniassance Unit 254 ID, 18.6.43
Helga W., Dortmund, 25.10.43
Corporal Rolf A., GR 328, 17.4.43
Private Karl Z., GR 328, 10.7.43
Private Heinrich R., Pi.Btl. 505, 29.1.44
Sergeant Karl S., 1. San. Kp. 126, 23.3.44
Sergeant Erich W., Gren. Rgt. 408, 5.4.44
Lt. Klaus W., Infantry Regiment 418, 6.7.41, 7.7.41, 17.7.41, 3.9.41, 10.10.41, 31.10.41, 18.11.41, 31.7.42

III. DEUTSCHE DIENSTELLE (WAST), BERLIN

Erkennungsmarkenverzeichnisse und Personalveränderungslisten
Folder 80549 1/405 GR
Folder 80588 1/407 GR
Folder 80744 1/415 GR

Folder 80763 1/416 GR
Folder 82026 1/422 GR
Folder 82066 1/424 GR
Verlustmeldungen
Verlustmeldung 2 Juni 41–Juli 42 I/IR u. GR 416
Infanterie Regiment 415 Namentliche Verlustmeldungen Nr. 7:
  7.12.1941–9.4.1942

IV. FELDPOSTARCHIV, BERLIN MUSEUM FÜR KOMMUNIKATION (MFK)

3.2002.0827: Heinz, 6.6.43, 13.6.43, 7.8.43, 1.9.43, 2.9.43, 6.9.43

V. GEHEIMES STAATSARCHIV PK (GSTA), BERLIN-DAHLEM

XX HA Rep. 240B Nr. 9, Gauleitung Ostpreußen der NSDAP, Der Gauleiter
XX. HA, Rep. 240, Nr. 31a–31g, Gauleitung Ostpreußen der NSDAP, Nationalsozialistische Frauenschaft Rundschreiben und Tätigkeitsberichte 1939–1944
XX 1 Rep. 240 Nr. 57a-e, Territoriale Gliederung der NSDAP Ostpreußen III, Kreis Labiau der NSDAP – Geschichte, Tätigkeitsberichte, Meldungen; Kreis Labiau der NSDAP – Kreisleitung. "Stimme der Heimat." Gruß der NSDAP des Kreises Labiau an die feldgrauen Kameraden Nr. 1–8 1940–1942
XX HA Rep. 240, C66 a-e, Territoriale Gliederung der NSDAP Ostpreußen III, Heimatbriefe der Ortsgruppe Kreuzingen der NSDAP 1942

VI. BUNDESARCHIV (BA), BERLIN-LICHTERFELD

R 70 Sowjetunion/20, Polizeidienstellen in der Sowjetunion.

VII. NATIONAL ARCHIVES RECORDS ADMINISTRATION (NARA), WASHINGTON, DC

Army files (microfilm)
Eighteenth Army: T-312, Rolls 763, 766
X Corps: T-314, Rolls 446, 449, 450, 496
XXXVIII Corps: T-314, Rolls 900, 902
L Corps: T-314, Roll 1234
SS and Police files (microfilm)
Ereignismeldung USSR: T-175, Rolls 233–5
Meldungen aus den besetzten Ostgebiete: T-175, Rolls 235–6

VIII. UNITED STATES HOLOCAUST MEMORIAL MUSEUM ARCHIVE (USHMM), WASHINGTON, DC

RG-22.002M: Extraordinary State Commission to Investigate German-Fascist Crimes Committed on Soviet Territory from the USSR, Archive of the October Revolution records, Reels 17, 1745
RG-18.00: Organizational and Administrative Correspondence Relating to the Wehrmacht, SS, SD, and SIPO in the Ostland

PUBLISHED PRIMARY SOURCES

Arad, Yitzhak, Shmuel Krakowski, and Shmuel Spector (eds.), *The Einsatzgruppen Reports: Selections from the Dispatches of the Nazi Death Squads' Campaign against the Jews in Occupied Territories of the Soviet Union, July 1941–January 1943* (New York, 1989).

Baade, Fritz (ed.), *Unsere Ehre heisst treue: Kriegstagebuch des Kommandostabes Reichsführer SS, Tätigkeitsberichte der 1. und 2. SS-Inf. Brigade, der 1. SS Kav.- Brigade und von Sonderkommandos der SS* (Vienna, 1965).

Bähr, W. and H.W. Bähr (eds.), *Kriegesbriefe gefallener Studenten 1939–1945* (Tübingen and Stuttgart, 1952).

Bock, Fedor von, *Generalfeldmarschall Fedor von Bock: The War Diary, 1939–1945* (ed. Klaus Gerbert) (Atglen, 2000).

Bolovchansky, Anatoli et al. (eds.), *"Ich will raus aus diesem Wahnsinn": Deutsche Briefe von der Ostfront 1941–1945* (Wuppertal, 1991).

Buchbender, Ortwin and Rheinhold Sterz, *Das andere Gesicht des Krieges: Deutsche Feldpostbriefe 1939–1945* (Munich, 1982).

de Beaulieu, Walter Chales, *Der Vorstoß der Panzergruppe 4 auf Leningrad 1941* (Neckargemünd, 1961).

Dönhoff, Marion, Countess, *Before the Storm: Memories of My Youth in Old Prussia* (New York, 1990).

Glantz, David (ed.), *The Initial Period of War on the Eastern Front, June 22–August 1941* (London, 1993).

Goebbels, Joseph, *The Goebbels Diaries, 1939–1941* (ed. and trans. Fred Taylor) (New York, 1983).

The Goebbels Diaries, 1942–1943 (ed. and trans. Louis P. Lochner) (New York, 1948).

Grossman, Vasily, *A Writer at War: Vasily Grossman with the Red Army 1941–1945* (ed. and trans. Antony Beevor and Luba Vinogradova) (New York, 2005).

Guderian, Heinz, *Panzer Leader* (New York, 1996).

Halder, Franz, *Kriegstagebuch: Tägliche Aufzeichnungen des Chefs des Generalstabes des Heeres 1939–1942* (ed. Hans-Adolf Jacobson), vols. I–III (Stuttgart, 1962–4).

Heer, Hannes (ed.), *"Stets zu erschießen sind Frauen, die in der Roten Armee dienen": Geständnisse deutscher Kriegsgefangener über ihren Einsatz an der Ostfront* (Hamburg, 1996).

Heesch, Wilhelm von, *Meine 13. Infanterie-Geschütz-Kompanie Grenadier- Regiment 408* (no place of publication, 1962).

Heiber, Helmut and David Glantz (eds.), *Hitler and His Generals: Military Conferences, 1942–1945* (New York, 2003).

Hill, Alexander (ed.), *The Great Patriotic War of the Soviet Union, 1941–1945* (Abingdon, 2009).

Hitler, Adolf, *Mein Kampf* (trans. Ralph Mannheim) (Boston, 1971).

Höhne, Gustav, "In Snow and Mud: 31 Days of Attack under Seydlitz during the Early Spring of 1942," in Steven Newton (ed.), *German Battle Tactics on the Russian Front, 1941–1945* (Atglen, 1994), pp. 109–35.

Bibliography

Hubatsch, Walther (ed.), *Hitlers Weisungen für die Kriegführung 1939–1945* (Frankfurt am Main, 1962).
Hughes, Daniel J. (ed.), *Moltke on the Art of War: Selected Writings* (Novato, 1993).
International Military Tribunal, *Trials of the Major War Criminals before the International Military Tribunal*, 42 vols. (Nuremberg, 1948).
Klee, Ernst, Willi Dreßen, and Volker Rieß (eds.), *"The Good Old Days": The Holocaust as Seen by Its Perpetrators and Bystanders* (New York, 1991).
Klein, Peter (ed.), *Die Einsatzgruppen in der besetzten Sowjetunion 1941/42: Die Tätigkeits- und Lageberichte der Sicherheitspolizei und des SD* (Berlin, 1997).
Klemperer, Victor, *I Will Bear Witness: A Diary of the Nazi Years, 1933–1941* (New York, 1999).
I Will Bear Witness 1942–1945: A Diary of the Nazi Years (New York, 2001).
Leeb, Wilhelm, Ritter von, *Tagebuchaufzeichnungen und Lagebeurteilungen aus zwei Weltkriegen* (ed. Georg Meyer) (Stuttgart, 1976).
Lubbeck, William, *At Leningrad's Gates: The Story of a Soldier with Army Group North* (Philadelphia, 2006).
Luck, Hans von, *Panzer Commander* (New York, 1989).
Mallmann, Klaus-Michael, Volker Rieß, and Wolfram Pyta (eds.), *Deutscher Osten: Der Weltanschauungskrieg in Photos und Texten* (Darmstadt, 2003).
Manoschek, Walther (ed.), *"Es gibt nur eines für das Judentum: 'Vernichtung'": Das Judenbild in deutschen Soldatenbriefen 1939–1944* (Hamburg, 1995).
Manstein, Erich von, *Lost Victories* (Novato, 1994).
Moritz, Erhard (ed.), *Fall Barbarossa: Dokumente zur Vorbereitung der faschistischen Wehrmacht auf die Aggression gegen die Sowjetunion (1940/41)* (Berlin, 1970).
Müller, Norbert (ed.), *Deutsche Besatzungspolitik in der UdSSR 1941–1944: Dokumente* (Cologne, 1982).
  (ed.), *Die faschistische Okkupationspolitik in den zeitweilig besetzten Gebieten der Sowjetunion (1941–1944)* (Berlin, 1991).
Müller, Rolf-Dieter (ed.), *Die deutsche Wirtschaftspolitik in den besetzten sowjetischen Gebieten 1941–1943: Der Abschlußbericht des Wirtschaftsstabes Ost und Aufzeichnungen eines Angehörigen des Wirtschaftskommandos Kiew* (Boppard am Rhein, 1991).
Newton, Steven (ed.), *German Battle Tactics on the Russian Front, 1941–1945* (Atglen, 1994).
Reisman, W. Michael and Chris T. Antoniou (eds.), *The Laws of War: A Comprehensive Collection of Primary Documents on International Laws Governing Armed Conflict* (New York, 1994).
Schramm, Percy (ed.), *Kriegstagebuch des Oberkommando der Wehrmacht 1940–1945*, vols. II–VI (Munich, 1982).
Statistischen Reichsamt (ed.), *Statistisches Jahrbuch für das Deutsche Reich, 1924/25* (Berlin, 1925).
  (ed.), *Statistisches Jahrbuch für das Deutsche Reich, 1928* (Berlin, 1928).
  (ed.), *Statistisches Jahrbuch für das Deutsche Reich, 1932* (Berlin, 1932).
US Government Printing Office (ed.), *Trial of War Criminals before the Nuernberg Military Tribunals under Control Council Law No. 10*, vol. X, *The High Command Case*, vol. XI, *The High Command Case* (Washington, DC, 1951).

Warlimont, Walter, *Inside Hitler's Headquarters, 1939–1945* (Novato, 1964).
Wehrmachtsverbrechen: Dokumente aus sowjetischen Archiven (Cologne, 1997).
Wilhelm, Hans-Heinrich, *Rassenpolitik und Kriegführung: Sicherheitspolizei und Wehrmacht in Polen und der Sowjetunion 1939–1942* (Passau, 1991).

SECONDARY SOURCES

"Abrechnung mit Hitlers Generälen," *Spiegel-Online*, 27 November 2001, available at www.spiegel.de/spiegel/print/d-20849227.html.
Adamy, Kurt and Kristina Hübener (eds.), *Adel und Staatsverwaltung in Brandenburg im 19. und 20. Jahrhundert: Ein historischer Vergleich* (Berlin, 1996).
Addison, Paul and Angus Calder (eds.), *Time to Kill: The Soldier's Experience of War in the West 1939–1945* (London, 1997).
Aly, Götz, *Hitler's Beneficiaries: Plunder, Racial War, and the Nazi Welfare State* (London, 2009).
Aly, Götz and Susanne Heim, *Architects of Annihilation: Auschwitz and the Logic of Destruction* (Princeton, 2002).
  "Deutsche Herrschaft 'im Osten': Bevölkerungspolitik und Völkermord," in Rürup and Jahn (eds.), *Erobern und Vernichten*, pp. 84–105.
Ambrose, Stephen, *Citizen Soldiers: The U.S. Army from the Normandy Beaches to the Bulge to the Surrender of Germany* (New York, 1997).
Anderson, Truman, "Incident at Baranivka: German Reprisals and the Soviet Partisan Movement in Ukraine, October–December 1941," *Journal of Modern History* (71) 1999, pp. 585–623.
Angrick, Andrej, "Das Beispiel Charkow: Massenmord unter deutscher Besatzung," in Hartmann, Hürter, and Jureit (eds.), *Verbrechen der Wehrmacht: Bilanz einer Debatte*, pp. 117–24.
  "Der Stellenwert von Terror und Mord in Konzept der deutschen Besatzungspolitik in Baltikum," in Lehmann, Bohn, and Danker (eds.), *Reichskommissariat Ostland*, pp. 69–87.
Ankum, Katharina von (ed.), *Women in the Metropolis: Gender and Modernity in Weimar Culture* (Berkeley, 1997).
Applegate, Celia, *A Nation of Provincials: The German Idea of Heimat* (Berkeley, 1990).
Arnold, Klaus Jochen, *Die Wehrmacht und die Besatzungspolitik in den besetzten Gebieten der Sowjetunion: Kriegsführung und Radikalisierung im "Unternehmen Barbarossa"* (Berlin, 2005).
Ashworth, Tony, *Trench Warfare 1914–1918: The Live and Let Live System* (London, 1980).
Atkinson, Rick, *An Army at Dawn: The War in North Africa, 1942–1943* (New York, 2002).
Bajohr, Frank and Michael Wildt (eds.), *Volksgemeinschaft: Neue Forschungen zur Gesellschaft des Nationalsozialismus* (Frankfurt am Main, 2009).
Baranowski, Shelley, *The Sanctity of Rural Life: Nobility, Protestantism, and Nazism in Weimar Prussia* (Oxford, 1995).
Barr, Niall, *Pendulum of War: The Three Battles of El Alamein* (London, 2005).

Bartov, Omer, "Brutalität und Mentalität: Zum Verhalten deutscher Soldaten an der 'Ostfront'," in Rürup and Jahn (eds.), *Erobern und Vernichten*, pp. 183–97.
  The Eastern Front 1941–1945: German Troops and the Barbarization of Warfare (London, 1985).
  "German Soldiers and the Holocaust," in Bartov (ed.), *The Holocaust: Origins, Implementation, Aftermath*, pp. 162–84.
  Hitler's Army: Soldiers, Nazis and War in the Third Reich (Oxford, 1992).
  (ed.), *The Holocaust: Origins, Implementation, Aftermath* (London, 2000).
  "The Missing Years: German Workers, German Soldiers," in Crew (ed.), *Nazism and German Society, 1933–1945*, pp. 42–66.
  "The Wehrmacht Exhibition Controversy: The Politics of Evidence," in Bartov, Grossman, and Nolan (eds.), *Crimes of War*, pp. 41–60.
  "Whose History Is It, Anyway? The Wehrmacht and German Historiography," in Heer and Nauman (eds.), *Vernichtungskrieg: Crimes of the Wehrmacht*, pp. 400–16.
Bartov, Omer, Atina Grossman, and Mary Nolan (eds.), *Crimes of War: Guilt and Denial in the Twentieth Century* (New York, 2002).
Bartusevičius, Vincas, Joachim Tauber, and Wolfram Wette (eds.), *Holocaust in Litauen: Krieg, Judenmorde und Kollaboration im Jahre 1941* (Cologne, 2003).
Baumgart, Winfried, *Deutsche Ostpolitik 1918: Von Brest-Litowsk bis zum Ende des Ersten Weltkrieges* (Munich, 1966).
Beck, Earl, *Under the Bombs: The German Home Front, 1942–1945* (Lexington, 1999).
Becker, Frank et al. (eds.), *Politische Gewalt in der Moderne: Festschrift für Hans-Ulrich Thamer* (Münster, 2003).
Becker, Peter W., "Fritz Sauckel: Plenipotentiary for the Mobilization of Labor," in Smelser and Zitelmann (eds.), *The Nazi Elite*, pp. 194–201.
Beevor, Antony, *Stalingrad: The Fateful Siege* (New York, 1998).
Berghahn, Volker, "NSDAP und 'Geistige Führung der Wehrmacht'," *Vierteljahresheft für Zeitgeschichte* (17) 1969, pp. 17–71.
Berkhoff, Karel Cornelius, *Harvest of Despair: Life and Death in Ukraine under Nazi Rule* (Cambridge, MA, 2004).
Bessel, Richard (ed.), *Fascist Italy and Nazi Germany: Comparisons and Contrasts* (Cambridge, 1996).
  Political Violence and the Rise of Nazism: The Storm Troopers in Eastern Germany, 1925–1934 (New Haven and London, 1984).
Blackbourn, David and James Retallack (eds.), *Localism, Landscape and the Ambiguities of Place: German-Speaking Central Europe, 1860–1930* (Toronto, 2007).
Blank, Ralf, "Kriegsalltag und Luftkrieg an der 'Heimatfront'," in Echternkamp (ed.), *Die deutsche Kriegsgesellschaft 1939 bis 1945: Politisierung, Vernichtung, Überleben*, pp. 357–461.
Böhler, Jochen, *Auftakt zum Vernichtungskrieg: Die Wehrmacht in Polen 1939* (Frankfurt am Main, 2006).
Boog, Horst, "The Strategic Air War in Europe and Air Defence of the Reich, 1943–1944," in Boog et al., *The Strategic Air War in Europe and the War in the West and East Asia 1943–1944/5*, pp. 9–458.

Boog, Horst et al., *Das Deutsche Reich und der Zweite Weltkrieg*, vol. IV, *Der Angriff auf die Sowjetunion* (Frankfurt am Main, 1991).
Germany and the Second World War, vol. VI, *The Global War: Widening of the Conflict and the Shift of the Initiative 1941–1943* (Oxford, 2001).
Germany and the Second World War, vol. VII, *The Strategic Air War in Europe and the War in the West and East Asia 1943–1944/5* (Oxford, 2006).
Brandon, Ray and Wendy Lower (eds.), *The Shoah in Ukraine* (Bloomington, 2008).
Brosatz, Martin and Elke Fröhlich (eds.), *Bayern in der NS-Zeit*, vols. I–VI (Munich, 1977–83).
Browning, Christopher, *Ordinary Men: Reserve Police Battalion 101 and the Final Solution in Poland* (New York, 1992).
Browning, Christopher and Jürgen Matthäus, *The Origins of the Final Solution: The Evolution of Nazi Jewish Policy, 1939–1942* (Lincoln, NE, 2004).
Bucheim, Hans et al., *Anatomy of the SS State* (New York, 1968).
Bücheler, Heinrich, *Hoepner: Ein deutsches Soldatenschicksal des Zwanzigsten Jahrhunderts* (Herford, 1980).
Bucholz, Arden, *Moltke, Schlieffen, and Prussian War Planning* (Providence, 1993).
Burleigh, Michael, *The Third Reich: A New History* (New York: 2000).
Burleigh, Michael and Wolfgang Wippermann, *The Racial State: Germany 1933–1945* (Cambridge, 1991).
Cecil, Robert, *Hitler's Decision to Invade Russia 1941* (London, 1975).
Chiari, Bernhard, *Alltag hinter der Front: Besatzung, Kollaboration und Widerstand in Weißrussland 1941–1944* (Düsseldorf, 1998).
  "Grenzen deutscher Herrschaft: Voraussetzungen und Folgen der Besatzung in der Sowjetunion," in Echternkamp (ed.), *Die deutsche Kriegsgesellschaft 1939 bis 1945: Ausbeutung, Deutungen, Ausgrenzung*, pp. 877–976.
  "Zwischen Hoffnung und Hunger: Die sowjetischer Zivilbevölkerung unter deutscher Besatzung," in Hartmann, Hürter, and Jureit (eds.), *Verbrechen der Wehrmacht: Bilanz einer Debatte*, pp. 145–54.
Chickering, Roger, *Imperial Germany and the Great War, 1914–1918* (Cambridge, 1998).
Childers, Thomas, *The Nazi Voter: The Social Foundations of Fascism in Germany, 1919–1933* (Chapel Hill, 1983).
Citino, Robert M., *The German Way of War: From the Thirty Years' War to the Third Reich* (Lawrence, KS, 2005).
  Path to Blitzkrieg: Doctrine and Training in the German Army, 1920–39 (Boulder, 1999).
  The Wehrmacht Retreats: Fighting a Lost War, 1943 (Lawrence, KS, 2012).
Clark, Alan, *Barbarossa: The Russian–German Conflict 1941–1945* (New York, 1985).
Clark, Christopher, *Iron Kingdom: The Rise and Downfall of Prussia, 1600–1947* (Cambridge, MA, 2006).
Classen, Peter and Peter Scheibert (eds.), *Festschrift Percy Ernst Schramm*, vol. II (Wiesbaden, 1964).
Collingham, Lizzie, *The Taste of War: World War II and the Battle for Food* (New York, 2012).

Confino, Alon, *The Nation as Local Metaphor: Württemberg, Imperial Germany, and National Memory, 1871–1918* (Chapel Hill, 1997).
Cooper, Matthew, *The German Army, 1933–1945* (Chelsea, 1990).
Corum, James, *The Roots of Blitzkrieg: Hans von Seeckt and German Military Reform* (Lawrence, KS, 1994).
Craig, Gordon, *Germany, 1866–1945* (Oxford, 1978).
Creuzberger, Stefan et al. (eds.), *St. Petersburg – Leningrad – St. Petersburg: Eine Stadt im Spiegel der Zeit* (Munich, 2000).
Crew, David F. (ed.), *Nazism and German Society, 1933–1945* (London, 1994).
de Goure, Leon, *The Siege of Leningrad* (Stanford, 1962).
Deist, Wilhelm, "The Rearmament of the Wehrmacht," in Deist et al., *Germany and the Second World War*, vol. I, *The Build-Up of German Aggression*, pp. 373–540.
 et al., *Germany and the Second World War*, vol. I, *The Build-Up of German Aggression* (Oxford, 1990).
Demps, Laurenz, "Die Provinz Brandenburg in der NS-Zeit (1933 bis 1945)," in Materna and Ribbe (eds.) *Brandenburgische Geschichte*, pp. 619–76.
Diamond, Hanna, *Fleeing Hitler: France 1940* (Oxford, 2007).
Dieckmann, Christoph, *Deutsche Besaztungspolitik in Litauen, 1941–1944* (Göttingen, 2011).
 "Deutsche und litauische Interessen: Grundlinien der Besatzungspolitik in Litauen 1941 bis 1944," in Bartusevičius, Tauber, and Wette (eds.), *Holocaust in Litauen: Krieg, Judenmorde und Kollaboration im Jahre 1941*, pp. 63–76.
Dieckmann, Christoph, Babette Quinkert, and Tatjana Tönsmeyer (eds.), *Kooperation und Verbrechen: Formen der "Kollaboration" im östlichen Europa 1939–1945* (Göttingen, 2003).
DiNardo, R.L., *Mechanized Juggernaut or Military Anachronism? Horses and the German Army of World War II* (Westport, CT, 1991).
Division Tradition Group (ed.), *Geschichte der 121. Ostpreussische Infanterie-Division 1940–1945* (Münster, Frankfurt am Main, and Berlin, 1970).
Doubler, Michael, *Closing with the Enemy: How GIs Fought the War in Europe, 1944–1945* (Lawrence, KS, 1994).
Dreetz, Dieter, Klaus Gessner, and Heinz Sperling, *Bewaffnete Kämpfe in Deutschland, 1918–1923* (Berlin, 1988).
Dunn, Walter S., Jr., *Hitler's Nemesis: The Red Army, 1930–1945* (London, 1994).
Düwell, Kurt and Wolfgang Kölmann (eds.), *Rheinland-Westfalen im Industriezeitalter*, vol. II, *Von der Reichsgründung bis zur Weimarer Republik* (Wuppertal, 1984).
 (eds.), *Rheinland-Westfalen im Industriezeitalter*, vol. III, *Vom Ende der Weimarer Republik bis zum Land Nordrhein-Westfalen* (Wuppertal, 1984).
Dwyer, Philip G. (ed.,) *Modern Prussian History, 1830–1947* (Harlow, 2001).
Echternkamp, Jörg (ed.), *Das Deutsche Reich und der Zweite Weltkrieg*, vol. IX/I, *Die deutsche Kriegsgesellschaft 1939 bis 1945: Politisierung, Vernichtung, Überleben* (Munich, 2004).
 (ed.), *Das Deutsche Reich und der Zweite Weltkrieg*, vol. IX/II, *Die deutsche Kriegsgesellschaft 1939 bis 1945: Ausbeutung, Deutungen, Ausgrenzung* (Munich, 2005).

"Im Kampf an der inneren und äußeren Front: Grundzüge der deutschen Gesellschaft im Zweiten Weltkrieg," in Echternkamp (ed.) *Die deutsche Kriegsgesellschaft 1939 bis 1945: Politisierung, Vernichtung, Überleben*, pp. 1–76.

Edele, Mark and Michael Geyer, "States of Exception: The Nazi–Soviet War as a System of Violence, 1939–1945," in Geyer and Fitzpatrick (eds.), *Beyond Totalitarianism: Stalinism and Nazism Compared*, pp. 345–95.

Ehlert, Hans, Michael Epkenhans, and Gerhard P. Groß, *Der Schlieffenplan: Analysen und Dokumenten* (Paderborn, 2006).

Ekstein, Modris, *Rites of Spring: The Great War and the Birth of the Modern Age* (New York, 1989).

Erickson, John, *The Road to Berlin* (London, 1998).

The Road to Stalingrad (London, 1998).

Evans, Richard, *The Coming of the Third Reich* (New York, 2004).

The Third Reich at War (New York, 2009).

Farrell, Kevin W., "'Culture of Confidence': The Tactical Excellence of the German Army of the Second World War," in Kolenda (ed.), *Leadership: The Warrior's Art*, pp. 177–203.

Fischer, Conan, *The Ruhr Crisis, 1923–1924* (Oxford, 2003).

Förster, Jürgen, "Geistige Kriegsführung in Deutschland 1919 bis 1945," in Echternkamp, *Die deutsche Kriegsgesellschaft 1939 bis 1945: Politisierung, Vernichtung, Überleben*, pp. 469–640.

"Hitlers Entscheidung für den Krieg gegen die Sowjetunion," in Boog et al., *Der Angriff auf die Sowjetunion*, pp. 27–68.

"Motivation and Indoctrination in the Wehrmacht, 1933–1945," in Addison and Calder (eds.), *Time to Kill*, pp. 263–73.

"Die Sicherung des 'Lebensraumes'," in Boog et al., *Der Angriff auf die Sowjetunion*, pp. 1227–87.

"Das Unternehmen 'Barbarossa' als Eroberungs- und Vernichtungskrieg," in Boog et al., *Der Angriff auf die Sowjetunion*, pp. 498–538.

"Verbrecherische Befehle," in Wette and Ueberschär (eds.), *Kriegsverbrechern im 20. Jahrhundert*, pp. 137–51.

"Die Weltanschauliche Erziehung in der Waffen-SS," in Matthäus et al., *Ausbildungsziel Judenmord?*, pp. 87–113.

Frei, Norbert et al. (eds.), *Ausbeutung, Vernichtung, Öffentlichkeit: Neuen Studien zur nationalsozialistischen Lagerpolitik* (Munich, 2000).

Friedrich, Jörg, *The Fire: The Bombing of Germany, 1940–1945* (New York, 2006).

Frieser, Karl-Heinz, *The Blitzkrieg Legend: The 1940 Campaign in the West* (Annapolis, 2005).

(ed.), *Das Deutsche Reich und der Zweite Weltkrieg*, vol. VIII, *Die Ostfront 1943/44: Der Krieg im Osten und an den Nebenfronten* (Stuttgart, 2007).

"Der Ruckschlag des Pendels," in Frieser (ed.), *Die Ostfront*, pp. 277–490.

"Die Schlacht im Kursker Bogen," in Frieser (ed.), *Die Ostfront*, pp. 83–208.

Fritz, Stephen, *Hitler's Frontsoldaten* (Lexington, 1996).

Ostkrieg: Hitler's War of Annihilation in the East (Lexington, 2011).

Fritzsche, Peter, *Life and Death in the Third Reich* (Cambridge, MA, 2009).

Ganzenmüller, Jörg, *Das belagerte Leningrad 1941–1944: Die Stadt in den Strategien von Angreifern und Verteidigern* (Paderborn, 2005).

"... die Stadt dem Erdboden gleichmachen": Zielsetzung und Motive der deutschen Blockade Leningrads," in Creuzberger et al., *St. Petersburg – Leningrad – St. Petersburg*, pp. 179–95.

Gay, Peter, *Weimar Culture: The Outsider as Insider* (New York, 2001).

"'Gegen Kritik immun.' Der Potsdamer Historiker Rolf-Dieter Müller über die Wehrmacht im Zweiten Weltkrieg und die Thesen des Hamburger Instituts für Sozialforschung," *Der Spiegel* (23) 1999, pp. 60–2.

Gellately, Robert, *Backing Hitler: Consent and Coercion in Nazi Germany* (Oxford, 2001).

Gentile, Carlo, *Wehrmacht, Waffen-SS und Polizei im Kampf gegen Partisanen und Zivilbevölkerung in Italien 1943–1945* (Paderborn, 2012).

Gerlach, Christian, " Extremely Violent Societies: An Alternative to the Concept of Genocide," *Journal of Genocide Research* (8, 4) 2006, pp. 455–71.

Kalkulierte Morde: Die deutsche Wirtschafts- und Vernichtungspolitik in Weißrussland, 1941–1944 (Hamburg, 1999).

Krieg, Ernährung, Völkermord: Forschungen zur deutschen Vernichtungspolitik im Zweiten Weltkrieg (Hamburg, 1998).

"'Militärische Versorgungszwänge', Besatzungspolitik und Massenverbrechen: Die Rolle des Generalquartiermeisters des Heeres und seiner Dienststellen im Krieg gegen die Sowjetunion," in Frei et al. (eds.), *Ausbeutung, Vernichtung, Öffentlichkeit*, pp. 175–208.

"Operative Planungen der Wehrmacht für den Krieg gegen die Sowjetunion und die deutsche Vernichtungspolitik," in Quinkert (ed.), *"Wir sind die Herren dieses Landes"*, pp. 55–63.

"Die Verantwortung der Wehrmachtführung: Vergleichende Betrachtungen am Beispiel der sowjetischen Kriegsgefangenen," in Hartmann, Hürter, and Jureit (eds.), *Verbrechen der Wehrmacht: Bilanz einer Debatte*, pp. 40–9.

"Verbrechen deutscher Fronttruppen in Weißrussland 1941–1944," in Pohl (ed.), *Wehrmacht und Vernichtungpolitik*, pp. 89–115.

Gerlach, Christian and Nicholas Werth, "State Violence – Violent Societies," in Geyer and Fitzpatrick (eds.), *Beyond Totalitarianism*, pp. 133–79.

Geßner, Klaus, *Geheime Feldpolizei: Zur Funktion und Organisation der faschistischen Wehrmacht* (East Berlin, 1986).

Geyer, Michael, *Aufrüstung oder Sicherheit: Die Reichswehr in der Krise der Machtpolitik, 1924–1936* (Wiesbaden, 1980).

"Civitella Della Chiana on 29 June 1944: The Reconstruction of a German 'Measure'," in Heer and Naumann (eds.), *War of Extermination*, pp. 175–216.

"German Strategy in the Age of Machine Warfare, 1914–1945," in Paret (ed.), *The Makers of Modern Strategy*, pp. 527–97.

"Restorative Elites, German Society and the Nazi Pursuit of War," in Bessel (ed.), *Fascist Italy and Nazi Germany*, pp. 134–64.

"The Stigma of Violence, Nationalism and War in Twentieth-Century Germany," *German Studies Review* (15) 1992, pp. 75–110.

"War, Genocide, Extermination: The War against the Jews in an Era of World Wars," in Jarausch and Geyer, *Shattered Past*, pp. 111–48.

Geyer, Michael and Sheila Fitzpatrick (eds.), *Beyond Totalitarianism: Stalinism and Nazism Compared* (Cambridge, 2009).

Gildea, Robert, *Marianne in Chains: Daily Life in the Heart of France during the German Occupation* (New York, 2003).
Gildea, Robert et al. (eds.), *Surviving Hitler and Mussolini: Daily Life in Occupied Europe* (New York, 2007).
Glantz, David, *Armageddon in Stalingrad: September–November 1942* (Lawrence, KS, 2009).
  The Battle for Leningrad 1941–1944 (Lawrence, KS, 2003).
  Colossus Reborn: The Red Army at War, 1941–1945 (Lawrence, KS, 2005).
  Stumbling Colossus: The Red Army on the Eve of the World War (Lawrence, KS, 1998).
  To the Gates of Stalingrad: Soviet–German Combat Operations, April–August 1942 (Lawrence, KS, 2009).
  Zhukov's Greatest Defeat: The Red Army's Disaster in Operation Mars, 1942 (Lawrence, KS, 1999).
Glantz, David and Jonathan House, *The Battle of Kursk* (Lawrence, KS, 1999).
  When Titans Clashed: How the Red Army Stopped Hitler (Lawrence, KS, 1995).
Golczewski, Frank, "Die Kollaboration in der Ukraine," in Dieckmann, Quinkert, and Tönsmeyer (eds.), *Kooperation und Verbrechen*, pp. 151–82.
Gorodetsky, Gabriel, *Grand Delusion: Stalin and the German Invasion of the Soviet Union* (New Haven, 1999).
Green, Abigail, *Fatherlands: State-Building and Nationhood in Nineteenth-Century Germany* (Cambridge, 2001).
Gregor, Neil, "A Schicksalsgemeinschaft? Allied Bombing, Civilian Morale, and Social Dissolution in Nuremberg, 1942–1945," *Historical Journal* (43) 2000, pp. 1051–70.
Grenkevich, Leonid D., *The Soviet Partisan Movement, 1941–1944: A Critical Historiographical Analysis* (London, 1999).
Grier, Howard D., *Hitler, Dönitz, and the Baltic Sea: The Third Reich's Last Hope, 1944–1945* (Annapolis, MD, 2007).
Groß, Gerhard P., "Das Dogma der Beweglichkeit: Überlegungen zur Genese der deutschen Heerestaktik im Zeitalter der Weltkriege," in Thoß and Volkmann (eds.), *Erster Weltkrieg, Zweiter Weltkrieg*, pp. 143–66.
Hamburger Institut für Sozialforschung (ed.), *Besucher einer Ausstellung* (Hamburg, 1998).
  (ed.), *The German Army and Genocide: Crimes against War Prisoners, Jews and Other Civilians, 1939–1944* (New York, 1999).
  (ed.), *Verbrechen der Wehrmacht: Dimensionen des Vernichtungskrieges 1941–1944* (Hamburg, 2002).
  (ed.), *Vernichtungskrieg: Verbrechen der Wehrmacht 1941–1944*, Austellungskatalog (Hamburg, 1996).
Hansen, Ernst Willi, Gerhard Schreiber, and Bernd Wegner (eds.), *Politischer Wandel, organisierte Gewalt und nationale Sicherheit: Beiträge zur neueren Geschichte Deutschlands und Frankreichs* (Munich, 1995).
Hartmann, Christian, "Massensterben oder Massenvernichtung? Sowjetische Kriegsgefangene im "Unternehmen Barbarossa." Aus dem Tagebuch eines Lagerkommandanten," *Vierteljahresheft für Zeitgeschichte* (49) 2001, pp. 97–158.

"Verbrecherisch Krieg – verbrecherische Wehrmacht? Überlegungen zur Struktur des deutschen Ostheeres 1941–1944," *Vierteljahreshefte für Zeitgeschichte* (52) 2004, pp. 1–75.
Wehrmacht im Ostkrieg: Front und militärisches Hinterland 1941/42 (Munich, 2009).
"Wie verbrecherisch war die Wehrmacht?", in Hartmann, Hürter, and Jureit (eds.), *Verbrechen der Wehrmacht*, pp. 69–79.
Hartmann, Christian, Johannes Hürter, and Ulrike Jureit (eds.), *Verbrechen der Wehrmacht: Bilanz einer Debatte* (Munich, 2005).
Hasenclever, Jörn, *Wehrmacht und Besatzungspolitik in der Sowjetunion: Die Befehlshaber der rückwärtigen Heeresgebiete, 1941–1943* (Paderborn, 2010).
Hass, Gerhart, "Deutsche Besatzungspolitik im Leningrader Gebiet 1941–1944," in Quinkert (ed.), *"Wir sind die Herren dieses Landes"*, pp. 66–81.
Hastings, Max, *Bomber Command* (London, 2010).
Haupt, Werner, *Heeresgruppe Nord, 1941–1945* (Bad Nauheim, 1967).
Heer, Hannes, *"Hitler war's": Die Befreiung der Deutschen von ihrer Vergangenheit* (Berlin, 2005).
"The Logic of the War of Extermination: The Wehrmacht and the Anti-Partisan War," in Heer and Naumann (eds.), *War of Extermination*, pp. 92–126.
Tote Zonen: Die deutsche Wehrmacht an der Ostfront (Hamburg, 1999).
"Verwischen der Spuren: Vernichtung der Erinnerung," in Heer, *Vom Verschwinden der Täter* (Berlin, 2004), pp. 67–104.
Vom Verschwinden der Täter: Der Vernichtungskrieg fand Statt, aber keiner war dabei (Berlin, 2004).
Heer, Hannes, Walter Manoschek, and Alexander Pollak (eds.), *Wie Geschichte gemacht ist: Zur Konstruktion von Erinnerungen an Wehrmacht und Zweiten Weltkrieg* (Vienna, 2003).
Heer, Hannes and Klaus Naumann (eds.), *Vernichtungskrieg: Verbrechen der Wehrmacht, 1941–1944* (Hamburg, 1995).
(eds.), *War of Extermination: The German Military in World War II 1941–1944* (New York, 2000).
Heiber, Helmut and David Glantz (eds.), *Hitler and His Generals: Military Conferences, 1942–1945* (New York, 2003).
Heilbronner, Oded, *Catholicism, Political Culture, and the Countryside: A Social History of the Nazi Party in South Germany* (Ann Arbor, 1998).
Herbert, Ulrich, *Hitler's Foreign Workers: Enforced Foreign Labor in Germany under the Third Reich* (Cambridge, 1997).
"Zur Entwicklung der Ruhrarbeiterschaft 1930 bis 1960 aus erfahrungsgeschichtlicher Perspektive," in Niethammer and Plato (eds.), *"Wir kriegen jetzt andere Zeiten"*, pp. 19–52.
"Zwangsarbeit in Deutschland: Sowjetische Zivilarbeiter und Kriegsgefangene 1941–1945," in Rürup and Jahn (eds.), *Erobern und Vernichten*, pp. 106–31.
Herwig, Holger, *The First World War: Germany and Austria–Hungary, 1914–1918* (New York, 1997).

The Marne 1914: The Opening of World War I and the Battle That Changed the World (New York, 2009).
"Strategic Uncertainties of a Nation-State: Prussia–Germany, 1871–1918," in Murray et al. (eds.), *The Making of Strategy*, pp. 242–77.
Herzog, Dagmar (ed.), *Brutality and Desire: War and Sexuality in Europe's Twentieth Century* (Basingstoke, 2009).
Hill, Alexander, *The War behind the Eastern Front: The Soviet Partisan Movement in North-West Russia 1941–44* (London, 2005).
Hillgruber, Andreas, *Hitlers Strategie: Politik und Kriegsführung 1940–1941*, 3rd edn (Bonn, 1993).
"'Nordlicht': Die deutschen Pläne zur Eroberung Leningrads im Jahre 1942," in Classen and Scheibert (eds.), *Festschrift Percy Ernst Schramm*, pp. 269–87.
"Das Russland-Bild der führenden deutschen Militärs vor Beginn des Angriffs auf die Sowjetunion," in Hillgruber, *Die Zerstörung Europas*, pp. 256–71.
Die Zerstörung Europas: Beiträge zur Weltkriegsepoche 1914 bis 1945 (Frankfurt am Main and Berlin, 1988).
Hirschfeld, Gerhard, *Nazi Rule and Dutch Collaboration: The Netherlands under German Occupation* (New York, 1992).
Hirschfeld, Gerhard and Tobias Jersak (eds.), *Karrieren im Nationalsozialismus: Funktionseliten zwischen Mitwirkung und Distanz* (Frankfurt am Main, 2004).
Horne, John and Alan Kramer, *German Atrocities 1914: A History of Denial* (New Haven, 2001).
Housden, Martin, *Hans Frank, Lebensraum and the Holocaust* (Basingstoke, 2003).
Howard, Michael, *The Franco-Prussian War* (New York, 1991).
Hull, Isabel, *Absolute Destruction: Military Culture and the Practices of War in Imperial Germany* (Ithaca, 2005).
Hürter, Johannes, *Hitlers Heerführer: Die deutschen Oberbefehlshaber im Krieg gegen die Sowjetunion 1941/42* (Munich, 2006).
"Konservative Mentalität, militärischer Pragmatismus, ideologisierte Kriegsführung: Das Beispiel des Generals Georg von Küchler," in Hirschfeld and Jersak (eds.), *Karrieren im Nationalsozialismus*, pp. 239–53.
"Die Wehrmacht vor Leningrad: Krieg und Besatzungspolitik der 18. Armee im Herbst und Winter 1941/42," *Vierteljahrshefte für Zeitgeschichte* (49) 2001, pp. 377–440.
Jäckel, Eberhard, *Hitler's World View: A Blueprint for Power* (Cambridge, MA, 1981).
Jackson, Julian, *France: The Dark Years, 1940–1944* (Oxford, 2001).
Jacobson, Hans-Adolf, "The Commissar Order and the Mass Execution of Soviet Prisoners of War," in Bucheim et al., *Anatomy of the SS State*, pp. 163–283.
(ed.), *Deutsch–russische Zeitenwende: Krieg und Frieden 1941–1945* (Baden-Baden, 1995).
Jahn, Peter (ed.), *Blockade Leningrads – Blockada Leningrada* (Berlin, 2004).
"Russenfurcht und Antibolschwismus: Zur Entstehung und Wirkung von Feindbildern," in Rürup and Jahn (eds.), *Erobern und Vernichten*, pp. 47–77.
Jarausch, Konrad and Michael Geyer, *Shattered Past: Reconstructing German Histories* (Princeton, 2003).

Jelavich, Peter, *Berlin Alexanderplatz: Radio, Film, and the Death of Weimar Culture* (Berkeley, 2009).
  Berlin Cabaret (Cambridge, MA, 1996).
Jüngerkes, Sven, *Deutsche Besatzungsverwaltung in Lettland 1941–1945: Eine Kommunikations- und Kulturgeschichte nationalsozialistischer Organisationen* (Constance, 2010).
Kaiser, Wolf (ed.), *Täter in Vernichtungskrieg: Der Überfall auf die Sowjetunion und der Völkermord an den Juden* (Berlin and Munich, 2002).
Karner, Stefan and Wolfram Dornik (eds.), *Die Besatzung der Ukraine 1918: Historischer Kontext – Forschungsstand – wirtschaftliche und soziale Folgen* (Graz, 2008).
Kassimeris, George (ed.), *The Barbarization of Warfare* (New York, 2006).
Kay, Alex J., *Exploitation, Resettlement, Mass Murder: Political and Economic Planning for German Occupation Policy in the Soviet Union, 1940–1941* (New York, 2006).
  "Germany's Staatssekretäre, Mass Starvation and the Meeting of 2 May 1941," *Journal of Contemporary History* (41) 2006, pp. 685–700.
Kay, Alex J., Jeff Rutherford, and David Stahel (eds.), *Nazi Policy on the Eastern Front, 1941: Total War, Genocide and Radicalization* (Rochester, 2012).
Kehrig, Manfred, *Stalingrad: Analyse und Dokumentation einer Schlacht* (Stuttgart, 1974).
Kershaw, Ian, *Fateful Choices: Ten Decisions That Changed the World, 1940–1941* (New York, 2007).
  Hitler, 1936–1945: Nemesis (New York, 2000).
  The Nazi Dictatorship: Problems and Perspectives of Interpretation, 4th edn (New York, 2000).
  Popular Opinion and Political Dissent in the Third Reich (Oxford, 1991).
Kilian, Jürgen, *Wehrmacht und Besatzungsherrschaft im russischen Nordwesten 1941–1944: Praxis und Alltag im Militärverwaltungsgebiet der Heeresgruppe Nord* (Paderborn, 2012).
Kitchen, Martin, *The German Officer Corps, 1890–1914* (Oxford, 1968).
Kleinfeld, Gerald R. and Lewis A. Tambs, *Hitler's Spanish Legion: The Blue Division in Russia* (Carbondale, 1979).
Klink, Ernst, "Die Landkriegführung," in Boog et al., *Der Angriff auf die Sowjetunion*, pp. 246–328.
  "Die Operationsführung," in Boog et al., *Der Angriff auf die Sowjetunion*, pp. 451–652.
Knox, MacGregor, *Common Destiny: Dictatorship, Foreign Policy, and War in Fascist Italy and Nazi Germany* (Cambridge, 2000).
  "Reading the Wehrmacht's Mind?" *Sehepunkt* (12) 2012, available at www.sehepunkte.de/2012/03/19936.html.
Koch, Magnus, *Fahnenfluchten: Deserteure der Wehrmacht im Zweiten Weltkrieg. Lebenswege und Entscheidungen* (Paderborn, 2008).
Kohl, Paul, *Der Krieg der deutschen Wehrmacht und der Polizei 1941–1944: Sowjetische überlebende Berichten* (Frankfurt am Main, 1998).
Kolenda, Christopher (ed.), *Leadership: The Warrior's Art* (Mechanicsburg, 2001).

Koonz, Claudia, *The Nazi Conscience* (Cambridge, MA, 2005).
Kossert, Andreas, *Ostpreussen: Geschichte und Mythos* (Munich, 2005).
Krausnick, Helmut, *Hitlers Einsatzgruppen: Die Truppe des Weltanschauungskrieges 1938–1942* (Stuttgart, 1985).
"Kommissarbefehl und 'Gerichtsbarkeiterlass Barbarossa' in neuer Sicht," *Vierteljahrshefte für Zeitgeschichte* (25) 1977, pp. 684–737.
Krausnick, Helmut and Hans-Heinrich Wilhelm, *Die Truppe des Weltanschauungskrieges: Die Einsatzgruppen der Sicherheitspolizei und des SD 1938–1942* (Stuttgart, 1981).
Kreutzmüller, Christoph, "Die Wirtschaft Berlins," in Wildt and Kreutzmüller (eds.), *Berlin 1933–1945*, pp. 83–95.
Kroener, Bernhard, "The Manpower Resources of the Third Reich in the Area of Conflict between Wehrmacht, Bureaucracy, and the War Economy, 1939–1942," in Kroener et al., *Organization and Mobilization of the German Sphere of Power*, pp. 789–1154.
"'Menschenbewirtschaftung,' Bevölkerungsverteilung und personelle Rüstung in der zweiten Kriegshälfte (1942–1944)," in Kroener et al., *Organisation und Mobilisierung des deutschen Machtbereichs*, pp. 777–1001.
Kroener, Bernhard et al., *Das Deutsche Reich und der Zweite Weltkrieg*, vol. V/II, *Organisation und Mobilisierung des deutschen Machtbereichs* (Stuttgart, 1999).
Germany and the Second World War, vol. V/I, *Organization and Mobilization of the German Sphere of Power* (Oxford, 2000).
Kronenbitter, Günter, Markus Pöhlmann, and Dierk Walter (eds.), *Besatzung: Funktion und Gestalt militärischer Fremdherrschaft von der Antike bis zum 20. Jahrhundert* (Paderborn, 2006).
Kühne, Thomas, "Der nationalsozialistische Vernichtungskrieg im kulterellen Kontinuum des Zwanzigsten Jahrhunderts: Forschungsprobleme und Forschungstendenzen der Gesellschaftsgeschichte des Zweiten Weltkrieges, Part II," *Archiv für Sozialgeschichte* (40) 2000, pp. 440–86.
"Der nationalsozialistischen Vernichtungskrieg und die 'ganz normalen' Deutschen: Forschungsprobleme und Forschungstendenzen der Gesellschaftsgeschichte des Zweiten Weltkrieges, Part I," *Archiv für Sozialgeschichte* (39) 1999, pp. 580–662.
Kunz, Norbert, "Das Beispiel Charkow: Eine Stadtbevölkerung als Opfer der deutschen Hungerstrategie 1941/1942," in Hartmann, Hürter, and Jureit (eds.), *Verbrechen der Wehrmacht: Bilanz einer Debatte*, pp. 136–44.
Latzel, Klaus, *Deutsche Soldaten – nationalsozialistischer Krieg? Kriegserlebnis – Kriegserfahrung 1939–1945* (Paderborn, 1998).
"Feldpostbriefe: Überlegungen zur Aussagekraft einer Quelle," in Hartmann, Hürter, and Jureit (eds.), *Verbrechen der Wehrmacht: Bilanz einer Debatte*, pp. 171–81.
Laub, Thomas, *After the Fall: German Policy in Occupied France, 1940–1944* (Oxford, 2008).
Leach, Barry, *German Strategy against Russia, 1939–1941* (Oxford, 1973).
Leetz, Antje and Barbara Wenner (eds.), *Blockade: Leningrad 1941–1944. Dokumente und Essays von Russen und Deutschen* (Reinbek, 1992).

Lehmann, Sebastian, Robert Bohn, and Uwe Danker (eds.), *Reichskommissariat Ostland: Tatort und Erinnerungsobjekt* (Paderborn, 2012).
Lehnstaedt, Stephan, *Okkupation im Osten: Besatzeralltag in Warschau und Minsk, 1939–1944* (Munich, 2010).
Lieb, Peter, "Aufstandsbekämpfung in strategischen Dilemma: Die deutsche Besatzung in der Ukraine 1918," in Dornik and Karner (eds.), *Die Besatzung der Ukraine*, pp. 111–39.
  Konventioneller Krieg oder NS-Weltanschauungskrieg? Kriegführung und Partisanenbekämpfung in Frankreich 1943/44 (Munich, 2007).
Lieberman, Benjamin, *Terrible Fate: Ethnic Cleansing in the Making of Modern Europe* (Chicago, 2006).
Liulevicius, Gabriel, *War Land on the Eastern Front: Culture, National Identity and German Occupation in World War I* (Cambridge, 2000).
Lohse, Gerhart, *Geschichte der rheinisch-westfälischen 126 Infanterie-Division* (Bad Nauheim, 1957).
"The Long Nineteenth Century," *German History* (26) 2008, pp. 72–91.
Lower, Wendy, *Nazi Empire-Building and the Holocaust in Ukraine* (Chapel Hill, 2005).
Lübbers, Gert C., "Die 6. Armee und die Zivilbevölkerung von Stalingrad," *Vierteljahreshefte für Zeitgeschichte* (1) 2006, pp. 87–123.
Lüdtke, Alf, "The Appeal of Exterminating 'Others': German Workers and the Limits of Resistance," *Journal of Modern History* (64) 1992, pp. 46–67.
  "'Fehlgreifen in der Wahl der Mittel': Optionen im Alltag militärischen Handeln," *Mittelweg* (36) 2003, pp. 61–75.
Lukas, Richard, *Forgotten Holocaust: The Poles under German Occupation, 1939–1944* (New York, 1997).
Maier, Klaus et al., *Germany and the Second World War*, vol. II, *Germany's Initial Conquests in Europe* (Oxford, 2000).
Mallmann, Klaus-Michael and Bogdan Musial (eds.), *Genesis des Genozids: Polen 1939–1941* (Darmstadt, 2004).
Mann, Michael, *The Dark Side of Democracy: Explaining Ethnic Cleansing* (Cambridge, 2005).
Manoschek, Walther, "'Coming Along to Shoot Some Jews?' The Destruction of the Jews in Serbia," in Heer and Naumann (eds.), *War of Extermination*, pp. 39–52.
  "Der Holocaust in Feldpostbriefen von Wehrmachtsangehörigen," in Heer, Manoschek, and Pollak (eds.), *Wie Geschichte gemacht ist*, pp. 35–58.
  "Partisanenkrieg und Genozid: Die Wehrmacht in Serbien 1941," in Manoschek (ed.), *Die Wehrmacht im Rassenkrieg*, pp. 142–67.
  "Serbien ist Judenfrei!" Militärische Besatzungspolitik und Judenvernichtung in Serbien, 2nd edn (Munich, 1995).
  (ed.) *Die Wehrmacht im Rassenkrieg: Die Vernichtungskrieg hinter der Front* (Vienna, 1996).
Mansoor, Peter, *The GI Offensive in Europe: The Triumph of American Infantry Divisions, 1941–1945* (Lawrence, KS, 1999).
Massie, Suzanne, *Pavlovsk: The Life of a Russian Palace* (Boston, 1990).

Materna, Ingo, "Brandenburg als preußische Provinz in der Weimar Republik (1918 bis 1933)," in Materna and Ribbe (eds.) *Brandenburgische Geschichte*, pp. 561–618.
Materna, Ingo and Wolfgang Ribbe (eds.), *Brandenburgische Geschichte* (Berlin, 1995).
Matthäus, Jürgen, "Kaunas 1941–1944," in Ueberschär (ed.), *Orte des Grauens*, pp. 83–91.
Matthäus, Jürgen et al., *Ausbildungsziel Judenmord? "Weltanschauliche Erziehung" von SS, Polizei und Waffen-SS im Rahmen der "Endlösung"* (Frankfurt am Main, 2003).
Mawdsley, Evan, *Thunder in the East: The Nazi–Soviet War, 1941–1945* (New York, 2005).
Mazower, Mark, *Hitler's Empire: How the Nazis Ruled Europe* (New York, 2008).
  Inside Hitler's Greece: The Experience of Occupation, 1941–1944 (New Haven, 1993).
  "Military Violence and the National Socialist Consensus: The Wehrmacht in Greece, 1941–1944," in Heer and Naumann (eds.), *War of Extermination*, pp. 146–74.
Megargee, Geoffrey, *Inside Hitler's High Command* (Lawrence, KS, 2000).
  War of Annihilation: Combat and Genocide on the Eastern Front, 1941 (New York, 2006).
Merridal, Catherine, *Ivan's War: Life and Death in the Red Army, 1939–1945* (New York, 2006).
Messerschmidt, Manfred, "Völkerrecht und 'Kriegsnotwendigkeit' in der deutschen militärischen Tradition," in Messerschmidt (ed.), *Was damals Recht war*, pp. 190–229.
  (ed.), *Was damals Recht war ... NS- Militär- und Strafjustiz im Vernichtungskrieg* (Essen, 1996).
  "Die Wehrmacht als tragende Säule des NS-Staates (1933–1939)," in Manoschek (ed.), *Die Wehrmacht im Rassenkrieg*, pp. 39–54.
  Die Wehrmacht im NS-Staat: Zeit der Indoktrination (Hamburg, 1969).
Moeller, Robert, *German Peasants and Agrarian Politics, 1914–1924: The Rhineland and Westphalia* (Chapel Hill, 1986).
Möller, Horst, "Preußen von 1918 bis 1947: Weimarer Republik, Preußen und der Nationalsozialismus," in Neugebauer (ed.), *Vom Kaiserreich zum 20. Jahrhundert*, pp. 149–316.
Mommsen, Hans, *The Rise and Fall of Weimar Democracy* (Chapel Hill, 1996).
Moore, Bob, "The Netherlands," in Noakes (ed.), *The Civilian in War*, pp. 126–49.
Mueller-Hillebrand, Burkhart, *Das Heer, 1933–1945: Entwicklung des organisatorischen Aufbaues*, vol. II, *Die Blitzfeldzüge 1939–1941: Das Heer im Kriege bis zum Beginn des Feldzuges gegen die Sowjetunion im Juni 1941* (Frankfurt am Main, 1956).
  Das Heer, 1933–1945: Entwicklung des organisatorischen Aufbaues, vol. III, *Der Zweifrontenkrieg: Das Heer vom Beginn des Feldzuges gegen die Sowjetunion bis zum Kriegsend* (Frankfurt am Main, 1969).
Mühlhäuser, Regina, "Between 'Racial Awareness' and Fantasies of Potency: Nazi Sexual Politics in the Occupied Territories of the Soviet Union, 1942–1945," in Herzog (ed.), *Brutality and Desire*, pp. 197–220.

Eroberungen: Sexuelle Gewalttaten und intime Beziehungen deutscher Soldaten in der Sowjetunion 1941–1945 (Hamburg, 2010).
Müller, Klaus-Jürgen, *The Army, Politics and Society in Germany, 1933–1945* (Manchester, 1987).
Das Heer und Hitler: Armee und nationalsozialistisches Regime 1933–1940 (Stuttgart, 1969).
Müller, Rolf-Dieter, *Der letzte deutsche Krieg* (Stuttgart, 2005).
"Liebe im Vernichtungskrieg: Geschlechtergeschichtlichtliche Aspekte des Einsatzes deutscher Soldaten im Rußlandkrieg 1941–1944," in Becker et al. (eds.), *Politische Gewalt in der Moderne*, pp. 239–67.
"Menschenjagd: Die Rekrutierung von Zwangsarbeitern in der besetzten Sowjetunion," in Heer and Naumann (eds.), *Vernichtungskrieg: Verbrechen der Wehrmacht, 1941–1944*, pp. 92–103.
"Das Scheitern der Wirtschaftlichen 'Blitzkriegstrategie'," in Boog et al., *Der Angriff auf die Sowjetunion*, pp. 1116–1226.
"Das 'Unternehmen Barbarossa' als wirtschaftlicher Raubkrieg," in Ueberschär and Wette (eds.), *Der deutsche Überfall auf die Sowjetunion 1941: "Unternehmen Barbarossa"*, pp. 173–96.
"Von der wirtschaftsallianz zum kolonialen Ausbeutungskrieg," in Boog et al., *Der Angriff auf die Sowjetunion*, pp. 141–245.
"Die Wehrmacht: Historische Last und Verantwortung. Die Historiographie im Spannungsfeld von Wissenschaft und Vergangenheitsbewältigung," in Müller and Volkmann (eds.), *Die Wehrmacht*, pp. 3–35.
Müller, Rolf-Dieter and Hans-Erich Volkmann (eds.), *Die Wehrmacht: Mythos und Realität* (Munich, 1999).
Mulligan, Timothy, *The Politics of Illusion and Empire: German Occupation Policy in the Soviet Union, 1942–1943* (New York, 1988).
Murray, Williamson, *The Change in the European Balance of Power* (Princeton, 1984).
(ed.), *German Military Effectiveness* (Baltimore, 1992).
"German Response to Victory in Poland. A Case Study in Professionalism," in Murray (ed.), *German Military Effectiveness*, pp. 229–39.
Murray, Williamson et al. (eds.), *The Making of Strategy: Rulers, States and War* (Cambridge, 1996).
Neitzel, Sönke and Harald Welzer, *Soldaten: Protokolle von Kämpfen, Töten und Sterben* (Frankfurt am Main, 2011).
Neugebauer, Wolfgang (ed.), *Handbuch der Preussischen Geschichte*, vol. III, *Vom Kaiserreich zum 20. Jahrhundert und Große Themen der Geschichte Preußens* (Berlin, 2001).
Niethammer, Lutz and Alexander von Plato (eds.), *"Wir kriegen jetzt andere Zeiten": Auf der Suche nach der Erfahrung des Volkes in nachfaschistischen Ländern*, vol. III, *Lebensgeschichte und Sozialkultur im Ruhrgebiet 1930 bis 1960* (Berlin and Bonn, 1985).
Noakes, Jeremy (ed.) *The Civilian in War: The Home Front in Europe, Japan and the USA in World War II* (Exeter, 1992).
"Germany," in Noakes (ed.), *The Civilian in War*, pp. 35–61.
Nolte, Ernst, *Der Faschismus in seiner Epoche* (Munich, 1963).
Nolzen, Armin, "Die NSDAP, der Krieg und die deutsche Gesellschaft," in Echternkamp (ed.), *Die deutsche Kriegsgesellschaft 1939 bis 1945: Politisierung, Vernichtung, Überleben*, pp. 99–193.

"'Verbrannte Erde': Der Rückzug der Wehrmacht aus den besetzten sowjetischen Gebieten, 1941/42–1944/45," in Kronenbitter, Pöhlmann, and Walter (eds.), *Besatzung*, pp. 161–75.

Oldenburg, Manfred, *Ideologie und militärisches Kalkül: Die Besatzungspolitik der Wehrmacht in der Sowjetunion 1942* (Cologne, Weimar, and Vienna, 2004).

Orlow, Dietrich, *Weimar Prussia, 1918–1925: The Unlikely Rock of Democracy* (Pittsburgh, 1986).

Overmans, Rüdiger, *Deutsche militärische Verluste im Zweiten Weltkrieg* (Munich, 1999).

Pabst, Klaus, "Der Vertrag von Versailles und der deutsche Westen," in Düwell and Kölmann (eds.), *Von der Reichsgründung bis zur Weimarer Republik*, pp. 271–90.

Paret, Peter (ed.), *The Makers of Modern Strategy: From Machiavelli to the Nuclear Age* (Princeton, 1986).

Pavlowitch, Stevan K., *Hitler's New Disorder: The Second World War in Yugoslavia* (New York, 2008).

Pennington, Reina, "Offensive Women: Women in Combat in the Red Army," in Addison and Calder (eds.) *Time to Kill*, pp. 249–62.

Peukert, Detlev, *Inside Nazi Germany: Conformity, Opposition and Racism in Everyday Life* (New Haven, 1987).

The Weimar Republic: The Crisis of Classical Modernity (New York, 1989).

Pine, Lisa, *Hitler's "National Community": Society and Culture in Nazi Germany* (New York, 2007).

Pohl, Dieter, *Die Herrschaft der Wehrmacht: Deutsche Militärbesatzung und einheimische Bevölkerung in der Sowjetunion 1941–1944* (Munich, 2008).

"The Murder of Ukraine's Jews under German Military Administration and in the Reich Commissariat Ukraine," in Brandon and Lower (eds.), *The Shoah in Ukraine*, pp. 23–76.

Pohl, Karl Heinrich (ed.), *Wehrmacht und Vernichtungpolitik: Militär im nationalsozialistischen Staat* (Göttingen, 1999).

Pomp, Rainer, "Brandenburgischer Landadel und die Weimarer Republik: Konflikte um Oppositionsstrategien und Elitenkonzepte" in Adamy and Hübener (eds.) *Adel und Staatsverwaltung in Brandenburg im 19. und 20. Jahrhundert*, pp. 185–218.

Primel, Kim C., "Sommer 1941: Die Wehrmacht in Litauen," in Bartusevičius, Tauber, and Wette (eds.), *Holocaust in Litauen*, pp. 26–39.

Quinkert, Babette, *Propaganda und Terror in Weißrussland 1941–1944: Die deutsche "geistige" Kriegführung gegen Zivilbevölkerung und Partisanen* (Paderborn, 2009).

(ed.), *"Wir sind die Herren dieses Landes": Ursachen, Verlauf und Folgen des deutschen Überfalls auf die Sowjetunion* (Hamburg, 2002).

Rass, Christoph, *"Menschenmaterial": Deutsche Soldaten an der Ostfront: Innenansichten einer Infanteriedivision 1939–1945* (Paderborn, 2003).

"Das Sozialprofil von Kampfverbänden des deutschen Heeres 1939 bis 1945," in Echternkamp, *Die deutsche Kriegsgesellschaft 1939 bis 1945: Politisierung, Vernichtung, Überleben*, pp. 641–741.

"Verbrecherisch Kriegführung an der Front: Eine Infanteriedivision und ihre Soldaten," in Hartmann, Hürter, and Jureit (eds.), *Verbrechen der Wehrmacht*, pp. 80–90.

Reese, Roger, *Stalin's Reluctant Soldiers: A Social History of the Red Army, 1925–1941* (Lawrence, KS, 1996).

Reid, Anna, *Leningrad: The Epic Siege of World War II, 1941–1944* (New York, 2011).

Rescheke, Oliver and Michael Wildt, "Aufstieg der NSDAP in Berlin," in Wildt and Kreutzmüller (eds.), *Berlin 1933–1945*, pp. 19–32.

Reuth, Ralf Georg, *Goebbels* (New York, 1993).

Richie, Alexandra, *Faust's Metropolis: A History of Berlin* (New York, 1998).

Richter, Timm C. (ed.), *Krieg und Verbrechen. Situation und Intention: Fallbeispiele* (Munich, 2006).

"Die Wehrmacht und der Partisankrieg in den besetzten Gebieten der Sowjetunion," in Müller and Volkmann (eds.), *Die Wehrmacht: Mythos und Realität* (Munich, 1999), pp. 837–57.

Röhr, Werner (ed.), *Okkupation und Kollaboration (1938–1945): Beiträge zu Konzepten und Praxis der Kollaboration in der deutschen Okkupationpolitik* (Berlin and Heidelberg, 1994).

Römer, Felix, *Der Kommissarbefehl: Wehrmacht und NS-Verbrechen an der Ostfront 1941/42* (Munich, 2008).

"Volksgemeinschaft in der Wehrmacht? Milieus, Mentalitäten und militärische Moral in den Streitkräften des NS-Staates," in Welzer, Neitzel and Gudehus (eds.), *"Der Führer war wieder viel zu human, viel zu gefühlvoll"*, pp. 55–94.

"The Wehrmacht in the War of Ideologies: The Army and Hitler's Criminal Orders on the Eastern Front," in Kay, Rutherford, and Stahel (eds.), *Nazi Policy on the Eastern Front, 1941*, pp. 73–100.

Rosenhaft, Eve, *Beating the Fascists? The German Communists and Political Violence 1929–1933* (Cambridge, 1983).

Rossino, Alexander B., *Hitler Strikes Poland: Blitzkrieg, Ideology, and Atrocity* (Lawrence, KS, 2003).

Rürup, Reinhard and Peter Jahn (eds.), *Erobern und Vernichten: Der Krieg gegen die Sowjetunion 1941–1945* (Berlin, 1991).

Rush, Robert Sterling, "A Different Perspective: Cohesion, Morale, and Operational Effectiveness in the German Army, Fall 1944," *Armed Forces & Society* (25) 1999, pp. 477–508.

Hell in Hürtgen Forest: The Ordeal and Triumph of an American Infantry Regiment (Lawrence, KS, 2001).

Rutherford, Jeff, "Life and Death in the Demiansk Pocket: The 123rd Infantry Division in Combat and Occupation" *Central European History* (41) 2008, pp. 347–80.

"'One senses danger from all sides, especially from fanatical civilians': The 121st Infantry Division and Partisan War, June 1941–April 1942," in Shepherd and Pattinson (eds.), *War in the Twilight World*, pp. 58–79.

"The Radicalization of German Occupation Policies: The Wirtschaftsstab Ost and the 121st Infantry Division in Pavlovsk, 1941," in Kay,

Rutherford, and Stahel (eds.), *Nazi Policy on the Eastern Front, 1941*, pp. 147–84.
Salisbury, Harrison, *The 900 Days: The Siege of Leningrad*, 2nd edn (New York, 1985).
Sammartino, Annemarie H., *The Impossible Border: Germany and the East, 1914–1922* (Ithaca, 2010).
Scheck, Raffael, *Hitler's African Victims: The German Army Massacres of Black French Soldiers in 1940* (Cambridge, 2008).
Schmider, Klaus, *Partisanenkrieg in Jugoslawien 1941–1944* (Berlin, 2002).
Schmiecken-Ackermann, Detlef, *Nationalsozialismus und Arbeitermilieus* (Bonn, 1998).
Schreiber, Gerhard, *Deutsche Kriegsverbrechen in Italien: Täter, Opfer, Strafverfolgung* (Munich, 1996).
Schröder, Hans Joachim, "Alltagsleben im Russlandkrieg 1941–1945: Eine deutsche Perspektive," in Jacobson (ed.), *Deutsch–russische Zeitenwende*, pp. 388–409.
  "German Soldiers' Experiences during the Initial Phase of the Russian Campaign," in Wegner (ed.), *From Peace to War*, pp. 309–24.
  Die gestohlene Jahre: Erzählgeschichten und Gesichtserzählung im Interview: Der Zweite Weltkrieg aus der Sicht ehemaliger Mannschaftsoldaten (Tübingen, 1991).
Schüler, Klaus A. F., "The Eastern Campaign as a Transportation and Supply Problem," in Wegner (ed.), *From Peace to War*, pp. 205–22.
  Logistik im Russlandfeldzug: Die Rolle der Eisenbahn bei Planung, Vorbereitung und Durchführung des deutschen Angriffs auf die Sowjetunion bis zur Krise vor Moskau im Winter 1941/42 (Frankfurt am Main, 1987).
Schulte, Bernd F., *Die deutsche Armee 1900–1914: Zwischen Beharren und Verändern* (Düsseldorf, 1977).
Schulte, Theo, *The German Army and Nazi Policies in Occupied Russia* (Oxford, 1989).
Schulze, Hagen, "Democratic Prussia in Weimar Germany, 1919–1933," in Dwyer (ed.) *Modern Prussian History*, pp. 211–29.
  Freikorps und Republik 1918–1920 (Boppard am Rhein, 1969).
Seaton, Albert, *The Russo-German War, 1941–1945* (Novato, 1993).
Sheehan, James, "What Is German History? Reflections on the Role of the Nation in German History and Historiography," *Journal of Modern History* (53) 1981, pp. 1–23.
Shepherd, Ben, *Terror in the Balkans: German Armies and Partisan Warfare* (Cambridge, MA, 2012).
  War in the Wild East: The German Army and Soviet Partisans (Cambridge, MA, 2004).
Shepherd, Ben and Juliette Pattinson (eds.), *War in the Twilight World: Partisan and Anti-partisan Warfare in Eastern Europe, 1939–45* (Basingstoke, 2010).
Shils, E.A. and Morris Janowitz, "Cohesion and Disintegration in the Wehrmacht in World War II," *POQ* (12) 1948, pp. 280–315.
Showalter, Dennis, "From Deterrence to Doomsday Machine: The German Way of War, 1890–1914," *Journal of Military History* (64) 2000, pp. 679–710.

Slepyan, Kenneth, *Stalin's Guerillas: Soviet Partisans in World War II* (Lawrence, KS, 2006).
Smelser, Ronald and Edward J. Davies II, *The Myth of the Eastern Front: The Nazi–Soviet War in American Popular Culture* (Cambridge, 2008).
Smelser, Ronald and Rainer Zitelmann (eds.), *The Nazi Elite* (New York, 1993).
Smith, Helmut Walser, *The Continuities of German History: Nation, Religion, and Race across the Long Nineteenth Century* (Cambridge, 2008).
Snyder, Jack, *The Ideology of the Offensive: Military Decision Making and the Disasters of 1914* (Ithaca, 1984).
Sorokina, Marina, "People and Procedures: Towards a History of the Investigation of Nazi Crimes in the USSR," *Kritika* (4) 2005, pp. 797–831.
Stahel, David, *Kiev 1941: Hitler's Battle for Supremacy in the East* (Cambridge, 2012).
  Operation Barbarossa and Germany's Defeat in the East (Cambridge, 2009).
  Operation Typhoon: Hitler's March on Moscow, October 1941 (Cambridge, 2013).
Stein, George H., *The Waffen SS: Hitler's Elite Guard at War* (Ithaca, 1994).
Steinberg, Heinz Günter, "Die Bevölkerungsentwicklung Nordrhein-Westfalens bis 1970," in Düwell and Kölmann (eds.), *Vom Ende der Weimarer Republik bis zum Land Nordrhein-Westfalen*, pp. 21–34.
Steinkamp, Peter, "Die Haltung der Hitlergegner Generalfeldmarschall Wilhelm Ritter von Leeb und Generaloberst Erich Hoepner zur verbrecherischen Kriegführung bei der Heeresgruppe Nord in der Sowjetunion 1941," in Ueberschär (ed.), *NS-Verbrechen und der militärische Widerstand gegen Hitler*, pp. 47–61.
Stephenson, Jill, *Hitler's Home Front: Württemberg under the Nazis* (London, 2006).
Stoneman, Mark R., "The Bavarian Army and French Civilians in the War of 1870–1871: A Cultural Interpretation," *War in History* (8) 2001, pp. 273–93.
Storz, Dieter, *Kriegsbild und Rüstung vor 1914: Europäische Landstreitkrafte vor dem Ersten Weltkrieg* (Hamburg, 1992).
Strachan, Hew, "Ausbildung, Kampfgeist und die zwei Weltkriege," in Thoß und Volkmann (eds.), *Erster Weltkrieg, Zweiter Weltkrieg*, pp. 265–86.
  "Time, Space and Barbarisation: The German Army and the Eastern Front in Two World Wars," in Kassimeris (ed.), *The Barbarization of Warfare*, pp. 58–82.
Streim, Alfred, *Die Behandlungen sowjetischer Kriegsgefangener im "Fall Barbarossa"* (Heidelberg, 1981).
Streit, Christian, *Keine Kameraden: Die Wehrmacht und die sowjetischen Kriegsgefangene 1941–1945* (Stuttgart, 1978).
Strohn, Matthias, *The German Army and the Defence of the Reich: Military Doctrine and the Conduct of the Defensive Battle 1918–1939* (Cambridge, 2011).
Sydnor, Charles, *Soldiers of Destruction: The SS Death's Head Division, 1933–1945* (Princeton, 1990).
Tauber, Joachim, "Vergangenheitsbewältigung in Litauen: Politik, Gesellschaft und der Holocaust nach 1945," in Lehmann, Bohn, and Danker (eds.), *Reichskommissariat Ostland*, pp. 331–48.

Tenfelde, Klaus, "Zur Sozialgeschichte der Arbeiterbewegung im Ruhrgebiet 1918 bis 1933," in Düwell and Kölmann (eds.), *Von der Reichsgründung bis zur Weimarer Republik*, pp. 333–48.

Tessin, Georg, *Verbände und Truppen der Deutschen Wehrmacht und Waffen SS 1939–1945*, vol. VI, *Die Landstreitkräfte 71–130* (Onasbrück, 1972).

Thiele, Hans-Günther (ed.), *Die Wehrmachtsausstellung: Dokumentation einer Kontroverse* (Bremen, 1997).

Thoß, Bruno and Hans-Erich Volkmann (eds.), *Erster Weltkrieg, Zweiter Weltkrieg: Ein Vergleich* (Paderborn, 2002).

Tooze, Adam, *The Wages of Destruction: The Making and Breaking of the German War Economy* (London, 2006).

Traba, Robert, *Ostpreußen – die Konstruktion einer deutschen Provinz: Eine Studie zur regionalen und nationalen Identität 1914–1933* (Osnabrück, 2010).

Traditionsverband der Division (ed.), *Geschichte der 121. Ostpreussische Infanterie-Division 1940–1945* (Berlin, 1970).

Ueberschär, Gerd, "Der Angriff auf Leningrad und die Blockade der Stadt durch die deutsche Wehrmacht," in Wenner and Leetz (eds.), *Blockade: Leningrad 1941–1944*, pp. 94–105.

Generaloberst Franz Halder: Generalstabschef, Gegner und Gefangener (Göttingen, 1991).

"Hitlers Entschluß zum Lebensraum Krieg im Osten," in Ueberschär and Wette (eds.), *Der deutsche Überfall auf die Sowjetunion 1941: "Unternehmen Barbarossa"*, pp. 13–43.

(ed.), *NS-Verbrechen und der militärische Widerstand gegen Hitler* (Darmstadt, 2000).

(ed.), *Orte des Grauens: Verbrechen im Zweiten Weltkrieg* (Darmstadt, 2003).

Ueberschär, Gerd and Wolfram Wette (eds.), *Der deutsche Überfall auf die Sowjetunion 1941: "Unternehmen Barbarossa"* (Frankfurt am Main, 1997).

Umbreit, Hans, "The Battle for Hegemony in Western Europe," in Maier et al., *Germany's Initial Conquests in Europe* (Oxford, 2000), pp. 229–326.

"Die deutsche Herrschaft in den besetzten Gebieten 1942–1945," in Kroener et al., *Organisation und Mobilisierung des deutschen Machtbereichs*, pp. 3–272.

Van Creveld, Martin, *Fighting Power: German and U.S. Army Performance, 1939–1945* (Westport, CT, 1982).

Supplying War: Logistics from Wallenstein to Patton (Cambridge, 1977).

Vardi, Gil-Li, "Joachim von Stülpnagel's Military Thought and Planning," *War in History* (17) 2010, pp. 193–216.

Vestermanis, Margers, "Local Headquarters Liepaja: Two Months of German Occupation in the Summer of 1941," in Heer and Naumann (eds.), *War of Extermination*, pp. 191–236.

Vinen, Richard, *The Unfree French: Life under the Occupation* (New Haven, 2006).

Voglis, Polymeris, "Surviving Hunger: Life in the Cities and Countryside during the Occupation," in Gildea et al. (eds.), *Surviving Hitler and Mussolini*, pp. 16–41.

Waite, Robert G.L., *Vanguard of Nazism: The Free Corps Movement in Postwar Germany 1918–1923* (New York, 1969).

Wallach, Jehuda, *The Dogma of the Battle of Annihilation: The Theories of Clausewitz and Schlieffen and Their Impact on the German Conduct of Two World Wars* (Westport, CT, 1986).
Wawro, Geoffrey, *The Austro-Prussian War: Austria's War with Prussia and Italy in 1866* (Cambridge, 1996).
  The Franco-Prussian War: The German Conquest of France in 1870–1871 (Cambridge, 2003).
Weber, Thomas, *Hitler's First War: Adolf Hitler, the Men of the List Regiment and the First World War* (Oxford, 2010).
Webster, Charles and Noble Frankland, *Strategic Air Offensive against Germany*, vol. II, *Endeavour* (London, 1961).
  Strategic Air Offensive against Germany, vol. III, *Victory* (London, 1961).
Wegner, Bernd, "Die Aporie des Krieges," in Frieser (ed.), *Die Ostfront*, pp. 246–74.
  "Defensive ohne Strategie: Die Wehrmacht und das Jahr 1943," in Müller and Volkmann (eds.), *Die Wehrmacht*, pp. 197–209.
  "Erschriebene Siege: Franz Halder, die 'Historical Divison' und die Rekonstruktion des Zweiten Weltkrieges im Geiste des deutschen Generalstabes," in Hansen, Schreiber, and Wegner (eds.), *Politischer Wandel, organisierte Gewalt und nationale Sicherheit*, pp. 287–302.
  (ed.), *From Peace to War: Germany, Soviet Russia, and the World, 1939–1941* (Providence and Oxford, 1997).
  "Von Stalingrad nach Kursk," in Frieser (ed.), *Die Ostfront*, pp. 3–79.
  "The War against the Soviet Union 1942–1943," in Boog et al., *The Global War*, pp. 842–1215.
Weinberg, Gerhard, *A World at Arms: A Global History of World War II* (Cambridge, 1994).
Weiss-Wendt, Anton, *Murder without Hatred: Estonians and the Holocaust* (Syracuse, 2009).
Welzer, Harald, Sönke Neitzel, and Christian Gudehus (eds.), *"Der Führer war wieder viel zu human, viel zu gefühlvoll": Der Zweite Weltkrieg aus der Sicht deutscher und italienischer Soldaten* (Frankfurt am Main, 2011).
Werth, Alexander, *Russia at War, 1941–1945* (New York, 1984).
Wette, Wolfram (ed.), *Deserteure der Wehrmacht: Feiglinge – Opfer – Hoffnungsträger? Dokumentation eines Meinungswandel* (Essen, 1995).
  "'Rassenfeind': Antisemitismus und Antislawismus in der Wehrmachtspropaganda," in Manoschek (ed.), *Die Wehrmacht im Rassenkrieg*, pp. 55–73.
  Die Wehrmacht: Feindbilder, Vernichtungskrieg, Legenden (Frankfurt am Main, 2002).
Wette, Wolfram and Gerd Ueberschär (eds.), *Kriegsverbrechern im 20. Jahrhundert* (Darmstadt, 2001).
  (eds.), *Stalingrad: Mythos und Wirklichkeit einer Schlacht* (Frankfurt am Main, 1992).
Wettstein, Adrian, "Operation 'Barbarossa' und Stadtkampf," *Militärgeschichtliche Zeitschrift* (66) 2007, pp. 21–44.
Wiener, Amir, "Something to Die For, a Lot to Kill For: The Soviet System and the Barbarisation of Warfare, 1939–1945," in Kassimeris (ed.), *The Barbarization of Warfare*, pp. 101–25.

Wildt, Michael and Christoph Kreutzmüller (eds.), *Berlin 1933–1945* (Munich, 2013).

Wilhelm, Hans-Heinrich, "Motivation and 'Kriegsbild' deutscher Generale und Offiziere im Krieg gegen die Sowjetunion," in Jahn and Rürup (eds.), *Erobern und Vernichten*, pp. 153–82.

Williams, Charles, *Adenauer: The Father of the New Germany* (New York, 2000).

Ziemke, Earl, *Stalingrad to Berlin: The German Defeat in the East* (Washington, DC, 1968).

Zuber, Terence, *Inventing the Schlieffen Plan: German War Planning 1871–1914* (New York and London, 2003).

Index

Aachen, 50
Adenauer, Konrad, 50
Adriatic Sea, 39
Allied strategic bombing, 347–8
Alsace, 323
Amsterdam, 168
antiguerilla policies. *See* anti-partisan warfare
Athens, 168
Austro-Hungarian Empire, 40

Backe, Herbert, 71–2, 174
Baden, 205
Balkans, 56, 66, 203
Baltic region. *See* Baltic states
Baltic Sea, 39, 359
Baltic states, 6, 16, 57–61, 96, 98, 101, 106, 132, 135, 345, 357, 370, 373–4, 381, 384. *See also* Estonia, Latvia, Lithuania
Bartenstein, 76
Battle of Berlin, 351
Battle of Britain, 56
Bauhaus school, 47
Belarus, 58, 132, 156, 171, 194, 336, 374
Belgium, 19, 56, 94, 378
Belgrade, 168
Berlin, 5, 31–2, 40, 42, 45–50, 54–6, 68, 70, 168, 205, 299, 308, 309, 348, 351, 386–7
Berlin-Brandenburg, 5, 32, 51, 55, 207, 277, 325, 385
Bismarck, Otto von, 53
Black Sea, 39
Bochum, 348
Bock, Fedor von, 238, 249
Bonaparte, Napoleon, 16, 197, 218, 371
Bonn, 50
Bormann, Martin, 350
Brandenburg, 5, 32, 40–7, 49, 51, 299
Brandenburg (city), 42
Brauchitsch, Walther von, 57, 79, 120, 155, 238, 248

Brecht, Bertolt, 47
Breslau, 322
British Bomber Command, 347, 351
Bucher, Wolfgang, 179
Busch, Ernst, 61, 78, 95, 99, 120, 123, 198

Catholic Workers' Union, 53
Caucasus, 8, 100, 250, 283
Center Party, 43, 53–5, 387
Chemnitz, 203
Christian Union, 53
Chudovo, 327, 374
collective measures, 17, 19, 88, 130–4, 163, 167, 214–15
Cologne, 50, 349
Commissar Order, 13, 75, 78, 212, 254
Crimea, 8, 166, 170, 194, 249, 267
"Customs of War on Land," 18

Demiansk, 7, 121, 126, 207, 217, 219–22, 224, 229, 234, 248, 256–71, 275, 278, 280–1, 287, 297–8, 301, 303, 306, 308–10, 313–17, 320, 330, 339, 341, 375, 380–1
  withdrawal from, 306
Denmark, 56
Dnieper river, 359
Dno, 308
DNVP. *See* German Nationalist People's Party
Donbas, 194
Donets basin, 8, 171
Dorochova, 92–4, 112
Dortmund, 348
Düsseldorf, 54, 348
Dvina river, 89
Dvinsk, 89

East Prussia, 5, 32, 40–6, 49, 51, 55, 66–7, 76, 100–1, 206, 276, 323, 370, 385–7

415

416 Index

Economic Staff East, 30–1, 71–2, 107, 151,
  157, 162, 165, 168, 170, 174,
  176, 178–82, 187, 193, 214,
  216, 251, 254, 287–8, 292,
  313–14, 330, 341, 355–7, 374,
  381, 385
  Conflicts with German Army, 179–81
  in Pavlovsk, 162, 165, 168
Eighth Air Force, 347
Einsatzgruppen, 31, 74–5, 163, 167, 213, 385
  agreement with army, 74–5, 213–14
  Einsatzgruppe A, 96, 99, 160–1, 174,
    182, 187, 193, 213
  Einsatzkommando 1B, 213
  and Poland, 74
  Sonderkommando 1B, 160
Essen, 348
Estonia, 106, 119, 344
Eupen-Malmedy, 323
Eydtkau, 78

Feldpostbriefe, 31
Feodosia, 156
Final Solution of the Jewish Question.
  See Holocaust
Finland, 358
  and the Winter War, 59
Finnish Army, 190
Finnish Sea, 217
First Battle of the Ruhr, 348, 351
First World War, 7, 16, 22, 25, 39, 49, 56,
    64–5, 121–2, 248, 352–3,
    377–8, 380
  effects on German policy in Second
    World War, 56
  German anti-partisan policies, 18
  labor deportations, 19
  and northern France, 19
Foch, Ferdinand, 49
forced evacuations, 381–2
  Demiansk pocket, 234–5
  and the German Army, 289
  Leningrad region, 1941–2, 176
  Pavlovsk, 1941, 158
  Pavlovsk/Pushkin, 1942, 288
  retreat to Panther Line, 368–9
Foreign Armies East, 251
Four-Year Plan, 30, 71
France, 10, 51, 62, 111, 199, 203, 272
  defeat in 1940, 56
  and First World War, 19, 21
  1940 invasion of, 25
Franco-Prussian War, 15–18, 25, 94, 378
Frankfurt an der Oder, 42
Freikorps, 20, 40, 46, 50, 101
Fremde Heere Ost, 357

Friedrichshain, 49
Fromm, Friedrich, 199, 272, 275

Geheime Feldpolizei. *See* Secret Field Police
Gehlen, Reinhard, 252
Geistige Betreuung 354
  and preparations for Operation
    Barbarossa, 79–81
General Government, 169
Generalquartiermeister-Programms, 287
Gerichtsbarkeitserlass (Curtailment of
    Military Jurisdiction Decree),
    75, 79, 83
German Army
  anti-partisan policies, 4, 20, 94, 384–5
  anti-partisan policies in Operation
    Barbarossa, 128–30
  anti-partisan policies in Yugoslavia, 66
  complicity in starvation plan, 384
  formations
    Armies
      Eighteenth, 60, 160, 240, 284, 308,
        358, 367, 370, 380
        and anti-partisan policies, 1943,
          384–5
        and civilian evacuations, 1943,
          331–2
        and Demiansk, 265–7
        and forced evacuations, 1943,
          344–5
        and the Holocaust, 98, 159, 383
        and military necessity, 8
        and Operation Barbarossa, 108,
          116, 119, 131–2
        and retreat to Panther Line, 364
        and siege of Leningrad, 153, 166,
          172, 175–6, 185, 187, 189, 191,
          193, 198
        and Volkhov pocket, 229
      Eleventh, 8, 166, 170, 235, 250–1,
        266–7
        and first Ladoga battle, 284
        and Operation Nordlicht, 283
      First Panzer, 250, 359
      Fourth, 121
      Fourth Panzer, 171, 201
      Ninth, 91, 126, 133, 263, 352
      Seventeenth, 8, 152, 170–1, 250–1,
        264, 266
      Sixteenth, 60, 78, 156, 330, 340,
        358, 380
        and Demiansk, 257, 262, 265,
          308
        and forced evacuations, 160, 343,
          345
        and the Holocaust, 98–9, 383

Index

and Operation Barbarossa, 61, 91,
  107–8, 116, 119–20, 123,
  126–8, 132, 144, 176, 198–9,
  210, 213, 215
and Volkhov pocket, 229
and winter crisis, 221
Sixth, 3, 170, 305, 308–9, 346
Third Panzer, 187
Army Groups
  Center, 6, 58, 60, 91, 106, 115–16,
    120, 124, 126–7, 132, 173,
    197–8, 206, 217, 219, 221–2,
    224, 228, 272–3, 306, 352, 358
  Kurland, 6
  North, 6, 31–2, 59–60, 87, 91, 95,
    115–16, 174, 217, 305, 325,
    336, 353, 357–8, 367, 374, 376,
    382, 384
    anti-partisan policies, 1943, 336
    anti-partisan policies in Operation
      Barbarossa, 131–3, 136
    and cancellation of Operation
      Nordlicht, 284
    casualties during Operation
      Barbarossa, 199
    combat in 1944, 364
    combat in opening phase of
      Operation Barbarossa, 94
    co-operation with *Einsatzgruppen*,
      213
    defensive orientation, 1942, 248,
      283
    and Demiansk, 260, 280, 315
    evolution of occupation policy,
      252
    and forced evacuations, 1943,
      344–6
    and the Holocaust, 97, 100, 383
    manpower issues, 273, 280, 302,
      319
    military necessity, 8, 193, 278–9
    morale problems, 1943, 307, 309,
      314, 347
    occupation policies, 1943, 330–1
    and Operation Barbarossa, 57, 61,
      87, 106–7, 110, 115–16, 120,
      123, 133, 191, 197, 206, 208–9
    and Operation Nordlicht, 283
    and positional warfare, 6
    and scorched-earth retreats, 382
    and siege of Leningrad, 173, 176,
      179, 185, 193
    and strategy, 1943, 358
    supply problems in Operation
      Barbarossa, 209–10
    and Volkhov pocket, 229–30, 241

  and winter crisis, 218–19, 221–2,
    224, 232, 379
  South, 6, 106, 115, 249, 305–6, 322,
    359
Battle Groups
  Laux, 230
  Rauch, 257
  Seydlitz, 259–60
Companies
  1.I/405th Infantry, 206, 275–7, 300,
    324
  1.I/407th Infantry, 275–7
  1.I/415th Infantry, 207–8, 276, 300,
    324
  1.I/416th Infantry, 208, 276–7, 300,
    324
  1.I/422nd Infantry, 207–8, 276–7,
    300, 324
  2.I/424th Infantry, 207, 276–7, 300,
    324
Corps
  I, 135–6, 146, 252–3, 255, 322, 327
  II, 75, 91, 107, 117, 120, 126–8,
    132–3, 141–2, 147, 149, 176,
    210
    anti-partisan policy, 1943, 340
    and collective actions, 144
    and Demiansk, 224–6, 228, 232,
      234, 260–1, 263, 266, 269,
      290
    withdrawal from Demiansk
      pocket, 309–10, 312, 315
  X, 76, 117, 120, 126, 225, 346
  XVIII, 369
  XXVI, 286, 318
  XXVIII, 60, 76, 87, 91, 117, 122,
    134, 153, 156, 164, 176–7, 183,
    190–1, 202, 317, 332–3, 361,
    367, 369
  XXXVIII, 175, 369–70
  XXXIX Panzer, 123
  L, 91, 155, 175–7, 192, 195, 288,
    353, 364, 366
  LIV, 284
Divisions
  1st Infantry, 240
  5th Light, 281
  12th Infantry, 127, 225, 233, 235,
    259, 310
  21st Infantry, 66–7, 103, 240, 371
  30th Infantry, 225, 258, 310
  32nd Infantry, 127, 225, 258
  45th Infantry, 63, 201
  58th Infantry, 155
  61st Infantry, 32, 96, 190
  81st Infantry, 322

Index

German Army (cont.)
  93rd Infantry, 32, 102, 149, 360
  121st Infantry, 5
    anti-partisan policies in 1943, 337
    anti-partisan policies in Pavlovsk, 163
    casualties and replacements, 1943, 320
    casualties in Operation Barbarossa, 200
    casualties in winter crisis, 272
    combat, 1943, 317
    combat, 1944, 367
    combat in Leningrad siege line, 193
    and commissars, 77
    confiscation of clothing in Pavlovsk, 190
    establishment of, 63, 65
    and first Ladoga battle, 286
    and forced evacuations, 1943, 333
    and ideological planning for Barbarossa, 76
    and ideological war, 96
    and interactions with civilians, 87, 134
    and labor procurement, 1944, 370
    occupation of Pavlovsk, 168
    occupation of Pavlovsk, 1942, 289
    occupation policies, 1942, 255
    and planning for Operation Barbarossa, 60
    regional composition, 66
    replacements 1941, 203
    replacements in winter crisis, 274
    replacements, late 1942, 297
    role in Operation Barbarossa, 60
    supply issues in Operation Barbarossa, 145
    and the Holocaust, 99
    and the Volkhov pocket battle, 245
    training, 1943, 327
  122nd Infantry, 202
  123rd Infantry, 5
    anti-partisan policies in Demiansk pocket, 271
    anti-partisan policies, late 1941, 145
    anti-partisan policies, 1943, 341
    casualties and replacements, 1943, 322
    casualties in Operation Barbarossa, 201
    casualties in winter crisis, 273
    combat, 1943, 359
    combat, 1944, 361
    and Demiansk offensive, 128
    and Demiansk pocket, 271
    discipline problems, 68, 126
    establishment of, 63, 65
    food policies within Demiansk pocket, 265
    and forced evacuations from Demiansk pocket, 343
    and forced evacuations, 1943, 343
    and the formation of the Demiansk pocket, 228
    ideological preparation for Operation Barbarossa, 80
    implementation of "criminal orders," 79
    morale problems, 351
    occupation policies, 1943, 331
    and planning for Operation Barbarossa, 60
    replacement policies, late 1942, 299
    replacements 1941, 203
    replacements in winter crisis, 273
    regional composition, 66
    role in Operation Barbarossa, 60
    supply crisis in Operation Barbarossa, 150
  126th Infantry, 5
    anti-partisan policies, 1943, 338
    anti-partisan policies in battle of Volkhov pocket, 236
    anti-partisan policies in Operation Barbarossa, 128–30, 141
    and battle for Volkhov pocket, 231
    casualties and replacements, 1943, 320
    casualties during winter crisis, 272
    casualties in Operation Barbarossa, 200
    and collective actions, 93, 141
    combat, 1943, 319
    combat, 1944, 364, 367
    and development of occupation policy, 1942, 293
    establishment of, 63, 65
    and forced evacuations, 1943, 333
    and ideological planning for Barbarossa, 77
    and ideological preparation for Operation Barbarossa, 80
    and ideology, 1943, 353
    massacre of Soviet POWs, 239
    morale problems, 245, 351
    occupation policies, 1943, 332

Index

occupation policies in Volkhov region, late 1942, 255
and Operation Michael, 283
and planning for Operation Barbarossa, 60
regional composition, 66
replacement policies, late 1942, 298
replacements 1941, 204
replacements in winter crisis, 275
role in Operation Barbarossa, 60
scorched-earth retreat from Demiansk pocket, 313
and supply crisis in Operation Barbarossa, 145
and the Volkhov pocket battle, 246
and Tichvin operation, 125
training, 1943, 328
215th Infantry, 228–9
221st Security, 131, 251
250th Infantry (Spanish Blue Division), 140
253rd Infantry, 4, 32, 67, 87, 136, 149, 232, 234, 255, 354
254th Infantry, 32, 67, 101, 150, 186, 246, 349
290th Infantry, 225, 258
296th Infantry, 63, 69, 111, 136, 201
4th Panzer, 201
12th Panzer, 364, 366
Ersatzheer (Replacement Army), 199
Korück 337
Volksgrenadier, 29
Panzer Groups
Four, 5, 7, 61, 84, 88, 90, 108, 116–17, 132, 173, 198, 213
Three, 116
rear army area 178, 292
Regiments
27th Infantry, 259
89th Infantry, 259
126th Artillery, 237
405th Infantry, 2, 84, 117, 121–2, 284
407th Infantry, 63, 95–8, 191–2, 210, 297
408th Infantry, 64, 86, 98, 133–4, 185, 203, 230, 297, 327
411th Infantry, 202
415th Infantry, 66, 119–20, 126–7, 144, 205, 227, 258, 299
416th Infantry, 66, 119–20, 127, 142, 191, 222, 258–9
418th Infantry, 91, 109, 120, 141, 258, 295, 299

422nd Infantry, 66, 124, 138, 231, 236, 281
424th Infantry, 66, 119, 140, 150, 230, 237
426th Infantry, 124, 135–6, 229, 241
ideological indoctrination of troops, 351–4
ideological war, 375–6
and Nazi ideology, 11
and occupation policy, 6, 9
and overconfidence towards the Soviet Union, 59–60
and preparations for ideological war, 73–5
and Reichswehr, 24
relationships with Soviet women in the Demiansk pocket, 265–7
soldiers' perceptions of Soviet citizens, 102–5, 155
soldiers' perceptions of Soviet Union, 100–2, 246–7
soldiers' perceptions of the Red Army, 92
and structure and tasks of infantry divisions, 61–3
training, 325–9
training comparison with American Army, 328
use of Soviet auxiliaries, 293–4
German Communist Party (KPD), 47–8, 52, 54–5
in Soviet Union, 169–72
German Nationalist People's Party (Deutschnationale Volkspartei or DNVP), 43–4
German Navy, 359
German Southwest Africa, 22, 378
and the Herero Revolt, 22, 25
and the Nama tribe, 22
Germany
food policy and the Soviet Union, 57, 169–72
food policy in Europe, 168–9
and food shortages, 56
and regionalism in, 27, 34–55
as violent society, 34–6, 55, 378
and *Volksgemeinschaft*, 34
Gestapo, 78
Goebbels, Joseph, 48, 168, 348
Göring, Hermann, 30, 71, 174–5
Great Britain, 56–7
Great Depression, 48
Greece, 10, 62, 66, 111, 169
Green Folder
and starvation plan, 73
Gropius, Walter, 47
Grossman, Vasily, 209
Grunewald, 309

guerilla warfare. *See* German Army, anti-partisan policies
Guidelines for the Conduct of the Troops in Russia, 75, 79, 83, 86

Hague, The, 168
Halder, Franz, 30, 69, 87, 108, 115–16, 120, 123–4, 131, 172–3, 178, 197–200, 209, 217, 221, 224, 229–30
Hamburg, 47, 274, 351
Hamburg Institute for Social Research, 10
Hannover, 205
Hartmann, Julius von, 16
Hasse, Gerhart, 178
Himmler, Heinrich, 30, 237–8
historiography of war of annihilation, 10–14
Hitler, Adolf, 38, 56, 58, 60, 71, 73–4, 124, 131, 163, 169, 177, 254, 256, 283–4, 358–9, 363–4, 366
  and anti-partisan policies, 129
  and Demiansk, 259–60, 281, 308, 310
  and forced labor, 268
  and Operation Barbarossa, 115
  and planning for Operation Barbarossa, 57
  and Tichvin offensive, 123
  view of Leningrad, 59, 172–3
  and war of annihilation, 69
  and winter crisis, 20, 221–4, 230, 232–3
Hoepner, Erich, 61, 95, 101, 131, 213
Holocaust, 96, 383–4
  in Pavlovsk, 160, 194
Holstein. *See* Economic Staff East
Hoppe, Harry, 302
Hoth, Hermann, 20, 264

imperial Germany, 38, 70
Italy, 10
Izhora river, 122

Jamburg, 327, 344
Jodl, Alfred, 60, 155, 197, 306
Junker class, 42

Kaiserreich. *See* imperial Germany
Kapp Putsch, 46, 50
Kazlai, 87–8, 133
Kazley-Ruda, 97
Keitel, Wilhelm, 93, 129–30, 173, 194, 266, 352
Kharkov, 169–70, 305–6
Kholm, 91, 117, 119–20, 125, 127, 146–7, 210, 225, 257
Kiev, 156, 169
Kleist, Ewald von, 250

Kluge, Günther von, 121
Knuth, Hans, 178
Kölnischen Volkszeitung, 50
Kommandostabes Reichsführer-SS, 99
Königgrätz, 21
Königsberg, 42
Kovno, 97–100, 383
Krakow, 169
Krasnogvardeisk, 180, 183, 187, 288–9
Krasnoje Selo, 344
Krefeld, 348
Kronstadt, 59
Küchler, Georg von, 60–1, 78, 81–2, 95, 131, 173, 176–8, 185, 224, 228, 240, 252, 279, 304, 308, 327, 339, 353, 357–8, 364, 366
Kulturkampf, 53
Kursk, 6, 306

Lake Chud (Lake Peipus), 358, 366
Lake Ilmen, 120, 126, 215, 219–20, 228
Lake Ladoga, 123, 294, 375
Lake Samra, 174
Lake Seliger, 126, 150, 210
Lake Stersh, 222
Lancelle, Otto, 83, 87, 94–5
Latvia, 6, 97
Laux, Paul, 218
Leeb, Wilhelm Ritter von, 60, 84–6, 91, 95, 99, 105, 115–16, 119–20, 123–4, 126, 131–2, 145–6, 173, 179, 191–2, 197, 208, 210, 217, 219, 222, 224, 228–9, 358
Leningrad, 8, 33, 58, 60, 73, 96, 113, 115–17, 119, 121–2, 126, 132, 134–5, 151, 153, 158, 161–3, 167, 172–3, 175, 177–8, 190, 192–3, 197–8, 202, 215, 217, 219, 228, 240, 263, 283, 289, 306, 308, 318, 337, 346, 359, 363, 367, 369, 373, 384
  as industrial center, 59
  siege of, 6–7, 172–3
  and starvation plan, 72
Lersner, Wilhelm Freiherr von, 352–3
Libau, 345
Liebknecht, Karl, 46
Lindemann, Georg, 237
Lithuania, 19, 40, 84, 88, 97–8, 100–1, 133, 344, 378
Liuban, 183, 186–7, 228–30, 287, 327, 367, 370, 374
Lorraine, 323
Lovat river, 259–60, 313, 315, 330, 339, 341

Index

Low Countries, 56, 62, 85, 199.
  See Belgium, Luxembourg, Netherlands
Luftwaffe 173, 199, 228, 368
  and the Battle of Britain, 56
  formations
    VIII Air Corps, 116
    9th Field Division, 363
    12th Field Division, 366
Luga, 174, 308, 344
Luga Line, 117–18, 133, 366–7
Luga river, 117
Luxembourg, 56, 323
Luxemburg, Rosa, 46

Mainz, 50
Malaia Vischera, 123, 124–5
Manstein, Erich von, 170–1, 267, 283–4, 305
Marcks, Erich, 58
Mediterranean Sea, 69
Mein Kampf, 80
Mga, 123, 228
military necessity, 7–10, 16, 20, 25, 377–80
  definition of, 7
  and development of German occupation policy, late 1942, 303–4
  development within Demiansk pocket, 267
  evolution in Prusso-German Army, 14–26
  and evolution of occupation policy, 248–52
  and First World War, 22
  and 121st Infantry Division's occupation of Pavlovsk, 151–93
  interaction with Nazi ideology, 4
  internal contradictions, 268, 290, 304, 330, 355–6, 381
  and Nazi ideology, 9, 82–3
  and Operation Barbarossa, 112, 130–1, 211–16
  and winter crisis, 239, 278–9
  and withdrawal from Demiansk pocket, 314
Minsk, 157, 171
Model, Walter, 366
Moltke, Helmuth von, the Elder, 17–18, 94
Moltke, Helmuth von, the Younger, 94
Molvotitsy, 235, 257, 263, 270
Montpellier, 168
Moscow, 6, 48, 58–9, 72, 115–16, 126–7, 172–3, 187, 198, 217, 256, 260
Müller, Eugen, 129
Murmansk, 248

Nagel, Hans, 71, 251
Narva, 308
Narva river, 240
National Socialist German Workers' Party (NSDAP), 44–5, 48, 54–5
Netherlands, 56, 168
Neukölln, 49
Neva river, 153
North Africa, 62
Norway, 56
Novgorod, 61, 117, 119, 367
Nuremberg, 347
Nuremberg trials, 10

Oberbefehlshaber Ost (Ober Ost), 15, 20, 378, 380
Oder river, 172
Oldenburg. *See* Economic Staff East
Operation Barbarossa, 1, 5, 9, 26, 28, 33, 69, 71, 80–1, 83, 108, 200, 212, 268, 291, 316, 346, 379–80
  failure of, 197–216
  and German Army's supply crisis, 105–8, 145–50, 209–10
  German casualties in, 85
  and German perceptions of Red Army, 86
  and ideological planning, 70
  and living off the land, 110
  and manpower issues, 199–202, 271–2
  strategic conflicts within German High Command, 57–9, 115–17
  and war of annihilation, 57, 94–5, 111
Operation Brückenschlag, 259
Operation Michael, 281
Operation Nordlicht, 283–4
Operation Pointblank, 347
Operation Polar Star, 308, 316
Operation Raubtier, 230
Operation Spark, 307–8
Operation Typhoon, 127
Operation Zitadelle, 306. *See* Kursk
Opotschka, 181
Oranienbaum, 162, 217, 318, 363
Ordesh, 314
Orša, 178
Ostashkov, 126
Ostland, 345
Ottoman Empire, 40

Panther Line, 33, 344, 357–8, 364, 366–70, 373, 382
Paris, 40
  and the Peace Conference, 40
Paulus, Friedrich, 346

Pavlovsk, 33, 122, 125, 133, 151, 213–14, 283, 287–9, 302–3, 313, 374, 381, 383–5
  cannibalism in, 184–5
  German attempts to win over population of, 163–5
  German occupation of, 151–2
  starvation in, 183–9
Pavlovsk Palace, 157–8
Petersburg. *See* Leningrad
Pogorelizy, 263–4
Pola river, 257
Poland, 40, 56, 59, 62, 70, 74, 169, 203, 323
  invasion of, 25
Polish Corridor, 40
Porchov, 369
Potsdam, 42
Pravda (German newspaper in Pavlovsk), 164–5
Pripet Marshes, 58
Protestant Union Church, 43
Prussia, 38–9
Pskov, 308, 367–9, 371, 373
Pushkin, 165, 175, 184, 283, 287–9, 302, 374

Red Army, 2
  formations
  Armies
    Second Shock, 229–30, 241–2
  Brigades
    1st Parachute, 257
    21st Partisan, 339
    204th Parachute, 257
  Fronts
    Leningrad, 219, 307
    Northwest, 219–20, 280, 308, 315
    Volkhov, 219, 307–8, 316
      performance in Winter War, 59
      and purges, 60
      training 329
Reich Ministry for Food and Agriculture, 70
Reichenau, Walther von, 170, 177, 195, 249
  and October 1941 order, 177
Remscheid, 348
Replacement Policy, 28–9, 33, 65–6, 202
  and Army Group North, 1943, 322–5
  and late 1942, 295, 301–2
  and winter crisis, 271–2, 277
Rhine, 49
Rhineland, 51, 348, 387
Rhineland-Westphalia, 5, 32, 45, 49–55, 66, 204–5, 245, 276, 385, 387

Roques, Franz von, 99
Royal Navy, 70
Ruhr industrial region, 49–52, 67, 347–9, 351
  Franco-Belgian occupation of, 50
Russian Empire, 40, 71, 102
Russian–German Museum, Karlshorst, 265
Rzhev, 305–6

Salonica, 168
Sauckel, Fritz
  and labor procurement in Soviet Union, 268
Saxony, 205
Scheidemann, Philipp, 46
Schirwindt, 76, 78
Schlieffen, Alfred von, 21
scorched-earth retreats, 3–4, 33, 336, 356, 385
  and destruction of Pskov, 373
  retreat to Panther Line, 366–7, 370–3
  Ukraine, 1943, 360–1
  during winter crisis, 232, 257
  during withdrawal from Demiansk pocket, 309–13
Second Empire. *See* imperial Germany
II SS-Infantry Brigade, 156, 237–8
Secret Field Police, 291. *See* Geheime Feldpolizei
Sedan
  battle of 1870, 17, 21
Seeckt, Hans von, 24
Serbia, 66, 168
Sevastopol, 283
Sicherheitsdienst (Security Service or SD), 8, 31, 161–3, 174, 187, 214, 291, 327, 338, 383
Simferopol, 8, 166
Siniavino, 284, 307–8, 316, 327
Slaviansk, 250
Šlissel'burg, 123, 307
Slutsk. *See* Pavlovsk
Smerdynia, 316
social Darwinism, 36
Social Democratic Party (SPD), 44, 48, 52–5
Sodki, 235
Soviet Extraordinary Commission, 183
Soviet High Command, 218–19, 359
Spartacist Revolt, 46
Speer, Albert, 295
SS, 13, 30–1, 35, 74–6, 78, 82, 151, 159–63, 193, 213, 237, 330, 374
SS-Polizei Division, 178, 284, 367

Index

SS-Totenkopf Division, 225, 227, 259–60
Stab Holstein. *See* Economic Staff East
Stahlecker, Walther, 213
Stalin, Joseph, 219
Stalin Line, 89
Stalingrad, 6, 305, 308–9, 346, 352
Staraia Russa, 61, 117–18, 120, 219–21, 259, 270, 291, 374
Starvation Plan, 72–3
   and Leningrad region, 172–89
   and Operation Barbarossa, 72–3
Stavka, 308
Stülpnagel, Joachim von, 24
Sudetenland, 323

Third Supreme Army Command, 15, 23
Thirty Years War, 175
Thomas, Georg, 71, 175
Thuringia, 268
Tichvin, 124
Tichvin operation, 124, 197, 201, 210, 217, 222
Tigoda river, 186
Tilsit, 42
Tobolka, 262–4
Todt Organization, 288–9
Tosno, 121, 228, 286, 308
Treaty of Versailles, 24, 49–51
Trier, 50
Truppenführung (unit command), 62

Ukraine, 6, 19, 57, 152, 164, 169, 249, 358, 360, 374
United States Army Historical Division, 30

Valdai Hills, 126
Vichy France, 168
Vienna, 323
Vilkoviszki, 2
Vitka, 136
Volga river, 309
Volkhov pocket, 241–54, 283, 296, 303
Volkhov river, 7, 123–5, 150, 217, 228–9, 241, 245, 252, 254, 259, 276, 280, 303, 316, 375

Wagner, Eduard, 75–6, 82, 175, 178, 180
Wandel, Martin, 283
War Economy and Armaments Office, 71
Warsaw, 169
Wedding, 49
Wehrmacht. *See* German Army
Weimar Republic, 24, 39, 42–3, 45, 48, 53, 55
Wellington, 16
West Prussia, 323
Wiesbaden, 50
Wilhelm II, 19
Wilhelmine Germany. *See* imperial Germany
winter crisis, 3, 28, 91, 107, 217–39
   radicalization of German behavior in, 9
Wirtschaftsstab Ost. See Economic Staff East
Wuppertal, 348
Württemberg, 205

Young Turks, 24
Yugoslavia, 10, 62

Zaporozhye, 359
Zeitler, Kurt, 308, 364
Zhukov, Georgii, 315